When Their World Falls Apart

When Their World Falls Apart

Helping Families and Children Manage the Effects of Disasters

Lawrence B. Rosenfeld

Joanne S. Caye

Ofra Ayalon

Mooli Lahad

NASW PRESS
National Association of Social Workers
Washington, DC

Gary Bailey, MSW, *President*
Elizabeth J. Clark, PhD, ACSW, MPH *Executive Director*

CHERYL Y. BRADLEY, *Publisher*
PAULA L. DELO, *Executive Editor*
ANDRE BARNETT, *Editor*
HEATHER BRADY, *Editor*
CHRISTINA BROMLEY, *Editorial Assistant*
ALISON PENA, *Copy Editor*
MARCIA ROMAN, SARAH LOWMAN, *and* FRANCES PETREY, *Proofreaders*
BERNICE EISEN, *Indexer*

Cover by Cohen Design
Interior design by Metadog Design Group, Washington, DC
Printed and bound by Port City Press, Baltimore, MD

Library of Congress Cataloging-in-Publication Data

When their worlds fall apart : helping families and children manage the effects of disasters /
 Lawrence B. Rosenfeld ...[et al.].
  p. cm.
 Includes bibliographical references and index.
 ISBN 0-87101-358-4 (pbk.)
 1. Disaster relief. 2. Disaster victims—Services for. 3. Family social work. I. Rosenfeld, Lawrence B.

 HV553.W48 2003

2003061078

CONTENTS

ABOUT THE AUTHORS

Lawrence B. Rosenfeld, PhD, is professor of communication studies and vice-chair of the Academic Affairs Institutional Review Board, University of North Carolina at Chapel Hill. He is the author or coauthor of 18 books on interpersonal, small group, and nonverbal communication and on conducting quantitative research. His most recent book is *Interplay: The Process of Interpersonal Communication*, a text for understanding and improving close relationships. He has written numerous articles and chapters in the areas of social work, communication, education, and psychology. He is a recipient of the National Communication Association's Donald H. Ecroyd Award for Outstanding Teaching in Higher Education, the University of North Carolina's Johnston Award for Teaching Excellence, and is listed as one of the 10 most prolific currently active scholars in the field of communication. He served as editor of the *Western Journal of Speech Communication* and of *Communication Education* and, most recently, as coeditor of the "Practice Highlights" section of *Children & Schools*.

Joanne S. Caye, MSW, is a clinical assistant professor at the University of North Carolina at Chapel Hill. She is the faculty liaison for the North Carolina Child Welfare Education Collaborative, housed in the School of Social Work in Chapel Hill. She teaches and mentors students earning master of social work degrees who plan to work in public child welfare after graduation. She has been involved with the social work field since 1970 as a direct practice social worker, supervisor, and program administrator at the local and state levels in Pennsylvania, Louisiana, and North Carolina. She has trained social workers and managers who assist families who have experienced trauma and who have lived through disasters. She has written several curricula focusing on family-centered social work and is a regular workshop presenter.

Ofra Ayalon, PhD, is a psychologist specializing in work with families and trauma survivors. She is the director of Israel's Nord Cope Center, a venue for creative training and developing coping resources in individuals, families, and communities. As an international traumatologist and consultant for UNICEF, the Red Cross, and other nongovernment organizations, she trains mental health professionals in countries around the world. After the 9/11 attacks on the World Trade Center, she consulted widely in American organizations on coping with trauma associated with suicide bombers. During her 35 years of teaching at Haifa University, she has authored numerous papers and chapters and 20 books on various aspects of stress and coping. Her book *Rescue: Community Oriented Prevention Education*, which has been translated into five languages, presents cognitive, imaginative, and metaphorical approaches for helping survivors and rescue workers deal internally with what they experienced externally in their chaotic world and turn their plight into might.

Mooli Lahad, PhD, is professor of dramatherapy at Tel Hai College in the Upper Galilee in Israel and at the University of Surrey Roehampton in London. He is director of the Community Stress Prevention Center, an organization he established in 1979 together with the Israeli Ministry of Education. Professor Lahad is the author or coauthor of 18 books and many articles on the topics of communities under stress, creative supervision, and coping with life-threatening situations. He is the recipient of the Israeli Psychology Association's Bonner Prize for outstanding contributions to Education in Israel, the Adler Institute's Award for the Welfare of the Child Prize (Tel Aviv University), and the Israeli Lottery Prize for Innovations in Medicine for developing telepsychology services. He serves as a consultant to many ministries and to UNICEF and has conducted numerous workshops and seminars worldwide. He is a member of the Israeli Prime Minister's Committee on Public Resiliency.

NASW Practice Resources Series

Our lives are punctuated by events. Some events are good. Births, graduations, and weddings are times for celebration. But some events are not good. When they strike, disasters such as hurricanes, airplane crashes, and violence set off processes of adaptation and adjustment that are poorly understood. However, recent research sheds light on how people recover from the loss of loved ones, the destruction of homes and workplaces, and the trauma accompanying these events that leads to loss. *When Their World Falls Apart* is a comprehensive and clear examination of the effects of disasters on children and families. It celebrates the resilience of people in their responses to adversity, and, as part of the Practice Resources Series of NASW Press, it is a guide for action when crises disrupt our lives, the lives of others, and routine services.

Mark W. Fraser, PhD, MSW
Series Editor

ACKNOWLEDGMENTS

A product as ambitious as *When Their World Falls Apart* does not spring to life without the help of many people. We are grateful to the students in our classes who, wittingly or not, helped shape the material presented here. We are indebted to the many people with whom we have had the opportunity (and pleasure) to work—the social workers and mental health professionals providing relief to disaster victims, disaster volunteers devoting themselves to helping others, the community leaders striving to create responsive government services, and the people whose lives were touched by the disasters we discuss in this volume. The ideas in this book were born out of necessity and tested in the real world of natural and technological disasters as well as disasters of human design, such as war and terrorism. And we are thankful for the input of colleagues, especially Robin Gurwitch and Conway Saylor, who waded through early drafts of this book and helped sharpen our perspectives and make clearer our ideas.

We thank Donna Campbell, director and editor of the documentary *Hard Rain*, and Bob Royster, director of production at UNC-TV, for their willingness to share their work with us. They helped bring the ideas in this book to life.

Jack Richman, dean of the School of Social Work of the University of North Carolina at Chapel Hill, and a grant he obtained from the North Carolina Division of Mental Health, Developmental Disabilities and Substance Abuse Services, instigated the projects that served as the groundwork for this book. Without him, and without it, this book never would have been written.

Finally, we express our gratitude for the support of our families. We appreciate their indulgence, both during the times when the ideas of this text were taking shape in the crucible of experience, and the many hours we locked ourselves away to write *When Their World Falls Apart*.

PART ONE

UNDERSTANDING DISASTERS

CHAPTER ONE

INTRODUCTION TO DISASTERS

CHAPTER OVERVIEW

WHY STUDY DISASTERS?

PERSPECTIVES OF THIS BOOK
Family-Centered Perspective
Integrated Model: Three Lenses
Cognitive or behavioral perspective
Family systems perspective
Ecological perspective

IMPORTANT TERMS USED IN THIS BOOK
What Is a Disaster?
Types of disasters
Phases of disasters
What Is a Child?
How Does a Victim Differ from a Survivor?

PLAN OF THIS BOOK

SUMMARY

REFERENCES

After studying the material in this chapter, you should

- understand the importance of studying the effects disasters have on children, families, and communities
- be able to identify the different types of disasters and understand the effects of each type
- be able to describe the predominant phases of disasters and understand how individuals and communities behave during each phase
- understand the family-centered approach and the integrated model (the "three lenses") used to study the effects of disasters
- be able to define and use the foundation terms of this book: *disaster, child, victim,* and *survivor*
- be familiar with the perspectives and plan of this book.

We are naturally fascinated by disasters. We stay glued to our televisions as pictures of crashed planes and nuclear power plant accidents, hurricanes and floods, wars and terrorism—near and far—are played and replayed on the 5:30 news, then on the 6:00 and 11:00 news. We often choose to spend the last moments of each day as witnesses to horrors in our communities and around the world.

And if we are somehow able to avoid televised disasters on the news and television movies, we spend our hard-earned money to watch movies that depict disasters—people fighting wars, combating terrorism, suffering from tornadoes, preparing for a tidal wave, digging out of earthquakes, or diverting meteors from destroying the earth. It seems that our appetite for disasters and potential disasters is insatiable.

Consider, though, what it might be like to be caught in any one of these disasters. Stop for a moment and think what it would *really* be like.

The activity on page 5—and the many others offered throughout this book—will help provide a "touch of reality" to the subject matter, to bridge the gap between cognitive and affective learning. For you to know how families and children respond to disasters and to truly understand how society may help those families and children to manage the effects of disasters requires the ability to pit the academic material of this book against reality. First, how would you feel, what would you think, and how would you behave if you were exposed to a disaster? Second, what are others likely to feel, think, and do? Touching Reality (see, for example, "Experiencing a Disaster") activities are presented to help make those connections, to begin to help you provide answers to these two important questions.

You will notice that some of the Touching Reality activities are written as if you are conducting a workshop or a training session or as if you and several colleagues are reading this book together. Regardless of how you are using and applying the material, you should read each Touching Reality activity and, at the least, "do it" in your mind. This book will be more meaningful and useful if you do so.

The news media confirm that disasters are common throughout the world. The stories fascinate us, whether they are of the destructive power of natural disasters, such as floods and fires; technological disasters, such as plane crashes and nuclear power plant accidents; or complex disasters—which is the name for disasters intentionally designed by humans—such as wars and terrorism. We want to understand what happened, to learn how people are responding, to be assured that something is being done to help, and to empathize with the families and children suffering from the effects of a disaster.

The study of disasters' psychosocial aspects—for example, what conditions mediate a child's and family's responses and why some children are resilient and experience a quick return to their everyday life while others may never resume normal functioning—has several benefits. The following section discusses some of these benefits.

WHY STUDY DISASTERS?

Why are we fascinated by disasters?

Is it our fear of death?

Is it our concern about others' suffering and our interest in being sympathetic and empathic to the victims and survivors?

Is it our need to be prepared in the event we experience a similar traumatic event?

Is it our awe at the destructive power of whatever causes the disaster?

Is it our fascination with the human reaction to disaster—how the victims, rescue workers, and caregivers react, how the media portray the disaster, and how groups—from the local, state, and national levels—coordinate their response efforts?

In recent years there have been increases in natural disasters reported by the United Nations Office for the Coordination of Humanitarian Affairs and the National Oceanic and Atmospheric Administration, in violent crime rates (Children's Defense Fund, 1994, Fitzpatrick & Boldizar, 1993), in community violence (Gullotta & McElhaney, 1999), wars (Rosenblatt, 1983; Solomon, 1995); and civilian war casualties (Boyden, 1994). Because of the increases in disasters, we need to understand what factors put children and families at risk to suffer some form of lasting psychopathology, and what factors serve to protect them and enhance their resiliency.

In her 1986 book, *When Disaster Strikes: A Handbook for the Caring Professions,* Beverley Raphael discussed five reasons for studying the psychosocial aspects of disasters. They are

1. to learn common themes from descriptions of individual and group responses to different disasters
2. to increase the effectiveness of strategies to counteract disasters' effects

---

TOUCHING REALITY

Experiencing a Disaster

The purpose of this activity is to provide a sense of what it is like to experience a disaster—to put you, the reader, "into" a situation so you can begin to understand your possible reactions. Commercial movies, available on video, are useful for this purpose. For example, several minutes of the recent film about a volcano, *Dante's Peak,* may be useful for depicting reactions when a disaster strikes a community. Take a look at the film, and note especially the section from the community meeting in the high school when the first serious tremors are felt, to shortly after the volcano's eruption. Other disaster films include *Twister, Titanic, Towering Inferno,* and *Daylight.* What is important is that you select a sequence in the film that depicts the onset of a disaster and people's initial reactions to it. A segment lasting up to five or seven minutes should be sufficient for this purpose.

Use your imagination to put yourself in the scene. If you use *Dante's Peak,* consider the following questions as a way to help yourself get the most out of the viewing:

1. Imagine you are a child in this scene.

   How do you feel emotionally?
   How do you feel physically?
   What are you thinking?
   What are you doing?

2. Imagine you are a helper or rescue worker who arrives at the aftermath of such a disaster.

   How do you feel emotionally?
   How do you feel physically?
   What are you thinking?
   What are you doing?

3. What questions are in your mind as you imagine yourself in the scene?

4. What are your other reactions to the scene?

3. to understand stress and its effects, in general, and stress connected with life events, in particular
4. to determine which factors affect the psychological and social problems associated with life events
5. to provide important information to researchers and others who support and train caretakers, rescue workers, and anyone else who intervenes when disaster strikes.

This book focuses on the effects of disasters on families and children, and its goal is to teach ways to improve preparations for their care in these extraordinary times of need. The goals of intervention after any disaster are to decrease immediate trauma and the chances of long-term damage; to decrease the time it takes for people to recover; and to facilitate recovery by enhancing ways of coping, and by decreasing risk factors.

To facilitate understanding and applying the concepts introduced in the chapters that make up this book, we refer you to a CD that can be found in the back of this book. This CD incorporates images and narratives from the documentary of Hurricane Floyd, *Hard Rain* (Campbell, 1999), which hit North Carolina in September 1999.

PERSPECTIVES OF THIS BOOK

It is important for you to understand the several perspectives guiding this book. Each person's perspective determines how she or he makes sense of the world. Since, during a disaster, we are exposed to more information than we can possibly manage, a person's perspective first determines what he or she focuses on. A carpenter might focus on how a house did or did not maintain its integrity during a hurricane, and we—as social workers, nurses, Red Cross workers, disaster relief workers, mental health professionals, firefighters, police officers, teachers, and so on—might focus on the human element and consider the extent to which people "maintain their integrity." Selecting what to focus on is not an objective process: When we pay attention to some things and ignore others our observations are invariably distorted. Consider what your answer would be if someone asked you to describe "what happened" at a disaster site—it would be impossible to describe everything that occurred and any description you were to give would tell the other person as much about you, and what you think is important, as it would about the event.

Our perspective determines what we choose to concentrate on, and it determines how we arrange what we focus on in our effort to make sense of the world. The raw data we perceive with our senses can be organized in more than one way. For instance, there are at least four ways to describe people suffering from the effects of a disaster (Andersen, 1993): (1) We could focus on physical constructs and classify them by their appearance, such as "starving" or "covered with infected blotches." (2) We could focus on role constructs, such as "victim," "survivor," or "military personnel." (3) We could describe them by focusing on interaction constructs—social behavior— such as "friendly," "helpful," or "aloof." (4) We could use psychological constructs to describe the people, such as "depressed," "anxious," "insecure," or "generous."

Once our perspective has guided our selection and organization of our perceptions, we interpret those perceptions in a way that makes some sort of sense to us.

Is the woman laughing because the flood destroyed her house and she is overwhelmed by the loss, or is she laughing because she had plans to raze the house and build a new one, and the flood strikes her as ironic? If our perspective—informed by our past experiences, assumptions about human behavior, expectations, and our understanding of human conduct—tells us to focus on problems, we might conclude that she is so overwhelmed and distraught by her loss that she is in shock, and her laughing is the same as crying. If our perspective tells us to focus on an individual's strengths, we might jump to the conclusion that she is laughing as a way to cope with her loss—without considering that, perhaps, from her perspective there may be no loss.

Two broad perspectives guide how we look at disasters. They also inform our vantage point for looking at the effects of disasters on families and children and on methods for helping them manage those effects. The first perspective is family-centered, and the second is an integrated model that combines three different perspectives. An understanding of these perspectives should help you appreciate how we have organized this book, the various activities and examples we offer, and the information we present.

Family-Centered Perspective

Although the primary focus of the chapters that make up this book is on children—how disasters affect them and how they can be helped to recover from disasters—the book also takes a family-centered perspective (Bailey et al., 1998; Dunst, 1997; Minuchin, Colapinto, & Salvador, 1998). This emphasis on families reflects several beliefs about helping individuals, especially children, cope with trauma:

- Children live in a context of families and not in isolation. Research often focuses on the effects family members have on each other when each is coping with trauma.
- Given the effects family members have on children, helping professionals should cooperate with families when considering interventions.
- It is crucial for the professional to secure the input and involvement of the family to ensure an intervention's success.

We can contrast the family-centered perspective with three other approaches social workers and other professionals might use to work with families.

In a professional-centered approach, the helping professional is viewed as an expert who determines a family's needs from her or his own perspective instead of the family's. The professional implements interventions because she or he perceives that the family is incapable of solving its own problem.

In a family-focused approach, the family is viewed as needing professional services, advice, and assistance. Unlike the professional-centered approach, however, where interventions are implemented by the professional who perceives a need, in this approach the family is encouraged to use professional networks of services to meet their own needs.

In a family-involved approach, the family members are viewed as agents of the professionals; the family members are enlisted to implement both child- and parent-level interventions that professionals see as necessary for the benefit of the family.

A family-centered approach shares some characteristics with the three other approaches, yet adds a different perspective

TABLE 1-1. SUMMARY OF KEY PERSPECTIVES AND APPROACHES

FAMILY-CENTERED PERSPECTIVE

Emphasis is on:	Can be contrasted to:
Children live in a context of families and not in isolation.	*Family-focused approach.* The family is viewed as needing professional services, advice, and assistance.
Given the effects family members have on children, helping professionals should partner with families when considering interventions.	*Family-involved approach.* The family members are viewed as agents of the professionals.
It is crucial for the professional to secure the input and involvement of the family to ensure an intervention's success.	*Professional-centered approach.* The helping professional is viewed as an expert who determines a family's needs.

INTEGRATED MODEL

Three lenses are:	Assumptions of an integrated model:
1. *Cognitive or behavioral perspective.* Focuses on the functioning of individual family members.	1. Intervention in any dimension of a family's life resonates across all dimensions.
2. *Family systems perspective.* Focuses on the family as an indivisible system of interrelating people.	2. The context in which a person lives affects her or his cognitive and thinking abilities.
3. *Ecological perspective.* Focuses on the larger context—school, neighborhood, work, and community—in which families are embedded.	3. A person's thinking processes mirrors his or her family processes.

to the interaction between the professional and the family. With a family-centered approach, the professional is viewed as the agent and instrument of the family (unlike the professional-centered approach in which the professional is viewed as someone who acts on the family). In a family-centered approach, the professional intervenes in ways that help the family develop its capabilities and competencies so that it can help itself (unlike the family-focused approach in which the family is dependent on professional services to meet its needs). Finally, interventions, including service delivery and resource provision, are driven by the family's needs and desires (unlike the family-involved approach in which the family implements what the professional deems necessary).

Integrated Model: Three Lenses

In addition to the family-centered perspective, the chapters in this book study the effects of disasters on families and children using the integrated model developed by Roger Friedman (1993). This model acknowledges that to understand, plan for, and respond most effectively to the needs of children and families, helping professionals must draw on several theoretical perspectives. Each perspective focuses on a different level or view of the situation; by combining the perspectives, we understand the "big picture." The result is an integrated model of intervention that allows us to understand and serve families in a multilevel, comprehensive way.

The three key theoretical perspectives we use in our integrated model are (1) the cognitive or behavioral perspective, (2) the family systems perspective, and (3) the ecological perspective.

Cognitive or behavioral perspective.
This perspective focuses on the functioning of individual family members. Cognitive theory states that our thinking and attitudes have a profound effect on our feelings and behavior. Behavioral theory states that scientific principles govern the development, maintenance, and change of behavior. Cognitive or behavioral strategies often focus on teaching new skills.

Family systems perspective.
This perspective focuses on the family as an indivisible system of interrelating people. Family-systems theory assumes that a family's process or context is a key variable in determining individual functioning. Problems are not located in people but in relationships. Since change takes place in a "rippling" effect (any change to one part of the system eventually effects changes in the entire system), to influence one family member is to influence the whole family.

Ecological perspective.
This perspective focuses on the larger context—school, neighborhood, work, and community—in which families are embedded. It assumes that we must first understand the social environment of formal and informal supports around the family before we can understand family functioning. An ecological perspective carefully assesses the network of relationships and institutions that link families to their environment.

Another way to think of the integrated model is to envision it as a sequence of three lenses, each of which successively broadens our focus. The first lens focuses on the individual and provides the narrowest point of view. The second opens up our focus by considering the family. The third provides the broadest view by focusing on the community. Information provided by all three lenses is necessary for humane, effective intervention that has the potential of helping individuals and families address their complex needs.

Following are the three key assumptions of an integrated model of family-centered services; these assumptions are drawn from the three "lenses"—cognitive or behavioral systems, family systems, and ecological perspectives:

1. *Intervention in any dimension of a family's life resonates across all dimensions.* To teach a behavior management skill to a parent that results in a child adjusting to relocation after a disaster affects the cognitive skills of the parent and child, affects the family's process, and eventually affects the family's relationship to the school and other microsystems in which it is found. Therefore, a behavioral intervention is also a family and an ecological intervention.

2. *The context in which a person lives affects her or his cognitive and thinking abilities.* Members of a chaotic, grief-stricken family find it difficult to focus on problem solving. When a helping professional intervenes in the family process and provides structure, the professional also reduces anxiety and improves communication. As a result, family members may be able to think more clearly, examine alternatives more calmly, and solve problems more effectively. For example, when family members are facing homelessness, they may not be able to process information clearly; thus, an ecological intervention might be effective in addressing immediate cognitive problems.

3. *A person's thinking processes mirror his or her family processes.* How someone thinks about problems reflects not only her or his individual cognitions, but also the attitudes and methods of dealing with problems in that person's family. Both cognitive or behavioral and family system approaches can be effective. When deciding which approach to use, the professional helper should consider the family's style, the helper's abilities, and what works for a particular family (Friedman, 1993).

IMPORTANT TERMS USED IN THIS BOOK

The terms *disaster*, *child*, *victim*, and *survivor* appear frequently in the literature on disasters. Before going any further, we look at each of these terms and define how they are used in this book.

What Is a Disaster?

It is not unusual for individuals to have their own accepted wisdom about what a disaster really is, depending on their own experiences. Often, what researchers define as disasters differ from the usual, everyday definitions. The purpose of the Touching Reality "Preconceived Notions of What 'Disaster' Means" activity is to provide you and those with whom you may be working the opportunity to examine your preconceptions of a disaster's defining elements.

It is likely that the events labeled as disasters that you listed during the Touching Reality activity involve destruction of property, loss of life, and widespread injury. Historically, labeling an event a disaster means that it has several characteristics in addition to these three. According to Saylor (1993), a disaster also "has an identifiable beginning and end; adversely affects a relatively large group of people; is

---

TOUCHING REALITY

Preconceived Notions of What "Disaster" Means

What types of events do you think of when you hear the word disaster?

List all your responses.

What do these events have in common? How could you use this list to begin to describe the defining characteristics of events commonly called disasters?

You might have listed a "tragic" car accident in which someone is injured, for instance, or a "disastrous" house fire that affects a single family. For the purposes of this book, we will limit the scope of what we mean when we use the word disaster.

'public' and shared by members of more than one family; is out of the realm of ordinary experience; and, psychologically, is traumatic enough to induce stress in almost anyone" (p. 2). Vogel and Vernberg (1993) added three characteristics to this list: Disasters are "events that are relatively sudden, highly disruptive, [and] time-limited (even though the effects may be longer lasting)" (p. 465).

The American Red Cross (1987) classifies disasters according to five "levels." A Level I disaster is one that is both local and recurrent. Disasters at levels II, III, IV, and V range in how much they cost the American Red Cross: level II costs the agency less than $50,000, level III costs from $50,000 to $250,000, level IV costs from $250,000 to $2.5 million, and level V costs more than $2.5 million. Most (in)famous disasters are of the level V variety. The 1993 Midwest floods, according to FEMA estimates, cost $802 million, and the 1992 Los Angeles riots cost $180 million. By classifying disasters according to cost as well as type (which will be discussed below), the American Red Cross is able to make decisions about staffing and other response needs.

By combing the several perspectives, we can describe a disaster as an event that exhibits the following seven characteristics. A disaster

1. involves the destruction of property, injury, or loss of life, or more than one of these
2. has an identifiable beginning and end
3. is relatively sudden and time-limited (even though the effects may be long lasting)
4. adversely affects a relatively large group of people

5. is "public" and shared by members of more than one family
6. is out of the realm of ordinary experience
7. is psychologically traumatic enough to induce stress in almost anyone (see Touching Reality "Common versus Scientific Definitions of 'Disaster'").

If we apply the seven defining characteristics of disasters, many events that people consider "disastrous" and "traumatic," such as job loss, an individual house fire, and the murder of an individual in a robbery, would not qualify as disasters.

Types of disasters. In addition to enumerating characteristics that qualify an event as a disaster, another useful approach to devel-

---

TOUCHING REALITY

Common versus Scientific Definitions of "Disaster"

Examine the events that you labeled as disasters in the previous Touching Reality experience. Which ones fulfill the definition used by researchers?

Which events on your list have all seven of the characteristics that researchers indicate define a disaster?

Which of the characteristics is missing from each event?

Which of the seven characteristics, in general, seem important to you and which seem unimportant in the everyday use of the word disaster?

---

oping a typology of disasters considers the origin or etiology of the event. Raphael (1986) discussed two broad classifications: "natural" and "man-made" disasters; and Vogel and Vernberg (1993) subdivided man-made disasters into two parts: "acts of human violence, such as sniper shootings," and "failures of technology or results of human error, such as plane crashes and toxic contamination" (p. 465). Parson (1995) divided disasters into three categories: natural disasters, "disasters of human unintentional occurrence" (similar to Vogel and Vernberg's "failures of technology"), and "disasters of intentional human strategy" (similar to Vogel and Vernberg's "acts of human violence," pp. 164–165).

This book classifies disasters into three categories, *natural* (such as earthquakes and hurricanes), *technological* (such as plane crashes and toxic spills), and *complex* (such as terrorism, wars, and gang violence), to allow consideration of the broad range of events covered in the literature on disasters (see Touching Reality "Types of Disasters").

It is important to distinguish among the different types of disasters so that we may understand the different effects each has on children, families, and communities. Although the effects of disasters are covered in more depth in other chapters of this book, we present here some of the most relevant differences among the types of disasters with respect to their effects on children.

We offer the following summary of current research—and others throughout this book—to provide a closer look at how researchers study and think about disasters than is typically offered. There are many ways to learn about disasters, including direct experience, observation, interaction with clients, and reading the results of others' research. The Spotlight on Research sections of this book summarize important research articles and chapters on disasters and, together with the Touching Reality activities and examples, provide another way for you to learn about the effects of disasters on families and children, and how professionals can help families and children cope. In the Spotlight on Research "Children's Reactions to Disasters," two researchers present their summary of findings on children's reactions to disasters and then detail some of the variables that influence how a child is likely to react.

Natural disasters, such as earthquakes, tornadoes, fires, floods, and hurricanes, are disasters that usually strike suddenly with little or

Children's Reactions to Disasters

In this article, the first of a two-part report, Juliet Vogel and Eric Vernberg reviewed the research on disasters to discover what factors influence how children respond. The article begins with defining disasters as "events that are relatively sudden, highly disruptive, time-limited (even though the effects may be longer lasting), and public (affecting children from more than one family)" (p. 465). This definition excludes events that are certainly "disastrous," such as family violence, but are not within the bounds of this definition.

Systematic research of children's responses to disasters is relatively recent. Researchers conducted one of the first systematic studies in 1953, after a tornado struck a Vicksburg, Mississippi, movie theater during a Saturday matinee. Two months after the tornado parents completed a questionnaire (and researchers interviewed many of them) about their children's reactions. Early studied disasters include:

  1972: Buffalo Creek Disaster (Buffalo Creek, West Virginia)—collapse of a slag-mining dam caused flooding
  1976: Chowchilla School Bus Disaster (Chowchilla, California)—three men hijacked a school bus and held the driver and children hostage

The American Psychological Association (APA) introduced posttraumatic stress disorder (PTSD) as a diagnostic category in the *Diagnostic and Statistical Manual of Mental Disorders* (Third Edition–Revised) (DSM-III-R); the APA later added PTSD symptoms specific to children. Beginning in the 1980s, researchers have investigated children's responses to extreme stress, including disasters, more extensively.

Most common disaster responses of children include "specific fears [fear of recurrence is the most common], separation difficulties, and symptoms that are on a continuum of stress response syndromes and PTSD [such as reenactment in play, sleep problems, increased irritability, regression, somatic complaints, guilt]" (p. 468). School performance often declines.

Factors that influence children's reactions to a disaster are:

- life threat and exposure to the grotesque
- bereavement (that is, more severe reactions by those whose family members or close friends were killed or injured)
- separation (not only from parents, but from familiar surroundings)
- injury
- physical losses and disruption of the environment
- child's age
- child's gender
- child's prior pathology and prior traumatic experiences
- parents' responses (child responses may be correlated with the severity of parent responses)
- availability of social support

Vogel, J. M., & Vernberg, E. M. (1993). Task Force Report, Part 1: Children's psychological responses to disasters. *Journal of Clinical Child Psychology, 22,* 464–484.

no warning, and are caused by forces of nature. According to the Federal Emergency Management Agency (FEMA, 2003), after a natural disaster, children from ages birth to two may become irritable or cry and want to be held and cuddled more than usual; they often remember the sights, sounds, and smells associated with the trauma. Very young children, under age four, have an underdeveloped level of consciousness that prevents them from fully appreciating the extent of a natural disaster—what is important is their mother's or primary caretaker's reaction to the natural disaster. Preschoolers (ages two to six) tend to feel helpless and powerless after a natural disaster, whereas school-age children (6 to 10) may become preoccupied with the details of the trauma and experience a variety of reactions, including guilt, failure, or fantasies of "playing rescuer." Preteens and adolescents typically react in a manner that contains both childlike and adult elements. Teenagers may survive with a feeling of invulnerability, or they may be overwhelmed by their wide range of emotions and feel unable to discuss them with their family. Although some reactions are the same regardless of the type of natural disaster, many reactions differ depending on the specific disaster—for instance hurricane or earthquake (La Greca & Prinstein, 2002), wildfire (McDermott & Palmer, 2002), flood (Jacobs et al., 2002), or a residential fire involving many people, such as a dormitory fire (Jones & Ollendick, 2002).

Technological disasters occur when something made by humans and intended for human use becomes defective with little or no warning, resulting in psychological or physical harm, or both (Breton, Valla, & Lambert, 1993; Vernberg & Vogel, 1993). Examples are a building collapse, a plane crash, a train derailment, or the poisoning

that follows an industry mishap. Toxic spills and accidents at nuclear power plants—which are of course relatively recent events—differ from many other types of disasters because of their significant long-term consequences for human health and environmental welfare (Wroble & Baum, 2002). Unlike natural disasters, with which children often have some familiarity and some coping mechanisms, technological disasters present a challenge to those trying to help children cope. Children typically have little or no guidance as to how they should react or what their feelings mean when an unfamiliar disaster occurs. For example, children had no model to follow to guide their reac-

Earthquake in Turkey

On August 17, 1999, one of the most powerful earthquakes to hit the world in the past 100 years, 7.4 on the Richter scale, jolted the city of Sakarya, Turkey. It is uncertain how many people died because many buildings were bulldozed in an effort to avoid epidemics, although there are estimates as high as 40,000. More than 350,000 people were left homeless, angry, and frightened, and fires from factories, power plants, houses, and oil refineries made the already difficult rescue missions even more difficult.

The international community and Turkish citizens have criticized the Turkish government for not responding to the disaster in a timely and effective manner. Prime Minister Bulent Ecevit said that telecommunications failures were one of the main problems that caused the government's slow response.

Chernobyl Nuclear Power Plant Accident

The explosion at the Chernobyl nuclear power plant, which occurred on the morning of April 26, 1986, resulted from a safety experiment: Plant operators were testing the ability of plant equipment to provide electrical power, and the team in charge of the test had not coordinated the procedure with those responsible for the safety of the nuclear reactor. The Chernobyl power plant did not have the containment structure common to most nuclear power plants, so radioactive material escaped into the environment. Chernobyl Unit 4 reactor contained about 190 metric tons of uranium dioxide fuel and fission products, of which 13 percent to 30 percent escaped.

Belarus received about 60 percent of the contamination, and a large area in the Russian Federation south of Bryansk was also contaminated, as were parts of northwestern Ukraine.

Officially, the total number of fatalities caused by Chernobyl is small; however, researchers have classified as many as 600,000 people as "significantly exposed." Participants at a 1988 conference in Kiev estimated that 50,000 people had received 50 rad and about 2,000 people had received around 200 rad—an exposure of about 100 rad causes symptoms of radiation sickness; about 10,000 people were exposed to that amount in this disaster. Professional observers continue to see effects in those who were exposed to the radiation.

tions to the *Challenger* explosion (Wright, Kunkel, Pinon, & Huston, 1989). Similarly, after a toxic spill, children have a difficult time processing the disaster because such accidents have no definitive end; after such a spill children are left in a state of relentless anxiety and fear (Wroble & Baum, 2002).

Complex disasters, catastrophic events of intentional human design, include a much broader range of events than those that define natural and technological disasters. Community violence (Kuperschmidt, Shahinfar, & Voegler-Lee, 2002), civil war, government-sponsored terrorism, terrorism between nations, and war between nations (Gurwitch, Sitterle, Young, & Pfefferbaum, 2002; Klingman, 2002) are all examples of complex disasters. Summarizing numerous studies of the effects of war and political violence on children, Swenson and Klingman (1993) found, for example, that many children exposed to the war in Lebanon had "symptoms of post-traumatic stress…and feelings of betrayal that altered their sense of trust" (p. 139) and that children exposed to the political violence in Cambodia who lived "in foster care were more likely to have a psychiatric diagnosis than children living with their family" (p. 148).

Researchers who study children's reactions to complex disasters often ask parents to judge their children's behavior. In a study of reactions to the September 11, 2001, terrorist attack on the World Trade Center, Schlenger and his colleagues (2002) found that more than 60 percent of the parents in the New York metropolitan area reported that their children were upset, with the symptoms of those who were most upset including trouble sleeping, irritable behavior, and separation anxiety.

Sitterle and Gurwitch's (1999) study of the bombing of the Murrah Federal

Building in Oklahoma City found responses associated with different age groups unlike those found with natural disasters; this was especially true for very young children. For example, infants experienced more sleep difficulties and displayed clingy behavior; toddlers showed these behaviors as well as a heightened response to loud noises; and children ages three to five displayed regressive behaviors, such as toileting accidents.

Phases of disasters. Finally, disasters may be considered from the point of view of their predominant phases. Kafrissen, Heffron, and Zusman (1975), for example,

Bombing of the Alfred P. Murrah Federal Building, Oklahoma City

On April 19, 1995, at approximately 9:03 am, Timothy McVeigh set off a 4,800-pound explosive that blasted through the Alfred P. Murrah Federal Office Building in Oklahoma City. One hundred sixty-nine people were killed, including 19 infants and children; 614 were treated in outpatient clinics; and 82 were hospitalized. In addition to the people who were physically wounded, an immeasurable number of people were indirectly harmed. Thirty-eight percent of the population of the area knew someone who was killed or injured in the blast, and people who were in areas near the blast, such as children in nearby schools, were traumatized by the disaster. In addition, children who did not live in Oklahoma City or know anyone harmed in the bombing were affected by the disaster through a loss of their sense of safety.

defined seven stages through which people and communities go, beginning with the moment a disaster is imminent: (1) The first phase is *alarm*, when disaster is predicted (disasters that occur suddenly skip this phase), followed by (2) *threat*, when an assessment is made of the possible danger (again, disasters that occur suddenly skip this phase). Next is (3) *impact*, when the disaster occurs, followed by (4) *inventory*, when people survey the damage and recovery begins. This is followed by (5) *rescue*, when helpers begin to assist people that have been exposed to the disaster, and then (6) *remedy*, when morale is high due to the large-scale relief efforts taking place. The final stage is (7) *restoration*, when people begin to see that recovery is possible and that the community will survive.

Another useful, and often quoted, phase perspective is one developed by Farberow and Frederick (1996). Their first phase is the *heroic phase*, which occurs at impact and immediately thereafter, during which emotions are strong and direct and people are called on to respond in heroic ways to save their own and others' lives. Next is (4) the *honeymoon phase*, which occurs about a week after a disaster and can last several months. During this phase, there is an influx of support from government agencies, people clear debris, and trust that they will be helped. Community groups care for the needs of community members: Optimism is high. The honeymoon phase dissolves into the *disillusionment phase*, which can last for a year or more. Strong feelings of disappointment and bitterness occur due to inevitable delays or failures in promised aid, as outside agencies pull out, as community groups weaken, and as people turn from helping others to helping themselves. The final phase, the *reconstruction phase*, may last for

Phases of a Disaster

Eric Vernberg and Juliet Vogel (1993) described four temporal phases in disaster intervention.

1. Predisaster preparation phase
(before disaster onset)

During this phase the emphasis is on reducing physical danger, primarily through enhancing perceived control. Education regarding reactions, enhancing coping mechanisms, developing reaction plans—all are methods for preparing for a disaster and increasing citizens' feelings of preparedness and control in a disaster situation.

2. Disaster impact phase interventions
(from disaster onset through disaster end)

This is a highly emotional time, requiring "emotional first aid." Effective intervention requires support for leaders and helpers. Tasks during this phase include gathering and providing information through factual updates and telephone hotlines, such as notification of deaths and injuries and making contact with children and adolescents who have witnessed traumatic events. This contact provides an opportunity for these individuals to ventilate and acknowledge their strong feelings.

3. Short-term adaptation phase interventions
(from 24 hours to three months postdisaster)

During this phase children work to accept the events, acknowledge their emotional reactions, regain a sense of control, and resume their age-appropriate roles.

- *Classroom interventions:* This is a common setting because it brings children together naturally. Helping professionals use methods to allow the children to express their thoughts and feelings, understand what happened, and plan a return to ordinary routines. (Some techniques might be free drawing, open or task-focused discussion, role playing, writing free-verse poetry and stories, and projects that are designed to increase mastery of disaster-related events.)
- *Small-group interventions:* Professionals may see four to 12 children, usually those considered at "high risk" of psychological problems, in small groups. These groups are particularly useful for grieving and intense treatment.
- *Family interventions:* Professionals provide families with educational materials, activities to use with the children, and brief family therapy. This is most useful when a family member has been killed or injured.
- *Brief individual interventions:* In this intervention professionals use debriefing interviews, wherein the affected child retells the trauma under controlled conditions; they may also use creativity rooms; drugs; and individual psychotherapy.

4. Long-term adaptation phase interventions
(three or more months postdisaster)

Most symptoms are under control by three months; typically, only the most severely affected individuals are still in need of help.

- Individual psychotherapy (such as play therapy, behavioral and cognitive approaches)
- Family therapy
- Memorials, rituals, and gatherings of survivors

Vernberg, E. M., & Vogel, J. M. (1993). Task Force Report, Part 2: Interventions with children after disasters. *Journal of Clinical Child Psychology, 22,* 485–498.

several years as community members realize that they will have to do most of the rebuilding themselves to re-establish predisaster living.

Of course, all of Farberow's and Frederick's phases (1996) may take on different configurations dealing with a chronic disaster, such as wartime, or when dealing with communal violence, that stretches on for years, or even decades. In those instances, the reconstruction phase is more complicated, and risk of emotional damage and long-term effects are increased.

These descriptions of the phases people and communities go through during and after a disaster are useful only insofar as they inform assessment and intervention strategies. Spotlight on Research "Phases of a Disaster" presents a model that combines the phases of children's and community reactions to a disaster. This model should be useful for helpers who plan disaster interventions. (For a model of children's reactions to a disaster, see the discussion of Silverman and La Greca's, 2002, five-phase model—preimpact, impact, recoil, postimpact, and recovery and reconstruction—which we present in chapter 3.)

What Is a Child?

If you were to ask the ages that define a "child," you would probably be given a definition typical of the majority of people raised in the United States: A child is a person who is younger than 18 years old. At age 18 a person is considered old enough to enter into a legally binding contract.[1]

By no means is 18 a universally accepted age for "adult." Researchers often warn their readers to explore each cultural context individually (Boyden, 1994), and Cairns pointed out some examples of exceptions that make the warning a very reasonable one:

In South Africa, childhood has generally been defined as spanning the period from birth to 10 years old. However, between 10 years and 18 years, the term "youth" has been commonly used. In Palestine on the other hand, during the Israeli occupation, presumably because of the active role played there by children in the Intifada, [according to Ushewr, 1991, p. 15] "the Israel military's definition of the legal criminal age has been remarkably fluid. In 1987, it was 16; by 1988, 14; more recently it has been 12." (Cairns, 1996, p. 9)

Child labor laws are flexible in their definition of "child," as are the laws that distinguish young members of society who can be tried as adults and those who will be tried as children (for example, age 14 is the cutoff for considering a person an adult if the crime is a particularly heinous one). Indeed, ideas about children and childhood have changed significantly over the years. This is obvious not only through analysis of historical writings, but by examination of the way children are portrayed in the artwork of different eras. For example, until the Middle Ages, there was no separate category labeled "childhood," and children were treated as small adults—painters gave

---

[1] An exception is that 17-year-old "children" may be recruited for military service. The U.N. Convention on the Rights of the Child specifies 15 years of age as the minimum age for military recruitment, although there is discussion about raising it. At this time, 44 countries recruit people younger than 18 for military service, and some have been reported to recruit children as young as eight. "The latest research on child soldiers estimates that more than 300,000 children under 18 years old are fighting in armed conflicts around the world. Although most recruits are over 15 years of age, significant recruitment starts at 10 years, and the use of even younger children has been recorded" (Human Rights Watch, 1998)

children faces that are almost indistinguish-able from those of adults. Children can be seen as small adults, or "innocents," or as people needing training and discipline to become full members of society, or as young people enjoying an age of exploration—all these views affect how children are per-ceived by a culture and what age defines a "child" (Heller, 1998).

When we refer to children in this book, we will be referring to people under age 18. In some cases, however, this age may change when we consider different cultures; any changes will be indicated.

How Does a Victim Differ from a Survivor?

Young (1998), in her book for the National Organization for Victim Assistance (NOVA), defined the roles of disaster victims and disaster survivors. According to her defini-tions, victims are

individuals who took the brunt of the catastrophe; those at the center. There are dead victims; seriously physically injured victims; victims with minor physical injuries; victims who were not physically injured but were at the center and lost property; witnesses who lost nothing tangible but were at the center of the catastrophe—perhaps witnessing the death of someone else. (Appendix A, p. 22)

Survivors, however

- are individuals whose loved ones were killed in the disaster. They may include family members, friends, partners, and so on. May be preoccupied with how the victims died—did they feel pain, were they conscious, how long did the pain last?

- may be angry at the victims who survived and find it difficult to talk to their signif-icant others
- often encounter practical problems in body identification, death notification procedures, funeral arrangements, body transportation, and reclaiming the deceased's property
- often are angry at God, particularly when God spared others and not the loved one
- imagine the pain, the anguish, the fear that their loved ones endured may cause horror and revulsion
- may feel guilt at something they did or did not do, when seeing or talking with the victim just before he or she died
- have grief as the predominant emotion; however, for some survivors, their grief is repressed in their anger at immediate problems or the disaster itself. (Young, 1998, Appendix A, p. 23)

The primary distinction between a victim and a survivor hinges on the answers to two questions: (1) Did the disaster directly affect the individual? (2) Is the individual in a crisis state? If the answers to both are yes, the individual is a victim, and if the answers are no, he or she is a survivor. Problems arise, however, when the answer to one question is yes and the other no. For instance, there are people who may have been directly affected but are not in a crisis state—how should they be labeled? How do we label a woman who loses her home to a hurricane but is not unhappy about it, since she planned to move and will receive substantial compensation for her lost property? And how do we label a man who was not direct-ly affected by a terrorist attack—who was not injured physically, did not lose any prop-erty, and so on—but who identifies so strongly with those directly affected that he is in a crisis state?

Clearly, when a disaster occurs there are those who are adversely affected, who are either clients or potential clients—people in need of intervention to minimize the impact of the disaster on their well-being. To avoid the pitfalls of labeling—which denies people their humanity by identifying them with a state of being that ignores everything else they are—we will name a person who is suffering from the effects of a disaster a "disaster client." A client is a person first and not simply a victim or a survivor. If a helper can see the individual as an individual client suffering from the effects of a disaster, he or she is less likely to assume the existence of a crisis state—less likely to view the person as a victim—and more likely to begin interacting with the client to determine just what "suffering from the effects of a disaster" means for this particular individual.

Nevertheless, the word "victim" is still the word most commonly used to describe people suffering from the effects of a disaster, and the word "survivor" is still the word most commonly used to describe people who no longer suffer a great deal from the effects of a disaster but who suffered at one time. Therefore, the words victim and survivor define endpoints of a continuum along which people may be arranged. Where on the continuum someone stops being a victim and starts being a survivor is uncertain; however, looking at each affected person as a client and not simply as a category helps clarify the individual's unique needs to the helper.

Throughout this book, when we use the word victim we mean it in the special sense described here: A victim is a disaster client for whom the effects of a disaster cannot be assumed but need to be determined.

PLAN OF THIS BOOK

At this point, after reading the heading for this section, you are probably thinking about skipping right to the next chapter. Please do not neglect to read the next few pages. The short summary below of each chapter should help orient you and facilitate reading and applying this book to your own work. The book is divided into three parts, the first of which contains two chapters—this one and chapter 2—that provide a framework for understanding disasters. The second part, The Effects of Disasters, consists of five chapters (chapters 3 through 7) that focus on children's, families', and communities' reactions to the three types of disasters. The third section, Disaster Intervention, contains seven chapters (chapters 8 through 14) that provide a thorough look at intervention, beginning with preventive intervention and finishing with helping the helpers.

Chapter 2, Models for Considering the Effects of Disasters, begins with a brief review of four general models for looking at children's reactions to disasters: Gibson's model; Vernberg, La Greca, Silverman, and Prinstein's model; DeWolfe's model; and the circles of vulnerability and support. The chapter then goes on to distinguish individual and collective trauma, and to describe three models for looking at the effects of disasters and the implications of each model for developing interventions. The first model focuses on PTSD, which considers children more or less passive victims of a disaster. The second, newer model, focuses on resilience, including risk and protective factors, and views children as active, resourceful agents possessing qualities or having access to environmental resources that make them less prone to suffering ill effects. The third model, BASIC-Ph, which falls within a resiliency framework, focuses exclusively on recognizing and developing six different types of coping mechanisms for responding to disasters and other traumatic events.

Chapter 3, Children and Disasters: The Child's Reaction, begins by discussing factors that influence children's reactions to disasters, then focuses on developmental stages, as defined by Erik Erickson, and makes the connection between a child's reactions to trauma and disaster and her or his developmental stage, biological sex, prior exposure to disaster, proximity to the event, and family and community influences. Then, building on the work in chapter 2, the chapter discusses children's specific resiliency characteristics and their usefulness in assessing a child's likelihood to recover from a disaster.

Chapter 4, Family and Community Reactions to Disasters, presents four perspectives on families: (1) family systems theory, (2) family life cycle development, (3) family cohesion and adaptability, and (4) family resilience. This is followed by discussions of the stages or phases of family response to disasters, of the parent–child disaster-response relationship, and of the double ABCX model. The chapter also discusses how helpers may use each perspective to assess multiple stressors on a family as they attempt to manage the effects of a disaster. Furthermore, the chapter details how characteristics in a family can become risk or protective factors when the family experiences a disaster, and how a family's culture affects perceptions of and responses to a traumatic event, including the willingness of family members to interact with helpers after the event occurs. Finally, the chapter concludes with a discussion on community involvement in disasters, including the attributes of a community; risk factors in communities; community responses to disaster; and community healing.

Chapter 5, Natural Disasters, defines "natural disaster" and describes how this type of disaster differs from other types; discusses factors affecting discrepancies in the effects of natural disasters; explains how children, families, and communities commonly respond to natural disasters; and details the factors that can influence responses to natural disasters. Next, it studies the effects of natural disasters on vulnerable populations—elderly people, people with cognitive disabilities, emotionally fragile people, and pets. The argument is made for predisaster planning for individuals, families, and communities and that to intervene effectively and help children cope with the effects of disasters requires working with families and communities. The chapter concludes with descriptions of mitigation for children, families, and communities to recover from natural disasters.

Chapter 6, Technological Disasters, defines "technological disaster," discusses the inevitability of technological disasters, enumerates the various types of disasters that fall within this category, cautions against underestimating children's reactions, and explains why survivors of technological disasters tend to have stronger reactions to their traumatic experience than survivors of natural disasters have to theirs. After a discussion of secondhand exposure and the effects of technological disasters, the connection is drawn between risk for technological harm and minority group membership and low socioeconomic status. The chapter concludes by facilitating the reader's identification of the reactions he or she might experience when faced with a technological disaster, and identifies specific risk factors with which certain populations have to contend.

Chapter 7, Complex Disasters, defines "complex disaster" and details the variety of disasters that fall in this category. The chapter also considers children as direct targets and the importance of protecting children from complex disasters and those who perpetrate them. Next, it looks at families in complex disasters, communal violence, and the effects of different types of complex disasters on children and their families. The chapter studies the different active and passive coping mechanism children may use to respond to complex disasters, as well as ways children can be empowered. An important step toward empowering children is, as the chapter discusses, the United Nations' bill of rights for children. These rights include the child's right to life, to education and recreation, to freedom of expression, to dignity, and to special protection. The chapter concludes with consideration of the ways we are taught to hate and fear those who are different, and how hatred and fear provide fertile ground for wars and terrorism.

Chapter 8, Preventive Intervention, introduces the three phases of preventive care: primary prevention, secondary prevention, and tertiary prevention. "Primary prevention" is addressed in this chapter; secondary and tertiary prevention are addressed in chapters 9 and 10, respectively. Primary prevention, cognitive and organizational preparation for an expected disaster, aims to provide organizations, families, and potential caregivers with the skills necessary to deal effectively with any potential disaster. This chapter pays special attention to the major role schools can play in primary prevention. Chapter 8 also discusses the BASIC-Ph model as a preventive blueprint for group work with children and includes a description of the goals, structure, and activities of the Community Oriented Preventive Education (COPE) program, a generic stress-prevention program that has been implemented in several countries. Finally, the chapter reviews a 10-step protocol for organizational primary prevention and primary intervention in the family, and concludes with recommendations for creating a family disaster plan.

Chapter 9, Crisis Intervention, highlights the needs of children and families during secondary prevention, which is during and immediately after a disaster, and the value of working with groups in these situations. It begins with a discussion of helpers' goals in crisis intervention, then addresses the dual-level model of secondary prevention: immediate first aid during the impact phase of a disaster, and early crisis intervention conducted during the first six weeks after the event. The chapter addresses group crisis intervention, including multidimensional strategies for crisis intervention. The chapter discusses intervention with families, describes methods of group crisis intervention adapted to different age groups, and concludes with a discussion of the role of the school as an agent for preparing intervention programs, training helpers, and helping both children and adults cope with a disaster.

Chapter 10, Postdisaster Intervention, presents detailed descriptions of tertiary intervention, that is, methods for use with children and families in the long range. The chapter offers guidelines for helpers and details posttrauma interventions, including posttraumatic family interventions. The chapter also describes criteria for distinguishing functional from dysfunctional families after a disaster, and offers examples of methods of working with families within the context of each of five treatment phases. The chapter concludes with a look at mourning, including the relationship between bereavement and trauma, and the special issues that arise when a child or family is bereaving the loss of a family member and simultaneously responding to the trauma of a disaster. The therapeutic attitude proposed in this chapter is that all interventions need to respect natural resilience and enhance individual coping resources.

Chapter 11, Disaster Recovery with Vulnerable Populations, presents a workshop, complete with Trainer Notes and a Participant Handbook. The workshop starts with participants reflecting on what it is they do and, importantly, why they do what they do. This, then, leads to a discussion of resiliency and Maslow's need hierarchy, both of which frame explanations for why helpers use the methods they use in disaster recovery work. The second part of the workshop builds on the first and makes the transition to working with vulnerable populations. Participants assume roles that provide them with an experience of "what it is like to be a member of a vulnerable population and be exposed to a disaster." Participants enacting the role of helper gather information on making the transition from "helper with disaster clients without specific vulnerabilities" to "helper with disaster clients with specific vulnerabilities."

Chapter 12, The Community Disaster Plan, focuses on community preparedness and organization as ways to mitigate disasters. By being well organized and well prepared—by having a community disaster plan—a community can help ensure that it will move from destruction to recovery. The chapter stresses that plans must be tested in a variety of simulations involving both local services and the public and need to be evaluated and revised periodically, even if they are put to the test of a real disaster and found to be effective. The goal of an effective community disaster plan is to help community members to help themselves. The chapter concludes with a discussion of disaster plan failures, when a community fails to cope successfully with a disaster.

Chapter 13, Disasters and the Media, focuses on the uses and deficits of media involvement at the time of a disaster. The chapter explains how working with the media requires planning, training, and patience, and how choosing not to work with them may cause additional hardships to communities trying to cope with and recover from a disaster. It is important to establish a relationship with the media before a disaster occurs, to develop media relations skills, and to have a well-developed and tested crisis communication plan that minimizes coverage that inflicts further damage on communities. Working effectively with the media can facilitate the recovery of a community by disseminating information that enables the community to move from disaster to recovery, and that fosters hope for the future. Productive press relations are an important part of successful disaster recovery, and this chapter is a guide to developing and navigating that relationship.

Chapter 14, Helping the Helpers, presents a second workshop—also complete with Trainer Notes and a Participant Handbook—designed to provide disaster recovery workers with methods of self-care. The workshop begins with a description of stress and burnout and the factors that contribute to burnout in the disaster context. Through self-assessments of stress and stress reactions, the workshop enhances both understanding and application of the concepts to a recovery worker's own situation. A description of characteristics of effective coping behavior connects burnout to the development of interventions, and a presentation of Danieli's principles of self-healing provides the framework for developing and critiquing effective coping methods. Specific self-help methods are practiced in the workshop, including the use of guided imagery to release pain and sadness from disaster experiences, Critical Incident Stress Debriefing (CISD), Group Defusing, and Multiple Stressor Debriefing (MSD). The workshop concludes with the facilitator leading discussion on the advantages and disadvantages of CISD, Group Defusing, and MSD, and on where helpers would be able to access continued support.

SUMMARY

Recent increases in disasters of all types make it imperative to study their effects. By studying disasters we can develop strategies to help children, families, and communities prepare for and respond effectively; studying disasters also leads to improved training of workers who assist with disaster recovery efforts.

Two broad perspectives guide this book. The first is the family-centered perspective, which argues that professionals should intervene in ways that help the family develop its capabilities and competencies so that it can help itself. The second is the integrated model, which includes the cognitive or behavioral perspective, the family systems perspective, and the ecological perspective. The integrated model increases its focus from the individual to the family to the community.

The term *disaster* as used in this book differs from its everyday use. To qualify as a disaster, the event has to meet particular criteria: It has to adversely affect a relatively large group of people, be out of the realm of ordinary experience, and be psychologically traumatic enough to induce stress in almost anyone. Three types of disasters may be distinguished: (1) natural, (2) technological (human error or the unintentional failure of

technology), and (3) complex (disasters of intentional human design).

Disasters typically occur in phases, beginning with when the disaster is predicted (if it is predicted), through when the disaster occurs, through recovery. Phases also may be conceptualized as *heroic* (impact and immediately thereafter), *honeymoon* (recovery and high optimism), *disillusionment* (disappointment and bitterness), and *reconstruction* (community members rebuild).

The term *child* refers to an individual younger than 18 years of age, although 18 is not conversely a universally accepted age for "adult."

The term *victim* refers to those who the disaster directly affects and who are in a crisis state—people suffering from the effects of a disaster. The word *survivor* refers to people who no longer suffer a great deal from the effects of a disaster but who suffered at one time. As used in this book, the word victim refers to a disaster *client* for whom the effects of a disaster cannot be assumed but need to be determined.

REFERENCES

American Red Cross. (1987, May). *The disaster services human resources system member's handbook* (ARC Publication 4473). Washington, DC: Author.

Andersen, P. A. (1993). Cognitive schemata in personal relationships. In S. Duck (Ed.), *Individuals in relationships* (pp. 1–29). Newbury Park, CA: Sage Publications.

Bailey, D. B., Jr., McWilliam, R. A., Darkes, L. A., Hebbeler, K., Simeonsson, R. J., Spiker, D., & Wagner, M. (1998). Family outcomes in early intervention: A framework for program evaluation and efficacy research. *Exceptional Children, 64,* 313–328.

Boyden, J. (1994). Children's experiences of conflict related emergencies: Some implications for relief policy and practice. *Disasters, 18,* 254–267.

Breton, J. J., Valla, J.-P., & Lambert, J. (1993). Industrial disaster and mental health of children and their parents. *Journal of the American Academy of Child and Adolescent Psychiatry, 32,* 438–445.

Cairns, E. (1996). *Children and political violence.* Oxford, England: Blackwell.

Campbell, D. (Producer). (1999). *Hard rain: Lessons learned from the flood of '99* [Documentary]. (Available from the University of North Carolina Center for Public Television, 10 T.W. Alexander Drive, P.O. Box 14900, Research Triangle Park, NC 27709-4900)

Children's Defense Fund. (1994). *The state of America's children 1994.* Washington, DC: Author.

Dunst, C. J. (1997). Conceptual and empirical foundations of family-centered practice. In R. Illback, C. Cobb, & J. Herbert, Jr. (Eds.), *Integrated services for children and families: Opportunities for psychological practice* (pp. 75–91). Washington, DC: American Psychological Association.

Farberow, N. L., & Frederick, C. J. (1996). *Training manual for human service workers in major disasters* (DHHS Publication No. SMA 90-538). Washington, DC: U.S. Government Printing Office. (Original work published 1978)

Federal Emergency Management Agency. (2003, February 11). *Helping children cope with disaster.* Retrieved February 24, 2004, from http://www.fema.gov/rrr/children.shtm

Fitzpatrick, K. M., & Boldizar, J. P. (1993). The prevalence and consequences of exposure to violence among African-American youth. *Journal of the American Academy of Child and Adolescent Psychiatry, 32,* 424–430.

Friedman, R. (1993). Review of draft North Carolina family-centered/family preservation services training curriculum, Units I and II. Silver Spring, MD: Unpublished report.

Gullotta, T. P., & McElhaney, S. J. (Eds.). (1999). *Violence in homes and communities: Prevention, intervention, and treatment.* Thousand Oaks, CA: Sage Publications.

Gurwitch, R. H., Sitterle, K. A., Young, B. H., & Pfefferbaum, B. (2002). The aftermath of terrorism. In A. M. La Greca, W. K. Silverman, E. M. Vernberg, & M. C. Roberts (Eds.), *Helping children cope with disasters and terrorism* (pp. 327–357). Washington, DC: American Psychological Association.

Heller, S. (1998, August 7). The meaning of children in culture becomes a focal point for scholars. *Chronicle of Higher Education,* pp. A14–A16.

Human Rights Watch. (1998). *HRW condemns recruitment of child soldiers in Congo.* Retrieved September 20, 2003, from http://www.hrw.org/press98/aug/cong0811.htm.

Jacobs, G. A., Boero, J. V., Quevillon, R. P., Todd-Bazemore, E., Elliott, T. L., & Reyes, G. (2002). Floods. In A. M. La Greca, W. K. Silverman, E. M. Vernberg, & M. C. Roberts (Eds.), *Helping children cope with disasters and terrorism* (pp. 157–174). Washington, DC: American Psychological Association.

Jones, R. T., & Ollendick, T. H. (2002). Residential fires. In A. M. La Greca, W. K. Silverman, E. M. Vernberg, & M. C. Roberts (Eds.), *Helping children cope with disasters and terrorism* (pp. 175–199). Washington, DC: American Psychological Association.

Kafrissen, S. R., Heffron, E. F., & Zusman, J. (1975). Mental health problems in natural disasters. In H. L. P. Resnick, H. L. Ruben, & D. D. Ruben (Eds.), *Emergency psychiatric care: The management of mental health crises* (pp. 157–170). Bowie, MD: Charles Press.

Klingman, A. (2002). Children under stress of war. In A. M. La Greca, W. K. Silverman, E. M. Vernberg, & M. C. Roberts (Eds.), *Helping children cope with disasters and terrorism* (pp. 359–380). Washington, DC: American Psychological Association.

Kuperschmidt, J. B., Shahinfar, A., & Voegler-Lee, M. E. (2002). In A. M. La Greca, W. K. Silverman, E. M. Vernberg, & M. C. Roberts (Eds.), *Helping children cope with disasters and terrorism* (pp. 381–401). Washington, DC: American Psychological Association.

La Greca, A. M., & Prinstein, M. J. (2002). Hurricanes and earthquakes. In A. M. La Greca, W. K. Silverman, E. M. Vernberg, & M. C. Roberts (Eds.), *Helping children cope with disasters and terrorism* (pp. 107–138). Washington, DC: American Psychological Association.

McDermott, B. M., & Palmer, L. J. (2002). Wilderness area and wildfire disasters. In A. M. La Greca, W. K. Silverman, E. M. Vernberg, & M. C. Roberts (Eds.), *Helping children cope with disasters and terrorism* (pp. 139–156). Washington, DC: American Psychological Association.

Minuchin, P., Colapinto, J., & Salvador, M. (1998). *Working with families of the poor.* New York: Guilford Press.

Parson, E. (1995). Mass traumatic terror in Oklahoma City and the phases of adaptational coping, part I: Possible effects of intentional injury/harm on victims' post-traumatic responses. *Journal of Contemporary Psychotherapy, 25,* 155–184.

Raphael, B. (1986). *When disaster strikes: A handbook for the caring professions.* London: Hutchinson.

Rosenblatt, R. (1983). *Children of war.* Garden City, NY: Anchor Press.

Saylor, C. F. (1993). Children and disasters: Clinical and research issues. In C. F. Saylor (Ed.), *Children and disasters* (pp. 1–9). New York: Plenum Press.

Schlenger, W. E., Caddell, J. M., Ebert, L., Jordan, B. K., Rourke, K. M., Wilson, D., Thalji, L., Dennis, J. M., Fairbank, J. A., Kulka, R. A. (2002). Psychological reactions to terrorist attacks: Findings from the National Study of Americans' Reactions to September 11. *JAMA, 288,* 581–588.

Silverman, W. K., & La Greca, A. M. (2002). Children experiencing disasters: Definitions, reactions, and predictors of outcomes. In A. M. La Greca, W. K. Silverman, E. M. Vernberg, & M. C. Roberts (Eds.), *Helping children cope with disasters and terrorism* (pp. 11–33). Washington, DC: American Psychological Association.

Sitterle, K. A., & Gurwitch, R. H. (1999). The terrorist bombing in Oklahoma City. In E. S. Zinner & M. B. Williams (Eds.), *When a community weeps* (pp. 160–189). Philadelphia: Brunner/Mazel.

Solomon, Z. (1995). *Coping with war-induced stress: The Gulf War and the Israeli response.* New York: Plenum Press.

Swenson, C. C., & Klingman, A. (1993). Children and war. In C. F. Saylor (Ed.), *Children and disasters* (pp. 137–163). New York: Plenum Press.

Vernberg, E. M., & Vogel, J. M. (1993). Task Force Report, part 2: Interventions with children after disasters. *Journal of Clinical Child Psychology, 22,* 485–498.

Vogel, J. M., & Vernberg, E. M. (1993). Task Force Report, part 1: Children's psychological responses to disasters. *Journal of Clinical Child Psychology, 22,* 464–484.

Wright, J. C., Kunkel, D., Pinon, M., & Huston, A. C. (1989). How children reacted to televised coverage of the space shuttle disaster. *Journal of Communication, 39*(2), 27–45.

Wroble, M. C., & Baum, A. (2002). Toxic waste spills and nuclear accidents. In A. M. La Greca, W. K. Silverman, E. M. Vernberg, & M. C. Roberts (Eds.), *Helping children cope with disasters and terrorism* (pp. 207–221). Washington, DC: American Psychological Association.

Young, M. A. (1998). *The community crisis response team training manual* (2nd ed.) [Online]. Washington, DC: National Organization for Victim Assistance. Retrieved September 20, 2003, from http://www.ojp.usdoj.gov/ovc/publications/infores/crt/welcome.html

CHAPTER TWO

MODELS FOR CONSIDERING THE EFFECTS OF DISASTERS

CHAPTER OVERVIEW

After studying the material in this chapter, you should

- understand the elements that make up general models for looking at the effects of disasters on children and families, including the disaster event, children's and families' personal characteristics, and the several environmental contexts in which the children live
- be able to distinguish individual from collective trauma
- know that reactions to disaster situations are highly individual but fall into general patterns that are affected by age, culture, and prior traumatic experiences
- be able to describe the symptoms of posttraumatic stress disorder (PTSD) in adults and children and understand the PTSD model
- know the factors included in the resiliency model and identify potential risk and protective factors in a simulated situation
- understand that the BASIC-Ph model is based on strengths and focuses on the strongest, most comfortable coping strategies that the individual uses when under the stress of a disaster.

OVERVIEW

GENERAL MODELS FOR LOOKING AT CHILDREN'S AND FAMILIES' REACTIONS TO DISASTERS

An engineer would be foolhardy to begin building a bridge without having some idea about the overall plan, a plan that spells out the various elements that go into constructing the bridge, and how the elements fit together. In a similar way, before looking at specific models that focus on how families and children are affected by and cope with disasters, we need to "draw" a picture of the disaster event and its elements—and of how these elements fit together. These elements should include the disaster's characteristics; the children's and families' personal characteristics that mediate experiences of the disaster; and the ecological factors, including social and political conditions, that create the context in which the child and family live. This "big picture" highlights the enormous complexity involved in predicting how a particular disaster may affect a specific child, a group of children, or a family.

Although there are several specific models that apply to a particular group of victims, such as disaster relief workers, or a particular setting, such as schools (Eaves, 2001), several general models are also available. One general model, developed by Gibson (1989), focuses on acts of political violence; another, developed by Vernberg, La Greca, Silverman, and Prinstein (1996), applies to natural disasters. A third, broader model, developed by DeWolfe (2000a, 2000b), describes key factors that mental health and human service workers need to know to predict responses to any type of major disaster; and a fourth model, which is also broad, considers several "circles of vulnerability" for predicting responses to a disaster. Together, these four

models provide insight into the numerous elements that make up the disaster situation.

Gibson's Model

Gibson's (1989) model drew attention to five levels to consider: (1) the immediate stressful event; (2) interpersonal factors, such as the child's biological sex, temperament, and coping strategies; (3) interpersonal and contextual variables, such as family support and the support available from others; (4) wider contextual variables, such as social, political, and economic conditions; and (5) the link between ideological structures of the society—the society's cultural beliefs—and the factors on the other four levels. Gibson was concerned with how these five levels interacted in a dynamic way.

This model's emphasis on contextual variables, such as political and economic conditions, and broader variables, such as cultural beliefs, makes it one of the few that go beyond the child's and family's immediate environment. De Jong (2002) argued that without an understanding of the broad context, without "contextual insight," it was difficult to mobilize resources and help people cope.

Vernberg, La Greca, Silverman, and Prinstein's Model

The integrative conceptual model developed by Vernberg and his colleagues (1996) enumerated four factors that determine a child's reaction after a natural disaster, and described how these factors interact to affect the whole child. The model is broad; although it was developed for natural disasters, it may be logically extended to both technological and complex disasters.

The first factor Vernberg and his colleagues (1996) described in their model is the child's level of exposure to the traumatic event. This is the most crucial factor in determining whether she or he will develop symptoms of posttraumatic stress disorder (PTSD—later in the chapter we will describe those symptoms). La Greca, Silverman, Vernberg, and Prinstein (1996) found that a child's level of exposure to a natural disaster was a significant factor leading to PTSD symptoms seven to 10 months after the event. Wang and his colleagues (2000) found that the level of exposure to an earthquake predicted impairment in quality of life and psychological well-being three months and nine months after the disaster. (People from two villages in northern China, one closer to the earthquake's epicenter than the other, participated in the study.) Ginexi (1997) found that the level of exposure to the 1993 floods in the Midwest of the United States was the most informative predictor of coping behavior. Part of the relationship between exposure and well-being may concern a natural disaster's influence on a child's access to social support and his or her ability to use coping strategies (Vernberg et al. 1996).

The second factor Vernberg and his colleagues (1996) described in their model considered the individual characteristics of a child, such as biological sex, ethnicity, and age. These variables may be the most widely studied of all pre-existing characteristics, most likely because of the ease with which they can be measured (Silverman & La Greca, 2002).

The third factor was the characteristics of the social environment, such as access to social support networks, the availability of natural disaster–related interventions, and the functional ability of the adults in the child's life. For example, children with strong social support networks typically cope better with trauma than isolated children, and although parents offer the most significant source of support to children, peers and teachers also serve vital roles (Vernberg et al., 1996).

The fourth element Vernberg and his colleagues (1996) described in their model is based on the coping skills of a child. The four different types of coping strategies used in the model—(1) positive coping, (2) blame–anger, (3) wishful thinking, and (4) social withdrawal—are all associated with PTSD symptoms (Vernberg et al.). For example, research findings indicate that children generally use several of these coping strategies, positive and negative, to deal with a specific traumatic event. However, use of the negative coping strategy of blame–anger has been shown to be a strong predictor of PTSD symptoms (La Greca et al., 1996); in contrast, wishful thinking is a harmless coping strategy typically used after a major natural disaster (Vernberg et al.). The coping model that Vernberg and his colleagues discuss is only one of several available; we consider a different one, developed by Lahad (1997, 1999), that is broader and, perhaps, easier to apply in a disaster situation.

Building on the model developed by Vernberg and his colleagues (1996), La Greca and her colleagues (1996) and La Greca, Silverman, and Wasserstein (1998) added a fifth factor—any intervening stressful life events in a child's life. Traumatic life events unrelated to the natural disaster, such as the death of a family member or a divorce in the family, negatively affect a child's post-disaster reaction. In an interesting study of the effect of the Gulf War's psychological outcomes on the responses of military personnel to a subsequent natural disaster (Hurricane Andrew), Sutker and her colleagues, 2002) found that prior war trauma was associated with greater fears for safety and heightened psychological symptoms during the disaster. Those military personnel with pre-existing war-related PTSD reported higher depression, anxiety, anger, PTSD symptoms, and physical symptoms and lower self-esteem than those free of pre-existing war-related PTSD.

DeWolfe's Model

A third model—which is similar to the models developed by Gibson (1989) and by Vernberg and his colleagues (1996)—was developed by DeWolfe (2000b) specifically to help mental health and human services workers respond effectively to major disasters. From her review of research on how people respond to disasters, DeWolfe found three considerations to be the most crucial when predicting responses.

Her first consideration was the *disaster's characteristics*, which included five parts. The first part was whether the disaster had a natural or a human cause, although these are not necessarily disconnected. For instance, low-quality housing, which has a human cause, may exacerbate the damage from a flood, which has a natural cause. Some may view natural disasters as beyond human control, which may help them cope, whereas others may take the natural disaster as evidence that the world is unsafe and uncontrollable.

The second part was the disaster's degree of personal impact, including the family's or child's direct exposure to the disaster and the exposure of significant others and the community. A child's trauma from direct exposure to an act of terrorism, for example, is compounded with grief when a parent is hurt or killed, his or her house damaged or destroyed, or community services disrupted (Pfefferbaum, Call, Lensgraf, Miller, & Flynn, 2001; Pfefferbaum et al., 1999). Benight and his colleagues (1999) found that recovery from and responses to Hurricane Andrew in Florida in 1992 were contingent on the loss of resources, such as pets and sentimental possessions. Victims who report-

ed more resource loss also reported higher levels of active and avoidant coping behaviors and greater psychological distress.

The third part was the disaster's size and scope—the level of devastation. Widespread community destruction, for example, produces more severe reactions than localized destruction. A widespread disaster affects the community's ability to marshal resources, to make those resources available to the entire community, and to sustain those resources over a long period.

How visible the disaster is and how clearly marked are its beginning and end was the fourth part of DeWolfe's (2000b) disaster characteristics. These characteristics highlighted the chronic stress and anxiety caused when the effects of a disaster are "invisible," as is the case in toxic waste spills, or when the disaster has no clear beginning or end. A clearly defined end point allows the child, family, and community to bring closure: The disaster is over, and healing can begin. A case in point is Love Canal, near the Niagara River in New York and the homes built on more than 200,000 tons of chemical waste (Kim, 1998). It took years for the "invisible" underground technological disaster to be connected to the community's high rates of miscarriage and birth defects. When the disaster began and when it will end—effects persist to this day—are unknown.

The fifth part of DeWolfe's "characteristics of the disaster" considers the possibility that the disaster will reoccur. Many natural disasters, such as earthquakes, hurricanes, and floods, reoccur, which keeps anxiety high. For example, from a child's perspective, experiencing even a few natural disasters means feeling as if they occur "all the time." In a study of suicide rates after a natural disaster, Krug and his colleagues (1999) found no rise in the rate after one disaster but found a dramatic rise after a reoccurrence: "When we compared rates before the disasters with rates in the first two years after the second disaster, we found an increase of 14.8 percent" (p. 149).

The second consideration in DeWolfe's (2000b) model was the "characteristics of those exposed to the disaster." She noted that "each survivor experiences the disaster through his or her own lens. The meaning the survivor assigns to the disaster, the survivor's inherent personality…world view and spiritual beliefs contribute to how that person perceives, copes with, and recovers from the disaster" (DeWolfe, sec. 2, p. 4). Do those exposed to the disaster have financial resources? Is a viable social support network in place?

The third consideration is disaster relief efforts. What pre-existing disaster plan did the community have in place? How do disaster relief efforts adapt to community members—for example, are broadcasts, emergency aid materials, and relief workers sensitive to the various groups and languages represented in the community? Do relief efforts change as the disaster's phases change? For example, efforts needed during the threat of a disaster, such as helping people evacuate an area, are different from those needed during the "disillusionment phase," when unrelenting stress may trigger a high need for counseling services.

Figure 2-1 is based on a figure developed by Rosenfeld, Lahad, and Cohen (2001). It depicts how the factors from the three models fit together to help predict a child's or a family's response to a disaster— a prediction that depends on consideration of all the factors simultaneously. The model's concentric circles start with the disaster itself—the trigger event—and broaden to the wider context within which the family and child live. At the same time, each circle

After Hurricane Fran in North Carolina

An interviewer spoke with family members who had been through Hurricane Fran and asked: What do you remember about Hurricane Fran? What did you do after the hurricane? Were you afraid?

The older sister, seven years old, remembers waking up at 4:00 A.M. to go to the bathroom and seeing a tree bending over, and then breaking, in the wind. She remembers being afraid and staying with her parents after that. She also has a stark memory of the noise of the glass breaking, as the wind came through the den. She remembers her sister waking up the following morning and, seeing tree limbs jutting into the room, asking, "Where are we?"

Both parents remember the inexhaustible questions that the girls asked: "Why does God make hurricanes? Why did it hit us? Why do some people get killed? Will this happen again?" They answered the questions as honestly as possible, without lying or making false promises. They focused on the low frequency of hurricanes in the past, but this came back to haunt them. While they were seasoned to expect a hurricane once in a lifetime, their children are experiencing a hurricane once every few years, with major hurricanes Andrew, Bertha, Fran, Hugo, and Floyd occurring in recent years.

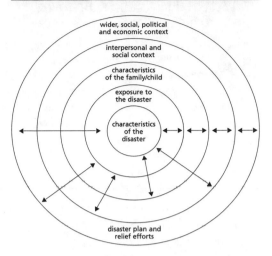

that it is possible to predict which people are most likely to experience inordinate problems and, therefore, the people who will need extended help. Predictions are based on consideration of three "circles of vulnerability" and one "circle of support." The three circles of vulnerability help assess a person's risk. The first circle considers the person's physical proximity to the disaster, the second considers her or his psychological or social proximity, and the third considers the extent to which she or he may be a member of a known at-risk population. The circle of support helps assess a person's available support systems, which is an important resource.

is connected with its adjoining circle and all the other circles in the diagram. While one factor may be more important than the others in a particular circumstance, it is only after consideration of all the factors and their interactions that a reaction to a disaster may be understood fully.

Circles of Vulnerability and Support

Professional helpers working with people who have experienced disasters recognize

Circles of physical vulnerability. There are four concentric circles of physical vulnerability (Figure 2-2). Each one describes a more intense level of vulnerability, ranging from the most vulnerable (the inner circle) to the least vulnerable (the outer circle):

1. People in the first, innermost circle are victims: They experience direct exposure to the disaster and are the most vulnerable.
2. People in the second circle are witnesses who have a near-miss experience. People in this circle are less vulnerable than those in the first circle but are still quite vulnerable.
3. People in the third circle are those within hearing, feeling, smelling, and so on of the disaster but who do not witness it. They are less vulnerable than those people in either of the first two circles.
4. People in the fourth circle are outside the disaster area, in distant neighborhoods and communities—potentially the whole nation for some disasters, such as the terrorist attacks in the United States on September 11, 2001. Typically, these people are the least vulnerable; however, it

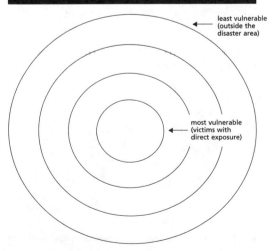

is difficult to assess what circle children—and adults—occupy who witness events on television, hear about them on radio, or read about them in newspapers. Although it seems logical to place those children in this fourth circle, highly sensitive children are more likely to occupy one of the other circles—that is, be more vulnerable to the disaster's effects.

Circles of psychological or social vulnerability. Three concentric circles describe levels of psychological or social vulnerability (Figure 2-3). These range from the most vulnerable in the inner circle to the least vulnerable in the outer circle:

1. People in the first, innermost circle are those socially close to people who experienced the disaster, such as family members, friends, and others with whom they have a close personal relationship. These people are the most vulnerable.
2. People in the second circle are those who know the victims as acquaintances or as friends who are not considered "close." These people are less vulnerable than those in the first circle, but they are still quite vulnerable.
3. People in the third circle are those who identify with the victims. They may see themselves as similar to the victims in age, ethnicity, occupation, or they may perhaps identify themselves as citizens of the same country. Although less vulnerable than those in the other two circles, people in this third circle are still vulnerable to the disaster's effects.

Circles of risk associated with prior experiences. There are four concentric circles of risk associated with a person's experiences and well-being before the

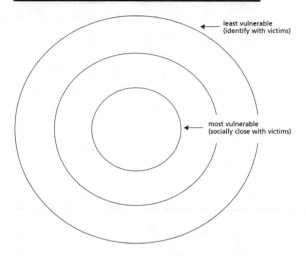

FIGURE 2-3. CIRCLES OF PSYCHOLOGICAL OR SOCIAL VULNERABLITY

least vulnerable
(identify with victims)

most vulnerable
(socially close with victims)

disaster (Figure 2-4). These range from most vulnerable, in the inner circle, to least vulnerable, in the outer circle:

1. People in the first, innermost circle—those who are the most vulnerable—experienced a similar trauma in the past. Children and adults who live in areas where there is an ongoing, yearly threat of hurricanes, for example, are continuously retraumatized. The effect often is cumulative.

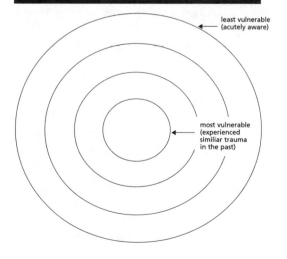

FIGURE 2-4. CIRCLES OF RISK ASSOCIATED WITH PRIOR EXPERIENCES

least vulnerable
(acutely aware)

most vulnerable
(experienced similiar trauma in the past)

2. In the next level of vulnerability are people who experienced a significant loss over the past year, such as the death of a family member, the loss of a job, or a divorce.

3. People in the third circle are those who are in the middle of a severe personal or social crisis, something that may be particularly relevant to preadolescent and adolescent children, characterized by their independence and search for identity. Disasters, especially those of human design, including terrorism, may trigger a loss of faith in adults. They may perceive the world as dangerous and unpredictable because those who are supposed to take care of things appear incapable.

4. People in the fourth circle are those who are particularly sensitive to or acutely aware of the events around them. Children ages from six to 11, for example, have an increasing awareness of the danger around them, both to themselves ("Can a terrorist come to our home?" "Will the floods on the coast reach our home?") and their family ("Will a bomb kill Daddy?" "Will Mommy make it home in her car if the streets are flooded?").

Circles of support. Just as there are circles that help conceptualize an individual's vulnerability to the effects of a disaster, there are circles that provide an indication of available support (Figure 2-5). Support serves as a protective factor; therefore, the larger and more dense the support network—beginning with the innermost circle and working outward to the fourth circle—the less vulnerable the person exposed to the disaster is.

1. People in the first circle are those who are most familiar with the victim and

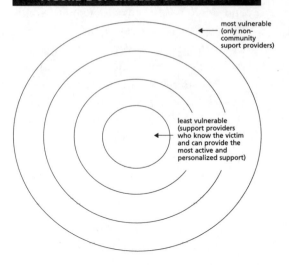

FIGURE 2-5. CIRCLES OF SUPPORT

most vulnerable (only non-community suport providers)

least vulnerable (support providers who know the victim and can provide the most active and personalized support)

available to provide the greatest degree of personalized and individualized support. Typically, people in this circle include family members and nearby friends and relatives.

2. People in the second circle may know the victim personally, although not as personally as do people in the innermost circle. People in the second circle can provide support to and are readily accessible by the victim, although not as accessible as family members. This group of support includes teachers, neighbors, mental health workers, and school counselors.

3. The third circle contains community members who provide both direct and indirect support for the victim, and who probably do not know the victim personally. People in this group include firefighters and police officers, school principals, the district superintendent, and other community members, such as the mayor.

4. The fourth circle contains agencies outside the community that provide support for disaster victims, such as the Red Cross and the Red Crescent, and FEMA.

A victim will probably have a variety of support providers. These include people who know the victim well and who provide direct and personalized support, such as a parent; people who know the victim, but not as well, such as a teacher; community members who do not know the victim personally at all, such as firefighters; and agency representatives from outside the local community, such as American Red Cross or FEMA representatives. The best circle in which to locate a victim is the one in which she or he can fit that is closest to the center. For example, if someone has family support, she or he is in the innermost circle, even if other support is available.

Considering all the factors used for predicting how a family or child will *most likely* respond to a disaster—those enumerated by Gibson (1989), Vernberg and his colleagues (1996), DeWolfe (2000b), and the several circles of vulnerability—it is evident that making predictions is a highly complex task and that any prediction has a chance of being wrong. To understand how the factors fit together and influence each other, it may be helpful to begin with self-examination: How might you respond to a disaster? What are your personal strengths and skills that help determine your reaction? Does your experience in other disaster situations prompt associations with this disaster? What in your social context helps you cope (support from relatives, neighbors, friends, coworkers, and others)? What in your social context works against your coping successfully? Does your community have a disaster plan, and are you familiar with it? The Touching Reality "Reacting to a Disaster" experience will help you answer these questions by presenting you with some disaster situations and having you record your responses.

The Explosion of Pan Am 103

On December 21, 1988, a disaster occurred when Pan Am flight 103— "Maid of the Seas"—exploded in midair over the small town of Lockerbie, Scotland.

The Pan Am 747-100 departed from London Heathrow Airport (LHR), running 25 minutes behind schedule. While the crew was preparing for the Atlantic crossing, approximately 35 to 40 minutes after departure from LHR, an explosion ripped through the fuselage. The plane broke into three pieces: the wings, the main plane fuselage, and the cockpit and first class lounge. Pieces of the plane landed on Lockerbie, killing 11 residents, and all 259 people onboard.

Eventually, investigators traced the explosion's source to a piece of luggage that was loaded onto an Air Malta flight that had departed from Malta, en route to Frankfurt Airport (FRA), in Germany. At FRA the piece of luggage, a suitcase, was transferred onto a waiting Pan Am 727 bound for LHR. Upon arrival at LHR, the suitcase containing the bomb was transferred to the doomed aircraft, the Pan Am clipper flight destined for New York. The criminal investigation indicated that if the 747 had taken off on time, the bomb would probably have blown up over the Atlantic Ocean, leaving little or no traces of explosive compound behind—and leaving an open question as to whether it had been a bomb that caused the accident.

The Buffalo Creek Flood

In the days preceding February 26, 1972, rain fell almost continuously on Buffalo Creek, West Virginia, although experts later claimed this was typical for late winter weather in the area. Buffalo Mining Company officials, concerned about the condition of the highest dam on the creek, measured water levels every two hours the night of the 25th. Although a Pittston official in the area was alerted to the increasing danger, the residents of the hollow below the dam were not informed. The Company sent away two deputy sheriffs, who had been dispatched to assist with potential evacuations. Despite the lack of warning from company officials, some residents sensed the danger and moved to higher ground.

Just before 8:00 A.M. on February 26, heavy-equipment operator Denny Gibson discovered the water had risen to the crest of the impoundment and noted that the dam was "real soggy." At 8:05 A.M., the dam collapsed. The water obliterated the other two impoundments, and approximately 132 million gallons of black wastewater rushed through the narrow Buffalo Creek hollow.

The 15- to 20-foot wave of black wastewater gushed at an average of seven feet

per second and destroyed one town after another. A resident of Amherstdale commented that before the water reached her town: "There was such a cold stillness. There was no words, no dogs, no nothing. It felt like you could reach out and slice the stillness" (Erikson, 1976).

Another resident commented on the rushing tide: "This water, when it came down through here, it acted real funny. It would go this way on this side of the hill and take a house out, take one house out of all the rows, and then go back the other way. It would just go from one hillside to the other" (Erikson, 1976).

In a matter of minutes, 125 people were dead, 1,100 were injured, and over 4,000 were left homeless.

The flood had destroyed 1,000 cars and trucks.

The flood demolished 502 houses and 44 mobile homes and damaged 943 houses and mobile homes. Property damage was estimated at $50 million.

Even a cursory view of the general model for looking at how children and others respond to a disaster should make it clear that different individuals respond to disasters in different ways; this fact should not be lost even though there may be commonalities between or among people. Your own reactions to the disasters in the Touching Reality experience may be similar to others', but the similarities should not mask the important differences that also exist. To determine whether a person or family is in crisis after experiencing a major stressor such as a disaster, it is essential to ascertain their perception of how serious or overwhelming that situation is for them.

INDIVIDUAL AND COLLECTIVE TRAUMA

In his book, *Everything in Its Path: Destruction of Community in the Buffalo Creek Flood*, Erikson (1976) described two types of disaster trauma—individual trauma and collective trauma. Individual trauma occurs when a disaster or trauma breaks through a person's defenses suddenly and with such force that she or he cannot react to it effectively. A state of shock ensues characterized by numbness, survivor's guilt, and a loss of faith in social order.

Collective trauma occurs when a disaster or trauma damages the bonds that connect people and destroys the basic tissues of social life and the prevailing sense of community. Moral anchors are lost; morale plummets. People feel disoriented, "torn loose from their moorings" (Erikson, 1976, p. 212), and disconnected from each other and their collective "self." They no longer perceive the world as being safe.

Abadian (2000) used the notions of individual and collective trauma to discover why Native Americans who live on reserves and reservations suffer disproportionately from poverty, poor health, violence, and alcohol and substance abuse. When individual and collective traumas occur together, Abadian argued, the capacity of people to heal is crippled, so the trauma persists from generation to generation.

In this and other chapters, we discuss both of these types of trauma at great length, how they connect, and how they affect each other. We begin by discussing three models used to study individual human reactions to disasters—the PTSD model, the resiliency model, and the BASIC-Ph model (which falls within a resiliency framework). While reactions vary from person to person, there are patterns that appear often enough to allow for a general assessment of the trauma a person experiences, as well as her or his coping strengths.

Until recently, studies of individuals and the communities where disasters occurred focused almost entirely on the negative effects the experience had on the people or community involved. For example, on the individual level, data typically are gathered on how many people are injured and how many need intensive counseling; at the community level, data are gathered on the breakdown of civil order. Although disaster-relief and mental health workers recognize that some people fare better than others, attention nevertheless remains primarily on damage done and injuries received. The PTSD model reflects this focus.

POSTTRAUMATIC STRESS DISORDER MODEL

According to Keppel-Benson and Ollendick (1993), "prior to the 1950s, there was little systematic investigation into the effects of traumatic events on children or adolescents.... This is not to suggest that children and adolescents were free from trauma; to the contrary, their lives were characterized by considerable turmoil that today would be described as 'out of the range of usual human experience'" (p. 29).

Observers have documented adult reactions to disasters for at least three centuries. For example, although PTSD as a formal mental health diagnosis first officially appeared in the psychiatric literature in 1980, Samuel Pepys's compilation of his own psychological symptoms following the 1666 Great Fire of London corresponds to our current description of PTSD (Daly, 1983; Lamprecht & Sack, 2002). Trimble (1985) documented the use of terms such as "shell shock" before 1900, although the term came into common use during World War I as a description for a combat-related syndrome; shell shock and war neuroses, however, soon expanded to include soldiers who developed certain symptoms even in the absence of explosions. It is interesting—and frightening—that during World War I some of the soldiers labeled as suffering from shell shock, who today would be diagnosed as having PTSD, were executed for cowardice (Joseph, 1997).

The first edition of the American Psychiatric Association *Diagnostic and Statistical Manual of Mental Disorders* (DSM–I), published in 1952, contains a diagnosis of "gross stress reaction," a designation later dropped. "Posttraumatic stress disorder" was first described in the 1980 DSM–III, probably because of studies conducted during the Vietnam War, and much of the scattered literature was compiled. The revised third edition, DSM–III–R, published in 1987, added PTSD symptoms specific to children. The description evolved with each edition of the DSM.

In the latest edition of the DSM, DSM–IV–TR (American Psychiatric Association, 2000), six diagnostic criteria for PTSD are presented. The first criterion is "exposure to a traumatic event" in which the person is threatened with death or injury to self or others and to which he or she responds with "intense fear, helplessness, or horror." A note is added to this section about children: Their reaction may include "disorganized or agitated behavior" instead of intense fear and the other "adult" reactions. It is important to note that one of the key variables in defining the event as traumatic is the individual's *subjective interpretation*.

The second diagnostic criterion for PTSD focuses on "persistent re-experiencing of the traumatic event." This includes intrusive distressing recollections (this may show up in children's play); distressing dreams; acting or feeling as if the event is reoccurring; and intense psychological or physiological distress when in the presence of reminders of the trauma.

The third criterion details "persistent avoidance of stimuli associated with the trauma and numbing of general responsiveness." A list of seven markers is presented, three of which need to be present for a diagnosis of PTSD. Markers include avoiding things that arouse recollections, disinterest in important activities, and a restricted range of emotions.

The fourth diagnostic criterion for PTSD centers on "persistent symptoms of increased arousal," as indicated by two of five marker behaviors, such as irritability and difficulty concentrating.

The fifth and sixth criteria are "duration of more than a month" ("acute" is less than three months, and "chronic" is more than three months) and "distress or impairment in functioning that is clinically significant," respectively.

Some effects can be quite long lasting. For example, Green and associates (1991) reported that 17 percent of the survivors of the 1972 Buffalo Creek flood disaster in

PTSD and the Aftermath of the Buffalo Creek Flood

On Saturday morning, February 26, 1972, the collapse of a slag dam resulted in a flood of black wastewater and sludge that caused 125 deaths and substantial community destruction in Buffalo Creek, West Virginia. Reports were collected two years later, and examined for symptoms of PTSD and possible relationships between children's PTSD symptoms and age, biological sex, flood experience, and parental responses.

Data from 118 families were collected through interviews. Bereavement was measured by the closeness of the person lost in the flood (0 = no loss; 4 = immediate family member lost). Flood stress was measured by assessing exposure, including degree of warning, contact with the flood, family separation, and the extent of exposure to the elements. The severity of parental reaction was assessed. "Family atmosphere" was assessed along the dimensions of depressed or gloomy, irritable, violent, and supportive.

PTSD symptoms routinely noted were "flood related dreams or nightmares, distress at exposure to reminders, sleep disturbances, restricted affect, avoidance of reminders, irritability, and difficulty concentrating" (p. 947). "Probable" PTSD was diagnosed in 37 percent of the children, with "distress at exposure to reminders" and "thinking about the flood" the most frequent symptoms (65 percent of the children).

The authors concluded that, "adolescents seem to be more influenced by parents' reaction than their latency age siblings. Perhaps they are the ones that endure the worst of parental reactions if parents are functioning poorly...or they may be more likely to identify with parental affects of survivor guilt or responsibility.... The strongest predictors of the number of symptoms across the three age groups [two to seven, eight to 11, and 12 to 15] were the overall level of functioning of the parents along with an irritable atmosphere in the home" (p. 950).

Green, B. L., Korol, M., Grace. M. C., Vary, M. G., Leonard, A. C., Gleser, G. C., & Smitson-Cohen, S. (1991). Children and disaster: Age, gender, and parental effects on PTSD symptoms. *Journal of the American Academy of Child & Adolescent Psychiatry, 30*, 945–951.

West Virginia still experienced PTSD symptoms 14 years after the event. (As indicated in the Spotlight on Research "PTSD and the Aftermath of the Buffalo Creek Flood," as many as 37 percent of the children had PTSD symptoms two years after the flood.) A study in 1992 and 1998 of Dutch veterans of World War II revealed no change in the percentage (approximately 28 percent) that experienced PTSD (Dirkzwager, Bramsen, & Van Der Ploeg, 2001). Some World War II veterans showed continued PTSD up to 40 years later (Joseph, 1997).

PTSD and Children

According to DeBord (2000) and DeWolfe (2000a), possible stressful reactions to a disaster vary from age group to age group. For example, preschool children (ages one to five) may react by exhibiting uncontrollable crying and by being excessively clingy, whereas children ages six through 11 are more likely to regress, have trouble sleeping, display irrational fears, and refuse to go to school. (Nightmares are common in both groups of children—from one to five and from six to 11 years of age.) Children in their early adolescence (12 to 14) and adolescence (14 to 18) may withdraw, become depressed, or display antisocial or delinquent behavior, such as aggression.

How many children should we expect to exhibit PTSD symptoms after a disaster? That depends on the type of disaster—not only on whether it was a natural, technological, or complex disaster, but more specifically on what particular type of natural, technological, or complex disaster it was. For example, Belter and Shannon (1993; see also Saylor, Belter, & Stokes, 1997), in their summary of research on the effect of natural disasters on children, reported large variations in the percentage of children who suffer both short- and long-term effects from a disaster. They found that it depends on the type of natural disaster, the child's age and biological sex, prior psychological problems, family reactions, and so on. They summarized their review by stating that "diagnosable psychopathology is not commonly seen in the great majority of children who experience a natural disaster" (Belter & Shannon, p. 99). In addition, long-term effects appear to be minimal. Then they offered this caveat: The more directly the child experiences the disaster and the more disruptive the disaster, the greater the psychological impact.

A recent investigation of children's reactions to a flood, including PTSD symptoms, provided estimates from school-age children three months after the disaster (Kreuger & Stretch, 1999). Approximately 9 percent of the students were identified as needing services by each school's counseling department, with 20 percent of students showing elevated anxiety and 6 percent showing signs of depression.

Green and his colleagues (1991) reported a much higher estimate of children in need of services reported in their follow-up examination of children who survived the Buffalo Creek flood of February 26, 1972. They noted routine PTSD symptoms two years later that were "flood related dreams or nightmares, distress at exposure to reminders, sleep disturbances, restricted affect, avoidance of reminders, irritability, and difficulty concentrating" (Green et al., p. 947). As noted in the Spotlight on Research "PTSD and the Aftermath of the Buffalo Creek Flood," "probable" PTSD was diagnosed in 37 percent of the children, with "distress at exposure to reminders" and "thinking about the flood" the most frequent symptoms (in 65 percent of the children).

Focusing on the diagnostic usefulness of 48 symptoms of PTSD, Lonigan, Anthony, and Shannon (1998) studied more than 5,000 children exposed to Hurricane Hugo. They found 5.5 percent had a diagnosis of PTSD. They concluded that the DSM–III–R numbing/avoidance cluster, and symptoms from the numbing/avoidance cluster, had the highest diagnostic efficacy, suggesting that avoidance may be the hallmark of severe posttraumatic reactions.

Results of a follow-up investigation of children's reactions to Hurricane Andrew (Vincent, 1998) indicated that the 43 children who reported high levels of PTSD symptoms 10 months after the hurricane were still showing signs of PTSD 44 months after the hurricane. Specifically, 16 children (40 percent) continued to qualify for a full

PTSD diagnosis. Re-experiencing symptoms were most frequently endorsed (92.5 percent), followed by hyperarousal (80 percent) and avoidance/psychic numbing symptoms (45 percent). According to the researcher, findings supported the conclusion that a substantial number of children may experience significant long-term disaster-related problems.

A great deal of new work is underway to develop tools for screening children for PTSD—prompted in part by the September 11, 2001, attacks. Assessing PTSD in children, however, is difficult (Drake, Bush, & van Gorp, 2001; Ronen, 2002), beginning with the controversy regarding whether children develop PTSD at all. Some argue yes, and some argue that children respond normally to traumatic experiences and, "after a time, return to their usual pattern of behavior" (Ronen, 2002, p. 89). As Ronen pointed out, assessment results are influenced by who does the assessment (parents and children often disagree on the children's reactions), who is present during the assessment (children may underreport their reactions in the presence of their parents), what is asked (children may not understand the language used in a self-report measure), and when an assessment is conducted (initial reactions and reactions at various times postdisaster may be different). Drake and associates (2001) proposed that the most effective way to assess PTSD in children is through a multidimensional approach, one that can include an assessment of a child's cognitive, emotional, behavioral, developmental, and academic functioning and interviews with parents.

The need for assessment tools, especially valid and reliable ones that are easy to use for screening and that can provide a first step in diagnosis, drives the continuous development of self-report measures. (For a review of standardized measures and procedures, see Drake et al., 2001, and Wilson & Keane, 1997.) A new instrument, developed by Greenwald and Rubin (1999), provides an example of a simple-to-use, efficient measure of PTSD for children eight through 13 years old—one for which there is preliminary evidence of validity. The measure has two parts. One is a self-report a child completes, and the other an instrument for parents to complete about their child. The child self-report instrument, CROPS (Child Report of Post-Traumatic Symptoms), developed using groups of third-grade through eighth-grade students, is made up of 25 items that a child rates 0 (none), 1 (some), or 2 (lots):

1. I daydream
2. I "space out" when people are talking to me
3. I find it hard to concentrate
4. I think about bad things that have happened
5. I try to forget about bad things that have happened
6. I avoid reminders of bad things that have happened
7. I worry that bad things will happen
8. I do special things to make sure nothing bad happens
9. It is hard for me to go to sleep at night
10. I have bad dreams or nightmares
11. I do some things that I am probably too old for
12. I get headaches
13. I get stomachaches
14. I feel sick or have pains
15. I feel tired or low energy
16. I feel all alone
17. I feel strange or different than other kids
18. I feel like there is something wrong with me

19. I feel like it is my fault when bad things happen
20. I am a jinx or bad-luck charm
21. I feel sad or depressed
22. I do not feel like doing much
23. Things make me upset or mad
24. I am on the lookout for bad things that might happen
25. I am nervous or jumpy

The parent self-report instrument, PROPS (Parent Report of Post-Traumatic Symptoms), developed using the parents of the same third- through eighth-grade students, was made up of the following 30 items that a parent rates with the child in mind, 0 (none), 1 (some), or 2 (lots):

1. Difficulty concentrating
2. Mood swings
3. Thinks of bad memories
4. Spaces out
5. Feels too guilty
6. Anxious
7. Irrational fears
8. Repeats the same game or activity
9. Clings to adults
10. Avoids former interests
11. Fights
12. Bossy with peers
13. Sad or depressed
14. Hyperalert
15. Feels picked on
16. Gets in trouble
17. Worries
18. Fearful
19. Withdrawn
20. Nervous
21. Startles easily
22. Irritable
23. Quick temper
24. Argues
25. Secretive

26. Does not care anymore
27. Difficulty sleeping
28. Nightmares or bad dreams
29. Stomachaches
30. Headaches

Suggested PTSD cutoff scores are 19 on the children's version (CROPS) and 16 on the parents' version (PROPS) (Greenwald & Rubin, 1999).

Case for Sleep Disturbances

In his review of research on sleep disturbances, Lavie (2001) argued that for both adults and children, "subjective problems with sleep are very common, in both the immediate and long-term aftermath of exposure to traumatic events" (p. 1825) and that this finding holds whether the disaster in question is natural, technological, or complex. Two sleep-related problems that are part of the list of PTSD symptoms are re-experiencing the trauma in nightmares and having difficulty getting to sleep and staying asleep.

Lavie's (2001) review covered a variety of disasters—such as hurricanes, floods, earthquakes, industrial accidents, and wars—and concluded that sleep disturbances, along with anxiety, fear, and physical problems, are the most common troubles described by victims (especially by women). Six months after the bombing of the Murrah Federal Building in Oklahoma City, for example, 70 percent of the victims reported having insomnia, and 50 percent reported having nightmares.

Objective findings conducted after a traumatic event—derived from the small number of sleep-studies in the laboratory, and studies in which participants wear devices at home to monitor their sleep—reveal a different picture. In many instances, subjective reports of sleep disturbances are exaggerated, both in their frequency and severity; this is true for subjective reports made soon after the trauma and those made in the long term. Traumatized individuals, it seems, misperceive how they sleep. Regardless, many traumatized people do experience sleep disturbances, and reports of such problems may be the signal of problems to come.

Poor sleep is a normal immediate response to trauma, and for most people it is a transient response. However, without objective evidence, it is not possible to know the extent to which a reported sleeping problem is "real." Therefore, an intervention may be a logical response; Lavie (2001) outlined several behavioral interventions, such as progressive muscle relaxation, sleep restriction, good sleep hygiene (meaning, for example, avoiding stimulants before bedtime), and paradoxical intention (persuading the patient to stay awake). He also outlined several pharmacological interventions, such as benzodiazepine hypnotics (he cautioned that there is little support for the use of sedating antihistamines and melatonin).

Many victims have benefited from the emergence of PTSD as a diagnosis. However, as a model for understanding and treating people exposed to a disaster, PTSD is reactive rather than proactive—its primary usefulness is to help assess postdisaster destructive effects rather than to predict an individual's possible response to an impending disaster—and in some ways it is too negative, emphasizing problems with the disaster victim. Studies of reactions to disasters beg the following question: If only a small proportion of any given population suffers extreme reactions to a disaster and requires extensive psychosocial (and medical) interventions, what is it about the rest of the population that allows them to return to normalcy?

RESILIENCY MODEL

With the question above, the focus shifts from a PTSD model to a resiliency model. Although each model presents a different perspective of disasters, the two models are not mutually exclusive. Studies that are clearly conducted within a PTSD framework can, with a slight shift, be reframed as resiliency research. For example, studies of PTSD that focus on children's personal characteristics and the attributes of their several ecosystems that predispose them to suffer or not to suffer from PTSD may be seen as falling into the category of resiliency research (Boyden, 1994; Rutter, 1987). These studies begin to delineate why it is that some people do not suffer the negative effects of disasters—that is, why some children are resilient.

"Resiliency is the child's capacity to bounce back from [or not succumb to] traumatic childhood events and develop into a sane, integrated, and socially responsible adult" (Apfel & Simon, 1996b, p. 1). According to Garmezy (1993), the "central element in the study of resilience lies in the power of recovery and in the ability to return once again to those patterns of adaptation and competence that characterized the individual prior to the pre-stress period" (p. 129).

Focus on the concept of resilience grew out of responses to two questions: (1) What in a child's personal and psychological makeup or ecosystem puts her or him at greater risk of suffering ill effects from experiencing a disaster? (2) What in a child's personal and psychological makeup or ecosystem serves to protect him or her from the ill effects of a disaster? So, when speaking about resilience, the discussion includes consideration of risk and protective factors; indeed, to define resilience, researchers have considered what characteristics of a child and a child's environment constitute risk factors and what characteristics constitute protective factors.

Risk factors are influences that increase the probability of negative outcomes or that help maintain negative outcomes that already exist (Kirby & Fraser, 1997; Vance & Sanchez, 1998). Parson (1995) discussed two different types of risk factors. The first type includes "intraself" characteristics. This translates to the absence of emotional support, low educational attainment, and prior traumatic exposure. The second type includes "socioenvironmental" characteristics. Within the context of disaster recovery, this means the abruptness of the disaster's onset, the degree of destruction and social network disruption, and the post-disaster community resources available.

Protective factors are internal and external influences that help people, including children, resist risk and poor outcomes, deal with disasters, and react to them in positive ways (Kirby & Fraser, 1997; Vance & Sanchez, 1998). According to Garmezy, Masten, and Tellegen (1984; see also Vance & Sanchez, 1998), protective factors fall into three categories: (1) the child's qualities (similar to Parson's "intraself" characteristics), such as above-average intelligence and a good sense of humor; (2) the family's qualities, such as warm and caring relationships and well-established routines; and (3) the qualities of support from outside the family, such as support from teachers, religious organizations, and work.

Lists are available of different risk and protective factors, and although some of the lists' contents may differ, many items regularly appear and reappear. The Touching Reality "Personal Risk and Protective Factors" experience invites you to think about your own risk and protective factors; do this exercise before looking at the lists that follow.

When the Tree Hit the House

During an interview of a family whose house was damaged in a recent tornado, the parents related how their two boys reacted when a tree crashed into the roof and branches poked into their bedroom. Both were in bed when it happened, and both were frightened and ran into the parents' bedroom. Differences in the boys' reactions emerged soon after the house was repaired. One son, the younger one, quickly adapted and treated the repaired bedroom as if nothing had happened—he expressed no fears about trees crashing down, and even mentioned how the whole evening was quite an adventure. The older boy responded very differently: He refused to sleep upstairs and expressed continuing fear about future tornadoes. The parents were surprised at the different reactions and were open to learning about how they might help their older son cope successfully with the trauma.

Sanchez and Vance (1995) developed a Brief Resiliency Checklist for use as a screening tool to assess the "net risk" for high-risk youths, such as those referred to Willie M. services. The instrument requires completing a checklist of 23 psychosocial risk factors and a checklist of 27 psychosocial protective factors. The total number of risk factors checked is assigned a negative number, the total of protective factors checked is assigned a positive number, and then the two numbers are combined. The sum is the "net risk," with a high negative net risk score indicating the likely need for intervention. With respect to a child's response to a disaster, a high negative net risk score may well indicate a high probability of psychosocial problems.

Psychosocial risk factors listed on the Brief Resiliency Checklist, which cover the range from personal characteristics to aspects of the ecological environment, include:

Personal Risk and Protective Factors

Consider a time in your life when you were under a great deal of stress or when you experienced some serious, perhaps traumatic, event. How would you describe your own risk and protective factors?

What were your intraself risk factors—for example, was this trauma one you had experienced before? What were your socioenvironmental risk factors—for example, did the trauma occur suddenly, or did it, to a large extent, disrupt your ability to work or maintain relationships?

What were the protective factors associated with your personal qualities at that time—for example, did you have an easy temperament and a well-developed ability to empathize? What about protective factors associated with your family—for example, did you have a caring spouse, and supportive people outside your family? Did you have a strong and well-integrated social support network?

- Does the child have an IQ of less than 70?
- Is the child currently failing school, or has the child dropped out of school?
- Is the family…living in poverty?
- Currently, do the parents (or does the single parent) have emotional or mental disorders or problems?
- Is the child currently neglected in any way?

Psychosocial protective factors on the assessment tool, also representing a range from personal to ecological characteristics, include:

- Is the child a good reader?
- Does the child show the ability to get along with most other children?
- Is the family presently involved with a religious group (such as a church, mosque, temple, synagogue) on a regular basis?
- Does the child have special support from any peers?
- Is the child confident that life events are under his or her control, rather than that they are controlled by luck or fate?

Kirby and Fraser (1997) provided another list of risk and protective factors on the basis of their literature review of studies of children in a variety of areas. Arguing that the factors they detail are common to many situations and children, they divided their risk and protective factors into three areas: (1) broad environmental conditions; (2) family, school, and neighborhood conditions; and (3) individual psychosocial and biological characteristics.

In the first category, risk factors include few opportunities for education and employment, racial discrimination and injustice, and poverty. Protective factors include educational opportunities and possibilities of employment, growth, and achievement.

In the second category, risk factors include child maltreatment, interparental conflict, parental psychopathology, and poor parenting. Protective factors include social support, presence of a caring and supportive adult, positive parent-child relationships, and effective parenting.

Finally, in the third category, risk factors include gender (some studies found that girls report greater distress levels than boys) and biomedical problems. Protective factors include an "easy" temperament, high self-esteem and self-efficacy, competence in typical roles, and high intelligence.

Focusing on the trauma associated with loss, the Minnesota Extension Service (Hokanson, 1993) lists common resilient characteristics of survivors of this type of trauma on their Web site:

- Almost without exception, those who survive a tragedy give credit to one person who stood by them, supported them, and offered them a sense of hope.
- Those who survive a tragedy understand the magnitude of what they have lost.
- Those who survive a tragedy learn to transcend their guilt. (They forgive themselves and define their own good qualities.)
- Those who survive a tragedy have a reason to go on living. (They do not live solely in the past and they see a real possibility of a future.)

Apfel and Simon (1996a) focused specifically on complex disasters, such as war and terrorism, and found that not all children succumb to the horrors of this type of disaster; some are resilient. Summarizing research across a variety of types of complex disasters, and considering data from interviews with survivors and clinicians, they outlined 11 factors they see as contributing to resiliency (Apfel & Simon, pp. 9–12):

1. *resourcefulness*—the ability to extract warmth and kindness in the worst of circumstances
2. *adult support*—the ability to attract and use adult support enhances feelings of power and competence
3. *curiosity and intellectual mastery*—being active rather than passive, seeking rather than denying
4. *compassion*—but with detachment
5. *conceptualization skills*—the ability to gain a broader view of the disaster, which makes it more than a personal struggle
6. *right of survival*—the conviction of one's right to survive
7. *images of good and sustaining figures*—the ability to remember and invoke these images, usually of parents, which offers standards and ideals that provide a sense of security, and of order
8. *sensitivity to affects*—the ability to be in touch with a variety of affects, not denying or suppressing major affects as they arise; the ability to compartmentalize the pain and postpone affect until it is safe to express pain
9. *a goal to live for*—the ability to summon a vision of the possibility and desirability of the restoration of a civilized moral order, which includes recognizing that "a need to act to restore moral order may take precedence over the need to get even" (Apfel & Simon, p. 11)
10. *affective repertory*—the need and ability to help others; an ability to laugh and to stay calm in difficult circumstances
11. *altruism*—recognizing that helping others also helps oneself and that being helpless to stop the disaster does not mean being helpless in dealing with its consequences.

Research is available to support the importance of particular risk and protective factors in particular disaster situations. For example, Galante and Foa (1986) found that children seem to be more resilient to psychological problems after a natural disaster if the following criteria are met: if they have family support systems that are able to respond to their needs; if their daily routine is quickly restored, including a return to school; and if they are given the opportunity to discuss and work through their fears and disaster experiences in a structured environment. In addition, Kiser and associates (1993) found that children who have an internal locus of control, a high level of dedication to tasks, and a perception of change as positive and challenging can improve their ability to cope with natural disasters.

Assessing the effect of war on children, Macksoud, Aber, and Cohn (1996) argued for a variety of variables affecting the relationship between war-related stress and outcomes. For example, children who believe they are secure and who are trusting (which is often the result of having responsive parents) appear more adaptive to stressors than those who are insecure and not trusting; and children who feel empowered and competent to deal with stress are more likely to cope effectively with a disaster.

Klingman (2002) reviewed the research on children's responses to war and concluded that "the impact of war stress on children depends considerably on both personal coping and environmental support…and their parents' and significant others' support….For adolescents, war often brings out a strength and energy unlike anything seen at other times" (p. 364). Some specific protective factors that emerge from the literature included having a "cause" or purpose to live for, having a sense of humor, having positive expectations, and staying active in helping others. In addition, an important protective factor is having access to adults who provide support, reassurance, and protection.

In his discussion of children and political violence, Cairns (1996; Muldoon & Cairns, 1999) reviewed the literature on children and disasters to extract factors that promote resilience. For example, passive, withdrawn children appear to be more vulnerable to the effects of political violence, whereas extroverted children are more likely to respond in an outgoing way, and so to be immune from the effects. In addition, social support appears to be a strong protective factor. However, Cairns pointed out a problem with studies focusing on children's resilience to political violence that is not unique to research with this particular type of disaster: Experts are still unsure what causes some children to have strong protective factors, while other children bend under the slightest strain—"a major problem with this whole area is the almost complete lack of studies in which children have been seen both before and after their exposure to political violence…. [S]tudies in this area often lack adequate (or any) control groups, while samples may be biased when they are obtained from clinical sources" (1996, p. 69).

Regardless of Cairns' valuable criticism, the conceptualization of the child as active (resiliency model) rather than passive (PTSD model) is a compelling one. Gibbs'(1994) research—highlighted in the Spotlight on Research "Resiliency in the Children of Mozambique"—although never using the word "resilience," invited readers to reframe the child as an active subject who has the ability and motivation to break patterns of trauma induced by exposure to warfare (described most frequently in PTSD models). In addition to this reclamation of power to each child, Gibbs asserted that people should consider each child's emotional, as well as physical and political, needs. Gibbs believed that it is important to acknowledge reconstruction of the heart and spirit at the same time that fields and homes are being rebuilt.

Resiliency models stress coping; how children and families cope and what in their ecological environments helps them to cope define many of the protective factors that contribute to resiliency. For example, Jeney-Gammon, Daugherty, Finch, Belter, and Foster (1992) found a relationship between children's means of coping with disaster and the development of depressive symptoms. They drew hypotheses from three different theories and supported them as follows:

- As predicted by psychoanalytic theory, children with feelings of anger and self-blame about a disaster were found more likely than other children to develop depressive symptoms.
- As forecast by Levinson's behavioral theory, children who withdrew from social interactions after a natural disaster developed higher

---

SPOTLIGHT ON RESEARCH

Resiliency in the Children of Mozambique

Beginning at the end of 1993, a year after signing the peace treaty that ended the war in Mozambique, Sara Gibbs conducted a three-month ethnographic study in the district of Milange. Her interest was in how the people were reconstructing their lives, especially "how the disrupted psychosocial world of children was understood and addressed as part of the process of community and individual healing" (p. 268). Western European tradition holds that children are vulnerable and dependent on the adults around them, and that certain stressors, such as witnessing violence and being separated from one's parents, create a traumatized state. Children, in other words, are seen as victims.

Childhood in Milange, however, is seen differently. "Children do not perceive themselves, nor are they perceived as passive, vulnerable, or being unable to work. This is not to say that they have not suffered during the war [in Mozambique] and its aftermath, only that they have suffered just as everyone else has suffered" (p. 272). Just as the process of suffering in Mozambique is the same for adults as it is for children, so is the process of healing.

For children and adults alike who witnessed the war's horrors and whose hearts were changed (suffering is embodied in the heart, unlike the Western conceptualization that embodies suffering in the mind), the healing process centers on productive activity, such as building houses and planting fields. Hearts needed to be "calmed."

Productive activity, healing medicines, and churches worked to reconstruct individual and community lives. Indeed, "it appeared that the focus of the healing process—for everyone—regardless of their individual well being, would come when the community celebrates the success of its harvest and thus 'true peace'" (p. 273).

Gibbs, S. (1994). Post-war social reconstruction in Mozambique: Re-framing children's experience of trauma and healing. *Disaster, 18,* 268–276.

levels of depressive symptoms than children who sought social support.

- As anticipated by cognitive theory, children who positively reframed circumstances had less depression than children who blamed themselves for the negative outcomes of disasters.

Lahad (1981, 1997) developed a coping schema useful for assessing people's responses to a disaster and for helping them increase their response effectiveness. The schema, called the "BASIC-Ph," describes six coping styles.

BASIC-PH MODEL

During the 1970s and 1980s, northern Israel was under continuous risk of rocket shelling. Although their lives, property, and daily routine were constantly threatened, the children and adults in northern Israel appeared to cope effectively. For example, a survey of referrals to the local mental health clinic and school psychology services in Kiryat Shmona, a town near the northern border, showed that they were at the same rate as referrals in the center of Israel—between 5 percent and 10 percent (Lahad, 1981). If such a small percentage of the population manifested acute stress reactions, what helped the rest of the population to continue their lives productively?

To answer this question, Mooli Lahad, the director of the Community Stress Prevention Centre in Kyriat Shmona, sought answers to two more specific questions: (1) What helps you to continue living in this situation? (2) What do you do to continue? The answers provided a simple explanation; he found that people often are stronger than expected, momentary disability does not predict pathology, and most people's responses are simply normal reactions to abnormal situations.

On the basis of his observations and interviews with hundreds of adults (parents, teachers, and community workers) and students (children and adolescents) living under constant and prolonged threat in Israel and elsewhere, Lahad and his colleagues (Lahad, 1997, 2000; Lahad & Cohen, 1997) developed a multimodal model to explain resilience in stressful situations. The BASIC-Ph model relates to six major characteristics or dimensions that Lahad (1997) argued are at the core of an individual's coping style.

1. **B**—*Beliefs and values*: A person copes by referring to self-reliance and her or his clear values, views, and beliefs. These references help the person "make sense" of the experience. This includes religious and political beliefs, as well as a sense of mission.
2. **A**—*Affect*: A person copes by expressing affect of all types. In the affective coping mode, the person uses emotions—crying and laughing—to tolerate the stress.
3. **S**—*Social*: A person copes by seeking support in friendships, social settings, and organizations. The person receives support from being a member of a group, from having specific tasks to accomplish, from taking on a role, and from being part of the organization.
4. **I**—*Imagination*: A person copes by using his or her imagination, such as creating imaginary playmates or situations. The person may daydream, pretend things are not all that bad, divert his or her mind through self-guided or external-guided imagery, or imagine new and innovative solutions to the problem; the person may use humor and improvisation.

5. **C**—*Cognitive*: A person copes by acting according to her or his knowledge, thoughts, and common sense. The person gathers information, solves problems, has internal conversations, makes lists, and uses rational thinking and appraisal skills.

6. **Ph**—*Physiological*: A person copes by engaging in physical activity, including eating, dancing, and traveling. Relaxation and desensitization also are expressions of physiological coping.

Coping with Hurricane Fran

The interviewer asked members of a family about the effects of Hurricane Fran on the family unit and how they responded when the hurricane hit. Their answers made it easy to explore the different coping styles of the family members. The teenage son exhibited a social coping style—he immediately sought his friends for companionship and entertainment—and a cognitive style—he made a list of what he needed to do to finish a project for school. Both the mother and father used a physiological coping style—they began to clean up their yard and then rushed to find out if their new house was intact. The father also used an imaginative coping style—he joked about being "Super Woodsman" as he cut fallen trees in his yard. The mother's continuous reference to "God spared us, we're lucky" is evidence of her using a belief coping style. These differences confirm Lahad's ideas that people can cope in different ways and use more than one mode in doing so.

Each individual has primary coping activities and resources and a style that may reflect a blending of all six dimensions (for example, a person whose primary coping style is SI, social and imagination, might seek social support from imaginary figures, such as Superman). Although each person can potentially use any of the strategies, each has a preferred mode of coping that is developed and refined in childhood. Certainly, a person's cultural background has a powerful affect on which BASIC-Ph areas dominate.

Lahad's BASIC-Ph model is a resiliency model because of its focus on strengths and the characteristics that assist a person to survive a disaster and return to (or maintain) stability and effectiveness. As Lahad (1997) stated: "It is essential to assess the way a person meets the world before we can start the intervention.... These ways of coping must be assessed in order to be able to 'speak' the client's language" (p. 124). The BASIC-Ph helps disaster response workers to understand the client's strengths. In addition, the BASIC-Ph framework helps workers develop intervention strategies. For example, a disaster victim may be helped to use those coping styles he or she is already predisposed to using, or he or she may be encouraged to use different coping styles, to expand his or her repertoire of coping styles.

Touching Reality "How Do You Cope?" invites you to explore your own coping styles by completing a questionnaire.

The BASIC-Ph model has been used in response to a variety of incidents. For example, Lahad and his colleagues worked with psychosocial teams in Tel Aviv during the Gulf War, during various military operations in the north of Israel, and during the "Intifada" in the West Bank and Gaza; they also worked with communities and

How Do You Cope?

What do you do to cope with stress? Most people develop a particular way, pattern, or style for coping. Each statement below describes a way of coping. Respond to each statement by indicating how often you are likely to use each way of coping or *one like it* when you are stressed (circle the number that indicates the likelihood you would use that style). Use the following scale:

0 = I *never* use this method or one like it to cope.
1 = I *rarely* use this method or one like it to cope.
2 = I *occasionally* use this method or one like it to cope.
3 = I *sometimes* use this method or one like it to cope.
4 = I *often* use this method or one like it to cope.
5 = I *almost always* use this method or one like it to cope.
6 = I *always* use this method or one like it to cope.

1. I defer—give up the problem—to a higher power or to fate.　0　1　2　3　4　5　6

2. I may not express how I feel directly, but I do it indirectly by, for example, crying or brooding "on the inside."　0　1　2　3　4　5　6

3. I seek out the support of other people.　0　1　2　3　4　5　6

4. I fantasize and let my mind wander—for example, I imagine myself in a calm, serene place.　0　1　2　3　4　5　6

5. I gather information to make sure what I do is the best approach for me.　0　1　2　3　4　5　6

6. I eat or sleep more than usual—or just the opposite, I eat or sleep less than usual.　0　1　2　3　4　5　6

7. I have faith in my own ability to get me through it.　0　1　2　3　4　5　6

8. I use a roundabout way to suggest my feelings, such as hinting, being sarcastic, or even being flirtatious.　0　1　2　3　4　5　6

9. I talk on the phone with friends.　0　1　2　3　4　5　6

10. I think about the theme of a favorite story, fable, parable, nursery rhyme, or fairytale as a way to help me with the problem.　0　1　2　3　4　5　6

11. I analyze the crisis and think about how it might be solved.　0　1　2　3　4　5　6

12. I keep myself busy doing physical things, such as cleaning, cooking, working with wood, fixing the car, or even building a model airplane.　0　1　2　3　4　5　6

cont'd

13. I tell myself something like, "I can get through this no matter what."   0 1 2 3 4 5 6

14. I release my feelings—for example, cry, laugh, or yell—instead of holding them in.   0 1 2 3 4 5 6

15. I seek out the support of a friend or family member.   0 1 2 3 4 5 6

16. I let my mind wander as I listen to music.   0 1 2 3 4 5 6

17. I make a specific plan to follow, and do what has to be done one step at a time.   0 1 2 3 4 5 6

18. I use relaxation exercises.   0 1 2 3 4 5 6

19. I pray for help.   0 1 2 3 4 5 6

20. I "pump up my feelings" as a way to motivate myself.   0 1 2 3 4 5 6

21. I involve myself with people in my community or an organization to which I belong.   0 1 2 3 4 5 6

22. I think about times when things were better, or about a time when they will be better.   0 1 2 3 4 5 6

23. I try to understand what is going on in the first place.   0 1 2 3 4 5 6

24. I relax by doing something, like showering or bathing, taking a walk, or jogging.   0 1 2 3 4 5 6

25. I use my spiritual beliefs or think about my philosophy of life.   0 1 2 3 4 5 6

26. I tell or listen to jokes and funny stories.   0 1 2 3 4 5 6

27. I look for people to hang out with.   0 1 2 3 4 5 6

28. I watch a sitcom, sports, or a movie, or read a book.   0 1 2 3 4 5 6

29. I think about the best solution and develop a problem-solving strategy.   0 1 2 3 4 5 6

30. I try to keep myself physically busy doing things.   0 1 2 3 4 5 6

31. I think about sayings like, "that which does not kill me, makes me stronger."   0 1 2 3 4 5 6

32. I let my emotions out.   0 1 2 3 4 5 6

cont'd

33. I write an e-mail or a letter to a friend in hopes of getting a response.   0 1 2 3 4 5 6

34. I tend to daydream about better times.   0 1 2 3 4 5 6

35. I think about as many solutions as possible and then pick the one I think is the best solution for the problem at hand.   0 1 2 3 4 5 6

36. I work off the energy by, for example, getting out of my apartment or house and being active.   0 1 2 3 4 5 6

Of the 36 items, which one do you use the most?
(put the number on the line)   _____

Which one do you use second most?   _____

Which one do you use third most?   _____

Add your responses to 1, 7, 13, 19, 25, and 31. This is your B score   _____

Add your responses to 2, 8, 14, 20, 26, and 32. This is your A score   _____

Add your responses to 3, 9, 15, 21, 27, and 33. This is your S score   _____

Add your responses to 4, 10, 16, 22, 28, and 34. This is your I score   _____

Add your responses to 5, 11, 17, 23, 29, and 35. This is your C score   _____

Add your responses to 6, 12, 18, 24, 30, and 36. This is your Ph score   _____

For the item you indicated as the method of coping you use the most, add 3 points to that dimension of coping (for example, if you wrote in #19 in the first space, add 3 points to your B score). For the item you indicated as the second-most used method, add 2 points to that dimension of coping. For the item you indicated as the third-most used method, add 1 point to that dimension of coping.

What is your BASIC-Ph profile?
Are there one or two types of coping styles you are most prone to use?
Does your BASIC-Ph profile fit with how you see yourself?
How can you expand the coping styles you use?

psychosocial services during suicide bomb attacks in 1996 and 1997. In addition to its usefulness with complex disasters, the BASIC-Ph model has been used after natural disasters. For example, it was used as part of a training program for disaster workers in Turkey after the country's northern section was hit with a series of devastating earthquakes in 1999.

Although planned and controlled studies of crisis interventions are scarce, children's coping styles were studied during two different incidents. The first involved the evacuation of children from Kiryat Shmona during Operation Accountability in 1993; the second involved junior high school students in Afula exposed to a suicide car bombing (the bomb exploded at the gates of their school, killing three girls and four adults, and injuring eight classmates). Results confirmed the structure of the BASIC-Ph model and its usefulness in working with children, both for helping them use their natural coping styles and for enhancing and expanding their coping mechanisms to reduce tension and prevent posttraumatic stress reactions.

Touching Reality "PTSD, Resiliency, and Disasters" invites you to take a moment and look at two video segments on the CD and compare the different responses of the people presented.

SUMMARY
General models of disasters presented by Gibson (1989), Vernberg and his colleagues (1996), and DeWolfe (2000a, 2000b) make it clear that a disaster event is highly complex. Attempts to predict reactions need to take into account the disaster's characteristics, the extent of exposure to the disaster, the characteristics of the child or family affected by the disaster, the interpersonal and social context, and the cultural context (for example, the social, political, and economic contexts), and the disaster plan and relief efforts available.

TOUCHING REALITY

PTSD, Resiliency, and Disasters

Segments 1 and 2 on the CD provide a means for applying the PTSD and resiliency models to help explain reactions to a natural disaster. Segment 1 presents two families who experienced Hurricane Floyd in 1999 in North Carolina. Both families lived in Princeville, North Carolina, which was completely flooded after the Hurricane. They respond differently. One of the women summarizes her coping skills this way: "I just keep prayin'... I feel like cryin'... and I hope for better things." Segment 2 shows how a couple with four children (one an infant born a week after the storm) is dealing with the loss of their home. The man is at the home daily, so far unable to return to work. The woman is grateful for what they do have "because everything else can be replaced." Imagine yourself in these circumstances. What coping skills and supports would be available to you? Would you leave or stay?

It is important for us to distinguish between two types of trauma: Individual trauma occurs when a person cannot respond effectively to a disaster or trauma, and collective trauma occurs when a disaster damages the bonds that attach people in a community.

Two major models are available for understanding the effects of disasters on children and families. The PTSD model focuses on enumerating the negative effects of a disaster, the aim of which is to determine the extent to which the person is in need of psychological intervention. The resiliency model, however, assesses an individual's risk and protective factors as the basis for predicting how she or he might respond to a disaster. Models that emphasize coping, such as the BASIC-Ph, fall within the resiliency model.

REFERENCES

Abadian, S. (2000). From wasteland to homeland: Trauma and the renewal of indigenous peoples and their communities. *Dissertation Abstracts International, 60,* 2591.

American Psychiatric Association. (2000). *Diagnostic and statistical manual of mental disorders* (4th ed., text rev.). Washington, DC: Author.

Apfel, R. J., & Simon, B. (1996a). Introduction. In R. J. Apfel & B. Simon (Eds.), *Minefields in their hearts: The mental health of children in war and communal violence* (pp. 1–17). New Haven, CT: Yale University Press.

Apfel, R. J., & Simon, B. (1996b). *Psychosocial interventions for children of war: The value of a model resiliency.* Retrieved August 20, 2003, from http://www.ippnw.org/MGS/V3Apfel.html

Belter, R. W., & Shannon, M. P. (1993). Impact of natural disasters on children and families. In C. F. Saylor (Ed.), *Children and disasters* (pp. 85–103). New York: Plenum Press.

Benight, C. C., Ironson, G., Klebe, K., Carver, C. S., Wynings, C., Burnett, K., & Greenwood, D. (1999). Conservation of resources and coping self-efficacy predicting distress following a natural disaster: A causal model analysis where the environment meets the mind. *Anxiety, Stress and Coping: An International Journal, 12*(2), 107–126.

Boyden, J. (1994). Children's experiences of conflict related emergencies: Some implications for relief policy and practice. *Disasters, 18,* 254–267.

Buffalo Creek. (n.d.). Retrieved August 20, 2003, from http://www.wvculture.org/history/buffcreek/buff1.htm

Cairns, E. (1996). *Children and political violence.* Oxford: Blackwell.

Daly, R. J. (1983). Samuel Pepys and post traumatic disorder. *British Journal of Psychiatry, 143,* 64–68.

de Jong, J. T. V. M. (2002). Public mental health, traumatic stress and human rights violations in low-income countries: A culturally appropriate model in times of conflict, disaster and peace. In J. de Jong (Ed.), *Trauma, war, and violence: Public mental health in socio-cultural context* (pp. 1–91). New York: Kluwer Academic/Plenum Press.

DeBord, K. (2000). *Recognizing stress in children.* Raleigh, NC: North Carolina State University Cooperative Extension. Retrieved August 20, 2003, from http://www.ces.ncsu.edu/depts/fcs/humandev/disas1.html.

DeWolfe, D. J. (2000a). *Field manual for mental health and human service workers in major disasters* (DHHS Publication No. ADM 90-537). Washington, DC: Center for Mental Health Services. Retrieved August 20, 2003, from http://www.mental-health.org/publications/allpubs-/ADM90-537/Default.asp

DeWolfe, D. J. (2000b). *Training manual for mental health and human service workers in major disasters* (DHHS Publication No. ADM 90-538). Washington, DC: Center for Mental Health Services. Retrieved August 20, 2003, from http://www.mentalhealth.org/publications/allpubs-/ADM90-538/Default.asp

Dirkzwager, A. J. E., Bramsen, I., & Van Der Ploeg, H. M. (2001). The longitudinal course of posttraumatic stress disorder symptoms among aging military veterans. *Journal of Nervous and Mental Disease, 189,* 846–853.

Drake, E. B., Bush, S. F., & van Gorp, W. G. (2001). Evaluation and assessment of PTSD in children and adolescents. In S. Eth (Ed.), *PTSD in children and adolescents. Review of psychiatry* (vol. 20, no. 1, pp. 1–31). Washington, DC: American Psychiatric Association.

Eaves, C. (2001). The development and implementation of a crisis response team in a school setting. *International Journal of Emergency Mental Health, 3*(1), 35–46.

Erikson, K. T. (1976). *Everything in its path: Destruction of community in the Buffalo Creek flood.* New York: Simon & Schuster.

Galante, R., & Foa, D. (1986). An epidemiological study of psychic trauma and treatment effectiveness for children after a natural disaster. *Journal of the American Academy of Child Psychiatry, 25,* 357–363.

Garmezy, N. (1993). Children in poverty: Resilience despite risk. *Psychiatry, 56,* 127–136.

Garmezy, N., Masten, A. S., & Tellegen, A. (1984). The study of stress and competence in children: A building block for developmental psychopathology. *Child Development, 55,* 97–111.

Gibbs, S. (1994). Post-war social reconstruction in Mozambique: Re-framing children's experience of trauma and healing. *Disaster, 18,* 268–276.

Gibson, K. (1989). Children in political violence. *Social Science and Medicine, 28,* 659–667.

Ginexi, E. M. (1997). Situational and psychological predictors of coping responses and mental health outcomes among flood victims. *Dissertation Abstracts International, 58,* 1593.

Green, B. L., Korol, M., Grace, M. C., Vary, M. G., Leonard, A. C., Gleser, G. C., & Smitson-Cohen, S. (1991). Children and disaster: Age, gender, and parental effects on PTSD symptoms. *Journal of the American Academy of Child & Adolescent Psychiatry, 30,* 945–951.

Greenwald, R., & Rubin, A. (1999). Assessment of posttraumatic symptoms in children: Development and preliminary validation of parent and child scales. *Research on Social Work Practice, 9,* 61–75.

Hokanson, R. L. (1993). *Regaining resiliency after loss.* Minneapolis: Minnesota Extension Service. Retrieved August 20, 2003, from http://www.extension.umn.edu/distribution/familydevelopment/components/ITT-09.html.

Jeney-Gammon, P., Daugherty, T. K., Finch, A. J., Belter, R. W., & Foster, K. Y. (1992). Children's coping styles and report of depressive symptoms following a natural disaster. *Journal of Genetic Psychology, 154,* 259–267.

Joseph, S. (1997). *Understanding post-traumatic stress: A psychosocial perspective on PTSD and treatment.* New York: John Wiley & Sons.

Keppel-Benson, J. M., & Ollendick, T. H. (1993). Posttraumatic stress disorder in children and adolescents. In C. F. Saylor (Ed.), *Children and disasters* (pp. 29–43). New York: Plenum Press.

Kim, S. (1998, September 21). Love Canal byproduct is tech disaster. *Disaster News Network.* Retrieved August 20, 2003, from http://www.disasternews.net/hot/9-21-98_ny-lovecanal.shtml

Kirby, L. D., & Fraser, M. W. (1997). Risk and resilience in childhood. In M. W. Fraser (Ed.), *Risk and resilience in childhood: An ecological perspective* (pp. 10–33). Washington, DC: NASW Press.

Kiser, L., Heston, J., Hickerson, S., Millsap, P., Nunn, W., & Pruitt, D. (1993). Anticipatory stress in children and adolescents. *American Journal of Psychiatry, 150,* 87–91.

Klingman, A. (2002). Children under stress of war. In A. M. La Greca, W. K. Silverman, E. M. Vernberg, & M. C. Roberts (Eds.), *Helping children cope with disasters and terrorism* (pp. 359–380). Washington, DC: American Psychological Association.

Kreuger, L. W., & Stretch, J. J. (1999, January). *A protocol for identifying long term PTSD in adolescent flood victims.* Presented at the meeting of the Society for Social Work and Research, Austin, TX.

Krug, E. G., Kresnow, M. J., Peddicord, J. P., Dahlberg, L. L., Powell, K. E., Crosby, A. E., & Annest, J. L. (1999). "Suicide after natural disasters": Retraction. *New England Journal of Medicine, 340,* 148–149.

La Greca, A. M., Silverman, W. K., Vernberg, E. M., & Prinstein, M. J. (1996). Symptoms of posttraumatic stress in children after Hurricane Andrew: A prospective study. *Journal of Counseling and Clinical Psychology, 64,* 712–723.

La Greca, A. M., Silverman, W. K., & Wasserstein, S. B. (1998). Children's predisaster functioning as a predictor of posttraumatic stress following Hurricane Andrew. *Journal of Consulting and Clinical Psychology, 66,* 883–892.

Lahad, M. (1981). *Preparation of children and teachers to cope with stress: A multi-modal approach.* Unpublished master's thesis, Hebrew University, Jerusalem.

Lahad, M. (1997). BASIC Ph: The story of coping resources. In M. Lahad & A. Cohen (Eds.), *Community stress prevention* (Vols. 1 & 2, pp. 117–145). Kiryat Shmona, Israel: Community Stress Prevention Center.

Lahad, M. (1999). Darkness over the abyss: Supervising crisis intervention teams following disaster. In O. Ayalon, M. Lahad, & A. Cohen (Eds.), *Community stress prevention* (Vol. 4, pp. 1–12). Kiryat Shmona, Israel: Community Stress Prevention Center.

Lahad, M. (2000). *Creative supervision.* London: Jessica Kingsley.

Lahad, M., & Cohen, A. (Eds.). (1997). *Community stress prevention* (Vols. 1 & 2). Kiryat Shmona, Israel: Community Stress Prevention Center.

Lamprecht, F., & Sack, M. (2002). Posttraumatic stress disorder revisited. *Psychosomatic Medicine, 64,* 222–237.

Lavie, P. (2001). Sleep disturbances in the wake of traumatic events. *New England Journal of Medicine, 345,* 1825–1832.

Lonigan, C. J., Anthony, J. L., & Shannon, M. P. (1998). Diagnostic efficacy of posttraumatic symptoms in children exposed to disaster. *Journal of Clinical Child Psychology, 27,* 255–267.

Macksoud, M. J., Aber, J. L., & Cohn, I. (1996). Assessing the impact of war on children. In R. J. Apfel & B. Simon (Eds.), *Minefields in their hearts: The mental health of children in war and communal violence* (pp. 218–230). New Haven, CT: Yale University Press.

Muldoon, O., & Cairns, E. (1999). Children, young people, and war: Learning to cope. In E. Frydenberg (Ed.), *Learning to cope: Developing as a person in complex societies* (pp. 322–337). Oxford England: Oxford University Press.

Pan American Airlines. (2000). Retrieved August 20, 2003, from http://history1900s.about.com/library/weekly/aa051800a.htmon

Parson, E. (1995). Mass traumatic terror in Oklahoma City and the phases of adaptational coping: I. Possible effects of intentional injury/harm on victims' post-traumatic responses. *Journal of Contemporary Psychotherapy, 25,* 155–184.

Pfefferbaum, B., Call, J. A., Lensgraf, S. J., Miller, P. D., & Flynn, B. W. (2001). Traumatic grief in a convenience sample of victims seeking support services after a terrorist incident. *Annals of Clinical Psychiatry, 13*(1), 19–24.

Pfefferbaum, B., Nixon, S. J., Tucker, P. M., Tivis, R. D., Moore, V. L., Gurwitch, R. H., Pynoos, R. S., & Geis, H. K. (1999). Posttraumatic stress responses in bereaved children after the Oklahoma City bombing. *Journal of the American Academy of Child and Adolescent Psychiatry, 38,* 1372–1379.

Ronen, T. (2002). Difficulties in assessing traumatic reactions in children. *Journal of Loss and Trauma, 7,* 87–106.

Rosenfeld, L. B., Lahad, M., & Cohen, A. (2001). Disaster, trauma, and children's resilience: A community response perspective. In J. M. Richman & M. W. Fraser (Eds.), *Children, families and disasters: A risk and resiliency perspective* (pp. 133–185). Westport, CT: Greenwood Press.

Rutter, M. (1987). Psychosocial resilience and protective mechanisms. *American Journal of Orthopsychiatry, 57,* 316–331.

Sanchez, H., & Vance, E. (1995). *Brief resiliency checklist.* (Available from Resiliency Inc., 12200 Glenlivet Way, Raleigh, NC 27613)

Saylor, C. F., Belter, R., & Stokes, S. J. (1997). Children and families coping with disaster. In S. A. Wolchik & I. N. Sandler (Eds.), *Handbook of children's coping: Linking theory and intervention* (pp. 361–383). New York: Plenum Press.

Silverman, W. K., & La Greca, A. M. (2002). Children experiencing disaster: Definitions, reactions, and predictors of outcomes. In A. M. La Greca, W. K. Silverman, E. M. Vernberg, & M. C. Roberts (Eds.), *Helping children cope with disasters and terrorism* (pp. 11–33). Washington, DC: American Psychological Association.

Sutker, P. B., Corrigan, S. A., Sundgaard-Riise, K., Uddo, M., & Allain, A. N. (2002). Exposure to war trauma, war-related PTSD, and psychological impact of subsequent hurricane. *Journal of Psychopathology and Behavioral Assessment, 24*(1), 25–37.

Trimble, M. R. (1985). Posttraumatic stress disorder: History of a concept. In C. R. Figley (Ed.), *Trauma and its wake: The study of posttraumatic stress disorder.* New York: Brunner/Mazel.

Vance, E., & Sanchez, H. (1998, February). *Willie M. services—Creating a service system that builds resiliency.* Raleigh: North Carolina Department of Mental Health, Developmental Disabilities, and Substance Abuse Services. Retrieved August 20, 2003, from http://www.dhhs.state.nc.us/mhddsas/sections/child/williem/risk_and_resiliency.htm

Vernberg, E. M., La Greca, A. M., Silverman, W. K., & Prinstein, M. J. (1996). Prediction of posttraumatic stress symptoms in children after Hurricane Andrew. *Journal of Abnormal Psychology, 105,* 237–247.

Vincent, N. R. (1998). Children's reactions to Hurricane Andrew: A forty four month follow up study. *Dissertation Abstracts International, 59,* 891.

Wang, X., Gao, L., Zhang, H., Zhao, C., Shen, Y. & Shinfuku, N. (2000). Post-earthquake quality of life and psychological well-being: Longitudinal evaluation in a rural community sample in northern China. *Psychiatry and Clinical Neurosciences, 54,* 427–433.

Wilson, J. P., & Keane, T. M. (Eds.). (1997). *Assessing psychological trauma and PTSD.* New York: Guilford Press.

PART TWO

The Effects of Disasters

CHAPTER THREE

CHILDREN AND DISASTERS: THE CHILD'S REACTION

CHAPTER OVERVIEW

After studying the material in this chapter, you should

- understand the connection between a child's reactions to trauma and disaster and her or his developmental age
- be able to apply concepts of child development to real situations to assess a child's behavior within the context of a disaster
- be able to identify general and individual characteristics and other risk and protective factors involved in children's reactions to disasters and any resulting trauma
- understand the effect of the family context on children's ability to cope with a disaster
- understand how culture can affect children's reactions to a disaster and the type of support children might experience during a disaster.

The natural, technological, and complex disasters described in the first two chapters of this book do not discriminate by age. Children are involved in disasters wherever they occur. The much-studied Buffalo Creek flood in West Virginia, for example, left 125 dead, 52 of them children. Victims of the 2000 earthquake disaster in western India included hundreds, perhaps thousands, of children. Of the 168 people killed in the bombing of the Alfred P. Murrah Federal Office Building in Oklahoma City, 19 were infants. Children are passengers on planes when they crash, are in buildings when they burn or are attacked by terrorists, and live in areas that are flooded. In complex disasters (such as gang shootings, wars, terrorist attacks, or kidnappings), children may be specifically targeted because of the emotional impact that their victimization has on the community.

Forced use of children in war has been discussed in the United Nations for many years. Children in war-torn countries have been taken from their homes and forced to become combatants and to commit atrocities against their own families and communities. Mutilation of children in war and during times of forced colonization has been performed to shock their parents and caregivers. For example, during the takeover of the Congo by Belgian King Leopold during the early 1900s, children's bodies were mutilated and the sev-

The Chowchilla Bus Kidnapping

On July 15, 1976, a school bus driver named Ed Ray and 26 children from Chowchilla, CA—19 girls and 7 boys, ages 5 to 14—were returning home from a swim outing when their bus was hijacked. The three hijackers were well-to-do young men who wanted to buy a large estate house they could share. Although they came from relatively wealthy families, none of them had enough to buy this house, so, they developed a detailed plan to kidnap a school bus full of children. They "decided the bus they would capture would have to be loaded with grammar school children. Older students were bigger and might resist" (Baugh & Morgan, 1978, p. 53). Their motive for the kidnapping was money; surely, they reasoned, adults would pay for their young children to be returned. Investigators found a rough draft of a ransom note for $5,000,000 in one of the kidnapper's homes.

Before the kidnapping, two of the hijackers bought an old moving van, 8 feet by 16 feet, and had buried it out in the desert. They stocked it with mattresses, a makeshift toilet, food, and water. After commandeering the school bus, they drove the children and Mr. Ray around for several hours, then forced them to transfer into the buried van.

After being buried for 16 hours, Mr. Ray and two sixth-grade boys dug their way out. Rescuers found the victims wandering around in a remote area near the Shadow Cliffs East Bay Regional Park. The hijackers were arrested, convicted, and sentenced to life in prison. The children showed very high indicators of PTSD, and several of them remained highly traumatized for years afterward. "The only remnant of the incident in Chowchilla today is a simple granite monument dedicated to the victims which is located at the Government Center" (City of Chowchilla, 2001).

ered parts shown to the parents to force them to comply with the powerful, foreign regime (Hochschild, 1998).

Closer to home, and closer to the present, violent crime in the United States continues to be an affair of the young. "Although juveniles (ages 12 to 17) accounted for one-tenth of the U.S. population, one in four violent crimes involved a juvenile victim in 1992" (Saigh, 1996). American youths are exposed to chronic, daily violence in their homes, in their neighborhoods, and on television. Morland (2000) investigated the relationship between exposure to bomb-related images on television and the severity of PTSD symptoms in a sample of more than 2,700 Oklahoma City students, seven weeks after the bombing of the Murrah Federal building. She found that watching bomb-related images was significantly related to severity of posttraumatic stress symptoms.

In their literature review related to children exposed to community violence, Kupersmidt, Shahinfar, and Voegler-Lee (2002) pointed out that "exposure to violence has become pervasive across our society and is not just restricted to adolescents or children living in inner cities" (pp. 383–384). Although the typical scenario of violence against youths in the 1970s and 1980s involved adults as perpetrators, in the 1990s "highly publicized events were more often committed by students shooting other students" (Nader & Mello, 2002, p. 301).

Even in the most stable of homes, communities, and situations, disasters—natural, technological, and complex—affect children.

PREDICTING CHILDREN'S REACTIONS TO DISASTERS

This chapter focuses specifically on the reactions of children to disaster. Children respond to disaster situations based on a variety of factors. Aptekar and Boore (1990) identified six factors that influence children's reactions, including:

1. the child's belief as to who or what caused the disaster
2. the degree of destruction
3. the child's developmental level
4. the child's premorbid mental health
5. the community's ability to offer support
6. the parental reactions to the disaster.

Green and her colleagues (1991) considered four factors that influence children's reactions:

1. the child's exposure to traumatic events during and after the disaster
2. the child's pre-existing characteristics
3. the levels of social support after the disaster
4. the child's coping skills.

Vernberg, and colleagues (1996) articulated four similar factors that influence children's reactions:

1. the child's exposure to trauma
2. the child's pre-existing characteristics
3. the occurrence of major life stressors in the child's life
4. the type of coping strategies the child uses to manage stress.

This chapter outlines children's reactions to disasters largely based on these three models. Specifically, we focus on four general categories, categories that subsume the factors in the three models described as well as those discussed in other models developed in an attempt to predict how specific children are likely to respond to a disaster:

1. the child's developmental level and his or her associated identified reactions
2. the child's ability to make sense of the disaster experience
3. the effect of the child's culture on her or his reactions to the disaster
4. previous traumas the child has experienced, including the predisaster life environment of the child.

Social support (or its lack) from both family and community members is clearly a significant factor when predicting the effects of a disaster on children (O'Donnell, Schwab-Stone, & Muyeed, 2002). Social support is discussed more fully in the next chapter, Family and Community Reactions to Disaster.

Children's Reactions to the Floods Following Hurricane Floyd

According to the director of the Boys and Girls Club of two eastern North Carolina counties, children's most common reaction to the flooding after Hurricane Floyd (which hit eastern North Carolina in September 1999), was confusion: "Why did this happen?" "How could God let this happen?" and "Is this the end of the world?"

Although questions like these were common, the most striking reaction was the intense fear the children felt with any disaster-related event. The first time it rained after the flooding, for example, "They freaked out," and asked questions like, "Is my house gonna flood again?"

The director also noted a great deal of separation anxiety, particularly for those who had been separated from a parent or sibling during the hurricane. "One particular seven-year-old boy screamed and cried hysterically when separated from his brother one afternoon at a Boys and Girls Club meeting. One van had left to return a group to a shelter. This van had had the boy's brother on it, and it took some serious convincing to make him realize that the second van would go to the same shelter where he and his brother would be reunited."

Like separation anxiety, antisocial behavior was also a common reaction of the child disaster victims (Weaver, 1995). The director reported that, for some time after the flooding, theft was a big problem around the clubs. They had never experienced this problem before, and they attributed it to the floods because the stolen items were usually clothing and similar materials that the children would have lost during the disaster.

Regression also was noted among the younger children: "One particular child was having severe toileting problems." Another reaction of the children to the flooding was found in their artwork. The director noted that there had been quite an increase, in all the clubs, of artwork consisting of water and boats. A year after the flood, such drawing still dominated the children's artistic expression.

DEVELOPMENTAL LEVEL AND ASSOCIATED REACTIONS

One benchmark used to predict the reactions of children to a disaster is their developmental age (Lerner, Volpe, & Lindell, 2003). Throughout this section, we discuss children's reactions based on their three capacities: physical, cognitive, and emotional. Changes in developmental level or developmental age (the terms "level" and "age" are used interchangeably here) signal changes in the child's three capacities. It is important to note that a child's chronological age may not correspond to the chronological ages typically associated with each developmental level. For many reasons, a child may be ahead of the curve of expected capacities, or may fall behind the "norm." Congenital problems, illness, family troubles, abuse, and accidents all may change the developmental curve for a particular child.

The degree to which a child is dependent on those around him or her to meet his or her needs depends in part on the child's age and capacity. Adults have different expectations regarding a child's ability to weather a difficult or traumatic situation depending on the child's developmental age. However, helpers should never take age

SPOTLIGHT ON RESEARCH

PTSD Symptoms in Children Following a Fire

According to the U.S. Census Bureau, each year more than 500,000 house fires result in approximately 5,000 deaths. Survivors must deal with the physical loss of place and belongings, the psychological trauma left by the fire, and any injuries or deaths. Helaine Greenberg and Anne Keane (1997) completed a study to understand and describe the symptoms of PTSD in children who experienced trauma after a fire that destroyed their homes.

Fifty-six children, ages six to 17, were interviewed at four to six months (T1), and eight to 10 months (T2) after the fire. Sixty-eight percent of the children were inside the home when the fire started, and 48 percent encountered smoke and flames. Seventy-one percent of the children at T1 and 57 percent at T2 showed some level of stress-related symptoms. Greenberg and Keane found that the symptoms differed according to the child's developmental age.

Younger children tended to withdraw and to fear separation. Younger children worried about the loss of personal possessions and favorite toys (many children in the study came from poor families, and replacement was difficult for the families). "School-age children may perform poorly in class…fantasize…regress…become hypervigilant" (p.13). Some fires were caused by human error, and some children worried about recurrence, and expressed concern about the effect of the extra stress the fire caused to their parent.

Symptoms suffered by adolescents are similar to those of adults, except that "adolescents, because of their egocentricity, have a great potential for acting out or feeling guilty" (p. 13). Children who were babysitters received blame if younger children under their care set the fires. The babysitters also felt a great deal of guilt for not doing more to put out the fire.

Greenberg, H. S., & Keane A. (1997). A social work perspective of childhood trauma after a residential fire. *Social Work in Education, 19,* 11–22.

as a sole determinant of a child's ability to cope. Making such assumptions can cause difficulties for an older boy, for example, who is expected to be independent and helpful after a disaster strikes, but who exhibits the emotional needs of someone younger and who needs a great deal of support. Similarly, expectations that a young girl will be dependent and require a great deal of nurturing may prevent her from filling a productive helper role simply because she is believed to be "too young."

Disasters, by definition, are sudden and unpredictable, which means that regardless of the stated function of your position—whether you are a social worker, nurse, Red Cross worker, teacher, or some other trained caregiver—you may find yourself in the role of a helper in a postdisaster situation. Helpers often work with children during and after a disaster. Given that a child's reaction is heavily dependent on his or her developmental age, it is important for you, the helper, to be familiar with the generally accepted characteristics and abilities associated with a particular life stage. You may be called upon to plan a disaster response at a school, or even within your own family, and it is difficult to plan a trauma-reducing response for a child exposed to a disaster without knowing basic developmental processes. Realistic and effective interventions require this information.

We could base this discussion on the work of several different child development experts and researchers. We chose to rely on Erik Erikson, because those who work with children generally know his stages and accept them as valid descriptions of children's developmental processes. Using one primary child development perspective encourages a common language and provides a baseline against which to consider research findings about children whose reactions are outside the norm. The discussion of Eriksonian stages is augmented with Piaget's theory of cognitive development and Kohlberg's schema of moral development.

Erik Erikson divided the years from birth to adolescence into five stages, each based on the primary focus, skill, or function being learned during that time (Erikson, 1999). For each stage, Erikson depicted an "either/or" situation. For example, in the first stage, oral-sensory, the child learns to trust the care and interaction that comes from others, or the child learns that his or her trust in adult caretakers is misplaced.

Erikson believed that the skill associated with a particular stage needed to be mastered before the child could go on to the next skill and the next stage. In this sense, the stages are organized in a developmental or hierarchical sequence, and the child who fails to develop a particular skill must revisit that skill later to reach full maturity. The notion of completing developmental stages in sequence has significance in disaster work because children may be forced by traumatic events to behave in ways that are advanced for their years, or they may become stuck in or regress to an earlier developmental stage because of trauma and fear. Most children who experience disasters eventually return to normal developmental stages.

A substantial decrease in children's symptoms occurs within months to a year after most disasters, with close to complete symptom remission by 16 months to three years, with the exception of symptoms of some children who experienced very high degrees of life threat and some who experience substantial continuing family disruption and distress (Vogel & Vernberg, 1993).

The Oklahoma City Bombing

The bomb that destroyed the Alfred P. Murrah Federal Building also "hit" the YMCA daycare center next door: It blew out windows, collapsed its ceiling, and unhinged its doors. Within a few days, a new facility was opened, several miles away. Although the new daycare location was isolated and serene, children's symptoms associated with trauma were noticed, with differences in symptoms related to age differences. Sitterle and Gurwitch (1999) noted that

> [p]arents of infants and infant care staff reported more sleep difficulties, more clingy behavior, and more difficulty with soothing and consoling a crying infant. In the toddler room, children also showed these behaviors as well as a heightened response to loud noises and more irritability. The increased startle response was particularly problematic for these very young children.... Parents also reported a change in affect in some of the children, particularly a more restricted emotional demeanor.

> In children between 3 and 5 years of age...regressive behaviors such as a return to a pacifier and toileting accidents were noted...[and also] separation anxiety and sleep disturbances. (p. 176)

Oral–Sensory Stage: Basic Trust versus Basic Mistrust

From birth to about one year of age, the major work of an infant is attachment. As an infant comes into contact with the primary people involved in her or his life, many questions are asked, some are answered, and a great deal is learned: "Am I cared for? Will I be fed? Will I be kept reasonably clean and dry? Will I be held so that I feel human skin and warmth?" The infant may learn that she or he can depend on others for care, food, and human warmth, or the infant may learn that people are not always available, or that care is sporadic, unpredictable, or insufficient.

Attachment is the foundation for the child's remaining developmental stages. Whether that foundation is solid or shaky is determined by many factors, including the parent's and child's physical, mental, and emotional health; separations that may occur between the infant and primary caretakers; and the absence or presence of effective parenting skills. An infant attaches, and in fact develops the ability to attach, when there is consistent positive care. When basic trust grows, the child develops a hopeful attitude: "This world must be an okay place because people here are taking care of me."

During the second six months of life, the child begins to reach out to the world and "demand" things. Trust is built, or fails to be built, depending on the primary caretaker's reaction to those demands.

Child development experts tend to agree that the infant's primary task during the oral-sensory stage is the development of attachment. Bowlby (1969, 1980), Fahlberg (1991), Erikson (1999), and others have all described the process in which an infant and her or his primary caretakers form strong connections. Bowlby described attachment as the push for human beings to develop strong emotional bonds to others.

Touching Reality "How Does Attachment Develop?" provides an opportunity for you to recognize how attachment develops.

How Does Attachment Develop?

How does attachment develop?

Stop for a moment and think of an infant you have seen. Bring up a mental image of that baby.

Now, visualize this baby hungry, or with a wet diaper, or craving human contact. What happens? Can you see the baby ball up his or her hands, tighten facial muscles, tense arm and leg muscles, turn red in the face, and let fly with the noises necessary to get some attention?

The world is strange to the infant, and the infant has neither the cognitive ability nor the capacity to alert the world to his or her needs in a language the world might understand.

Now, what happens if the baby in your mind has caretakers who are willing, able, and at least somewhat skilled at deciphering the messages? Often, there is instant silence! The need of the moment is met, and the baby relaxes; the face changes to a more usual color, the tears stop, and sometimes there is cooing or a smile.

Repetition of this cycle—awareness of a need, frustration and rage in trying to get the need met, a response that meets or reduces the need, followed by relaxation—creates the building blocks from which attachment is built.

Over time, the habitual sufficient meeting of the infant's needs results in the establishment of a bond of trust between the infant and caretakers. This bond is the foundation of an optimistic worldview and positive self-esteem. The infant begins to believe that the caretakers are trustworthy people because they respond consistently to his or her needs: "My needs are met; I feel okay." In addition, the infant is given the message that he or she is a "worthy" person, a loveable person who merits receiving continuous care.

Separation is the temporary or permanent loss of the trusted "object" person who is involved with the infant in the attachment process. Bowlby (1969, 1980) described responding with anxiety to an unwilling separation as a normal reaction for a human being. The younger the child, the more severe is the impact of separation—the child may not understand the reason for the separation, or the attachment process may be incomplete, or new and fragile.

Disasters can cause major disruptions to this critical attachment process. Parents and children can become separated through injury, death, or simply the chaos of a disaster's aftermath. In some instances, caretakers may be present but so distressed or traumatized by the disaster experience that they are not available for the child. Separation from parents and loved ones as a result of a disaster can be much worse for infants and small children than the loss of property or the lack of food.

When at all possible, helpers in the disaster situation must remain aware of the need to support infants and young children's attachment to a primary adult. This means that the helper must be keenly aware of the distress felt by a child when his or her parent or other primary caretaker cannot be located. Helpers might also need to encourage the child to bring the parent to mind if the parent is unavailable.

There are several ways to offer support to the infant or young child. Is there any clothing belonging to a parent that is available in which to dress or wrap the child? Are there any extended family members who have had contact with this child previously? Do the people caring for the child speak the family's language? What are this child's routines and usual foods? Can they be replicated? The helper looks for any small ways to help the child feel a sense of normalcy.

Because infants and early toddlers cannot speak in words, they find other ways to exhibit their distress when regular needs are not met. Anxiety or fear may show up as an inability to sleep, an inability to sleep without a light, night terrors, irritability, aggressiveness, sadness, speech difficulties, or eating problems. The child may become irritable, cry more than usual, and want to be cuddled more. Because the child may still be largely or completely nonverbal, certain sights, sounds, or smells may be associated with the trauma. Memories are attached to physical anchors that may be a lifelong unarticulated sensory perception on the adult's part. An adult who experienced a disaster in childhood may experience mysterious physical pains in connection to the early life event (Young, 1998).

Significant absence or the death of a parent is, obviously, a critical loss. The infant who has not yet reached the developmental stage of object constancy—the ability to hold an image of an object or person in mind even in its absence, which is a stage usually reached between seven and 10 months—does not know that people continue to exist if they are out of sight. As a result, the child may experience feelings of abandonment almost immediately. The child

may withdraw from his or her surroundings and become numb, unfeeling, or mute. The risk of growing up and becoming independent may be too frightening.

Fear is a typical reaction among children to trauma and disaster. Because the infant's cognitive abilities are still largely undeveloped, it may seem difficult to determine if the child is experiencing fear. "Kagan (1982) has shown in studies of normal infant development that when confronted with new and different information infants may smile if the information is successfully integrated, and they show fear by crying or withdrawing if they cannot make sense of the information" (Speier, 2000, p. 4).

Encouraging children and adults to draw pictures and then talk about them is one way to help them begin to make sense about what has happened—the trauma may not be available for verbal descriptions. Frequently, when children experience something traumatic, scary, or sad, they are at a loss for words to adequately describe what has happened to them, and pictures open the door to the sharing of useful and accurate information about reactions to disasters. "Young children may have only physical memories of an event, without words to put to the memory. Even if verbal, they may not be able to integrate sensory perceptions into a narrative understanding of what happened. Hence, often a memory may focus on one specific impression associated with the threat or harm" (Young, 1998). As a result, an intervention that helpers frequently use with children is an activity called "It Happened to Me." To experience some small sense of a child's nonverbal reaction to a trauma or a difficult situation, you can try this activity for yourself in Touching Reality "Recapturing a Nonverbal Experience: It Happened to Me."

Recapturing a Nonverbal Experience: It Happened to Me

Gather a piece of paper and some markers, crayons, or pencils. Recall an experience that was scary, sad, or difficult for you. You can choose a recent experience or one from your childhood. Were you ever in a hurricane? Did a loved pet die? Were you in a scary car accident? Did friends or relatives experience a house fire? Was a member of your family or a relative in the military or law enforcement and in danger? Recall as much detail as you can of that time. What feelings do you remember? How did those around you behave? Did their reactions affect your own?

Whatever event you have chosen, do you have it in your mind?

Now draw a picture of that event. Drawing skill is not important here. Instead, try to experience what it might be like to be nonverbal, and to put on paper what you might not be able to explain in words. Try to demonstrate your reactions to the event by what you draw.

Look at your picture. Are there reactions and feelings that come back to you as you remember the event? Do you recall your own clarity or confusion about the incident that accompanied the feelings? If you were a child at the time of your remembered event, what were you able to understand? Did other people around you explain things or acknowledge your reactions? Even in adult situations, some events can cause confusion about roles and the order of things in the universe.

Consider sharing your picture with someone else—describe the picture and tell the person how old you were. What did you learn about your own reactions by drawing this picture? Consider what this experience might be like for a child or a youth who feels powerless in the face of a sudden trauma or long-term community violence.

End this activity by reminding yourself of the stability you have in your life now, and of your capability as an adult who is doing well in your world.

A series of pictures may show a child's ongoing attempt to understand and make sense of an event that seems senseless. As we have already said, trauma tends to be nonverbal, and picture drawing may be helpful to an adult as well as a child.

Muscular–Anal Stage: Autonomy versus Shame and Doubt

Children at this stage of life—from about one year to three years old—begin to develop some independence. They gain and quickly develop language. How delightful that they can begin to communicate needs in a way that is more easily understood by caretakers! Adult reaction to this nascent self-control, coupled with the child's feelings of successful navigation of her or his world, affect the child's development of autonomy or doubt.

In his studies of child cognitive development, Piaget (2000) noticed that children at this stage make intellectual deductions by using their senses. Because they understand what they can see, hear, smell, taste, and touch, he labeled what takes place sensorimotor learning. Abstract concepts are not part of their repertoire, nor are they able to generalize. Each case is separate until there have been many, many repetitions. Each sunrise is a surprise, to be noticed and appreciated until it has been seen so many times that the expectation becomes ingrained. Hallmarks of this developmental stage include

- learning to walk, feed oneself, and talk
- muscular maturation, which sets the stage for the "holding on and letting go" necessary to learn appropriate use of the toilet
- beginning to develop a sense of self-esteem and self-efficacy—the ability to operate successfully—"I can pick up and put down, over and over"
- shame, which occurs when the child becomes self-conscious (through negative exposure), especially if the parents overly shame or blame the child (for example, with regard to toilet training and self-feeding in a messy way).

A disaster that occurs when a child is becoming aware of his or her own power and control over the environment can frustrate the child's sense of autonomy. The disaster may have destroyed accustomed possessions and may cause accustomed places or people to be unavailable. It may have disrupted patterns—of eating, using the toilet, and bathing. The disaster situation demonstrates clearly to the young child that her or his sense of control of the world is, at best, shaky.

The toddler exhibits fear in many ways. A common sign that the toddler is anxious and fears the trauma's reoccurrence is sleep disturbance. These disturbances might manifest as fear of sleeping alone or of the dark. The child who had been sleeping through the night may wake up frequently, or rise at very early hours, be watchful, and appear to be making sure that "bad things" will not happen again. If toilet habits have been established, accidents and regression to pretoilet training behaviors may occur.

Locomotor–Genital Stage: Initiative versus Guilt

At three to five years of age, children are egocentric, which is not the same thing as selfish. Egocentric behavior describes the reality that children measure their understanding of an event against a restricted number of experiences, and that they focus on their immediate life. They focus on the present and seldom think of yesterday or tomorrow.

Children at this age have difficulty taking another person's point of view and would be unlikely to think through the reasons for the other person's actions. They see themselves as the "cause of things" and, in their "magical thinking," believe that their wishing really can "make it so." During this stage, which Piaget calls "preoperational," children grow to realize that they can be the "cause" of more and more things. The encouraging reaction of important others in their world, coupled with facets of their own personality, can draw them out to try more things, or make them pull back, be cautious, and work to achieve invisibility. During this developmental stage:

- the child takes more initiative in both motor and intellectual tasks ("Me do it!"). In fact, with increasing large and small motor skills, the child can physically do more things. Language increases exponentially. The child begins to understand the power of words and starts to play with them. The beginning foundation for reading is developed at this time.
- guilt may arise over contemplated goals (especially aggressive fantasies). At this age, children engage in a great deal of magical thinking. They fantasize having grand notions and doing amazing things. The guilt for children at this age arises when they imagine dire consequences for another person who wronged them in

some way. These are the children who in very normal, uncivilized four-year-old behavior, vehemently wish Mama dead, or gone forever; who wish the beloved family dog who just ate their candy would get run over; or who wish that their sibling would be kidnapped by pirates. Guilt arises when the child stops (usually with adult prodding) and really pays attention to the scenario he or she has imagined. No! They do *not* really want all those things to happen.

- the child wants to mimic the adult world and begins to develop social role identification. Wearing Mommy's high heels or Daddy's hat, "working in the kitchen" at playschool, playing with papers like the older sister does after school—all these are ways that the child tries on adult roles. The child is beginning to classify behaviors and roles as those belonging to girls or boys and is usually inflexible in this way.

- sibling rivalry is common; a child might wish that other family members would leave so that she or he can have more attention, things, or food. The child is not heavily invested in sharing at this point in his or her existence. Alfred Adler, the well-known psychologist, is often quoted with regard to the child's thinking at this stage: "I want, what I want, when I want it."

The child at this stage of development, faced with a disaster event, may feel powerless and overwhelmed with fear and insecurity. As Keppel-Benson and Ollendick (1993) pointed out, a key variable in the child's reaction to the disaster is his or her subjective interpretation of the trauma. The child uses his or her short pool of experience to determine and understand what is happening. The conclusions the child draws may be incorrect and completely unfounded, but they are often hard to shake and may be long lasting. Children at this developmental stage may not be able to discuss events in terms of time, but rather in terms of how they relate to personal concerns, such as a birthday or a trip (Young, 1998). For instance, they will remember a fire that occurred just after Christmas; the loss of someone significant around a child's birthday may affect his or her birthday memories for a lifetime.

Preschool-age children do not have the cognitive ability to understand clearly what is happening to them. The usual predictable routines of their lives may be disrupted, the people they turn to for explanations and protection may not be available at all if they have been injured or killed, or they may be so emotionally upset themselves that they are not emotionally available to the child and cannot comfort the child adequately. The child may feel lost, alone, and unconnected.

Play is a key form of communication for children, and they are much more likely to act out their experience than they are to explain it verbally. Given the opportunity, children will demonstrate what they are worrying about inside. After hurricanes, or earthquakes, disaster volunteers may see children acting out burying scenes or playing "rescuer." Children who have experienced floods may show extreme fear at the approach of another storm or the first signs of rain. A child who has lost someone important in an airplane crash may crash toy planes, break them apart, or show anger at the sight of a crash seen on television.

The University of Illinois Cooperative Extension Service (1995a, 1995b) provides a variety of activities to help preschool and elementary school children express their feelings. Diffusing the feelings of children who are uncomfortable with talking, or whose verbal ability is limited, requires using techniques that depend on other modes of expression. For example, helpers can encourage children to play with toys such as ambulances, bulldozers, and blocks to re-enact in play what they saw and experienced during a disaster. Helpers might also help them ventilate their feelings through physical activity, such as playing Ring Around the Rosie, to relieve stress or through drawing pictures about what they saw (alone or in a group) and then talking about their product.

Children in the locomotor–genital stage of development may believe that thinking about something will cause it to happen. With their growing sense of power, it is perfectly logical from their perspective to believe that they caused the tornado, the flood, the hurricane, or the plane crash or train derailment, or the shooting or terrorist attack to occur. Children who wish ill on someone who is subsequently injured during a disaster may firmly believe that they caused the disaster. The resulting guilt can be overwhelming, and the child may not be cognitively capable of understanding that the disaster had nothing to do with her or him. The child's fantasy constructs another reality, and she or he may be unable to distinguish fact from fantasy.

Typical reactions of children in this stage of development include regressive behaviors such as bedwetting, whining, and separation anxiety (Lerner et al., 2003), or thumb sucking, fear of darkness or animals, inability to dress or eat without assistance, or excessive clinginess. The child may be unusually irritable, confused, and sad about the loss of prized possessions or pets, and he or she may exhibit speech difficulties.

Finally, television has a greater impact on three- and four-year-old children than it does on older children and adults, which means that monitoring their watching behavior after a disaster is especially important. Preschool children are more suggestible and fail to discriminate whether an event was seen live or on television (Thierry & Spence, 2002).

Latency Stage: Industry versus Inferiority

Children's cognitive abilities and social competencies develop at a tremendous rate at this time in their development, during the ages of six to 11 years old. They begin to understand that there are rules in life and in their families and that order is normal. The elementary school teacher discovers this affinity when she breaks one of her own rules, only to hear howls from the students who call her attention to the transgression. Children may remind their parents how something is supposed to be done, whether it is how to put clothes in the drawer (underwear on the left, socks on the right, naturally), when to go to Grandma's house (on Sunday afternoons, of course), where the dog sleeps (outside, as you would expect), and when to shop for food for the family (Friday, after school, obviously). The child—who is busy building, creating, and accomplishing—enjoys and is comforted by dependability and order.

During this developmental stage, the child develops an understanding of the physical construction of his or her universe and the fundamentals of social interaction. This is the time in the child's life when he or she uses tools alongside the parent. The child will plant seeds and watch them grow, help build a shed, sew a dress, raise a calf from birth, or begin to understand how a computer program is put together. Normally, the child is not doing

The Effects of Warlike Trauma on Children

Until recently, much research about responses to the stress of war and violence has focused on the adults who were combatants during the conflict. Lately, more attention is being paid to the effect of chronic violence on civilians, especially children. Salman Elbedour, Robert ten-Bensel, and David Bastien (1993) developed an ecological integrated model detailing the dimensions of children and their environment that researchers need to consider to understand the effects of war and chronic violent conditions on children.

Elbedour and his colleagues (1993) suggested that the "ability of children to integrate their traumatic situations is dependent upon the child's own resources and the child's developmental characteristics at the time of the situation" (p. 809). Although every child exposed to the horrors of war and chronic violence is likely to experience emotional upheaval, some children will overcome the effects and continue with their lives in a reasonably healthy way, whereas others will be profoundly hurt and suffer long-term damage. To determine the amount of suffering a child may experience, Elbedour and his colleagues suggested researchers need to consider the dynamic Interaction among five processes:

1. *The child's psychobiological makeup.* A child's age, gender, intelligence, imagination, and outlook are all personal characteristics that affect how she or he will deal with a traumatic situation. Previous traumas, or physical or mental disabilities, may make it harder to cope with the current situation. Continuous violence may overwhelm even the most resilient child's coping repertoire, and if the well of energy is almost empty

anyway, the crisis will take an even heavier toll.

2. *The disruption of the family unit.* Children pay attention to the reactions of the adults they know and trust when gauging the seriousness of a situation. When adults are emotionally overwhelmed, children become especially frightened. In addition, when family members are injured or killed, or when children are forced to become combatants themselves, the family unit begins to disintegrate. As a result, there is no psychological mantle of protection for the child. It is hard for young children, especially, to understand why the adults in their lives sometimes cannot make the danger or disruption go away.

3. *The breakdown of the child's community.* Communities provide another level of routine and protection for the child. The child derives comfort from known rituals, locations, neighborhoods, persons, and accepted ways of behaving. Chronic violence destroys the networks upon which the child depends for safety and familiarity by physically destroying places and damaging the connections between people. Fearful people tend to become less trusting and more isolated. In his book, There Are No Children Here, Alex Kotlowitz (1991) describes the effect chronic neighborhood violence has on the lives of two boys and their family living in the Henry Horner Housing Project in Chicago. Gangs divide the streets into safe zones and danger zones. Law enforcement officers are the enemy, not protection, and are to be avoided at all costs. Most of the boys did not expect to live to see 20 years of age. Because so many of the young died,

cont'd

having friends was a great risk. The two boys in this story had what they called acquaintances. Friends were too close, and too risky. There was little sense of community or mutual assistance among neighbors.

4. *The ameliorating effects of culture.* Culture can provide structure when other institutions are damaged or destroyed in chronic violence. A strong sense of community within a particular culture can assist a child to find stability and familiarity even if immediate family is unavailable. The culture can provide the necessary sense of belonging. When that culture is diminished or destroyed through disaster or chronic violence, it represents yet another loss for the child and his or her family,

5. *The intensity, suddenness, and duration of the warlike or violent experience.* The longer a child lives with trauma, the more likely he or she is to have lost family members, lost property, and seen violence close up. Sudden, violent altercations in different locations make whole neighborhoods or communities unsafe. The tension and risk may appear to be everywhere. The child never gets to relax or find a place that is "normal."

The researchers strongly suggest that institutions in such violent areas do what they can to create a safe haven for children, at least for a period. Whole families need support and education about the effects of violence on the family. The cultural heritage of a neighborhood should be supported and enhanced when possible so that communities will maintain a sense of belonging.

Elbedour, S., ten Bensel, R. & Bastien, D. T. (1993). Ecological integrated model of children of war: Individual and social psychology. *Child Abuse and Neglect, 17*, 805–819.

these things alone. There are others, who teach, suggest new ways to accomplish the task, and encourage the child toward the project's completion. Adults or children form sports teams for children during these years. Children get together with others (usually of the same sex) and play "grown-up" games, like "store," or "school," or "family." They practice how adults interact with one another and argue when their perspectives differ.

If a child despairs of his or her tools or skills and status among peers, there is a danger of developing a sense of inadequacy and inferiority. Some children do not fit in with those around them. They think, act, sound, or look different from the others. Some children learn more slowly, lack some physical attributes necessary to play sports or the strength to do farm chores well, or are very short in a family or community of Titans. These are the children who move to the sidelines, speak rarely or too loudly, and are not often rewarded for their presence. These may be the children who have adequate skills but who simply do not measure up to parental expectations or who have trouble following successfully in a sibling's footsteps. However, these also may be the children who suddenly carry all the family's hopes when an older sibling is lost through death, injury, or bad choices (such as drug involvement, marriage to an unacceptable person, and so on). When children do not believe that they are capable of meeting their own or others' expectations, they may give up, believe that they are unworthy, and avoid risks or chances to increase involvement in the world around them.

Piaget (2000) described children at this age as being solidly in "concrete operations." Children at this stage have an understanding of linear cause and effect and of the order of things in the world. They are usually able to solve concrete problems in a logical way. Rules and predictability are the foundation of a sense of security. However, there is still some magical thinking left over from the previous stage. For example, death is real, but how it occurs is quite mysterious, and the child may think it is reversible.

A child's sense of order is shaped by her or his notions of right and wrong—this is the child's morality—as it is shaped by the rules learned and the logic used. Kohlberg and his colleagues (Colby, Kohlberg, Gibbs, & Lieberman, 1994; Kohlberg, Levine, & Hewer, 1994) described this as parent-based morality. Because the child's experience of the world is limited, she or he uses the parent or parent figure as a compass when determining appropriate actions (Eisenberg & Valiente, 2002). The child may ask reflexively: "What would Mom or Dad say I should do?" In addition, most children at this stage want to stay out of trouble, above all else. "Trouble" could be loosely defined as anything that causes pain, embarrassment, punishment, or shame. Because the parent or parent figure is often the determinant of the consequences for wrong actions, the child again borrows parental thinking: "How much trouble would I get in if I did this thing that I know is wrong?" or "What will Grandma say if I do this thing?"

Cognitively and psychologically, most children at this stage do not have the skills to juggle several diverse concepts at one time. Actions and decisions are right or wrong, good or bad. Imagine a conversation you might have with an eight-year-old child after she or he heard you tell Aunt Emma that her new hair color is attractive but had earlier heard you tell another adult that Emma's choice in hair coloring is ridiculous. The child might ask, "Why did you lie? Is it okay to lie? When is it okay to lie? The teacher said lying is never okay." There is not a lot of room for ambiguity at this age. Things are right or wrong.

Children are usually fairly mobile at this age. They are at school, making friends, possibly joining clubs or doing more "adult" chores at home. The child's life develops a rhythm, a sense of routine.

Disasters are disorderly. The child understands that they are without purpose, that they randomly injure loved ones and destroy special things. Adults cannot prevent the disaster from happening or, usually, explain why it happened. In the disaster's aftermath, the child may believe that adults, who once seemed so powerful, had no control over the situation. When a child witnesses violence and violent death, for example, issues of human accountability, trust, and betrayal are raised, which may intensify the trauma's challenge to the child's moral development and sense of ongoing safety (Nader, 2002).

Children in this latency age have access to a much greater range of emotions than they did at the preschool age. In a disaster, fear, however, is the predominant emotion, but now it is attached to a much greater awareness of real danger and destruction to family and home. The child may develop fear of a dangerous future, real or imagined, or become frightened when the weather is reminiscent of the recent hurricane, tornado, or floods.

Grief is another common emotion after a disaster, and school-age children may have long-term difficulty dealing with this complex and strong emotion. Children may experience guilt if they believe, on some level, that they caused the disaster, or the injury or death of someone because they had harbored anger or maybe even "wished' it to happen. Children who are babysitters, who are responsible for the care of others, often feel guilt when their charges are hurt or frightened.

The younger children in this stage of development typically do not have the ability to express their emotions verbally, orally, or by writing, so they may instead act out how they feel behaviorally. According to Lerner and his colleagues (2003), Speier (2000), and Young (1998), behavioral reactions to disasters identified in school-age children include

- sleep problems, including nightmares and bedwetting
- sadness and crying
- disobedience
- refusal to attend school
- poor school performance
- interruption of school friendships, resulting in self-imposed isolation
- withdrawal of interest in activities
- inability to concentrate, confusion
- physical complaints, such as headaches
- distractibility
- peer problems, including aggressive behavior or withdrawal.

The disaster may be one a child witnesses second hand, perhaps on television, and not one experienced personally. Many children witnessed the explosion of the Challenger space shuttle, both as it occurred and in the countless news programs that aired the video repeatedly for days following the explosion; the children felt a strong empathy with the crew because of the schoolteacher aboard, Christa McAuliffe. Terr and her colleagues (1996) studied the disaster's "secondhand" effects on children (this study is the subject of a Spotlight on Research in chapter 6). They conducted two interviews, 14 months apart, with children living on the east and west coasts of the United States. During the first interview, the majority of children reported an ongoing tendency to visualize the explosion when they heard it

mentioned or if they received a visual reminder. By the second interview, most symptoms dramatically faded, although adolescents' expectations for the future, in general, were diminished after the disaster.

Because of children's limited verbal ability in this stage, play is an appropriate way to help them cope postdisaster. Painting, drawing, working with clay, and playful exercise are often useful interventions; this is especially true for the younger children. For the older children in this stage, writing in a journal, reading, and discussing and telling stories are constructive interventions.

Preadolescence and Adolescence: Identity versus Role Confusion

As any parent can tell you, preadolescence and adolescence—ages 12 through about 19—are periods of great change, upheaval, and usually some awkwardness. The adolescent revisits some of the rules and assumptions from her or his younger years and begins to question edicts that were once accepted without hesitation. The youths may trust some adults but not others. They may perceive some adults as having a real connection with the adolescent's world— these adults seem to understand their issues and listen to their concerns—and others as being out of touch, old fashioned, rigid, and a barrier to growth. The youths' search for identity leads to experimentation with different roles, dress, personal styles, and ways of behaving.

Regardless of the questioning and the search for identity (and despite their protests to the contrary), adolescents continue to have a strong connection to adult caretakers, who provide ongoing support, course direction, and suggestions for behavior. Klingman (2001b), for example, found that in the context of ongoing massive missile attacks that took place along Israel's northern border, adolescents' parents emerged as the most-approached and most-valued source of support for adolescents, followed by their friends.

This is a time of strong emotions. Anger can quickly become rage and sadness can become despair. Commitments are a sacred trust at the time they are made. Life seems to stretch ahead in an endless stream. Youths in this developmental stage often have feelings of ambiguity and self-consciousness. Other characteristics of this age:

- Youths at this age struggle to develop ego identity, to answer the question, "Who am I?" especially in terms of how that "who" is perceived by others. The youth is looking for continuity between the inner perception and his or her meaning for others.
- Adolescents are preoccupied with appearance. The psychological spotlight (that is, thinking that everyone in the world is watching you) is on.
- Group identity is paramount, and friends are immensely important. Groups can be clannish and exclusionary in cruel and insensitive ways. Anyone considered different is ostracized, left to form his or her own group, or to stand alone.
- Roles are confusing at this age: "Am I grown up or am I still a child?"
- Youths have a psychosocial moratorium between the morality learned as a child and the ethics of an adult—and have a strong radar for anything that seems like hypocrisy that is always in the "on" position.

Disasters are sudden, frightening, and sometimes overwhelming. Youths who have come to see themselves as competent, "grown" people might respond in a "childish" way and need support and protection despite their chronological age. Fear is a powerful emotion during a disaster, and youths may be embarrassed by their feelings.

Often, children in this stage of development want a meaningful role in disaster recovery and may not be permitted to take on such a role if adults are focused on other things or if they view the youths as too young. The disaster may cut the adolescent off from usual methods of checking reality—meeting friends at school, working at the grocery store, practicing with the team or the band. Identity confusion may be exacerbated.

Adolescents may place themselves in situations that are risky in an attempt to experience new and different actions, emotions, and people. This can increase their likelihood of being in areas where violence occurs, or where they may be in greater danger. Heightened emotionality can propel them to act in impulsive ways, possibly resulting in injury or death. Given the risk of any type of disaster for the general population and the increased risk from youthful behavior, the chances for stress reactions also may increase. Results of a random survey of 1,245 adolescents in the United States can be extrapolated to suggest that approximately 1.07 million adolescents currently suffer from PTSD (van der Kolk & MacFarlane, 1996). It is unclear how many of this estimated number need some kind of treatment and how many actually receive it.

Adolescents who can intellectually understand the reality and finality of death may be shocked when confronted with the actuality of death, especially if it involves a peer. The adolescent may move into denial, to avoid being overwhelmed by painful awareness of the destruction of special people, places, and pets. The adolescent may experience the death as a personal betrayal, drawing outrage and hurt: "How could you do this to me?" "You have purposefully made my life terrible, and I will hate you forever!"

Other adolescents may deal with the strong emotions evoked after a trauma by withdrawing, becoming secretive, and holding their feelings inside. They may not see adults as acceptable confidants, and if other young people are not available, adolescents may believe themselves to be cut off and alone. Depression is a predominant reaction at this age.

According to Lerner and his colleagues (2003), Silverman and La Greca (2002), and Speier (2000), specific behaviors identified for the adolescent include

- withdrawal and isolation
- somatic complaints, such as headaches and stomachaches
- depression
- school problems, including behavioral problems and a decline in academic performance
- antisocial behavior, avoidance of others
- sleep disturbances
- high risk-taking behavior
- alcohol or other drug use
- suicidal thoughts, gestures, conversations
- avoidance of developmentally appropriate separations (for example, not wanting to go away to boarding school or summer camp).

Silverman and La Greca (2002) argue that, when working with adolescents, it is critical to consider the disaster's phase—(1) preimpact, (2) impact, (3) recoil, (4) postimpact, or (5) recovery and reconstruction—although we know very little about adolescents' reactions during the first two phases. Shock, disbelief, and "feeling strange" are characteristic immediate responses to a disaster—the recoil phase. Postimpact responses—during the several weeks after the disaster—may include feelings of intense fear and helplessness and perhaps symptoms of acute stress disorder (for example, a sense of numbing or detachment and a reduced awareness of one's surroundings). Reactions during recovery and reconstruction—weeks, months, and perhaps years after the disaster—may include re-experiencing the disaster in dreams or when reminded (this is the most commonly reported PTSD symptom), difficulty sleeping, angry outbursts, and hypervigilance. However, "most children who develop PTSD or its symptoms following disasters do so in the first weeks or months following the event" (Silverman & La Greca, p. 18).

The Spotlight on Research "Children's Development of PTSD after a Disaster at Sea" focuses on the reactions of children to a disaster at sea. Many of these children were in the latency stage of development when their British cruise ship, Jupiter, sank. Several years later, in their preadolescent and adolescent stage of development, researchers interviewed the children to assess what characteristics best predicted ongoing PTSD.

Most of the emotional turmoil and behavioral responses to disasters associated with the different developmental stages tend to diminish and, often, go away altogether when adults and the community in which the child lives are supportive and when the child is resilient. If, however, symptoms continue or increase a month after the disaster, further assessment is recommended (Speier, 2000).

ADDITIONAL FACTORS INFLUENCING CHILDREN'S REACTIONS TO A DISASTER

Although predictions can be made for how a child will react to a disaster depending on her or his developmental age, the predictions are not very accurate. Researchers are aware of and sometimes perplexed by the tremendous variance in reactions to trauma exhibited by children as well as adults.

SPOTLIGHT ON RESEARCH

Children's Development of PTSD after a Disaster at Sea

On October 21, 1988, the cruise ship Jupiter set sail from Athens, with about 400 British students (ages six through 12—the latency period) and their teachers on board. On the night of the sailing an Italian tanker struck it, fatally damaging the ship. As the Jupiter sank, children became separated from friends and teachers, and although many were able to jump to tug boats that had come alongside, and some were able to cling to wreckage until rescued, many had to swim in the dark, oily, sometimes burning waters. All but one child and one teacher survived.

From 1993 to 1996, that is, five to eight years after the disaster, Orlee Udwin and his colleagues (Udwin, Boyle, Yule, Bolton, & O'Ryan, 2000) examined risk factors for the development of PTSD in a group of 217 survivors (then ages 11 to 17—preadolescence and adolescence). They found three main categories of risk factors—predisaster child and family vulnerability features, objective and subjective disaster-related experiences, and postdisaster dimensions. Developing PTSD was significantly associated with the following:

- being female
- having learning or psychological difficulties, or both, before the disaster
- experiencing violence in the home before the trauma
- the severity of exposure to the disaster
- the youth's subjective appraisal of the experience
- adjustment back to "normal" after the disaster
- significant life events after the disaster
- social support after the disaster.

The best predictors of developing PTSD were degree of exposure and subjective appraisal rated five months after the disaster. Adolescents who had PTSD symptoms longest were usually the ones who had significant predisaster vulnerability factors; they scored high for depression at the five-month mark after the disaster, as well.

Udwin, O., Boyle, S., Yule, W., Bolton, D., & O'Ryan, D. (2000). Risk factors for long-term psychological effects of a disaster experienced in adolescence: Predictors of post traumatic stress disorder. *Journal of Child Psychology and Psychiatry and Allied Disciplines, 41*, 969–979.

Trauma studies have been carried out with adults and most commonly with soldiers, for several decades (Adler, 1943; Howorth, 2000; Jones & Wessely, 2000; Joseph, 1997; Leys, 2000; Shephard, 2001). Only recently have researchers focused on determining what specific variables are most salient for predicting children's reactions to a disaster, and what interventions best mitigate the trauma they experience. It is crucial for disaster relief workers to be able to predict reactions to a particular type of disaster or trauma successfully, if they and other helpers are going to bring effective trauma reduction techniques to bear quickly and efficiently.

Proximity to the Disaster

The most vulnerable to the effects of a disaster are those who are directly exposed to it; the least vulnerable are those who are outside the disaster area and who are not directly exposed. The child's proximity to the disaster is one of the most important variables for predicting the degree of trauma reaction. Vernberg and his colleagues (1996) cited several studies supporting the belief that exposure is "considered to be the primary and most critical factor for the emergence of posttraumatic stress symptoms in most models of trauma.... Frightening, life-threatening events during the disaster and loss-disruption resulting from the disaster are two aspects of exposure that have frequently been linked to psychological distress in children" (p. 238).

According to Pfefferbaum (1997), physical proximity is the "physical distance from the event and witnessing injury or death. Emotional proximity is measured by features of the event that represent emotional involvement such as injury or death of a loved one. Emotional proximity is measured by the event's features that represent emotional involvement such as injury or death of a loved one" (p. 1504). The least-vulnerable and least-affected people are those who identify with victims but who do not know them personally; they may also be students, for instance, or members of the same ethnic, religious, or racial group.

Based on their review of research related to traumatic exposure, Silverman and La Greca (2002) noted that a particularly important (and perhaps essential) aspect of exposure is whether the child perceives the disaster as a threat to her or his life or the lives of family members. Also important are whether exposure to the disaster results in the loss of possessions and the disruption of everyday routines, whether it is over a longer period of time (floods usually take place over several days or weeks, unlike hurricanes that may last only several hours), and whether the disaster includes multiple incidents or one single incident.

Gender

On November 4, 1995, a fanatic opposed to Israel's peace policy toward the Palestinians assassinated Prime Minister Yitzchak Rabin. Klingman (2001a) was interested in children's reactions to the event and studied fourth-grade students' feelings and thoughts about the assassination. The students were boys and girls about nine years old. Almost all the children grieved and were anxious. However, boys and girls differed in their reactions: girls had higher scores for emotional expressiveness, coping and adaptation, perceived social support, and grieving—all of which, taken together, leads to the prediction that girls should deal more effectively with the trauma than boys.

The findings regarding the impact of gender on children's reactions to disaster and trauma are mixed, and what differences have been found appear to be small and of questionable clinical significance (Silverman & La Greca, 2002). Pfefferbaum (1997) suggested that sex influences many ways a child responds to a disaster, including defensive and coping styles, use of support networks, and expectations for response and recovery learned from his or her culture (Norris, Perilla, Ibanez, & Murphy, 2001). Vogel and Vernberg (1993) posited that gender differences in reactions to traumatic events often are based on variations in the acceptability of different expressions of psychological distress for boys and for girls.

Studies have found both more symptom expression and symptom severity in girls than in boys (Burke, Moccia, Borus, & Burns, 1986; Green et al., 1991; Lonigan, Shannon, Finch, Daugherty, & Taylor, 1991; Yule, 1993) and higher levels of anxiety and acting out in boys (Burke, Borus, Burns, Milstein, & Beasley, 1982; Gillis, 1993; Gleser, Green, & Winget, 1981). Udwin and his colleagues (2000), in their study of the Jupiter ship disaster, found that being female was a major risk factor.

Saylor and his colleagues (Saylor, Belter, & Stokes 1997) suggested that studies using more rigorous methodology indicate that gender differences may interact with other factors to influence the type of symptoms displayed by children exposed to disasters, with girls expressing emotional reactions and boys expressing cognitive and behavioral reactions. Overall, in the research to date, gender differences "pale in comparison to effects for exposure and characteristics of the postdisaster recovery environment" (Vernberg, 1999, p. 199). Vernberg cautioned disaster workers to be sure that boys' less-overt response did not preclude them from receiving needed posttrauma support.

Making Sense of the Disaster Experience

In addition to developmental age, proximity to the disaster, and gender, another influence on how children respond is their capacity to comprehend the disaster. Cognitive and social capacities shape the lens through which the child views the disaster. As Macksoud, Aber, and Cohn (1996) pointed out, the level of stress or trauma that a child exhibits is heavily determined by her or his subjective understanding of the experience.

Young children tend to internalize their meaning for the disaster and to see themselves as somehow having caused the event. You might hear such explanations as, "The fire happened because I wanted to see lightning," or "Mommy was hurt in the airplane crash because I was very mad at her for leaving me behind." The moral stages of development and how a child begins to understand justice, according to Kohlberg and his colleagues (1994) and Colby and her colleagues (1994), would place young children in the premoral stage. This means that a young child views the world from a punishment and obedience orientation; trouble is bad and the child knows to avoid it. A disaster definitely spells trouble, and the child may well see its effects as punishment for some naughty act. As a result, the child may feel guilt and may regress out of fear and a desire to avoid trouble. The abstract randomness of a tornado or flood and the nationalism of a war are meaningless to the young child. To a child, the disaster is personal.

The school-age child finds comfort and stability in order, consistency, and structure. The randomness of disasters or the malicious intent of terrorism may be incomprehensible to the child. The child may ask, "Why?" and not be able to answer it, or find adults who are able to answer it adequately. Making sense

What Children Can Tell Us About Living in Danger

Garbarino, Kostelny, and Nancy Dubrow (1991) asked the question, "How do children react to danger?" They provide some answers from their review of the research.

The majority of children "appreciate the thrill that comes with moderate danger and seek it out in their play" (p. 377). However, these children can leave the scene of danger and return to normal—they can return to their everyday life, which is not dangerous. Other children use involvement with extreme danger as a way of exhibiting psychopathology. Still others are paralyzed by the mere hint of anything that might involve risk or danger; this paralysis is usually caused by personal temperament or parental perspectives. All of these reactions require what Garbarino and his colleagues called "situational adjustment" by normal children leading normal lives.

What happens to children when there is no "normal life" to which they can return? How do they make sense of the world when the world is nonsensical? Chronic danger may result in a developmental or life-long adjustment. "There is a growing body of research and clinical observation based on a concern that children and youth caught up in war and other forms of social crisis will adapt in ways that produce developmental impairment, physical damage, and emotional trauma, and will be mis-socialized into a model of fear, violence, and hatred as a result" (p. 378). Children forced to cope with chronic danger may develop PTSD, exhibit hyperaggression when they feel threatened, or develop emotional withdrawal, even after the danger is long past.

Chronic danger, it seems, truncates moral development and creates a vendetta mentality: The child never moves away from a rather bifurcated worldview—good/bad, useful/not useful, enemy/friend. The child is especially vulnerable if he is male and lives in an environment where the political realities and the family social climate are both authoritarian and antidemocratic.

However, there is a hopeful side to this research. "Families can provide the emotional context for the necessary processing to make positive moral sense of danger" (p. 380). Three elements sustain a minimum positive standard of care for children: "If parents can sustain a strong attachment to their children, maintain a positive sense of self, and have access to rudimentary shelter, food, and medical care, then children will manage" (p. 380).

Garbarino, J., Kostelny, K., & Dubrow, N. (1991). What children can tell us about living in danger. *American Psychologist, 46,* 376–383.

of a disaster is very difficult when few can explain to the child why it occurred in language that the child understands. Sometimes the child is able to use tangible tools, such as maps, pictures, and coloring books to begin to develop some understanding of "Why here?", "Why now?", "Why me?"

School-age children are in the process of developing strong role conformity—they derive comfort from knowing their role and from receiving approval from others for their actions within those roles. They look to the adults around them for role models on how to behave during and after a disaster. They feel confused by the disruption or breakdown of usual routines; they respond with fear. In addition, adults may not be able to continue fulfilling their appropriate roles as guide, moral compass, and interpreter of the outside world; the child is unclear about how he or she is expected to behave in a situation. Anxiety, depression, and regression are responses to this confusion and ambiguity.

The older child or adolescent is frequently able to understand concepts such as war and terrorism, the randomness of storms, and the chance that technology will fail. The youth's explanation tends to be more externalized than those of younger siblings; adolescents are cognitively and psychologically mature enough to know that they did not cause a terrorist act, a flood, or a plane crash. Adolescents are able to postulate several possible outcomes to a situation and follow the postulates to their apparent and logical conclusions. There may be confusion, but they are also able to use reason as a tool to mitigate the confusion. Adolescents usually demonstrate the same types of responses to a disaster as do adults.

Because youths are closely aligned with friends, any disruption in being able to see them or talk with them may be very distress-ing. Regardless of the level of understanding of the disaster's cause, there may well be an "irrational" response to the closing of school, the inability to get together with friends, and the possibility of relocating. The adolescent may behave somewhat like the much younger and egocentric sibling.

The adolescent's growing emancipation from the family—the beginning stages of separation and individuation—may be disrupted as family members work together to survive and heal from the disaster.

The adolescent's need to trust in her or his own competence—and to appear to be competent, especially to friends and family—may be disrupted as the disaster creates an ambiguous situation to which the adolescent is unsure how to adapt.

Ultimately, the adolescent may experience a loss of self, of the family, and even of the whole community.

Complicating the matter further is the adolescent's feeling that no one feels as he or she does, that no one has ever experienced the depth of feeling he or she feels, and that no one has had to grapple with the issues with which he or she has to grapple. These strong emotions increase the chances that the adolescent may become depressed or attempt suicide.

Youths at this stage of moral development are "questioners" and "experimenters" (Colby et al., 1994; Kohlberg et al., 1994). They begin to re-examine and relearn lessons of right and wrong and to question the role of spirituality and religion in their lives. The disaster may enhance that normal questioning. A youth may become angry at the deity that his or her parents worship. ("How could God let this happen? What type of ineffective power have my parents taught me to believe?") Although the family may be using their faith and belief system as a coping tool, the adolescent may be unable to use that method. Instead, the young person may decide to deal with the disaster in ways that appear to be very unfamiliar to the family. The youth may, for instance, join a different spiritual group, declare a belief in atheism, or become involved with a political group that is strange to the family. The adolescent's struggle and questioning may cause a separation from the family at a time when the youth may need extra support. Conversely, the disaster may shake the youth's self-confidence, making asking questions appear to be too risky.

In war situations, the meaning that adolescents derive from their role in the conflict partly determines if the conflict ultimately has a positive or negative effect (Macksoud et al., 1996). Is the adolescent on the "right side" of the conflict? Does the youth believe that the actions being taken by his or her family and community in this conflict are congruent with his or her developing beliefs? Atrocities committed by combatants in a war may strongly offend the moral stance of adolescent fighters, leading them to question their own beliefs. Is the opponent really in the right in this situation? Adolescents who believe that their perspective is at least reasonably correct suffer fewer negative effects than those who believe their perspective may be wrong or misguided.

Culture's Effect on Children's Reactions

Although many of the factors that determine how children respond to a disaster exist within the cultural context from which they gain their meaning, one of the most understudied areas of disaster research concerns the topic of multicultural issues in the response of children to disasters

(Rabalais, Ruggiero, & Scotti, 2002). Culture—the language, values, beliefs, traditions, and customs that binds people together (Samovar & Porter, 2001)—"plays a key role in how individuals cope with potentially traumatizing experiences by providing the context in which social support and other positive and uplifting events can be experienced" (de Vries, 1996, p. 398). In addition, values, beliefs, customs, and so on "create meaning systems that explain the causes of traumatic events" (de Vries, p. 402). Does the child live in a community that explains flooding with reference to the properties of hurricanes and the cyclical nature of weather patterns? Does the child's community explain flooding by referring to supernatural forces that affect all humans? Does the community attribute the flooding to a lack of governmental planning and teach that anger and finger-pointing are appropriate responses?

Cultures vary in the emphasis they place on different facets of a person's life. The importance of privacy, whether an individual or group perspective is "right," how to comfort others, which emotions are appropriate to express under different conditions, how adults and children are supposed to interact, and whether asking for help is acceptable—all are culturally defined, and all are involved in predicting a child's reaction to a disaster. The Spotlight on Research on page 90 discusses the ways that cultural perspectives on natural bodily functions can affect young people.

de Vries (1996) cited several studies that found that individuals who identified strongly with cultural values benefited from the social support provided by those cultures. Their cultural connections became a buffer against the trauma's impact. The Bangladeshi girls mentioned in the

Notions of Honor, Shame, Purity and Pollution During the Bangladesh Floods

Adolescence is a relatively new concept in Bangladesh; culturally, many adolescents, especially girls, are married soon after the onset of puberty, so that the concept of this as a time of exploration and questioning is not present. Before the Bangladeshi girls are married, they are watched closely, and tend to be confined to limited surroundings and to contacts with family and close relations. Parents fear premarital sexual activity and any resultant pregnancies. The girl's "purity" is closely safeguarded, because without it, marriage prospects diminish to almost nothing, and marriage remains the only socially acceptable option for women, especially those living in rural areas. Both the girls and their families take extreme care of their reputation, which influences their behavior and attitudes.

In 1998 there were devastating floods in Bangladesh. Almost two-thirds of the country was under water for approximately nine weeks. Thirty million people were affected. Sabina Faiz Rashid and Stephanie Michaud (2000) interviewed nine girls between the ages of 15 and 19. The girls interviewed were from the poorer areas and were especially conscious of the repercussions of not following social norms or of not behaving acceptably. Unacceptable behavior included being seen in any public space, laughing or talking with boys or men, and being dressed immodestly—for example, with bare arms or legs.

The floods caused these young women shame and trouble because social norms hold regardless of the circumstances. Suddenly, the girls had to share living space in refugee camps or the rooms of houses. Bathing and toileting became public activities. One girl was afraid to sleep for fear that her legs would be exposed while she slept. Some of the girls were expected by their families to remain in the house until the floodwaters receded. One adolescent said, "It was so bad to be stuck inside the house for three months during the floods.... my mother would get angry with us for going outside of the house.... People think that young girls going around might be doing bad things,

you know, *prem* [romance]!" (p. 60). Many of the girls would only use the toilet late at night when no one else was around. Sometimes their fathers or older brothers would watch over them to be sure that no one was looking.

In the shelters, the girls were at risk of being harassed by men and boys from other families. "Most of the girls in this study expressed a general feeling of helplessness in the face of such harassment and believed that the best response was to ignore it" (p. 63). If men accosted a girl who was out, generally the result, even if it included molestation, was considered to be the girl's fault.

Menstruation, which is a private topic, was particularly difficult for these young women, who were just starting their menses. Culturally, it was critical to hide the fact that they were menstruating from all family members, even from their mothers. With their homes surrounded by dirty water, the girls had to keep clean and wash their underwear in public, and they were very much ashamed during menstruation. Many of the young girls interviewed had developed infections, or knew other young women who had, because of their lack of ability to wash their sanitary supplies.

Another effect of the flood was that some girls, recently married, were afraid that their husbands would leave them because their families had lost their crops and farm animals, and their dowry could not be paid in full. Under such circumstances, the husband could return the girl to her family. If this happens, further marriage prospects are limited because she is no longer "pure."

The young women's experience of the 1998 floods was profoundly affected by cultural notions of "honour, shame, purity and pollution, which regulated their sexuality and gender relations....Female adolescents' attempts and sometimes inability to follow these norms made them particularly vulnerable, and has had far-reaching implications on their health, identity, family and community relations" (p. 69).

Rashid, S. F., & Michaud, S. (2000). Female adolescents and their sexuality: Notions of honour, shame, purity and pollution during the floods. *Disasters, 24*, 54–70.

Spotlight on Research fared better if their families were able to maintain a sense of privacy and protection for them. The girls received social support from their family and relatives when they were able to maintain their expected cultural role, despite the floods. When the girls and their families could not maintain those social norms, both the girl and her family were shamed and lost community support.

Rabalais and her colleagues (2002) described important culturally relevant risk and protective factors, based on their review of the research on culture and disasters. For example, culture may be a risk factor when youths are members of an oppressed group or a group that is discriminated against. If health-care providers are members of a dominant group that is perceived to be prejudiced and, perhaps, hostile, youths have less motivation to seek help from them; and if government agencies are perceived as favoring one group over another, the less-favored group is unlikely to apply for postdisaster financial aid. Another risk factor is "acculturation stress," the stress that occurs when the values and practices of the majority culture conflict with those of the minority culture. What is a member of a culture that teaches "Do not discuss family business with strangers" supposed to do when the government employee who handles disaster-related grants asks what the individual perceives are highly personal questions?

Culture also can be a protective factor. A culture may protect against negative psychological outcomes by providing

positive parental or family relationships (African American and Hispanic Americans), reliance on extended kin networks (Hispanic Americans and African Americans), and spirituality (African Americans).... [And a] fourth protective factor: ethnic and racial socialization, which is multidimensional and includes the active teaching of cultural values, instillation of pride in one's culture, preparation of youth for coping with discrimination, and maintenance of cultural traditions. (Rabalais et al., 2002, p.78)

If the disaster is of such a magnitude that the very culture begins to fail, then individuals are left on their own to determine a course of action and to decide what behaviors are acceptable. This situation can create profound upheaval and discontinuity in the lives of children. What happens when children are torn from their culture and forced to live in an alien environment? Melville and Lykes (1992), studying the effects of Guatemala's civil war on the ethnic identity of children forced to live in refugee camps in Mexico, found that most of the children stopped speaking their native language, Mayan, in favor of Spanish; there was a decline in girls' attachment to traditional dress; and children could not learn the traditional tasks of farming, weaving, child care, and housework. In sum, the children lost their cultural roots. This research on state-sponsored terrorism is the subject of a Spotlight on Research in chapter 7.

Previous Traumas the Child Experienced, Including Level of Functioning before the Disaster

It is hard to determine the relationship of predisaster to postdisaster functioning because reports of predisaster behavior are usually collected retroactively. Also, at the time of a disaster, it is more likely that information regarding demographic characteristics will be gathered rather than particulars concerning the child's temperament, stated anxiety level, or prior trauma experiences (Vernberg, 1999). However, there are clear indications that pre-existing psychiatric conditions or anxiety are associated with postdisaster symptoms (Earls, Smith, Reich, & Jung 1988). When Handford and his colleagues (1986) studied reactions of children and their families to the nuclear accident at Three Mile Island, Pennsylvania, they found that four children with previously diagnosed psychiatric disorders "fell at either extreme of the reaction continuum, with three at the upper, or more severe end, and one at the extreme lower end" (p. 351). This incident is the subject of a Spotlight on Research in chapter 4.

There is little research relating prior conditions such as poverty, child abuse, and physical disability with postdisaster reactions, although recommendations for helping children and adults with these prior conditions are available (FEMA, 2003). Hearing-impaired participants in a disaster-recovery workshop, which was facilitated by the authors, spoke of the special difficulties faced by people who cannot hear disaster-related information that is broadcast over the radio or disseminated from trucks equipped with loudspeakers—two common methods for circulating information—or who lack access to interpreters (Mindy Hopper, personal communication, February 15, 2000). Illiterate children or adults also may have difficulties receiving information in a disaster.

Rolf Blizzard (2000), assistant director of the governor's Hurricane Floyd Redevelopment Center in North Carolina, described how prior conditions such as deafness and illiteracy can affect people's reactions to a disaster—as well as affect the success or failure of relief efforts:

It is truly amazing how easy it is to take for granted the basic ability to communicate. When disaster strikes, even the ability to communicate becomes paramount to the protection and recovery process. Imagine what it would be like if you could not hear the emergency broadcast warning on the radio or if the only way you could get basic advisory weather information was to actively look for it on the television. One of the many things we learned in disaster response was that we might have great assistance programs, but if they are not communicated to the disaster victim, they are of no use. At our first regional meeting to explain the disaster programs, the community for the deaf and hard of hearing reached out to us. They helped to get the message out to a community that our original efforts had neglected. In addition, as we registered folks that attended our regional outreach meetings, the reality of illiteracy in a developed state slapped us in the face when we met folks that could not read the material we had so intently drafted. (p. 1)

By its very definition, disasters interrupt, destroy, or permanently alter the life patterns of the children and families who experience them. Whether or not resources and options for recovery are available has an impact on the family's ability to regain some degree of normalcy after a disaster. Speier (2000) suggested that for children who experience a relatively normal childhood and who have support systems available, the trauma of a disaster can slowly be assimilated into their world; however, for other children, recovery is a complex and time-consuming process.

SUMMARY

In this chapter we focused on the specific reactions children tend to display in times of disaster and trauma. It is critical for you, as a helper, to assess a child who has experienced trauma by taking into account the child's stage of development, biological sex, prior living situation, prior traumatic experiences, and aspects of the child's culture. All of those factors change the "mix" for the child and require thoughtful responses from helpers. Research referred to in this chapter high-lighted many of the items to be considered, but also showed clearly that each child is a separate entity to be assisted in those ways that make the most sense within his or her unique context.

The most comforting conclusion from research on children who experience disasters is this: Most children bounce back to full health within a short period. With the support of family, friends, and the community, they are able to bend and adapt to their new life situation.

REFERENCES

Adler, A. (1943). Neuropsychiatric complications in victims of Boston's Coconut Grove disaster. *JAMA, 123*, 1098–1101.

Aptekar, L., & Boore, J. A. (1990). The emotional effects of disaster on children: A review of the literature. *International Journal of Mental Health, 19*(2), 77–90.

Baugh J. W., & Morgan, J. (1978). *Why have they taken our children? Chowchilla, July 15, 1976.* New York: Delacorte Press.

Blizzard, R. (2000). *Hurricane Floyd response and recovery: One public administrator's perspective.* Retrieved from August 20, 2003, http://www.iog.unc.edu/-uncmpa/alumni/newsletter/impact13.-htm#floyd on

Bowlby, J. (1969). *Attachment and loss: I. Attachment.* New York: Basic Books.

Bowlby, J. (1980). *Attachment and loss: III. Loss, sadness and depression.* New York: Basic Books.

Burke, J., Borus, J., Burns, B., Millstein, & Beasley, M. (1982). Change in children's behavior after a natural disaster. *American Journal of Psychiatry, 139,* 1010–1014.

Burke, J. D, Moccia, P., Borus, J. F., & Burns, B. J. (1986). Emotional distress in fifth-grade children ten months after a natural disaster. *Journal of the American Academy of Child Psychiatry, 25,* 536–541.

City of Chowchilla. (2001). *History of the 1976 bus kidnapping.* Retrieved August 20, 2003, from http://www.ci.chowchilla.ca.us/history.html on

Colby, A., Kohlberg, L., Gibbs, J., & Lieberman, M. (1994). A longitudinal study of moral judgment. In B. Puka (Ed.), *New research in moral development* (pp. 1–124). New York: Garland.

de Vries, M. W. (1996). Trauma in cultural perspective. In B. A. van der Kolk, A. C. McFarlane, & L. Weisaeth (Eds.), *Traumatic stress: The effects of overwhelming experience on mind, body, and society* (pp. 398–413). New York: Guilford Press.

Earls, F., Smith, E., Reich, W., & Jung, K. G. (1988). Investigating psychopathological consequences of a disaster in children: A pilot study incorporating a structured diagnostic interview. *Journal of the American Academy of Child and Adolescent Psychiatry, 27,* 90–95.

Eisenberg, N., & Valiente, C. (2002). Parenting and children's prosocial and moral development. In M. H. Bornstein (Ed.), *Handbook of parenting: Vol. 5: Practical issues in parenting* (2nd ed., pp. 111–142). Mahwah, NJ: Lawrence Erlbaum.

Elbedour, S., ten Bensel, R., & Bastien, D. T. (1993). Ecological integrated model of children of war: Individual and social psychology. *Child Abuse and Neglect, 17,* 805–819.

Erikson, Erik. (1999). *Erikson's stages of psychosocial development*. Retrieved April 9, 1999, from http://idealist.com/children/erk.html on

Fahlberg, V. I. (1991). *A child's journey through placement*. Indianapolis, IN: Perspectives Press.

Federal Emergency Management Agency. (2003, February 11). *Assisting people with disabilities in a disaster*. Retrieved August 20, 2003, from http://www.fema.gov/rrr/assistf.shtm on

Garbarino, J., Kostelny, K., & Dubrow, N. (1991). What children can tell us about living in danger. *American Psychologist, 46*, 376–383.

Gillis, H. (1993). Individual and small-group psychotherapy for children involved in trauma and disaster. In C.F. Saylor (Ed.), *Children and disasters* (pp. 165–186). New York: Plenum Press.

Gleser, G. C., Green, B. L., & Winget, C. (1981). *Prolonged psychological effects of disaster: A study of Buffalo Creek*. New York: Academic Press.

Green, B. L., Korol, M., Grace, M. C., Vary, M. G., Leonard, A. C., Gleser, G. C., & Smitson-Cohen, S. (1991). Children and disaster: Gender and parental effects on PTSD symptoms. *Journal of the American Academy of Child Psychiatry, 25*, 346–356.

Greenberg, H. S., & Keane A. (1997). A social work perspective of childhood trauma after a residential fire. *Social Work in Education, 19*, 11–22.

Handford, H. A., Mayes, S. D., Mattison, R. E., Humphrey, F. J., Bagnato, S., Bixler, E. O., & Kales, J. D. (1986). Child and parent reactions to the Three Mile Island nuclear accident. *Journal of the American Academy of Child Psychiatry, 25*, 346–356.

Hochschild, A. (1998). King Leopold's ghost: *A story of greed, terror and heroism in colonial Africa*. Boston: Houghton Mifflin.

Howorth, P. W. (2000). The treatment of shell-shock: Cognitive therapy before its time. *Psychiatric Bulletin, 24*, 225–227.

Jones, E., & Wessely, S. (2000). Shell shock. *Psychiatric Bulletin, 24*, 353.

Joseph, S. (1997). *Understanding post-traumatic stress: A psychosocial perspective on PTSD and treatment*. New York: John Wiley & Sons.

Keppel-Benson, J. M., & Ollendick, T. H. (1993). Posttraumatic stress disorder in children and adolescents. In C. F. Saylor (Ed.), *Children and disasters* (pp. 29–43). New York: Plenum Press.

Klingman, A. (2001a). Israeli children's reactions to the assassination of the prime minister. *Death Studies, 25*(1), 33–49.

Klingman, A. (2001b). Stress responses and adaptation of Israeli school-age children evacuated from homes during massive missile attacks. *Anxiety, Stress and Coping: An International Journal, 14*, 149–172.

Kohlberg, L., Levine, C., & Hewer, A. (1994). Moral stages: A current formulation and a response to critics: 3. Synopses of criticisms and a reply; 4. Summary and conclusion. In B. Puka (Ed.), *New research in moral development* (pp. 126–188). New York: Garland.

Kupersmidt, J. B., Shahinfar, A., & Voegler-Lee, M. E. (2002). Children's exposure to community violence. In A. M. La Greca, W. K. Silverman, E. M. Vernberg, & M. C. Roberts (Eds.), *Helping children cope with disasters and terrorism* (pp. 381–401). Washington, DC: American Psychological Association.

Lerner, M. D., Volpe, J. S., & Lindell, B. (2003). *A practical guide for crisis response in our schools* (5th ed.). New York: American Academy of Experts in Traumatic Stress.

Leys, R. (2000). *Trauma: A genealogy*. Chicago: University of Chicago Press.

Lonigan, C. J., Shannon, M. P., Finch, A. J., Jr., Daugherty, T. K., & Taylor, C. M., (1991). Children's reactions to a natural disaster: Symptom severity and degree of exposure. *Advances in Behaviour Research & Therapy, 13*(3), 135–154.

Macksoud, M. J., Aber, J. L., & Cohn, I. (1996). Assessing the impact of war on children. In R. J. Apfel & B. Simon (Eds.), *Minefields in their hearts: The mental health of children in war and communal violence* (pp. 218–230). New Haven, CT: Yale University Press.

Melville, M. B., & Lykes, M. B. (1992). Guatemalan Indian children and the sociocultural effects of government-sponsored terrorism. *Social Science and Medicine, 34*, 533–548.

Morland, L. A. (2000). The Oklahoma City bombing: An examination of the relationship between exposure to bomb-related television and post-traumatic stress symptoms following a disaster. *Dissertation Abstracts International, 60*, 4239.

Nader, K. (2002). Treating children after violence in schools and communities. In N. B. Webb (Ed.), *Helping bereaved children: A handbook for practitioners* (2nd ed., pp. 214–244). New York: Guilford Press.

Nader, K., & Mello, C. (2002). Shootings, hostage takings, and children. In A. M. La Greca, W. K. Silverman, E. M. Vernberg, & M. C. Roberts (Eds.), *Helping children cope with disasters and terrorism* (pp. 301–326). Washington, DC: American Psychological Association.

Norris, F. H., Perilla, J. L., Ibanez, G. E., & Murphy, A. D. (2001). Sex differences in symptoms of posttraumatic stress: Does culture play a role? *Journal of Traumatic Stress, 14*, 7–28.

O'Donnell, D. A., Schwab-Stone, M. E., & Muyeed, A. Z. (2002). Multidimensional resilience in urban children exposed to community violence. *Child Development, 73*, 1265–1282.

Piaget, J. (2000). Piaget's theory. In K. Kang (Ed.), *Childhood cognitive development: The essential readings* (pp. 33–47). Malden, MA: Blackwell.

Pfefferbaum, B. (1997). Posttraumatic stress disorder in children: A review of the past 10 years. *Journal of the American Academy of Child and Adolescent Psychiatry, 36*, 1503–1511.

Rabalais, A. E., Ruggiero, K. J., & Scotti, J. R. (2002). Multicultural issues in the response of children to disasters. In A. M. La Greca, W. K. Silverman, E. M. Vernberg, & M. C. Roberts (Eds.), *Helping children cope with disasters and terrorism* (pp. 73–99). Washington, DC: American Psychological Association.

Rashid, S. F., and Michaud, S. (2000). Female adolescents and their sexuality: Notions of honour, shame, purity and pollution during the floods. *Disasters, 24*, 54–70.

Saigh, P. A. (1996). Posttraumatic stress disorder among children and adolescents: An introduction. *Journal of School Psychology, 34*(2), 103–105.

Samovar, L. A., & Porter, R. E. (2001). *Communication between cultures* (4th ed.). Belmont, CA: Wadsworth.

Saylor, C. F., Belter, R., & Stokes, S. J. (1997). Children and families coping with disaster. In S. A. Wolchik & I. N. Sandler (Eds.), *Handbook of children's coping: Linking theory and intervention* (pp. 361–383). New York: Plenum Press.

Shephard, B. (2001). *A war of nerves: Soldiers and psychiatrists in the twentieth century*. Cambridge, MA: Harvard University Press.

Silverman, W. K., & La Greca, A. M. (2002). Children experiencing disasters: Definitions, reactions, and predictors of outcomes. In A. M. La Greca, W. K. Silverman, E. M. Vernberg, & M. C. Roberts (Eds.), *Helping children cope with disasters and terrorism* (pp. 11–33). Washington, DC: American Psychological Association.

Sitterle, K. A., & Gurwitch, R. H. (1999). The terrorist bombing in Oklahoma City. In E. S. Zinner & M. B. Williams (Eds.), *When a community weeps* (pp. 160–189). Philadelphia: Brunner/Mazel.

Speier, A. H. (2000). *Psychosocial issues for children and adolescents in disasters* (2nd ed.). Washington, DC: U.S. Department of Health and Human Services.

Terr, L. C., Block, D. A., Michel, B. A., Shi, H., Reinhardt, J. A., & Metayer, S. (1996). Children's memories in the wake of Challenger. *American Journal of Psychiatry, 153*, 618–625.

Thierry, K. L., & Spence, M. J. (2002). Source-monitoring training facilitates preschoolers' eyewitness memory performance. *Developmental Psychology, 38*, 428–437.

Udwin, O., Boyle, S., Yule, W., Bolton, D., & O'Ryan, D. (2000). Risk factors for long-term psychological effects of a disaster experienced in adolescence: Predictors of posttraumatic stress disorder. *Journal of Child Psychology and Psychiatry and Allied Disciplines, 41*, 969–979.

University of Illinois Cooperative Extension Service. (1995a, June). *Classroom activities to help children express feelings.* Retrieved August 20, 2003, from http://www.ag.uiuc.edu/~disaster/teacher/csndact2.html

University of Illinois Cooperative Extension Service. (1995b, June). *Examples of activities that promote the sharing of experiences and the sharing of feelings.* Retrieved August 20, 2003, from http://www.ag.uiuc.edu/~disaster/teacher/csndact7.html

van der Kolk, B. A., & McFarlane, A. C. (1996). The black hole of trauma. In B. A. van der Kolk, A. C. McFarlane, & L. Weisaeth (Eds.), *The effects of overwhelming experience in mind, body, and society* (pp. 3–23). New York: Guilford Press.

Vernberg, E. M. (1999). Children's responses to disaster: Family and systems approaches. In R. Gist & B. Lubin B. (Eds.), *Response to disaster: Psychosocial, community, and ecological approaches* (pp. 193–209). Philadelphia: Brunner/Mazel.

Vernberg, E. M., La Greca, A. M., Silverman, W. K., & Prinstein, M. J. (1996). Prediction of posttraumatic stress symptoms in children after Hurricane Andrew. *Journal of Abnormal Psychology, 105*, 237–248.

Vogel, J. M., & Vernberg, E. M. (1993). Task force report, part 1: Children's psychological responses to disasters. *Journal of Clinical Child Psychology, 22*, 464–484.

Weaver, J. D. (1995). *Disasters: Mental health interventions.* Sarasota, FL: Professional Resource Press.

Young, M. A. (1998). *The community crisis response team training manual* (2nd ed.). Washington, DC: National Organization for Victim Assistance. Retrieved August 20, 2003, from http://www.ojp.usdoj.gov/ovc/publications/infores/crt/welcome.html

Yule, W. (1993). Technology-related disasters. In C. F. Saylor (Ed.), *Children and disasters* (pp. 105–121). New York: Plenum Press.

FAMILY AND COMMUNITY REACTIONS TO DISASTERS

After studying the material in this chapter, you should

- be able to identify characteristics of a family
- be able to describe how family characteristics can become risk or protective factors when the family is faced with stress or a disaster
- be able to describe the ways that families take on systemic characteristics, and how those characteristics are important in times of disaster
- identify community characteristics that increase the potential for greater stress and trauma in a disaster
- understand the ways that the community can either offer support to families during times of disaster, or be the cause of even more stress when community infrastructure is damaged or destroyed
- identify ways that community culture and family culture affect family members' reactions to a disaster
- be able to describe how models of stress and "pileup" are applicable to disaster work, and explain some of the special vulnerabilities of people exposed to a disaster.

In the preceding chapter, we used our most narrowly focused lens to look at the effects of disasters on children. In this chapter, we use a wider-angle lens and broaden our focus as we consider the reactions of families to a disaster; then we use our most-powerful wide-angle lens to consider the community's role in reducing or exacerbating the stress felt by individuals and families in the face of a disaster.

There are almost as many definitions of "family" as there are groupings that use the word to define themselves. Some families include children, and others do not. A family may be formed intentionally when groups of like-minded people decide to share living space, or unintentionally, perhaps by force or arrangements made by others. Families can encompass one generation or many, and be held together by legal, blood, or emotional ties. How many kinds of family configurations can you describe?

Families also function in very diverse ways around the world. They can have a tight or loose organization, be smooth or bumpy, or be funny or serious. People may be wanted and supported by their family, or be ostracized and left out. For some, family is the place to go in times of trouble; for others, family is the place to leave to escape trouble. The Touching Reality on page 101 asks you to consider your own definition of "family."

Whatever the make-up of a particular family, we know that "the ways that children and adolescents cope with disasters cannot be understood solely in individual terms.... The family stands out as preeminent in understanding coping processes in response to disasters" (Compas & Epping, 1993, p. 21). In this chapter, we consider families as systems with certain characteristics, patterns, and methods of operation. Just as a child's age, culture, developmental level, gender, and personality have profound effects on her or his reaction to trauma and disaster, so too do the characteristics, patterns, and culture of that child's family.

Your Family: Who Is In, Who Is Out?

As we begin this chapter, think about the family that you know best, your own—the family in which you now live, or the family in which you spent some portion of your childhood—your family of origin. The first question to ask yourself is: What is your definition of "family"? Fill in the blank. A family is

_____

_____

_____ .

Now, who are the members of your family? Do you include extended family, friends, neighbors, and pets? Do you need to go back and change your original definition of "family" to better fit who is in and who is out?

As we go through descriptions of family characteristics, consider the families with whom you have been connected in your lifetime and see how the descriptions fit.

WHAT IS A FAMILY?

Before discussing family characteristics, we must first define "family" (Jurich & Johnson, 1999). One way to define family would be to review some of the definitions put forth by important figures in the helping professions. Mary Richmond (1917), an early pioneer in social work, defined family as all those sitting around a common table.

Bowen (1978) identified family as those connected on a family tree. We could use the U.S. government's definitions, such as those used for conducting a census, or social service agencies' definitions, such as those used to determine if various members of a group of people are eligible for a particular benefit. These definitions tend to count only those people who share the same legal address and are connected by blood, marriage, or adoption. Do these definitions fit the ones you use when you think about family? Who might be left out by these definitions? How do these definitions fit communal families, such as the Kibbutzim, or the special "family" relationships some have with their pets? Have we left out families formed by homosexual couples? foster families? older nonrelated people who choose to live together? Each consideration broadens our definition of family (Crawford, 1999); in fact, some proponents of family-centered approaches suggest that groupings who call themselves a family are, by definition, a family, and whoever is included in that definition is a family member.

Why should we take the time to struggle with what a family is when our topic is the effects of disasters? The answer is that when people experience a trauma, their first reaction is to look for connection and support from those who are most important to them: their families. For our purposes here, what is critical is to determine who is their family, who can comfort them, or whom might they have lost in the trauma. Sometimes, a disaster client is concerned with the family cat's welfare, and movement forward is not possible until the question of "How is the cat?" is answered. It is important that helpers take into account how each person defines his or her family.

There are many characteristics that can describe families. How might you describe your neighbors? Are they loud? polite? Are they the first to offer help when there is a difficulty, or are they last in line? As descriptions of family characteristics are presented here—characteristics associated with looking at the family as a system, as at a particular stage in the family life cycle, and as a unit responding to a disaster—pause to consider your current family or your family of origin and "touch reality," so that you connect the concepts and theories you read about here with your life.

Families as Systems

A system is a set of components that interrelate to form a whole. Elements in a system interact in relation to one another in reciprocal fashion so that the movement or condition of another. The most common example of a system is a mobile. Consider a child's toy mobile of circus animals. It is suspended in the air with all sections connected but each able to move, to a certain degree, on its own. If you push the tiger suspended from the frame, you notice that the giraffe, the monkey, and the other animals begin to jiggle around. Remove the zebra and the rest of the animals hang lopsided. The mobile demonstrates many of a system's characteristics. Galvin and Brommel (2000) described family systems as having four major characteristics: (1) components, (2) attributes, (3) relationships among components, and (4) existence in a specific environment.

Family systems have components or parts. Visualize the mobile once again. Mobiles have an internal frame or skeleton from which its elements—animals, airplanes, or angels—swing. In families, these "parts" are the members, defined by the family itself. In times of trauma, people focus on their family connections.

Researchers who studied child disaster survivors during World War II found that breaking up families during a disaster may have caused even more trauma than the disaster itself. In his book, *Children and Political Violence*, Cairns (1996) quoted from a 1943 work by Freud and Burlingham regarding children caught up in the war:

> War acquires comparatively little significance for children so long as it only threatens their lives, disturbs their material comfort, or cuts their food rations. It becomes enormously significant the moment it breaks up family life and uproots the first emotional attachments of the child within the family group. (p. 41)

Vogel and Vernberg (1993) described separation anxiety postdisaster in terms of the child-caretaker attachment relationship. They cited Bowlby's work supporting the notion that the child uses the caretaker as a "secure base" physically and sometimes psychologically. Raphael (1986) argued that the tendency to protect children postdisaster by sending them away from the place where the disaster has occurred adds to rather than alleviates the children's trauma.

Family systems have attributes. The attributes of a system are its qualities or properties. They are those actions, habits, or the "usual ways of doing things" that distinguish one family from another. The extent to which a family is open or closed, for example, can profoundly affect how it responds to disasters. When families expect members to keep difficulties "inside" the family, or to find internal resources to deal with a trauma, family members may be unable or unwilling to ask for or receive assistance from outside the family. As a result, the interviews required to apply for disaster assistance can seem intrusive in a way that prevents the family from receiving aid that is justifiably theirs. If a family member is having particular difficulty recovering from a disaster, the family may attempt to deal with the problem inside the family, even if they also are feeling overwhelmed. They may not arrange for the family member to seek outside help, possibly causing that person's pain to be prolonged.

On the positive side, strong family connections are powerful protective factors. The belief that the family will find a way to overcome trauma is one of the prerequisites to postdisaster recovery. The family can demonstrate another system characteristic when it is strong: The system is greater than the sum of each of its parts. Recall some famous families, such as the Kennedy, Ghandi, or Windsor families. The family's aura may seem larger than any individual members' lives. You may have met families who have such a presence. In disaster situations, each member may draw from that overarching sense of presence and gain from the whole family's strength. (For additional discussion of family protective and risk factors, see Walsh's, 2002, application of the resilience model to families, and Patterson's, 2002, discussion of family risk and protective factors.)

System parts relate to one another. Relationships vary between and among family members. Family members often have assigned roles to play: One person may be the funny one who keeps everyone laughing, another the serious one who wins academic awards, another the athlete, the outcast, the risk taker, and so on. One way to determine relationships among family members is to notice how they communicate with each other. How do people address one another in the family? How do angry family members interact? If a member receives a bad grade in school, who is the family member that the person first trusts with the news? Why this person?

The types of relationships that exist among family members also will have an effect on the way a family responds to disaster or trauma. "The stress of the threat or impact will intensify the bonds between members and often the family will respond as one unit—a system" (Raphael, 1986, p. 170). Members may often find comfort and stability in familiar roles or relationships within the family. Family members also may become confused or anxious when other family members do not respond in usual or anticipated ways.

In their review of the literature, Green and her colleagues (1991) cited several studies that emphasize the especially significant impact that parental reactions have on children's stress response in the family. A 1989 study completed by Bryce, Walker, and Peterson considered the relationship between the psychological functioning of mothers and children who were living in Beirut, Lebanon, during wartime. One of the findings was that mothers' level of depressive symptomatology was the best predictor of reports of child morbidity. Dawes, Tredoux, and Feinstein's (1989) study of 71 families in South Africa who experienced forced removal from a squatter community found that children were as likely to develop a single symptom of stress whether their mothers showed stress reactions or not. However, children whose mothers had diagnoses of PTSD were significantly more likely to have multiple symptoms of stress than children whose mothers were not diagnosed with PTSD. Breton, Valla, and Lambert (1993) studied the responses of families who lived around a PCB warehouse in St-Basile-le-Grand, Quebec, which was deliberately set on fire, forcing the families to evacuate in the middle of the night. Findings indicated that the fathers' as well as mothers' mental health were correlated with the children's symptoms. (This study is the subject of a Spotlight on Research in chapter 6.)

Hunter (1988) reviewed data on the effects on children of their parents' prolonged captivity during World War II, the Korean war, the Vietnam War, and Israel's Yom Kippur War. The data suggest, she argued, that if mothers were able to function during the prolonged absence and the continuing ambiguity of the fathers' missing in action (MIA) or prisoner of war (POW) status, then the children also tended to cope adequately. As Raphael (1986) concluded:

The experiences of children, particularly younger children, are usually inextricably interwoven with those of their parents and families, unless, at the time of the disaster, they have been separated. The fear and threat are experienced both directly and indirectly through identification with and response to parental reactions. (p. 149)

Garbarino, Kostelny, and Dubrow (1991) found through observations of Sudanese families in refugee camps in 1988 that children remain resilient as long as their parents are not pushed beyond what the authors called their "stress absorption capacity" (p. 380). When that occurs, infant mortality rates increase alarmingly, and the normal, daily care of children breaks down. According to Garbarino and his colleagues, if parents in situations of chronic violence and stress can sustain strong attachment bonds with their children, keep a positive sense of self, and maintain access to basic necessities to sustain life, then the children will also manage to cope.

Of course, it is not simply that parents' reactions influence their children's reactions, but also that children affect the parents. Mirzamani and Bolton (2002) studied the PTSD symptoms of 37 mothers whose adolescent children were directly involved in the 1988 sinking of the Jupiter (see the Spotlight on Research in chapter 3), including 20 whose children developed PTSD and 17 whose children did not. They found that 13 of the mothers were diagnosed with PTSD three months after the disaster, three of them were diagnosed with PTSD six years afterward, and that the PTSD diagnosis was more likely in the subgroup of mothers whose children had developed postdisaster PTSD.

Children's and Parent's Reactions

During the early morning hours of March 28, 1979, a plume of radioactive steam was released from Three Mile Island Nuclear Power Plant in Pennsylvania. Two days later, the governor of Pennsylvania advised the evacuation of pregnant women and young children (less than five years of age) who lived within a five-mile radius of Three Mile Island. This situation presented an opportunity for researchers to study psychological reactions to a disaster that had no recorded direct injury, loss of life, or property damage. H. Allen Handford and his colleagues wanted to systematically study children's reactions under the stress of disaster, both during 1979, and subsequently, because most families continued to live in the same area after they were allowed to return to their homes. Children and their parents were interviewed; they completed several psychological tests. Some results of the study were as expected. For example, 66 percent of the 35 children interviewed reported such effects as being upset, worried, or scared. Most parents, however, did not perceive any personality changes in their children after the incident. The parents themselves showed an increase in anxiety and hostility right after the incident; these reactions subsided within 18 months.

An unexpected finding had to do with children's reactions compared with their parents' reactions. Children who lived with single parents, or children whose parents reacted the *same way*, had a significantly lower intensity of reaction than did those children whose parents reacted in a *different way* to the disaster. "A child whose parents both revealed a high intensity of reaction was more likely to have a lower intensity of reaction than a child with one parent showing a low intensity response and the other a response of medium intensity" (p. 351).

Another interesting finding was that children consistently reported stronger and more symptomatic responses to the experience than their parents perceived them as having. Whereas 75 percent of the children reported initial fear after the disaster, only 33 percent of the parents reported seeing this fear in their children.

Handford, H.A., Mayes, S.D., Mattison, R.E., Humphrey, F.J., Bahnato, S., Bixler, E.O., & Kales, J.D. (1986). Child and parent reactions to the Three Mile Island nuclear accident. *Journal of the American Academy of Child Psychiatry, 25*, 346–356.

Family systems exist in a particular environment. The final systemic dynamic to consider has to do with context—that is, a family's culture and beliefs. (We discuss the family's involvement with the community or neighborhood in more detail later in this chapter.) "Culture plays a key role in how individuals cope with potentially trauma-tizing experiences by providing the context in which social support and other positive and uplifting events can be experienced" (deVries, 1996, p. 400). People who are connected strongly with family and with other family-like groups tend to experience a greater sense of support and belonging during times of disaster.

This finding was confirmed by the experience of a family-like group during Hurricane Andrew. Clubhouse members, a psychosocial residence and daycare facility for adults with severe and persistent mental illness, were forced to cope with the hurricane's devastation (Treuer, 1993). During interviews, these members, residents and staff alike, repeatedly mentioned their sense of belonging during the disaster, of their need to take care of each other, and to check on those not present to be sure they were doing well.

Culture can provide familiar supports for families who must deal with death and grief. It can offer some assistance in finding meaning for incomprehensible events, or at least validate that meaning is hard to find. After the 1999 Egypt Air Lines crash off the east coast of the United States, helpers realized it was critical to make available support people who were familiar with the spiritual and cultural realities of the survivors and who would understand the Egyptian family members' reactions to sudden loss, without a body to mourn and bury.

Strong belief systems within families may sustain the family's ability to function under extreme stress. Garbarino and his colleagues (1991) described several traumatic war and violence situations in which intense ideology buffered the individuals from stress. They noted Bettelheim's writings that indicated those who coped the best in the concentration camps of the Holocaust were those whose intense ideological commitments (ultrareligious or communists) offered meaning "impervious to day-to-day brutalization" (Garbarino et al., p. 381). Strong ideology can be a buffer against the grinding stress of a disaster.

Culture, however, may serve as either a risk or a protective factor (Rabalais, Ruggiero, & Scotti, 2002). Strong ideological beliefs or nationalism, as one aspect of culture, can pose difficulties. Punamaki (cited in Garbarino et al., 1991), for example, reported that more democratic, or humanistic, individuals on either side of the Palestinian–Israeli conflict paid a price for their moral sensibility and inclusiveness: They felt increased stress and moral tension. Whereas strong beliefs often mitigate reactions to stress and trauma, they also can prolong or intensify the very basis for continuing the conflict, thus exposing families and children to stress over a longer period. Those with intense beliefs are less available for the negotiations necessary to end war, and they find it much harder to compromise or change positions, even when faced with a different situation.

In addition, Gillard and Patton (1999), looking at the influence of religion on disaster stress in Fijian Islanders after Hurricane Nigel in 1997, found differences among Christian Fijians, Indians who follow Islam, and Indians who practice Hinduism. The religious organizations offered different assistance to each group, respectively, and made different demands on them. Religious denomination, in other words, exercised a differential impact on vulnerability, in some instances serving as a protective factor, and in others as a risk factor.

Family Life Cycle Development

The final family characteristic to consider has to do with changes experienced in any family, over time. Single people may choose to live together; they may choose to marry; they may choose to have children. Children grow and develop during the years they live in a family group, and their needs and abilities change based on their age, cognitive and emotional development, physical abilities, life experiences, and temperament. As already noted, the child is affected by the family context and culture within which he or she lives, and the family is affected by the changes occurring in each of its members. A family's response to a disaster tends to change depending on at what point in the life cycle the family may be.

A single individual may rejoin an earlier family constellation for support in a time of trauma, or perhaps connect with a family-like group instead. Pets may be part of the individual's definition of family. A couple may follow the same pattern as a single individual. The relationships they maintain with their respective families of origin affects their behavior during and postdisaster. On the one hand, they might self-identify as support providers for more vulnerable family members, such as those who are much younger or older. On the other hand, they may see themselves as being in need of help or protection from other family members.

A family unit with small children tends to put priority on the safety of its small, vulnerable members. Shielding children from further trauma or attempting to reduce or prevent long-term consequences are priorities. As children within the family grow, they may be more interdependent players in a disaster.

Children with previous traumatic experiences often are especially vulnerable to a current disaster and may need special care and attention. Children who experience pervasive calamity often are aware that the adults around them are unable to stop the flood, the tornado, or the war. This exacerbates their anxiety and tends to leave them feeling alone, without protection, and fearful.

As young family members reach adolescence, they may be viewed as equal helpers in times of trouble, depending upon family patterns or culture. In her study of children in Mozambique, Gibbs (1994) described the inclusion of adolescent children in the recovery of their villages (see the Spotlight on Research in chapter 2.). They were active members in their families, sometimes enacting the role of the oldest living male. The need for their valued work promoted healing—both of the youths and of the village as a community.

Typically in the United States and in other Western cultures, adolescents are engaged in the work of separating from their family of origin. During a disaster, they may be as concerned with friends, peers, and other family-like groups as they are with their family of origin. This "divided loyalty" may be the source of additional stress for the family. A disaster may, however, leave adolescents feeling ill equipped to deal with a hostile world, and the disaster may delay their normal separation from their family.

As the family ages, older adults become more vulnerable. Fragile, elderly, sick, or disabled members can experience particular disorientation during and postdisaster (we discuss this more at length in chapter 11). Predisaster conditions may hamper easy mobility, and disasters frequently create even more barriers to mobility. Inability to obtain medicines, the loss of electricity when the vulnerable member is dependent on medical devices that require electricity, or the unavailability of necessary assistance can cause added anxiety. The intrusiveness and sudden changes involved in many disasters may exacerbate preexisting memory impairment or dementia.

Family members, including the vulnerable members themselves, may find the needs of vulnerable family members to be distressing during and postdisaster because caretaking needs and decision-making responsibilities may increase.

Family members use different skills to function successfully as they move through the family life cycle. Disasters can disrupt the progression of a family or hasten changes in expected roles and interactions.

Family Cohesion and Adaptability

For a disaster relief worker to help a family means he or she must work with a unique system—the family—at a particular stage in its development. In addition, it means recognizing and working within the family's own mix of cohesion and adaptability.

Cohesion is the emotional bonding that family members have toward one another (Olson, 1986, 2000). Cohesion ranges from disengaged (very low) to enmeshed (very high). Midrange levels of cohesion—separate and connected—mean that family members are able to be both independent from and connected to their family; when enmeshed, there is too much consensus and too little independence; and when disengaged, there is limited attachment or commitment to the family.

Adaptability is the family's ability to change its power structure (for example, its assertiveness, control, or discipline), role relationships, and rules in response to situational and developmental stress. A rigid family (very low adaptability) is one in which one family member is highly controlling, roles are strictly defined, and the rules do not change; a chaotic family (very high adaptability) has erratic or no leadership, decisions are impulsive, and roles are unclear. Midrange levels of adaptability—structured and flexible—mean family relationships are, overall, less rigid; leadership may be shared; and rules could change in response to family needs. For example, Munton and Reynolds (1995), in their study of the relationship between family

functioning and adaptability to change within families that relocate, found that families that made minor changes in response to their move adapted to the new geographical location more successfully than those that did not change or those that made major changes.

Crossing the levels of cohesion and the levels of adaptability, families can be described as *balanced*, with midlevels of both cohesion and adaptability; *midrange*, with an extreme level of either cohesion or adaptability and a midrange level of the other; and *extreme*, with extreme levels of both cohesion and adaptability. Balanced family systems tend to be more functional than unbalanced, extreme systems, and are more likely to exhibit supportive communication and positive affect. Extreme families are more likely than other types to have members with emotional problems.

A number of studies have documented the effects of stressors—such as war, wartime captivity, and disasters—on families. Addington (1997) studied marital satisfaction in the United States Coast Guard (USCG) and how USCG marriage partners coped with stress. He found that marriage partners experiencing stress required more coping skills and adaptability in order for them to enjoy marital satisfaction.

Laor and his colleagues (Laor, Wolmer, & Cohen, 2001; Laor, Wolmer, Mayes, & Golomb, 1996) looked at cohesion and adaptability as a moderator of the devastating effects of traumatic events on children—specifically, SCUD missile attacks during the Persian Gulf War. Three groups of families were studied: (1) families displaced after the missiles damaged their houses, (2) families without home damage who were not displaced, and (3) families from a city that was threatened but not attacked. Among other things, results revealed two risk factors: displacement (displaced children and mothers had the most severe stress reactions); and inadequate family cohesion (low cohesion predicted symptomatic reactions for three- and four-year-old children but not for older ones). It is important to note that these risk factors were still predictive of symptoms five years later. Parallel findings were reported by Sutker and her colleagues (1995), who found that perceived family cohesion emerged as a consistent predictor of PTSD diagnosis among Persian Gulf veterans after the war.

Family Resilience

Families fulfill certain functions, functions that provide a variety of benefits to their members (Patterson, 2002). For example, one function of families is to provide membership, which gives a sense of belonging, identity, and direction. Another function is economic support, which gives members food, clothing, shelter, and so on. Nurturance is a third function, which provides members with social values and a context for psychological growth. Finally, families protect vulnerable members, whether they are young, ill, or disabled.

A family is resilient to the extent that it has the capability to fulfill its functions in light of demands made on it. Of course, those families that have trouble meeting normative demands (that is, normal changes during the family life cycle) are usually classified as at-risk; when unusual demands occur—when the family is exposed to significant risk, such as a disaster—the at-risk family is likely to experience a decrease in family functioning.

Few studies look at characteristics of resilience at the level of the family, although there are some recent exceptions (Allen, Whittlesey, Pfefferbaum, & Ondersma, 1999; Patterson, 2002). Patterson reviewed research,

and outlined several family protective factors. First, she discussed cohesion (as conceptualized by Olson, 2000) and noted that, whereas no particular level of cohesion is best at all times, a strong sense of family cohesiveness serves to protect the family from the negative consequences of significant stressors. Second, she discussed Olson's notion of adaptability, concluding that, whereas "some degree of resistance to change may actually be a sign of family health" (Patterson, 2002, p. 241)—such resistance may help the family maintain its stability and sense of identity—in the face of significant risk, flexibility is important to ensure that the family is safe. "Practitioners should be encouraged to take prior family routines into account when educating families about new demands.... Achieving a balance... contributes to the protective processes in any given family" (Patterson, p. 242).

Two other protective factors that Patterson (2002) discussed are family communication and family meanings. A significant stressor can affect a family's communication, especially the expression of affect; for example, family members may repress expressing negative emotions because they believe such expression would add to the family's stress. When communication decreases—both the expression of feelings and the discussion of ideas about how things should be done—the family may be less effective in responding to the new demands of the trauma it faces. Decreased and guarded communication reduces a family's ability to be adaptive and to remain cohesive.

Families literally construct the meaning that members should assign to stressful events, the family, and their worldview. The meaning assigned to a disaster, for example, influences how the family copes. Resilient families believe they have the ability to cope, to adapt, and to overcome obstacles, and they view the new demands placed on them by the trauma as a positive challenge. A worldview that helps families to function may include cultural or religious beliefs that allow them to make sense of trauma and to have a goal or a vision for which to strive.

STAGES OR PHASES OF RESPONSE TO DISASTERS IN FAMILIES

Raphael (1986), describing common reactions of families to disasters, suggested that there are identifiable stages or phases that families who experience a disaster move through.

1. At the time of the *threat* of a disaster, families attempt to stay in one place together. The intention is to face the threat as an intact unit. Evacuation may be a choice or a necessity depending on the situation, and, if possible, family members will try to sort out what is best together. For example, during the Three Mile Island nuclear incident, small children and pregnant women were told to evacuate, while other family members had a choice to leave or not; neighborhoods close to the World Trade Center in New York City were required to evacuate on September 11, 2001, after terrorist attacks destroyed the two buildings. If evacuation is the plan, family members will most frequently choose to evacuate to kin, if that is an option. If family members are not together, they will actively try to reunite, sometimes at some real risk. The movie *Dante's Peak* showed this effort, when the two children in the family chose to take the family truck and drive toward the erupting volcano to find their grandmother who lived up the mountain from them.

2. At the time of *impact*, the family tries to remain together and to ensure the safety of all. Care for the youngest, or most vulnerable, is a top priority. According to Raphael (1986), "Most families share the enormous sense of relief at personal survival and at the intact status of the family group. When members are absent, there is an intense preoccupation with insuring that they, too, have survived and are safe: arousal and active searching will continue until this has been established" (p. 153).

3. *Immediately after impact*, families first care for their own, but then reach out to others to offer care and support. There are several studies of families' efforts to find each other postdisaster. Raphael (1986) cited John Hersey's description of families searching for loved ones after the bombing at Hiroshima, amid thousands of dead. In the recent World Trade Center tragedy, the media showed family after family searching for members. The New York City disaster also highlights a nontraditional "family" in the connections that exist among the members of the fire and police departments, and the grief at the loss of so many emergency service workers. When the family searches for absent members, law enforcement personnel find it difficult to keep them away from the disaster site, especially if there is belief that a family member might be trapped or in need of assistance.

4. *Long-term recovery* tends to involve extended family if they are available. After Hurricane Andrew in Florida, for example, some people drove hundreds of miles with food, water, and clothing for their relatives. If a community is unable to maintain essential support, outside organizations such as the American Red Cross, Salvation Army, religious organizations, and FEMA, offer assistance.

On occasion, members of a particular group may not be able to locate each other for mutual assistance and support after a disaster. For example, after Hurricane Floyd struck eastern North Carolina, members of the hearing-impaired community had difficulty locating hearing-impaired individuals who needed assistance. Adding to the confusion for this community, mail delivery was disrupted, families were relocated all over the region, electricity needed for TTD phone connections was not available, and emergency shelters seldom had staff conversant in sign language (Mindy Hooper, personal communication, November 29, 2000).

A return to the usual way of doing things is a critical step that families need to take before they can recover from a disaster (Cohan & Cole, 2002). Most families are able to take this step successfully rather quickly. Vogel and Vernberg (1993) described interventions after disasters that focus "on dealing with the children's and parents' anxieties, and then helping the parents take charge of reestablishing normal routines and boundaries, such as normal sleeping arrangements" (p. 470).

Some families may be more vulnerable and, therefore, less able to care for themselves over time. Families that are isolated, poor, elderly, dependent, members of a minority language group, experiencing homelessness, or illiterate may all experience special difficulties. Families lose members tend to recover more slowly. Destruction of structures such as schools, homes, and roads, and permanent injury and disability for a family member all have a profound negative affect on a family's ability to recover speedily. Permanent personal relocation causes particular disruption to a family's wishes to return to familiar routines.

Raphael (1986) described several specific stressors that affect families unable to return home, including dealing with strange and often less-than-satisfactory shelter arrangements, loss of neighborhood and known services, and struggling with inflexible bureaucratic and administrative rules and requirements. In addition, an important issue that often arises with dislocation is a perceived loss of human dignity and centeredness. "Whatever his culture or society, there are roles, possessions, and rituals of behavior that contribute to an individual's perception of himself as a human being" (Raphael, p. 132). Self-image depends, in part, on performing certain roles, roles that may be altered during a disaster. Disasters are "great equalizers" in that they reduce people to a concern for their basic needs—the need for food, a safe shelter, and sanitary facilities. Given a familiar comfort with occupying a certain strata in society, most people are not comfortable for long with this "level field."

THE PARENT–CHILD DISASTER-RESPONSE RELATIONSHIP

It seems natural that children, whose physical and psychological disadvantages are pronounced during a disaster, would turn to adults (especially their parents) for disaster assistance; indeed, research supports the conclusion that children are much more dependent on their parents during a disaster situation. For example, a study was made of a group of children ages five and six whose school bus was caught in the crossfire of two rival drug dealers; during the violence, one six-year-old boy suffered a shot to the head. The case study of their first reactions to this complex disaster found that the children were preoccupied with their mothers and continuously asked where they were and when they would arrive (Marans, Berkman, & Cohen, 1996). Numerous other research documents list other indications of depend-

dependency as children's primary responses to disaster exposure, including clinging, separation anxiety, and anxiety about leaving the home (for example, see Saylor, Belter, & Stokes, 1997; Vogel & Vernberg, 1993).

Given children's dependency on their parents, it is logical that children's reactions to a disaster would relate to their parents' responses, if only because of the increased salience of the parent–child relationship during stress. Green and her colleagues (1991) provided evidence of this phenomenon based on their examination of the relationship between "parental functioning" and children's adaptation to a disaster. They found that elements of the home environment, especially parental functioning or the severity of parents' responses, were predictive of the severity of children's reactions. Another study—presented earlier in this chapter in the "Children's and Parents' Reactions" Spotlight on Research—found that children whose parents' responses were highly incongruous had significantly poorer outcomes (Handford et al., 1986).

It is interesting to note that this effect may not be limited to North American or even to Western culture. Gibbs'(1994) research in Mozambique suggested that during that society's postwar reconstruction process, both parents and children react, in similar ways, and use, similar methods of recuperation. Gibbs suggested that the children would recuperate once the parents had done so.

Explanations for the child-parent disaster-response relationship fall under three general headings: (1) child's deficits, (2) parental deficits; and (3) postdisaster environmental effects on both the child and the parent.

Child's Deficits

This explanation focuses on the cognitive immaturity of the child who must look for parental guidance as he or she processes the unusual and frightening effects of the disaster. This explanation best applies to younger children rather than adolescents who are more cognitively able to make sense of the disaster without guidance. Indeed, Green and her colleagues (1991) suggested that:

[t]he very young child's experience of a disaster is undoubtedly limited by his or her cognitive capabilities. The traumatic experience is probably not understood in a coherent conceptual way, thus producing a more generalized, disorganized posttraumatic state, which is likely to be strongly influenced by how the parents react to the event, and how they interact with the child after the event. (p. 949)

Thus, parent and child reactions are similar because young children must look to adults (and the adults they look to would presumably be those they were most exposed to, usually parents) for cues on how to process the postdisaster environment and challenges.

Parental Deficits

Other research findings point to the parents, and their postdisaster difficulties in providing adequate care for their children, as the primary catalyst in the parent–child disaster-response relationship. A disaster's numerous effects are overwhelming to the family and compromise parents' ability to properly provide for their children's increased needs (we discuss this more fully later when we look at the double ABCX model). Thus, a parent's negative outcomes translate to negative child outcomes through flawed parenting.

Green and her colleagues (1991) suggested that adolescents would have outcomes similar to their parents because they essentially take on parental roles during the postdisaster period, thus literally enduring "the brunt of parental reactions if parents are functioning poorly" (p. 950). Younger children would suffer because their needs increase due to disaster-related demands, while parents' abilities to provide for those needs often decrease. Using the example of intergenerational communal violence, Marans and his colleagues (1996) described the inability of many parents, who had themselves been traumatized, to provide for the needs of their traumatized children; he also described the resulting danger to the community at large. Similarly, Garbarino and Kostelny (1996) found that children of clinically depressed mothers suffered setbacks such as insecure attachments, neglect, and malnourishment.

In addition, poor parental outcomes may translate to poor child outcomes because of the loss of a normal routine, which is a known aide to the recovery process. When parents function at a substandard level, it is difficult for them to reintroduce their children's normal routine; parents' inability to return to a normal routine could indicate that they themselves are functioning poorly, as much as it limits their children's recuperation.

Postdisaster Environmental Effects

From a community perspective, both parents and children are highly, and similarly, susceptible to the formidable postdisaster environment. This argument suggests that it is neither the children's nor the parents' deficits, but rather the vulnerability of both to environmental demands that lead to negative disaster outcomes. Thus, parents and children can react negatively to a disaster because they both suffer from a change in their way of life, from disaster relief that is inadequate or insufficient, and from a lack of resiliency. In a similar way, both groups would maintain positive outcomes if the disaster fails to completely disrupt the family's way of life, if disaster relief services are adequate or superior, and if the family has resiliency characteristics enabling it to "bounce back" (Walsh, 2002).

Although this explanation probably does not completely account for the striking similarity in parent and child disaster responses, the environment does have a role in the recovery process. Marans and his colleagues (1996) provided evidence of this, especially in areas where a society is burdened by constant disaster-like symptoms. In such areas, people exposed to disaster, child and parent alike, seem doomed to poor responses and outcomes because the "victim orientation" is so ingrained. For example, inner cities in the United States, they argue, are "characterized not by consistent reminders of a more stable past but by multigenerational poverty, academic failure, political and economic disenfranchisement, and pervasive absence of expectations that the future will be better than the present" (Marans et al., p. 123). Similarly, such areas are plagued with overburdened social institutions called on to aid in the recovery process. It is easy to see, then, why both children and parents would have the same negative outcomes in such environments.

THE ABCX MODEL: AN EXPLANATORY MODEL FOR ASSESSING MULTIPLE STRESSORS ON A FAMILY

When families experience a disaster, they must deal with significant changes that may be temporary or permanent. "The hallmark of disasters is that they immediately plunge the child and family into situations in which they are exposed to multiple stressors" (Saylor et al., 1997, p. 363).

Families face these experiences with their coping skills and the presence or absence of social supports.

In the late 1940s, Hill (1949) developed a model of family crisis that is multivariate, and that simultaneously considers intrafamilial, psychological, and social variables. Based on the assumption that family outcomes are a by-product of multiple factors of interaction, the model's purpose was to assess how much of what types of stressors could be mediated by how much and what types of resources.

McCubbin and Patterson's expansion (1983) of Hill's ABCX model (1949) helps us visualize the risk and protective factors active in any family at the time they begin dealing with a traumatic experience, and the resultant stress overload that can occur over time.

The double ABCX model is presented in Figure 4-1. In this model, uppercase A (located in the middle of Figure 4-1) is the stressor event, which "has the potential to alter the family's social system" (McCubbin & Patterson, 1983, p. 8). This stressor event places demands on the system to which it needs to respond. *a* interacts with *b*, which denotes those resources the family brings to the event. Resources are external (such as economic interdependence) and internal (such as family adaptability, family sense of organization, and mutual affection among members). *c* stands for the meaning that the family gives to the event in their lives. Does the family see this stressor as a challenge to be navigated, or an overwhelming event over which they have little or no control? Do family members believe that this event might cause the demise of the family system as they know it? In Hill's ABCX model, the interaction of a, b, and c results in family stress or distress.

In the figure, *x* is the crisis that occurs in the family when the demands expected from the family because of the stressor event are not matched with concomitant resources available to the family. The family cannot restore stability as it is presently configured, and as family members presently interact with one another. The event applies continuous pressure for the family to make changes in structure or patterns of interaction.

McCubbin and Patterson (1983) expanded Hill's model, and developed the double ABCX model. They noted that stressors rarely come one at a time, but rather usually come in groups, causing a "pileup" of stressors. In Figure 4-1, this is shown by considering lowercase a and uppercase A in the same square. Stressor pileup has several possible sources:

- *The initial stressor and its consequential hardships.* When a disaster, such as a tornado, occurs, a variety of hardships will result. One such hardship is the need to continue to pay bills after the tornado destroys the primary earner's workplace and effectively eliminates any income. The company that financed the car still expects payment, even if the car has been damaged and is unusable.
- *Normative transitions.* Predictable changes that would have been "normal" predisaster take on new meaning or create new challenges. An example might be a teenage child's decision to quit school and get a job. This decision might have occurred with or without the initial stressor; however, the decision postdisaster may place additional demands for decision making and change on a family that is already in distress. Consider the situation of a family whose members are expected not only to complete high

school, but also to go on to college. What happens when the family's teenager quits school? Dealing with the decision of this child's break from family tradition, on top of untold disaster-related decisions, may overwhelm the parents' usual coping skills and cause extra distress and heightened reactions.

- *Prior strains.* Previous stressors and how the family responded to them, together with its perceptions of the current situation, affect a family's response to a disaster. For example, the current crisis might resurrect feelings associated with a previous decision to relocate the family, and all the changes that decision caused. For instance, a young daughter's resentment that she lost the chance to be captain of her middle school soccer team because of the move could resurface postdisaster.

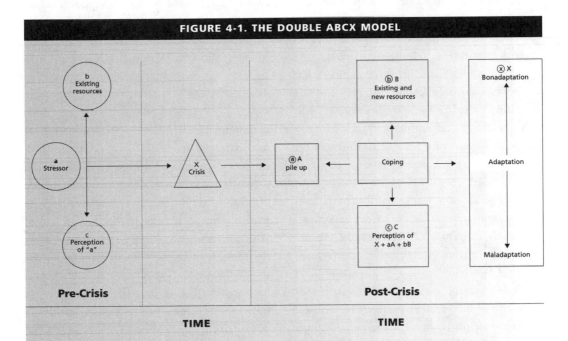

FIGURE 4-1. THE DOUBLE ABCX MODEL

a = life event or transition that has the potential to change a family's system, its life course

b = existing internal resources and external resources the family can use to keep an event from causing a crisis

c = how the family perceives the stressor, such as its importance

X = the amount of disruption to the system, the experienced anxiety and demands that the family cannot assimilate

aA = the immediate stressor plus the demands or changes that may emerge from individual system members, the system as a whole, and the extended system

bB = the family's ability to meet its needs with new and existing individual resources, system resources, and community resources

cC = the family's interpretation of the crisis, including the meaning given to the stressor event and the added stressors caused by the original crisis, plus its perception of how to bring the family into balance

xX = effect of the family's adaptation on the individual system and community levels, where a balance between member and family, and between family and community, is *bonadaptation*, and where a lack of balance is *maladaptation*.

- *Consequences of family efforts to cope.* Different family members may respond differently to a disaster and, if their different ways are not complementary, they may unwittingly undermine each other's ability to cope. For example, if a family member took a great deal of pride in being the primary wage earner predisaster, he or she might experience additional stress rather than relief if other family members step forward to help financially postdisaster. The primary wage earner would probably prefer that family members continue to rely on him or her, even if that is unrealistic. In this instance, what works as a useful coping strategy for one family member (stepping forward to help earn the family's income) results in a greater sense of upheaval and distress for another (who might believe he or she is being displaced).
- *Changes in intrafamily and social relationships that cause roles to become ambiguous.* Family roles may change, causing boundary alterations; for example, the teenage child who becomes a wage earner may expect changes in restrictions on his or her behavior, such as a later curfew. If the family needs to move, social relationships become ambiguous if a new school or new friendships come into the picture. If the family must seek outside help, or if the family must relocate to live with relatives, the family's social standing may alter, and one or more family members may lose face or independence.

When McCubbin and Patterson (1983) considered family coping in their expanded model, they noted existing resources available to the family and, in addition, new resources that become available during or after the disaster. Existing resources might include past successful parent experiences with teenagers growing up and separating from the family. New resources might include work groups that help former employees of a company find other employment, and social support groups that help deal with the grief and loss that accompany all the changes. McCubbin and Patterson perceived social support as a resource of primary importance in a family's ability to resist major crises and to recover from recurrent crises.

The *cC* factor listed in the ABCX model refers to the family's redefinition of the crisis, and the way that redefinition gives it new meaning. Usually, a family's new perspective shows the crisis to be manageable and increases the family's belief that they can carry on successfully. For example, after the loss of a business and job as a result of a tornado, family members may see each other as more independent and mature. The primary wage earner may develop closer affective ties to family members after spending more time with them. The family may redefine the experience as "a challenge to restructure our priorities," and emerge with a better fit between their beliefs about how family and work should interrelate and how family members should structure their time.

Because of both stressor pileup and the coping resources a family brings to bear on them, the family may now reach a level of adaptation that is good, useful, and healthy (bonadaptation) or negative, ineffective, and unhealthy (maladaptation). McCubbin and Patterson (1983) described these adaptations as determining a balance between individual family members and the whole family system, the fit between the community and the family, and the family's ability to work out the tension between control and trust within the family organization itself. In some situations, the family can exert some measure of control and, therefore, influence the outcome. In other situations, the family has little or no measure of control and has to trust that things will work out to their satisfaction. A family can begin to determine its best course of action and make its own decisions about the future, or it may have to trust that the employers and insurance companies, for example, will follow their own rules and trust that they will pay out as expected.

The process of a family moving from crisis toward adaptation and achieving a new balance in family functioning is a central concept of the ABCX model. The choices that a family makes in light of stressors and resources will have both immediate and lasting consequences. Touching Reality "The Double ABCX Model and a Natural Disaster" provides you with a chance to apply the double ABCX model to a family experiencing a natural disaster.

COMMUNITY INVOLVEMENT IN DISASTERS

For this section, we use our widest lens to consider the effects of disasters on the community; we also discuss some ways that communities can begin to heal. Our first challenge is to define "community;" it is just as difficult to define this word as it was to define "family."

Defining "Community"

Community evades precise definition in the research literature because the word is used in many ways in different contexts (Galbraith, 1990; Magrab, 1999). Community might be used to refer to a location in which people live—such as a neighborhood, or it might refer to a group of people

with similar interests or spiritual beliefs—such as the community of environmentalists, or people who have a similar culture or language—such as the Jewish community. Inhabitants of Tribeca or Harlem in Manhattan, members of the Triangle Baptist Church, Cubans living in Miami or Mexicans living in California, gay and lesbian people worldwide, and the hearing impaired—all these groups use the word "community" to identify themselves.

In times of disaster, communities can be a source of support for those who have experienced trauma; they can provide, for example, emotional support, housing, and money for food. They also can become additional stressors; for example, by labeling some sources of support as "good" and others as "bad," thus placing limits on where someone can or should seek support.

Attributes of a Community

In his chapter describing the Enniskillen Remembrance Day Bombing in Northern Ireland, David Bolton (1999) argued that

to understand the impact of a disaster on a community, it is necessary to have some means of judging how well it can endure the impact and consequences of a major traumatic experience, and, specifically, to enumerate those characteristics of community that are inherently supportive and which, if threatened or overwhelmed, can lead to serious consequences for the community as a whole and for individuals within it. (p. 194)

Bolton (1999) named several attributes by which one may assess the health of a community. These are *belonging; communality; segregating and integrating choices;* and *preparation, resilience, and competency in coping.*

The Double ABCX Model and a Natural Disaster

Imagine that you are in a family that has five members: two adults and three children, ages four, nine, and 12 years old. You have two pets, a cat and a dog. The adults are at work, the youngest child is in daycare in a neighbor's house, and the older children are in school.

Family members hear on the radio or from colleagues and schoolmates that there is a line of severe thunderstorms headed their way. Because there have already been several tornadoes spawned from this weather system, the chances of tornadoes are high. The storm system itself is carrying torrential rains, and high winds. Sudden flash floods are also a possibility. It is daytime.

Imagine that you are an adult in the family. What decisions do you make about the other family members? Have you had previous experiences with intense storms or tornadoes? If not, what have you heard about them? What would you most likely do in this situation? What are your first reactions?

Imagine that you are a child in the family. Have you had previous experiences with scary storms or tornadoes? If not, what have you heard about them? What are you worried about? What would you most likely do in this situation?

Tornadoes touch down, causing damage to your house and car. Trees are falling and flooding is occurring in parts of your neighborhood.

Imagine that you are an adult in the family. You hear that trees are falling in your neighborhood and that some houses are being flooded. Your place of employment plans to close early. What decisions do you make about the other family members now? What are your primary concerns and fears? What are you likely to do first? How might your feelings change if you were able to bring your family together in one place?

Imagine that you are a child in the family. You overhear school officials telling teachers to bring everyone to the gymnasium, which is the school building most likely to withstand the storm and offer protection. Televisions are turned on, and you hear that there is flooding and trees are falling in your neighborhood. What are you worried about now?

Jump ahead and imagine that it is now a few days after the storms. Family members are physically safe. Your house and possessions were not so lucky, however.

Imagine that you are an adult in the family. Your car is a total loss, your business is temporarily closed because of water damage, and you have been laid off. At home, a tree hit the side of the house causing part of the roof to collapse; there is water damage to your furniture. You realize that you do not have enough insurance to pay for the damage. There are tarps over the roof's damaged section. Your family is living in two rooms on the side of the house farthest from the damage. There is no electricity.

Will you ask for help? If you are willing, whom do you ask? How do you feel about asking for any kind of help? Do you have extended family? Is any transportation available to you? What previous struggles with finances or other challenges do you think about in this current situation?

During these events, usual problems do not disappear. Doctors' appointments, medication, and personal care assistance are still issues to be dealt with on a regular basis.

cont'd

Assuming the schools are open, children have an ongoing need for assistance with their schoolwork. The youngest child's fears about starting kindergarten are still a problem for the family.

Are you connected to any outside supports, such as a religious community, close friends, or employee associations? Do people in your neighborhood know who you are, or care how you are doing?

Imagine that you are child in the family. You overhear your parents talking about the possibility of having you stay with your cousins because your bedroom is damaged, and the electricity and water services are off. The school is being used as a shelter, so classes have been cancelled. You can tell people are upset around you, but all they say is that things will be okay. You are not so sure of that. Your parents act angry but are not explaining why to you. The kid who lives behind your house is still a bully, and you still want another pet.

It is now several weeks later.

Imagine that you are an adult in the family. It begins to look like your company may not reopen very soon, if at all. The roof has a very rough patch on it that will not last too long; however, it is just solid enough to have convinced the authorities to turn on the electricity again. You have been working at a few fast food restaurants just to bring in some money, while waiting for your previous employment to return. You liked that job. Now, however, you are more skeptical. Your severance package, should you choose to take it, is quite small. Should you apply for unemployment insurance? You have cut back on everything you can think of. You are riding the bus and trying to figure out how to buy an old car to drive to job interviews. On the radio, the announcers warn about unethical car dealers who will sell you a car that has been flooded and cleaned up. On the positive side, you hear about a company that is hiring, but it is about 50 miles away.

The pay is better, and so are the benefits. What about moving? What decisions might you make? How will these decisions affect the other family members?

Imagine you are a child in the family. You cannot go anywhere or do anything that costs money—not even to a movie. You are afraid in your bedroom because another tree might come in and "get you." Every time the wind blows, you hide under the kitchen table or sit in the bathtub. No one notices you are afraid. You wonder what will happen next.

When you imagine yourself in this scenario—as the adult and as the child—what coping skills do you have available to bring to your situation? What would be your attitude to all these changes? What could you do to keep yourself from feeling overwhelmed by the situation?

What support systems would help you and the other family members achieve bonadaptation, as opposed to maladaptation? Can you imagine other issues that might arise that would add to your difficulty, or that would provide more support? What would be the stressor pileup issues in your family?

Consider how recovery would be affected if you were illiterate, or were a diabetic on insulin, a person diagnosed with attention deficit disorder, or someone who drives a long-distance truck and is away from home several nights a week. How would your situation change if a family member had been hurt in the storm?

The questions you have been asking yourself in this exercise highlight the stressors that engage families after disasters. The family will change behaviors resulting in bonadaptation (good, healthy, or useful change) or maladaptation (negative, unhealthy, or ineffective change) depending on many variables including age, family members' physical and emotional state predisaster, external support systems, and so on.

Belonging. People describe themselves as belonging to a group because of their geographical location or mutual interests, or both. People can belong to several groups, and may hold to their "membership" in one more tightly if another group is threatened. Erikson (1994) labels communities that pull together in times of trauma and disaster "therapeutic communities" (p. 236). Indeed, the strength of citizens' bonds—the extent to which they describe themselves as "belonging" together—is a critical factor in a community's recovery. Some disasters can destroy or damage "belongings," as Bolton (1999) puts it, leaving survivors without communities and without a sense of connection.

Communality. Communality refers to the cohesive threads that bind a community together to create a familiar and positive environment. Postdisaster, a drop in communality may result in increases in uncertainty and unpredictability and, therefore, heightens the risk of negative social, emotional, or psychological consequences. Erikson (1994) calls the situation when people split into factions that work against each other or that highlight their separateness a "corrosive community," a community in which "those not touched try to distance themselves from those touched, almost as if they are escaping something spoiled, something contaminated, something polluted" (p. 236). The factions in Northern Ireland are a "corrosive community," as are the communities that formed after the Love Canal and Three Mile Island disasters. "In such circumstances, traumatic experiences work their way so thoroughly into the grain of the affected community that they come to supply its prevailing mood and temper, dominate its imagery and its sense of self, govern the way its members relate to one another" (p. 237).

Teddy Bears and the Kobe Earthquake

After a traumatic experience such as a disaster, people often assign special significance to items that come into their possession during recovery—items that help them maintain their sense of belonging to a nurturing, caring community. This is a story about some teddy bears that took on that significance in Japan.

The January 1995 Kobe Earthquake in Japan killed more than 6,000 people and injured almost 15,000. Dr. Robert Baker was in the country shortly after the disaster occurred. He described the experience of being at the scene and seeing hundreds of very young children who had lost homes, sometimes families. As a clinical consultant for the National Center for Post-Traumatic Stress Disorder in Palo Alto, CA, he knew the effects and disorientation that these young children would experience in the wake of such a disaster. Dr. Baker, his family, and other concerned Americans brought 10,000 donated teddy bears with them to Japan. A Japanese Sports Club housed all the bears at no charge. The bears were given to children in Kobe, along with a story about each bear's experience in the disaster. The story explained what happened and focused on the process of rebuilding in the future. The children learned of teddy bears of all types (firefighters, police officers, rescue workers) who were around to help and protect them. The bears were given along with efforts at normalization and validation of the children's behavior. "The bears became a symbol of love, support, and hope for the Japanese children as well as for the adults who cared for them" (Williams, Baker, & Williams, 1999, p. 104).

Segregating and integrating choices. When subgroups within a community disagree about certain cultural or government issues, helpers attempting to assess the community's health must first determine if and how these diverse groups interact and integrate in certain key areas. When two or more distinct cultural groups live in the same geographical space, we can judge the level of their integration by indicators of their mutual acceptance, such as the extent of intermarriage. Bolton (1999) warned that politeness and kind words between groups are no measure of integration—these niceties simply make the divisions invisible. Healthy communities can integrate successfully in critical areas, despite segregation in other areas.

Traumatic situations can exacerbate divisions between or among community groups, especially if the trauma may be attributed to one of the groups. Bolton (1999) described the struggles between Protestants and Catholics in Northern Ireland. When the population has deep perceptions of differences, "painstaking work aimed at achieving integration or mutual acceptance can be rapidly undone by relatively short-lived but negative political or violent events" (p. 196). According to Williams, Zinner, and Ellis (1999), current events between Israelis and Palestinians support the truth of this statement: "If communities cannot move past intracommunity struggle and blaming and cannot find positive meaning in catastrophic events, stagnation or regression may occur" (p. 9).

Preparation, resilience, and competency in coping. To determine how well a community might weather the experience of a disaster, Bolton (1999) argued that in addition to looking at belonging, communality, and segregating and integrating choices, it is important to assess a community's preparation, resilience, and competency in coping. What decisions has a community made (or not made) predisaster to be ready for a "what if"? What is the community's ability (or lack of ability) to rebound after a traumatic experience? How abundant (or how scarce) are the community's—and its leaders'—coping strategies when responding to different phases of the disaster experience? Answers to these questions highlight the markers that increase or decrease a community's chances of emerging from the disaster strong and viable.

Bolton (1999) used the term "preparation" to mean two things. One concerns passive preparation, preparation that is part of a community's regular infrastructure, including its reserves. For example, a farm family community that lives in an area prone to tornadoes in the United States may have root cellars with which all members are familiar. The second meaning refers to active preparation: The tragedy is somehow anticipated, even if the date is unknown. For example, a town community may train emergency workers, predetermine shelter locations, and analyze the vulnerability of its water supply.

"Resilience" concerns a community's ability to absorb tragedy and return to normal (although "normal" will most likely be redefined postdisaster). Raphael (1986) stated that resilience usually involves changes and adaptations for both individuals and their communities. Some communities, such as communities along the flood-prone Mississippi River in the United States, must cope with regular interruptions of life caused by floods. Repeated tragedies can quickly tap a community's resilience because the level of required change might become overwhelming. People whose resources are exhausted may emigrate from their community, or stay but become hardened, disassociated from, or numb to their feelings, or they might behave impulsively and possibly dangerously.

Rosenfeld (1997) pointed out that, although the resiliency model, as discussed in chapter 1, typically focuses on individual risk and protective factors, it can be adapted to discuss these factors at the community level. For example, one community-level protective factor may be for people to be accustomed to, or perhaps even comfortable with, accessing social services, which would make social service agencies' work more effective postdisaster. Another such protective factor may be for the community to have a strong identity, which should enhance the mobilization of search and rescue teams, support teams, and the sharing of resources such as water and shelter. A third community-level protective factor may be a community's degree of literacy: A community of people able to read and write facilitates the dissemination of information that is used to respond to a disaster. Preparation and resilience together enhance a community's chances for successfully working through a disaster situation and regaining a sense of normalcy without significant delay.

"Competency in coping" refers to the ability of a community's leaders to be flexible enough to meet the needs of their community when a disaster occurs. Will community structures be able to assist residents in understanding the disaster's meaning in their lives, and will they be able to support and care for those who have been affected? "How sensitively will the various parts of the community... address the implications of the disaster, and, specifically, the needs of those individuals, groups, and communities that have suffered directly?" (Bolton, 1999, p. 198). Sensitivity and flexibility were both apparent in responses to the World Trade Center attacks. Through television and print media, we followed the moment-to-moment adaptations that needed to be made as police officers, firefighters, and other city workers and officials responded to the disaster. The mayor and the governor spent much of their time out of their offices consoling families of those killed and injured and encouraging rescuers. Local and national animal rescue societies suspended their other activities to focus on finding and caring for pets left behind by the sudden evacuation. Hospitals reached out to rescuers and local populations by setting up emergency locations.

Risk Factors in Communities

In the preceding section, we mentioned community attributes that are useful for predicting the likelihood that a community will move through a disaster experience successfully. Just as there are risk factors that increase potential long-term negative effects of disasters on individuals, there are risk factors that affect a community's ability to respond to a disaster.

Prolonged exposure to events. When a community is exposed to a disaster over a prolonged period, it will probably experience a breakdown of significant portions of its infrastructure, and thus have a much more difficult recovery. As Williams and her colleagues (1999) summarized: "If the tragedy involved massive dislocation or relocation, long-term unemployment, and/or widespread property destruction, the catastrophe may challenge the identity and even the structure of that community" (p. 8).

For example, after the accident at the Chernobyl nuclear power plant (see disaster account in chapter 1), the government-forced an evacuation of apartments and businesses in a radius of several miles around the plant. People in the area continue to be exposed to radioactivity; it is unknown when, or even if, people will be allowed back to their homes. Even though families have relocated from the reactor's vicinity, they are continually reminded of the nuclear emission because of the high rates of cancer among both adults and children who were exposed. Memories of Chernobyl stay with them, wherever they may be.

Repetitive events. Communities recover when there is a belief that things can return to normal. Communities located along rivers or oceans that periodically flood, or communities with ongoing civil war or terrorism, do not have the luxury of anticipating normalcy. These communities run the risk of recurrent loss and damage. Sometimes government bodies do not permit rebuilding in areas where there is a risk of continuous damage. That was the decision of the North Carolina state government regarding Topsail Beach, after the second major hurricane in two years tore out homes and businesses along the coastline.

Intentionality of traumatic events. Communities have a higher risk for more intense grief or traumatic reactions when they sense, or know, that their trauma was intentional (Gurwitch, Sitterle, Young, & Pfefferbaum, 2002). This is often the case with complex disasters—history is laden with intense ethnic struggles and civil wars in which groups specifically unleash destruction and fear on each other.

Events damaging or threatening to life and physical integrity. Disasters that threaten community-members' lives pose a greater risk of trauma or intense grief than disasters that threaten only property. Nevertheless, extensive loss of property, whether public and private, creates barriers to a return to normalcy. For example, when the tidal waves of July 1998 hit Papua, New Guinea, they decimated outlying villages, killing most of the inhabitants. More than 2,000 people perished in the disaster. Much of the island's water supply became unusable because sewage leaked from the sanitation plants and flooded the few freshwater lakes and streams available to the residents. In addition, the decomposition of hundreds of drowned bodies contaminated the available water. The communities that had been hit by the waves were overwhelmed by the damage's extent, and were unable to provide water or sewerage service to their residents. People from Oxfam's Community Aid Abroad arrived and provided the materials to rebuild sewerage systems for some of the shelters and the hospital, and dug new wells to access water uncontaminated by surface waste. Once the initial assistance and focus were provided, local communities were able to begin providing their own needed resources.

Events damaging to the community support system. Some events—such as the Chernobyl nuclear meltdown, the Armenian earthquake, Hurricane Mitch in Honduras and Nicaragua, and the civil war in Rwanda—inflict such widespread damage and destruction that whole communities lose the ability to function, including the ability to provide community members with support. Infrastructure and support systems on which people depend may be

Community Risk Factor:
The Assassination of John F. Kennedy,
the Explosion of the Space Shuttle Challenger,
and the Terrorist Attacks in 2001

Three types of community risk factors appear most relevant in a comparison of the assassination of President Kennedy on November 22, 1963, a complex disaster; the Challenger explosion on January 28, 1986, a technological disaster; and the terrorist attacks on September 11, 2001, another complex disaster. These risk factors are prolonged exposure, the repetitive nature of the disaster, and intentionality.

There was prolonged exposure to all three events, due primarily to the involvement of television, although coverage increased from the first disaster to the third, because of the increase in both media personnel and technology. Television coverage had a significant effect on widespread reaction and the creation of a sense of national survivorship of a disaster. When Kennedy was assassinated, news coverage provided detailed pictures and descriptions of the location of the assassination in Dallas, the funeral, and President Johnson's confirmation ceremony. When the space shuttle Challenger exploded, network television left normal programming within six minutes of the disaster. Television reports included vivid pictures of the space shuttle itself, the faces of the witnesses, and reactions from around the country: "A survey conducted by the National Science Foundation determined that 95% of Americans had viewed some of the Challenger explosion coverage at the end of the day of loss" (Zinner, 1999, p. 35).

When the first plane struck the World Trade Center on September 11, coverage on the major news channels changed almost immediately, and pictures of subsequent events, including the second plane crashing into the second tower, were caught on camera and aired continuously.

Repetitive disastrous events put a community at greater risk for trauma than when the event is not repetitive. The assassination of President Kennedy, although not the first assassination of a U.S. president, was a rare enough event to be considered nonrepetitive. Similarly, shuttle explosions are rare events, although the possibility of similar technological disasters is higher than another assassination. The 9/11 terrorist attacks, however, although rare in U.S. history, may be viewed, perhaps, as the starting point for similar "repetitive events."

Finally, intentionality is a risk factor for increased traumatic reactions. The explosion of the Challenger was unintentional—an accident. The assassination of President Kennedy was intentional, but the target was specific—not the American people, but one particular person. The terrorist attacks also were intentional, but the target included all Americans, whether or not they worked in the World Trade Center or the Pentagon. With this switch from "him" as the target of a complex disaster, to "us," the risk for community trauma is heightened.

unable to carry out their functions, as happened in Armenia when hospitals could not treat all the injured people. In some disaster events, food, medicine, information, and support do not reach their targeted population because transportation is unavailable, or because people fear injury or reprisal if they enter certain, perhaps hostile, communities to receive support. The more the disaster prevents usual, expected, and timely responses from health, information, and protective systems within the community, the greater the perceived trauma among those affected by the disaster and the greater the damage to community support systems.

During disasters, people typically seek support from trusted community members rather than mental health professionals from outside their communities (North & Hong, 2000), which results in loss of support for the community. This loss of community support may be attributed to the type of disaster the community experienced. For example, complex disasters may affect community members' trust in the local government (after all, people may reason, it failed to protect them from the event) and this, in turn, may affect both the availability of support and the willingness of people to accept it. Sidhoum and his colleagues (2002) offered case examples from Algeria of the effects of violence on a community; these effects include a lack of trust and feelings of hopelessness, which in turn appear to have caused the observed decline in social cohesion and support. They speculated that the effects would last many years and extend to generations who were not directly exposed to the crisis.

Community Responses to Technological and Complex Disasters

Zinner (1999) described five response phases from the U.S. community after the Challenger disaster on January 28, 1986. The phases also describe reactions to the September 11, 2001, terrorist attacks on the World Trade Center in New York and on the Pentagon outside Washington, DC, and the associated plane crash in Pennsylvania. Many Americans compared their reactions to the Challenger disaster with reactions to the news about the assassination of President Kennedy, just as many compared the terrorist attacks to other traumatic experiences in the national memory, such as the attack on Pearl Harbor.

The five community response phases to national disasters are as follows (Zimmer):

1. *People's routine stops.* After the Challenger disaster everything seemed to stop as people who watched the explosion first-hand continued watching and listening to reports; others turned on their television sets to get the news and see the explosion replayed on tape.
2. *People are stunned, disbelieving.* People watched and listened in stunned silence as the explosion was played and replayed, unable to reconcile their feelings of optimism associated with the Challenger's historic voyage, which included a teacher among the crew, with their feelings of grief and confusion, and the challenge to their faith in "technology."
3. *People question the event, and need to know the cause.* Questions such as "How could this happen?" and "Who or what is to blame?" lead authorities to promptly convene investigations into the cause. If people know the cause, they might believe they are more in control of the disaster.
4. *Community leaders set the tone for national mourning.* For example, President Reagan postponed his State of the Union address after the Challenger disaster.

A Community Response to an Earthquake in Armenia

On December 7, 1988, a series of shocks measuring 6.9 on the Richter scale rocked the Republic of Armenia for 40 seconds. More than 25,000 people died, and more than 500,000 people were severely injured or left homeless, or both. The physical devastation was so severe that survivors had no services from which to request help or buildings left standing in which to find refuge. Anie Kalayjian (1999) conducted research in the area four to six weeks after the quake, and found the following reactions.

- Ninety-eight percent of the people interviewed expressed feelings of fear and shock; 58 percent experienced numbness.
- Once disbelief and denial faded, a deep, enduring sadness prevailed in the country. The cultural connection between Armenians and their land, exemplified by their referring to the land as "holy" and "sacred," was challenged.
- The connection the Armenians shared with their land also was challenged by two months of aftershocks. As a result, their belief in the security offered by the land was decreased by the threats of more lethal quakes. They were fear-

ful about the uncertainty of life in general and, specifically, the lives of members of their families.

- The people expressed anger: toward the Turks (87 percent), the buildings' engineers (83 percent), the Soviet government (85 percent), and God (11 percent). Part of their anger took the form of guilt for surviving (61 percent). Because they are forbidden by their culture to express anger toward those who have died, they targeted other victims with their anger.
- Victims felt helpless and frustrated, unable to control much of anything about their lives. They believed that they could do nothing to repair the damage.
- Feelings of emptiness and meaninglessness prevailed. It was difficult after the earthquake for most Armenians to find a reason for such a life-altering disaster.
- However, of the people interviewed, 20 percent had discovered positive meanings in their experiences. When people attributed a positive meaning to the earthquake, they focused on the present moment, and considered the help they had received from so many people.

Kalayjian, A. (1999). Coping through meaning: The community response to the earthquake in Armenia. In E. S. Zinner & M. B. Williams (Eds.), *When a community weeps: Case studies in group survivorship* (pp. 87–101). Philadelphia: Brunner/Mazel.

---

5. Multiple national memorial services take place. For example, many schools, streets, and public buildings were renamed after the Challenger or members of the crew; a national monument was erected at Arlington National Cemetery; and the day before the 10-year anniversary, President Clinton spoke about the disaster in his Saturday radio broadcast.

Group Survivorship

Zinner (1999) mentioned that there are no established ways for community members to respond when members are lost. Members often have a need for a guided or directed response when their community's survival might be uncertain after the loss of a key member or members. Zinner suggested that group members have both rights and obligations because of their group survivorship. Rights include the right to be acknowledged as survivors of a trauma, survivors who have experienced a significant loss; the right to receive facts about the loss and subsequent actions by leadership; and the right to take part in traditional or creative leave-taking ceremonies. Obligations include the obligation to publicly acknowledge one's membership in the surviving group; the obligation to respond to the survivors' family on behalf of the group; and the obligation to plan a response that benefits other members.

How can a person be deeply affected by an event that may not have any clear or direct link to her or him as an individual, but that does connect the person in some specific way to a community? Zinner's (1999) notion of group survivorship considered the impact of loss and death on a well-defined, socially recognized group. The Circles of Vulnerability (see Figure 2-3), however, especially the circle that considers psychological proximity, help us understand the process of group identification more clearly. With the advent of extended and in-depth news coverage of disasters, the opportunity to "feel as if" you are a part of a community increases, no matter how far away or physically removed you may be.

Community Healing

After a community has experienced a trauma, it has two choices. It can cease to exist, or it can move forward from the event into some new configuration. Community leaders can help their community heal in several ways (Williams et al., 1999):

- *Step back.* Leaders in a community that has suffered from a disaster should take a visual break from the traumatic experience. They should literally "step back" from the scene, perhaps even (temporarily) going away.

- *Acknowledge the crisis.* Leaders can acknowledge the disaster by giving information to the public in their area. They can bring a sense of calm, a sense that things are being handled, by offering as full a disclosure as possible. By doing so the leaders give permission for the public to express their emotions about the incident.

- *Present facts.* The leaders should give honest and open information to the public. It is important in times of crisis for them to lessen rumors that engender panic and anxiety.

- *Educate the public.* The leaders need to educate people about the disaster's possible effects to ensure that community members are able to identify signs of acute stress that they and others may experience. It is important for each community to assess how best to disseminate that information, given that different organizations carry different levels of trust within a community.

- *Develop a plan in the event of another disaster.* It is essential for leaders to plan ahead with effective responses to future disasters. Community members will accept help more readily if that help is perceived as being normal within the context of the crisis. One of the purposes of help is to restore equilibrium, and help will be more readily accepted and effective if leaders make it clear that support is the way the community can regain equilibrium.

- *Restore at least minimal functioning.* It is important for community leaders to help community members gain a sense of control and normalcy. The more normal the environment, the sooner the community will heal. There may be traditional rituals that will provide the group with a sense of self-identity, as well as some methods each particular community's culture uses to begin healing.

SUMMARY

Families come in all shapes and sizes. They have systemic characteristics that can assist or that can prove problematic at the time of a traumatic event, such as a disaster. Their relationships can be supportive, or can be barriers to postdisaster survival and recovery. Children's responses to disasters are largely based on the observed reactions of their parents. A child is more likely to respond in a positive way if the child has a single parent, or when both parents respond in similar ways, even if those ways are negative. Children are more confused, and are more likely to have long-term problems, when the responses of the primary adults around them are diverse. The family's culture also affects their response and help-seeking behaviors.

The double ABCX model for explaining the aftereffects of disasters on families helps visualize the process families move through during and after a disaster, and takes into account the family's internal and external resources in coping successfully with the trauma that a disaster forces on a family.

Similar to families, communities have characteristics that make them more or less vulnerable to a disaster's effects. Communities that engender a strong sense of belonging may be quicker to recover. That sense of belonging, or connection, may be overwhelmed, however, by the degree to which the community is exposed to the event's destruction. Healing comes with adaptation to the postdisaster world, as well as rapid a return to normalcy as possible.

In these last two chapters, we used three lenses to view the effects of disasters. Our first lens assessed the adult or child as a way to understand individual reactions to the event, and to focus on how personal characteristics—such as age, biological sex, intelligence, and coping styles—can affect a person's response to and recovery from a disaster. We began this chapter by switching to a wider lens to consider the reactions of a family to a disaster. Finally, we ended this chapter by using our widest angle lens, so that we could examine whole communities, the effects of disasters on those communities, and how communities respond to disasters. What happens with the individual, and what internal resources she or he has, affects her or his ability to respond in a positive way to the family; the community, in turn, is affected by and responds to the family.

REFERENCES

Addington, F. E. (1997). Marital satisfaction in the United States Coast Guard: Coping with stress in USCG marriages. *Dissertation Abstracts International, 57,* 5058.

Allen, J. R., Whittlesey, S., Pfefferbaum, B., & Ondersma, M. L. (1999). Community and coping of mothers and grandmothers of children killed in a human-caused disaster. *Psychiatric Annals, 29*(2), 85–91.

Bolton, D. (1999). The threat to belonging in Enniskillen: Reflections on the Remembrance Day bombing. In E. S. Zinner & M. B. Williams (Eds.), *When a community weeps: Case studies in group survivorship* (pp. 191–212). Philadelphia: Brunner/Mazel.

Bowen, M. (1978). *Family therapy in clinical practice.* New York: Jason Aronson.

Breton, J. J., Valla, J.-P., & Lambert, J. (1993). Industrial disaster and mental health of children and their parents. *Journal of the American Academy of Child and Adolescent Psychiatry, 32,* 438–445.

Bryce, J. W., Walker, N., & Peterson, C. (1989). Predicting symptoms of depression among women in Beirut: The importance of daily life. *International Journal of Mental Health, 18*(1), 57–70.

Cairns, E. (1996). *Children and political violence.* Cambridge, MA: Blackwell Publishers.

Cohan, C. L., & Cole, S. W. (2002). Life course transitions and natural disaster: Marriage, birth, and divorce following Hurricane Hugo. *Journal of Family Psychology, 16*(1), 14–25.

Compas, B. E., & Epping, J. E. (1993). Stress and coping in children and families: Implications for children coping with disaster. In C. F. Saylor (Ed.), *Children and disasters* (pp. 11–28). New York: Plenum Press.

Crawford, J. M. (1999). Co-parent adoptions by same-sex couples: From loophole to law. *Families in Society, 80*, 271–278.

Dawes, A., Tredoux, C., & Feinstein, A. (1989). Political violence in South Africa: Some effects on children of the violent destruction of their community. *International Journal of Mental Health, 18*(2), 16–43.

deVries, M. W. (1996). Trauma in cultural perspective. In B. van der Kolk, A. C. McFarlane, & L. Weisaeth (Eds.), *Traumatic stress: The effects of overwhelming experience on mind, body, and society* (pp. 398–413). New York: Guilford Press.

Erikson, K. (1994). *A new species of trouble: Explorations in disaster, trauma, and community.* New York: W. W. Norton.

Galbraith, M. W. (1990). The nature of community and adult education. In M. W. Galbraith (Ed.), *Education through community organizations* (pp. 3–11). San Francisco: Jossey-Bass.

Galvin, K. M., & Brommel, B. J. (2000). *Family communication: Cohesion and change* (5th ed.). New York: Longman.

Garbarino, J., & Kostelny, K. (1996). What do we need to know to understand children in war and community violence? In R. J. Apfel & B. Simon (Eds.), *Minefields in their hearts: The mental health of children in war and communal violence* (pp. 104–127). New Haven, CT: Yale University Press.

Garbarino, J., Kostelny, K., & Dubrow, N. (1991). What children can tell us about living in danger. *American Psychologist, 46*, 376–383.

Gibbs, S. (1994). Postwar social reconstruction in Mozambique: Re-framing children's experience of trauma and healing. *Disasters, 18*, 269–276.

Gillard, M., & Paton, D. (1999). Disaster stress following a hurricane: The role of religious differences in the Fijian Islands. *Australasian Journal of Disaster and Trauma Studies, 3*(2).

Green, B. L., Korol, M., Grace, M. C., Vary, M. G., Leonard, A. C., Gleser, G. C., & Smitson-Cohen, S. (1991). Children and disaster: Age, gender, and parental effects on PTSD symptoms. *Journal of the American Academy of Child & Adolescent Psychiatry, 30*, 945–951.

Gurwitch, R. H., Sitterle, K. A., Young, B. H., & Pfefferbaum, B. (2002). The aftermath of terrorism. In A. M. La Greca, W. K. Silverman, E. M, Vernberg, & M. C. Roberts (Eds.), *Helping children cope with disasters and terrorism* (pp. 327–357). Washington, DC: American Psychological Association.

Handford, H. A., Mayes, S. D., Mattison, R. E., Humphrey, F. J., Bagnato, S., Bixler, E. O., & Kales, J. D. (1986). Child and parent reactions to the Three Mile Island nuclear accident. *Journal of the American Academy of Child Psychiatry, 25*, 346–356.

Hill, R. (1949). *Families under stress: Adjustment to the crises of war separation and reunion.* New York: Harper & Row.

Hunter, E. J. (1988). Long-term effects of parental wartime captivity on children: Children of POW and MIA servicemen. *Journal of Contemporary Psychotherapy, 18*, 312–328.

Jurich, A., & Johnson, L. N. (1999). The process of family therapy: Defining family as a collaborative enterprise. *Marriage and Family Review, 28*(3–4), 191–208.

Kalayjian, A. (1999). Coping through meaning: The community response to the earthquake in Armenia. In E. S. Zinner & M. B. Williams (Eds.), *When a community weeps: Case studies in group survivorship* (pp. 87–101). Philadelphia: Brunner/Mazel.

Laor, N., Wolmer, L., & Cohen, D. J. (2001). Mothers' functioning and children's symptoms 5 years after a SCUD missile attack. *American Journal of Psychiatry, 158,* 1020–1026.

Laor, N., Wolmer, L., Mayes, L. C., & Golomb, A. (1996). Israeli preschoolers under Scud missile attacks: A developmental perspective on risk-modifying factors. *Archives of General Psychiatry, 53,* 416–423.

Magrab, P. R. (1999). The meaning of community. In R. N. Roberts, & P. R. Magrab (Eds.), *Where children live: Solutions for serving young children and their families,* (pp. 3–29). Stamford, CT: Ablex.

Marans, S., Berkman, M., & Cohen, D. (1996). Child development and adaptation to catastrophic circumstances. In R. J. Apfel & B. Simon (Eds.), *Minefields in their hearts: The mental health of children in war and communal violence.* (pp. 104–127). New Haven, CT: Yale University Press.

McCubbin, H. I., & Patterson, J. M. (1983). The family stress process: The Double ABCX Model of adjustment and adaptation. *Marriage and Family Review, 6*(1–2), 7–37.

Mirzamani, M., & Bolton, D. (2002). PTSD symptoms of mothers following occurrence of a disaster affecting their children. *Psychological Reports, 90,* 431–438.

Munton, A. G, & Reynolds, S. (1995). Family functioning and coping with change: A longitudinal test of the Circumplex Model. *Human Relations, 48,* 1055–1072.

North, C. S., & Hong, B. A. (2000). Project CREST: A new model for mental health intervention after a community disaster. *American Journal of Public Health, 90,* 1057–1058.

Olson, D. H. (1986). Circumplex Model IV: Validation studies and FACES III. *Family Process, 25,* 338–351.

Olson, D. H. (2000). Circumplex Model of marital and family systems. *Journal of Family Therapy, 22,* 144–167.

Patterson, J. M. (2002). Understanding family resilience. *Journal of Clinical Psychology, 58,* 233–246.

Rabalais, A. E., Ruggiero, K. J., & Scotti, J. R. (2002). Multicultural issues in the response of children to disasters. In A. M. La Greca, W. K. Silverman, E. M. Vernberg, & M. C. Roberts (Ed) (Eds.), *Helping children cope with disasters and terrorism* (pp. 73–99). Washington, DC: American Psychological Association.

Raphael, B. (1986). *When disaster strikes: A handbook for the caring professions.* London: Hutchinson.

Richmond, M. (1917). *Social diagnosis.* Troy, NY: Russell Sage Foundation.

Rosenfeld, L. B. (1997, September). *Adapting the individual-based resiliency model to a community-based model: A response to Sir Michael Rutter.* Paper presented at the Conference on Violence and Trauma in Childhood, Chapel Hill, NC.

Saylor, C. F., Belter, R., & Stokes, S. J. (1997). Children and families coping with disaster. In S. A. Wolchik & I. N. Sandler (Eds.), *Handbook of children's coping: Linking theory and intervention* (pp. 361–383). New York: Plenum Press.

Sidhoum, M. O. A., Arar, F., Bouatta, C., Khaled, N., & Elmasri, M. (2002). Terrorism, traumatic events and mental health in Algeria. In J. de Jong (Ed.), *Trauma, war, and violence: Public mental health in socio-cultural context* (pp. 367–404). New York: Kluwer Academic/Plenum.

Sutker, P. B., Davis, J. M., Uddo, M., & Ditta, S. R. (1995). War zone stress, personal resources, and PTSD in Persian Gulf War returnees. *Journal of Abnormal Psychology, 104,* 444–452.

Treuer, E. (1993). *Hurricane Andrew and Fellowship House* (D. Treuer, Director). Fellowship House under contract with US Department of Health and Human Services, emergency services and Disaster Relief Branch (Producer). Miami, FL: Camelot Video Productions, Inc. (Available from National Mental Health Services Knowledge Exchange Network, P.O. 42490, Washington, DC 20015, 800-789-2647)

Vogel, J. M., & Vernberg, E. M. (1993). Task Force Report, part 1: Children's psychological responses to disasters. *Journal of Clinical Child Psychology, 22*, 464–484.

Walsh, F. (2002). A family resilience framework: Innovative practice applications. *Family Relations, 51*, 130–137.

Williams, M. B., Baker, G. R., & Williams, T. (1999). The great Hanshin-Qwaji earthquake: Adapted strategies for survival. In E. S. Zinner & M. B. Williams (Eds.), *When a community weeps: Case studies in group survivorship* (pp. 103–118). Philadelphia: Brunner/Mazel.

Williams, M. B., Zinner, E. S., & Ellis, R., R. (1999). The connection between grief and trauma: An overview. In E. S. Zinner & M. B. Williams (Eds.), *When a community weeps: Case studies in group survivorship* (pp. 3–16). Philadelphia: Brunner/Mazel.

Zinner, E. S. (1999). The Challenger disaster: Group survivorship on a national landscape. In E. S. Zinner & M. B. Williams (Eds.), *When a community weeps: Case studies in group survivorship* (pp. 23–47). Philadelphia: Brunner/Mazel.

Natural Disasters

Chapter Overview

After studying the material in this chapter, you should

- be able to define *natural* disaster and describe how it differs from other types of disasters
- understand that natural disasters affect nations and communities differently and that the effect is often based on socioeconomic status
- understand the way children, families, and communities commonly respond to natural disasters
- know the factors that can influence responses to natural disasters
- understand what special effects natural disasters can have on vulnerable populations and what might mitigate those effects
- describe the need for natural disaster mitigation and identify the barriers to a successful completion of a mitigation plan.

From Cyclone Tracy in Australia, to the mudslides in Honduras and Nicaragua, to Hurricane Floyd in the United States—natural disasters' effects on people and property are often on people's minds. Read newspaper headlines or study the titles and subject of current movies and you will notice the level of fascination people have for natural disasters.

To this point in the book, we have discussed individuals', families', and communities' responses to all types of disasters. This chapter focuses specifically on natural disasters, which affect millions of people around the world every year. We look at interesting information regarding natural disasters' seeming discrimination, when they kill people and destroy property and livelihoods in what appears to be a nonrandom way. We study some of the international community's suggestions regarding preparedness for future disasters and response to disasters in developing nations. Children, individuals, families, and communities respond in specific ways to natural disasters, and these responses can be differentiated from how they respond to technological and complex disasters.

DEFINING "NATURAL DISASTER"

Broadly defined, as we discussed in chapter 1, a disaster involves destruction of property, loss of life, and widespread injury. Historically, labeling an event a disaster means that it has several characteristics in addition to these three. According to Saylor (1993), a disaster also "has an identifiable beginning and end; adversely affects a rela-

The Turkey Earthquake of 1999

On August 17, 1999, one of the most powerful earthquakes in the past 100 years jolted Turkey.[1] The earthquake's epicenter, which measured 7.4 on the Richter scale, was in Izmit, but the shock ravaged the entire country. The earthquake affected a 280-kilometer stretch of land in northern Turkey, starting in Istanbul and continuing eastward about 174 miles. The death toll (an estimated 20,000 people) was 10 times greater than the past earthquake of this size close to Izmit, which occurred in 1754 with a reported 2,000 deaths. The land in this area of Turkey is very active, with frequent temblors. For example, in 1970 a magnitude 7.1 earthquake, near Gediz (160 kilometers, or about 100 miles, to the south) killed over 1,000 people.

The earthquake occurred on the northern Anatolian fault, a fault very similar to California's San Andreas Fault. It left over 350,000 people homeless, angry, and frightened, and an estimated 1 million sleeping in the streets, because they were afraid to sleep inside the buildings. Damage, however, was disproportionate, with the most densely populated cities and towns suffering the most. Structures in some areas were completely demolished, whereas in other areas most buildings were left standing. The effects seemed almost random, initially.

As people began to examine the damage, however, they began to notice discrepancies from area to area, which led them to accuse the buildings' engineers of faulty construction and inadequate work. They extended blame to the government, and accused them of having responded too slowly.

[1] The most powerful earthquakes can be over magnitude 8.5, such as Alaska's 1964 earthquake (magnitude 9.2), and Chile's 1960 earthquake (at magnitude 9.5, the strongest quake ever recorded). The Richter scale is exponential, so that a magnitude 8.5 quake moves the ground 10 times more than a magnitude 7.5 quake.

tively large group of people; is 'public' and shared by members of more than one family; is out of the realm of ordinary experience; and, psychologically, is traumatic enough to induce stress in almost anyone" (p. 2). Vogel and Vernberg (1993) added three characteristics to this list: Disasters are "events that are relatively sudden, highly disruptive, [and] time-limited (even though the effects may be longer lasting)" (p. 465).

According to Belter and Shannon (1993), a *natural* disaster is a disaster "caused by the forces of nature, rather than by the actions or products of humans" (p. 85). These include floods, earthquakes, hurricanes, cyclones, blizzards, mudslides, droughts, windstorms, tornadoes, hailstorms, volcanic eruptions, lightning strikes, residential fires, and wildfires. Compared with other types of disasters, people may not have the opportunity to place blame with natural disasters; placing blame is sometimes part of the healing process and without it, people may find it harder to achieve closure and may be left with questions such as "Why?" or "Why me?"

The definition of "natural disaster" is not as clear as it may first appear. *The World Disasters Report 2001* quotes an African proverb that says, "God makes drought. Man makes famine" (International Federation of Red Cross and Red Crescent Societies [IFR-CRCS], 2001, p. 1). Humans may be the root cause of some natural disasters: widespread deforestation by humans may result in flooding and mudslides in the absence of trees to hold back the land; levee construction along rivers can cause spring rains to overwhelm their channels and flood communities that were built in floodplains. Is the result a natural disaster or something else?

According to the IFR-CRCS (2001), from 1991 to 2000, an average of 211 million people annually were killed or otherwise affected by natural disasters. On average, natural disasters accounted for 88 percent of all disaster deaths in that decade; 83 percent of all those killed by natural disasters were in Asia (Walter, 2001). Approximately 500,000 residential fires occur each year in the United States, resulting in 5,000 deaths; in fact, burn injuries are the third leading case of death for children (Jones & Ollendick, 2002).

Costs associated with natural disasters have increased significantly. The IFR-CRCS's *World Disasters Report 2001* estimates that since the 1950s, "costs have rocketed 14-fold" (IFR-CRCS, 2001, chap. 1, p. 1). For example, Hurricane Mitch's effect on the Honduran economy in 1998 was equivalent to three-quarters of its annual gross domestic product (GDP) (IFR-CRCS, chap. 2, p. 2).

LETHALITY, COST, AND FREQUENCY COMPARISONS

Disasters often precipitate discussions about the increase or decrease of natural disaster events worldwide. For instance, the IFR-CRCS reports: "While the number of geophysical disasters has remained fairly steady, the number of hydro-meteorological disasters since 1996 has more than doubled" (2001, chap. 8, p. 1). The average number of deaths by natural disasters is seven times greater than the number of persons killed or affected by conflict.

Both the cost and the lethality of natural disasters vary by type. From 1991 through 2000, more than 90 percent of deaths from natural disasters came from events such as droughts, windstorms, and floods. Floods affected over 66 percent of the 211 million touched by natural disasters each year in that decade; flood deaths resulted in 15 percent of all natural disaster deaths. However, famine is much more deadly, accounting for 42 percent of all natural disaster deaths. In the same decade, earthquakes accounted for 9 percent of all natural disaster deaths. The decade 1991 to 2000 was less deadly than 1981 to 1990 for natural disasters. Although fewer people died (75,252 compared with 86,328), more people were affected, showing an increase from an average of 147 million a year affected in the 1980s to 211 million a year affected in the 1990s (IFR-CRCS, 2001, chap. 8, p. 2).

It is very difficult to calculate the real costs associated with natural disasters; on the basis of available information, however, floods, earthquakes, and windstorms are the most expensive types of natural disasters. Earthquakes accounted for 30 percent of estimated damage, whereas famines (which are responsible for the most deaths) accounted for just 4 percent of the estimated damage (IFR-CRCS, 2001). Large natural disasters can overwhelm national economies. For example, the 1999 earthquake in Turkey was equivalent to between 7 percent and 9 percent of Turkey's GDP.

The Spotlight on Research "Volcano Fatalities" presents research on volcanic fatalities, including the variety of ways volcanoes kill people.

DO NATURAL DISASTERS DISCRIMINATE?

Most of us assume that natural disasters are similar to rain or sunshine—forces of nature that affect rich and poor alike. Read these

---

SPOTLIGHT ON RESEARCH

Volcano Fatalities

Tom Simkin, Lee Seibert, and Russell Blong (2001) documented over 400 fatal volcanic eruptions to determine what lessons can be learned so authorities can reduce future deaths by volcanoes.

Volcanoes kill people in many ways: Pyroclastic flows (hot ash that sweeps downslope at hurricane speeds, ahead of lava flow) have killed the most people. The researchers discovered, however, that the most common killer is the fragmental material thrown from volcanoes called tephra. The most common type of tephra is the ash that can accumulate on and collapse roofs (the most deaths from tephra occur this way). Tephra can also kill by projectile impact. Other fatalities occur during volcanic eruptions from tsunami and mud-flows, which are high-profile events that tend to receive much attention from the media, but which cause fewer deaths.

Simkin and his colleagues found that the timing of the deaths was interesting. The first 24 hours after the eruption are extremely dangerous. After the initial surprise, people are very aware of the crisis and willingly evacuate. However, within a few weeks, people usually decide to return home and simply live with the threat. Sometimes people become curious and climb close to the volcano's mouth. People become cynical about scientific information and choose to ignore it. "Nearly two-thirds of the fatalities and half the fatal events have taken place more than one month after the eruption's start."

Simkin, T., Siebert, L., & Blong, R. (2001, January 12). Volcano fatalities—Lessons from the historical record. *Science, 291*, 255.

figures (Table 5-1) taken from an article by Anthony Oliver-Smith (1986), which are, in turn, based on data from Thompson (1982).

To put these numbers a different way, between 1947 and 1981, approximately 92.8 percent of the deaths from natural disasters, excluding droughts, occurred in the developing countries of Asia, Africa, and Latin America. Between 1991 and 2000, 98 percent of those killed or injured by disasters were in nations of low or medium human development. According to the IFR-CRCS (2001):

TABLE 5-1. COMPARISON BY REGION OF DEATH TOLL FROM DISASTERS	
Region	**Deaths per million**
North America	31.50
Europe	38.57
Central America/Caribbean	918.16
South America	341.33
Asia	376.28
Africa (excluding droughts)	117.05
Australia/Oceania	323.50

TABLE 5-2. TWO EARTHQUAKES COMPARED		
	Managua	**San Fernando Valley**
Richter scale reading	5.6	6.6
Extent of destruction	100 km² (≈ 62 square miles)	1,500 km² (≈ 930 square miles)
Population of affected area	420,000	7,000,000
Dead	5,000	60
Injured	20,000	2,540

By comparing the totals reported killed with the total number of disasters, the effect of development on disasters becomes stark. On average, 22.5 people die per reported disaster in highly developed nations, 145 die per disaster in nations of medium human development, while each disaster in low human development countries claims an average of 1,052 people. (chap. 8, p. 2)

Stop for a moment and consider: Why are there high numbers of fatalities in low human development countries, as opposed to the fatalities in countries with medium or high human development?

Could it be a question of severity? You might guess that the type or severity of natural disasters is greater in developing countries.

Table 5-2 compares the 1971 earthquake in Managua, Nicaragua, with the 1972 earthquake in the San Fernando Valley, California (Seaman, 1984).

According to the Richter scale reading for the two earthquakes, the San Fernando Valley earthquake was 10 times more powerful and the area of destruction much greater, yet the number of dead and injured was much higher in Managua. So, what else might account for the tremendous discrepancy in numbers of fatalities in developing and developed countries?

Could it be a question of frequency? You might think that disasters occur more often in developing countries. Remember, however, that as we discussed earlier, the average number of natural disasters per year has not increased, with one possible exception: North Atlantic hurricanes and monsoons.

This activity was very high from 1995 to 2000 compared with the generally low activity from 1971 to 1994 (Goldenberg, Landsea, Mestas-Nuñez, & Gray, 2001); in addition, the number of monsoons has been increasing over the past 400 years (Black, 2002). The number of hydrometeorological events has also increased, but it is highly unlikely that the frequency could be different enough in different parts of the world to account for the 92.8 percent discrepancy mentioned above.

Could it be a question of geographic vulnerability? You might guess that, in countries with lower human development, more people may live in areas prone to natural disaster. This is partially true now, and it will certainly be truer in the future, as populations grow. Nevertheless, it is not a good explanation—see the Managua–San Fernando Valley comparison. In our example, there is a much greater population in the San Fernando Valley, and San Fernando Valley is as geographically vulnerable as Managua.

Factors Affecting Discrepancies in the Effects of Natural Disasters

Some researchers (for example, Oliver-Smith, 1986; Reice, 2001) suggest numerous factors that contribute to the severity of the disasters' effects on human populations. As you read the list that follows, note that countries with low human development are likely to experience more of these risk factors than countries with medium or high human development. Think also about your own community. Are there some areas, perhaps as small as neighborhoods, that seem to be hit more frequently with flooding or fires, or suffer more devastating effects from hurricanes or tornadoes? What are the distinguishing characteristics of those areas?

Researchers have suggested the following factors as explanations for natural disasters' apparent discrimination against certain people.

- *Inadequate housing quality*, such as poor construction, increases chances of death or injury during and after disasters and increases the number of people who will left homeless and at risk of disease, exposure, and so on. People who are poor often live on land that is unattractive to people who are richer. Hence, poor people will erect shanties, poorly constructed houses or tents on floodplains, mountainsides, and landfills.

- *A population's pre-existing poor health and nutritional status* make it vulnerable to stress and disease caused by disaster. Compromised physical and mental health are risk factors for increased negative effects of trauma.

- *Marginalized populations* in countries that have a great disparity between rich and poor may live in vulnerable areas without basic amenities or a well-developed infrastructure. In low development areas, for example, populations may have little or no sanitation or sewage disposal or have little access to shelters, hospitals, or medicine after a disaster. Clean water may not be available. In times of drought in parts of Africa, people may have to walk several kilometers for their water and then stand and wait for hours to fill a single bucket (Georgieva, 2000). After Hurricane Mitch—the fourth strongest hurricane ever recorded in the Atlantic Basin, with sustained winds of 180 miles per hour—hit Honduras on October 28, 1998, helpers were unable to reach entire villages in Nicaragua and Honduras because the few roads that had existed were destroyed.

- *Political instability* may also interfere with distribution of aid and relief efforts after a disaster. During the winter of 2001–2002, aid workers in Afghanistan had to wait for hostilities to stop before they could bring supplies and medicine to noncombatants who were without any food and who were coping with the harsh winter weather. According to reports, one combatant group or another robbed aid caravans before they could reach the starving civilians for whom they were intended.

- *Increasing urbanization and unplanned development*, especially in geographically vulnerable areas, combined with poor housing construction, can contribute greatly to the human cost of disaster. In many countries there has been a major population shift toward the coastlines. Florida's population in 2001, for example, was five times the number of residents in 1950, and 80 percent of Floridians live within 21 miles of the coast.

- *An inadequate social welfare infrastructure* means inadequate resources to provide basic human services and health care, increasing the likelihood of disease outbreaks after a disaster. In her summary of the work of the World Food Programme (WFP) of the United Nations, Judit Katona-Apte (1999) described North Korea as being in the grip of a "famine in slow motion." Every year, she said, programs and coping mechanisms fail. "Over 8 million people depend on WFP food aid, distributed through the (inadequate) Public Distribution System to schools, centers and food-for-work projects." The food shortage is growing. People who are starving are prey to many opportunistic diseases.

- *Population size and population growth* affect virtually all other explanations for natural disasters' apparent discrimination. Populations of the medium and low human development countries are increasing at a faster rate than the populations of high development countries; therefore, a greater percentage of the world's inhabitants are living in inadequate housing in locations of greater risk for natural disasters.

- *Pressures on the natural environment* result when populations increase and countries struggle to modernize, for example, "reclaiming" wetlands or engaging in agricultural or industrial practices that reduce the amount of land on which people can live increase the chances of certain types of natural disasters.

In the 1976 earthquake in Guatemala, 1,200 people were killed and 90,000 were left homeless. The majority of these were from poorer neighborhoods (Glass & Urrutia, 1977). Some researchers have gone so far as to call this event a "classquake" (Oliver-Smith, 1986). It is reasonable to predict that as the world's population grows, so will the impact of natural disasters. Today, 1.1 billion people fall into the category of the world's "poorest poor"—living on less than $700 annually per person. By 2050 there will be 1.5 billion, and by 2150, 2 billion of these "poorest poor" (Quammen, 1998).

REACTIONS TO NATURAL DISASTERS

Children's Reactions to Natural Disasters

Children's reactions to natural disasters are similar to the general trauma reactions described in chapter 3; there is no evidence to suggest that the severity of their reactions varies according to the type of natural disaster (La Greca & Prinstein, 2002). Most people, and that includes children, are considered "normal" at the time they experience a disaster. Normal children react to abnormal events, such as natural disasters, in ways that research shows to be somewhat predictable. We discuss some of the common reactions in this section.

Children often exhibit some or all of the following reactions to natural disasters, although it is important to keep in mind, especially from a resiliency perspective, that some children may not present any diagnosable psychopathologies at all (Scott, Knoth, Beltran-Quiones, & Gomez, 2003):

- *Fear and anxiety.* Children are afraid that the disaster will reoccur, that someone else will be injured or killed, that they

The Loma Prieta, California, Earthquake, October 1989

Many children were involved in the Loma Prieta, California, earthquake, that occurred in October 1989. The earthquake, which registered a 7.1 on the Richter scale, killed over 62 people—a remarkably low number given the time and size of the earthquake; most of the casualties were caused by the collapse of the Cypress Street section of highway I-880, because it hit during rush hour. At least 3,700 people were reported injured and over 12,000 were displaced. Over 18,000 homes were damaged and 963 were destroyed, and more than 2,500 other buildings were damaged and 147 were destroyed.

One of the lessons learned from disaster research is that a rapid return to some normalcy can reduce long-term trauma in victims and survivors. The school system in the Loma Prieta area reacted quickly and opened schools as soon as it was safe to do so. The administration provided training to teachers and staff on how to support the students and help them cope with their feelings. There is a video available that was created about one school's response to Loma Prieta; it shows the sensitivity of Ms. Frances Joe, a teacher, and

Ms. Coeleen Kiebert, an art therapist, following the disaster.[2]

The school children struggle in different ways, with bravado, tears, questions, continuing concerns for other family members, and fears for the future. Ms. Joe is able to react with comfort, information, humor, and support. She validates their concerns. She also gives the students information so that they can monitor reactions that endure, or are too strong, and understand that they might need additional help.

Ms. Kiebert, the art therapist, shows children's pictures and demonstrates how to move children from their fear and anxiety to more hopeful thoughts about the future. She emphasizes that we must help the children focus on what they learned, how they are stronger, and how they will be better prepared next time they have to deal with some serious difficulty. She describes ways to help the children draw pictures about how they are "prepared and ready" for the future. Both professionals identify behaviors that indicate a particular child might need more attention.

---

[2] The video, *Children and Trauma: The School's Response,* is available at no charge from National Mental Health Services Knowledge Exchange Network, P.O. Box 42490, Washington, DC 20015; 800-789-2647.

will be separated from their family, or that they will be abandoned (FEMA, 2003a). In studies on young children who had experienced hurricanes (La Greca et al., 1996; Swenson et al., 1996), more than half the children interviewed believed that they would die. Similar to other reactions, fear and anxiety responses depend on the child's level of exposure. La Greca, Silverman, and Wasserstein (1998) examined children's anxiety levels before and after Hurricane Andrew and found that anxiety increased in those with high exposure to the disaster.

- *Depression.* Some children express sadness and hopelessness by crying and acting lethargic after a natural disaster; that is, they experience depressive symptoms. The degree of depression, similar to most other symptoms, seems to depend on the degree of exposure and loss experienced by the child (Rustemli & Karanci, 1996; Swenson et al., 1996; Vogel & Vernberg, 1993). The Spotlight on Research "Coping Styles and Depressive Symptoms Following a Natural Disaster" describes such symptoms after a hurricane in the southern United States.

- *Poor school performance.* Some difficulties with school performance are common among children who have experienced a disaster. For example, Jurgens, Houlihan, and Schwartz (1996) completed a study to determine how students between the ages of 12 and 18 reacted when they were required to move to

SPOTLIGHT ON RESEARCH

Coping Styles and Depressive Symptoms Following a Natural Disaster

In September 1989, Hurricane Hugo hit the coast of South Carolina with winds of 175 miles per hour. The storm, which brought with it a tidal surge of up to 23 feet, caused 35 deaths. Hugo caused billions of dollars of property damage, cut off utilities for a million people, and, in general, disrupted life everywhere it went.

Patricia Jeney-Gammon and her colleagues (1993) arranged to study the reactions of 257 third-, fourth-, and fifth-grade students five months following the hurricane. They were specifically looking at the coping styles of the children; their goal was to understand the relationship between certain types of coping and the existence of depressive symptoms after a natural disaster.

Using standardized tests (Children's Depression Inventory, and Kidcope), findings suggested that several coping strategies were positively related to depression. Children who used emotional regulation (yelling, getting mad, or consciously trying to make themselves calm down) had more symptoms of depression than those who did not. Those who sought out social support experienced fewer depressive symptoms than those who withdrew. Positive reframing behaviors decreased depressive symptoms, while self-blame for the disaster increased depression. Results of the study strongly suggest that how children think about themselves and the disaster have a clear connection to their experience of depressive symptoms.

Jeney-Gammon, P., Daugherty, T. K., Finch, Jr., A. J., Belter, R. W., & Foster, K. Y. (1993). Children's coping styles and report of depressive symptoms following a natural disaster. *Journal of Genetic Psychology, 154*, 259–267.

another school district after their school was destroyed by a tornado that swept through southern Minnesota in June 1992. "Relocated students were found to differ significantly from their non-relocated peers in the area of grades and scores on the Child Behavior Check List. Relocated students had lower grades" (Jurgens et al., p. 4). The researchers postulated that the significant differences in scores might be caused by pre-existing differences. However, the teachers from the two districts also were merged so some of the relocated students had the same teachers, and all of the students experienced changes in teachers and class configurations.

- *Acting out, irritability, or aggression.* In the same study of children's reactions after the tornado in southern Minnesota (Jurgens et al., 1996), relocated students showed higher incidents of problem behavior, as reported by their parents. Corroborating evidence is available from a study completed after the 1992 earthquake in Erzincan, Turkey (Rustemli & Karanci, 1996), which suggested an increase in the level of irritability and hostility among both children and adults researched.

- *Separation anxiety.* Children who experience disasters frequently express fear that they will be separated from their parents, and those who are separated—for whatever reason—show distress and anxiety. Results of studies presented in chapter 4 indicate that children are strongly affected by their parents' reactions both during and after a trauma.

- *Sleep difficulties or nightmares, regression* (for example, thumb-sucking and bedwetting, primarily in younger children), and somatic complaints (for example, physical problems such as colds, rashes, headaches, allergies, or the flu). Sleep disturbances are common among children who have experienced trauma. Fourteen months after Hurricane Andrew, Swenson and her colleagues (1996) compared preschool children, two-to-six-years-old, who had experienced the hurricane with those who had not, and found that the former group were more likely to act whiny, be demanding, have trouble going to sleep, have disturbing dreams, and resist being left alone. However, according to the mothers surveyed, most children had a steady decrease in these behavior problems during the six months after the storm. Children who experienced further life stressors (for example, a marriage or a death in the family) or whose families' lost property in the hurricane, showed longer-term behavioral and emotional problems than those who had not.

Few studies focus exclusively on nightmares, but one was conducted after the 1989 Loma Prieta earthquake. Wood, Bootzin, Rosenhan, and Nolen-Hoeksema (1992) found the frequency of nightmares to be twice as high among area college students as among a control group in Tucson, Arizona. In addition, more of their nightmares were about earthquakes, but, contrary to popular belief, these nightmares were not more emotionally intense than other nightmares.

- *Playing disaster "games" as a way of processing the event.* Keppel-Benson and Ollendick (1993) cited early PTSD literature that suggests that young children are especially likely to act out memories of the trauma they experienced. Some researchers and scholars, however, consider this unhelpful, and believe that it keeps the child stuck in the repetitious replay of the traumatic experience. Others view the dramatization as a therapeutic way for children to work through their difficult experiences. In Swenson and colleagues' study (1996) of Hurricane Andrew, even 14 months after the storm, 9 percent of the children continued to create games, stories, or pictures about it. (Chapter 9 presents a discussion of the usefulness of games in disaster intervention.)

- *Guilt.* Lindy (1985) described guilt as an "organizer against helplessness," and as a "self-oriented manner to begin to place incomprehensible events into some frame of reference" (p. 160). The child who experiences an overwhelming event, such as a disaster, may assume responsibility for the event, as well as the damage and death it caused. In her study of the effects of Hurricane Hugo on nine elementary school children of St. Croix, the Virgin Islands, Ayot (1995) found guilt among the major themes in their responses, along with fear, worry, grief, and denial. Burke, and colleagues (1982) suggested that sufferers of natural disasters "may feel more personally responsible for their suffering than do victims who can blame an external agent such as a war or other manmade disaster" (p. 1013).

- *PTSD.* Before being diagnosed with PTSD, a child must have experienced an event that is outside her or his "usual experience." Children with symptoms of PTSD may experience intrusive thoughts of the trauma that prevent them from sleeping or carrying on regular activities. They may be afraid to return to school, or they may become clingy and demanding. Some children become numb to feelings, avoiding any experience that might remind them of the disaster. The most common PTSD symptoms after natural disasters are intrusive thoughts or dreams about the disaster (La Greca and Prinstein, 2002).

In their summary of the research linking PTSD and natural disasters, La Greca and Prinstein (2002) stated that "existing evidence suggests that rates of PTSD symptoms decline over the first year following natural disasters.... Nevertheless, even a year or more after hurricanes and earthquakes, many children continue to exhibit severe PTSD symptoms...and somewhere between 2% and 6% meet the criteria for a diagnosis of PTSD" (p. 119).

- *Concern for others.* When a natural disaster strikes, especially if it strikes with little or no warning, children may have to deal with abrupt separations from parents and caretakers. They may see people hurt or killed, and they may worry about their family. They may see adults whom they perceive as being "all-powerful" unable to control the forces of nature, or even as being unable to control their own responses to the event (Gillis, 1993). It may take some time for children to bounce back from these experiences. As they adjust, they may be very clingy, unable to separate easily, or at all, from their parents. They may be afraid of developing connections to any other adults for fear of losing them as well.

Stress, coping, PTSD, and grief are important issues with any disaster. However, specific to natural disasters is a child's ability to comprehend the disaster. As Belter and Shannon (1993) pointed out, "there is often not a clear and concrete explanation which fits the child's developmental level" (p. 88).

Belter and Shannon's (1993) summary of several early studies indicated a number of factors that predict the negative experiences of children from natural disasters. These factors include "the extent of exposure to the disaster, personal injury to self or significant others, predisaster history of stressful events, age or developmental level of the child, and the effectiveness of parental coping with the disaster" (p. 90). More recent—and more reliable and valid—studies have been conducted to examine responses to natural disasters, such as fires, earthquakes, and hurricanes. These studies have found varying degrees of emotional and behavioral consequences. Some of the general conclusions follow:

- After a natural disaster, children do not show diagnosable psychopathology, but most do report significant levels of emotional distress. Younger children appear to be more affected than older children, especially when there is disruption of their routine or family functioning after the event.
- "There is a general trend for the acute effects to diminish over time, with long-term effects for most children being minimal" (Belter & Shannon, 1993, p. 99).
- The more direct the experience is, and the more threatening it is personally or the more disruptive it is, the more the child is affected.
- Children's reports of the level of emotional distress tend to be higher than their parents' report for their distress.
- There is an association between a child's adjustment before the natural disaster and the extent to which she or he has difficulty coping with the disaster.
- The disaster's impact on the child is often related to its effect on the parents—the extent to which the impact is negative and the degree to which the parents are able to cope. Increased parental distress is associated with higher ratings of behavior problems.

- Researchers need to look at the distinctions among different types of disasters to determine the nature of their unique psychological impact on children.

Families' Reactions to Natural Disasters

Rubonis and Bickman (1991) examined the relationship between disaster occurrence and psychopathology outcomes for 52 studies. Their goal was to examine relationships among the characteristics of those exposed to a disaster, the characteristics of the disaster, the study methodology, and the type of psychopathology. They found a small but consistently positive relationship between disasters and psychopathology—with differences in the powerfulness of findings attributable to differences in research methodology.

Research findings regarding children's reactions to natural disasters make it clear that children do not react in isolation, and that many of the risk and protective factors for children are equally salient for adults and for families. The degree of exposure to the disaster (as described by the circles of vulnerability—see Figures 2-1 through 2-6), the loss of significant others, and pre-existing conditions can increase or decrease the probability of negative effects from a disaster. As adults struggle with a traumatic experience, children watch and take their cues.

Raphael (1986) described individuals' reactions during and after the impact of a disaster. During a disaster people often experience heightened arousal as they push to save themselves. Fear is a dominant reaction when the survival of one's self or family is threatened. It is common to feel helpless, especially when faced with an overwhelming situation over which there is little or no control. It is also common to feel abandoned: "How could this have happened to me? Where is God? Where are people to help me? How can I be relieved of all this?"

After the initial impact, feelings of intense relief are common: "I survived!" Raphael (1986) stated that release from the tension felt during the disaster is demonstrated as quiet, elation, laughter, or "hysterical" behaviors. People share their experiences with others, trying to make sense of what has occurred.

After the initial reaction, people exposed to disaster may experience any or a combination of the following:

- *shock*—They may feel numb and dazed.
- *anxiety*—They may feel nervous or dizzy; they may tremble and be unable to slow down, relax, concentrate, or sleep properly; or they may have a pounding heart or trouble breathing.
- *anger, irritability, or depression*—They may have loss of appetite, fatigue, restlessness, or a sense of hopelessness or worthlessness, or they may withdraw or show other depressive symptoms.
- *fear*—They may fear for their own continued safety and for the future.
- *guilt*—They may believe they are responsible for outcomes that may have been mitigated, feel awkward at receiving help, or believe that others have not been helped enough.

Spotlight on Research "Families' Reactions to Hurricane Andrew" provides a summary of an interesting study based on in-depth interviews with families who experienced Hurricane Andrew.

From their literature review, Briere and Elliott (2000) found a variety of examples of psychological symptoms that have been associated with natural disasters, such as posttraumatic stress, anxiety, depression, anger, dissociation, aggression and antisocial behavior, and substance abuse. They focused on these psychological symptoms in relation to specific types of natural disasters in a national survey of the prevalence, characteristics, and long-term consequences of exposure to a natural disaster of 935 randomly chosen people. (The people interviewed came from a sample of approximately 1,500 U.S. residents who were registered as automobile owners or who had a listed telephone. The average time between the disaster experience and the survey was 13 years.) The lifetime prevalence of natural disasters among the participants was a self-reported 22 percent, with a range of 4 percent having experienced a hurricane, and 8 percent an earthquake. All participants completed a Trauma Symptom Inventory (TSI), which measured specific psychological responses to the traumatic experience. The highest TSI scores among the participants came from people who had been exposed to fires; their scores were especially high in the areas of depression, intrusive experiences, defensive avoidance, and dissociation. Although there were different TSI scores associated with different types of natural disasters, the authors found no relationship between hurricanes and later TSI scores.

Briere and Elliott (2000) found that there were certain aspects of a person's disaster experience that seemed to predict later symptoms. People who endured physical injury and witnessed death or injury of others and had lost property "had scores in the clinical range for six of 10 TSI scales: Anxious Arousal, Depression, Intrusive Experiences, Defensive Avoidance, Dissociation, and Tension Reduction Behavior" (p. 670). These three characteristics—physical injury, witnessing death or injury of others, and property loss—were

Families Reactions to Hurricane Andrew

Coffman (1996) conducted in-depth interviews with 13 parents—eight mothers and five fathers—representing nine families, who lived in south Florida and who had first-hand experience of Hurricane Andrew that hit land on August 24, 1992. The hurricane killed 39 people, caused an estimated $20 billion of damage, destroyed 63,000 homes, left 250,000 people homeless, and caused the evacuation of 700,000 people. Coffman conducted the interviews two to three months after the disaster. The method used was phenomenological, that is, interviews were open-ended and explored the parents' realities from their own perspective regarding "the essence of being a parent after the hurricane" (p. 358). Rebuilding family life was at the heart of their experience after the hurricane.

Themes that described the experience were:

- Thankful for what we have (family safety was the most important issue)
- Overwhelmed by damage and demands
- Limited by aftereffects (such as no electricity)

- Balancing needs and roles (balancing the needs of their children with their own needs, and their role of parent with the demands of work)
- Constantly changing amid uncertainty (families still experiencing multiple changes, such as changes in child care)
- Responsible for children's well-being (their decision making was most affected by their feelings of responsibility for their children's physical and psychological well-being)
- Finding meaning and growing stronger (all parents reaffirmed the importance of family and their role as parents)

A seemingly obvious point but important nonetheless because of the probability of missing it is this: Ongoing demands, such as job requirements, illness, and childcare arrangements, were not displaced by the hurricane, but the demands of the hurricane were superimposed on top of them. Equally important is that "disaster victims are normal people encountering abnormal circumstances. Therefore, interventions for families should be planned not only to compensate for deficits, but to build on strengths and reaffirm them" (p. 365).

Coffman, S. (1996). Parents' struggles to rebuild family life after Hurricane Andrew. *Issues In Mental Health Nursing, 17,* 353–367.

better predictors of the symptoms someone might have than was the type of disaster.

Most research on the effects of disasters is limited by the lack of predisaster information—information necessary for drawing the best-supported conclusions. With access to formal records and agency reports, Adams and Adams (1984) compared data from before and after the 1980 volcanic eruption of Mount Saint Helens in Washington State. They studied the illnesses, family problems, aggression or violence, and adjustment problems of people living in the relatively isolated town of Othello, Washington.

Stress-related illnesses and visits to the mental health clinic increased significantly in the seven months following the eruption (198 percent and 235 percent, respectively), as did psychiatric commitment investigations (33 percent) and crisis line calls (79 percent). Hospital admissions decreased (7.2 percent), although there were increases in emergency room visits (21 percent).

Child abuse decreased (89.5 percent), as did divorce cases (6.3 percent). However, police-reported domestic violence cases increased (45.6 percent). Other increases in aggressive behavior included juvenile and adult bookings (2.4 percent and 22.7 percent, respectively), disorderly conduct (10 percent), and vandalism (24 percent).

Community Reactions to Natural Disasters

The most influential variables in determining how a community responds to a natural disaster are its degrees of poverty, deprivation, underdevelopment, and socioeconomic vulnerability (Raphael, 1986). In addition, a community's willingness or preparedness to cope with a natural disaster depends on its sense of vulnerability to the threat of natural disasters, the trust of its citizens in public authorities, its communication system, and the costs of preparedness and response.

Weinstein and colleagues (2000) completed a study to identify ways that disasters affect a community's biases concerning personal risk and vulnerability to harm. They were interested in the impact of a disaster even on people who had come to no personal harm but who were in the affected area. They decided to focus on "optimistic bias"—how high the levels are of perceived personal risk, behavioral control, and cognitive control, and a change in emotion—in three towns that had experienced severe tornadoes compared with control towns without such experiences. Optimistic biases were evident in the control towns, whereas "tornado-specific depression and anxiety were

significantly higher in impacted than control towns" (Weinstein et al., p. 383). In addition, people in the affected towns were significantly more worried about when the next tornado was coming. "The largest tornado effect we observed was the decrease in optimism on questions that directly asked people to compare their personal risk to the average risk, with optimism being practically eliminated after the tornadoes struck" (Weinstein et al., p. 389). The researchers suggest that mere proximity to damage was sufficient for the disaster to have adverse psychological effects on community members.

Natural disasters cannot be prevented, but preventive measures can be taken to lessen their effects. Skitka (1999) studied whether individual ideologies—liberal versus conservative—affect people's reactions to the need for assistance after a natural disaster. She developed three scenarios of three different communities devastated by the 1993 floods in the midwestern United States. The towns, which were given hypothetical names, varied in the degree to which inhabitants of the town took preventive measures to protect themselves from the floods. The 1,015 participants in the study were asked to give their reactions to the three different communities.

More than 73 percent of the respondents strongly believed that it was the responsibility of individual communities to build their own floodwalls and levees and to buy flood insurance. About 50 percent felt that the government should help with these plans and that the government should help people find low-cost flood insurance. Respondents in the study self-identified as liberal were more in favor of providing federal disaster aid in all forms than those self-identified as conservatives. "Even in the context of a disaster, perceivers still sought out and used information about personal responsibility when judging how deserving needy individuals were of public assistance, and other results supported the links between political orientation and judgments of being deserving" (Skitka, 1999, p. 799).

Respondents assessed communities in terms of perceived responsibility for self-protection. The respondents saw the communities more sympathetically and believed they were more deserving of assistance than were individuals. Liberals and conservatives were equally supportive of providing humanitarian aid to the town that planned ahead, but conservatives were less supportive of providing aid to those towns that had not taken preventive measures. Both groups, however, were "unenthusiastic about using federal disaster assistance to provide assistance beyond immediate humanitarian aid" (Skitka, 1999, p. 805).

Touching Reality "Hard Rain" presents four video segments from *Hard Rain* (Campbell, 1999), a documentary of responses to Hurricane Floyd by children, families, and communities located in eastern North Carolina.

THE EFFECTS OF A NATURAL DISASTER ON VULNERABLE POPULATIONS

What are the effects of a natural disaster on populations less well equipped to cope with the disaster's intrusion and destruction? As we know, people dealing with serious difficulties before a disaster have a greater likelihood of experiencing negative responses during and after a disaster.

Elderly People

As you will read in chapter 11, "Disaster Recovery with Vulnerable Populations," elderly people can have some particular difficul-

---

TOUCHING REALITY

Hard Rain

Segment 3 on the CD presents a portion of the section of Hard Rain titled, "The World's Still Turning—Pollocksville." The segment shows one family's sorrow at the loss of meaningful symbols of who and what they are and their sense of history; it also shows their resiliency. Think back to our discussion about coping and resiliency in chapter 2. What supports were in place that assisted this family in their response to the flood?

Segment 4 on the CD presents a portion of the section titled, "When Sorrows Come—Princeville." As you watch this segment, notice how the floods caused by Hurricane Floyd did more than destroy a city: They destroyed a community and a culture. Also consider the question posed earlier in this chapter: Do natural disasters discriminate?

Segment 5 on the CD presents a portion of the section titled, "FEMAville," filmed in a makeshift community of 350 trailers located in the shadow of a women's prison on the outskirts of Rocky Mount, North Carolina. As you play this segment, listen to the descriptions of the effects of living in FEMAville on the children and elderly people. What do you think might be the combined effects on the people evacuated to FEMAville of the floods, followed by a period living in this community of trailers?

---

ties dealing with the disruption that accompanies disasters. Havens and Hall (1999) completed a qualitative study on the experiences of 102 older Manitobans who survived the 1997 Red River Flood. The flood was the second largest in Manitoba, Canada, in more than 170 years. All the participants in the study were over 70 years of age. The authors cited Hutchins and Norris (1989), who found that older adults exposed to a flood tended to experience more social disruption, were less likely to have adult children available to help clean up, and were more affected by the loss of their homes and other property damage than younger victims. Havens and Hall found that "only a few respondents felt they had any long-term effects of the flood, and these were all individuals who had been evacuated or received notices" (p. 18). Despite this statement, however, several respondents felt their health was worse after the flood and that the flood had caused them a great deal of stress and worry. The majority of older flood victims maintained the same level of physical functioning after the experience. Stress levels were higher, especially for evacuated people. Temporary moves caused disruptions in routines. Some described bad dreams that were made worse by images seen on television. Unlike participants in the Hutchins and Norris study, the Manitobans described receiving the bulk of their emotional and physical support from family members. They also described receiving help and information from volunteers, the army, personal care home staff, and local municipal officials.

In general, respondents did not find much benefit from the flood, although some believed that the community came together to deal with the challenges presented by the disaster. The researchers found that cognitive status and self-related health were positively

affected for those in the study who were evacuated or threatened with evacuation. Finally, the findings suggest that "older women in particular may need more assistance during times of crises to guard against declines in activities of daily living...others take over these tasks in order to protect the individual from decline, perhaps to their detriment" (Havens & Hall, 1999, p. 34).

Not all presumed differences between elderly people and their younger counterparts are supported by research findings. For example, Arie (1998) investigated whether elderly people (defined here as those ages 65 and older) whose homes were destroyed by a tornado responded differently to the loss from the way their younger counterparts (under 65) responded. Although Arie hypothesized that elderly victims were more likely than younger victims to ascribe symbolic, rather than pragmatic, meanings to their losses, results did not support this conjecture.

People with Cognitive Disabilities

It might be expected that people with cognitive disabilities would have special difficulty adapting because of the disruptions—changes in living arrangements, routines, possible unavailability of caretakers, and so on—of a natural disaster. However, in the Manitoba study (Havens & Hall, 1999), those with significant mental impairment did not seem to be affected by the disaster, possibly because of lack of external awareness of their environment. Is awareness of the environment the important consideration?

A study completed in Japan after the 1995 Hanshin earthquake focused on people who were able to function to some degree and thus had more external awareness (Takahashi, Watanabe, Oshima, Shimada, & Ozawa, 1997). Those studied were living at home with their families and riding a bus to a day care center or workshop during the day. Some of the people from the workshops were brought to a refuge—a shelter. They appeared to have some difficulty adapting to refuge life: "There were no private spaces in such refuges, and people with intellectual disability were rejected and segregated by their neighbours in the refuges because of their strange behaviour and noisy utterances. This was another severe stress for these people" (Takahashi et al., p. 194). A significant positive difference in the ability of the disabled person to receive help and reduce trauma was the extent to which previous relationships and helpful neighbors were available, especially when other more formal connections were cut off.

McMurray and Steiner (2000) studied service delivery to individuals with severe mental illness (SMI) during and after a major ice storm that hit southeastern Canada in 1998. A questionnaire about the impact of the ice storm was administered to a group of patients in a community treatment program. The researchers found that service use during this natural disaster was consistent with that described in the literature: Those SMI patients studied were no more likely to be admitted to or visit an emergency room during the disaster than other patients. McMurray and Steiner concluded that SMI patients who have ongoing access to support and psychiatric services during disaster situations tend to cope well.

Emotionally Vulnerable People and Suicide

Krug and his colleagues (1998, 1999) studied 377 counties (12 percent of all counties in the United States) that had each been beset by a single natural disaster between 1982 and 1989. All the counties, with a combined pop- ulation of approximately 19.5 million, had been declared federal disaster areas. The researchers then determined the suicide rates in each county 36 months before the disaster and 48 months after it occurred. Whereas the change was not statistically significant, inter- estingly, for two types of natural disasters— floods and hurricanes—the rate increased, whereas for three types—severe storms, tor- nadoes, and earthquakes—it decreased. Specifically, the suicide rate after a flood increased from 12.22 to 12.46, and after a hurricane it increased from 12 to 12.17, per 100,000 people. After severe storms, the rate decreased from 11.27 to 10.29, for tornadoes it decreased from 12.24 to 12.15, and for earthquakes from 19.2 to 18.96. Whereas these figures are not statistically significant, they do imply changes that affect many lives.

In an analysis of the suicide rate in 70 counties that had two disasters separated by no more than two years, Krug and his colleagues (1999) found a significant and rather startling result. The suicide rate increased 14.8 percent from the predisaster rate to the rate during the first two years after the second disaster. (Results for each type of natural disaster are not presented.) This is important information for disaster workers in areas where natural disasters occur frequently, such as the midwest (tornadoes), southeast coastal region (hurricanes), and northern California (earthquakes).

Pets

Families often consider their pets as part of the family. A study completed in California after the 1997 Yuba County flood (Heath, 1999) looked for the risk factors associated with household evacuation failure and the possible connection to pet ownership. A risk factor was defined as the unwillingness to evacuate after an order or a willingness to leave but then an attempt to return and rescue the pet. The risk of household evacuation failure was higher in pet-owning households without children than in pet-owning households with children—and the more pets the person had the greater the likelihood of evacuation failure. In addition, the evacuation of families with cats was twice as likely to fail as families with dogs. Overall, the problem is a great one because "more than 80% of persons who re-entered the evacuated areas did so to rescue their pet" (Heath, p. 2).

It is easy to overlook that during times of disaster pets are quite vulnerable. They are vulnerable to the frightening noises that accompany disasters, and to poor planning that may characterize postdisaster recovery. Touching Reality "Pets and Natural Disasters" provides a chance to "reality test" your thinking about what needs to be considered when family pets are involved in a natural disaster.

NATURAL DISASTER MITIGATION

Natural disasters cause more deaths and, in general, do more damage than other types of disasters. Floods and droughts associated with the El Niño event of 1982–1983, for instance, resulted in losses of 10 percent of the gross national product of Bolivia, Chile, and Ecuador, and 50 percent of the annual public revenue of Peru (McCarthy, Canziani, Leary, Dokken, & White, 2001). Moreover, the cost of natural disasters has steadily increased over time. For example, the National Interagency Fire Center in Boise,

TOUCHING REALITY

Pets and Natural Disasters

It is very difficult for disaster responders to deal with pets—either their own or those belonging to others exposed to a disaster. What would you do with your dog, horse, cat, bird, hamster, lizard, or snake if you were suddenly faced with an evacuation notice? Remember that shelters do not normally accept anything other than guide dogs, and hotels have strict regulations regarding the housing of animals. So, do you leave them behind and wish them well, or bring them with you and try to find a place for them to be safe?

It is important to make plans for your pets before a disaster, to assess what needs to be done if a disaster occurs, and to make an action plan that could be put into place if needed. FEMA (2003b) suggested ways to care for pets before and during a disaster. How do these suggestions fit with your own plans? Are you prepared?

Before a disaster occurs, you need to contact your local animal shelter, humane society, veterinarian, or emergency management office for information on caring for pets in an emergency. Some questions to ask are, "Would shelters be available to take pets? Where can you leave your pet? Will local motels or hotels accept pets? Does your pet need medicine, and do you have enough on hand? Does your pet have an identification tag?"

During a disaster, can you bring your pet indoors? (most animals are sensitive to severe weather and noise) If you evacuate, can you prepare a place for your pet and take food and water for several days? Do you have medical information available? Do you have the space to separate dogs and cats, even ones that typically get along?

Idaho, estimates the cost of suppressing fires in the United States during 2000 was more than $1.6 billion, which is more than the preceding three years combined (Perkins, 2001).

Because of these death tolls, the UN declared the 1990s as the International Decade for Natural Disaster Reduction. The natural hazards specified by the UN were earthquakes, windstorms, tsunamis, floods, landslides, volcanic eruptions, wildfires, grasshopper and locust infestations, and drought and desertification. Member nations were to form national committees to coordinate national activities. Several organizations in the United States work toward reducing natural disaster fatalities and destruction, the most well known of which is FEMA. Another organization active in this area is under the National Research Council and is called the Board on Natural Disasters (BOND). Much of the information in this section comes from BOND's 1999 report, "Mitigation Emerges as Major Strategy for Reducing Losses Caused by Natural Disasters" (BOND, 1999)

Response Versus Mitigation

According to the members of BOND (1999), there are two basic approaches to reduce natural disasters—response and mitigation. Response begins once a natural disaster event is occurring and involves all the actions taken to reduce suffering and hasten the recovery of people and communities. Response includes both the short-term crisis activities taken by police, firefighters, medical, and other personnel, and the long-term actions taken by governmental and nongovernment organizations (NGOs) to provide food and shelter and to rebuild and restore the community.

Conversely, "mitigation includes all those actions that are taken before, during, and after the occurrence of a natural event that minimize its impacts" (BOND, 1999, p. 1944). Mitigation efforts, designed to avoid hazards, include building outside floodplains, away from seismic fault lines, and off steep mountain slopes that are subject to mudslides. Mitigation also includes building with construction materials that are fire retardant and earthquake or hurricane resistant, and improving a community's ability to warn and educate the populace about safe actions in the face of an imminent natural disaster. Some earthquake-prone regions, for example, have early warning systems: Earthquakes create several different types of seismic vibrations, the quickest of which, P-waves, can be "read" to make predictions about the dangerous S-waves that follow. Allen and Kanamori (2003) found that they only needed four seconds to make an assessment of P-waves, which means people could be warned about 16 seconds ahead of time regarding S-waves, allowing for utility companies to shut down pipe lines, trains to stop, school children to dive under their desks, and so on.

Effective, speedy, postdisaster response profoundly decreases trauma. Because a primary indicator of trauma reaction is the level of exposure to the event, response teams strive for interventions that allow people to move away from the disaster and back to some degree of normalcy as quickly as possible. Both response and mitigation activities are important in dealing with disasters; however, in the past, response has predominated in practice (BOND, 1999). As BOND pointed out, reliance on response and recovery strategies—instead of mitigation—means incurring the continuously escalating costs that go along with the escalating damage associated with natural disasters. Response and recovery are necessary for humanitarian, economic, and political purposes; however, effective mitigation programs aimed at reducing losses must accompany response and recovery.

Following the charge from the UN, FEMA established a Mitigation Directorate, and a National Mitigation Strategy office. FEMA also established Project Impact that oversees demonstration sites in 118 cities and communities. This initiative, called Building Disaster Resistant Communities, has as one of its goals to change the way people in the United States deal with disasters. Project Impact bases its work on three simple princi-ples: "preventive actions must be decided at the local level; private sector participation is vital; and long-term efforts and investments in prevention measures are essential" (FEMA, 2003c). The Project points to the efforts and forward thinking of the Anheuser Busch brewery in California as a model of the posi-tive outcomes resulting from disaster mitiga-tion. In the early 1980s, the company recog-nized that its plant in earthquake-prone California was at high risk of damage. They invested $15 million in retrofitting the facili-ties to make them quake resistant. In 1994 an earthquake that measured 6.7 on the Richter scale struck the area, with its epicenter a mere 12 miles away from the brewery. Operations at the brewery never stopped, and the Busch Company estimates that it saved $300 million in damages and lost production. Other initia-tives include the Outstanding Task Force Award, given to the Kitsap County Fire Safety Advisory Committee. Through collab-oration of local disaster response committees, real estate associations, housing authorities, and interested citizens, the Kitsap Committee focuses on reducing the number of multifam-ily fires in their area. Through a focused inves-tigation of the causes of fires and using build-ing codes and support from property owners, the Committee's task force was able to make clear recommendations to tenants and prop-erty owners to reduce the risk of fire.

In a 2001 reorganization of FEMA, the flood insurance section of FEMA and the Mitigation Directorate were merged into the Flood Insurance and Mitigation Administra-tion (FIMA). FIMA awards grants to people, to communities, and to organizations that are intent on reducing the risk of loss of proper-ty and loss of life caused by disaster. You can search through a list of success stories by state at FEMA's Web site (http://fema.web4.fema. gov/cgi-shl/web_evaluate.exe).

Disaster Mitigation in Kurantatuth, India

John Sparrow (2001), writing for the IFR-CRCS, described an example of mitigation at work. The people in the village of Kurantatuth, in Orissa state, India, experienced the worst cyclone in living memory during October 1999. Cyclones are common in this part of the world, and the Indian Red Cross had built several cyclone shelters with the support of the German gov-ernment. Volunteers warned people, helped evacuate as many as possible, and tied ropes from tree to tree to help people feel their way to the shelter when visibility was poor. In one shelter, 2,000 people crowded into a building that had a maximum capacity of 1,500—crowding that was common in other shelters. Winds reached over 180 miles per hour. After the storm, people in shelters realized that their entire village had been flooded by tidal waves. Hundreds of corpses floated in the water, and almost all the houses in the village were destroyed. Neverthe-less, government officials estimated that the shelters saved 40,000 people.

Coordinating Mitigation with Land-Use Planning

For disaster mitigation to work, it must be coordinated with land-use planning. The helper's goal should be to learn four key pieces of information.

Location and nature of potential hazards. What are the location and nature of potential hazards? What is the likelihood that a particular type of natural hazard will strike an area? How often is that likely to occur? Some places in the United States are known for the frequency with which they deal with tornadoes (notably Kansas and Texas), hurricanes (notably North Carolina and Florida), and earthquakes (notably California and Alaska). What is the best response to the likely hazards? For example, if it is known that cyclones are a regular and fatal occurrence in Orissa, India, the authorities should place a high priority on the construction of shelters to mitigate the cyclones' effects on residents.

Hazards and populations. What current and future populations are vulnerable to specific hazards? Approximately 80 percent of Florida's population lives within 21 miles of the coastlines. Nationally, the population of the United States has been migrating toward its coastlines, building increasingly on the earthquake-prone Pacific and the hurricane-prone Atlantic and Gulf Coasts. The same population movement is apparent in Pakistan and India, although it has a much denser population than the United States.

Part of the population assessment includes an understanding of the nature of the housing within which people live. Do people live in earthquake- or fire-resistant homes or in dwellings that will come apart quickly in the wind and rain? Are there ways for the populace to move quickly when warned of imminent danger? How often have we seen pictures of the gridlock of cars inching their way off the North Carolina coastline, over the only bridge to the mainland, in the face of a threatening hurricane?

Acceptable levels of risk. What are acceptable levels of risk? Researchers have joined with government officials to develop ways of estimating risk, and thus determining what is considered an acceptable level of risk to a given population. If hurricanes, for example, are rare in a given area, it may be an acceptable risk to build non–hurricane–resistant homes. Tests of various stressors on buildings, discussions of allocations of resources, the development of tools that can estimate the cost of a disaster, and the benefits of certain mitigation strategies, are all part of the study of acceptable risk.

Determining acceptable levels of risk is an extremely sensitive topic—what, after all, is an acceptable level of risk, and to whom is it "acceptable"? This issue is highly relevant to our discussion, later in this chapter, of barriers to disaster mitigation.

Costs and benefits. How do you develop mitigation strategies based on realistic costs and benefits? Land-use plans that avoid hazards in an attempt to reduce loss of life and costly damage tend to be a catalyst for strong disagreement among administrators and the general population alike. Safety is an issue that, when moderated by fiscal limitations, brings strong opinions to the floor. Those who see themselves as possible victims of disasters may consider "safety at any price" an option. Governments, corporations, and donor nations, with their priorities that span the "big picture," may not agree.

Touching Reality "Disaster Mitigation at Home" provides the opportunity to consider disaster mitigation in your own neighborhood.

Disaster Mitigation at Home

For a moment, consider disaster mitigation on a very personal, local level. As you do the following activity developed for elementary school children, think about applying what you learn to begin the mitigation process for your own locality, and consider some of the issues mitigation might raise for your neighborhood and neighbors.

Begin by walking or driving around your neighborhood or community. What is the topography like? Are there hills, low-lying areas, small streams, ponds, or lakes? Is the land flat and wide open, with few places to take refuge from a storm or the wind? Are there reservoirs for drinking water? Do residents get their water from a government source or from private wells?

What happens in your area when there is a very heavy rain or snowfall? Does the water flow in certain areas, or collect somewhere (the flood plains)? Are there storm drains in the area that can carry the water, or does the water back up, creating sudden lakes? Are there certain places that flood, such as underpasses? Do farm fields flood? Is livestock endangered? Can people and animals find refuge from tornadoes?

If your community has streams, rivers, or large drainage ditches, do you know where they start and end? What other communities are on the same streams or ditches? Are there any dams or levees built along these streams?

Draw a map of your community that shows the information you have gathered. What areas are most vulnerable? Would there be ways for families to evacuate if the water rose suddenly?

Now consider fires or tornadoes. Are these common occurrences? Does vegetation grow close to dwellings? Are there chemical plants or nuclear plants in your area that might be vulnerable to flooding or fires?

Last, what are the dwellings like in your area? Are they old farmhouses, mobile homes, or high-rise buildings? Is the construction "solid"? How many homeowners, renters, and other community members have insurance to cover possible losses? Are there people in your neighborhood who are particularly vulnerable to unplanned events, such as elderly persons who live alone, people who are illiterate, those who are hearing or sight impaired, or who are not mobile?

All these questions and more must be answered in the process of disaster mitigation planning. It might make for some interesting conversations among your family members and friends. What might you do about dwellings that are on flood plains, or that are especially vulnerable to fires? What would you do if one of those dwellings was yours? How would you respond, then?

The growing awareness of the need for mitigation, as well as response and recovery efforts, has made some changes in the way countries react to natural disasters. For instance, the Colombian government received strong condemnation from its citizens following a 1985 mudslide. Citizens ridiculed the government's response, which was named *resurgir* by the government, meaning "rising up again," by renaming it *resufrir* or "re-suffering," complaining that it was slow, ineffective, and unhelpful. In response, the Colombian government created a disaster organization that better planned response and recovery and focused on mitigation. Colombia had a chance to try out its new response after only eight years. In an earthquake in Paez, a remote village, in 1993, not only was initial response faster, but long-term recovery efforts included reducing the potential risks of future earthquakes during the reconstruction phase (LaFranchi, 1998). Public reaction was much more favorable and threat to loss of life was reduced.

Disaster Mitigation and "Acting Smart"

According to biologist Seth Reice in his book, *The Silver Lining: The Benefits of Natural Disasters* (2001), "Disturbances are natural. Fires and floods and hurricanes will happen. Let's get smart. Let's try to get out of their way." In this book he offered a few ideas about how to "get smart," most of which have to do with ensuring the survival of endangered ecosystems, not just endangered species. His first recommendation, however, spoke directly to the notion of natural disaster mitigation—ecologically sound plan development.

He offered two zoning guidelines for ecologically sound planning, guidelines that should help minimize losses caused by inevitable natural disturbances. First, restrict development in areas prone to fires, floods, and erosion, and build with an eye toward protecting natural ecosystems. What this means, for example, is that we should not build on beaches or barrier islands (which, in a natural process, continuously erode at one end and reform at the other), regardless of the great view of the ocean and the immediate access to the beach.

Second, we should not build in a river's floodplain. Rivers will flood—that is what they do—and building in a floodplain ensures the destruction of property as well as compromising the function of the wetland ecosystem.

Barriers to Mitigation

Unfortunately, disaster mitigation, despite strong support, moves slowly. Touching Reality "Landslides in Venezuela" features a story by Sayagues (2001) that describes the difficulties of designing effective mitigation strategies. His story, "Trapped in the Gap—Post-Landslide Venezuela," begs for solutions. What would you recommend?

The process involved in reducing human vulnerability to natural disasters faces significant barriers, in spite of the UN's focused effort, at the beginning of the 1990s, to bring current research and disasters knowledge to bear on such a reduction. The UN charged all its member countries with completing a comprehensive assessment of vulnerability to natural disasters and with initiating a determination of options for reduction of that vulnerability. Barriers continue to prevent countries from moving forward with mitigation efforts, regardless of their worthy intent.

Predisaster prevention. Often, mitigation efforts occur at a time when life is normal and disasters are not the highest priority, so

Landslides in Venezuela

Two years' worth of rain fell along the coastline during two days in December 1999, in Venezuela. Witnesses described 50-foot high walls of mud that swept whole neighborhoods from Vargas—a very densely populated urban area that attracts poor rural workers to its fishing and tourism industries—into the sea. Approximately 30,000 people died, more than 80,000 people were affected, and 5,500 homes were completely wiped out by landslides. Another 25,000 homes were damaged. Economic damage was estimated at US$1.9 billion.

Community and international response after massive disasters are always complex and difficult. Venezuelans not in the disaster responded generously. Aid came from around the world. The military evacuated 70,000 people during and after the disaster, and more than 70,000 self-evacuated.

Within eight months after the landslides, the initial rush of food and financial aid from both international and domestic sources had ended. About 33,000 people were still homeless, living in shelters, with no jobs and no homes. The "shelter people" were angry: They expected more help and felt that the government was more interested in road reconstruction than in finding homes for them. The government of Venezuela was concerned about the large numbers of people living in shelters and shanties in Vargas who were banding together demanding a response. Officials wondered if their presence would cause problems for tourism, which paid for the services they

demanded. Officials asked, "Don't we need roads in the country to re-establish commerce, and allow visitors to move about the country?"

Many people in the country were asking questions about mitigation. The area had been the sight of landslides before. Surely, something could be done to prevent this from happening again. How many times would the country have to deal with such loss of life and the costs of recovery? The government wanted the shelter people of Vargas to move away from the landslide-prone areas—and away from public view. They worked to resettle the shelter people in rural districts, offering a 70–square meter home (approximately 750 square feet). Many people did not want to leave their urban location, believing that there was greater chance for employment in Vargas than out in the rural districts.

The Venezuelan government chose to pressure people to move to the country. Most of the people who still had no homes were taken to the rural districts regardless of their preferences. However, many of the people could not find work there and are now moving back to the risky land areas. Once again, they live in substandard housing, on the mountainsides, ripe for further landslides and floods.

Who can stop them from returning?

What is the Venezuelan government to do?

How can the government achieve mitigation in this situation?

other tasks take priority over spending time, energy, and finances on an uncertain future event. As a result, it can be difficult for anyone to initiate mitigation efforts. In developing countries, where the gross national product may not cover basic needs of food and shelter for the population without external assistance, the authorities find it hard to justify spending money for a possible future occurrence. Despite the fact that mitigation prevents deaths and the devastation of infrastructure, many organizations and governments are reluctant to make current expenditures in the face of other realities, especially during a general economic slow down.

Financial resources. Most of the deaths from natural disasters occur in low or medium development countries. These countries have little or no money to use for disaster prevention. Countries' contributions specifically for the International Decade for Natural Disaster Reduction amount to only a few million dollars a year, worldwide. Japan is the largest contributor, along with Sweden, Netherlands, Norway, and Denmark. According to BOND (1999, 1944), "the United States contributed relatively little in funds, although the knowledge and expertise of U.S. scientists and engineers provided an important resource."

Land-use planning and restriction from disaster-prone locations. Although communities can reduce losses significantly by adopting land-use plans that avoid disaster-prone areas, residents are frequently outraged when told that they cannot return and rebuild on the same land where their home originally stood. Sometimes, too, damaged corporate structures cannot be repaired. For example, a multimillion dollar, multistory, condominium on the North Carolina coast is entrenched in lawsuits and political struggles

because the local government made the decision that the landowners could not have sand pumped from the nearby lagoon to reestablish the beach in front of the condominium—beach that has been washed away after repeated storms. Without such beach replenishment, the building will eventually fall into the sea.

People who are poor frequently live in less-desirable places, where they can afford to build. These sites often are less desirable because they are on floodplains, or mountainsides or are remote from services and supports. Houses may be less well constructed, making them especially prone to damage or destruction from natural disasters.

People prohibited from returning to their homes or communities may have significant difficulty finding other places to live. Even if they could afford to live elsewhere, people frequently do not want to move from familiar places where they are close to possible employment and social support systems. Officials' resistance to using government money to begin to retrofit private structures to better withstand natural disasters complicates the issue. Conversely, advocates point out that governments end up paying to rehouse many displaced persons after the disaster occurs, so subsidizing such mitigation efforts might be justifiable because it is cost-effective. There might also be tax incentives made available to residents who engage in mitigation efforts. In 1990, California voters passed Proposition 127; Prop 127 exempted seismic rehabilitation improvements to buildings from being reassessed, thus precluding them from increased property taxes.

Building codes. Building codes can be very important in guiding the development of structures resistant to natural disasters' damage. Several states have codes to accomplish this goal, although "more than half of the 30,000 communities in the United States have not adopted a building code at all" (BOND, 1999, p. 1945). Usually, building codes are established at the state level but enforced at the local level, although local governments are sometimes left to set their own building code standards. Local boards have been extremely reluctant to set higher standards for existing structures in the absence of money to pay for upgrades. Developers lobby against codes that increase the cost of new structures, especially in lower-cost housing.

Politics. LaFranchi (1998) described ways that disasters can put leaders on trial. For example, citizens who experience a disaster frequently berate political leaders whom they perceive as inadequately protecting them or helping them achieve recovery. (After Hurricane Mitch swirled through Nicaragua, people charged the government of President Arnaldo Alaman with corruption, favoritism, and ineptitude during the emergency.) With such attention to a government's response to disaster and recovery, it may be even more difficult to set aside funds to support prevention and mitigation planning activities.

John Twigg (2001), Research Fellow at the Genfield Greig Hazard Research Centre in London, leads a team researching NGO involvement in natural disaster mitigation and preparedness. With funds from the Department for International Development managed by the British Red Cross, the team studied international relief and development NGOs based in the United Kingdom, Bangladesh, Nicaragua, the Philippines, and Zimbabwe. Twigg's team found that disaster mitigation activities are not mainstreamed into regular NGO planning activities but are handled on an ad hoc basis. Emergency response work is specific, concrete, and time limited; mitigation work seems less so. Among their recommendations is this: Advocates for mitigation efforts need to lobby more forcefully within their own organizations and put pressure on other agencies that are donor agencies.

Communication technologies. Reliable communication is essential to dependable and cost-effective disaster mitigation (School of Law–Bloomington, 1998). Regardless, communication technologies and resources have historically faced legal obstacles caused by national customs regulations about movement of advanced technologies across borders, and national broadcasting regulations and frequency assignments that can limit use of communication technologies that compete with national communications service providers. Exporting countries wish to control dissemination of their product to maintain copyrights: the regulation of telecommunications touches on national sovereignty.

What do these restrictions have to do with the reduction of the loss of human life within the focus of disaster mitigation? Communication media and technologies link the people involved in disaster mitigation, such as scientists, government officials, and the public (School of Law–Bloomington, 1998). The public can learn how to prepare for disasters, can be warned of the proximity and intensity of a particular event, and can experience more coordinated response and recovery activities once the disaster has arrived. Restrictions on communication technology, such as satellite receivers, cellular phones, and walkie-talkies, obstruct relief efforts and hamper the quick dissemination of early warnings of hurricanes and other natural hazards (School of Law–Bloomington).

Organizations involved in planning for disaster mitigation may not know about the availability or location of communications equipment that might be available to them in times of disaster. Buying equipment during the chaos and uncertainty of a disaster situation is much more expensive (if equipment is available at all). Purchasing radio frequencies is even more financially prohibitive during a disaster.

Seventy-six nations participating in the 1998 Intergovernmental Conference on Emergency Telecommunications, in Tampere, Finland, developed a framework to reduce regulatory barriers to the use of telecommunications in disaster mitigation and relief (School of Law–Bloomington, 1998). It created ways to identify and evaluate the model practices of disaster mitigation organizations and explored ways to share them with others. One of the most noteworthy items in the conference report was the article that extended privileges and immunities to relief workers on assignment that heretofore had been extended only to diplomats. This means that different countries will agree on ways for relief workers to carry telecommunication equipment and use it during disaster response.

Touching Reality "Life without Communication Devices" invites you to think about what your life would be like without access to all the communication devices you use daily. What would it be like responding to a disaster without the taken-for-granted communication tools at your disposal?

SUMMARY

In this chapter, we discussed the differences between natural disasters and other types of disaster events. Natural disasters—forces of nature—can be anticipated or completely unexpected, which tends to make a difference in how we react to them, as does the fact that there is no one to blame. The strongest negative responses are usually associated with tornadoes, fires, and earthquakes, although famines are the most deadly of natural disasters.

We looked at why natural disasters have a much higher death toll among developing nations. Risk factors for the apparent discrimination shown by natural disasters include inadequate housing quality, pre-existing poor health and nutritional status, increasing urbanization and unplanned development,

---

TOUCHING REALITY

Life Without Communication Devices

Easy and regular access to communication tools may be something you take for granted in your daily life. Stop for a moment and imagine the complications involved in trying to carry on your regular day without reliable communication devices. How much more difficult would it be to complete activities if telephones, radios, televisions, computers, and fax machines—to name but a few communication devices—were no longer available to you? If a disaster occurred and you were not with your children, partner, or friends, how would you know where they were, if they were safe, or how to protect them? How would you know if the storm was widespread, still in the area, or coming your way? Where are shelters, if you need them? How do you arrange for the protection of your pets, property, and other belongings?

and political instability that may interfere with the distribution of relief efforts

Children have varying reactions to natural disasters, as do adults, and seem to recover over time. Degree of exposure, fear for one's life, and (for children) reactions of significant adults affect the likelihood of negative responses to disaster. In a similar way, communities recover more quickly depending on the level of damage and the extent to which the disaster reoccurs with some regularity.

Persons who have physical or mental disabilities may have greater difficulty with natural disasters than other persons. Pets are particularly vulnerable during a disaster. The presence of supportive others—and prior planning—can mitigate the effects.

Mitigation is the process of planning so that disasters take fewer lives and damage less property. Although mitigation is a popular notion, there are many barriers to mitigation, including national, state, and local laws that inhibit mitigation efforts.

REFERENCES

Adams, P. R., & Adams, G. R. (1984). Mount Saint Helen's ashfall: Evidence for a disaster stress reaction. *American Psychologist, 39*, 252–260.

Allen, R. M., & Kanamori, H. (2003, May 2). The potential for earthquake early warning in Southern California. *Science, 300*(5620), 786–789.

Arie, J. C. (1998). Motivation in elderly disaster victims during recovery from loss of home. *Dissertation Abstracts International, 58*, 4459.

Ayot, G. (1995). An exploration of the hurricane experiences of nine elementary school children of St. Croix, United States Virgin Islands. *Dissertation Abstracts International, 55*, 2258.

Belter, R. W., & Shannon, M. P. (1993). Impact of natural disasters on children and families. In C. F. Saylor (Ed.), *Children and disasters* (pp. 85–104). New York: Plenum Press.

Black, D. E. (2002, July 26). The rains may be a-comin'. *Science, 297*, 528–529.

Board on Natural Disasters. (1999). Mitigation emerges as major strategy for reducing losses caused by natural disasters. *Science, 284*, 1943–1947. Retrieved August 22, 2003, from http://www.sciencemag.org/cgi/content/full/284/5422/1943

Briere, J., & Elliott, D. (2000). Prevalence, characteristics and long-term sequelae of natural disaster exposure in the general population. *Journal of Traumatic Stress, 13*, 661–679.

Burke, J. D., Borus, J. F., Burns, B. J., Millstein, K. H., & Beasley, M. C. (1982). Changes in children's behavior after a natural disaster. *American Journal of Psychiatry, 139*, 1010–1014.

Campbell, D. (Producer). (1999). *Hard rain: Lessons learned from the flood of '99* [Documentary]. (Available from the University of North Carolina Center for Public Television, 10 T. W. Alexander Drive, P.O. Box 14900, Research Triangle Park, NC 27709–4900)

Children and trauma: The school's response [Video]. (n.d.). (Available from: National Mental Health Services Knowledge Exchange Network, P. O. Box 42490, Washington, DC 20015, 800-789-2647).

Coffman, S. (1996). Parents' struggles to rebuild family life after Hurricane Andrew. *Issues in Mental Health Nursing, 17*, 353–367.

Federal Emergency Management Agency. (2003a, February 11). *Helping children cope with disaster.* Retrieved August 22, 2003, from http://www.fema.gov/rrr/children.shtm

Federal Emergency Management Agency. (2003b, February 12). *Pets and disasters.* Retrieved August 22, 2003, from http://www.fema.gov/library/petsf.shtm

Federal Emergency Management Agency. (2003c, February 12). *Mitigation division, library, footnotes.* Retrieved August 22, 2003, from http://www. fema.gov/ library/pp2foot.shtm

Georgieva, K. (2000). *Disproportionate effects.* Our Planet. Retrieved December 19, 2001, from http://www.ourplanet.com/imgversn/111/ kristin.html

Gillis, H. M. (1993). Individual and small-group psychotherapy for children involved in trauma and disaster. In C. F. Saylor (Ed.), *Children and disasters* (pp. 165–186). New York: Plenum Press.

Glass, R., & Urrutia, J. J. (1977). Earthquake injuries related to housing in a Guatemalan village. *Science, 197*, 638–643.

Goldenberg, S. B., Landsea, C. W., Mestas-Nuñez, A. M., Gray, W. M. (2001, July 20). The recent increase in Atlantic hurricane activity: Causes and implications. *Science, 293*, 474–479.

Havens, B., & Hall, M. (1999). *Experiences of older Manitobans with the 1997 Red River flood.* Manitoba: Department of Community Health Sciences, University of Manitoba.

Heath, S. E. (1999). *The public and animal health consequences of pet ownership in a disaster: The January 1997 flood of Yuba County, California.* Purdue University, West Lafayette, IN. Retrieved August 22, 2003, from http://ndms.umbc.edu/ conference2001/2001con68/Heath.pdf

Hutchins, G. L., & Norris, F. H. (1989). Life change in the disaster recovery period. *Environment and Behavior, 21*(1), 33–56.

International Federation of Red Cross and Red Crescent Societies. (2001). *World disasters report 2001.* Retrieved August 22, 2003, from http://www.ifrc.org/publicat/wdr2001/

Jeney-Gammon, P., Daugherty, T. K., Finch, A. J. J., Belter, R. W., & Foster, K. Y. (1992). Children's coping styles and report of depressive symptoms following a natural disaster. *Journal of Genetic Psychology, 154*, 259–267.

Jones, R. T., & Ollendick, T. H. (2002). Residential fires. In A. M. La Greca, W. K. Silverman, E. M. Vernberg, & M. C. Roberts (Eds.), *Helping children cope with disasters and terrorism* (pp. 175–199). Washington, DC: American Psychological Association.

Jurgens, J. J., Houlihan, D., & Schwartz, C. (1996). Behavioral manifestations of adolescent school relocation and trauma. *Child & Family Behavior Therapy, 18*(1), 1–8.

Katona-Apte, J. (1999). *Natural disasters and policy response in Asia: Implications for food security.* Harvard University Asia Center on the World Wide Web. Retrieved January 4, 2002, from http://www. fas.harvard.edu/~asiactr/fx_katona.htm

Keppel-Benson, J. M., & Ollendick, T. H. (1993). Posttraumatic stress disorder in children and adolescents. In C. F. Saylor (Ed.), *Children and disasters* (pp. 29–43). New York: Plenum Press.

Krug, E. G., Kresnow, M.-J., Peddicord, J. P, Dahlberg, L. L., Powell, K. E., Crosby, A. E., Annest, J. L. (1998). Suicide after natural disasters. *New England Journal of Medicine, 338*, 373–378.

Krug, E. G., Kresnow, M-J, Peddicord, J. P, Dahlberg, L. L., Powell, K. E., Crosby, A. E., Annest, J. L. (1999). "Suicide after natural disasters": Retraction. *New England Journal of Medicine, 340*, 148–149.

La Greca, A. M., & Prinstein, M. J. (2002). Hurricanes and earthquakes. In A. M. La Greca, W. K. Silverman, E. M. Vernberg, & M. C. Roberts (Eds.), *Helping children cope with disasters and terrorism* (pp. 107–138). Washington, DC: American Psychological Association.

La Greca, A. M., Silverman, W. K., Vernberg, E. M., & Prinstein, M. J. (1996). Symptoms of posttraumatic stress in children after hurricane Andrew: A prospective study. *Journal of Consulting and Clinical Psychology, 64*, 712–723.

La Greca, A. M., Silverman, W. K., & Wasserstein, S. B. (1998). Children's predisaster functioning as a predictor of posttraumatic stress following Hurricane Andrew. *Journal of Consulting and Clinical Psychology, 66*, 883–892.

LaFranchi, H. (1998, November 19). *How disasters put leaders on trial.* Christian Science Monitor. Retrieved January 4, 2002, from http://www.csmonitor.com/durable/1998/11/19/fplslcsm.shtml

Lindy, J. D. (1985). The trauma membrane and other clinical concepts derived from psychotherapeutic work with survivors of natural disasters. *Psychiatric Annals, 15*(3), 153–160.

McCarthy, J. J., Canziani, O. F., Leary, N. A., Dokken, D. J., & White, K. S. (2001). *Climate change 2001: Impacts, adaptation, and vulnerability* [Web site]. Working Group II to the Third Assessment Report of the Intergovernmental Panel on Climate Change. Retrieved December 21, 2001, from www.ipcc.ch/pub/tar/wg2/001.htm

McMurray, L., & Steiner, W. (2000). Natural disasters and service delivery to individuals with severe mental illness—Ice storm 1998. *Canadian Journal of Psychiatry, 45*, 383–385.

Oliver-Smith, A. (1986). *Disaster context and causation: An overview of changing perspectives in disaster research.* In V. H. Sutlive, N. Altshuler, M.D. Zamora, & V. Kerns (Eds.), *Natural disasters and cultural responses: Studies in third world societies* (pp. 1–34). Williamsburg, VA: College of William and Mary, Department of Anthropology.

Perkins, S. (2001). A nation aflame: After last year's conflagrations, can we learn to live with wildfire? *Science News, 159*, 120–122.

Quammen, D. (1998, October). Planet of weeds: Tallying the losses of Earth's animals and plants. *Harper's Magazine, 297*, 57–69.

Reice, S. R. (2001). *The silver lining: The benefits of natural disasters.* Princeton, NJ: Princeton University Press.

Raphael, B. (1986). *When disaster strikes: A handbook for the caring professions.* London: Hutchinson.

Rubonis, A. V., & Bickman, L. (1991). Psychological impairment in the wake of disaster: The disaster-psychopathology relationship. *Psychological Bulletin, 109*, 384–399.

Rustemli, A., & Karanci, A. N. (1996). Distress reactions and earthquake-related cognitions of parents and their adolescent children in a victimized population. *Journal of Social Behavior and Personality, 11*, 767–780.

Sayagues, M. (2001). *Trapped in the gap—post-landslide Venezuela.* Retrieved December 16, 2001, from www.ifrc.org/publicat/wdr2001/chapter4.asp

Saylor, C. F. (1993). Children and disasters: Clinical and research issues. In C. F. Saylor (Ed.), *Children and disasters* (pp.1–9). New York: Plenum Press.

School of Law–Bloomington. (1998, August 3). *Disaster communication.* Retrieved February 23, 2002, from http://www.law.indiana.edu/webinit/disaster/

Scott, R. L., Knoth, R. L., Beltran-Quiones, M., & Gomez, N. (2003). Assessment of psychological functioning in adolescent earthquake victims in Colombia using the MMPI-A. *Journal of Traumatic Stress, 16*, 49–57.

Seaman, J. (1984). *Epidemiology of natural disasters.* New York: Karger Bazel.

Simkin, T., Siebert, L., & Blong, R. (2001). Volcano fatalities: Lessons from the historical record. *Science, 291*, 255.

Skitka, L. J. (1999). Ideological and attributional boundaries on public compassion: Reactions to individuals and communities affected by a natural disaster. *Personality and Social Psychology Bulletin, 25*, 793–808.

Sparrow, J. (2001). *Relief, recovery and root causes.* International Federation of Red Cross and Red Crescent Societies. Retrieved December 16, 2001, from http://www.ifrc.org/publicat/wdr2001/chapter1.asp

Swenson, C. C., Saylor, C., Powell, M. P., Stokes, S. J., Foster, K. Y., & Belter, R. W. (1996). Impact of a natural disaster on preschool children: Adjustment 14 months after a hurricane. *American Journal of Orthopsychiatry, 66,* 122–130.

Takahashi, A., Watanabe, K., Oshima, M., Shimada, H., & Ozawa, A. (1997). The effect of the disaster caused by the great Hanshin earthquake on people with intellectual disability. *Journal of Intellectual Disability Research, 41,* 193–196.

Thompson, S. A. (1982). *Trends and developments in global natural disasters,* 1947–1981. (Working Paper No. 45). Boulder: University of Colorado, Institute of Behavioral Science.

Twigg, J. (2001). *Risk reduction needs to move up policy agenda.* Our Work-International Activities— NGO Disaster Mitigation and Preparedness Project. Retrieved January 4, 2002, from www.alternet.org/thefacts/reliefresources/231364.

Vogel, J. M., & Vernberg, E. M. (1993). Task Force Report, part 1: Children's psychological responses to disasters. *Journal of Clinical Child Psychology, 22,* 464–484.

Walter, J. (2001). *Disaster data: Key trends and statistics.* International Federation of Red Cross and Red Crescent Societies. Retrieved December 16, 2001, from http://www.ifrc.org/publicat/wdr2001/chapter8.asp

Weinstein, N. D., Lyon, J. E., Rothman, A. J., & Cuite, C. L. (2000). Changes in perceived vulnerability following natural disaster. *Journal of Social and Clinical Psychology, 19,* 372–395.

Wood, J. M., Bootzin, R. R., Rosenhan, D., & Nolen-Hoeksema, S. (1992). Effects of the 1989 San Francisco earthquake on frequency and content of nightmares. *Journal of Abnormal Psychology, 101,* 219–224.

Technological Disasters

After studying the material in this chapter, you should

- be able to compare natural and technological disasters
- understand arguments for the "inevitability" of technological disasters
- know the definitions and types of technological disasters
- be able to identify the reasons why people tend to have stronger reactions after exposure to technological disasters than to natural disasters
- be able to identify the reactions and effects one might experience when faced with a technological disaster
- understand that there is an established connection between risk for technological harm and persons who are members of minority populations, or of lower socioeconomic status.

DEFINING "TECHNOLOGICAL DISASTER"

Three Mile Island meltdown. Bhopal, India, chemical spill. Exxon Valdez oil spill. Challenger explosion. Chernobyl meltdown. Love Canal toxic waste. Apollo I explosion. Titanic sinking. Hindenburg explosion.

The mere mention of these places and events causes people to cringe—and secretly give thanks that they were not present. These names also may evoke anger and give rise to difficult questions: "Who is to blame? Why did this happen? How can we make sure this does not happen again?" Technological disasters tend to evoke different responses from people than natural disasters.

> Since the dawn of human history, communities have faced numerous types of catastrophic events originating from natural processes. Events such as floods, volcanic eruptions, earthquakes, hurricanes, blizzards, droughts, and the like have been socially defined as disasters within a context of human communities and the natural environment. Although these events are outside the realm of ordinary daily activities, societal experiences suggest that these disasters conform with an ordinary course of nature. Thus, natural disasters follow a consistent sequence of events and impact a community's social structure at identifiable levels. (Gill & Picou, 1998, p. 795)

Technological disasters are different from other disasters—they are not "natural" but are instead the result of a breakdown in something made by humans that is not expected to break down; it is a failure of technology or some human error. Instead of assigning blame to "natural forces" or a "spiritual deity," culpability for these disasters' devastating consequences to children, families, and communities are assigned to technology, organizations, or even to particular people. As White (2001) reminded us, at one time in the history of humankind, natural disasters were blamed on "a fellow human being in the hope of assuaging the anger of the gods by appeasing them with a sacrificial scapegoat" (p. 24).

Technological versus Natural Disasters

Early research tended to ignore differences between natural and technological disasters, and discussed both as similar chronic stressor events. Differences in their effects, however, soon made it apparent that whereas both are, indeed, chronic stressor events, each has characteristics that make it unique. Baum, Fleming, and Davidson (1983; see also Prince William Sound Regional Citizen's Advisory Council, 2000) were among the first to compare natural and technological disasters in an attempt to explain people's different reactions to them. Differences between the defining characteristics of natural and technological disasters help explain their different effects.

Baum and his colleagues (1983) distinguished natural and technological disasters along five points of comparison. They are suddenness, power, predictability, low point of the disaster, and effects.

Suddenness. Natural disasters begin suddenly—forewarning is often possible, although predictions are not always accurate; technological disasters also begin suddenly, but unlike many natural disasters, there is little advance warning—indeed, there is no expectation that anything will "go wrong."

In addition to the suddenness with which a disaster may begin, there is the suddenness with which it ends. Most natural disasters have definitive end points: The hurricane or tornado passes, the aftershocks of an earthquake stop, the rivers crest. Conversely, whereas some technological disasters have clear beginnings and endings, such as disasters involving mass transportation, many have no easily recognized end point: Radiation and toxic waste, for example, may affect people and soil for an unknown period of time.

Power. Natural disasters and technological disasters are both powerful; however, with technological advances come the possibility of greater devastation from technological than from natural disasters. There are few natural disasters with the potential for destruction—and, in fact, of the **lingering** destruction—of a nuclear power plant accident. Radiation from the 1986 Chernobyl nuclear power plant accident, for instance, spread around the world and continues to affect the health of large numbers of people (Bequette, 1996).

Predictability. Many natural disasters are predictable. The paths of hurricanes and tornadoes can be traced with increasing accuracy, and assessments of their strength can be used to help people prepare. Although avalanches and volcanic eruptions are less predictable, their possible locations may be predicted with increasing accuracy. Conversely, technological disasters are unpredictable because they are not supposed to happen. Airplanes are not supposed to fall from the sky, dams are not supposed to rupture, nuclear power plants are not supposed to leak or melt down, and people are not supposed to dispose of toxic waste irresponsibly.

Low point of the disaster. This is the moment that can be pointed to as "the worst or lowest moment," after which conditions improve. The low point for natural disasters often is clear, even if only in retrospect: The hurricane or tornado moves away, the last aftershock of the earthquake occurs, floodwaters reach their apex, the volcano belches its final eruption, and so on. At this point, the threat of more destruction decreases significantly, damage is not likely to increase, and disruption is likely to end. Spirits begin to lift, and enhanced relief efforts are set in motion. In comparison, the low point for many technological disasters is often hard to define, especially for those that threaten a large number of people, such as toxic spills and nuclear power plant accidents. When an immediate threat ceases—for example, the nuclear power plant accident is contained and the reactors have been shut down—attention turns to long-term consequences. Long-term consequences of many technological disasters make a clear low point elusive—the point at which things begin to get better is not usually apparent. For example, 10 years after the March 24, 1989, Exxon Valdez oil spill in Prince William Sound, AK, "much of the ecosystem and many of the people have yet to fully recover. Oil persisting on beaches and in intertidal sediments continued to contaminate nearshore habitat and biota" (Prince William Sound Regional Citizen's Advisory Council, 2000, p. 10). And, as Bequette (1996), wrote, 10 years after the Chernobyl disaster:

> The ecological effects—apart from the harm done to human life—are still largely unknown. Grassy plains and fields and flat, bare ground are the kinds of terrain that are most seriously contaminated. Radionuclides concentrated in the sediment at the bottom of standing water (lakes, swamps, reservoirs and the like), are absorbed by animal and plant life. In

the forest radioactivity concentrates in tree bark, moss, lichen and mushrooms and in leaves and pine needles, which contaminate the soil when they fall to the ground. In some areas it is forbidden to gather firewood. When burned, the wood contaminates ovens, and its ash used as fertilizer contaminates soil and crops. (p. 44)

Effects. The effects of the two types of disasters differ. For example, natural disasters typically have traumatic social–psychological effects that are short lived, whereas technological disasters create chronic social and psychological disorder that, in turn, cause chronic community stress (Gill & Picou, 1998). In addition, natural disasters tend to create what is called a "therapeutic community," in which people pull together for the common good. Technological disasters tend to drive apart community members, as they debate different notions of what happened, what should be done, and who should be held responsible.

In their investigation of the chronic stress produced by technological disasters at the community level, Gill and Picou (1998) compare natural and technological disasters along five points of comparison that are different from those considered by Baum and his colleagues (1983). The points are responsibility, uncertainty, social constructionism, corrosive community, and chronic stress.

Responsibility. Whereas the processes that produce natural disasters are seen as uncontrollable, those that produce technological disasters are seen as controllable. As a result, people can assign blame for a technological disaster—blame is assigned to the person, group, or organization that should have exercised control to preclude a disaster. This ability to assign blame results in litigation and, usually, compensation. For example, because of litigation following the deadly gas leak in Bhopal, India, in 1984, Union Carbide agreed to pay $470 million as part of an out-of-court settlement (Tangri, 1999). (Unfortunately, according to Leonard, 2000, much of the money has yet to reach the affected families, and the people of Bhopal continue to seek restitution from the company and the then chief executive officer.)

Uncertainty. The second of Gill and Picou's (1998) point of comparison considers that, whereas the damage from natural disasters is highly visible—piles of rubble that had once been buildings after a monsoon or tidal wave, cars strewn haphazardly around the landscape after a tornado, roads buckled and distorted after an earthquake—damage from many types of technological disasters may not be obvious. It is not always easy to identify the problem and define the technological disaster when the problem is not obvious, or there is a long time lag between the point at which the disaster may have begun (for example, when toxic waste was dumped) and when it was recognized as a disaster (Kim, 1998). Radioactive gases are invisible, and toxic waste may not change the landscape immediately. This "invisibility," coupled with the ambiguity of long-term effects, creates uncertainty and raises questions: "How will health be affected and how long will people in the community have to worry about disaster-related health problems? Will property become contaminated and lose value? What effects will the disaster have on local resources and jobs? What will it take to restore the children, families, and community to their predisaster state, if such restoration is even possible?"

Social constructionism. The third dimension of comparison considers the potential effects of experiencing a technological disaster on an individual's worldview. Most people in the United States and other industrial countries do not routinely think about the safety of their water, air, food, soil, and homes (Kroll-Smith & Couch, 1993). After a disaster that contaminates the water and air, pollutes the food, spoils the soil and natural resources, or makes homes unsafe, their worldview is challenged and activities formerly taken for granted are re-examined. For example, after a disaster people may question whether they should drive their cars less to reduce pollution or whether they should reduce their dependence on electricity so that nuclear reactors are a less attractive source of energy. In addition, when there is a lack of clear evidence of contamination, or when evidence may be interpreted more than one way, disputes arise between sufferers and those blamed for the disaster over whether a problem exists at all.

Corrosive community. Unlike natural disasters, technological disasters have the potential for creating a corrosive community in which people fail to reach consensus regarding the existence and nature of the disaster. Natural disasters have a tendency to strengthen bonds between neighbors as they reach out to help one another—they create a therapeutic community. Technological disasters, conversely, have a tendency to weaken relationships in communities. Uncertainty regarding the disaster—how extensive it is, whether there is contamination, what problems the community might experience in the future—produces fear and anger and different definitions of the disaster. Conflict between community members and long, drawn-out litigation increases uncertainty and, ultimately, may undermine the social fabric of the community.

Chronic stress. The fifth point of comparison that Gill and Picou (1998) made considers the chronic stress likely to result from a technological, but not a natural, disaster. Similar to the point made by Baum and his colleagues (1983), the two types of disasters have

Uncertainty of the Effects of the Three Mile Island Nuclear Power Plant Accident

America's worst commercial nuclear power plant accident occurred on March 28, 1979, at 4 A.M., at which time there was a partial meltdown of the nuclear core of one of the reactors at Three Mile Island Nuclear Power Plant, near Harrisburg, Penn. Radioactive gas escaped and people in a five-mile radius were evacuated. Within five days, the 140,000 evacuees returned home.

A special report by National Public Radio's *Living on Earth*, "Three Mile Island: 20 Years Later" (Curwood, 1999b), made it clear that debate continued about whether radiation releases harmed the public. "Dr. Kenneth Miller at Penn State University Hospital in nearby Hershey, Penn., says there are no long-term health effects.... However, researchers from the University of North Carolina have recently found an alarming incidence of cancer near the plant....This is life today in the shadow of Three Mile Island. Some residents live in fear. And whenever a neighbor or family member becomes seriously ill, they question if the accident somehow caused it."

different consequences that may be explained by factors already considered. For instance, natural disasters disrupt a community but do not corrode its social fabric as technological disasters are apt to do; it is less likely that litigation and uncertainty will follow a natural disaster, as it often does a technological disaster, because blame cannot usually be assigned; and natural disasters, perceived as uncontrollable, do not raise the ontological questions that technological questions raise, such as how people relate to their technological creations, how people's lifestyles relate to the technology to sustain that lifestyle, or to larger questions of what is best "for the planet." A loss of faith in technology, in the ability to create technological advances that are safe and do not break down, raises questions that natural disasters do not raise and produces a chronic, long-term stress for children, families, and communities that natural disasters are not likely to produce.

A final point on the difference between natural and technological disasters concerns environmental advocacy. Whereas environmental advocacy is rarely a response to a natural disaster, it is a common response when the technological disaster damages the environment. An "environmental justice" perspective considers technological disasters to be crimes, not accidents, from which vulnerable people need to be protected (Kim, 1998).

Touching Reality "Reacting to a Technological Disaster" provides you with an opportunity to explore your own possible reactions to a technological disaster and to consider the reasons technological disasters affect people as they do.

INEVITABILITY OF TECHNOLOGICAL DISASTERS

To help us deal with technological disasters—to help us feel better after one occurs—we tend to ascribe them with characteristics such as "rare" and "fixable" (Miller, 1999). If a technological disaster is rare, then we do not have to worry about reoccurrence, and if it can be fixed, then we are in control. Charles Perrow (1999; Clarke & Perrow, 1999), a Yale University sociologist and organizational theorist, argued that technological disasters are not rare and, indeed, for some complex technologies they are inevitable. His theory rests on three assumptions:

Three Mile Island Nuclear Power Plant Accident Created a Corrosive Community

Twenty years after the Three Mile Island nuclear power plant accident, Steve Curwood, the executive producer of *Living on Earth* (1999a), interviewed Bonnie Valentine, a long-time resident of the Harrisburg, Pennsylvania, area, whose family homestead was sold and torn down to make room for the Three Mile Island Nuclear Power Plant. Ms. Valentine evacuated the area when the meltdown occurred and spent two weeks in a motel 15 miles away. Following is an excerpt of that interview:

Curwood: How would you say things are now between the power plant and the community?

Valentine: (sighs) I think we would be reluctant to believe anything they said, really, I would say there's a real credibility issue, because we know that they weren't totally honest with us 20 years ago when it happened. And once that trust is destroyed and you can't believe in the honesty of a corporation, you know, you're just not real comfortable with hearing what they have to say.

1. The components of complex systems, including the safety systems they contain, interact in ways that are too varied to understand or predict. (He calls this "interactive complexity.")

2. Small problems may trigger other problems so quickly that there is not enough time to determine what is happening and to respond quickly enough to prevent a disaster. (He calls this "tight coupling.")

Reacting to a Technological Disaster

On March 24, 1999, a fire that began in a truck carrying margarine and flour blazed through the Mont Blanc Tunnel connecting France and Italy. "The blaze reached temperatures of 1000 degrees Celsius and killed 35 people, who could not be rescued. The fire services had previously warned the company operating the tunnel that it would be extremely difficult to carry out rescue operations. The tunnel was used by 766,000 heavy goods vehicles in 1998" (UNEP, 2002).

What are your reactions? Would you react differently if you knew one of the 35 people who died in the disaster? How do you think people who travel through the tunnel on occasion are likely to react?

Now, consider this quote from William Yule (1993, p. 105): "It is widely accepted that human made technological disasters are associated with higher levels of later distress than are natural disasters."

Consider the following points:

- In technological disasters, the bereaved may never see their dead (for example, when a plane crashes in the ocean, when people in a fire are burned beyond the ability to identify them, or when an explosion destroys the bodies of those killed).
- If people believe that the disaster was caused by the negligence of another

person, or purposeful withholding of information about a dangerous substance, and so on, then there is a person, group, organization, or even government to blame.

- We fear being dependent on machines and processes that cause harm. Machines make our lives better in so many ways that we do not want to think about or deal with their negative aspects.
- Often, a technological disaster may cause those exposed to feel that they made an error in judgment that might have been corrected (for example, "Why did I have to be in that building, or on that plane/ship/bus?").
- Experiencing a technological disaster may significantly alter a person's lifestyle (for example, a survivor may no longer be willing to fly in an airplane, or travel on the local commuter train).
- A technological disaster may affect the lives of people not directly involved in the disaster. For example, reading about an airplane crash may alter a person's plans to travel by plane, or the collapse of a parking deck at a mall may influence people who were not involved in the disaster to avoid using a parking deck.

Have you ever been involved in a technological disaster? What were the long-term consequences? What changes to your lifestyle did you make?

For example, Weick's (1991) analysis of the 1977 Tenerife air disaster, in which two Boeing 747s collided and 583 people were killed, suggested that several processes amplified the effects of small events—such as the interruption of important routines and the breakdown of coordinated action—into disastrous events. These events, in turn, resulted in more errors and a reduction in the means to detect those errors.

3. Organizational plans to avert failure are "fantasy documents" because there is little experience on which to base them. In fact, as Clarke and Perrow (1999) argued, the probability of organizational failure actually increases because of the plans to avert disaster. This is because plans, based on insufficient information and experience, become the focus of attention; whereas they can provide comfort ("We're safe—we have a plan!"), they divert attention from the reality of critical situations. For example, after the Exxon Valdez oil tanker ran aground in Alaska's Prince William Sound, the plan that was used to respond to the 11 million gallons of spilled oil was based on an expected spill of 4,000 barrels because the planners had experience with that quantity.

Other problems contribute to the likelihood of technological disasters:

- Individuals and organizations may be concerned with appearing smart, or knowledgeable, which can prevent them from admitting that there is something they do not understand. This might have been the case when engineers who worked with the Challenger launch were reluctant to acknowledge that they did not know how the booster rockets would perform in extremely cold weather (Vaughan, 1996).

- Individuals and organizations may be concerned with appearing "in control," which can prevent them from admitting when something goes wrong or malfunctions.

- Someone may feel uncomfortable speaking up or arguing forcefully if he or she perceives the need to do what leaders and others want. According to Thomas White (2001), during the hearings conducted to investigate the Challenger explosion,

> it became clear that a teleconference the night before the Challenger launch between Morton Thiokol executives and NASA managers was the "smoking gun" that was needed to assign blame. During the teleconference, Morton Thiokol engineers argued that Challenger should not launch because they did not have sufficient data to predict the functionality of the rocket-motor seal in low-temperature conditions. After much debate (and coercion on the part of the NASA managers), Morton Thiokol executives overrode the engineers' assessment and recommended the launch. . . . Those who were blamed were doing what they thought their leaders and their nation wanted them to do. (White, p. 28)

- Bennett (2000) found a host of other "human factors" in his studies of small-boat sailors, airline pilots, train conductors, and motorists. He found, for example, that people who "see" the color traffic signal they want to see (it may be red, but the desire to see a green light "makes it" green) can turn accidents into disasters; people who are preoccupied with remote matters, such as relationship difficulties, financial worries, and health problems, can precipitate disasters; and people who are under the influence of alcohol or drugs can be the triggers for disastrous events.

The picture may be bleak; the solution, however, is neither to bury our heads in the sand and ignore the pervasive possibility of technological disaster nor to abandon the development of new technologies or innovative uses for existing technologies, nor to accept that disasters are inevitable and resign ourselves to them. Some "high-reliability organizations" (Miller, 1999; Pool, 1997) encompass technological systems that have avoided disasters and that have increased their safety records. Miller cited examples of the air traffic control centers at airports in Oakland and San Francisco, the nuclear power plant at California's Diablo Canyon, and the aircraft carriers U.S.S. Enterprise and U.S.S. Carl Vinson. In each instance, the organization was able to create a "culture of safety," to learn from—and not ignore—mistakes, to permit those most familiar with operations to make decisions in times of crisis, and to assign redundant supervision to critical tasks (such as monitoring radar screens). Pool added, drawing from the examples of aircraft carriers, that open and constant communication is important, as is the establishment of a nonpunitive culture regarding employees who make mistakes—punishment keeps people from learning everything they need to know and discourages open communication.

The way to avoid technological disasters, then, includes effective planning—and making any plan an open system, one that can adapt and change as new information becomes available, as new contingencies are recognized, and as new circumstances alter old conditions.

TYPES OF TECHNOLOGICAL DISASTERS

Technological disasters include a total or partial building collapse; mass transit accidents or disasters, such as coach and bus accidents; shipping disasters; and airplane, train, and major automobile accidents (Yule, 1993; Yule, Udwin, & Bolton, 2002). Such disasters also include toxic waste spills, nuclear power plant accidents (Wroble & Baum, 2002), and dam breaks (Korol, Kramer, Grace, & Green, 2002). Research into technological disasters is new, partly because many of the types of disasters studied are relatively recent. Nuclear power plant accidents and certain plastics fires or chemical spills are examples of situations for which risk did not exist a few decades ago. As use of these manufactured products increases, so does risk of misuse or unplanned complications.

Nuclear Power Plant and Toxic Spill Disasters

Research shows that it is only in relatively recent times that people are afraid of and concerned about the long-term effects of exposure to the toxins emitted or spilled from industrial or nuclear power plants; this fear and concern has definitely had an effect on our children. It is difficult for a parent or helper to address a child's anxiety and fear regarding nuclear power plant accidents because there are no definitive answers about the effects of current or continued exposure to nuclear chemicals. The young child, who is less informed about the subject, has greater fears about these accidents. However, whether or not a child has directly experienced a nuclear incident, a decade ago Klingman, Goldstein, and Lerner (1991) found that children reported nuclear war among their three worst fears. Studies of children's and adolescents' fears about nuclear war showed that just the threat of such an occurrence is a contributing factor to anxiety and other disorders found in teenagers (Thompson, 1986).

Handford and his colleagues (1986) focused on the relationship between children's ages and their reactions to the Three Mile Island nuclear power plant disaster. They found, for example, that younger children's responses were "vague and undifferentiated" (that is, they responded that Three Mile Island "might be dangerous"), whereas older students were more focused and explicitly relayed fears of their own and others' deaths, anger related to Three Mile Island interfering with their play space, concern about other people's feelings (such as their mother and father being worried), and worry about future consequences.

Children and adults tend not to discuss nuclear issues. Rather, there appears to be a general habit of avoidance. In certain countries, nuclear power is the primary power source for electricity. The inherent danger from misuse has come into the news once again with the fall of the Soviet Union and the questions about care and control of radioactive products in newly formed countries that are in political disarray and suffering from economic instability.

The public is becoming generally aware of the tremendous toxicity of the chemical dioxin, which is found in many industrial plants and which is connected to the production of plastics. As a result of the 1984 chemical leak at the Union Carbide plant in Bhopal, India, which dispersed dioxin throughout the area, approximately 2,500 people died and 200,000 were injured (Sinha, 1990). Accidents of this nature bring into question the role of multinational corporations, such as Union Carbide, in developing countries.

In 1997, a major industrial fire in Hamilton, Ontario, Canada, at an abandoned plastics recycling plant (Plastimet) poured toxic smoke and ash laden with dioxins onto the surrounding town. According to Ali (2002)

a very large and highly visible plume of dense black smoke formed and drifted across the city, leaving in its wake a thin film of toxic black soot on all outdoor articles, houses and properties in the vicinity. In response to the risk of exposure to these airborne and deposited toxins, the municipal government issued an emergency evacuation order and 650 residents fled their homes. The residents were permitted to return the next day, but were warned by government health officials not to allow their children to play on lawns and sandboxes in the area; not to consume any of the vegetables or fruits grown in their home gardens; and to wash all outdoor items very thoroughly before use (p. 129).

What makes situations such as these so complex is that there is usually no obvious aggression, and the scientific community does not agree about the long-term effects of exposure. In Ontario, for example, the minister of health was unwilling to open an inquiry because he saw no obvious criminal behavior to investigate.

Toxins can be spewed into the air as they were in Bhopal, Chernobyl, Three Mile Island, and Hamilton, or in the case of the Love Canal off the Niagara River in the state of New York, they can be dumped or buried. Before homes were built near the Love Canal in the 1970s, more than 200,000 tons of chemical waste were buried in the canal (Kim, 1998). The spring thaw after the blizzard of 1977 (a natural disaster) caused the canal and its waste to overflow (a technological disaster). Until the thaw exposed the problem, the "invisible" technological disaster took place mostly underground, and the connection of high rates of miscarriage and birth defects to the chemical waste was not apparent. However, "mandatory evacuation was issued after residents of the 230 homes and 250 apartments in the Love Canal community began noticing a dark ooze appearing in their sump pumps, basements, backyards, and swimming pools. They were replacing their sump pumps abnormally often due to rapid corrosion. Swimming pools were being eaten away" (Kim, 1998, p. 1). People who grew gardens and canned vegetables unwittingly spoon-fed their children toxins. Twenty years later, children and grandchildren of the original residents continue to suffer from the dumping of toxic waste into the Love Canal.

The extended example below is from a personal account of a technological disaster in Libby, Montana, by one of the residents.

Asbestos Contamination in Libby, Montana

Libby, Montana, is famous for many things—the spectacular scenery, the special glacial melt color of the Kootenai River, the huge trout—and now we are both famous and infamous for having the horrific stigma of being more poisonous than Love Canal because of the asbestos contamination in our town.

Trees (huge evergreens), line the streets and mountains and have furnished our town with jobs and America with wood products for over 200 years. And underneath the mountains lie rich ores of many types. One of these ores is vermiculite, and Zonolite Mountain is full of it. This is the mountain we refer to as the mountain of life, and the mountain of death.

We call it the mountain of life because the vermiculite mined here was a lucrative ore used for insulation, potting soil, fill and fiberglass fireproofing, and concrete, and because the mine provided jobs for many residents and fed families for many years.

We call it the mountain of death because, horrifically, the vermiculite is so toxic that is has killed over 200 residents of Libby so far. In fact, due to the exposure of the citizens of Libby, the whole town was encouraged to be screened for asbestos exposure. Regrettably, 18% of those tested, over 1,000 people, have lung abnormalities and other health problems due to breathing asbestos fibers. The asbestos present in Libby is the worst kind, tremolite, which causes asbestosis, lung cancer, and mesothelioma. Even residents who did not work at the mine have been diagnosed with asbestosis as well.

Twenty times the lethal dose of asbestos fibers "rained" on Libby for over 40 years.

I have lived in Libby since 1976 and have been exposed to tremolite asbestos for the entire time I have lived here. Since asbestos has a latency period from 10 to 40 years, I do not know if I will have the dreaded disease or not. My son, who was born and raised in Libby, has been diagnosed with lung problems. The schools have asbestos in the football fields, the baseball fields, running tracks, underneath the bleachers, and inside the building itself, so all the children of Libby have a latency period that started when they attended school if not before.

The EPA has a huge project in Libby, and has been "cleaning up" the city for almost two years.

Few studies have examined the consequences of technological disasters on children, although a great deal is available on adults' reactions (Wroble & Baum, 2002).

Spotlight on Research "Mental Health after an Industrial Fire" provides a closer view of the effects of a PCB fire on the mental health of children and adults.

SPOTLIGHT ON RESEARCH

Mental Health After an Industrial Fire

Most research on the effects of disasters suffers from a lack of a control group—people such as those exposed to the disaster in many ways but who were not directly exposed. Researchers can determine the effects of a disaster with greater surety if there is such a control group. This study is one of the few that has a control group, adding validity to the results.

On August 23, 1988, a PCB warehouse in St-Basile-le-Grand, a community 20 miles south of Montreal, caught fire, producing a thick black cloud of smoke containing dioxins and furans. Three communities were evacuated (1,663 families) at night: Families were woken and given only a few minutes to leave their homes.

A year after the fire, Jean-Jacques Breton and his colleagues (1993) conducted structured interviews with 87 children who they selected at random from those evacuated, and with a control group of 87 children matched for age, biological sex, and socioeconomic status selected at random from families living a few miles north of Montreal. Four groups of variables were assessed: (1) child-related variables (such as mental and physical health), (2) parent-related variables (such as mental health and level of education), (3) family-related variables (the family's structure and composition), and (4) disaster-related variables (including the events, anxieties, and personal reactions).

The mental health of parents who were exposed and those who were not exposed did not differ. In addition, there were no differences in behavioral problems, or the proportion of behavioral problems, for the group of younger children between ages three and five. Differences, however, were found between the exposed and unexposed older children, six to 11 years old. The children exposed to the disaster had higher overall internalized symptoms scores (that is, a major depressive episode, unspecified depression, separation anxiety, panic disorder, or social phobia) and posttraumatic stress disorder (PTSD) index. In addition, girls had higher internalized symptoms scores than boys.

Explaining the lack of differences between the exposed and unexposed younger children, the authors argued, "the immature cognitive development of preschoolers may prevent recognition of an industrial disaster that presents no visible or concrete consequences" (p. 443). In addition, "the fire took place in a wealthy area, and most children in the study came from upper-class families. This has, according to recent epidemiological surveys, a protective effect on children's mental health" (p. 443). They elaborated on this point, saying that because upper-middle-class adults are used to controlling their environment, the sudden vulnerability created by the disaster was brief.

Breton, J.-J., Valla, J.-P., & Lambert, J. (1993). Industrial disaster and mental health of children and their parents. *Journal of the American Academy of Child and Adolescent Psychiatry, 32*, 438–445.

Mass Transport Disasters

Late in 1988, the cruise ship *Jupiter* set sail from Athens, with about 400 British students, from 20 different schools, on an educational cruise of the eastern Mediterranean. As the ship took off in the late evening in the dark, it was struck by an Italian oil tanker, 20 miles out of harbor. As the Jupiter sank, children became separated from friends and teachers and had to swim in the dark, without adults, in oily water laden with debris. All but one child and one teacher, whose bodies were never recovered, survived. According to Yule, Udwin, and Murdoch (1990), specific stressors included fears related to boats, water, swimming, the anxiety of returning to school, and the guilt of being a survivor. In a related study, Yule and Udwin (1991) compared the fears of three groups of 14- to 15-year-old girls in one school—those who were on the cruise and traumatized, those who wanted to go but could not because of a lack of space, and those who had no interest in going. They found that only the girls who were on the cruise showed an increase in reported fears related to the events of the cruise. No differences were found in their fear of events unrelated to the cruise, indicating that fear was conditioned by the event and not generalized to other events. For example, a common result of disasters relating to transport is a fear of using that type of transportation in the future.

A follow-up study conducted by Yule and his colleagues (2000) five to seven years later found that 51.5 percent of the victims developed PTSD after the disaster (compared with 3.4 percent in a control group), most within several weeks and about 10 percent within six months of the disaster. The duration of PTSD varied; for example, it lasted less than a year in 30 percent of the victims. Five to seven years later, however, 38 of the 111 victims diagnosed with PTSD (34 percent) still had it.

Two studies of children who were in, witnessed, or knew someone who had been in a bus accident that took place in Israel, provide an interesting perspective on the effects of this type of technological disaster. The incident involved 450 seventh-grade students in 13 buses on their way to celebrate the end of the school year. A train at a railroad crossing hit one of the buses. Of the 33 children on the struck bus, 19 of them and three accompanying adults were killed. Children in three following buses witnessed the accident, and those in the remaining nine buses were told of the accident immediately after it occurred.

For the first study (Milgram, Toubiana, Klingman, & Raviv, 1988), questionnaire data were obtained one week and then nine months after the accident. Analyses indicated that being a friend of a classmate who was killed was more important for predicting both acute and chronic stress reactions than which bus a respondent was on—in other words, psychological proximity was more important than physical proximity. In addition, the incidence of moderate and severe stress reactions in the initial testing decreased markedly by the second testing, nine months after the incident.

In a follow-up study focusing on other effects of the disaster, Milgram and Toubiana (1996) examined the antecedents and consequences of two externalizing behaviors exhibited by children during the week following the disaster: confronting behavior versus avoidant coping behavior and receiving help from specific support individuals. Results indicated that personal loss, primarily, and exposure to the disaster, secondarily, were related to stress levels and that the atmosphere that encouraged children to engage in confronting behaviors raised stress levels further.

Perceived helpfulness of different types of support persons was related to current stress levels, context of the disaster, and prior helping relationships.

Dam Disasters

On February 26, 1972, the Pittston Company's refuse pile dam in Buffalo Creek, West Virginia, collapsed, unleashing 132 million gallons of water and coal waste materials (black wastewater) on the residents of 16 small towns along Buffalo Creek. The water and sludge traveled down the creek in 15- to 20-foot waves and at speeds up to seven feet per second. The disaster, which killed over 125 people and left more than 4,000 homeless, has been studied several times over more than two decades—partly because of the litigation that resulted. (A fuller description of the Buffalo Creek Disaster is presented in chapter 2.)

Erikson (1977) conducted the most extensive study of survivors' reactions to the Buffalo Creek Disaster; he published his findings in his book, *Everything in Its Path: Destruction of Community in the Buffalo Creek Flood*. In a recent revisiting of the original interviews, Erikson (1998) detailed the effects of the disaster revealed in the themes he found in interviewees' stories. His article began with a description of the results of psychiatric examinations of 615 survivors that took place 18 months after the disaster. He found that 93 percent (570) were suffering from depression, anxiety, phobia, apathy, and other indications of PTSD—"the nearest expressions in everyday English would be something like confusion, despair, and hopelessness" (p. 153). Even allowing for an overestimate (as Erikson pointed out, psychiatrists look for mental illness, so they are apt to find it), the number of people suffering so long after the disaster is alarming.

Themes revealed in Erickson's stories depicted people with feelings of

- *numbness and depletion* (as if in a dream state, limp)
- *survivor guilt*
- *a lost sense of self as house and furniture are destroyed* (The house was considered an extension of self, and the items in it represented one's life history.)
- *loss of faith in the social order* (a loss of faith in both nature and the company that built the dam, a company that should have "taken care of" the community of which it was a part)
- *loss of community* (which includes a loss of the structure that "cushions pain" and serves as the "repository for old traditions")
- *lack of morale accompanied by suspicion of moral standards* (Boys and girls became involved in "nameless delinquencies," and adults behaved in ways that the community moral order, if it had been in place, would not have approved.)
- *disorientation as a result of shock* (Survivors continued to feel disoriented for months after the disaster.)

Overall, there was a *loss of connection* between family members and between family members and the community, which created fertile ground for troubled marriages, troubled families, and the loss of good relationships with neighbors and acquaintances.

Studies of a more typical social science nature than the in-depth interviews Erikson collected have been conducted over the years since the disaster. For example, Green and her colleagues (1991) found that older children were more affected by parental reactions than younger ones, perhaps because they endured the strongest effects of their parents' emotional imbalance. In other words, if parents are emotionally ill-equipped to cope with a technological disaster, such as the Buffalo Creek flood, older children tend to take on parenting roles for younger siblings. In addition, older children may be more likely to relate to their parents' feelings of survivor guilt or the need to rectify the situation.

Seventeen years after the disaster, Green and her colleagues (1994) re-evaluated 99 survivors who, at the time of the catastrophe, were from two to 25 years old. They used a battery of instruments, including the Psychiatric Evaluation Form, and the Impact of Event Scale, and a structured clinical interview from the DSM–III–R. In general, compared with data collected two years after the disaster, analyses indicated significant decreases in overall severity ratings as well as in anxiety, belligerence, somatic concerns, and agitation—findings that were confirmed by Richard Honig and his colleagues (Honig, Grace, Lindy, & Newman, 1993). Honig and his colleagues found that among the original children studied after the disaster, the rates of PTSD and other forms of psychopathology had sharply declined. Significantly, however, Green and her colleagues (1994) found that a few symptoms that were not found in the child sample increased during the 15-year interval since the first evaluation, such as drug and alcohol abuse and suicidal ideation. In addition, whereas 32 percent of the population after the flood suffered from posttraumatic stress, the rate 17 years later was down to 7 percent, although a larger proportion of women than men evidenced PTSD-related symptoms.

Using a different methodology than that used by Green and her colleagues (1994), Honig and his colleagues (Honig, Grace, Lindy, Newman, & Titchener, 1999a, 1999b) assessed the long-term effects of the Buffalo Creek disaster on the child and adolescent survivors (now young adults). Although they uncovered PTSD symptoms that Green and her colleagues did not find, their most significant finding was that the long-term effects often took the shape of persistent character traits. Specifically, the coping responses children used as their immediate response to the trauma affected their subsequent emotional development and their capacity to confront later stressful events.

Bridge and Building Collapse Disasters
Given the frequency with which the media report disasters related to the collapse of bridges and buildings (other than those collapses that are part of a complex, not technological, disaster), we would expect a large number of studies detailing the effects of these disasters on people exposed to them. A perusal of journals in psychology, sociology, social work, and other related areas, however, indicates this is not the case. Most of the research on these types of technological disasters focuses on the technical aspects; articles are published in journals such as the *Journal of Structural Engineering* discussing, for example, how to build better bridges or how to construct safer buildings.

This lack of research is interesting, given the prominence of disasters of these types. Why is there so little research on their psychosocial effects? Perhaps it is because they are *too* frequent, *too* hard to dismiss as "rare," especially in the case of bridges. Unless prior experience tells us it is important, we do not think, "This bridge I'm driving on may collapse" or "This hotel may crumple." After we check into a hotel, we see a sign on the back of the room's door that tells us what to do in case of a fire—but no mention is made of what to do if the building begins to collapse. "What to do in the event this building begins to collapse" is too hard to imagine, the consequences too dire to contemplate. Therefore, except for the comfort offered in the notions that we can build better bridges and buildings, we ignore the psychosocial damage as an object of investigation. Practitioners are left to bring their notions of "best practice" to the disaster, to extrapolate from other experiences as they help disaster clients cope.

The 1857 Great Western Railway disaster at the bridge over the Desjardins Canal, Canada (Johnson, 1990–1991), is one of the earliest bridge disasters about which we have a great deal of technical information but no information about psychosocial effects. (The only information that can be gleaned is that there were "tens of thousands" of people at the funeral and there was a "great outpouring of melancholy"). The bridge collapsed and the train fell 60 feet onto the ice. Many died instantly from their injuries or were burned by fires started by the stoves on board the train; others drowned in the freezing water when the ice gave way. In all, about 35 people jumped off, escaped, or were rescued; 59 people died. The jury vindicated the railway, finding that the engine had been properly inspected and that the bridge was sufficiently strong. The jury recommended, however, that an iron bridge be constructed over the canal, and one was built a few years later. For several years, many passengers on the line would only cross the bridge on foot.

Blom (1986) studied the responses to an accident in which a crane struck a school skywalk in one of the few social science studies of a building collapse. Although there were 20 children on the overpass, only six fell, and of these six, five were seriously injured. A few hundred schoolchildren witnessed the accident. Interventions were offered on the individual, the group, and the community levels, with the overall goal of assisting people to assimilate the unanticipated disaster. Questionnaires completed 13 days after the accident indicated considerable distress, although within seven months only a few children were mildly upset. The primary anxiety for both girls and boys was with walking near walkways. Other reactions were different for each sex: Boys showed more sleep disturbance and fighting, and girls showed more startle reactions and thought more about the accident. Young children between five and eight years old experienced less stress than older children (the predominant complaints were somatic problems), whereas older children between nine and 12 experienced more sleep disturbances, worried about friends, and thought about the accident.

UNDERESTIMATING CHILDREN'S REACTIONS TO DISASTERS

Several studies have documented that parents and teachers underestimate their children's reactions to disasters. It is common for parents to minimize the distress their children experience after a trauma, and the older the children the more likely they are to underestimate (Monahon, 1993).

On December 21, 1988, debris from the bombed Pan Am Flight 103 fell on the town of Lockerbie, Scotland. Referencing a study of the effects of the disaster on the children of Lockerbie, Yule (1993), noted, "the teachers grossly underestimated the levels of psychopathology among the children"(p. 111).

Similarly, Handford and his colleagues (1986), in their study of the effects of the disaster at the Three Mile Island (TMI) nuclear power plant, found that "parent and child perceptions of the children's reactions to TMI revealed a marked discrepancy between what the children claimed to have felt and experienced and what the parents perceived as their children's feelings and experiences" (p. 349), with parents underestimating the children's responses. Whereas widespread fear was common among the children, according to their own accounts, for example, only a third of the parents reported noticing their fear.

The same held true for a study of natural disasters. Belter, Dunn, and Jeney (1991) found that parents reported significantly fewer symptoms of PTSD in their children than their children self-reported. They suggested that parents did not necessarily know how to detect signs of posttraumatic stress in their children.

Not every study looking at parents' and teachers' estimates of children's reactions find these discrepancies, but many do. Several reasons in addition to the one posed by Belter and his colleagues (1991) can account for the discrepancies. That is, children may try to hide their distress from their parents because they do not wish to add to their parents' anxiety (Sleek, 1998), or they may find it difficult to talk to their parents after a disaster (Stallard & Law, 1993). The parents may be overwhelmed with their own reactions and minimize their children's reactions to minimize their own burden, which may explain why within a year the parents become more accurate in their assessment of their children's reactions (Pynoos & Nader, 1988).

Perhaps a better question than "Why?" however, is, "What are the possible repercussions of parents and teachers underestimating the trauma's effects on children?"

SECONDHAND EXPOSURE TO TECHNOLOGICAL DISASTERS

Research concerned with secondhand exposure to a disaster—meaning, for example, watching the disaster on television either as it occurs or in repeated newscasts—has focused mostly on complex disasters, such as wars and terrorism. Recently, Pfefferbaum (2001; Pfefferbaum et al., 2001) studied a group of middle-school students in Oklahoma City following the 1995 bombing; they looked specifically at the effects of bomb-related television viewing on the students' posttraumatic stress symptoms (symptoms such as intrusion, avoidance, and arousal). The students were surveyed seven weeks after the incident. Bomb-related television viewing was associated with posttraumatic stress; among children who had not been physically or emotionally exposed to the disaster, the degree of television exposure was directly related to their posttraumatic stress symptoms.

When a child witnesses but does not experience a disaster, that child's processing of the disaster largely depends on her or his cognitive level. For example, Terr and her colleagues (1996, 1999) found that, whereas about 30 percent of all the children misunderstood something about the Challenger explosion and incorporated these misunderstandings into their memories as false details, only the latency age children (that is, those from approximately five to 11 years old) continued to harbor false details for 14 months afterward. Spotlight on Research "The Effects of Secondhand Exposure to the Challenger Explosion" details the important research that Lenore Terr and her colleagues conducted.

Wright and colleagues (1989) isolated three major stressors associated with secondhand exposure to the Challenger disaster

The Effects of Secondhand Exposure to the Challenger Explosion

"On January 28, 1986, the Challenger space shuttle 'malfunctioned' shortly after liftoff. Six astronauts—McNair, Onizuka, Resnik, Scobee, Smith, and Jarvis—and one high school teacher—McAuliffe—were killed" (Terr et al., 1996, p. 618). How did children with varying degrees of involvement respond to the event? How did those who watched the liftoff from Cape Canaveral, those who watched the liftoff on televisions in Concord, NH, where Christie McAuliffe lived and taught, and those living in California who did not see the liftoff on television but who first heard about it respond? (It was too early, and they were on their way to school.)

Lenore Terr and her colleagues selected children randomly for the study who lived in Concord, New Hampshire, or Portercille, California, these two cities served as good matches for each other because they had about the same populations, both had large mental hospitals, neither had heavy industries, and both were in good economic health. The study involved a total of 153 children, most of whom were ages eight or 15, and included students from those two cities who had traveled to Cape Canaveral for the launch and had watched it there. Children were interviewed twice—five to seven weeks after the disaster, and again 14 months later.

No differences were found between the Cape Canaveral and Concord groups, who had watched the event on television, with respect to their memory of the event, so the two groups were combined.

In their interviews, children described in a free narrative what happened to the space shuttle, as well as their own circumstances when they saw or heard about the tragedy. The interviewers then asked specific questions about "what the child was doing when the explosion occurred, where the child was... who else was there, how others had reacted, how the child had felt, and what the child then did" (p. 621).

After 14 months, the narratives of the older children and the more involved children were clearer than those of the younger and less involved children. In addition, whereas only 2 percent of the East Coast children varied the essence of their stories from the first interview to the second interview, 17 percent of the West Coast students did so. Mental mistakes, such as assuming that some strange human had destroyed the Challenger or that the child caused the explosion, continued to be made by only 8 percent of the older children as compared with 29 percent of the younger children. The researchers speculated that the adolescents tended to correct their memories over time through conversation, whereas the younger children did not. Terr and her colleagues found that, over the 14-month study, most symptoms dramatically faded, although adolescents' diminished expectations for the future in general increased.

During the first interview, the majority of children reported an ongoing tendency to visualize the explosion when it was brought up or when they received a visual reminder. Fourteen months later, 95 percent of the more involved East Coast group visualized on cue, versus 65 percent of the West Coast group.

"Flashbulb memories"—memories etched in after a national shock—do not have total veracity. Only those children who were more emotionally involved in the event had "clear, bright, detailed memories, emphasizing personal location, who else was there, and personal narrative" (p. 624)

Terr, L. C., Bloch, D. A., Michel, B. A., Shi, H., Reinhart, J. A., & Metayer, S. (1996). Children's memories in the wake of Challenger. *American Journal of Psychiatry, 153*, 618-625.

(that is, by watching the televised explosion). First, there was the initial shock of watching the disaster, followed by substantial emotional distress, especially because of the repeated media broadcasts. Distress reportedly subsided approximately six days after the explosion. Second, there was sadness at the loss of a teacher and friend by the children at the school in Concord, New Hampshire, where Christa McAuliffe taught. It is arguable that the rest of the nation's reaction was less severe than that felt by people in Concord, although it was still significant. Third, there was anger at not knowing whom to blame for the deaths of the crew. Young children particularly expressed anger, needing someone to blame, whereas older children saw the explosion as partially a technical error and not necessarily the result of human error.

The explosion of Challenger was a national disaster, and national responses were manifest. For example, flags were lowered to half staff, people shared moments of silence publicly and privately, daytime motorists in Atlanta turned on their headlights, outside lighting on the Empire State Building in New York was dimmed, and 20,000 people along the Florida coast shone flashlights into the sky (Zinner, 1999). On January 31st, following the disaster, President Reagan and his wife, 90 members of Congress, 6,000 National Aeronautic and Space Administration (NASA) employees, 4,000 family members and guests, and millions of television viewers attended a national memorial service held in Houston at the Johnson Space Center.

The marking of the disaster continued across the country. Buildings and sites were named after members of the crew, new schools were named Challenger, the Astronauts Memorial Foundation was established in Florida and money raised for it through the sale of commemorative license plates, monuments were erected, and so on. Commemorations throughout the country continue to mark the day of the explosion.

In her analysis of the disaster, Ellen Zinner (1999) discussed the extent to which different groups were vulnerable to the effects of the event—an important distinction for understanding both the effects of the disaster and for planning interventions. According to Zinner, there were four "survivor groups" (similar to representing different circles of vulnerability; see chapter 2). *Primary level survivorship* consisted of family members and intimates of those killed. *Secondary level survivorship* consisted of friends and acquaintances of those killed. *Tertiary level survivorship* consisted of all those people who identified with the deceased because they shared some social characteristics with those killed, such as ethnicity or occupation. Finally, *quaternary level survivorship* consisted of those who may have shared one broad characteristic with those killed (for example, being a citizen of the United States) but who did not feel particularly connected to them. People in these four survivor groups differed along three dimensions that helpers should consider when developing psychosocial interventions. They differed (1) in the extent to which they saw it as their right to be recognized as a survivor, (2) as to their right to be informed of what was known about the disaster and what was being done, and (3) as to their right to participate in ceremonies.

EFFECTS OF TECHNOLOGICAL DISASTERS

The Prince William Sound Regional Citizens' Advisory Council (2000) provides a list of 20 questions people ask after a disaster occurs, many of which are more relevant for technological disasters (and, even more specifically, disasters involving the release of oil or toxins into the environment) than some other type. A few of the questions follow (p. 34):

- What is really happening here?
- Why am I so angry?
- When is it going to end?
- Is this threatening my health or that of my family?
- How will I ever be able to live here now?
- What about lawsuits? How long will they take?
- Should I work with the responsible party or not (moral choices, guilt)?

Many of the effects of technological disasters on families and children are similar to those for natural disasters, including the defining characteristics of PTSD, fear, somatic complaints, and worry about the loss of one's lifestyle and routine. Many mental health problems persist. Arata and colleagues (2000) surveyed commercial fishers in Cordova, Alaska, six years after the Exxon Valdez oil spill and found that current symptoms of depression, anxiety, and PTSD were associated with resource loss and avoidant coping strategies. Havenaar, Rumiantseva, and van den Bout (1994), summarizing observations recorded by Dutch and Russian researchers studying the mental health aftereffects of the 1986 Chernobyl disaster, found that people's reactions in the affected area included loss of confidence, anxiety, and depression.

Wroble and Baum (2002) observed that few studies have examined the consequences of technological disasters on children, although many have examined their effect on adults. Nevertheless, Wroble and Baum indicated that typical effects of toxic waste spills and nuclear power plant accidents include nightmares about technological accidents, fear about nuclear power plant disaster (in children as young as four), anxiety (often associated with evacuation), and depression. They also noted, however, that predicting the effects of a technological disaster requires considering the extent of damage, the child's age and proximity to the disaster, and other contingencies.

There are effects more common to technological than other types of disasters. These include, for example,

- a loss of faith in technology, the organizations responsible for the technology, or the government that was supposed to regulate and control the technology
- anger directed at those blamed for the disaster
- concerns about litigation and compensation
- a change in lifestyle, such as no longer using the technology that was involved in the disaster
- unspecified fear of the unknown (questions such as, "What are the effects, and how long will they last?" and "Will this happen again?").

Finally, the effects of a technological disaster on a community distinguish this type of disaster from others. For example:

- Different community groups may define the disaster differently, leading to community conflict.
- Different groups may be able to make different claims for compensation, thus pitting community groups against each other (Prince William Sound Regional Citizens' Advisory Council, 2000, offered this example: "Some members of the community may have a clear claim against the

responsible party, while others may not. For example, if a fishery closes due to the disaster [Exxon Valdez oil spill], a fisherman can demonstrate he lost income. However, the supplier who sells the fishermen their nets and gear is not a direct victim and may not be able to recoup losses from the decline in business" [p. 12]).

- The ambiguous nature of what is needed to return to a predisaster state causes community conflict.
- Misunderstandings of the effects of the disaster delay community groups from acting in concert.
- Trust is eroded between community members and the organizations or groups held responsible for the disaster—distrust that impedes cooperative action.
- The overwhelming demands of responding to the disaster cause collective hopelessness and depression, which hamper community action.
- The community may not be able to return local natural resources, such as a river or farmland, to a predisaster state, thus changing the nature of the community forever.

Although it is possible to enumerate pertinent questions and to outline the effects of technological disasters on individuals and communities in general, the effects of a particular disaster depend on what type it is. The immediate and long-term effects of a plane crash, for example, are quite different from the effects of a toxic waste accident. The former has identifiable beginnings and end points, unambiguous outcomes for those directly exposed, and geographical and psychological damage that is highly circumscribed; the latter has hard-to-define beginnings and end points, ambiguous outcomes for those directly exposed, and geographic and psychological damage that is impossible to describe fully.

The history of failed technology is long, and the number of failures is rising rapidly as technological advances and reliance on technology increase—Cable and Benson (1993; cited in Evan & Manion, 2002), for instance, estimated that there is an average of four toxic spills every day in the United States. With technological disasters come blame, especially when there is loss of life (White, 2001). The process of inquiry follows a logical pattern: "What happened? How did it happen? Why did it happen?" And, then, blame: "Who or what is responsible?"

For blame to be assigned, three conditions must be met (White, 2001): (1) Something terrible happened that could have been prevented by one or more people; (2) those people had a moral duty to undertake measures to prevent the disaster; and (3) they could have taken those measures and had no legitimate reason for not doing so.

Of course, the person or group meeting these conditions and subsequently blamed may or may not actually be blameworthy. Not every technological disaster has an identifiable cause, and even if there is one, it may not be related to negligence. But assigning blame and exacting justice provide a measure of confidence that "technology is not to blame," "whatever the problem is it can be fixed," and that disasters are not—Perrow's (1999) analysis notwithstanding—inevitable.

SOCIAL VULNERABILITY TO TECHNOLOGICAL DISASTERS

Do county-level population characteristics predict social vulnerability to toxic risk? Focusing on eight southeastern U.S. states, Rogge (1996) found that population density was the critical factor driving exposure to toxic risk and that social factors varied in their effects, with some increasing risk in some circumstances and decreasing it in others. Her review of literature, however, indicated that there is a consistent relationship between poverty and environmental hazards. In general, communities that suffer from the effects of toxic waste are characterized by low socioeconomic status and various social problems, such as high unemployment, high school dropout, high dependency on government-sponsored social programs, and family and community disruption. According to Rogge (1996), "These are places where 'disposable waste' is dumped among 'disposable people' to generate 'disposable income' for others" (p. 110).

Spotlight on Research "Technological Disaster on the Pigeon River" details an almost century-long battle between a low socioeconomic community and the company that is its primary source of jobs—and the cause of a technological disaster.

Many environmental policies exploit the vulnerability of economically and politically disenfranchised communities; therefore, low-income communities and communities composed predominantly of members of ethnic minority populations receive a disproportionate burden of pollution problems (Bullard, 1994). For example, the Love Canal population consisted of blue-collar workers, low-income families, and many African American residents. People moving into the Love Canal area were not told of any dangers when they purchased their homes and, when the disaster became known, they had their life savings and equity tied up in their homes. They could not leave their homes, sell them, rent them, or give them away.

SPOTLIGHT ON RESEARCH

Technological Disaster on the Pigeon River

Hussein Soliman (1996) chronicled the struggle between the people of Cocke County, Tennessee, a community in the Appalachain mountains and the Champion Paper Company of Canton, North Carolina. This is a poor community: In 1990, almost 26 percent of the entire population of Cocke County received food stamps, there was a high percentage of low birthweight babies, and there was a high infant mortality rate. In 1908, the Champion Paper Company began production near the Pigeon River, which flows into Tennessee. Immediately, the water below the plant became hot and colored; it had a low level of oxygen and smelled like rotten eggs. The fish started dying out. Above the plant, the water was clear and teeming with fish.

The battle between the people who lived along the Pigeon River and the company has spanned more than 90 years. Studies have been done of the river numerous times, followed by promises from the company to reduce the pollution. After a communitywide lawsuit in 1991, Champion offered a settlement. The plaintiffs refused when the offer came to less than $1,200 per property owner.

People need to work and, in our market economy, companies have to make enough profit to remain in business. Where do we draw the line between the risk of technological disaster and the well-being of a community?

Soliman, H. H. (1996). Community responses to chronic technological disaster: The case of the Pigeon River. In C. L. Street & S. A. Murty (Eds.), *Research on social work and disasters* (pp. 89–107). New York: Haworth Press.

Ali (2002), from his analysis of the toxic fire in Hamilton, Ontario, discussed several key features of "disaster incubation"—issues surrounding environmental risks that increase the probability of a technological disaster. These features include (1) lax enforcement of regulations related to land use and building and property codes; and (2) the desire for industry, with its jobs and capital, makes "special deals" reasonable, such as tax incentives, rezoning, and the suspension of some land-use regulations. The result is a climate in which "growth machine entrepreneurs" (Ali, p. 143) can flourish. Sometimes, because of an industry's role in the economic survival of a community, there may be passive toleration of practices that have long-term negative consequences on the health and well-being of the people and environment. Ultimately, practices that set the stage for technological disaster are likely to occur in areas with the greatest poverty and among people without the political influence to fight back effectively or to recognize early that the seeds for a future disaster are being sown.

Touching Reality "Living with a Technological Disaster" invites you to imagine what it would be like for you to experience a technological disaster; then, it invites you to consider what it would be like to be poor, without transportation, and so on, and experience the same disaster.

SUMMARY

Technological and natural disasters differ in a variety of ways, all of which point to the differences in their effects: suddenness, power, predictability, low point, effects, responsibility, uncertainty, social constructionism, corrosive community, and chronic stress. In addition, for many types of technological disasters, environmental advocacy becomes part of a community's response.

According to some researchers, technological disasters may be inevitable, not avoidable—whether they are nuclear and toxic spills, mass transport disasters, dam disasters, or the collapse of bridges and buildings. They cite three primary reasons: (1) technological advances are too complicated and varied to understand fully, (2) small problems trigger other problems in a quickly escalating cascade of events impossible to predict or control, and (3) plans to avert failure are inherently flawed because of a lack of information. These problems, however, do not argue against planning; rather, they mean that plans must be flexible and open to change.

Secondhand exposure to technological disasters is a by-product of the extensive news coverage such disasters typically receive. Technological disasters often are national in scope, as people tune in to television reports that provide on-site and up-to-date coverage for long periods. "Flashbulb memories," regardless of their fidelity to the disaster, etch the event into the national consciousness.

The effects of technological disasters can be seen in the kinds of questions they raise for people exposed to them, and their short- and long-term outcomes for both those exposed and their communities. Whereas natural disasters tend to provoke a "therapeutic community" in which citizens help one another, technological disasters tend to create a "corrosive community" in which different community factions argue about how the disaster should be defined, what long-term outcomes are likely, how the disaster should be dealt with, and how litigation should proceed.

Finally, evidence is available to support the conclusion that technological disasters occur with greater frequency in low rather than high socioeconomic areas.

Living with a Technological Disaster

If possible, complete this Touching Reality with several people with whom you can share reactions.

Either read the following guided imagery slowly, imagining each part as you read, or tape-record it and, with your eyes closed to help you visualize events, listen to your recording.

Merle Smith, Chapel Hill, North Carolina, Fire Department, provided technical assistance for this exercise. All of the facts of this event are technically correct and could unfold as described here.

> A truck loaded with liquid chlorine is traveling south on the major road into your city. The truck's brakes have failed, and the driver is losing control. There are several other vehicles on the road, not far from the truck. As they realize that the driver is having difficulties, they give the truck more space.
>
> The driver sideswipes some utility poles to see if he can start decreasing the truck's speed. The poles break off. Imagine that you are at home, unaware of the unfolding events.
>
> Your electricity goes out. What is your reaction?
>
> [Pause.]
>
> The driver loses control of the truck. The truck hits a pole and flies off the road; its tank ruptures. Liquid chlorine starts pouring out onto the road. As the chlorine meets the air, it goes through a chemical reaction, expanding into a gas 400 times greater than the volume of the liquid.

> The gas billows out from the truck, but because the gas is much heavier than air, it does not move quickly, even though there is a breeze.
>
> When the truck hit the pole, it dug deep holes in the ground, and broke the telephone cables buried underground.
>
> Your phone goes out, in addition to your electricity. What is your reaction now?
>
> [Pause.]
>
> As the chlorine gas billows around the area, any vegetation it touches immediately dies. The driver is overcome quickly by the gas, and will die soon.
>
> Birds start falling out of the sky when the gas reaches them. The drivers of the cars near the accident run away from their vehicles, coughing, and experiencing problems with their eyes, as they try to escape the gas. The outside finish of their cars begins to bubble where the gas is very thick.
>
> Someone has called law enforcement. Hazardous Material (Haz-Mat) personnel realize very quickly that this situation is life threatening, and begin an immediate, mandatory evacuation of the area where the cloud of chlorine gas may float.
>
> Your home is in that area. A law enforcement officer comes to your home and tells you that you have to leave in the next five to 10 minutes before you are overcome by chlorine gas, and that it will kill you if you stay.

cont'd

You can take small pets but nothing else that you cannot fit in your car in five minutes.

Now you are hurrying to get to your car and move what you can. The officer cannot tell you how long you will be gone. You decide to look for a hotel because you do not know too many people in the area.

What is your reaction as you pack hurriedly to escape from the danger?

[Pause.]

Town administrators do not have enough time to open shelters because the evacuation is so fast.

Officials realize that the cloud is heading for the area elementary and middle schools. They make the decision to line up buses and drive the children to a nearby safe city. Parents are not allowed to pick up their children from school, to ensure better control of the children and their locations.

Consider that you have children in school; what is your reaction now?

[Pause.]

Traffic out of town is backing up. People are nervous.

Local businesses start shutting down as the gas begins to move toward the center of town.

Farmers fear for their crops. Their livestock are in mortal danger.

Officials realize now that when the truck crashed, chlorine spilled into the area's water supply. They make the decision to shut down the outlet valves that supply water to people in the city and nearby towns.

[Pause.]

Time passes. It has been almost a week since the chlorine gas leak occurred. The cloud is dissipating very slowly. It has been around for several days. You have been staying with friends or in a hotel, and you are running out of money. Officials are saying that it may take as long as two more weeks for the cloud to go away completely.
What is your reaction now?

If you complete this Touching Reality with others, discuss your reactions. If you complete this alone, think about your reactions to this type of disaster.

Now, consider how you (and others, if you are in a group) might respond to this situation if you were:

- Hearing or sight impaired, mobility impaired, or mentally disabled?
- Poor, without transportation or money to stay in a hotel, or with no family to turn to?
- A foster parent, or foster child without clear connections to your birth family, and with some legal restrictions regarding movement out of the area?
- A person who works or lives in a nursing home, detention facility, hospital, or prison?
- A person who does not speak the local language, or does not speak it adequately?
- A farmer, or a businessperson?
- A child who is frequently left alone, or whose parents are alcohol or crack addicts?

What kind of planning might you think is necessary to deal with this type of incident?

REFERENCES

Ali, S. H. (2002). Disaster and the political economy of recycling: Toxic fire in an industrial city. *Social Problems, 49*, 129–149.

Arata, C. M., Picou, J. S., Johnson, G. D., & McNally, T. S. (2000). Coping with technological disaster: An application of the Conservation of Resources model to the Exxon Valdez oil spill. *Journal of Traumatic Stress, 13*, 23–39.

Baum, A., Fleming, R., & Davidson, L. M. (1983). Natural disaster and technological catastrophe. *Environment and Behavior, 15*, 333–354.

Belter, R., Dunn, S., & Jeney, P. (1991). The psychological impact of Hurricane Hugo on children: A needs assessment. *Advanced Behavioral Research Therapy, 13*, 155–161.

Bennett, G. (2000). Railway signals passed at danger: Psychology matters. *British Medical Journal, 7248*, 1549.

Bequette, F. (1996, April). Chernobyl today. *UNESCO Courier, 49*, 43–45.

Blom, G. E. (1986). A school disaster: Intervention and research aspects. *Journal of the American Academy of Child Psychiatry, 25*, 336–345.

Breton, J.-J., Valla, J.-P., & Lambert, J. (1993). Industrial disaster and mental health of children and their parents. *Journal of the American Academy of Child and Adolescent Psychiatry, 32*, 438–445.

Bullard, R. D. (1994). *Unequal protection: Environmental justice and commentaries of color.* San Francisco: Sierra Club Books.

Clarke, L., & Perrow, C. (1999). Prosaic organizational failure. In H. K. Anheier. (Ed.), *When things go wrong: Organizational failures and breakdowns* (pp. 179–196). Thousand Oaks, CA: Sage Publications.

Curwood, S. (Executive Producer). (1999a, March 26). A resident reminisces. *Living on earth.* Washington, DC: National Public Radio.

Curwood, S. (Executive Producer). (1999b, March 26). Three Mile Island: 20 years later. *Living on earth.* Washington, DC: National Public Radio.

Erikson, K. T. (1977). *Everything in its path: Destruction of community in the Buffalo Creek Flood.* New York: Simon and Schuster.

Erikson, K. T. (1998). Trauma at Buffalo Creek. *Society, 35*, 153–160.

Evan, W. M., & Manion, M. (2002). *Minding the machines—Preventing technological disasters.* Englewood Cliffs, NJ: Prentice Hall.

Gill, D. A., & Picou, J. S. (1998). Technological disaster and chronic community stress. *Society and Natural Resources, 11*, 795–816.

Green, B. L., Grace, M. C., Vary, M. G., & Kramer, T. L. (1994). Children of disaster in the second decade: A 17-year follow-up of Buffalo Creek survivors. *Journal of the American Academy of Child and Adolescent Psychiatry, 33*, 71–79.

Green, B. L., Korol, M., Grace, M. C., Vary, M. G., Leonard, A. C., Gleser, G. C., & Smitson-Cohen, S. (1991). Children and disaster: Age, gender, and parental effects on PTSD symptoms. *Journal of the American Academy of Child and Adolescent Psychiatry, 30*, 945–951.

Handford, H. A., Mayes, S. D., Mattison, R. E., Humphrey, F. J., Bagnato, S., Bixler, E. O., & Kales, J. D. (1986). Child and parent reactions to the Three Mile Island nuclear accident. *Journal of the American Academy of Child Psychiatry, 25*, 346–356.

Havenaar, I. M., Rumiantseva, G. M., & van den Bout, J. (1994). Mental health problems in the Chernobyl area. *Journal of Russian and East European Psychiatry, 27*(2), 83–91.

Honig, R. G., Grace, M. C., Lindy, J. D., & Newman, C. J. (1993). Portraits of survival: A twenty-year follow-up of the children of Buffalo Creek. *Psychoanalytic Study of the Child, 48*, 327–355.

Honig, R. G., Grace, M. C., Lindy, J. C., Newman, C. J., & Titchener, J. L. (1999a). Assessing the long-term effects of disasters occurring during childhood and adolescence: Questions of perspective and methodology. In M. Sugar (Ed.), *Trauma and adolescence* (pp. 203–224). Madison, CT: International Universities Press.

Honig, R. G., Grace, M. C., Lindy, J. C., Newman, C. J., & Titchener, J. L. (1999b). Assessing long-term effects of trauma: Diagnosing symptoms of avoidance and numbing. *American Journal of Psychiatry, 156,* 483–485.

Johnson, I. C. (1990–1991). Nightmare on the Great Western, 1957. *Beaver, 70*(6), 17–22.

Kim, S. (1998, September 21). Love Canal by-product is tech disaster. *Disaster News Network.* Retrieved August 23, 2003, from http://www.disasternews.net/hot/9-21-98_nylovecanal.shtml

Klingman, A., Goldstein, Z., & Lerner, P. (1991). Adolescents' response to nuclear threat: Before and after the Chernobyl accident. *Journal of Youth and Adolescence 20,* 519–530.

Korol, M., Kramer, T. L., Grace, M. C., & Green, B. L. (2002). Dam break: Long-term follow-up of children exposed to the Buffalo Creek disaster. In A. M. La Greca, W. K. Silverman, E. M. Vernvberg, & M. C. Roberts (Eds.), *Helping children cope with disasters and terrorism* (pp. 241–257). Washington, DC: American Psychological Association.

Kroll-Smith, J. S., & Couch, S. R. (1993). Technological hazards: Social responses as traumatic stressors. In J. P. Wilson & B. Raphael (Eds.), *International handbook of traumatic stress* (pp. 79–91). New York: Plenum Press.

Leonard, D. (2000, April 3). Bhopal ghosts (still) haunt Union Carbide. *Fortune, 141,* 27–28.

Milgram, N. A., & Toubiana, Y. H. (1996). Children's selective coping after a bus disaster: Confronting behavior and perceived support. *Journal of Traumatic Stress, 9,* 687–702.

Milgram, N. A., Toubiana, Y. H., Klingman, A., & Raviv, A. (1988). Situational exposure and personal loss in children's acute and chronic stress reactions to a school bus disaster. *Journal of Traumatic Stress, 1,* 339–352.

Miller, D. W. (1999, October 15). Sociology, not engineering, may explain our vulnerability to technological disaster. *Chronicle of Higher Education,* p. A19.

Monahon, C. (1993). *Children and trauma: A guide for parents and professionals.* New York: John Wiley & Sons.

Perrow, C. (1999). *Normal accidents: Living with high risk technologies.* Princeton, NJ: Princeton University Press.

Pfefferbaum, B. (2001). The impact of the Oklahoma City bombing on children in the community. *Military Medicine, 166*(12, Suppl. 2), 49–50.

Pfefferbaum, B., Nixon, S.-J., Tivis, R. D., Doughty, D. E., Pynoos, R. S., Gurwitch, R. H., & Foy, D. W. (2001). Television exposure in children after a terrorist incident. *Psychiatry, 64,* 202–211.

Pool, R. (1997, July). When failure is not an option. *Technology Review, 100*(5), 38–45.

Prince William Sound Regional Citizen's Advisory Council. (2000). *Coping with technological disasters: A user friendly guidebook.* Anchorage, AK: Author. Retrieved December 15, 2001, from http://www.pwsrcac.org/CWTD/thebook.html

Pynoos, R. S., & Nader, K. (1988). Psychological first aid and treatment approach to children exposed to community violence: Research implications. *Journal of Traumatic Stress, 1,* 445–473.

Rogge, M. E. (1996). Social vulnerability to toxic risk. In C. L. Streeter & S. A. Murty (Eds.), *Research on social work and disasters* (pp. 109–129). New York: Haworth Press.

Sinha, M. M. (1990, July). *Technological risk and public policy: A case study of the Bhopal gas disaster.* Paper presented at the meeting of the International Sociological Association, Madrid.

Sleek, S. (1998, June). After the storm, children play out fears. *APA Monitor,* p. 12.

Soliman, H. H. (1996). Community responses to chronic technological disaster: The case of the Pigeon river. In C. L. Streeter & S. A. Murty (Eds.), *Research on social work and disasters* (pp. 89–107). New York: Haworth Press.

Stallard, P., & Law, F. (1993). Screening and psychological debriefing of adolescent survivors of life threatening events. *British Journal of Psychiatry, 163,* 660–665.

Tangri, N. (1999, November 16). Bhopal victims sue Union Carbide over '84 disaster. Retrieved August 23, 2003, from http://lists.essential.org/dioxin-l/msg01318.html

Terr, L. C., Bloch, D. A., Michel, B. A., Shi, H., Reinhardt, J. A., & Metayer, S. (1996). Children's memories in the wake of Challenger. *American Journal of Psychiatry, 153,* 618–625.

Terr, L. C., Bloch, D. A., Michel, B. A., Shi, H., Reinhardt, J. A., & Metayer, S. (1999). Children's symptoms in the wake of Challenger: A field study of distant-traumatic effects and an outline of related conditions. *American Journal of Psychiatry, 156,* 1536–1544.

Thompson, J. (1986). Psychological consequences of disaster: Analogies for the nuclear case. In F. Solomon & R. Q. Marston (Eds.), *The medical implications of nuclear war* (pp. 290–316). Washington, DC: National Academy Press.

UNEP [United Nations Environment Programme]. *Technological disasters.* Retrieved January 11, 2004, from http://www.uneptie.org/pc/apell/disasters/lists/technological.html

Vaughan, D. (1996). *The Challenger launch decision: Risky technology, culture, and deviance at NASA.* Chicago: University of Chicago Press.

Weick, K. E. (1991). The vulnerable system: An analysis of the Tenerife air disaster. In P. J. Frost & L. F. Moore (Eds.), *Reframing organizational culture* (pp. 117–130). Newbury Park, CA: Sage Publications.

White, T. G. (2001). The establishment of blame in the aftermath of a technological disaster. *National Forum, 81*(1), 24–29.

Wright, J. C., Kunkel, D., Pinon, M., & Huston, A. C. (1989). How children reacted to televised coverage of the space shuttle disaster. *Journal of Communication, 39*(2), 27–45.

Wroble, M. C., & Baum, A. (2002). Toxic waste spills and nuclear accidents. In A. M. La Greca, W. K. Silverman, E. M. Vernvberg, & M. C. Roberts (Eds.), *Helping children cope with disasters and terrorism* (pp. 207–221). Washington, DC: American Psychological Association.

Yule, W. (1993). Technology-related disasters. In C. F. Saylor (Ed.), *Children and disasters* (pp. 105–121). New York: Plenum Press.

Yule, W., Bolton, D., Udwin, O., Boyle, S., O'Ryan, D., & Nurrish, J. (2000). The long-term psychological effects of a disaster experienced in adolescence: I. The incidence and course of PTSD. *Journal of Child Psychology and Psychiatry, 41,* 503–512.

Yule, W., & Udwin, O. (1991). Screening child survivors for post-traumatic stress disorders: Experiences from the "Jupiter" sinking. *British Journal of Clinical Psychology, 30*(2), 131–138.

Yule, W., Udwin, O., & Bolton, D. (2002). Mass transportation disasters. In A. M. La Greca, W. K. Silverman, E. M. Vernberg, & M. C. Roberts (Eds.), *Helping children cope with disasters and terrorism* (pp. 223–239). Washington, DC: American Psychological Association.

Yule, W., Udwin, O., & Murdoch, K. (1990). The "Jupiter" sinking: Effects on children's fears, depression, and anxiety. *Journal of Child Psychology and Psychiatry, 31*, 1051–1061.

Zinner, E. S. (1999). The Challenger disaster: Group survivorship on a national landscape. In E. S. Zinner & M. B. Williams (Eds.), *When a community weeps: Case studies in group survivorship.* (pp. 23–47). Philadelphia: Brunner/Mazel.

COMPLEX DISASTERS

CHAPTER OVERVIEW

After studying the material in this chapter, you should

- be familiar with the range of events that fall under the heading "complex disaster"
- be conscious of the nature of threat to personal and social well-being that is posed by complex disasters
- understand the psychosocial needs of children who have been traumatized by organized violence
- be familiar with a variety of examples of psychosocial outcomes of war-affected and forced-migrant populations
- be familiar with the effects of complex disasters on children and families
- be familiar with the transgenerational effects of trauma
- understand the variety of active and passive methods children have for coping with complex disasters
- be aware of the dangers of "hate education"—the lessons learned about hating and fearing others—and the need for peace education.

The range of events included under the heading "complex disaster" is much broader than the range of events for natural or technological disasters. The many types of community violence, civil war, government-sponsored terrorism, terrorism between nations, and war between nations are all examples of complex disasters, of events that are the result of human design or motivation.

From one perspective, we may argue that natural disasters are caused by "a god" or "nature," that technological disasters are caused by people's unintentional (not purposeful) actions, and that complex disasters are caused by people's intentional (purposeful) actions—that they are, in fact, "unpredictable acts of human violence" (Vogel & Vernberg, 1993, p. 485). This is not to imply, however, that natural, technological, and complex disasters are unrelated. A disaster can be a mix of two, or even of all three. Consider these examples:

- Pan Am Flight 103 that exploded over Lockerbie, Scotland, was a plane crash (technological disaster) caused by a bomb placed on the plane for the explicit purpose of blowing it up (complex disaster). The cause was human and the event was purposeful and intentional.
- Famines (natural disaster) may occur when crops are destroyed by bad weather (natural disaster). However, many famines that have occurred in recent years, for example, in Mozambique, are the result of civil strife and large-scale refugee movements within the country (complex disaster).
- Houses that fail to withstand the wind and rain of a hurricane may collapse. Did the natural disaster (the hurricane) cause the technological disaster (the building collapse)? Perhaps the houses were not built

"up to standard" because the builder wanted to increase profits. Does the builder's motivation make the disaster "complex"?

THE COMPLEX DISASTER OF ORGANIZED VIOLENCE

For the past 100 years, human-made violence has been rampant, manifesting itself in many shapes and forms, and with an escalating impact on noncombatant (as well as combatant) populations. Consider the following statistics compiled by the United Nations Children's Fund (UNICEF, 1996a) and the U.S. Agency for International Development (1997):

- In World War I, civilians accounted for 14 percent of the victims, by World War II it was close to 70 percent, and by the 1990s almost 90 percent of those afflicted by war and its aftermath were civilians.
- Most contemporary wars are not between states but within them—that is, they are civil wars. Today's conflicts are often bound up with ethnic differences; under these circumstances, warring groups target any member of the other group as a present or future enemy, which can lead to genocide and what is called "ethnic cleansing."
- Many combatants target civilians by damaging hospitals, schools, water supplies, and food-production areas. As a result, far more children die slow deaths from malnutrition and disease than die from bombs and bullets.
- In 1960 there were an estimated 2 million refugees in the world. By 1997, 14.5 million people were refugees outside their own borders as a result of war and violence, and an additional 5.4 million people were internally displaced; that is, although they did not leave their country, they fled from their homes.

The wars in the former Yugoslavia and in Rwanda created situations in which adults and children were exposed to violence and terror on an unprecedented scale, with a reality of war for which they and the international community were unprepared, a reality that involved new instruments of war and new social categories of victims (Miosso, 1996).

War, terrorism, and other forms of organized violence damage our ability to trust others and invalidate the assumption that we live in a relatively safe world. If we cannot trust with impunity, any stranger could be our enemy.

If a person is exposed to cruelty—especially if in close proximity to an attacker who appears to be sadistic—that person's basic comprehension of acceptable human behavior is destroyed. Exposure to the brutality of a complex disaster evokes the danger of emotional leakage or contagion of aggression from perpetrator to victim (Ayalon, 1998a). The child–victim's surging aggression is fed by frustration and reinforced by perceptions of the aggressor as an authority whose power is derived from absolute physical advantage. Ongoing encounters with such perceptions of authority may damage or even break a person's acquired fragile psychological barrier against his or her innate aggressive drives, which is the barrier that safeguards the very heart of civilization. This breakdown is especially dangerous for children who may identify with the aggressor and, in a paradoxical way, cast the terrorists into the children's role models (Ayalon & Waters, 2002).

Hate sows the seeds of complex disasters. Spotlight on Research "Teaching Hatred" describes how children living in Northern Ireland are taught to hate.

SPOTLIGHT ON RESEARCH

Teaching Hatred

How do Roman Catholic and Protestant children in Northern Ireland come to hate each other? To answer this question, Paul Connolly (1998) surveyed 352 children, between ages three and six, at 44 elementary schools and nurseries throughout Northern Ireland. He showed the children pictures and objects and asked them what they knew about each and whether they liked or disliked what they saw. Subjects with sectarian connotations included Irish and British flags, Protestant Orangemen parading, different soccer teams' uniforms, and Catholic girls in an Irish dancing class.

Results indicated that children as young as three years old had already learned to fear and loathe each other's communities. Connolly (1998) blamed this hatred on the children's parents, and on Northern Ireland's religiously segregated school system (only 4 percent of primary-age children in Northern Ireland are educated in religiously mixed schools). His research team found that by age five, boys and girls from the British Protestant and Irish Catholic sides of society have absorbed their communities' prejudices. (Children at the age of five enter the elementary schools that keep them almost entirely segregated, in two separate systems.) The proportion of children making overtly sectarian statements rises exponentially when they are five and six, that is, during the first two years of formal schooling.

The Northern Ireland report concluded that youngsters in divided societies need specially designed educational packages to counter the parochial prejudice of their immediate environment.

Connolly, P. (1998). *Racism, gender identities and young children: Social relations in a multi-ethnic, inner-city primary school.* London: Routledge.

CHILDREN AS DIRECT TARGETS

Graça Machel (2001), Mozambique's Minister for Education until 1989, and a vehement advocate for children's human rights, claimed that there is a war on children, that children (and their families) are not merely "collateral damage" but are being deliberately killed, mutilated, and violated by people who consider them their future enemies. During the 1990s, some 2 million children were killed in wars—333,000 in Angola alone—and 490,000 children were killed in wars in Mozambique between 1982 and 1986 (Bellamy, 1996). During the same time, more than 4 million children were physically disabled because of bombings, land mines, and torture; 12 million were displaced by wars and other violence; 5 million were in refugee camps; and more than 1 million were orphaned or separated from their parents (Bellamy; UNICEF, 1996a). A study on the effects of land mines in 206 communities in Afghanistan, Bosnia, Cambodia, and Mozambique found that one household in 20 reported a member of the household had been a victim of a land mine, with a third of those victims dying as a result; one in 10 was a child (Andersson, Palha da Sousa, & Paredes, 1995).

Child Soldiers

Children, including very young children, are being deployed as soldiers in over 30 countries (Goodwin-Gill & Cohn, 1994). More than 200,000 children under the age of 16 fight in wars in 25 countries every year, taking part in torture and executions, sometimes of their own relatives. Most of them go through a process of indoctrinations, of dehumanizing the enemy and preparing to die for a cause that is often beyond their understanding. Boothby (1992) reported that Iranian children as young as eight years old have been recruited and trained as martyrs for Islam and have been compelled to walk in rows in front of tanks to clear the land of mine fields.

Children volunteered, or were coerced, into active involvement in 33 conflicts during 1995 and 1996 alone (Brett, McCallin, & O'Shea, 1996). During the early years of the war in Afghanistan, for example, 10 percent of combatants were under age 16, and 17 percent were between 16 and 18. Such "war apprentices" were abundant in Sri Lanka, the Iran–Iraq war, the Palestinian Intifada, in Northern Ireland, Angola, and Zambia (Hundeide, 1994).

For children taken from their families to be trained as soldiers, either by "their" side of the armed conflict or by the "other" side, the world of the war is the reality that gives structure and meaning to their lives and defines their identity. Socialization into "war culture" may render them incapable of being socialized into the postwar civil society when weapons are set down and peace is negotiated. As one child soldier put it, "The first time you are forced to kill, it is terrible and you feel guilty afterwards, then after a few killings it becomes a matter of routine. Now sometimes I enjoy the killing, it gives me a feeling of power" (Hundeide, 1995, p. 5).

Children separated from their families are at high risk of underage military recruitment. Because of their participation in conflict, they lose opportunities for education. On demobilization, lack of education may mean that they are drawn into child labor or commercial sexual exploitation.

Many child soldiers, having lost their parents and relatives, become deeply attached to their leaders, who are seen as their sole source of food, shelter, and protection. When their leaders are killed or abandon them, the child soldiers may regress into utter helplessness. In addition, because these child soldiers have been compelled to commit violent atrocities and murders against unarmed civilians, often as a ceremonial "rite of passage" into the combat forces, they have great difficulty returning to their families and communities. On re-entry, they may be prosecuted and sent to prison (Cantwell, 1997).

Sexual War Crimes against Women and Girls

Violence against women, especially rape, has added its own brand of shame to recent wars. Girls have been singled out for rape, imprisonment, torture, and execution (Korn, 1999; Yuksel, 1993). Rape is a common part of violent conflict but is almost invisible (Swiss & Giller, 1993). Underreporting of rape by its victims is probably universal because of rape's association with stigma and shame. In Arab or Islamic cultures, for example, the honor of a family is located in the bodies of the women, in their virginity, and in their modest deportment. To rape a woman is thus a way of penetrating the inner sanctum of her entire family's honor (Makiya, 1993).

Military and other powerful males often target women and girls for abuse and exploitation. Sexual violence sometimes occurs with the collusion of the community's male members, in the form of bartering women or girls for arms, ammunition, and food, or in exchange for documentation. Unaccompanied children are particularly susceptible to exploitation and may suffer sexual abuse by camp workers or from members of their foster families (Boothby, 1992).

Research conducted by UNICEF (1996a, 1996b) found that systematic rape is often used as a weapon of war in ethnic cleansing. More than 20,000 Muslim girls and women have been raped in Bosnia since fighting

began in April 1992; their families have forced many impregnated girls to bear the enemy's child. In some raids in Rwanda, virtually every adolescent girl who survived an attack by the militia was subsequently raped; their families and communities ostracized many of those girls who became pregnant. Ultimately, some abandoned their babies; others committed suicide. Children conceived in rape and born into violence often suffer social ostracism. Added to this trauma is that sexual violence brings with it a high risk of infection from sexually transmitted diseases, including HIV/AIDS, for the young mothers and their infants.

In his report on Rwanda, Cantwell (1997) wrote that even many years after they witnessed genocide and suffered systematic rape, girls who suffered this abuse, and the children born as a result, live with unresolved problems. Many of the children born as a result of rape are abandoned at birth, and many are stigmatized and persecuted by their own people. This is the case in Angola, Bosnia-Herzegovina, and most other warring countries (Ayalon, 1995).

Indirect Exposure to Organized Violence

Responses to living in dangerous environments differ from child to child, depending on individual factors such as age, biological sex, loss of family members, relatives, or home, and the availability of family, friends, and community support systems. Differences in findings of outcome studies of war's impact on children reflect the different degrees of exposure to stressors and even the manner in which stressors are perceived and defined (Kuterovac, Dyregrov, & Stuvland, 1994). Some children can be sheltered and protected from the actual fighting, and information about it may be mediated by parents and peers or filtered through mass media. Some may be proud of their fighting fathers and brothers; others may mourn the death of these family members. Children may be randomly targeted by terrorists, taken hostage, or crowded in shelters to hide from air raids and rockets. In countries involved in prolonged military conflicts, such as Israel (Ayalon, 1989a, 1989b), Lebanon (Bredy, 1983), and Northern Ireland (Cairns, 1987; Fraser, 1973), countries where children are relatively protected in a functioning community, they are nevertheless aware of the looming danger and carnage and are traumatized by vicarious exposure to war damages. Children may be exposed when their homes, schools, and neighborhoods are destroyed by shelling; they may live under the threat of terrorism; they may participate in random evacuations from a community in peril; and they may witness casualties directly or secondhand (that is, through mass media) (Macksoud, Dyregrov, & Raundalen, 1993; Rosenblatt, 1992; Schlenger et al., 2002).

Ripple Effects of the Traumatic Experience of Organized Violence

When acts of organized violence or terrorist attacks affect people directly, an immeasurable number of them are caught up in the traumatic ripple effects. Just as a stone cast into a pool of water causes ripples to spread, the disaster causes ripples to spread throughout the entire community (Ayalon, 1993). Families who lost their loved ones and friends are victimized, as are the rescue workers who come in close contact with the horrors of death and injury, including medical staff, social workers, teachers, and psychologists. Eyewitnesses, including journalists, also are traumatized (Feinstein, Owen, & Blair, 2002).

Many children become "near miss" victims by their physical or psychological proximity to their dead, injured, or orphaned

peers: Their subconscious minds realize indelibly that "it could have happened to me." Many of them are hidden victims who carry unseen scars. Neither they nor their parents may realize how wounded they are, how the damage inflicted on them when they watched a lethal attack is compounded by the imposed passivity of having to watch or listen helplessly to the sights and sounds of death and destruction. Family, school, law enforcement agencies, and mental health professionals are frequently at risk of neglecting the needs of witnesses. It is important for helpers who plan services to identify those vicariously affected by their geographical proximity to the incident's site or by their social or psychological proximity to those directly affected because they, too, are at risk (Soskis & Ochberg, 1982). At the same time, it is paramount to identify those agents in the community who are available to give support, ranging from professional caretakers to volunteers and peers.

FAMILIES IN COMPLEX DISASTERS

Complex disasters often create profound social changes in family composition and customs, in patterns of labor, in the distribution of rural and urban populations, and in agricultural and industrial patterns. To understand the impact of complex disasters, a helper must have a family-oriented understanding of traumatization, which includes new categories of families: families of the missing, families of the killed, families of the wounded, families of detainees or ex-detainees, refugee or displaced families, and returnee families. Reactions differ for each type of family (Jensen, 1994).

Families from which children or adults have disappeared insist on hoping for the return of the missing family member,

Postwar Devastation:
Evidence from Three Countries

Angola: After achieving independence from Portugal in 1975, Angola entered a 16-year civil war between government forces (FMLA) and rebel forces (UNITA). Of the total population of 10.5 million, more than 3 million people were either displaced or directly affected by the war in some other way. An estimated 100,000 children were orphaned, and large numbers of children suffered the shock of attack, displacement, separation from parents, destruction of home, pervasive hunger, inadequate health care, and crippling accidents from land mines. Nearly 10,000 children were forcibly mobilized. In the first years of the 21st century, tensions have risen, and fighting has begun again between FMLA and UNITA forces. USAID and Save the Children® work with the government of Angola to help document, trace, and reunite children with their families. By 2003, USAID had helped reintegrate more than 300,000 traumatized children in eight provinces.

Kosovo: Following 10 years of political oppression and two years of war, the prevalence of PTSD in Kosovo is estimated to be 25 percent, which is an extremely high percentage for any population. The most frequent symptoms observed in children from ages five through 18 are concentration problems, separation anxiety, enuresis, hyperactivity, nightmares, various somatic complaints (which are seen especially in older adolescents), generalized anxiety, and behavioral problems associated with alcohol and substance abuse. More than 400 international aid agencies operated in Kosovo immediately after international forces entered the country; some worked directly with children, some trained teachers and other professionals to deal with traumatized children and symptoms, and some trained parents to deal with their children. The intervention programs lasted two years; there was no strategy to sustain them (Areliu, 2002).

Croatia: Although war ended in 1995, Croatia still carries the negative consequences of a five-year period of war (Miljevic-Ridicki, 2002). During the war, 303 children were registered as killed, 1,280 as wounded, and 35 as imprisoned or missing. Heavy and light artillery weapons, shrapnel bombs, and rocket fire inflicted the majority of injuries. During the war, there was the stress caused by displacement, and after the war, there is the stress caused by return. The most frequent behavioral symptoms observed by psychologists include nightmares; difficulty falling asleep; heart, stomach, and allergy problems; tics; speaking difficulties; and enuresis. Other problems include withdrawal, aggression, weakening of contact with family members, spitefulness, hyperactivity, self-inflicted injuries, and problems concentrating. The primary emotion is fear—fear of separation, general fearfulness, and fear of certain objects and situations. Symptoms depend on age, with younger children having more separation fears and adolescents showing more aggression and spite.

although often the family member is dead. Without a body, or other significant proof of the death, the family continues searching for their loved one, which makes it impossible for them to begin the mourning process and to heal.

Families in which a member has been killed, and which has proof of the killing such as a body, can begin the mourning process; however, their reactions are usually a mixture of sorrow and anger. In addition, the loss of the family member may trigger devastating social and economic changes to the family.

Families with a wounded member, who is often the father, may suffer from the wounded member's unemployment, retreat into alcoholism, and disappointment. The family dynamic may shift dramatically compared with predisaster conditions, both between the spouses and between the parents and their children.

Refugee and displaced families are preoccupied with their loss of home, neighbors, and country (internal refugees also "lose their country," but in more of a metaphoric than actual sense). These refugees are uncertain if they will ever return home. Social and economic conditions of families living in collective centers, camps, or even private accommodations are often dreadful compared with their lives before the disaster. Refugee families that survive the transfer and adapt to the host country face new problems. Plans for repatriation and resettlement are the necessary bridges to avoid a repetition of violence (Arcel, 1994; Stuvland, 1994).

Children and Families Facing Threats of Unconventional War

During the Gulf War, which occurred in the first two months of 1991, the Israeli population was subjected to threats of chemical warfare, threats that were taken very seriously with the launching of "conventional" missile attacks. Civil defense orders confined the general population to their homes for long hours in sealed rooms during air raids, with special instructions for them to wear gas masks as protection against possible chemical missile attacks.

The use of gas masks activated the worst fears of total annihilation: Panic symptoms caused approximately 12 deaths by suffocation or heart attack. Milder panic cases occurred when "mask refusal" symptoms developed.

Family members, who sometimes included extended family members, were confined to their homes for long periods, during which time they were disconnected from friends and other support systems.

Living under these conditions created "forced intimacy" that increased the possibility of family conflict and disrupted the precarious balance between togetherness and separateness that each family system tries to maintain. Teenagers, busy with disengaging themselves from the family grip, reacted with rage or regression to the imposed intimacy and return to dependency. Divorced or separated parents were drawn back into the family home, driven by an obligation to protect their children, thus interfering with their efforts to draw apart and establish a new independence. The confinement became a hothouse for aggression, especially in families where prewar interaction had been unstable (Ayalon, 1997; Ayalon & Zimrin, 1992).

Family members coped in a variety of ways, but two methods were prominent: (1) They took an active leadership or assistance-to-others role; and (2) they found comfort in a support group, most often within the increased cohesiveness in the family.

Families returning from exile or displacement may find that their house and land no longer exist and that old friends and neighbors are gone. Someone else may occupy their home. In addition to these problems, returnee families may be met with hostility from their former neighbors and friends, who consider them deserters, as ones who left to "live a life of luxury elsewhere while we stayed back here in danger."

Touching Reality "The Flight of Leila Habibi," on page 200 which uses fictitious names, presents the true story of a girl and her family's flight from Iran in 1983, when they were forced to leave their homeland because of religious persecution. Their flight took them to Pakistan, then to Spain, and finally to the United States. As you read their story, think about what it would be like to make their journey, and what helped them survive their ordeal.

Intergenerational Transmission of Trauma

Do parents transmit their trauma to the next generation? Research with second-generation victims of the Holocaust and the Vietnam War supports the notion that the distress felt by those exposed to a complex disaster can be transmitted to the next generation (Danieli, 1980, 1998; Wardi, 1992), although the evidence is not consistent (Major, 1996). Natan Kellerman (2001), writing in a special issue of the *Israel Journal of Psychiatry and Related Sciences* on children of Holocaust survivors, noted that there is a disparity between what clinicians report and what researchers discover. Whereas clinicians offer accounts of distress in the second generation, researchers offer mixed findings. It seems that second-generation children of Holocaust survivors who do not seek therapy do not show any more signs of psychopathology than do others; however, the clinical population of offspring tends to share a particular profile including, among other things, a predisposition to posttraumatic stress disorder (PTSD).

In an interesting study on transgenerational effects, Zahava Solomon and her colleagues (Solomon, Kotler, & Mikulincer, 1988–1989) compared Israeli soldiers in the 1992 war in Lebanon, who were the children of Holocaust survivors, with a control group of soldiers who were not children of Holocaust survivors. Results showed that two and three years after their participation in the war in Lebanon, the children of Holocaust survivors suffered higher rates of PTSD than did the soldiers in the control group.

The question, of course, is "*How* is this intergenerational trauma transmitted?" Three studies provide some similar answers. One study described the communication of parental Holocaust survivors as often being characterized by obsessive retelling of stories or all-consuming silence and suggested that this, coupled with strong family ties, sets the stage for vicarious, secondary traumatization of children (Baranowsky, Young, Johnson-Douglas, Williams-Keeler, & McCarrey, 1998). A second study (Stein, 1995) found that the sons of those Vietnam War combat veterans who discussed their combat experiences with them in graphic, vivid language fell within the clinically disturbed range on a symptom checklist test. In addition, some of these sons exhibited PTSD symptoms that were similar to their fathers'. The third study confirmed the importance of parental communication. Children of Holocaust survivors may develop PTSD symptoms in response to hearing about their parents' traumatic experiences (Yehuda, Halligan, & Grossman, 2001). However, this study also found that in relation to a comparison

The Flight of Leila Habibi

In 1983, Leila Habibi was five years old. She and her parents and younger sister lived in Iran. Their life in Iran was comfortable and interesting. Mr. Habibi was a successful accountant, and Mrs. Habibi worked in the admissions office of the local university.

Life in Iran was very good for the Habibis, except for one thing. They were Baha'i, in a country where Moslem fundamentalists were moving into total control. Harassment, persecution, and "disappearances" were increasingly possible events. The Habibi family was in a very uncomfortable position.

Five-year-old Leila was told that her family was going on a "vacation." She did not understand why they could only take two bags for the entire family. She noticed there was a lot of crying. When she came into a room, people talked in hushed voices. Her mother was definitely in distress. The family maintained a façade of hopefulness when everyone knew something was wrong.

She remembers crying a lot, because she knew she was leaving many wonderful things.

The time came to leave. They left quietly and secretly, in the night. Leila had her small purse, into which she squashed all the treasures a five-year-old child would want. She learned that they were to go across the desert at night, by camel. She rode for nine very cold hours with her father. She remembers complaining and crying. Her father was curt, and kept saying, "Quiet or I'll be taken away." What Leila did not know until years later was that the guides had told her father that if she did not keep quiet they would kill her rather than allow her to risk all their lives.

When they finally stopped, Leila realized that all her treasures had fallen out of her purse. She cried and cried.

The family stopped in Pakistan. Leila did not like this strange place where she had to share a room with many people she did not know. There were large lizards everywhere, as common as cockroaches are in crowded cities. The man whose house they were in was domineering and required a strict adherence to the Muslim religion. She was afraid. The Habibis remained in Pakistan for 10 months. Next, the Habibis moved to Spain. This was much better. Leila found Spain quite beautiful and warm. She had her own room. About a month and a half after they arrived in Spain, though, they moved to Oklahoma to her uncle's home. After three months with her uncle, the Habibis moved to Texas, to a city near Dallas.

Leila immediately started school. She spoke no English. She went to the cafeteria, tried to eat green beans that she had never seen before, and got sick. She sensed that people were making fun of her, and she hated everything about the school. Leila had a grandmother back in Iran, and she missed her terribly. She kept asking to return to Iran to the life and the people she knew.

Mr. and Mrs. Habibi struggled very hard in the United States. Leila recollects that she learned English much faster than they did. Their first job on arriving in Texas, and for quite some time, was at a fast food restaurant.

cont'd

Leila remembers advice from her parents about succeeding and always doing her best. By second grade, things began to feel better. She describes herself as extremely competitive and somewhat arrogant. "If someone puts me down, I work harder to show the person I can do anything," she says.

Leila graduated from high school in Texas as class valedictorian. Her younger sister recently took her SATs and received a perfect score. Leila thinks that she will be valedictorian as well.

Leila is now in college. She describes herself as having a "crazy imagination." She sees herself as fiercely independent. When she was in high school, she was sure that she wanted to go to college far away from home. She does not get homesick. "I don't feel particularly tied to any place. I'm going to survive. I'll take care of me."

- Consider the risk and protective factors that you read about in previous chapters, especially chapter 2. What are the risk and protective factors exhibited by the family and by Leila?
- What issues are of the most concern to you about this family's resiliency?
- Westermeyer and Wahmanholm (1996), writing about refugee families, argued that children are both more vulnerable to psychological problems and more adaptive. They said, for example, that such families are able to learn the language and culture of the new country more quickly and easily than other family members. Does this seem to be true for the Habibi family?

group, adult offspring of Holocaust survivors showed significantly higher levels of self-reported childhood trauma, particularly emotional abuse, and neglect, which is largely attributable to parental PTSD.

Parents who are traumatized by a complex disaster, whether or not they suffer from PTSD, may communicate their trauma to their children in many ways. They may tell stories of their trauma—stories of combat, of cruelty suffered at the hands of an enemy, and of the death and destruction they witnessed—or they may not. The stories could traumatize their children, especially if the stories are extremely graphic and vivid. However, even if stories are not told, traumatized parents may behave in ways that hurt their children's psychological well-being.

Spotlight on Research "Children's Responses to Their Parents' Victimization" presents a researcher's analysis of the stories of children of Holocaust survivors.

COMMUNAL VIOLENCE

Children's development is damaged when they live in situations of chronic war or unrest—consider the following:

- *Children need to be rooted in the life of their community*. The unpredictability of war and terrorism make this stability very difficult, if not impossible.
- *Children need to be socially competent*. The constant danger of war and civil violence undermine this competence. Children may cease to believe that adults will be able to protect them. Basic trust is intrinsically damaged when the child cannot depend on the continuity of care from adults.
- *Children need to learn many ways to communicate with each other*. The stress of war may

SPOTLIGHT ON RESEARCH

Children's Responses to Their Parents' Victimization

Thirty years after the Holocaust, Robert Prince (1999), speaking with children of Holocaust survivors, was struck that "Not one child could remember a time when he did not have at least a dim awareness of his parents' experiences of persecution" (p.185). Whether the parents withheld all information about their experiences, or whether they repeated the same stories from the time their children were little, most children had only fragmentary knowledge of isolated details.

The responses of children to their parents' Holocaust accounts included "isolation, denial, horror, guilt, anger at the world, and anger at the parents for subjecting them to the horrors of the past" (Prince, 1999, p.186). Most children were extremely hesitant to question their parents directly and seemed to feel that to do so might cause their parents harm. Some children reported that knowledge of the parents' suffering was very painful for them and produced in them a need to distance themselves. At the same time, many children were in awe of their parents' ability to endure in the face of the horrific conditions in the concentration camps.

Several themes concerning the parent–child relationship emerged from the interviews: "the unavailability of the parents for their children's emotional needs, the extremely controlling and overprotective behavior of parents, and the induction of guilt feelings in the children" (Prince, 1999, p. 187). The most outstanding feature of all was the parents' communicating that the only thing of value left in their lives was their children.

The constant presence of concentration camp imagery and evidence of their parents' suffering constituted a prolonged, day-by-day exposure to the Holocaust and "exposure to their parents' state of having been traumatized was for at least some children of survivors, psychologically close to their having been in a concentration camp themselves" (Prince, 1999, p.190).

Prince, R. M. (1999). *The legacy of the Holocaust: Psychohistorical themes in the second generation.* New York: Other Press.

limit their capacity to adapt their communication to the variety of situations they encounter.

- *Children need a sense of wonder to sustain their cognitive development.* The horror of sustained violence erodes the sense of wonder a child may have and replaces it with disillusionment (Garbarino & Kostelny, 1996)

The need for stability, family strength, and hope for the future are necessary components of resiliency; however, "unfortunately, for many poor children in urban America, it is precisely this sense of past stability, historical continuity and hope for the future that is missing from the family and community environments in which their chronic exposure to communal violence takes place" (Marans, Berkman, & Cohen, 1996, p. 123). When the child experiences chronic violence, he or she gives up expecting safety within the family.

Continual traumatic events result in accumulated damage.

Normal development describes the toddler moving from direct enactment of his or her aggressive tendencies (such as biting and hitting), to the preschooler's fantasies of destruction, to the school-age child's acting out aggressive tendencies in sports, to the balance of affection and anger that mark adult relationships. Marans and his colleagues (1996) described situations in urban America in which a child's capacity to develop normally, to sublimate his or her aggressive tendencies, is undermined because the child's basic preconditions for feeling competent—including physical safety, stable relationships, and goal achievement—"are overwhelmed by poverty, family dysfunction, overstimulation and actual or threatened danger" (p. 107).

According to neurologists, chronic overstimulation affects brain functioning (Cohen, Perel, DeBellis, Friedman, & Putnam, 2002). Trauma arises when the child, whose brain stem development is not complete until age eight or nine, "cannot give meaning to dangerous experiences in the presence of overwhelming arousal" (Garbarino & Kostelny, 1996, p. 39). After continuous experiences of arousal, panic responses, and ongoing danger, the child begins to lose the ability to calm back down and remains continuously in a state of hypervigilance and heightened awareness. The downward spiral damages the hippocampus, and the deterioration continues. Children in a constant state of hypervigilance—continuously in "fight or flight" mode—have serious difficulty concentrating in school. They discontinue looking to adults for protection and lose opportunities for learning normal social competence. Even sleep is affected, and this, in turn, affects growth, health, and cognitive development.

Many children experience violence on a daily basis. They may live in neighborhoods where gun fighting is a regular occurrence; they may have seen relatives killed; they may live in households where they witness regular drug use, which places them close to people who have a history of violence; they may be abused or live with family members who are abused; they may live in households in which fighting is constant; or they may be members of gangs.

Certain groups of children may be most vulnerable to these daily exposures to violence, such as children who are very young, who have disabilities that affect their mobility or their ability to think clearly, and who have been separated from their primary caretakers. As access to social support decreases, these children experience decreases in their self-esteem, the feeling that they have the right to survive, their belief in their ability to help others, and their assurance of their own effectiveness.

THE EFFECTS OF COMPLEX DISASTERS ON CHILDREN

Swenson and Klingman (1993) offered a guide for looking at the direct, long-term, and indirect effects of these complex disasters by summarizing numerous studies of the effects of war (including the 1973 Yom Kippur War in Israel and the 1992 war in Lebanon) and political violence on children (including Palestinian children, children in South Africa, Mozambique, and Central America, and children in a Cambodian concentration camp). For example, many children exposed to the war in Lebanon had "symptoms of post-traumatic stress ... and feelings of betrayal that altered their sense of trust" (Swenson & Klingman, p. 139), and children exposed to the political violence in Cambodia who lived "in foster care were more likely to have a psychiatric diagnosis than children living with their family" (Swenson & Klingman, p. 148). The accumulated evidence drives home one truth: Childhood is devastated by war.

Children who grow up in a dangerous environment, whether the stress is continuous or intermittent, see the world differently from those who are raised in relative safety. For the former group of children, the world is not a safe place, and they cannot rely on parents, the primary source of their security, for their constant protection. After all, how can parents be relied on when they leave their children in times of danger (such as when fathers are conscripted), allow them to be separated from familiar surroundings (such as when they are evacuated), and let horrific things happen?

For child survivors of terrorist attacks, one of the most stressful elements of the traumatic experience is the perceived failure of their meaningful adults to shield them or themselves from danger. Ayalon (1982) found that toddlers who survived a night of terrorist captivity in their nursery and saw one infant shot to death expressed a great deal of anger and resentment at their parents for having "abandoned" them. Their desperate accusations signified a breech in the developing ability to trust adults and to bond securely with their parents.

Children are influenced by the moods of their parents and absorb feelings of worry, pain, anger, and frustration. Studies first conducted during World War II attested to the relationship between long-term disorders in children and the agitation and confusion in the adults looking after them. For example, Freud and Burlingham (1943) found that nervousness, bed-wetting, and other anxiety reactions that appeared in children after aerial bombings were related to their parents'

overanxious reactions. Children who have immature coping styles and are dependent on adults to understand external events are even more vulnerable.

The loss of family, caretakers, and friends may shatter children's worlds and put them at high risk. Children tend to regress, suffer from sleep and eating disorders, lose trust in others, have impaired concentration, and do poorly in their schoolwork. Some become aggressive and violent. Small children repeatedly re-enact the trauma in their games and have recurrent nightmares (Terr, 1990).

When families live in areas where frequent dangerous incidents occur, the constant turmoil and lack of security affect them. The need to hide in shelters disrupts daily routines and often disturbs their sleep. Forced evacuations sometimes separate children from their parents. Close proximity to where the incident occurred increases stress and anxiety, but geographical distance does not always provide protection from these feelings because immediate reports on television narrow psychological distance and increase general feelings of insecurity. Thus, children living in different regions from where the incident took place become indirectly involved.

Once battles subside, the stress does not completely disappear. Even in times of calm, there are elements of emergency. A situation of "neither peace nor war," where the threat of violence is chronic, imposes a constant emotional burden on anyone living in the area. Under these conditions of constant threat, children tend to exhibit signs of distress, expressed in behavioral signs of insecurity, anxiety, dependence, difficulty concentrating, frustration, anger, and aggression.

The literature on the effects of war on children yielded several important conclusions (Swenson & Klingman, 1993):

1. *Females tend to show higher levels of anxiety than males.* Several explanations are available for this finding. Females, because of their socialization, may be better able to show their emotions, and this ease with expression is taken as a sign of being more anxious. Females may live with more anxiety to begin with, and this is not taken into account when assessing their anxiety in the midst of a complex disaster. Females tend to be more empathic than males, which might contribute to their feeling greater anxiety. Finally, males may have more obvious, concrete tasks to complete during and after a complex disaster, and this activity may reduce their anxiety.

2. *Unlike natural disasters, younger children exposed to complex disasters show higher anxiety levels than older children exposed to the same disasters.* This is most likely because of the higher cognitive functioning of the older children. In addition, younger children have more trust in adults, and the complex disaster has a greater potential than a natural disaster to shatter this trust.

3. *Anxiety decreases over time, except for children of political or communal violence, who may maintain high anxiety levels.* Children who experience political violence eventually lose the ability to predict (as well as their confidence in being able to predict) when and where incidents may occur; therefore, they are left with the knowledge that violence may occur at any time and in any place, and their anxiety level is constantly high.

4. *Parents' psychological symptoms are related to psychological symptoms in the children.* Children, especially small children, have a tendency to spend more time with their mothers, and so draw their reactions from them. Children may look to both parents, whether they react similarly or differently, to determine an "appropriate" response. Chapter 4 presented several alternative explanations for the parent-to-child disaster-response relationship, such as whether it concerns deficits of the child or the parents.

5. *Social support, especially by family members, serves as a buffer against psychological difficulties.* Social support provides a way to vent feelings and a way for those exposed to a disaster to have their perspective of it confirmed. In addition, people who provide social support offer information that helps the support recipient understand the disaster and recognize potential sources of aid or help (Rosenfeld, Richman, & Bowen, 2004).

6. *Children of adult survivors show psychological difficulties similar to those of their parents.* Patterns of behavior, including coping mechanisms, are handed down through families. Earlier in this chapter, we considered the intergenerational transmission of trauma.

Spotlight on Research "Children Exposed to State-Sponsored Terrorism" presents a research study of two groups of Mayan children, one group in two orphanages and a rural Guatemalan village, and the other in refugee camps in urban Mexico. How did the children, who were between the ages of two and 11, respond to their refugee status and to the terrorism they witnessed?

Children's Fears

For the children that Melville and Lykes (1992) interviewed, fear was their overwhelming response to their refugee status and the terrorism they witnessed. Of what were they afraid? What are children frightened

Children Exposed to State-Sponsored Terrorism

From 1981–1983, Mayan Indians in Guatemala suffered state-sponsored terrorism as part of the government's counterinsurgency strategy in its 30-year civil war. The aim of the state-sponsored terrorism was to stop potential support for guerrilla forces and to prevent a generalized popular uprising. Over 400 rural villages were destroyed, and 50,000 to 100,000 villagers were killed. About 1 million people became "internal refugees" (out of a population of 8.5 million), and an estimated 150,000 sought refuge in Mexico (where they were typically unrecognized and unwanted), 6,000 sought refuge in Belize, 1,000 in Honduras, and up to 200,000 in the United States. Over 200,000 children lost one or both parents and were exposed to extreme violence. "When civil war is waged ... the clear identification of the enemy, as well as the organization of self-defense, is more problematic. And when a population faces government-sponsored terrorism, human rights and due process of law are suspended by the very institutions claiming to be their guardians" (Melville & Lykes, 1992, p. 534).

During the summer of 1988, Margarita Melville and Brinton Lykes (1992) studied Mayan children, between two and 11 years old, in two locations: (1) two orphanages and a rural village in Guatemala (36 children) and (2) refugee camps in urban Mexico (32 children). Children were interviewed for approximately two hours, during which time they "told their story," completed (orally) a structured questionnaire, drew pictures, were shown five pictures and told to make up a story about each, and answered questions about their emotional responses to what they experienced. The focus was on the effects of the civil war on the children's ethnic identity, and the factors that helped them survive.

Asked what was the worst thing that happened to them, most of the children in the Guatemalan orphanages said the death of a parent or relative, and several mentioned "war" and "violence," in general. Half the children in Mexico identified the death or kidnapping of a parent or relative, another 25 percent mentioned exile from Guatemala, and 14 percent mentioned hunger.

The strongest emotion felt by the children in Guatemala and Mexico was fear (*susto*). Two-thirds of the children in Guatemala added *miedo*, which means "pervasiveness": For the children in Guatemala, pervasive fear was their overwhelming emotion. A second emotion mentioned by children in both locations was sadness.

In response to questions concerning what they found helpful in recovering from the trauma they experienced (and, for many, continued to experience), the children's "overall responses confirmed that parents and close relatives were the most helpful, particularly for children in Mexico [seven of whom lost one or both parents; in Guatemala, 31 lost one or both parents]" (Melville & Lykes, 1992, p. 543). If support from parents and relatives was not available, support from friends, caretakers, and God was thought most helpful in their recovery.

Sociocultural changes occurred in three areas considered principal markers of cultural identity: (1) traditional dress—there was a decline in attachment to traditional dress by the girls in Mexico; (2) language—most of the children in Guatemala and Mexico still spoke Spanish and a Mayan language, but some had either not learned Mayan or had discontinued its use and spoke only Spanish; and (3) sex-related work—whereas the boys in Guatemala received better preparation for peasant life in Guatemala, the boys in Mexico received only training in farming, which was not feasible.

To help the children regain their psychic health, the authors mentioned an intervention project that includes opportunities to overcome fear by talking about the traumatic events, support for maintaining the elements of cultural identity, and preparation for future occupations that take into account real opportunities.

Melville, M. B., & Lykes, M. B. (1992). Guatemalan Indian children and the sociocultural effects of government-sponsored terrorism. *Social Science and Medicine, 34*, 533–548.

of in times of a complex disaster? Are their fears different from those related to the normal process of growth and change? Through careful observation of children's signs of distress during tense security situations, six types of fear can be identified.

First, there are *fears because of circumstances*. Fear following threat is "healthy fear," common to both adults and children (Janis, 1968). It warns the person to be careful, thus increasing chances of survival. However, when circumstances interfere with the fearful person being able to take the appropriate means of defense, such as finding a weapon, or when circumstances inhibit flight reactions, then physical symptoms of confusion and psychological problems ensue and are usually accompanied by regressive behavior.

Second, there are *imaginary fears*. The realistic fear of violence, whether connected with war or drive-by shootings, is often mixed with fears of imaginary creatures, such as monsters and aliens. Young children may find it difficult to distinguish between real and imaginary dangers.

Third, *contagious fears* may be caused by the behavior of those around the child. Young children experience the world through the significant adults in their life. Children in the care of adults who are themselves frightened and who are, perhaps, overreacting to the danger around them, become afraid. Sometimes adults pretend not to be distressed, to hide their suffering "for the children's sake," but this rarely is successful. The children recognize that the adults are distressed and become even more afraid. Unfortunately, because the adults are hiding how they feel, the children are deprived of necessary support and are denied the opportunity to have their perception of danger validated. Instead of being allowed to express their feelings, the children may suffer shame,

guilt, confusion, and isolation. An open discussion of feelings and thoughts, combined with expectations for a better future, may counter these fears.

Fourth, *fear of separation from parents*, increases as unavoidable separations increase. Watching a parent leave to confront a dangerous situation, whether a war, a fire, or a collapsing building from which people need to be rescued, is anxiety provoking, especially if it occurs during the first years of a child's life.

Fear of death, of its ominous mystery, preoccupies children at various developmental stages. Complex disasters may expose children to the experience of loss of life before they have the means to deal with it, and the presence of death around them increases feelings of their own vulnerability. Preparing children to cope with the subject of death, expressing feelings of distress and mourning, comforting those who are bereaved, and understanding their own and others' bereavements are an urgent social–educational issue (Ayalon, 1978, 1992; Lahad & Ayalon, 1995). However, children's frequent exposure to death can cause a flattening of their emotions, apathy, and a depreciation of the value of life.

The sixth type of fear is *traumatic fear*. In extreme cases, exposure to life-threatening incidents or loss of loved ones may cause PTSD. Symptoms of PTSD are likely to include flashbacks, phobic avoidance of places or activities triggering memories of the traumatic event, hyperarousal, nervousness, psychic numbing, disruption in one's sense of identity, memory impairment or trouble concentrating, sleep disturbance, self-blame and survivor guilt, and suspicion and alienation with regard to society and its institutions. These symptoms are unlikely to diminish or disappear without special treatment (Ayalon, 1993).

Children's Responses to Terrorist Activity

Terrorist activity calculatedly and systematically fosters fear in the defenseless civilian population. By demonstrating their ability to strike noncombatants any place and at anytime, terrorists intensify psychological demoralization. Those killed and injured are not the real targets but are used as a form of blackmail and as a demonstration of destructive power (Schreiber, 1979).

Terrorists' direct and indirect threats create traumatic situations that necessitate therapeutic intervention to minimize psychological damage. The main feature of such trauma is "rupture"—the trauma ruptures continuity in time, relations, and attachments; in perceptions of self and others; in basic assumptions about the world; and in future expectations (Gordon & Wraith, 1993). Above all, it ruptures the fabric of meaning. The traumatized are unable to grasp the full implications of the loss or come to terms with the reality of the situation because it is inexplicable, unbelievable, and incomprehensible. The imagery of terrorist violence can become an unconscious organizing principle, determining how people see the world and how they choose to act. Some might develop a militaristic coping strategy, tinted with paranoid suspicions that may precipitate a new round of violence; others may "give up" and suffer from feelings of anomie and helplessness.

Ayalon and Soskis (1986) and Desivilya, Gal, and Ayalon (1996) conducted studies over a 17-year period that provided an in-depth analysis of how children and adolescents are affected by terrorism. They chose to study the Maalot Massacre. On May 5, 1974, 105 children in Maalot, Israel, were on their school's spring outing when they were captured in a school building and held hostage by three terrorists. Before the army rescued them, 22 of the children had been killed; many others had been wounded.

The young hostages' immediate reactions during the attack included the following:

- The arbitrariness of the attack intensified fears and shook their sense of personal identity.
- The loss of their ability to defend themselves and others, and the obstruction of escape routes, increased their frustration.
- The frustration, in turn, bred aggression that had no way of being diffused, so the children directed it inward and the aggression became desperation.
- Ambivalent attachment to the terrorists occurred when some hostages felt totally dominated and dependent on them for the most basic and private daily functions, such as their mobility, speaking, nourishment, and using the bathroom.
- Communicating and interacting with the terrorists damaged some victims' self-image and burdened them with guilt and self-disgust. After the rescue, one girl, who shared some bread with one of the captors, developed an aversive reaction to eating bread, which for her became contaminated and repulsive.

The long-term effects of this act of terrorism included a perpetual disruption of their sense of self and the integration and continuity of their personal history. The brush with death shattered their illusion of invulnerability; years later, one boy who survived with an injury said, "I feel dead. I go every day to the cemetery to visit my dead friends" (Ayalon & Horowitz, 1996, p. 56).

Some responded to the trauma with violence—perhaps in an attempt to overcome their worst inner fears, to awaken a sense of feeling in an otherwise "frozen" psyche, or to find a legitimate outlet for massive grief and anger. One of the hostages who, by volunteering to carry the terrorists' messages out of the building, was spared several hours of the ordeal and its harrowing termination, described a perpetual preoccupation with his guilt and a great need to act out his hostility. Years later, during a military action against terrorists in which he participated as a regular soldier, it became well known that he was "carrying out a private war of revenge for his murdered mates" (Ayalon & Horowitz, 1996, p. 57). According to this young man, he succeeded in releasing an enormous personal pressure by being able to participate in the military operation.

Some survivors suffered guilt, became chronically suspicious or angry, or turned their unspent aggression inward, damaging themselves mentally or physically. Some emerged from the disaster with a bleak outlook on life, feeling depressed and helpless, whereas some adopted a heroic attitude and sought to become "saviors." Others shifted toward forgiveness and altruism.

One major change that was prominent across the group of young victims was the emergence of a "survivor identity" that became the subjective measure of all subsequent life experiences. Some started their life narrative from the day of the attack, as if all previous life experiences were wiped out. An examination of the personal meaning associated with retaining a survivor identity revealed that it converged with two distinct outlooks on life, one generally optimistic and the other predominantly pessimistic. The former identity was based on the belief that through their traumatic experience and rescue they had been chosen for life by supreme powers and hence were protected and immune. By contrast, their pessimistic counterparts viewed their ordeal as proof of some unknown guilt, condemnation, or punishment and nurtured catastrophic expectations for the future.

Seventeen years after the event, well into young adulthood, more than half of the survivors still suffered from some frequency of the following symptoms: hyperalertness, sleep disturbances and recurrent dreams, intrusive images and thoughts, reliving the catastrophe through fantasy, avoidance of objects and places that reminded them of the event, startle reactions to abrupt noises, and nervousness. A minority of the survivors complained about depressive reactions, numbing of sensations (psychic numbing), social withdrawal, memory blocks, and problems with concentrating. A few had feelings of persecution and expectations that the event will reoccur. Some searched for prophetic signs (omens and portents), felt regret and guilt toward those who perished, and were suspicious and alienated ("A stranger could never understand what I've been through"). A few showed a great drive for excellence, achievement, and altruistic contributions to society, whereas some took great pains to hide their past predicament even from their own children. In sum, different individuals adopted different survival strategies, demonstrating that *we cannot deduce adult behavior from childhood trauma.*

COPING WITH COMPLEX DISASTERS

Coping with a complex disaster takes many forms, which can be divided into two groups—active and passive. There is some evidence that active coping, active resistance, and demonstration may be more helpful than passive coping for managing the stress of a complex disaster. In addition, altruistic behavior involving actively helping others seems to enhance positive coping (Apfel &

Simon, 1996). In uncontrollable and over-whelming situations, however, denial—of both the threat and of unpleasant feelings—is a healthy way of coping (Lazarus & Folkman, 1987; McCarroll, Ursano, Wright, & Fullerton, 1993; Rofe & Levin, 1982).

Active Coping

There are many anecdotal stories of how children, even very young ones, saved their own and others' lives by coping actively with their traumatic situations (Ayalon & Soskis, 1986). These are stories of a five-year-old girl, who had been wounded, who clung to her dead father and pretended to be dead, as terrorists shot her mother and younger brother; a six-year-old girl, captured by a terrorist on a dark stairway, who kicked her captor in the leg, managed to free herself, and hid under a piece of furniture from the terrorist who searched for her; an 11-year-old girl who used a secret code language to

SPOTLIGHT ON RESEARCH

Resilience in the Face of a Dangerous Environment

Children living in conditions of political violence constantly experience loss, danger, and threat to their lives, and may subsequently suffer from psychological distress. Researchers have found high levels of anxiety, emotional, and behavioural symptoms, and post-traumatic stress disorder (PTSD) among children and adolescents exposed to military violence in the Middle East ... in Africa ... and in Europe. (Punamäki et al., 2001, p. 256)

With this as the backdrop, Raija-Leena Punamäki, Samir Qouta, and Eyad El-Sarraj (2001) asked: What resiliency factors can protect the well-being of Palestinian children living in the middle of political violence? They looked at several possible factors: intelligence; creativity; perceived parenting styles (loving and caring versus rejecting and hostile); traumatic events (for example, witnessing assaults, or serious familial illness); and the extent to which the child responds actively (confronts) versus passively (observes, escapes)

to violence. How do these variables predict mental health outcomes, such as PTSD?

Children (*n* = 103) were assessed in 1993, during the political violence of the Intifada; they ranged in age from 10 to 12 years old. Three years later, during a more peaceful time, 86 of the original children, now 13 to 15 years old, participated in follow-up testing. Analyses were limited to the 86 children who completed measures both times.

Results reveal several protective factors, factors that enhance resilience: "active response to military violence, creativity, and good and harmonious perceived parenting" (Punamäki et al., 2001, p. 264). As for PTSD, the researchers found it was high for children who had both been exposed to a high level of Intifada violence and who responded passively rather than actively. PTSD also was high for those children who perceived their mothers, but not their fathers, as being loving and caring.

Punamäki, R.-L., Qouta, S., & El-Sarraj, E. (2001). Resiliency factors predicting psychological adjustment after political violence among Palestinian children. *International Journal of Behavioral Development, 25*, 256–267.

fool her captors and call the military for help; a 12-year-old girl running for her life in the middle of the night, dodging bullets and explosions, who stopped, ignoring her own safety, to help a younger child who was lost and frightened. Spotlight on Research "Resilience in the Face of a Dangerous Environment" presents a study of Palestinian youths and the usefulness of their actively responding to the violence around them.

Punamäki (2000) studied the coping behavior of Palestinian children traumatized by violence and political oppression under Israeli military occupation through an analysis of the content of dreams of 185 children, 10 to 13 years old. Their dreams revealed a compensatory dynamic. Children who were courageous and actively engaged in throwing stones at Israeli military vehicles during the day reported a search for safety and security in their dreams; children who were withdrawn and afraid during waking hours dreamed aggressive and heroic dreams.

In another study focused on Palestinian children's resilience and coping skills, Punamäki (2000) used two tools: (1) a verbal sentence completion test and (2) a projective test of pictures showing military violence, humiliation, threat, and loss. Children showed a combination of coping methods: *behavioral*, such as actually participating in the fighting; *emotional*, such as expressing hatred and anger; *cognitive*, such as problem solving; and *social*, such as looking for support from parents and partners. Some responses indicated the use of the *belief* coping channel: prayers and wishful martyrdom. Others indicated the use of *imagination*: "I wish I were somewhere else," or "I imagine I have a machine gun." Coping modes that aimed at changing the external situation, such as cognitive problem solving and active fighting, were most effective in alleviating children's stress.

Passive Coping

Stories of bravery and heroism notwithstanding, the evidence is not consistent that an active coping style is always the best. Findings from Northern Ireland, for example, indicated that aggressive behavior of children toward the military during the day resulted in nightmares and other regressive nocturnal symptoms (Fraser, 1983).

Earlier we discussed some of the findings from research conducted over a 17-year period with the children and adolescents of the Maalot Massacre (Ayalon & Soskis, 1986; Desivilya et al., 1996). In addition to the effects already summarized, the researchers learned a great deal about how the children coped by asking them these questions: "What did you think, what did you feel, what did you do during the hostage event that either upset you or helped you?" (this was repeated for the time period shortly after being taken hostage by the terrorists, and then again for the long range of the children's lives); and "What did others do during the event or in the aftermath that either helped you or disturbed you?" (referring to people such as the terrorists, classmates, teachers, parents, medical staff, and therapists). These questions were the first step in the rehabilitative process because they helped fulfill the disaster clients' need to regain identity and mastery, whether in a symbolic or a tangible fashion, and to view themselves as capable of choosing and shaping their own fate.

Several palliative passive coping styles were evident from the hostages' reports of what helped them during their ordeal. Denial and dissociation, for example, abated the unbearable anxiety they felt: daydreaming about hearth and home, fantasizing a beloved person, and ruminating over childhood memories. A very helpful strategy mentioned by a survivor was the effort to record and bear witness: "In the hospital, with bandaged hands, I kept writing my diary" (Ayalon & Soskis, 1986, p. 263).

The ability to imagine, fantasize, and have "out of body" experiences that put one in a different time and space can save those exposed to disasters from unbearable pain. Saban (1990) described hostages who spent many hours in captivity, surrounded by wired explosives and guns pointed at the children by the terrorists. Magical thinking, taking vows, and bargaining with fate ("If I survive, I will always be good") reinforced hope in some of them, who also found consolation in prayer and religious rituals.

Empowering Children to Cope

Children are affected deeply by human-made disasters. They are vulnerable, they suffer, and they need protection. The good news, however, is that they also seem to be resilient. Studies of children in complex disasters around the world found that many of them maintain an active and positive attitude in the face of adversity (Apfel & Simon, 1996, 2000; Garbarino, Kostelny, & Dobrow, 1991; Govender & Killian, 2001; O'Donnell, Schwab-Stone, & Muyeed, 2002), and resilience can be developed and maintained by systematically enhancing both intrapsychic and action–oriented coping resources (Lahad & Cohen, 1998).

Emerging in the international community is a fight to eliminate or at least reduce factors that jeopardize children. On November 20, 1989, the United Nations' Convention on the Rights of the Child adopted and opened for signature a "bill of rights" for children (http://www.unhchr.ch/html/menu3/b/k2crc.htm). Some of the provisions of this document include

Traditional Healing for Traumatic Responses

Van der Veer, Somasundaram, and Damian (in press) have studied examples of traditional healing. Tamils have their traditional resources for help. In the community of Jaffna, there are healers who are able to ameliorate psychosocial problems and minor mental health problems. Among these healers are mediums who go into a trance and then come under the influence of a Hindu god(dess) such as Amman or Kali or, in the case of Christian mediums, the Christian God. The medium then makes movements with the head or the whole body and starts to speak in a different, louder voice, calling the assembled clients one by one, answering their questions, or predicting their future. The medium also gives advice about what herbal medicines the clients should take or hands out a prepared mixture. At last, the medium falls unconscious and, when awakened, asserts that he or she is unable to recollect what was said during the trance.

Oracles provide another form of traditional healing. They use various procedures, such as lighting camphor, breaking a coconut, or reading betel leaves. After performing one of these procedures, they close their eyes and meditate for a while. Then, they give advice. Families of people who "disappeared" after being taken away by armed men often seek the help of an oracle to find out the fate of their loved one. Surrounded by family members, the oracle tells them what has happened to their loved one—by acting out the torture the disappeared person might have suffered, reporting that the person died, or revealing that the person is surviving somewhere. If the disappeared person is being detained, one of the family members will make a vow to the god or temple asking for his or her release and will fulfill it if the family member is released.

- "The child shall be registered immediately after birth and shall have the right from birth to a name, the right to acquire a nationality and, as far as possible, the right to know and be cared for by his or her parents" (Article 7).
- "Where a child is illegally deprived of some or all of the elements of his or her identity, States Parties shall provide appropriate assistance and protection, with a view to re-establishing speedily his or her identity" (Article 8).
- "States Parties shall take all appropriate legislative, administrative, social and educational measures to protect the child from all forms of physical or mental violence, injury or abuse, neglect or negligent treatment, maltreatment or exploitation, including sexual abuse" (Article 19).
- "States Parties shall take appropriate measures to ensure that a child who is seeking refugee status or who is considered a refugee in accordance with applicable international or domestic law and procedures shall, whether unaccompanied or accompanied by his or her parents or by any other person, receive appropriate protection and humanitarian assistance" (Article 22).
- "The development of respect for the child's parents, his or her own cultural identity, language and values, for the national values of the country in which the child is living, the country from which he or she may originate, and for civilizations different from his or her own" (Article 29)
- States Parties shall take all feasible measures to ensure that persons who have not attained the age of fifteen years do not take a direct part in hostilities .... [S]hall refrain from recruiting any person who has not attained the age of fifteen years into their armed forces .... In accordance with their obligations under international humanitarian law to protect the civilian population in armed conflicts, States Parties shall take all feasible measures to ensure protection and care of children who are affected by an armed conflict" (Article 38).

On May 25, 2000, the UN adopted an "Optional Protocol to the Convention on the Rights of the Child on the involvement of children in armed conflicts" (http://www.unhchr.ch/html/menu2/6/protocolchild.htm), to go into effect February 2002. Several of its articles make clear that children under the age of 18 should not be recruited into the military and, if someone under the age of 18 voluntarily joins, she or he should "not take a direct part in hostilities" (Article 1).

As of November 4, 2002, 191 countries had signed the declaration affirming that each child has the right to life, a name, a home and a family, a nationality, an education and recreation, freedom of expression, dignity, and special protection and care in situations of armed conflict. It is important to note, as Article 8 and the Optional Protocol states, that children should never be allowed to play an active role in warfare, and they must be offered immediate protection and assistance when conflicts erupt.

CAN WE LIVE WITHOUT AN ENEMY?

The provocative question posed in the title of this section—asked by Rowe (1985)—touches on a most important source of terrorism and violence. The dichotomy between "good" and "evil" and the projection of everything evil onto the "other," the "one who is different." Touching Reality "Creating the Fertile Ground for Terrorism and Violence" provides the opportunity to examine the ways you were taught to hate and fear those who are different.

Creating the Fertile Ground for Terrorism and Violence

Take a few minutes to write down all the ways you probably were taught to hate and fear those who are different. Think about the following, which are only a few of the areas to consider:

- Can you recall the early rhymes and expressions used in your family that taught you to look down on, hate, or fear people of other racial or ethnic backgrounds?
- What goes through your mind when you are in a rush and "those people" seem to be holding you back—the people who cut you off when you are driving, or make you wait in line too long?
- Who are the people with whom you associate the fear of losing your job?
- Who are the people with whom you associate your loss of material possessions—the people who are most likely to rob you, mug you, or terrorize you?

What connections do these attitudes have with family violence, communal violence, war, and political violence?

Depth psychology maintains that the "enemy" image is constructed from denied aspects of the self (Volkan, 1990). "In the beginning we create the enemy. Before the weapon comes the image. We are driven to fabricate an enemy as a scapegoat to bear the burden of our denied enmity" (Keen, 1986, p. 1). When we project our denied aspects of personality onto others, we try to destroy the other as a way of unknowingly getting

rid of what we hate in ourselves. The interface between external hostile encounters, such as war and terrorism-induced violence, and projections of inner rejected parts, generates a persistent psychosocial fear–hate combination that is very resistant to change (Ayalon, 1998b, 1999). Whereas the trauma caused by terrorist attacks is real and needs to be tended to (Gurwitch, Sitterle, Young, & Pfefferbaum, 2002), prolonged exposure to terrorism as a psychosocial phenomenon harbors long-range dangers for the moral development of the attacked society and its value system. It creates an overriding atmosphere of suspicion and demonization of the "other" that may permeate all levels of development and contaminate basic humanistic values of society.

At the collective level, whether between groups or nations, we see not only the above symptoms assailing individuals and their families, but also polarized thinking between different groups, demonizing and dehumanizing the other. Seeking justice through violence and revenge appears logically to be the only choice. We ruminate only on our traumatic narrative, which becomes increasingly distorted over time. Massive projection becomes a developmental danger for children, because it is too absolute, too final, too irreversible. (Flashman, 2002, p. 3)

The result, according to Flashman (2002), is impaired moral judgment and social irresponsibility, lack of empathy, constriction of creative imagination, and invasion of demonic frightening fantasies.

It is difficult enough to conduct encounters between antagonistic groups in the **aftermath** of hostilities, but it is usually impossible to do it **during** active hostility

(Ayalon & Shacham, 2000). Tolerance for "otherness" happens when both individuals and the community acknowledge and own those inner "rejected" aspects of themselves and when encounters with representatives of the "other side" transcend stereotypical and biased perceptions of those regarded as enemies.

SUMMARY

This chapter deals with the effects of complex disasters—including war, terrorism, and political and community violence—on children and their families. In addition to being "collateral damage," children may be the direct targets of organized violence. Traumatization may occur by witnessing death and destruction, either firsthand or secondhand (through the media) or by the extreme poverty, exile, and bereavement that often results from complex disasters.

Complex disasters destroy families by causing the death or injury of family members, by causing the loss of social status and economic standing, and by forcing families into refugee status. Forced evacuations may separate children from their parents. Family trauma may be passed on to future generations. Children of adult survivors show psychological difficulties similar to those of their parents.

For children who grow up in a dangerous environment the world is not a safe place, and parents cannot be relied on for protection. Children tend to regress, suffer from sleep and eating disorders, lose trust, and have impaired concentration. Some become aggressive and violent; small children re-enact the trauma in their games. Females tend to show higher levels of anxiety than males; younger children show higher anxiety levels than older children. Children also may show any of six types of fear (such as imaginary fears). The long-term effects of a massive act of terrorism include the emergence of a "survivor identity."

Coping with a complex disaster takes many forms, although they may be divided into two groups, active (those who express anger and fight actively) and passive (those who use denial and dissociation). Studies found that although children are vulnerable, many also are resilient.

When children grow up in dangerous environments, they are denied their elementary rights, which are crucial for healthy development. A major challenge is to implement the UN's bill of rights for children, including the child's right to life, education, and recreation, and freedom of expression, dignity, and special protection. However, the ways we are taught to hate and fear those who are different provide fertile ground for wars and terrorism. The interface between external hostile encounters and projections of inner rejected parts generates a psychosocial fear–hate combination that is resistant to change.

REFERENCES

Andersson, N., Palha da Sousa, C., & Paredes, S. (1995). Social costs of land mines in four countries: Afghanistan, Bosnia, Cambodia and Mozambique. *British Medical Journal, 311,* 718–721.

Apfel, R. J., & Simon, B. (1996). Introduction. In R. J. Apfel & B. Simon (Eds.), *Minefields in their hearts: The mental health of children in war and communal violence* (pp. 1–17). New Haven, CT: Yale University Press.

Apfel, R. J., & Simon, B. (2000). Mitigating discontents with children in war: An ongoing psychoanalytic inquiry. In A.C.G.M. Robben & M. M. Suarez-Orozco (Eds.), *Cultures under siege: Collective violence and trauma* (pp. 102–130). New York: Cambridge University Press.

Arcel, L. A. (1994). Building bridges is creating hope for the future. In L. A. Arcel (Ed.), *War victims, trauma and psycho-social care* (pp. 26–29). Zagreb, Croatia: European Community Humanitarian Office.

Areliu, A. (2002, June). *Supporting children experiencing war and terrorism.* Paper presented at the 25th International School Psychologist Conference, Nyborg, Denmark.

Ayalon, O. (1978). *Emergency kit.* Haifa, Israel: University of Haifa Press. (Hebrew)

Ayalon, O. (1982). Children as hostages. *The Practitioner, 226,* 1771–1773.

Ayalon, O. (1989a). Coping with terrorism—The Israeli case. In D. Meichenbaum & M. Jaremko (Eds.), *Stress reduction and prevention* (pp. 293–339). Cambridge, MA: Perseus.

Ayalon, O. (1989b). The psychological price of the security situation. *Chetz Journal, 2,* 32–40. (Hebrew).

Ayalon, O. (1992). *Rescue! Community oriented preventive education handbook.* Ellicott City, MD: Chevron.

Ayalon, O. (1993). Death in literature and bibliotherapy. In R. Malkinsom, S. Rubin, & E. Vitztum (Eds.), *Loss and bereavement in Israeli society* (pp. 155–175). Jerusalem: Ministry of Defense. (Hebrew)

Ayalon, O. (1995). *Training Angola youth leaders/therapists in post traumatic stress management.* Lisbon: International Child Development.

Ayalon, O. (1997). Sealed rooms and gas masks. In M. Lahad & A. Cohen (Eds.), *Community stress prevention 2* (pp. 191–198). Kiryat Shmona, Israel: Community Stress Prevention Center.

Ayalon, O. (1998a). Community healing for children traumatized by war. *International Journal of Psychiatry, 10,* 224–233.

Ayalon, O. (1998b). Reconciliation: Changing the face of the enemy. In O. Ayalon, M. Lahad & A. Cohen (Eds.), *Community stress prevention 3* (pp. 62–66). Kiryat Shmona, Israel: Community Stress Prevention Center.

Ayalon, O. (1999). Reconciliation—A holistic peace curriculum. In M. Iverson & D. Broen (Eds.), *Reconciliation anthology* (pp. 45–61). Copenhagen: Danish Refugee Council. (Danish)

Ayalon, O., & Horowitz, M. (1996). *Survivors of Ma'a lot: A handbook.* Tel Aviv: The Israeli Educational Television. (Hebrew)

Ayalon, O., & Shacham, Y. (2000). Helping the helpers in war trauma. In A. Klingman, A. Raviv, & B. Stein (Eds.), *Children in stress and crisis situations* (pp. 462–484). Jerusalem, Israel: Ministry of Education. (Hebrew)

Ayalon, O., & Soskis D. (1986). Survivors of terrorist victimization. In N. A. Milgram (Ed.), *Stress and coping in time of war: Generalizations from the Israeli experience* (pp. 257–274). Philadelphia: Brunner-Routledge.

Ayalon, O., & Waters, F. (2002). The impact of terrorism on Jews in Israel. *Journal of Trauma Practice, 1*(3–4), 133–154.

Ayalon, O., & Zimrin, H. (1992). *Painful childhood: A second look at child abuse.* Tel Aviv: Sifriat Poalim Publishers. (Hebrew)

Baranowsky, A. B., Young, M., Johnson-Douglas, S., Williams-Keeler, L., & McCarrey, M. (1998). PTSD transmission: A review of secondary traumatization in Holocaust survivor families. *Canadian Psychology, 39*(4), 247–256.

Bellamy, H. (1996). *State of world children.* Oxford: Oxford University Press.

Boothby, N. (1992). Children of war: Survival as a collective act. In M. McCallin (Ed.), *The psychological well-being of refugee children: Research, practice and policy issues* (pp. 169–184). Geneva: International Catholic Child Bureau.

Bredy, L. (1983). Children and war: Experiences from Lebanon. In M. Kahnert, D. Pitt, & I. Taipale (Eds.), *Children and war* (pp. 121–123). Helsinki, Finland: Kirjapaino.

Brett, R., McCallin, M., & O'Shea, R. (1996). *Children: The invisible soldiers. Report on the participation of children in armed conflicts and internal disturbances and tensions for the United Nations study on the impact of armed conflict on children.* Geneva: Quaker United Nations Office and International Catholic Child Bureau.

Cairns, E. (1987). *Caught in crossfire: Children and the Northern Ireland conflict.* Belfast: Appletree Press.

Cantwell, N. (1997). *Starting from zero: The promotion and protection of children's rights in post-genocide Rwanda–July 1994–December 1996.* Florence, Italy: UNICEF, International Child Development Centre.

Cohen, J. A., Perel, J. M., DeBellis, M. D., Friedman, M. J., & Putnam, F. W. (2002). Treating traumatized children: Clinical implications of the psychobiology of posttraumatic stress disorder. *Trauma Violence and Abuse, 3*(2), 91–108.

Connolly, P. (1998). *Racism, gender identities and young children: Social relations in a multi-ethnic, inner-city primary school.* London: Routledge.

Danieli, Y. (1980). Families of survivors of the Nazi Holocaust: Some long-term effects. In N. Milgram (Ed.), *Psychological stress and adjustment in times of war and peace* (pp. 67–79). Washington, DC: Hemisphere.

Danieli, Y. (Ed.). (1998). *International handbook of multigenerational legacies of trauma.* New York: Plenum Press.

Desivilya, S. H., Gal, R., & Ayalon O. (1996). Long-term effects of trauma in adolecence: Comparison between survivors of a terrorist attack and control counterparts. *Anxiety, Stress and Coping: An International Journal, 9*, 135–150.

Feinstein, A., Owen, J., & Blair, N. (2002). A hazardous profession: War, journalists, and psychopathology. *American Journal of Psychiatry, 159*, 1570–1575.

Flashman, A. (2002). *Demon in the mirror: The price of projection.* Unpublished manuscript, Middle East Children Organization, Jerusalem.

Fraser, M. (1973). *Children in conflict.* New York: Basic Books.

Fraser, M. (1983). Childhood and war in Northern Ireland. In M. Kahnert, D. Pitt, & I. Taipale (Eds.), *Children and war* (pp. 124–128). Helsinki, Finland: Kirjapaino.

Freud, A., & Burlingham, D. T. (1943). *War and children.* New York: Medical War Books.

Garbarino, J., & Kostelny, K. (1996). What do we need to know to understand children in war and community violence? In R. J. Apfel & B. Simon (Eds.), *Minefields in their hearts: The mental health of children in war and communal violence* (pp. 33–51). New Haven, CT: Yale University Press.

Garbarino, J., Kostelny, K., & Dobrow, N. (1991). *No place to be a child: Growing up in a war zone.* San Francisco: Jossey-Bass.

Goodwin-Gill, G. S., & Cohn, I. (1994). *Child soldiers: The role of children in armed conflict.* New York: Oxford University Press.

Gordon, R., & Wraith, R. (1993). Responses of children and adolescents to disaster. In J. P. Wilson & B. Raphael (Eds.), *International handbook of traumatic stress syndromes* (pp. 561–575). New York: Kluwer Academic/Plenum.

Govender, K., & Killian, B. J. (2001). The psychological effects of chronic violence on children living in South African townships. *South African Journal of Psychology, 31*(2), 1–11.

Gurwitch, R. H., Sitterle, K. A., Young, B. H., & Pfefferbaum, B. (2002). The aftermath of terrorism. In A. M. La Greca, W. K. Silverman, E. M. Vernberg, & M. C. Roberts (Eds.), *Helping children cope with disasters and terrorism* (pp. 327–357). Washington, DC: American Psychological Association.

Hundeide, K. (1994). *Children's life-world and their reaction to war.* Oslo, Norway: International Child Development Programs.

Hundeide, K. (1995). *A critical note: Balancing trauma therapy with social realities.* Oslo, Norway: International Child Development Programs.

Janis, I. (1968). When fear is healthy. *Psychology Today, 1,* 46–49.

Jensen, S. B. (1994). Psycho-social stresses and protective factors in families under war conditions and peace building in former-Yugoslavia. In L. A. Arcel (Ed.), *War victims, trauma and psychosocial care* (pp. 72–79). Zagreb, Croatia: European Community Humanitarian Office.

Keen, S. (1986). *The faces of the enemy.* New York: Harper & Row.

Kellerman, N. P. F. (2001). Psychopathology in children of Holocaust survivors: A review of the research literature. *Israel Journal of Psychiatry and Related Sciences, 38*(1), 36–46.

Korn, D. A. (1999). *Exodus within borders.* Washington, DC: Brookings Institution Press.

Kuterovac, G., Dyregrov, A., & Stuvland, R. (1994). Children in war: A silent majority under stress, *British Journal of Medical Psychology, 67,* 363–375.

Lahad, M., & Ayalon, O. (1995). *On life and death.* Haifa, Israel: Nord. (Hebrew)

Lahad, M., & Cohen, A. (1998). Eighteen years of community stress prevention. In O. Ayalon, M. Lahad, & A. Cohen (Eds.), *Community stress prevention 3* (pp. 1–9). Kiryat Shmona, Israel: Community Stress Prevention Center.

Lazarus, R. S., & Folkman, D. (1987). Transactional theory and research on emotions and coping. *European Journal of Personality, 1*(3, Special Issue), 141–169.

Machel, G. (2001). *The impact of armed conflict on children: A critical review of progress made and obstacles in increasing protection for war-affected children.* New York: Palgrave Macmillan.

Macksoud, M. S., Dyregrov, A., & Raundalen, M. (1993). Traumatic war experiences and their effects on children. In J. P. Wilson, & B. Raphael (Eds.), *International handbook of traumatic stress syndromes* (pp. 625–633). New York: Plenum Press.

Major, E. F. (1996). The impact of the Holocaust on the second generation: Norwegian Jewish Holocaust survivors and their children. *Journal of Traumatic Stress, 9,* 441–454.

Makiya, K. (1993). *Cruelty and silence: War, tyranny, uprising and the Arab World.* London: Jonathan Cape.

Marans, S., Berkman, M., & Cohen, D. (1996). Child development and adaptation to catastrophic circumstances. In R. J. Apfel & B. Simon (Eds.), *Minefields in their hearts: The mental health of children in war and communal violence* (pp. 104–127). New Haven, CT: Yale University Press.

McCarroll, J. E., Ursano, R. J., Wright, K. M., & Fullerton, C. S. (1993). Handling bodies after violent death: Strategies for coping. *American Journal of Orthopsychiatry, 63,* 209–214.

Melville, M. B., & Lykes, M. B. (1992). Guatemalan Indian children and the sociocultural effects of government-sponsored terrorism. *Social Science and Medicine, 34,* 533–548.

Miljevic-Ridicki, R. (2002). *Supporting children experiencing war and terrorism.* Paper presented at the 25th International School Psychologist Conference, Nyborg, Denmark.

Miosso, A. (1996, June). *Emergency unit*. Paper presented at the Conference on Europe's Contribution to Safeguarding Children's Rights in Situations of Armed Conflicts, Firenze, Italy.

O'Donnell, D. A., Schwab-Stone, M. E., & Muyeed, A. Z. (2002). Multidimensional resilience in urban children exposed to community violence. *Child Development, 73*, 1265–1282.

Prince, R. M. (1999). *The legacy of the Holocaust: Psychological themes in the second generation*. New York: Other Press.

Punamäki, R.-L. (2000). Personal and family resources promoting resiliency among children suffering from military violence. In L. van Willigen (Ed.), *Health hazards of organized violence in children 2* (pp. 29–42). Utrecht, Netherlands: Pharos Foundation for Refugees.

Punamäki, R.-L., Qouta, S., & El-Sarraj, E. (2001). Resiliency factors predicting psychological adjustment after political violence among Palestinian children. *International Journal of Behavioral Development, 25*, 256–267.

Rofe, Y., & Lewin, I. (1982). The effects of war environment on dream habits. In N. A. Milgram (Ed.), *Stress and coping in time of war: Generalizations from the Israeli experience* (pp. 67–79). Philadelphia: Brunner-Routledge.

Rosenblatt, R. (1992). *Children of war*. New York: Doubleday.

Rosenfeld, L. B., Richman, J. M., & Bowen, G. L. (2004, February). *In the face of a dangerous community: The moderating effects of social support on high school students' school outcomes*. Paper presented at the annual meeting of the Western States Communication Association, Albuquerque.

Rowe, D. (1985). *Living with the bomb*. London: Routledge & Kegan.

Saban, S. (1990). *To live again*. Tel Aviv: Ministry of Defense Publications.

Schlenger, W. E., Caddell, J. M., Ebert, L., Jordan, B. K., Rourke, K. M., Wilson, D., Thalji, L., Dennis, J. M., Fairbank, J. A., Kulka, R. A. (2002). Psychological reactions to terrorist attacks: Findings from the National Study of Americans' Reactions to September 11. *JAMA, 288*, 581–588.

Schreiber, J. (1979). *The ultimate weapon*. New York: Wm. Morrow.

Solomon, Z., Kotler, M., & Mikulincer, M. (1988–1989). Combat related post-traumatic stress disorder among the second generation of Holocaust survivors: Transgenerational effects among Israeli soldiers. *Psychologia: Israel Journal of Psychology, 1*, 113–119.

Soskis, D., & Ochberg, F. (1982). Concepts of terrorist victimization. In F. Ochberg & D. Soskis. (Eds.), *Victims of terrorism* (pp. 105–135). Boulder, CO: Westview Press.

Stein, D. H. (1995). Intergenerational effects of PTSD: A hypothesis concerning mode of transmission. *Dissertation Abstracts International, 55*, 4134.

Stuvland, R. (1994). School-age children affected by war: The UNICEF program in former Yugoslavia. In L. A. Arcel (Ed.), *War victims, trauma and psycho-social care* (pp. 111–126). Zagreb, Croatia: European Community Humanitarian Office.

Swenson, C. C., & Klingman, A. (1993). Children and war. In C. F. Saylor (Ed.), *Children and disasters* (pp. 137–163). New York: Plenum Press.

Swiss, S., & Giller, J. (1993). Rape as a crime of war: A medical perspective. *Journal of the American Medical Association, 270*, 612–615.

Terr, L. (1990). *Too scared to cry*. New York: Harper & Row.

United Nations Children's Fund (UNICEF). (1996a). *The state of the world's children*. Oxford, England: Oxford University Press.

United Nations Children's Fund (UNICEF). (1996b). *UNICEF survey documents horrors experienced by Rwandan children during 1994 genocide* (CF/DOI/PR/1996-08). New York: Author.

U.S. Agency for International Development. (1997, January). *Disaster facts*. Retrieved August 30, 2003, from http://www.info.usaid.gov/press/releases/9701.htm.

van der Veer, G., Somasundaram, D., & Damian, S. (in press). Counselling in areas of armed conflict: The case of Jaffna. *Sri Lanka Journal of Mental Health, Psychosocial Work and Counselling in Areas of Armed Conflict*.

Vogel, J. M., & Vernberg, E. M. (1993). Task Force Report, part 1: Children's psychological responses to disasters. *Journal of Clinical Child Psychology, 22*, 464–484.

Volkan, V. (1990). Psychoanalytic aspects of ethnic conflicts. In J. V. Montville (Ed.), *Conflict and peacemaking in multiethnic societies* (pp. 81–92). Washington, DC: Lexington Press.

Wardi, D. (1992). *Memorial candles*. London: Tavistock/Routledge.

Westermeyer, J., & Wahmanholm, K. (1996). Refugee children. In R. J. Apfel & B. Simon (Eds.), *Minefields in their hearts: The mental health of children in war and communal violence* (pp. 75–103). New Haven, CT: Yale University Press.

Yehuda, R., Halligan, S. L., & Grossman R. (2001). Childhood trauma and risk for PTSD: Relationship to intergenerational effects of trauma, parental PTSD and cortisol excretion. *Development and Psychopathology, 13*, 733–753.

Yuksel, S. (1993). Sexual abuse of children (case from Turkey). In L. van Willingen (Ed.), *Health hazards of organized violence in children: Conference proceedings* (pp. 77–89). Utrecht, Netherlands: Pharos Foundation for Refugees.

PART THREE

DISASTER INTERVENTION

PREVENTIVE INTERVENTION

After studying the material in this chapter, you should

- be familiar with the three phases of preventive care
- understand the benefits of primary prevention in coping with imminent disasters
- realize the difficulties in planning and implementing primary prevention programs
- have a model for setting up prevention programs in schools
- understand the role of the facilitator in conducting group interventions with children
- realize the role of the family in preparing to cope with disaster
- know how to mobilize families to take part in primary prevention.

PHASES OF PREVENTIVE CARE

Helpers seek to prevent or alleviate morbid responses to distressful and traumatic events, to restore disrupted continuities, to enhance natural resilience, and to emphasize and develop new coping skills in the individual, in the family, and in the community. They do this through the implementation of disaster-intervention programs, and the best interventions are pre-emptive.

Public health research documents three phases of preventive care, which provide the blueprint for disaster-care delivery (Caplan, 1964): (1) *primary prevention* occurs before the event, (2) *secondary prevention* occurs during and immediately following the event, and (3) *tertiary prevention* occurs in the aftermath. Each phase has different foci, different time spans, and different strategies.

Primary prevention, sometimes referred to as "anticipatory intervention," focuses on cognitive and organizational preparation for an expected or possible disaster. Of course, the notion of anticipatory intervention is conceptually murky: To be truly anticipatory, the intervention would have to be used in a community in which no disaster has ever occurred. This kind of community may be very hard, if not impossible, to find, so it may be more appropriate to think of primary prevention as taking place in a community where a disaster may have occurred at one time and the intervention is less related to the past disaster than it is to a possible future disaster. The problem is one of word order: Does living through a disaster kindle the desire for primary prevention, or does the desire for primary prevention arise from the anticipation of living through a disaster?

Regardless of the source of motivation, the main purpose of primary or preventive intervention is to provide organizations and potential caregivers with the necessary skills to deal with any potential disaster effectively; this phase does not concern helping people to respond to a previous or current disaster. In the case of children, this phase involves the entire educational system. Anticipatory activities include training rescue workers and caregivers in educational institutions, creating protocols of rescue and first aid, teaching about children's expected behavior in disasters, identifying ahead of time vulnerable individuals who may need special attention, and rehearsing responses to simulated disasters.

The main purpose of secondary prevention, often referred to as "crisis intervention," is to identify pathological reactions as they form and to minimize the danger of fixating on traumatic stress responses. The main goal of secondary prevention is to prevent chronic PTSD. Secondary prevention is a brief and target-oriented psychoeducational intervention targeting at-risk groups and individuals. According to the "PIE" principle, crisis intervention tactics should be used as close as possible to the original location (proximity), as fast as possible, focusing on the "here and now" (immediacy), with an active, positive, and hopeful orientation (expectancy). The critical period for secondary preventive intervention is typically within six weeks of the onset of the disaster.

Tertiary prevention focuses on rehabilitative-therapeutic intervention that principally treats individuals with PTSD and reactions of delayed mourning and applies a wide range of therapeutic methods. This phase's duration depends on the severity of the symptoms, the individual's pace of recovery, and the therapeutic ideology.

This chapter focuses on primary prevention, chapter 9 focuses on secondary prevention, and chapter 10 focuses on tertiary prevention.

PRIMARY PREVENTION

The following Touching Reality "Being Wise before the Event" provides an opportunity to understand the benefits of being "wise before the event" (Yule, 2001).

People who benefit most from primary prevention are those who might be exposed directly or indirectly to the effects of the disaster, those who have close physical or psychological proximity to sufferers, and those who come in contact with disaster clients, including rescue workers, medical staff, and other helping professionals.

TOUCHING REALITY

Being Wise before the Event

When you notice your house burning down, it is too late to think about buying a fire extinguisher, to start selecting the items you wish to rescue, or to plan escape routes for you, your family, and your pets.

Think of a time in your life when you had an emergency, when it was too late to take preventive action. Maybe it was something as simple as having a flat tire and no spare, or maybe it was something life threatening. What happened? What did you do? What did you think? How did you feel?

Now, think of an emergency for which you were well prepared with a plan of action, a list of phone numbers to call, people to appeal to for help, and information that could guide your actions. What happened? What did you do? What did you think? How did you feel?

Compare the two narratives and the advantages of being "wise before the event."

EDUCATIONAL SYSTEMS AND CRITICAL INCIDENTS

Anticipatory prevention of emergencies in schools operates on two levels. First is the organizational level, which involves the intervention's physical and personnel structure and is systemwide. The second is the psychoeducational level, which is targeted at caregivers, counselors, teachers, small groups, and individual children. The aim of anticipatory, or primary, prevention in schools is to create school crisis teams responsible for

- developing crisis prevention curricula adapted to children's ages and needs
- creating predisaster social support networks
- encouraging leadership and responsibility
- addressing issues related to communication, transportation, school design and safety, and crisis drills and readiness activities. (Poland, 1997)

At the heart of anticipatory prevention lies a paradox: Decision makers and individuals are asked to plan for an "invisible" eventuality. That is, the demand for financial and human resources to be used in dealing with threatening ideas and images, as well as the motivation to make those resources available, occurs at a time of relative stability, when those involved wish to carry on with life as usual and not envision a possible disaster. There is also the belief that exposing children to issues related to disasters before they occur (to "inoculate" them) may increase fear and, perhaps, be harmful in the same way that inappropriate media exposure is harmful to children. There is a great deal of evidence that points to the effectiveness of anticipatory prevention with regard to complex disasters, especially in communities where stress from complex disasters, such as war, is relatively high (Klingman, 2002a; Lahad & Abraham, 1983). There is less evidence, however— because there has been little research—that points to the effectiveness of anticipatory prevention with regard to natural and technological disasters. Nevertheless, the continued use of a large variety of inoculation programs supports their usefulness—including inoculating students against stress and PTSD (Ursano, Grieger, & McCarroll, 1996), against the effects of natural disasters FEMA, 2001), and against the repercussions of school violence (Aber, Brown, & Jones, 2003; Flannery et al., 2003).

School, because of its unique role in the lives of most children, can play a major role in primary prevention (Brock, Lazarus, & Jimerson, 2002; Klingman, 1989, 2002b). For much of childhood and adolescence, most children spend the greatest part of the day in school. This is true whether the children are growing up in poverty, are abused, and have inadequate parental care as a result of, among other factors, death or divorce, or, at the other end of the spectrum, whether they are growing up in affluence but have inadequate parental contact. In many children's lives, school is the only stable influence, which maintains predictable continuity and an expected set of rules, roles, and reliable human contact. Many studies have established that the role of school in a child's life should be comprehensive: School addresses cognitive growth and socialization, is responsible for each child's physical health and emotional well-being, and helps to heal emotional wounds (Ayalon & Flasher, 1993; Garmezy & Rutter, 1983; Goleman, 1995; Johnson, 1993, 1998). In spite of these expectations, current research and abundant experience reveal that there is much to be accom-

plished before the school system as a whole is able to respond most effectively in times of disaster and trauma (Brock et al., 2002; Capewell, 1992).

Disaster, trauma, and loss are seldom considered appropriate subjects of discussion with children in the school environment. School authorities manifest a prevailing tendency to carry on as usual in the wake of a disaster, even at the cost of ensuing repression, distortion of memories, depression, and mounting aggression among the children. Disasters challenge the prevailing attitude that adults should be able to protect young people from harm, and if harm should come to the young ones, then adults should be able to rescue them. Moreover, when distress affects children, it reminds adults of their own vulnerability and may trigger their own deeply repressed memories.

Attitudes expressed by school personnel often mirror attitudes in the general adult population: They reflect social taboos, "magical thinking," denial of anxiety, and the need to maintain a "stiff upper lip." Once reawakened, memories of loss, fear, and confusion may threaten adults' vulnerable self-image and shatter their own sense of security.

Repeated experience has shown how difficult it is to mobilize an educational system to think and act proactively (Ayalon, 1993; Lahad & Abraham, 1983; Vernberg & Vogel, 1993). Teachers often ask: "What if the anticipated disaster does not take place? How can we assess individual benefits of the intervention if we cannot compare children's reactions before and after the disaster? How can we separate children's natural resilience from the benefits of learned coping skills? When is the crucial time for post-disaster assessment of the anticipatory prevention—during the disaster, immediately afterward, or in the long run?"

Reactions to Primary Prevention

In the wake of a series of terrorist attacks on the Israeli civilian population between 1974 and 1979, it became apparent to the authorities that preventive intervention was needed. Ayalon (1979) conducted a survey among primary school counselors and school psychologists to examine their attitudes regarding implementing preventive programs in the school curricula. Survey questions asked:

1. Is the school responsible—and equipped—to deal with issues of security hazards in the classroom?
2. Is death a proper subject of discussion for the classroom?
3. Are teachers and school counselors qualified to address issues concerning security hazards in the classroom?
4. Should school-age children be exposed to training and simulations to prepare for possible security hazards?
5. What are the counterindications for including children in stress prevention programs (age, prior traumatic experience, parental consent, and so on)?

Of the 60 primary school counselors and school psychologists who took part in the survey, 38 (63 percent) indicated they were opposed to involving schools in primary prevention. Their reasons fell into six areas:

1. They did not want to upset the children ("Children must not think about death").
2. They did not want to disrupt the existing curriculum ("We must catch up with the basics—reading, writing, and arithmetic").
3. They felt that children should forget bad times and focus on positive experiences.
4. They thought it best to avoid the issue if there was no call to address it, that is, "to let sleeping dogs lie."
5. They felt that talking about troubles increases the probability that the troubles will occur ("Don't tempt trouble").
6. They felt that because, as children, they never had psychological intervention and never missed it, today's students could do without it, also.

Of the same 60 primary school counselors and school psychologists, 19 (32 percent) indicated they were in favor of involving schools in primary prevention. Their reasons fell into four areas:

1. They had seen children's behavior following disasters get out of hand ("Some were too depressed, some too aggressive"), and they wanted to learn how to help them cope.
2. They needed to have reasonable and useful answers to children's difficult and sometimes embarrassing questions, such as those concerning death, life after death, and "divine justice."
3. They believed in expanding children's experience to include both pleasant and unpleasant events, as an enrichment of the child's inner resources.
4. They trusted children to be able to process harsh realities if properly guided by a reliable adult.

Ayalon, O. (1979). Community oriented preparation for emergency. *Journal of Death Education, 3*, 222–244.

Prevention demands an extended time perspective. Cowen (1977), in an address to the American Psychological Association, introduced this notion and discussed the groundwork necessary to develop primary prevention:

If we wish to understand behavior in relation to primary prevention we will need to do more work with people over time. This is so for several reasons: the manipulations and processes of primary prevention are intrinsically complex, their means-end contingencies are often below the surface, and target behaviors are ones that tend to change very slowly. In several studies anticipated preventive effects that failed to appear initially became clearer as time passed. (p. 10)

However, the price for neglecting preventive preparation may be even higher than the costs involved in running it. If crisis intervention is offered only *during* critical incidents, chaos, panic, role confusion, and overlapping instructions cause secondary damage (Ayalon, 1982).

PRIMARY PREVENTION AND THE GROUP

"Psychological immunization" and "stress inoculation" are the terms for any therapeutic intervention intended to reduce the psychological damage that may be caused by an impending trauma. Stress inoculation, as in medical inoculation, is designed to build "psychological antibodies" and enhance resistance to extreme stress by exposure to powerful stimuli that arouse psychological defenses without the threat of actual breakdown. The experience of successfully coping with manageable levels of stress enables us to develop a sense of

"learned resourcefulness" that prepares us to deal effectively with impending dangers and loss (Meichenbaum, 1983).

Anticipatory prevention has two important features. First, preparation for excessive or traumatic stress is best conducted in times of minimal or normal stress—a good time to become more aware of one's own modes of response to extreme stress and to acquire new coping skills (Ayalon, 1983; Ursano et al., 1996). Second, stress inoculation as a method of primary prevention suggests ways to simulate not only the traumatic events, but also the physical, cognitive, and emotional responses accompanying such events, and to practice appropriate modes of reaction (Meichenbaum & Jaremko, 1983).

Building resilience and developing coping skills are best done in a group setting. There are five benefits to using the group as the arena for primary prevention:

1. We are all members of some groups, and each of those groups influences us in some way, sometimes a great deal. The primary group—the family—is the basic social system into which most human beings are born and in which they grow and develop their full potential as people. In the family system, children shape their capacities for intimacy, empathy, and mutual caring. Later, the peer group (classmates and neighborhood friends) offers the meaningful figures with which children interact and develop. Securing for a child a place in a group saves the child from loneliness.

2. Children are accustomed to learning and working in groups. Consider that some preventive interventions, such as fire drills, already take place in the "natural group," which most often is the class-

room. Other interventions target smaller groups, such as those for children who have trouble learning certain math concepts and so spend time with a tutor.

3. The small group is an efficient setting in which to develop problem-solving strategies. In the supportive and helpful atmosphere of a small group, children and adults can raise questions for discussion, role-play new behaviors, learn coping techniques in simulation games, and counsel and be counseled. A group that nurtures mutuality and multidirectional communication frees participants from inhibitions, shame, and hesitation and motivates them to participate in the activities. When youngsters believe that their contribution to the group is meaningful, their involvement in group assignments is enhanced.

4. The small group is most suitable for tasks connected with emotional learning, counseling, and therapy and for the development of skills for coping with threatening situations. A well-conducted support group provides intimacy, attention, encouragement, and security. In this environment, the child can summon the courage to express and share perceptions and memories of the traumatic experience, as well as her or his fears, doubts, and expectations of catastrophe. In the final analysis, small groups typically allow children to express themselves without having to be afraid of censure or criticism. Each participant has a unique story with regard to previous traumatic experiences and, while listening to other group members' personal stories, each realizes that she or he does not have to be emotionally crippled by the trauma and is no different from the others. Group members measure the normality of their reactions against those of their friends and gradually adjust a self-concept that has been distorted by their traumatic experiences and repair their damaged self-esteem. Hearing others speak of events similar to what the child has experienced is very often the boost she or he needs to accept that hardships can be overcome. Such modeling from the group is often more effective than encouragement from grown-ups, whether parents, teachers, or therapists (Hammond, 1981).

5. Group participation provides for each individual child a variety of models of problem solving and expressive behavior. Johnson (1989), a developer of trauma prevention curricula, highlighted that "children learn best from modeling experience; this format of gradual assumption of responsibility allows children to evaluate information, recognize alternatives and take action" (p. 209)—skills that are critical to building resilience.

An advantage of group interventions with children who have had a traumatic experience is that the members of the group can actually present different stages of recovery. Thus, group members reflect varied experiences in a wide range of trauma-related situations, providing for each other an opportunity to reconsider the disaster and its effects and to find a range of suitable behavioral, emotional, and cognitive responses that they can emulate or adapt.

Spotlight on Research "Violence Prevention in Elementary Schools" highlights both the effectiveness of a primary intervention and the usefulness of classroom groups for putting the intervention into practice.

Violence Prevention in Elementary Schools

The Resolving Conflict Creatively Program (RCCP)—a school-based preventive intervention program focused on school violence—has served more than 200,000 children in New York City public schools since 1985. The goal of the program is to teach students constructive conflict resolution strategies and to promote positive intergroup relations. This goal is accomplished, among other things, by:

- making the children aware of the different choices available for responding to conflicts, and helping them to develop skills for making those choices;
- encouraging respect for their own culture and the culture of others;
- teaching children how to recognize and stand up against prejudice; and
- making "children aware of their role in creating a more peaceful world" (Aber, Brown, & Jones, 2003, p. 326).

To test the usefulness of the program, J. Lawrence Aber, Joshua Brown, and Stephanie Jones (2003) recruited four schools in each of four districts in New York City to use the curriculum over two years. A highly representative sample of 11,160 children in grades 1 to 6 participated.

The results were extremely positive. For example, children whose teachers taught more lessons in the program's creative conflict resolution (not all the teachers used the program in their classes the same way, although all were trained identically) "demonstrated (a) slower rates of growth in hostile attribution bias, aggressive interpersonal negotiation strategies, [and] self-reported conduct problems... and (b) faster rates of growth in teacher-reported prosocial behavior" (Aber et al., p. 344). The effect of the intervention was essentially the same for girls and for boys and for children from different economic and racial or ethnic backgrounds.

The researchers pointed out some of the limitations of their study—for example, the teachers self-selected to learn and use the RCCP and decided on their own how much to implement it in their classes. These realities of the research make it impossible to be certain about cause and effect relationships. However, given the robustness of the findings even with these limitations, the RCCP clearly is a powerful prevention intervention. In fact, following its success in New York, it is being implemented in a dozen school systems across the U.S.

Aber, J. L., Brown, J. L., & Jones, S. M. (2003). Developmental trajectories toward violence in middle childhood: Course, demographic differences, and response to school-based intervention. *Developmental Psychology, 39*, 324–348.

Foundation for Group Support

In her book *Blitz Kids*, Mordaunt (1941) described a nine-year-old girl who is stranded in the middle of a London street in the middle of a German air attack, during World War II. Having lost contact with family members, the girl starts spiraling into panic. At her most anxious moment, she spots a much younger child, alone and lost, who is crying in panic. As the girl takes the child by the hand and runs to find shelter, she experiences a total mood change: Whereas before she felt lost, she now feels in control; whereas before she felt confused and panicked, she now feels calmer, as she focuses on caring for the younger child in need.

This mechanism of gaining control over panic and grief by bestowing help to someone needy has been identified and labeled by Alfred Adler (1927/1998) as "social interest" and by Sol Gordon (1988) as "Mitzva Therapy" (*mitzva* is the Hebrew word meaning to transcend oneself by offering help to someone else). Helping others with the ultimate aim of helping oneself is at the root of building a group support system. According to Figley and McCubbin (1983), "support is often not an altruistic act. We derive considerable pleasure from helping others. For example, we may feel appreciated, needed; we may have more confidence that when we are in need those we are supporting will become *our* supporters" (p. 12).

In laying the principles for creating a prevention curriculum, Johnson (1989) emphasizes the difficulties facing children in crisis when their need for a support group is hampered by their lack of emotional and conceptual capability to build, maintain, and reconstruct a support system.

> When crises occur the personal situation changes and new needs arise, and this means that new supports must be sought. Yet during crisis the individual is usually the least able to assess personal needs, evaluate the types of support available, and to embark upon a project to enlist the appropriate support.... The time to engineer an adequate support system is *before anything happens*. (pp. 210-211) [emphasis in the original]

Group Interventions

There are at least two steps to setting up a group intervention: establishing ground rules and using familiarizing techniques to allow the group members—the children—to get to know each other.

Establishing ground rules. The early establishment of group structure and rules is very important, especially with children in the latency period (roughly ages five or six to puberty) who have boundless energy and are likely to disrupt the sessions. A focused structure (rather than the freewheeling chaos typical of children's groupings) helps children to learn and interact, enhances group cohesion, and encourages commitment to common goals.

The group, following the facilitator's succinct suggestions, usually decides on the ground rules of the contract. Although rules will differ from one group to another, most groups will agree on the following basic rules of interpersonal communication:

- The group will maintain an atmosphere of tolerance and mutual respect by accepting each other as she or he is and by listening to each other without judging or criticizing.
- Group members will speak about themselves in the first person.
- If someone wants to offer a remark or comment about something another group member has said or done in the group, she or he will address the other group member directly rather than discussing the matter in the third person.
- Conversations and sharing secrets are not allowed while another member of the group is speaking. Everyone listens to the person speaking.
- A group member may not choose to "not be on speaking terms" with another group member. It is all right to be angry with someone, but it is preferable to express this anger verbally.
- Anything said in the group is confidential: No one will share personal stories heard in the group with people outside the group.

In addition, it is against the rules to turn a group member's feelings or thoughts into weapons against her or him or to gossip about anyone.

- No one will be forced to speak. Group members who sit quietly in the group may be emotionally involved, enjoying themselves, and learning from others' stories.
- Each group member has the right to speak; no one is permitted to dominate discussions.

Developing group familiarization techniques. A facilitator may help the group begin its development by using warm-up activities that require physical, verbal, or dramatic actions. These activities have three goals: (1) to build trust in the facilitator, therapist, or group leader; (2) to develop trust and encourage communication among the children; and (3) to create a "conflict-free zone" in which creative activities can take place (Ayalon & Flasher, 1985). Creative activities provide a relaxing diversion and help group members search for alternative solutions for distressing situations. Music, games, relaxation exercises, comfortable chairs, and light refreshments help create the appropriate atmosphere.

Children should enjoy participating in group activities, even when the theme for the group intervention is preparing for disaster. Any activity that helps the children make meaningful contact with each other prepares the ground for successful intervention (Jennings, 1986; Liebmann, 1986).

Part of helping the children get to know each other is providing the opportunity for them to express their emotions. To express their emotions accurately, often it is necessary for them to enrich their "feelings vocabulary." This may be accomplished by helping them identify the spectrum of feelings connected with different behaviors and social situations. The "Feelings Wheel"

FIGURE 8-1. THE FEELINGS WHEEL

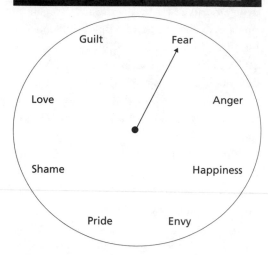

(Ayalon & Flasher, 1985) is one efficient way of learning the vocabulary of feelings.

The Feelings Wheel (Figure 8-1) passes from hand to hand, with each participant spinning it as if it were a roulette wheel until it comes to a stop at one of the feelings named on the wheel. The participant who spun the wheel then calls to mind some incident where he or she experienced this feeling, and shares the story with the group. The group leader then develops these themes, encouraging discussions and role-playing.

BASIC–PH MODEL: PREVENTIVE BLUEPRINT FOR GROUP WORK WITH CHILDREN

Even when it is impossible to foresee the details of an imminent critical event, programs for stress inoculation can be developed in advance based on the idea of enhancing generic resilience and coping skills, according to the BASIC-Ph model described in chapter 2. Each of the six dimensions of this model of coping resources may be looked at as a "bridge" to resilience. The working assumption is that resilience to stress can be developed systematically in individuals, groups, and systems by enhancing existing coping strategies and expanding coping repertoires to include new strategies (Ayalon & Lahad, 1991).

- **B**—*Beliefs and values channels*: The foundation of many groups is their ability to clarify and build their group identity by referring to and reinforcing their beliefs and values. This often requires creating group symbols, group ethos, and positive images of group competence. Some of these beliefs and values stem from the group history and belief system—for example, national identity, anthems, flags, and stories of ancestral bravery in the face of hardships—and some can be generated from group activities that create symbols and rituals to maintain the myth of togetherness. Religious beliefs, social ideals, moral values, and faith in self and in the group are all tested and reinforced in primary prevention simulations and role-playing.
- **A**—*Affective channels*: Affect (emotional experiences and expressions) mediate between our outer and inner worlds, unite and separate people, modify behaviors, and help give meaning to life. When we are able to express emotions, we create a sense of continuity of experience during changing times and a sense of belonging, caring, and containment in the group. The goal of opening this channel in preventive intervention is to promote "emotional intelligence" (Goleman, 1995) and to exercise the power of affective expression in building trust in the ability of the group to contain the individuals' distress if disaster strikes.
- **S**—*Social channels*: Building social structure and assigning roles are very important parts of every preventive program. Building the group's ability to maintain its normalcy when facing crisis or during

prolonged times of uncertainty helps stabilize group members. Simulations of possible impending crises can achieve this goal as leadership (on various levels) and other social-stability maintenance roles are rehearsed in the preventive phase. Most people maintain contact with various social groups at school, at play, at work, where they live, and with others who share a common interest or a common history. Important social channels include family bonds; the reciprocal commitment to family provides a safety net in situations of radical change. Family roles, family rituals, and multigenerational traditions stabilize a person's function in situations of uncertainty and are an important part of any preventive program.

- **I**—*Imagination channels*: Through the gift of imagination and fantasy, we connect the past, present, and future. In primary prevention activities, group members share their dreams and aspirations and strive to create a joint image of the desired future. Enhancing the group's ability to use imagination and creativity can serve as an essential element in unexpected situations when improvisation is needed to find alternative solutions to problems of safety and security.
- **C**—*Cognitive channels*: In early, or primary, prevention, the group learns the "rules of the game," including how to accumulate experience and predict what is going to happen. The bridge of logical reality testing enables group members to trust the world as rational and predictable. Group activities reinforce group members' recognition of the natural order in science and society, knowledge of social procedures, practices, and regulations, and their knowledge of the world in general and the close surroundings in particular. Discriminating and

appraising threatening cues, acquiring information about threats, and devising strategies of problem solving enhance group members' sense of control when facing situations of uncertainty.

- **Ph**—*Physical channels*: Helping group members learn to help themselves is a fundamental part of any prevention program. Being active, learning how to use physical exercises, relaxation, and focusing on practical solutions is part of the prevention effort. Taking care of basic survival needs is another aspect of this Ph mode.

SCHOOL–BASED STRESS PREVENTION PROGRAM: COPE

Before anyone can design a blueprint for diagnosis, needs assessment, or the building of intervention programs to enhance coping skills and resources, he or she must have a fundamental understanding of the six BASIC-Ph channels and the importance of practicing prevention activities in support groups to enhance individual resilience. These are the main features of the Community Oriented Preventive Education (COPE) program, a generic stress-prevention program initially developed for the Israeli school system and later translated and implemented in several other countries (Ayalon, 1978). For example, COPE has been used to enhance coping with stress and trauma associated with technological transitions and disasters in Thailand, domestic violence in England (Ayalon, 1987a, 1987b) and Finland (Ayalon, 1995a), war-related disasters in former Yugoslavia (Ayalon, 1995b), terrorism in Argentina (Ayalon & Lahad, 1995), and earthquakes in Turkey (Ayalon & Lahad, 2000).

COPE was developed as a preventive educational program in the 1970s to fit into the school curriculum and to be conducted by facilitators selected from the teaching and counseling staff (Ayalon, 1979). It is best to enhance schoolchildren's resilience in groups because children in schools are naturally in a variety of group combinations, from typical classroom peer groups to natural "tribelike" groups composed of children of various ages. Groups of children with shared experiences (for example, children with special needs, orphaned children, and immigrant children) also can become the training module for resilience building.

COPE was designed to be a comprehensive program with the following five goals:

1. To help children develop skills for coping with any sort of traumatic experience
2. To provide opportunities for children to rehearse specific modes of behavior useful in foreseeable situations of danger, ranging, among others, from an earthquake to a school fire to an air raid attack
3. To present children with information about typical stress-related physical and emotional reactions, so that they are not embarrassed or bewildered by their own reactions
4. To help children acquire techniques useful for gaining control over panic and distress
5. To train children in communication skills so that they are able to describe their inner turmoil, express their distress, ask for help, and offer help to others in need (helping others reduces the helper's own sense of helplessness and increases feelings of control).

COPE was first developed and implemented in a small urban town close to Israel's northern border, whose population consisted almost entirely of immigrants of a low socioeconomic level. There was a dual problem in choosing this particular community as the launching ground of the first COPE project. In addition to being overburdened with socioeconomic stress on top of the occasional disasters that hit it (usually in the form of rocket attacks), there were the challenges of upgrading the level of input of the local educational system and confronting problems associated with working with an ethnically diverse population. The project encompassed the entire school system, including nine preschools, three elementary schools, and two high schools.

The greatest challenge was to overcome the population's resistance to change and particularly the resistance to implement a primary-stress and disaster-prevention program in the school system. To reduce resistance, a holistic strategy was used that included sharing information, interacting, and communicating with community leaders and educational personnel, as recommended by Bennis, Benne, and Chin (1985). This strategy was introduced in five steps.

Step 1: The first step was to create an interdisciplinary emergency network within the community. Anticipated resistance from policymakers, local officials, and educators was dealt with by recruiting representatives from all the community's helping professions (education, welfare, health, and security departments) on both the ministerial and municipal levels. Interdisciplinary "emergency teams" were recruited to screen the specific local problem areas, map the community for resources, and act as catalysts among their colleagues.

Step 2: The second step was to gain entrance to and mobilize the school system by conducting meetings with educational personnel from the ministry and the community and with parents' representatives. The meetings were designed to allow teachers to express doubts and reservations, to reduce general

anxiety, to clarify attitudes toward the program, to "sell" the idea of the benefits of intervention, and to obtain the necessary formal clearance and consent from parents.

Step 3: The third step was to introduce COPE methods to the entire educational community. A conference on primary prevention was held for all of the school principals, teachers, counselors, school nurses and doctors, social workers, youth group leaders, and several parents. Following the plenary presentation on the educational benefits of conducting primary prevention in schools, the audience broke into small experiential workshop groups with trained facilitators. These groups discussed the use of COPE methods for enhancing better coping skills in students facing disaster-related issues. Some issues discussed were: children's needs to deal with uncertainty and threats to their security; children's worries and feelings of abandonment when parents, who may be nurses, doctors, firefighters, police, military, or other emergency personnel, are on call during a critical event; children's attitudes toward people who are injured or disabled by disasters and accidents; and children's fears of death following a critical event.

Step 4: The next step was to demonstrate how children of different ages engage in classroom and small group COPE activities. These demonstrations took place simultaneously in all affected schools: nine kindergartens and five public schools (three elementary schools, and two high schools).

Step 5: The last step was to evaluate and assess the project as a whole, and to use this information for revising the community plan. (See chapter 12 for several different approaches to developing a community disaster plan.)

Creative Techniques

The introduction of COPE intervention programs into the educational system inspired innovative research (Klingman & Ayalon, 1977) and a series of handbooks, such as *Rescue!* (Ayalon, 1992), *Life on the Edge* (Ayalon, & Lahad, 1991), and *On Death and Life* (Lahad ,& Ayalon, 1995). These publications provide preventive curricula for teachers and counselors who wish to prepare their students for natural, technological, and complex disasters. The activities, based on the BASIC-Ph resilience and coping model, offer creative means for developing a wide range of coping skills.

Imagination and emotional expression.

Imagination and emotional expression are tapped by narrative-metaphoric methods, using stories, myths, legends, and poems (Bettelheim, 2000; Gersie & King, 1990; Mills & Crowly, 1986). After a well-chosen story is presented, the group participates in performing a prescribed task, thus composing individual stories parallel to the presented one. The whole process remains within the metaphoric discourse.

For example, "Leave Taking" (Saltan, 1929), which presents a dialogue between the two last leaves about to fall from an oak tree in the autumn, is a story carefully chosen to reflect the many faces of separation, death, and bereavement. The following is an example of the text read to the students, after which the teachers or other helpers ask them to fill in the conversation between the leaves and provide an ending for the story:

"Why must we fall?" asked the trembling leaf. "What will happen to us when we fall down?"... The second leaf was silent for a while, then said: "I don't know....Let's remember how beautiful it was to feel the sunshine and the morning dew....You've always been so kind to me."...Then both were silent. Hours passed.

The story, similar to a make-believe play, exists in a "transitional space" (Winnicott, 1982) where facts and fiction are mixed. It allows the listeners to examine issues that usually arouse conflicts and anxiety from a relatively safe distance. The narrative healing process follows the story's structure step-by-step. First, the story presents the problem of encountering death—distressful feelings are formulated, such as fear, grief, anger, longing, regret, and the need to find meaning in disaster. Following this narrative, the group discusses various solutions. Third, the group offers a symbolic solution in a form of a parting ritual or a written eulogy. Finally, the group members achieve some level of acceptance of the inevitability of loss and death, and then they reflect on the entire process (Ayalon, 1993). The group acts as a "safe container" for the release of the individuals' intense emotions.

Free writing.

Free writing helps discharge emotions, gain self-awareness, and project future expectations. Free writing allows a person to learn about her or his masks and, perhaps, to look at what is under them.

Cappacione (2001) suggested that by writing questions with their dominant hand and then letting free associations emerge by writing with the nondominant hand, children are given an opportunity for an inner dialogue to emerge that opens up previously hidden resources. Lahad (Lahad, 2000) suggested writing with closed eyes so that cognitive criticism is delayed, allowing a free flow of thoughts and feelings. A third method of free writing consists of writing a letter that will never be sent—a method that can provide closure for an unfinished or disrupted relationship with a meaningful person in the child's life (Ayalon & Flasher, 1993). In addition to these methods, sentence completion is another way to elicit "stuck" emotions.

Dramatic play. Dramatic play is useful for solving interpersonal and intrapsychic conflicts (Lahad, 2000). Drama, which mirrors social processes and encourages change (Grainger, 1990), consists of acting "as if I am someone else whereas I know that I am not." This position increases people's capacity to take risks. It encourages them to choose among a range of different ways of perceiving the world or the specific traumatic event. Drama therapy is a way of rehearsing and practicing skills children need to face life's adversities.

Different dramatic techniques include "re-enactment" and "an empty chair." Re-enactment involves the recreation of a traumatic incident, leading to an exploration of areas of distress, confusion, anger, helplessness, and so on, as well as an exploration of what went well, what helped, and what gave a sense of control. Other group members may take different roles. With "an empty chair," an empty chair is used to represent a missing person, and the group member is encouraged to address this person (the chair). In addition, the group member changes places (sits in the chair) and acts as if she or he is the missing person. Other group members may support or join in (Winn, 1994).

Nonverbal methods. Nonverbal methods, such as drawing, sculpting, movement, dance, play, and relaxation, are well suited for children who have difficulty articulating their thoughts and feelings (Robbins, 1994).

Cognitive and social restructuring. Preventive intervention support groups are an excellent place to rehearse cognitive and social restructuring methods, such as stress inoculation, affirmations, problem solving, and conflict resolution (Meichenbaum, 1985). Stress inoculation methods are based on the belief that even when children cannot change their external reality, they can be helped to transform their internal reality, the way they think and feel and interpret the events in their lives (Ellis, 1991).

Simulations. Simulations provide highly motivational training opportunities for meeting an unexpected, complicated situation (Inbar, 1968). By using simulations as part of a preventive intervention strategy, helpers can provide an opportunity for the redirection of individual and community energies toward growth and development. On the individual level, simulations can help protect against stress-induced depression, anxiety, and feelings of loneliness and abandonment.

For a simulation of COPE to be successful, facilitators need to be familiar with the following five principles, which form COPE's basic procedures:

1. Distress can lead to the individual or the group discovering hidden strengths.
2. Existing coping patterns can be enhanced and new ones can be acquired, suitable to the individual ages and temperaments of the participants.
3. Creative activities can alleviate tension; help participants integrate emotions; cognitions, and actions; reinforce a positive self-image, and serve to minimize the perception of the threat.
4. Subgroups within the class can become a support group, with an emphasis on shared

Mock Disaster at a High School

On March 20, 2001, mock terrorists stormed Beulah High School in Lee County, Alabama. The event, a large-scale disaster preparedness exercise, took place while security cameras captured the terrorists' actions and transmitted them in real-time via the Internet to school and law enforcement officials. The goal of the simulation was to test the usefulness of the information provided by remote video surveillance. Can this information help school officials, emergency medical personnel, and police respond quickly and safely to the crisis? The answer the simulation provided was yes. The equipment provided video access that allowed officials to determine, within minutes, where the terrorists were, what weapons they carried, and how many hostages were being held.

Although disaster preparedness is not new to schools, the use of video surveillance is—especially video surveillance that uses the Internet. This means any computer can be used to gain access to live images, making access to a "control room" unnecessary.

fate. The participants in these smaller groups can serve as mirrors and role models for each other, and the group can subsequently foster open communication and self-expression without fear of judgment, criticism, or rejection by peers.

5. Spontaneous and imaginative expression triggered by projective techniques helps children gain access to suppressed worries; alleviating such worries serves to release additional creative energies.

In *Rescue!* Ayalon (1992) applied COPE, and presented structured guided units with instructions for a facilitator and explicit suggestions for participants; this structure facilitates operation by mental health professionals, educators, and paraprofessionals. To check the usefulness of *Rescue!*'s "Rescue Emergency Kit," Ayalon set up a disaster simulation, code named D Day (Ayalon, 1979). One elementary school became the target school; high school students were assigned to the school as group leaders and facilitators for the younger children. Helpers instructed the high school students beforehand and prepared them for their role by means of a simulation game designed for that purpose.

The Touching Reality "A School's Impending Disaster" provides you with an opportunity to experience the D Day simulation.

Evaluations of COPE

Researchers initially assessed the effectiveness of COPE through observation of the D Day simulation. Their reports supported the following six conclusions: (1) The availability and clarity of the instructions included in the Rescue Emergency Kit contributed to the successful operation of COPE. (2) A lot of dynamic activity went on in the groups, with a free interplay between reality and imagination. (3) The observers noted a high degree of involvement by all the children, as well as intensive interpersonal communication. (4) The availability of both verbal and nonverbal modes of expression enabled children to choose activities that best suited them. (5) Role-play activities provided even the most inhibited children with the opportunity to vent their feelings from behind borrowed identities. (6) The children exercised their skills for coping with stress as they looked for unusual solutions and experienced new behaviors.

A School's Impending Disaster

As you read the following description of a school's impending disaster, consider that you are in a position to assume responsibility for the safety of the schoolchildren, and although there is no immediate danger to any of them, you realize that they are under stress. They cannot exit their classrooms. They have no information about what is going on. They cannot make contact with their families.

Because you are already familiar with several COPE activities, you decide to facilitate some of these activities in the classrooms, to be conducted by the teachers. Your aim is to help the children alleviate their tensions and for them to be active and cooperative for as long as the crisis lasts. Remember that children can enjoy being active in more than one way: They need to engage in physical actions and group interaction; and they need to engage in Intellectual activities that trigger their imaginations, challenge their cognitive skills, allow them to ventilate emotions, and strengthen their self-esteem and trust in others.

D Day Scenario

The school is in a state of siege. Convicts from a nearby jail have broken out and are hiding somewhere near the school grounds. They are armed, desperate, and considered very dangerous. To keep the students and staff safe, there is an emergency alert. Transportation and phones are either cut off or overloaded. Children are confined to their classrooms, and all outside play is curtailed. The situation is murky and tension is high, although there is no immediate life-threatening danger. The teachers have a fairly complete understanding of the BASIC-Ph coping channels, but they may benefit from being reminded that these letters stand for Beliefs and values, Affect (emotions), Social interaction, Imagination and creativity, Cognition—thinking and problem solving, and Physical actions and relaxation.

Take some time to plan activities for at least two or three different age groups. Write down the instructions for these activities. You can make them up or use some of the previously described creative techniques. After you (and any others with whom you may be doing this Touching Reality experience) write your suggestions for the classroom activities, go on to read the following examples of COPE activities. You can add them to your own list.

Some Vignettes of D Day Events

Magic Shop. Sixth-grade students open a "magic shop" that sells "solutions." Participants play the roles of customers and vendors.

The following is one example of the game. Client: "My brother's a police officer and he's been missing since yesterday. I'm frightened of what might happen to him. Can you sell me something so I won't be so scared?"

The sellers offer different solutions, such as:

1. "Trust your friends to help you out."
2. "Write all your worries in a letter to God and pray to God to take care of him."
3. "Put an ad on the Internet—someone who knows his whereabouts will get in touch."

The sellers compete, trying to get their advice sold to the client. The winning solution is the one best liked by the customer. As the atmosphere warms up, both "customers" and "merchants" learn to pay careful attention to each other, to help and to be helped.

(BASIC-Ph Note: The customer's plea reflects the use of imagination, plus an expression of feeling and social concerns for a family member. Solution 1 taps the Social channel, solution 2, the Belief channel, and solution 3, the Cognitive channel.)

Like a House on Fire. A "fire" breaks out in the first-grade classroom. Some children become the flames and threaten to burn

Cont'd

everything, some role-play frightened victims and run away, and some role-play firefighters and volunteer to "extinguish" the flames. There is a great commotion, cries, and laughter. After some struggle, the "firefighters" succeed in overcoming the fire. The helper guides the children to a quiet corner and to calm themselves with deep breathing relaxation.

(BASIC-Ph Note: This activity encourages the use of three channels, Physical activity and relaxation, Imagination, and Social role fulfillment and cooperation.)

Our Shelter. Children build a shelter out of existing furniture and scrap wood. The shelter is decorated to be comfortable and secure. When an "alert" siren is heard, participants hurry into the "shelter." Inside the "shelter," children initiate fun activities, such as singing and games, until the "all clear" siren sounds. Participants process the experience using a "draw and tell" activity.

(BASIC-Ph Note: This activity encourages the use of the Physical channel, with building the shelter, playing games, and singing; the

Imagination channel, with singing, playing games, and drawing, as well as designing the shelter; the Affect channel, with the search for security; and the Social channel, with planning, cooperation, group singing, social listening, and acceptance.)

Where Is Daddy? Children improvise a short play: Mother and daughter go out to search for the father who went to the army and did not send any letters home. On their search, they encounter different creatures (imaginary and real); some of these "creatures" are helpful, and some put obstacles in their way. As they meet each creature, they need to negotiate and convince it of their quest's importance. The helper leads a group discussion following the short play that focuses on allowing the children to share personal experiences that they have never before had a chance to share.

(BASIC-Ph Note: This activity uses three channels, with its emphasis on Affective expressions, Imaginary encounters with creatures, Social role playing, and social sharing of experiences.)

When the observers reflected on the D Day simulation they became aware of a concern that needs to be addressed when conducting a preventive intervention simulation. Stress inoculation promotes vigilance, which is positive, but it also raises a problem: How do you balance downgrading threat cues sufficiently without inviting the children to become callous, and how do you encourage alertness without inviting the children to be overwhelmed by anxiety?

Lahad and Abraham (1983) conducted a formal research study in Kiryat Shmona, Israel, to test the effectiveness of COPE in reducing anxiety and enhancing schoolchildren's ability to cope when exposed to stress and threat. The research population included 168 pupils (86 in the experimental group and 82 in the control group) in grades

3, 5, 6, and 7, and a group of eight teachers and three school administrators. The researchers carried out the classroom interventions over nine weekly two-hour meetings (18 hours total for each class). All children completed several measures, including a measure of situational anxiety before and after the intervention.

The results indicated a considerable decrease in students' antisocial behavior and fear-induced responses, such as screaming and somatic complaints, and an increase in children's cooperative behavior, such as mutual support. In addition, the experimental groups scored higher on expressive behaviors: Children willingly shared personal thoughts and feelings about what was happening in their lives. Although situational anxiety tested higher in the experimental group than in the control group, students in the program showed an increase in their effective use of coping skills. The results in the experimental classes, tested after one year, remained stable. These outcomes have been corroborated by more-recent research (Ayalon, Lahad, & Cohen, 1998, 1999).

The intervention model developed in Kiryat Shmona was later adapted for the entire Israeli school system (Ayalon & Lahad, 1991; Klingman & Ayalon, 1977) and has since been used in preparing for natural and complex disasters in other countries around the world (Ayalon, Lahad, & Cohen, 1998, 1999; Krkelijic & Pavlicic, 1998; Lugovic, 1999).

Lessons Learned

An important lesson learned from these pioneering steps in the area of prevention is that to succeed in implementing a primary prevention program in schools, helpers must gain the school principals' consent and active leadership. This is a prerequisite to forming an emergency team that includes key personnel, including the vice principal, senior teachers, school nurse or doctor, counselor, school psychologist, parents' representatives, and a teacher appointed as safety and security officer. The emergency team goes through in-service training in planning for a disaster, both on the organizational level and on the psychoeducational level.

It may seem obvious that the best time to invest in these preparations is the relatively peaceful time before a disaster strikes, but it seems that a sense of approaching threat is the best trigger to motivate school personnel and to reduce antagonism directed toward the program. In many cases, the need for prevention arises *after* a disaster hits a community, as was the case following the explosion of the space shuttle Challenger and the

attacks on the World Trade Center in New York and the Pentagon in Virginia. For example, a group intervention protocol, suggested by the principal of River Dell High School in Oradell, New Jersey (Stevenson, 1986), was written so that River Dell High, as well as other schools, would have a written plan to follow if an incident such as the Challenger explosion were to reoccur. In addition to a school-based intervention, the program includes a detailed outline of the protocol that River Dell High adopted for individual student intervention.

In light of the growing awareness of the central role that schools play in the life of children, and the increase of crises both in schools and out of schools, but affecting school populations, the time is ripe to propose a generic approach to prevention intervention. Anticipatory planning must include organizational considerations, training of emergency teams, and the rehearsal of possible solutions. At the same time, it must be clear that disasters have a way of surprising even the most meticulous of planners, so fostering a flexible and open attitude is essential in preparing for crisis and disaster.

10–STEP PROTOCOL FOR ORGANIZATIONAL PRIMARY PREVENTION

The following 10-step protocol is developed from a school-based model for preventive disaster intervention planning (Ayalon & Lahad, 1991). Although it is based on experience and experimentation within the Israeli school system in border areas that are under severe stress, the model has been subsequently elaborated and tested in various other school disasters. These disasters include a school bus collision (Klingman, 1989), a terrorist suicide bus bombing (Shacham, Lahad, Sela, &

Shacham, 2000), a school bus accident (Toren, 2000), a terrorist attack on a Buenos Aires community center (Stein, Green, Terlyuk, & Horacio, 2000), and an earthquake in Turkey (Ayalon & Lahad, 2000).

1. The first step involves *mapping targets for crisis management during an anticipated disaster* to minimize casualties and maximize feelings of security. This entails locating the most likely areas where disasters may occur and identifying the personnel to be trained first.

2. The second step requires *monitoring weak points in the physical and social structure* of the school. This step calls for identifying high-risk groups vulnerable individuals and marking unsafe or hazardous spaces on the school premises.

3. Planning begins with the third step, which requires *preparing a contingency plan* for crisis management and intervention, and training school staff in applying the contingency plan. This may include evacuation to a safe location and the establishment of emergency communication networks.

4. The fourth step focuses on *preparing alternatives* to conducting school activities in the event of a critical incident. For example, if a school building becomes unsafe, an alternative location needs to be available, and if a staff member is absent or dead, a replacement may come from among parents or volunteers. It is essential for authorities to recruit and train community members (including parents, retired professionals, and young adults) to stand in for absent personnel, if necessary.

5. The fifth step involves *training small, efficient target teams* of staff, parents, and students to deal with designated functions,

such as evacuating classes and securing safe gathering places; obtaining electricity, water, and medical supplies; arranging substitute activities for children for the duration of the incident; and screening for people who show signs of malfunctioning, such as those who are sick, panicked, or severely distressed.

6. The sixth step focuses on *designating a crisis headquarters* with full authority for decision making during the critical incident, including the development of practical staff aids and the in vivo practice of their use.

7. Step 7 focuses on *educating staff and students in the basic understanding of human behavior under stress*, and preparing materials for quick reference when needed. Information may include what to look for—common reactions of children to disasters, distinguished by age—and helpful ways to respond to those reactions.

8. Step 8 considers the interaction between the school and the children's parents. It is important to *designate representatives to respond to and help worried parents*, and to guide parents in ways to help their distressed children, such as remaining calm and reassuring their children that they are safe.

9. In addition to designating school personnel who will work with parents, administrators also need to *designate school personnel who will work with the local media and social services agencies*—this is the focus of Step 9. Some disasters may bring national media and social services agencies to the area, and these national representatives need to have designated personnel with whom to communicate.

10. Step 10 considers *developing stress inoculation curricula*, rehearsing it, and reassessing it periodically.

Before building a scenario for a school's response to a pending disaster, administrators must depend on an analysis of previous responses to critical events in the school. This analysis should provide the necessary information to correct past mistakes and to highlight the school's strengths in dealing with a crisis. Finally, it is important to refresh the intervention plan periodically by organizing simulation exercises. This keeps the staff in a state of preparedness, maintains staff motivation, and allows for the assessment of the process and for the correction of mistakes.

PRIMARY INTERVENTION IN THE FAMILY

As a stress-buffering environment, the family forms the first line of defense against post-traumatic stresses precipitated by a disaster. The family's traditional ways of dealing with daily stress and its repertoire of coping resources can be directed to meet the challenges of a disaster. The most effective adjustment the family can make to lower the toll of a disaster is to prevent as much physical and mental damage as possible. "Prevention includes family planning for possible emergencies, knowledge of the best ways to survive, some form of psychological preparation, and overt actions to prepare" (Smith, 1983, p. 145). Planning in the family context reduces uncertainties, gives the family more appropriate procedures for coping, prepares psychological defenses, helps reduce anxiety to manageable levels, and provides for basic needs.

Touching Reality "Before and After a Disaster" provides you with an opportunity to consider the advantages of primary prevention and some of the obstacles that need to be considered for primary prevention to become a reality.

TOUCHING REALITY

Before and After a Disaster

Imagine that you are sitting with your family on Monday night, September 10, 2001, when you get a phone call (or a letter, an e-mail, a visit) from the local disaster watch group. You are asked to join a project called "Families Preparing for a Future Disaster." The type of disaster, its duration, and its impact are vague, but you are told that a supervisor will come to your home on the following day to explain the program to your family. What do you think? What do you feel? Do you discuss it with members of your family, and if you do, with whom? How is the family going to reach a decision? Do you wish to talk to other candidates of the proposed program? What, in the end, do you decide to do? (Write whatever comes to mind and fold the paper.)

Now, it is late evening on Tuesday, September 11, 2001. All day you have been watching the "Attack on America" broadcasts, the collapse of the World Trade Center in Manhattan, and the Pentagon burning outside Washington, D.C. You are sitting with your family, talking of yesterday's offer to participate in the Families Preparing for a Future Disaster. Think of the interaction in your family. Who says what?

What are the pros and cons of involving families in primary prevention programs?

Families in Primary Prevention Programs

The first part of this chapter described the issues involved in primary prevention in social and educational systems. Comparing the progress achieved in implementing disaster primary intervention in educational systems with that achieved in family primary prevention, the latter still lags behind. It is important to bridge this gap and enhance family prevention programs.

Family primary intervention programs should provide knowledge about disasters and typical reactions to them. In addition, they should provide information on how to deal with crises in general and with specific disasters common to the area in which the family lives (for example, earthquakes in the northern part of California and hurricanes along the east coast of Florida). It is vital for helpers to supply practical strategies to deal with an impeding disaster, because offering information about disasters without providing appropriate coping skills is likely to induce fear and promote feelings of helplessness. This is true both for individuals and for families.

It is important to realize that each family, as a living system, has a unique way of coping with adversities. Therefore, primary intervention programs are best conducted by facilitators who focus on family coping resources, and who have a basic understanding of family dynamics. When applying a program to a specific family, facilitators need to consider the existing leadership and communication style of the family, and use the family's problem-solving methods for enhancing predisaster coping skills.

Planning disaster prevention programs for families must consider issues of gaining access to families, dealing with resistance, raising motivation, giving supervision, and monitoring the preparation processes. The following are fundamental questions that need to be addressed in order for a comprehensive family-based plan to be operative.

- "Is the family unit capable of being a basic unit around which overall disaster planning can be tied?" (Smith, 1983, p. 146).

Family characteristics. On the one hand, because protecting its members is one of the basic roles of a functional family, it is only natural for facilitators to equip the family with life-saving knowledge and instructions that they can use during a disaster. On the other hand, many families are not functioning at their optimum level and may be unable to take on these responsibilities. For example, many families are overburdened with economic problems, and others may suffer from health deficiencies, addictions, or violence. Numerous families are fragmented because of death or divorce, and others are marginalized socially (Figley & McCubbin, 1983). Not all families will have appropriately supportive interrelations and helpful communication among the family members.

- How do I reach out and gain entree to the family system: How can "family disaster preparedness" be fostered in spite of the natural reluctance of people to deal with the unpleasantness it suggests, and to allocate the resources it requires?

Gaining access and overcoming resistance. Families, in sharp contrast to other organized social systems, are private entities. For example, schools and other community services, because they are public organizations, are relatively accessible to helpers who wish to conduct predisaster programs; also, they have a defined and identifiable leadership and are committed to act for the benefit of the community. Families, however, may have loose connections to the community, and may have other priorities that may seem to them more pressing than preparing for a future disaster.

Several preconditions are needed for a facilitator to be able to introduce a planned program of "family disaster preparation." First, families need to opt for the program, that is, they have to choose to be active participants, to follow instructions, and to agree to be trained in specific methods of domestic crisis organization. Second, they need to agree to be supervised and to expose themselves to some form of monitoring or assessment.

For many families, family disaster preparation may seem an uncalled–for burden on the family's schedule, an additional and unwanted strain on the parents, or an infringement of the family's privacy. Having "outsiders" dictate certain aspects of the household organization and family members' behaviors may violate the family's sense of autonomy. Moreover, emergency instructions, including an open discussion of emotionally loaded issues, may be experienced as an interference with family norms and values.

Clinical experience has shown that gaining access to families and mobilizing them to change their routine for a cause that holds some vague future benefits has only a small chance of success. There is no proven way for implementing family primary prevention, but some attempts have been shown to be quite fruitful. For example, Figley and McCubbin (1983) suggested the use of public, private, and religious educational programs, as well as the use of the media, to help families become aware of "the importance and effectiveness of educating families about emergency prepared-

ness for avoiding the negative impact of disasters" (p. 189). FEMA in the United States (FEMA, 2003a, 2003b) issued recommendations for parents to create their own family disaster plan *before* a natural disaster occurs, and provided details about how to develop such a plan.

Mental health professionals, who usually act as agents for implementing primary prevention, frequently encounter families' passive or active resistance to disaster education. Resistance can be cognitive (such as rejection of the information about an impending disaster or regarding it as irrelevant, because of the belief that "it won't happen to us"), emotional (such as parents' unwillingness to deal with threatening themes, as well as their attempt to protect their children from ideas or images that may arouse their anxiety), and behavioral (such as unwillingness to engage in any activity or to make the necessary preparations). Resisting parents will not be willing to allocate their time or money for the purpose of preparation. Facilitators have to encourage communities to make efforts, and they have to find "change agents" to motivate parents to participate in family disaster preparedness programs.

- How can schools help introduce family disaster planning and motivate families to engage in them?

Schools as agents of change for the family. In view of these impediments, facilitators need to find effective channels to reach and motivate families to take part in prevention. For families with school-age children, school may be one of these channels. Parents will be drawn to the "prevention program" by their children's participation in a school primary prevention curricula, something, perhaps, such as COPE. (It is imperative, of course, to receive parents' consent before including a child in any group process that is not an integral part of the school's curriculum.)

Family involvement in disaster planning may start with protests: Parents may have religious, cultural, political, or personal objections to their child participating in a disaster intervention group and discussing subjects such as disaster, war, terrorism, death, separation, evacuation, or even uncertainty. The best way for school authorities to handle such resistance is to call group meetings with parents. The first part of these meetings should address reasons for such refusal. Common reasons include (1) parents distrust the capacity of school personnel to handle emotional problems, (2) parents wish to protect their child from exposure to disaster-related threatening materials, and (3) parents feel incapable of dealing with their children's distress and questions following the school intervention.

Group meetings can be used to change parents' objections into cooperation. Parents' trust in the school's facilitators can be built during these direct encounters, and parents can be briefed on the educational importance and behavioral benefits of pre- and postdisaster interventions with children. When appropriate, parents can be invited to participate in certain parts of the intervention as observers or trained to be facilitators—recruiting them, in essence, into the family prevention programs.

- Are there other community services that can help foster family engagement and commitment for disaster preparation?

Family guidance groups as agents of change for the family. An alternative entree into the family can be initiated through parents' guidance groups, groups that promote family well-being and teach family members how to deal with everyday stresses and expected crises. When parents turn to professionals to learn more about childrearing or to seek specific enlightenment regarding developmental issues of their children, they may be open to accept a module on crisis and disaster intervention as part of the general course. Parent and family guidance programs have a wide outreach, and their guidelines can be implemented in the pre-disaster planning. For example, Parent Effectiveness Training (Gordon, 2000) provides tools for parents to improve their leadership of and communication with their children from birth to young adulthood. Effective leadership and open communication can prove to be very important tools in developing the family's capabilities to respond to disaster.

Developing a Family Disaster Plan

Information about helping resources that are available, and specific instructions for developing a disaster plan are of great practical value to a family preparing for a disaster. The following extended example presents material from two FEMA publications, "Your Family Disaster Plan" (2003a) and "Your Family Disaster Supplies Kit" (2003b). "Your Family Disaster Plan" begins with the following questions: "What would you do if basic services—water, gas, electricity or telephones—were cut off?... Where will your family be when disaster strikes?... How will you find each other?... Will you know if your children are safe?," then reminds readers, "Local officials and relief workers will be on the scene after a disaster, but they cannot reach everyone right away" (FEMA, 2003a, p. 1).

Your Family Disaster Plan
FOUR STEPS TO SAFETY

1. Find Out What Could Happen to You

- Ask authorities for information on what types of disasters are most likely to happen. Request information from the police, firefighters, and so on as to how to prepare for each.
- Learn about your community's warning signals—their sound and what you should do when you hear them.
- Ask a community leader for information on how to help elderly or disabled persons in your community, if needed.
- Next, talk to your employer, your children's school or day care center, and authorities at other places where your family spends time for information about disaster plans at each location.

2. Create a Disaster Plan

- Meet with your family and discuss why you need to prepare for disaster. Explain the dangers of fire, severe weather, and earthquakes to children. Make a plan to share responsibilities and to work together as a team.
- Discuss what to do in an evacuation. Plan how to take care of your pets, if any.

- Pick several locations you could meet outside the home or elsewhere if you cannot return home, and prioritize them (that is, "First go to the Smiths; if their house is also damaged, go to the Millers," and so on).

3. Complete This Checklist

- Postemergency telephone numbers by phones (fire, police, ambulance, and so on).
- Teach children how and when to call 911 or your local Emergency Medical Services number for emergency help.
- Show each family member how and when to turn off the water, gas, and electricity at the main switches.
- Stock emergency supplies and assemble a Disaster Supplies Kit (this should include supplies for three days of confinement: two quarts of water per person per day, ready-to-eat canned food, high-energy food, comfort food, a first aid kit, nonprescription drugs, tools and supplies, sanitation items, clothing and bedding, and important documents In waterproof containers).
- Determine the best escape routes from your home. Identify two ways out of each room.
- Identify the safe spots in your home for each type of disaster.

4. Practice and Maintain Your Plan.

When a disaster is impending, parents can be motivated to introduce measures of preparation into their homes. For example, it is typical when a meteorological warning of an impending hurricane or flood is given for parents to seal their house, prepare necessary kits for a hasty evacuation, and encourage their children to pack personal belongings and some games to take if an evacuation is necessary. It is usual to see the shelves in supermarkets stripped bare as family members rush to buy staples, comfort foods, and foods that do not require cooking (electricity may be out and gas lines broken).

By staying alert to broadcasts to gather the latest news, parents are able to provide their children with accurate information and direct instructions, which are both important in helping their children cope with the coming event.

A Parent–Child Tool for an Impending Disaster

During the warning stage before "Desert Storm" (the Gulf War) in 1991, the Israeli civilian society was threatened by a chemical warfare attack from Iraq as retaliation for the U.S. coalition against Saddam Hussein. Gas masks were distributed to the bewildered population with minimal instructions on how to use them. Following the gas mask distribution, authorities broadcasted instructions to families to seal one room in their house and stay in it until the anticipated missile attack had ended. The nation needed a nationwide preventive intervention tool; this was especially true for families with young children, to help parents help their children. To meet the parents' need for tools to explain what was happening, and to help them train their children to wear the masks, Mooli Lahad, Vered Lahad, and Ofra Ayalon published and distributed a coloring book using child's language.

The coloring book, *Space-Kids in Search of Clean Air* (Lahad, Lahad, & Ayalon, 1991), which included a guide for parents, is an example of a parent-focused stress inoculation program for young children that can be used in cases of threat of any impending disaster, such as chemical and biological warfare, earthquakes, floods, road accidents, industrial disasters and terrorist attacks. The booklet can be used for storytelling, dramatization, and coloring, and can also be used as a trigger for children's verbalizing their fears, anger, and other emotions.

The story creates a psychological framework for talking about disasters in a playful manner. It facilitates a gradual exposure to concepts that are familiar to the child and helps develop coping skills. The framework of the story is geared to helping parents and teachers to deal with their own uncertainties, by providing them with an effective tool to regain a sense of control.

THE SPACE-KIDS IN SEARCH OF CLEAN AIR: A GUIDEBOOK FOR PARENTS AND CHILDREN

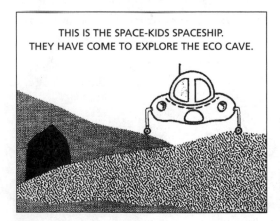

THIS IS THE SPACE-KIDS SPACESHIP. THEY HAVE COME TO EXPLORE THE ECO CAVE.

THE CAVE IS BIG, VERY BIG. WHEN THEY ARE DEEP INSIDE, THEY SEE A SIGN: POLLUTED AIR!!!

POLLUTED AIR!

cont'd

IT'S HARD TO BREATHE. THE AIR IS SO BAD. IT IS POLLUTED.

SUDDENLY THEY SEE BUNNY BIGNOSE, HAPPY AND CHEERFUL. THEY COUGH AND SAY: WHAT A FUNNY NOSE! HOW COME YOU ARE SO HAPPY?

BUNNY BIGNOSE SAYS: WHEN IT RAINS, WE USE RAINCOATS AND UMBRELLAS. WHEN IT IS SUNNY AND HOT WE STAY UNDER A SUNSHADE. AND WHEN THE AIR IS BAD, IT'S SMART TO USE A MASK.

YOU CAN ALSO BE HAPPY AND FEEL SAFE TO EXPLORE THE CAVE IF YOU PUT ON THE MASK. AT FIRST IT MAY BE A BIT TIGHT AND DIFFICULT TO BREATHE, BUT SOON YOU'LL GET USED TO IT.

NOW THEY ARE PUTTING ON THEIR MASKS. THEY DO LOOK FUNNY, DON'T THEY? BUT NOW THEY CAN BREATHE CLEAN AIR AND FEEL HAPPY.

LET'S EXPLORE THE CAVE, UNTIL THE AIR IS CLEAN AGAIN.

WHEN YOUR PARENTS OR TEACHER TELL YOU THAT THE AIR IS SO BAD YOU MUST ALSO PUT ON THE "CLEAN AIR MASK" JUST LIKE BUNNY BIGNOSE. YOU CAN PUT YOUR OWN PHOTO ON THE MASK, OR DRAW YOUR FACE INSIDE THE MASK.

Source: Lahad, M., Lahad, V., & Ayalon, O. (1991). *Space Kids in Search of Clean Air*. Haifa, Israel: Nord.

SUMMARY

Primary prevention, which focuses on cognitive and organizational preparation for an expected disaster, aims, above all, to provide organizations, families, and potential caregivers with the skills necessary to deal with a potential disaster effectively. Schools, with their predictable routines and as the place where many children spend the greatest part of the day, can play a major role in primary prevention. School authorities, however, often mirror attitudes and fears in the general adult population that make it difficult to engage schools in primary prevention.

The group can serve as the arena for primary prevention, whether organized in schools or other organizations, or the family. Setting up a group intervention requires a facilitator to establish ground rules to create a focused structure and promote cohesion, and to use "get acquainted" activities to promote the development of trust and create a "safe space" to interact.

The COPE program is a generic stress prevention program initially developed for the Israeli school system but which has since been used in various countries throughout the world. Its goals, structure, and activities—as well as the problems it encountered being implemented and how those problems were resolved—may serve as a model for the development of other preventive education programs. The 10-step protocol presents a generic model to guide preventive disaster intervention planning.

The family, as the first line of defense against posttraumatic stresses precipitated by a disaster, is an important site for primary prevention. Planning disaster prevention programs for families must consider issues such as gaining access to families and dealing with resistance. FEMA's recommendations for a Family Disaster Plan include suggestions that each family

- find out what could happen to them during a disaster
- create a plan that meets the needs of the particular family and ensures that the family members work together as a team
- complete a disaster checklist and put together a Disaster Supply Kit
- practice and maintain the plan.

To be realistic, preventive programs that follow a disaster have a greater appeal—and, therefore, a greater chance of implementation—than those that are an "early warning." Regardless, preventive intervention is the first step to ensuring the best possible outcome when a disaster strikes.

REFERENCES

Aber, J. L., Brown, J. L., & Jones, S. M. (2003). Developmental trajectories toward violence in middle childhood: Course, demographic differences, and response to school-based intervention. *Developmental Psychology, 39*, 324–348.

Adler, A. (1998). *Understanding human nature* (C. Brett, Trans.). Oxford, England: Oneworld. (Original work published 1927)

Ayalon, O. (1978). *Emergency kit*. Haifa, Israel: Haifa University Press. (Hebrew)

Ayalon, O. (1979). Community oriented preparation for emergency. *Journal of Death Education, 3*, 222–244.

Ayalon, O. (1982). Children as hostages. *Practitioner, 226*, 1771–1773.

Ayalon, O. (1983). Coping with terrorism: The Israeli case. In D. Meichenbaum & M. Jaremko (Eds.), *Stress reduction and prevention* (pp. 293–339). New York: Plenum Press.

Ayalon, O. (1987a). Living in dangerous environments. In M. Brassard, R. Germain, & S. Hart (Eds.), *Psychological maltreatment of children and youth* (pp. 171–182). New York: Pergamon Press.

Ayalon, O. (1987b). *C.O.P.E: Community Oriented Preventive Education*. Haifa, Israel: Nord.

Ayalon, O. (1992). *Rescue! Community oriented preventive education handbook*. Ellicott City, MD: Chevron.

Ayalon, O. (1993). Death in literature and biblio-therapy. In R. Malkinsom, S. Rubin, & E.Vitztum (Eds.), *Loss and bereavement in Israeli society* (pp. 155–175). Jerusalem: Ministry of Defense. (Hebrew)

Ayalon, O. (1995a). *Selvidyn*. Jyvaskyla, Finland: Gummerus Kirjapaino. (Finnish)

Ayalon, O. (1995b). *Help our children*. Zagreb, Croatia: Skolska Knjiga. (Croatian)

Ayalon, O., & Flasher, A. (1985). Educational and therapeutic intervention methods for increasing psychological resilience in children of divorce. In M. Horowitz & H. Ashdot (Eds.), *One-parent families* (pp. 51–115). Jerusalem: Ministry of Education. (Hebrew)

Ayalon, O., & Flasher, A. (1993). *Chain reaction: Children and divorce*. London: Jessica Kingsley.

Ayalon, O., & Lahad, M. (1991). *Life on the edge*. Haifa, Israel: Nord.

Ayalon, O., & Lahad, M. (1995). *Enfrentando situaciones de estres [Confronting stressful situations]*. Jerusalem: Ministry of Education. (Spanish)

Ayalon, O., & Lahad, M. (2000). *H.A.N.D.S. workbook—Helpers assisting natural disaster survivors: Surviving the quake in Turkey 2000*. Istanbul: JDC.

Ayalon, O., Lahad, M., & Cohen, A. (Eds.). (1998). *Community stress prevention 3*. Kiryat Shmona, Israel: Community Stress Prevention Center.

Ayalon, O., Lahad, M., & Cohen, A. (Eds.). (1999). *Community stress prevention 4*. Kiryat Shmona, Israel: Community Stress Prevention Center.

Bennis, W. G., Benne, K. D., & Chin, R. (Eds.). (1985). *The planning of change*. New York: Holt, Rinehart & Winston.

Bettelheim, B. (2000). *The uses of enchantment: The meaning and importance of fairy tales*. Magnolia, MA: Peter Smith.

Brock, S. E., Lazarus, P. J., & Jimerson, S. R. (Eds.). (2002). *Best practices in school crisis prevention and intervention*. Bethesda, MD: National Association of School Psychologists.

Capewell, E. (1992, March). Disaster: The role of education. *Home & School*, 37–41.

Caplan, G. (1964). *Support systems and community mental health*. New York: Behavioral Publications.

Cappacione, L. (2001). *Living with feeling: The art of emotional expression*. New York: Tarcher/Putnam.

Cowen, E. L. (1977). Baby-steps toward primary prevention. *American Journal of Community Psychology, 5*(1), 1–22.

Ellis, A. (1991). The revised ABC of rational-emotive cognitive therapy. *Journal of Rational-Emotive Cognitive Therapy, 3*, 39–172.

Federal Emergency Management Agency. (2001, June). *Julia and Robbie: The disaster twins*. Retrieved August 30, 2003, from http://www.fema.com/kids/twins/juliarobbie2.pdf

Federal Emergency Management Agency. (2003a, February 11). *Your family disaster plan*. Retrieved August 30, 2003, from http://www.fema.gov/rrr/displan.shtm

Federal Emergency Management Agency. (2003b, February 12). *Your family disaster supplies kit*. Retrieved March 26, 2004, from http://www.fema.gov/library/diskit.shtm

Figley, C., & McCubbin, H. (1983). *Stress and the family 2: Coping with catastrophe*. New York: Brunner/Mazel.

Flannery, D. J., Vazsonyi, A. T., Liau, A. K., Guo, S., Powell, K. E., Atha, H., Vesterdal, W., & Embry, D. (2003). Initial behavior outcomes for the PeaceBuilders universal school-based violence prevention program. *Developmental Psychology, 39*, 292–308.

Garmezy, N., & Rutter, M. (1983). *Stress, coping, and development in children*. New York: McGraw-Hill.

Gersie, A., & King, E. (1990). *Storymaking in education and therapy*. London: Jessica Kingsley.

Goleman D. (1995). *Emotional intelligence—Why it can matter more than IQ*. New York: Bantam Books.

Gordon, S. (1988). *When living hurts*. New York: Dell.

Gordon, T. (Ed.). (2000). *Parent effectiveness training: The proven program for raising responsible children*. New York: Three Rivers Press.

Grainger, R. (1990). *Drama and healing*. London: Jessica Kingsley.

Hammond, J. M. (1981). Loss of the family unit: Counseling groups to help kids. *Personnel and Guidance Journal, 59*, 392–396.

Inbar, M. (1968). Individual and group effects on enjoyment and learning in a game simulating community disaster. In S. Baccoc & E. Schild (Eds.), *Simulation games in learning* (pp. 169–190). Beverly Hills, CA: Sage Publications.

Jennings, S. (1986). *Creative drama in groupwork*. London: Winslow Press.

Johnson, K. (1989). *Trauma in the lives of children: Crisis and stress management techniques for counselors and other professionals*. Alameda, CA: Hunter House.

Johnson, K. (1993). *School crisis management*. Alameda, CA: Hunter House.

Johnson, K. (1998). *Trauma in the lives of children: Crisis and stress management techniques for counselors and other professionals*. Alameda, CA: Hunter House.

Klingman, A. (1989). School-based emergency intervention following an adolescent suicide. *Death Studies, 13*, 263–274.

Klingman, A. (2002a). Children under stress of war. In A. M. La Greca, W. K. Silverman, E. M. Vernberg, & M. C. Roberts (Eds.), *Helping children cope with disasters and terrorism* (pp. 359–380). Washington, DC: American Psychological Association.

Klingman, A. (2002b). Schools and war. In S. E. Brock, P. J. Lazarus, & S. R. Jimerson (Eds.), *Best practices in school crisis prevention and intervention* (pp. 577–598). Bethesda, MD: National Association of School Psychologists.

Klingman, A., & Ayalon, O. (1977). Preparing the education system for emergency. *Israeli Journal of Psychology and Counseling in Education* [Chavat Da'at], *15*, 135–148. (Hebrew)

Krkelijic, L., & Pavlicic, N. (1998). School project in Montengro. In O. Ayalon, M. Lahad, & A. Cohen, (Eds.), *Community stress prevention 3* (pp. 51–60). Kiryat Shmona, Israel: Community Stress Prevention Center.

Lahad, M. (2000). *Creative supervision*. London: Jessica Kingsley.

Lahad, M., & Abraham, A. (1983). Preparing teachers and pupils for coping with stress situations: A multi-modal program. *Israeli Journal of Psychology and Counseling in Education, 16*, 196–210.

Lahad, M., & Ayalon, O. (1995). *On life and death*. Haifa, Israel: Nord.

Lahad, M., Lahad, V., & Ayalon, O. (1991). *Space-kids in search of clean air*. Haifa, Israel: Nord Publications.

Lahad, S., & Abraham, A. (1983, September). Preparing teachers and pupils for coping with stress situations: A multi-model program. *Israeli Journal of Psychology and Counseling in Education, 16*, 196–210.

Liebmann, M. (1986). *Art therapy for groups*. London: Croom Helm.

Lugovic, G. (1999). Skradin children post-trauma study. In O. Ayalon, M. Lahad, & A. Cohen (Eds.), *Community stress prevention 4* (pp. 52–56). Kiryat Shmona, Israel: Community Stress Prevention Center.

Meichenbaum, D. (1983). *Coping with stress*. London: Century

Meichenbaum, D. (1985). *Stress inoculation training*. New York: Pergamon Press.

Meichenbaum, D., & Jaremko, M. (1983). *Stress reduction and prevention*. New York: Plenum Press.

Mills, J. C., & Crowley, R. J. (1986). *Therapeutic metaphors for children*. Philadelphia: Brunner-Routledge.

Mordaunt, E. (1941). *Blitz kids*. London: Oxford University Press.

Poland, S. (1997). School crisis teams. In A. P. Goldstein & J. C. Conoley (Eds.), *School violence intervention: A practical handbook* (pp. 127–159). New York: Guilford.

Robbins, A. (1994). *A multi-modal approach to creative art therapy*. London: Jessica Kingsley

Saltan, F. (1929). *Bambi*. New York: Simon & Schuster.

Shacham, Y., Lahad, M., Sela, M., & Shacham, M. (2000). Community preparations for unremitting emergencies and evacuations. In A. Klingman, A. Raviv, & B. Stein (Eds.), *Children in stress and emergency situations* (pp. 434–449). Jerusalem: Ministry of Education. (Hebrew)

Smith, S. M. (1983). Disaster: Family disruption in the wake of natural disaster. In C. Figley & H. McCubbin (Eds.), *Stress and the family: Coping with catastrophe* (pp. 120–147). New York: Brunner/Mazel.

Stein, B., Green, D., Terlyuk, N., & Horacio, L. (2000). Psychological community intervention in Argentina. In A. Klingman, A. Raviv, & B. Stein (Eds.), *Children in stress and emergency situations* (pp. 450–461). Jerusalem: Ministry of Education. (Hebrew)

Stevenson, R. (1986). The shuttle tragedy, "community grief," and schools. *Death Studies, 10,* 507–518.

Toren, Z. (2000). School bus accident—First four hours. In A. Klingman, A. Raviv, & B. Stein (Eds.), *Children in stress and emergency situations* (485–499). Jerusalem: Ministry of Education. (Hebrew)

Ursano, R. J., Grieger, T. A., & McCarroll, J. E. (1996). Prevention of posttraumatic stress: Consultation, training, and early treatment. In B. A. van der Kolk, A. C. McFarlane, & L. Weisaeth (Eds.), *Traumatic stress: The effects of overwhelming experience on mind, body, and society* (pp. 441–462). New York: Guilford Press.

Vernberg, E. M., & Vogel, J. M. (1993). Task Force Report, part 2: Interventions with children after disasters. *Journal of Clinical Child Psychology, 22,* 485–498.

Winn, L. (1994). *Post-traumatic stress disorders and drama therapy*. London: Jessica Kingsley.

Winnicott, D. W. (1982). *Playing and reality*. London: Tavistock.

Yule, W. (2001). When disaster strikes—The need to be "wise before the event": Crisis intervention with children and adolescents. *Advances in Mind Body Medicine, 17*(3), 191–196.

CRISIS INTERVENTION

After studying the material in this chapter, you should

- understand the need to ask questions to analyze the disaster situation before implementing crisis intervention
- understand the primary goals of crisis intervention
- understand key concepts of emotional first aid and early crisis intervention
- be able to help families maintain their important continuities
- identify the basic beliefs about interventions with families and children following their experiences of a disaster
- use body awareness for safe trauma therapy
- be able to define crisis intervention and understand guidelines for its use, including the importance of involving parents in the support of their children's recovery from disaster
- be able to identify a range of intervention activities that may be used with children's groups in disaster situations, according to the BASIC-Ph model of coping resources
- be able to define group crisis intervention in a disaster context and describe the role of the group facilitator
- be able to describe the steps of the group intervention session procedure
- understand the rationale for school-based interventions with children
- understand the process of group crisis intervention with children and identify the six-phase intervention model
- be able to apply group crisis–intervention process models in the classroom.

WHEN DISASTER STRIKES: SECONDARY PREVENTION

Secondary prevention—crisis intervention—occurs during and immediately after a disaster. As we stated in chapter 8, the main purpose of secondary prevention is to identify pathological reactions as they form and to minimize the danger of fixating on traumatic stress responses. Secondary prevention is a brief and target-oriented psychoeducational intervention for at-risk groups and individuals. Crisis intervention tactics are employed as close as possible to the original location, as fast as possible, focused on the "here and now," with an active, positive, and hopeful orientation. The critical period for secondary preventive intervention is typically within six weeks of the onset of the disaster.

To determine the most appropriate response to a disaster, we need to ask ourselves several questions. The answers help determine our best course of action.

1. *What is the duration of the impact phase of the disaster?* Some disasters have a short impact duration: They strike and disappear, leaving havoc behind them; an example is the terrorist attacks on the United States on September 11, 2001. Other disasters occur over a prolonged period; an example is flooding, kidnappings, and the continuous violence and carnage found in war-stricken zones.

2. *How many people need immediate attention, how many people are in the innermost circles of physical, psychological or social vulnerability, and how many have experienced disasters previously, making them most vulnerable to the present disaster?* Those who occupy the outer circles of vulnerability may be "hidden victims," those who identify with the sufferers or experience a reawakening of old traumatic experiences. Mental health professionals need to respond to those immediately affected by a disaster, but they also need to respond to children who live in surrounding communities, who

may be psychological "near-miss" victims (Shaw et al., 1995). Children in peripheral areas may also suffer, but are often overlooked by mental health professionals who tend to provide aid only to children who have been directly affected.

3. *How predictable is the disaster?* A one-time occurrence, such as the 1976 bus kidnapping in Chowchilla, California, may be entirely unpredictable. Even if a disaster tends to happen repeatedly, its reoccurrence may or may not be predictable; for example, although hurricanes and floods are predictable, earthquakes are less predictable. Uncertainty augments the traumatic effects of disaster. If victims are left wondering when and where the next act of terrorism will occur, for example, they will be more anxious, and the devastating effects of this complex disaster is increased. Predictable reoccurrences have different dynamics. While the pending threat may increase anxiety and, even over a short period of time, exhaust people emotionally, it also may allow for the mobilization of a well-developed crisis intervention response that decreases physical and psychological casualties.

4. *What losses, damage, and devastation does the disaster cause immediately, and what effects may occur in the next several weeks?* When planning a disaster response, helpers need to consider both the immediate consequences of the disaster and how these effects are likely to multiply postdisaster. Many disasters set off other catastrophes, confounding the choice of appropriate intervention. Consider, for example, the enormity of the task of planning interventions in major disasters such as the genocide in Rwanda. That complex disaster was complicated by the millions of orphaned and homeless children in a

The Northridge, California, Earthquake

On January 17, 1994 at 4:30 A.M., an earthquake hit Northridge, California, registering a magnitude 6.7 on the Richter scale, and lasting for 15 seconds—the strongest quake ever recorded under a major U.S. city. The quake occurred on a blind thrust fault under the greater Los Angeles area. The existence of the fault was previously unknown. Over 9,000 people were injured, and 51 were killed. Over 22,000 were left homeless. Reported damages exceeded $44 billion. There was massive damage to roadways and transportation systems. Nine bridges collapsed over freeways and interstates, and 11 major roads in the greater Los Angeles area were closed. Nine hospitals were closed, with the loss of 2,500 beds. Natural gas mains ruptured, and 3,000 water system ruptures were reported. Ten days after the quake, 47 schools were still closed, affecting 640,000 students.

A massive emergency response was launched and served over 300,000 people out of the 3 million people affected by the quake. Shelter, food, and welfare services were provided to 33,000 people. Over 9,000 persons were deployed in the rescue and recovery efforts from local, state, and federal agencies.

country experiencing famine (which was principally a natural disaster) and by the minefields that continued to cause additional deaths and injuries even after the cessation of hostilities. Disasters that destroy the national infrastructure of a country and cause the loss of numerous lives, such as natural disasters and chemical or biological warfare, call for an innovative approach to crisis intervention and disaster management. In such cases, the entire society may be left with no resources with which to carry out any kind of effective intervention, especially when the caregivers are as traumatized as the rest of the population. In this and similar situations, external help from less beleaguered societies or international organizations is necessary. Such disasters often require an international effort for rescue and healing.

External Help in Former Yugoslavia

In 1992 Imam of Zagreb appealed to the United Kingdom Jewish Aid and International Development (UKJAID) for help for the communities and children in former Yugoslavia traumatized by a prolonged complex disaster. The United Nations Children's Fund (UNICEF) enlisted the psychological teams of the Community Stress Prevention Center and the Carmel Center in Israel to run an intervention program (Gal, 1997). The four-year-long intervention was focused on empowering local teams of caregivers by providing collegial support, sharing the experience of coping with war traumas, enriching their repertory of intervention techniques, and supervising their work in their local communities (Ayalon, Lahad, & Cohen, 1998, 1999). Dutch teams (Pen, 1997) and Danish teams (Juul, 1997), among others, created an international helping umbrella needed to respond to this kind of disaster, when the infrastructure of local helping services was damaged.

Touching Reality "Join an International Disaster Team of Helpers" provides an opportunity for you to think about what you would do if you joined an international disaster team of helpers.

HELPERS' GOALS IN CRISIS INTERVENTION

Helpers and those who need help often view the process of crisis intervention from two different perspectives. Typically, the main wish of those who need help is to restore themselves to their precrisis level of well-being and ability to function and to regain control over their lives. For caregivers who realize the low probability of life being the same as before, the immediate goals of crisis intervention are to reduce individual suffering and to reinforce the use of active emergency coping skills. Caregivers need to establish a sense of safety and security, give survivors a chance to ventilate their feelings, and predict any possible problems survivors may face.

Safety and Security

The first goal of caregivers immediately after the disaster's impact is to help people establish a sense of safety and security. Until safety is addressed, other issues and concerns will remain tangential.

To help establish a sense of safety and security, helpers must deal with physical security, which could mean helping a family leave its damaged home, and urgent medical needs, which could mean obtaining immediate medical assistance. Helpers also need to ensure the availability of food, clothing, and shelter. Sometimes, protecting disaster clients from unwanted invasion of their personal space becomes necessary, as is the case when media personnel arrive on the scene. Finally, caregivers need to help clients find a comfortable place to express their emotions.

Join an International Disaster Team of Helpers

Read the following description of the earthquake disaster in Turkey (Ayalon & Lahad, 2000b).

On August 17, 1999, a major earthquake hit Turkey. The death toll was an estimated 20,000 people, and it left over 350,000 people homeless, angry, and frightened. The regional school structure was destroyed. The desperate situation required that a multinational task force be engaged in the immediate and intermediate intervention. Such a multinational approach required the coordination and training of local helpers—those familiar with the local language, culture, and religion of the children and their families. As in all such situations, local caretakers are the ones most likely to know the most appropriate ways to instill necessary survival skills.

Consider that you have been asked to join an international group of volunteers to help displaced Turkish children who have been relocated to a makeshift camp after the earthquake. Your mission is to join with local workers in the camp, to share your knowledge of the effects of disasters on children, and to help the children cope.

- What are the skills and life experiences that will help you work with traumatized children?

- What are your skills in nonverbal communication? These skills are important, given that you will work in a non-English speaking country and you will probably not be able to communicate with the Turkish children with words. Can you decipher body language and facial expressions? Do you have the ability to silently empathize with children? Can you use nonverbal play-therapy-oriented activities with traumatized children?

Write down your responses, and if possible, brainstorm with your colleagues. After you and the colleagues with whom you are doing this Touching Reality have written down responses, share your concerns. Use the following questions to help guide your discussion:

- What are your strengths, knowledge, experiences, and skills that would help you cope with the challenge of being a part of an international group of caregivers?
- Do you think you could successfully cooperate with other volunteers from different countries?
- What supplementary preparation would you need before setting out on this mission? Would you need support from friends and family? Would you need to learn more about the target country and its culture? Would you need to know more techniques for working with children?

Additional ways to help people feel safe and secure include assisting them in their attempts to contact family and loved ones who would be willing to support them; facilitating their problem solving immediate challenges that have been caused by the tragedy; and helping them re-establish a sense of control, first over the small issues, then over the larger ones. When helpers remind survivors of the need for rest and proper eating, they also help create a sense of safety and security.

When helping disaster survivors feel safe and secure, caregivers must avoid making assumptions that others feel safe because they, the helpers, feel safe. In addition, caregivers need to respond to the need for nurturing but be wary of becoming "rescuers" on whom the client could become dependent.

Ventilation and Validation

Survivors need to tell the story of the disaster repeatedly to ventilate their feelings and reactions. They need to be heard and to have their shocking experiences validated. As Brison (1998) put it, "Narrating memories to others (who are strong and empathic enough to be able to listen) empowers survivors to gain more control over the traces left by trauma. … [Telling their story is] a speech act that defuses traumatic memory, giving shape and a temporal order to the events recalled, establishing more control over their recalling, and helping the survivor to remake a self" (p. 40).

One way caregivers can help peoples' storytelling process and provide them with validation is to ask them to describe the disaster, where they were at the time they heard of the event or saw, heard, or felt it happen, and their reactions and responses. Effective listening, which encourages the victim to talk by communicating the caregiver's caring and concern, requires that you, the caregiver, do the following:

- ask questions only to facilitate the flow of storytelling
- believe that the disaster clients' impressions and reactions are your most important concern
- echo key words or phrases to acknowledge what is important to the disaster client
- support and honor silence by waiting for disaster clients to decide when they want to continue their story
- clarify what is being said by asking disaster clients if they can retell those parts of their story that are confusing, or if they can remember other things that might help you understand what they are saying
- keep personal values, beliefs, biases, and judgments to yourself; avoid imposing them on the disaster clients
- listen, summarize, and remember that the objective is to help disaster clients develop a narrative for the event and to find words to describe their emotional reactions.

When working with disaster clients and listening to their anguished stories, it is absolutely necessary to ensure the confidentiality of such communications, to reassure them that their reactions are acceptable and not uncommon (that their responses are a normal reaction to an abnormal situation), and to support the storyteller's efforts to achieve a sense of emotional control.

Prediction and Preparation

An important step to rebuilding peoples' lives after a disaster is to aid them to predict and prepare for postdisaster eventualities. Helpers need to have access to information about the possibilities of relocation, financial help, medical or legal assistance, body identification, and funeral procedures. It is also important for the helper to educate survivors about trauma, and to enlighten them about normal crisis and stress reactions that might occur among family members or friends, especially among children. Because it is not uncommon for parents to underestimate the effects of a disaster on children (see discussion in chapter 6), special care must be given to explain overt and hidden children's trauma responses and to provide parents with some basic suggestions of how to deal with a traumatized child.

During supportive encounters, helpers can encourage people

- to focus on daily planning and setting small, achievable goals
- to eat, sleep, and exercise regularly
- to explore new options for rehabilitation
- to use simple problem-solving techniques as they try to sort out the postdisaster chaos
- to talk and write about the event as a way of bringing some coherence to their chaotic feelings
- to plan time for memories and memorials
- to find someone in their community who can support them in practical and emotional hardships.

DUAL–LEVEL MODEL OF SECONDARY PREVENTION

Secondary prevention can be divided into two stages (Slaikeu, 1990). The first stage is *immediate first aid*, which may last only a few hours but will probably occupy the first few days after a disaster. The second stage is *early crisis intervention*, which may last several days and as long as six or eight weeks after the onset of the disaster. Any intervention beyond six to eight weeks falls into the category of tertiary prevention.

Immediate First Aid
The first stage in any secondary prevention intervention is to get people to safety and to ensure their physical security. Once children

and adults are out of danger, human contact and support are needed. "Mental health staff need to set aside traditional methods, avoid the use of mental health labels, and use an active outreach approach" (Myers, 1994, p. 3). *Psychological first aid* should be brief, adjusted to the severity of the crisis, and focused on the immediate needs of the survivors. Although each single strategy of immediate first aid reflects the particular circumstances surrounding the disaster, five elements are common to immediate first aid strategies:

1. reuniting family members and verifying information about losses are the most immediate and urgent needs.
2. giving clear directions of "what to do, where to go." When adults assume a leadership role they provide a model of behavior for the children in their care; therefore, direct guidance for parents about how to deal with their own disaster responses provides indirect but effective guidance for their children.
3. helping children understand what has happened during and after the crisis.
4. providing physiological relaxation and tension reduction (in a safe location).
5. providing a clear (even if faint) sense of the future and hope for improvement.

Contrary to the common expectation that children are needy and passive immediately after a disaster, helpers have found that when children take an active role in caring for themselves, their younger siblings, or domestic chores they gain a sense of control and enhance their resourcefulness (Ayalon, 1983a, 1983b; Gibbs, 1994; Speier, 2000). Adults can help children build group support, allow for and accept a variety of emotional expressions, and engage in systematic problem solving and planning.

Early Crisis Intervention

During this second stage of secondary prevention, helpers may use a broad spectrum of brief beneficial methods with individuals, families, and groups. This is the time for triage, the process whereby helpers screen for children who may be at high risk for severe emotional problems because of the enormity of their loss, their youth, their previous vulnerability, and other factors. Some children will manifest signs and symptoms of distress, whereas others may seem untouched by the disaster. Lindy (1989) noted that children who do not immediately show signs of psychological distress may nevertheless be badly shaken. The variety of children's immediate responses demands that helpers use flexible approaches when they conduct crisis intervention.

The need for flexibility in choosing a method of intervention was reinforced in a study conducted by Handford and his colleagues (1986). This group of researchers, who studied children involved in the Three Mile Island nuclear power plant disaster, noted that children used a variety of coping mechanisms as they worked through their trauma.

Professional helpers believed for a long time that early crisis intervention helps reduce or even eliminate posttraumatic stress disorders (PTSD). However, evidence now indicates that people with severe and chronic PTSD are not just manifesting a "normal reaction to an abnormal situation"; instead, they are responding in ways that reflect severe underlying problems. Helpers should not expect to eradicate totally the danger of posttraumatic syndrome by means of "crisis intervention." Rather, crisis intervention aims to reduce acute symptoms (for example, acute stress disorder or acute stress response). Such intervention can help people who are moderately affected to use their natural coping recourses, to rebuild the lives that had been disrupted by the traumatic events, and to resume functioning at a normal level (Myers, 1994).

Spotlight on Research "Early Crisis Intervention and the Sinking of the Jupiter"—which concerns the same disaster as reported in a Spotlight on Research in chapter 3 ("Children's Development of PTSD after a Disaster at Sea")—highlights a study that provides empirical support for the importance of early crisis intervention.

"To Describe the Devastation is Like Trying to Define Infinity"

The Oakland–Berkeley Hills firestorm of October 20, 1991, was the worst urban fire that the United States has ever witnessed. Within six hours it had destroyed 3,642 homes and 400 apartments. Twenty-five people died, 150 were injured, and 6,000 were left homeless—95 percent of the homeless lost virtually everything they owned. The damage was estimated at 1.5 billion dollars.

"I am one of those survivors. I lost my home. I lost my clothing, furniture, photographs, heirloomes, artwork, beloved objects, one car and two pets. I also lost twenty-five years of anthropological research, seven manuscripts not yet into publishers, all my other writings, ideas, projects in development, the slides and photos of travels, lectures and course notes, and my entire library. Thankfully, I lost no family, no friends, no people, still to describe the devastation both physical and psychological of this kind of loss is like trying to define eternity or infinity. It defies words, evades phrase, and renders mute any euphemistic catchall" (Hoffman, 1994, p. 15).

Early Crisis in Intervention and the Sinking of the Jupiter

In sudden disasters, the recommended time span for early crisis intervention is within six to eight weeks from the onset of the event. This is supposedly the crucial period after which posttraumatic symptoms may become fixed and, perhaps, chronic. The effects of not providing help during this period were studied by William Yule (1992), who looked at the psychopathology of child survivors of a sea disaster involving a ship, the Jupiter, carrying 400 British students (from 20 different schools) and their teachers, and an Italian oil tanker.

Yule (1992) found that some of the students' schools supported the quick organization of mental health teams, whereas other schools decided not to pursue help until nearly a year later. He compared the different approaches and found that the children in the schools who pursued immediate help fared better than those who got help much later, as seen from lower scores on the Fear Survey Schedule and the Impact of Events Scale (IES). The IES measures two main aspects of the impact of events on people exposed to a disaster: (1) intrusive memories (pictures, sounds, and thoughts); and (2) avoidance behavior.

Yule (1992) offered the following suggestions for the most effective intervention. First, it is paramount for helpers to assist children to "make sense of what happened to them and to gain mastery over their feelings" (p. 224). The most efficient way to go about this process is to treat the children in small groups and to ask them to write out their complete recollection of the disaster. Besides writing, it is extremely helpful to let children talk about their experience in a safe environment, especially to their parents. Teachers can facilitate discussion by encouraging children to bring in photos and newspaper articles of the disaster, and by speaking with other children who have lived through the disaster. The dialogue between children can help them gain some perspective about their feelings of anxiety, survivor's guilt, sadness, and shame. Children who were friends of students who had survived the ordeal also seemed to have been affected by the tragedy, as witnessed by a marked decline in their end-of-year examination scores.

Yule, W. (1992). Post-traumatic stress disorder in child survivors of shipping disasters: The sinking of the "Jupiter." *Psychotherapy and Psychosomatics, 57*, 200–205.

Mending Disrupted Continuities

Dr. Susanna Hoffman (1994) lamented the severe disruption of the most meaningful continuities of her life. Her story is typical: Omer and Alon (1994) analyzed many survivors' stories and identified four areas in which "continuity," usually perceived vital for conducting a normal life, is disrupted by disaster:

- *Functional continuity*. In a disaster-scarred reality, people may be troubled by the question of how to maintain their usual routines during or even after the disaster.
- *Historical continuity*. Having lost their home, community, place of work, memorabilia, and personal objects, people may feel as if they have lost their identity and a sense of their history.

- *Interpersonal continuity.* In cases of relocation following the loss of home and neighborhood, people may be troubled by fears of not being able to patch up their broken social network.
- *Spiritual continuity.* Feeling a loss of faith in a stable and just world, people may be exposed to a lasting sense of vulnerability and despair, not being able to deal with a world which is no longer good, safe, or predictable.

Crisis intervention is focused on enhancing the recovery process of lost or broken continuities and involves a physical, emotional, and spiritual rebuilding. The rebuilding process involves three aspects. Mental health professionals must help survivors to recognize and appreciate (1) *talk*, the need to teach people of the healing that comes from talking with friends, family, and counselors; (2) *tears*, the need for people to recognize that tears are a natural and essential way to heal from their losses, including their loss of the feeling that the world is a safe place; and (3) *time*, the need for people to understand the necessity of taking time for reflection and to recognize all the challenges that they met and overcame (Myers, Zunin, & Zunin, 1990).

Early crisis intervention responds to the perceived disruption of functional, historical, interpersonal, and spiritual continuities by enhancing and broadening natural resilience and by teaching new coping skills. It helps survivors to work through perceptions and responses to the disaster so that the event may be integrated into the fabric of life and remembered—without reawakening traumatic reactions—similar to working through loss and bereavement (Parkes & Weiss, 1995); and helps survivors find new ways to bridge the disrupted continuities. This process is much more extensive and therapeutic than psychological first aid. It requires more time and calls for a caregiver with a higher level of training than what is necessary for immediate first aid. (For an elaboration of how to deal with disrupted continuities through narrative therapy, see chapter 10.)

Some of the most frequent methods and strategies used in early crisis intervention follow:

- conducting mourning and memorial rituals that promote positive affirmations of resilience
- recognizing and accepting verbal and nonverbal emotional responses
- talking through dreams, nightmares, and other traumatic reactions
- reprocessing traumatic reactions by a variety of techniques, such as eye movement desensitization and reprocessing (EMDR is described in chapter 10, since typically it is used in tertiary prevention; sometimes, however, it is used in secondary prevention—crisis intervention.)
- de-freezing the somatic trauma by body awareness, expression, and regaining body–mind control

Using Body Awareness for Safe Trauma Therapy

In their recent brain research, van der Kolk, McFarlane, and Weiseth (1996) shed new light on the biological components of trauma. During an emotional emergency, part of our "old brain," the amygdala, controls much of the rest of the brain, including the rational mind, and stores frightening, life-threatening experiences. Similar to a psychological sentinel, the amygdala scans incoming sensory signals—every experience—for trouble, challenging every situation and every perception with the most primitive survival question: "Is this dangerous, frightful, or painful to me?" When it detects danger, it triggers bodily secretions that mobilize a fight or flight stress response. If a fight or flight stress response is not activated, these patterns are frozen into the body and stay there as "trauma memories" that are not directly accessible to our conscious awareness.

The trauma stored in the body evokes involuntary responses, such as crying and trembling. Levine and Frederick (1997) suggested that helpers should allow these natural reactions to occur and to physically support the shaken (and perhaps shaking) child and provide emotional reassurance until the tension stored in the body is totally spent. They also recommended helping the child pay attention to what is going on in his or her body and, when the shock is over, helping the child reprocess the event, either by telling the story or by enacting it in play. For the enactment to be therapeutic, the child needs guidance to reach a safe solution and to regain lost control. Levine and Frederick called this process "negotiation with the trauma." To provide an opportunity to gain body awareness, it is helpful for the facilitator to ask the following questions—this would create an intervention that would treat the traumatized body as well as the traumatized mind:

- Where were you at the time of the disaster?
- What did you first hear?
- What did you first see?
- What happened in your body (tension, numbness, and so on)?
- What is happening in your body now when you remember the disaster?

- When you remember the disaster now, what is the primary mode in which you are experiencing it? Do you hear it? See it? Touch it? Feel it? Smell it?

Somatic interventions, interventions involving the body, may be useful as an adjunct to other trauma therapies. Body-oriented means of containing or reducing arousal are the equivalent of brakes on an accelerating car (Rothchild, 1999).

The first step in body awareness is learning to identify signs of increased arousal. Body awareness refers to the precise awareness of skin, muscles, bones, organs, breathing, movement, position in space, temperature, tension, relaxation, sweat, heart rate, and so on. Somatic techniques that are meant to reduce hyperarousal use guided re-experiencing of body postures, sensations, and movements experienced at the time the trauma occurred, with holding and supportive contact with the therapist. Careful guidance helps the child experience safety within her or his body (van der Kolk et al., 1996).

GROUP CRISIS INTERVENTION

Group crisis intervention builds on the lessons from the long tradition of group dynamics as a powerful tool for changing attitudes and behaviors (Jagodic, Kontac, & Zubenko, 2002; Turner, 2000; Yalom, 1985). The guidelines for group work presented here are adapted from a model for group crisis intervention originally developed by the National Organization for Victim Assistance (NOVA) (Young, 1998).

Group work allows disaster workers to address the needs of many adults and children efficiently, and to guide them to release their extreme emotions after a traumatic event. Peer-group participation and sharing of painful experiences and responses encourages the validation of individuals' feelings and reactions. Group crisis intervention is useful both as an immediate response to acute crisis and as a way to continue to integrate the trauma into the individual and the community posttrauma period.

Well-trained group facilitators seek to accomplish the following:

- to enhance an environment of social support among group members and to help rebuild community bonds
- to enhance the group's sense of safety and security
- to provide ample opportunity for ventilation and validation by using a variety of techniques and tools to address all types of adults and children, with their varied needs and their wide-ranging experiences
- to take care of each individual within the group setting and to enhance the group's coping resources to build individual coping skills
- to provide a cognitive learning experience by contributing to the group participants' knowledge about trauma and its aftermath
- to affirm or reaffirm hope in a safe future.

Ground Rules for Group Sessions

Apart from the particular group crisis intervention used, participants need to be informed of three ground rules for interacting (Ayalon & Flasher, 1993): confidentiality, the agenda for the session, and boundaries (freedom of expression).

Confidentiality. The facilitator assures the group that all discussion in the group is confidential. This does not mean that issues raised in the group cannot be talked about outside the group, but rather that no story or concern will be attributed to any specific group member. Confidentiality cannot be guaranteed, but the facilitator can encourage group members to make a sign of assent to confidentiality to help underscore its importance.

Agenda for the session. The facilitator informs the group that the sessions are designed to help group members understand typical crisis reactions; to provide some crisis intervention; and to predict and to prepare the group for possible future disaster events. Time limits for the group meeting, perhaps 60 or 90 minutes, also are announced at the start of the session.

Boundaries (freedom of expression). The facilitator gives permission to participants to express any thoughts or reactions they have and reassures them that these will be contained and accepted within the group. The facilitator makes it clear that no physical violence or verbal abuse is allowed and that participants are safe and protected in the group.

Group Intervention Format and Procedure

NOVA divides a typical group intervention format into six parts. Part 1, the introduction, takes approximately 10 minutes. During this part, the facilitator introduces herself or himself and the supporting group members, including the scribe (the person who takes notes on a flipchart, assists any group member who goes into crisis, and takes over as facilitator if for some reason the facilitator cannot continue), other crisis intervention–team members, and local caregivers who may assist during the intervention. The facilitator then reviews the guidelines for discussion, noting rules of confidentiality and the boundaries of expression, including issues of safety, and finishes with an overview of the agenda, including the time limit set for the group intervention.

Part 2, the longest part of the group meeting (about 35 minutes), is organized around a series of questions that review physical and emotional reactions to the disaster. Questions NOVA recommends include: Where were group members when the disaster happened? Who were they with? What did they see, hear, smell, taste, or touch at the time? What did they do? How did they react at the time? (Young, 1998, chapter 11). All of the questions are posed initially, and then the facilitator asks if any participant would like to volunteer to tell what he or she remembers. People who respond are thanked for their contribution and their experience is validated. The facilitator also points out similarities between and among responses.

Part 3, approximately 25 minutes, builds on Part 2 by asking group members to describe what has happened to them in the aftermath of the event, including the two days before the group intervention. Emotional reactions of shock, disbelief, anger, fear, frustration, confusion, shame, guilt, grief, and so on are ventilated and validated.

Parts 4, 5, and 6 are each approximately 10 minutes. During Part 4, the facilitator poses questions to help participants recognize their expectations: Participants think about what has happened, what they think will happen at work and with their family in the next few days or weeks, and what their possible reactions will be. What are their concerns, their worries about what will happen next? How do they think they will deal with future problems?

Part 5 focuses on coping strategies. What coping strategies have participants used in the past that they might use now? What information is needed? The facilitator highlights positive coping strategies and suggests alternatives to the negative ones.

Part 6 focuses on a summary of what has been said, including descriptions of sensory perceptions, emotional turmoil, and concerns about the future. The facilitator indicates that the reactions experienced are all reflective of crisis or trauma reactions. In addition, the facilitator talks about expectations for the future that were mentioned during the intervention and adds others not addressed that may arise, and reassures participants of useful coping strategies. If future meetings are planned, the days and times for these are mentioned.

A postgroup session, lasting 15 to 30 minutes, is used for distributing handouts (for example, "typical reactions to trauma," telephone numbers and locations of community caregivers, and where to get accurate and up-to-date information), answering individual questions, talking to individuals, and saying good-bye to individual participants.

Adaptations of Group–Crisis Intervention Procedures for Children

In recent years different protocols, built on the original concept but varying in their techniques, have been used for crisis intervention with victims of all kinds, especially children of all ages and stages of development. Although NOVA allows children to be participants in group–crisis intervention sessions *with their parents*, group–crisis intervention strategies designed for use specifically with children are still needed. This need has inspired experimentation with different forms of adaptations for groups of children involved in disasters (Ayalon & Soskis, 1986; Galliano & Lahad, 2000)— new protocols designed to provide age-appropriate understanding and naming of the events, emotional processing, ventilation, and normalization. These new procedures take into account the needs of traumatized children for re-establishing a sense of belonging and support in the very preliminary stages after the event (Boatright, 1985). The new procedures are specifically geared to mobilize group solidarity and promote individual strength and coping, and to prepare children for possible future disaster events.

A recently adapted protocol for children, called Critical Incident Processing and Recovery (CIPR) (Galliano & Lahad, 2000), stressed the need to establish the children's sense of "continuity of experience." To anchor the children in their relative predisaster stability, when their world was familiar and predictable, facilitators for individual or group interventions focus their first questions on activities and experiences during the hours before the incident. Striking the same note, the sessions end with an emphasis on looking for signs of returning to some level of routine or normalcy. Another revision, pertinent for children but also recommended for adults, is to include in the process family members and relatives available for support and nurturance, either in the session or just outside the room where the group crisis intervention takes place (Lahad & Cohen, 1998). As a safeguard, short individual interviews and assessments follow the group encounter.

A further adaptation of CIPR for young children (ages three to six) introduced toys in the group–crisis intervention procedure (Lahad, 1999). Young children have a limited ability to process information cognitively and verbally, but engage spontaneously in imaginative and make-believe play with toys. They also have a shorter attention span than older children or adults. To elicit a trauma story from a group of young children, the facilitator uses hand puppets representing different human and animal figures. When interviewed, the puppets "tell their story," expressing their feelings during the event and at present. The facilitator directs suggestions on how to cope, how to sleep better, how to fight back fears and bad dreams, how to express anger, and so on, to the puppet.

The whole group–crisis intervention procedure is carried out on a metaphoric level, using the language of the children and projective play techniques. The intervention takes place within the metaphor, as the children identify with the puppets and, at the same time, the puppets provide a safe distance from which the children can touch their own frightening experience (Ayalon, 1993a, 1993b). To ensure the group process is successful, it is highly recommended that the facilitators be known to and trusted by the children.

Within a few days following one metaphorical CIPR intervention (see the extended example on p. 291), parents told the teacher and Dr. Lahad that there was a noticeable reduction in the children's symptoms. The CIPR adaptation was added to the protocol (Lahad, 2000).

Special Issues in Working with Children

Children of all ages, first and foremost, must sense that they are safe (Herman, 2000). What young children need postdisaster is to return to their secure "home base" and to resume their contact with their parents or other caregivers. This requires that parents or other caregivers be involved and supportive during the process of crisis intervention. When safety is restored, the children's natural coping skills can emerge; however, it is not easy to ensure parental involvement. Often, the exposure of children to a disaster may trigger parental guilt and a sense of failure to

Puppets as Representational Figures in Group Crisis Intervention

Following a shooting attack on a school, the kindergarten teacher, a significant adult in the children's lives, realized the need to help the frightened children in her care. Most of the children heard the shooting and heard the story of the attack from their parents and older siblings. The teacher reported that on previous similar occasions, the children had expressed their experience mostly through aggressive play and spontaneous drawing, but during the verbal processing, they tended to mimic each other and avoid telling their own individual stories.

The kindergarten teacher and a psychologist, Mooli Lahad, acted as co-facilitators and conducted a series of gamelike sessions for the children. The facilitators each picked a hand puppet and encouraged the children to each pick one. Next, the teacher sang a favorite song and described the rules of a new game: Each child tells the story of his or her puppet, talking only when his or her turn comes. The teacher's puppet was a bird and Lahad's puppet was a monkey, and they modeled the story-game for the children:

Bird (teacher): Good morning [and Bird named the various puppets]. I am a bird and my name is Nuli. I live in this village on a high tree from which I can see the whole place. Last night I was on my tree and I heard a loud noise of shooting and immediately I went into my nest and peeped outside to see what was going on. I felt my heart beat and I felt my wings hold very tight to my body. Did any of you puppets hear that noise?

Then each child told her or his puppet's version.

Following the bird's expression of her feelings and fears, all the other puppets told their reactions and feelings. Then the bird asked the monkey (Lahad) what helped him during last night's ordeal. The monkey said it was his mother and the little penlight that he had under his pillow. Each child then had his or her puppet share and describe what helped them survive the experience.

protect the child, particularly for the father (Dembert & Simmer, 2000). Parents may be extremely unsettled by the disaster. Monahan (1995) suggested that parents need group or individual support to reconcile their own issues, before being able to support their children's healing.

As children mature, their preferred sources of support may shift. In preadolescence and adolescence, children rely primarily on peer support and acceptance and may regard the teacher as a reliable source of protection and knowledge. But if the teacher conducts the group crisis intervention with the classroom group, self-disclosure may have negative effects, because it is unlikely that confidentiality and empathy among peers can be assured. Classroom interventions may expose a vulnerable child to ridicule, to being bullied, or to being ostracized, all of which constitute secondary dramatization. An additional hazard to classroom interventions lies in the traditional teacher's training: Teachers may lack the skills for conducting a nonjudgmental process such as group crisis intervention, and need either training or outside help. Finally, verbal processing may be just a partial method, because young children will find it easier and more age appropriate to express themselves in symbolic play, in physical activities, and in nonverbal methods such as movement, music, or art (Ayalon, 1978, 1992; Davis, 1995).

Multidimensional Methods of Crisis Intervention for Children

To ensure maximum effectiveness, crisis interventions should include all channels of interpersonal and intrapersonal coping skills. This may be accomplished by using the multidimensional BASIC-Ph model as a guide (for a comprehensive discussion of this model, see chapters 2 and 8). In addition, crisis interventions should be carried out as near as possible to the disaster site and as soon as possible after the disaster; that is, to ensure being most effective, it is important to adhere to the PIE principle, as discussed in chapter 8. The optimal conditions for a successful intervention include *proximity*—the intervention should be as near as possible to the disaster site; *immediacy*—it should be offered as soon as possible after the disaster; and the helper should have *expectancy*—an active, positive, hopeful orientation, focused on recovery and a return to normalcy (Salmon, 1919).

There is a distinct difference between offering help to an individual and offering help to a group of children. When working with groups of children, who may be victims or near-miss victims of a disaster, it is not always possible to make clear distinctions between "first aid" and "early crisis intervention," as it is when working with a single person. In the same group of children, some may need first aid and others may need early crisis intervention, depending on their individual experiences. An additional complexi-ty in choosing an appropriate method of intervention is that groups of children often are composed of mixed ages and different developmental stages. Therefore, it is recommended that the group facilitator be familiar with a variety of methods and be able to apply them as dictated by the observed needs of the group.

Spotlight on Research "Managing the Complexity of Helping Children after a Disaster" details one useful approach for managing the complexity of working with children after a disaster; it was developed by a team of researchers and clinicians at the University of California at Los Angeles.

Table 9-1 presents various intervention methods that are widely practiced in crisis intervention. The purpose of the table is to serve as a "toolbox" from which intervention methods can be gleaned and applied according to the need at hand. Many of the intervention strategies and methods mentioned in the table have their roots in the practice of child group therapy (Gardner, 1993; Oaklander, 1978). Whereas some of the tools and techniques on the list, such as EMDR (Shapiro & Forrest, 1997) and neuro-linguistic programming (NLP) (Bandler, 1985; Overdorf & Silverthorn, 1996) need specialized professional training, most other techniques listed may be safely used by trained professional and paraprofessional facilitators, such as youth leaders, nurses, counselors, educators, psychologists, social workers, art and expressive therapists, and others in the helping professions.

As you read the table, keep the following in mind:

- Each method refers to one or more of the following phases of intervention, as marked by the code letters I, E, and R. The initial I stands for *immediate first aid,*

Managing the Complexity of Helping Children after a Disaster

According to Pynoos and his colleagues (Pynoos, Goenjian, & Steinberg, 1998), three levels of organization are necessary to implement an effective postdisaster, population-based intervention for children. Level 1 is the government level, which focuses on the mobilization of public, private, and volunteer resources. Level 2 is the school level, which focuses on interventions such as assisting principals and teachers, and outreach programs providing educational and therapeutic interventions to parents regarding their children. Finally, level 3 is the intervention team level, including professionals and paraprofessionals, responsible for subpopulations of children, such as those who are severely traumatized.

It is a complex task for helpers to screen children to determine how a disaster has affected them. It requires looking at objective and subjective exposure, loss exposure, acute difficulties, ongoing adversities, traumatic reminders, traumatic prior exposure or loss in the past year, and current level of distress.

Based on a developmental psychopathology model of traumatic stress, the University of California at Los Angeles (UCLA) Trauma Psychiatry Program developed a treatment approach that addresses five areas. (1) The first area is "traumatic experiences," such as internal and external dangers, and a child's self-protective efforts to downplay certain dramatic details or moments. (2) The second area is "traumatic reminders," which includes identifying significant reminders, increasing the child's awareness, and increasing tolerance. (3) The third area focuses on bereavement and the interplay of trauma and grief, addresses the child's memories of last moments with the deceased, and promotes skills to communicate about the loss. (4) The fourth area is "post-disaster stresses and adversities." (5) The fifth area is "developmental impact," such as a decline in educational achievement, and poor peer relationships.

Pynoos and his colleagues present a case study of their use of the five-area approach with a 12-year-old girl in Armenia after the Armenian earthquake. In addition, they describe a prevention-intervention program in an elementary school in an inner city community that had extremely high rates of crime and gang-related violence.

Pynoos, R. S., Goenjian, A. K., & Steinberg, A. M. (1998). A public mental health approach to the postdisaster treatment of children and adolescents. *Child and Adolescent Psychiatric Clinics of North America, 7*, 195–210.

the initial E stands for *early crisis intervention*, and the initial R stands for *rehabilitative therapeutic intervention*, which is often referred to as tertiary prevention (the subject of chapter 10).

- The methods mentioned are boxed according to the BASIC-Ph coping channels.
- A recommendation guide by age group is provided for each activity.

TABLE 9-1. MULTIDIMENSIONAL METHODS OF CRISIS INTERVENTION FOR CHILDREN IN GROUPS

COPING CHANNEL	METHOD	WHEN	WHO
	Enhancing natural coping resources Guiding with coping tools and strategies	**Immediate first aid** **Early crisis Intervention** **Rehabilitative therapeutic intervention**	Recommmended age of participants **I** = 4–7; **II** = 8–11; **III** = 12–17; **IV** = 18–22
B: Beliefs	Assisting faith and prayer (to a "higher power") for protection and rescue	I	ALL
	Promoting positive affirmation of resilience ("we shall overcome")	I, E	III, IV
	Fostering loyalty to national and ethnic identity symbols	E	IV
	Clarifying values	E, R	ALL
	Searching for meaning (logotherapy—see chapter 10)	I, E, R	III, IV
	Appraising values	R	II, III
	Engaging in story and poetry therapy	R	ALL
	Mourning and engaging in memorial rituals	R	III, IV
	Maintaining continuity and routine to regain self-esteem and control	E, R	ALL
A: Affect	Enhancing emotional intelligence and identifying feelings (feeling vocabulary)	E	I, II, III
	Expressing feelings nonverbally: drawing, drama, music, movement	I, E, R	ALL
	Legitimizing and ventilating feeling by telling and writing	E, R	ALL
	Engaging in metaphoric expression through therapeutic storytelling cards	R	ALL
S: Social	Promoting reliable leadership	I	III, IV
	Modeling on adults	I, E	II, III, IV
	Receiving dyadic support (one to one)	E	III, IV
	Sharing and support in a group	I, E	II, III, IV
	Taking a caring role in groups ("Mitzvah" therapy)	E, R	II, III, IV
	Sharing experiences (CIPR)	I, E, R	II, III, IV
	Using a help line	E, R	III, IV
I: Imagination	Diverting attention	I	ALL
	Fantastisizing reality: "as-if" games	I, E, R	I, II, III

COPING CHANNEL	METHOD	WHEN	WHO
I: Imagination (continued)	Using dissociative transcendence	I	III, IV
	Imagining a friend (hero)	I, E	I, II
	Engaging in creative activities	E, R	ALL
	Desensitizing by fantasy	I, E	ALL
	Using humor	E, R	II, III, IV
	Playing games	E, R	ALL
C: Cognition	Learning reliable information about the incident	I	II, III, IV
	Curbing the "rumor industry"	I	ALL
	Following directions: "what to do when . . ."	I	ALL
	Making a look-draw-tell (scrapbook)	E, R	I, II
	Mapping alternatives— planning a safer future	E, R	III, IV
	Desensitizing by gradual exposure	E	ALL
	Solving problems	I, R	II, III, IV
	Reframing	E, R	III, IV
	Encouraging self-talk	I	II, III, IV
	Ranking order of priorities	E	III, IV
	Pacing and leading	E, R	III, IV
	Engaging in paradoxical intervention	E, R	III, IV
	Playing simulation games for planning a safer future	R	II, III, IV
	Renarrating the personal "disaster" story	R	III, IV
	Working through dreams and nightmares	E, R	ALL
Ph: Physiology	Using breath and muscle relaxation	I	ALL
	Relaxing by physical exhaustion	I	I, II
	Engaging in biofeedback	I, E, R	ALL
	Eating well (nutrition for stress reduction)	E	ALL
	Resting	E, R	III, IV
	Engaging in psychobiological cues (NLP—see chapter 10)	E, R	II, III, IV
	Using EMDR (see chapter 10)	E, R	II, III, IV
	Biodynamics		

A Multidimensional Intervention with a Group of Traumatized Children*

Three armed gunmen raided a beach house in a small resort town in the north of Israel. A father and his two small girls (ages two and four) were brutally murdered while neighbors, who heard the commotion and thought the whole area was under attack, either hid or fled from their homes.

A survey of the area schools the next morning indicated that 54 children were absent. Authorities went to their homes and found them hiding there; they were escorted to school. An assessment found them to be near-miss and high-risk traumatized children. They manifested a host of symptoms that included acute anxiety, flashbacks, catastrophic expectations, fear of the dark and of loud noises, and a strong aversion to the beach, which was the scene of the crime.

The children in this high-risk group found it impossible to concentrate in class, because they were haunted by images of the two murdered girls. They experienced crying spells, headaches, stomachaches, sleeplessness and tended to cling to their parents. Ofra Ayalon suggested, and then supervised, a group crisis intervention.

The children were divided into three groups according to age, to be observed, supported, and treated by the school crisis team. The school allocated special rooms to this intervention; the homeroom teachers were informed and asked to cooperate and support the process. Members of the school crisis team conducted each group for five consecutive days, approximately two hours each day. The following is a description of how one group was conducted for children ages 12 to 14.

Initial Ventilation of Feelings
As they assembled in the room, the children were crying and could hardly speak. They were offered finger paint and asked to use it to express their experience and feelings. Some children seemed flooded with frightening images of past and present experiences, which were reflected in their drawings.

Enactment of the Traumatic Experience
The next day communication was a bit more coherent. The children relived the traumatic events of the night by role-play and excited narration. They shared stories of sights and sounds, of their flight from home and hiding under furniture. They relived every move, thought, and feeling with detailed descriptions, and they discharged excessive affect. In the role-play of the event, some children chose to play the victims' roles, letting themselves be "captured" and "killed," and others played the aggressors, imitating the terrorists' shouts and shootings. The facilitators granted full legitimization to all expressions, even the most idiosyncratic; these expressions were normal for this stage of processing the trauma.

Channeling Aggression
During the first two days, violent emotions surged. The facilitators helped the children turn these emotions into scenarios of vengeance and retaliation against the aggressors, allowing the children to act out these new scenarios in drama and puppet shows. The facilitators noticed the first signs of relief when the children mimicked an execution of the "puppet terrorists." At that stage, the children's anger and accusations also were aimed at the adults who failed to protect them and who exposed them to such horrid dangers. When their feelings became too frightening, the children invented fantasy solutions in make-believe games, in which the attackers were captured before having a chance to perpetrate their crime.

Gradual in–Vivo Exposure
Whereas the participants showed signs of regaining control, their fear of the beach prevented them from going out of homes that faced the sea. To respond to this, parents were invited the next day and were guided to help treat the "beach phobia" on site. They walked with their children on the beach, held and comforted them, and assured them that the danger was over. The children needed a great deal of support and encouragement to restore

cont'd

them to their predisaster level of confidence. One 14 year old stated, "My father took me to the sea shore. I saw the terrorists' boat and the blood on the rocks on which they smashed the head of the little girl. I'm sorry I have seen all this, it haunts me in my dreams. But I am not afraid of the sea any longer."

Cognitive Reappraisal of the Experience

On the following day, children were active and creative. They created road maps and clay models of the scene, with detailed reconstruction of the sequence of events. At this stage, they discussed their recollections in a more age-appropriate manner, trying to evaluate each reaction in the light of retrospective knowledge: Those who hid or fled could appreciate the survival value of their actions, and not feel any more shame for them.

Creative Means for Dealing With the Trauma

Day by day, the children expressed themselves in more structured ways. As they regained their feelings of security and control over their fears, they added writing as another means of expression. They became engaged in a kind of "poetic dialogue," writing poems to each other. Some of the writing explicitly expressed grief and mourning, and some expressed shock, rage, and the loss of trust in a "just world," as is evident in the following example written by a 14-year-old girl.

> *If There's a God*
>
> *If there's a God*
> *and yes, many claim there is*
> *then how come little kids get killed?*
>
> *And how is it*
> *that children*
> *who have not yet managed to do anything in their lives*
> *are the ones to be shot and the ones to die?*
> *Yet there still are those who claim*
> *that there is a God.*
> *If there is a God then how does this happen?*
> *Who even needs it?*
> *Let's get it over with.*
> *Let's finish this matter.*

> *If there is a God*
> *and yes, many claim there is,*
> *then how come*
> *little kids get killed?*

Problem Solving and Mapping Alternatives

Whereas the children initially drew chaotic drawings of the scene, they gradually began to, instead, draw illustrative portrayals of the victims and what happened to them. Based on all the information they had about the event, participants were now ready to come up with suggestions for future encounters with threat and danger. The feelings that had been expressed in the earlier phases of the intervention were now, at the final stage, channeled into a group problem-solving activity, producing a plan for future eventualities. The children slowly came to terms with the stress of being near-miss victims.

Mourning and Memorial Rituals

On the day of the last meeting, the group assembled pieces of broken glass to create a memorial, which they captioned, "So Life was Broken." Building the memorial signified the beginning of their accepting loss.

Family Counseling

During this period, the facilitators counseled families on how to respond to their children. Parents were encouraged to share their own feelings with their children and, together, to work through the difficult period of recuperation. Traumatic symptoms gradually subsided, and the children resumed their daily activities.

Follow–Up Assessments

Teachers conducted follow-up surveys and interviews two months and eight months later. They found no persistence of symptoms in most children; posttraumatic intervention was suggested for those who were exceptions.

---

* Information on the attack, the case, and the interventions are available in Ayalon (1993b).

Whether performing a communitywide intervention or working with children on an individual basis, it is widely believed that facilitators need to allow children to express their feelings and emotions about the experience (Breton, Valla, & Lambert, 1993). Children usually profit from sharing their experiences and feelings with others who have lived through the disaster. "Shared fate" (Kirk, 1984) creates a common ground for those who try to put into perspective their bewildered feelings, and to deal with their anxiety, survival guilt, sadness, and shame (Monaco & Gaier, 1987; Yule, 1992). Children often express themselves through play, creative devices, symbols, and metaphors, so facilitators should offer them a wide variety of verbal and nonverbal modes for expression.

The extended example on pages 274–275 presents a description of a multidimensional crisis intervention with a group of traumatized school children. The process, conducted during five consecutive days following a disaster, used eight distinct crisis intervention methods: (1) ventilation of feelings, (2) enactment, (3) channeling aggression, (4) gradual exposure, (5) cognitive reappraisal, (6) creative expression, (7) problem solving, and (8) mourning rituals.

As in every case of crisis intervention, issues of assessment are complicated. Generally, when facilitators terminate early crisis interventions, they assume that "nature will take its course" and that everything will be fine. In some cases, they use structured evaluation tools in the follow-up, such as self-report questionnaires, feedback checklists, and reports by family members, teachers, and clinicians. The picture that emerges of the effectiveness of the intervention may change depending on when the evaluation takes place—whether it is immediately after the termination of the intervention or several weeks or months later. Regardless of when it is conducted, an evaluation should address the following three questions:

1. How did the re-entry to routine take place and at what price?
2. Are the children functioning at their pre-crisis level or better?
3. Are there residual traumatic responses or reawakened old traumatic wounds (for example, nightmares, fears, and depression) that may indicate the need for tertiary intervention?

INTERVENTION WITH FAMILIES

A family is a living system that continuously seeks to balance itself while facing perpetual changes from inside and pressures from outside. As systems behave under stress, so do families: Some adapt and survive, some even flourish, whereas others crumble or disintegrate. A crisis can be detrimental to a family or it can serve as a stimulus for reshuffling resources and creating greater cohesion and growth.

A disaster's effects on the family depend on the family's resources, and on its predisaster level of mutual bonds, communication, cohesiveness, and values. Other factors include the degree of the family's flexibility in reallocating roles and adapting rules according to situational demands, its general physical and mental health, and the availability of crucial support from within and without (Ayalon, 1983b). In terms of the double ABCX Model (McCubbin & Patterson, 1983), explained in chapter 4, stressors rarely come one at a time, but rather usually come in groups, causing a "pileup" of stressors. As stressors pile up, a family's coping resources are mobilized to respond. The family may now reach a level of adaptation that is good and healthy (bonadaptation) or negative and unhealthy (maladaptation), with "good" meaning a balance is achieved between individual family members and the family system as a whole, between the community and the family, and so on. In some situations, the family can exert some measure of control and, therefore, can influence the outcome.

A disaster-induced crisis triggers a series of changes in the structure and function of the family as a system. It changes the emotional distance between family members, its communication patterns, and its established role relationships. As a result of these changes, mutual trust and support may be disrupted. Families sometimes lack the resources to adapt on their own to crisis-induced changes. When this happens, it is time for the family to seek professional help.

Touching Reality "How Is Your Family?" will help you analyze your family of origin's response pattern to crisis or disaster.

The primary purpose of family crisis intervention is to help the family re-establish the balance lost because of the crisis or disaster. To accomplish that, family crisis intervention has three aims: (1) to decrease the likelihood that negative, long-term mental health problems of one of its members will disrupt family functioning; (2) to enlist the family as a support system for one or more of its traumatized members; and (3) to treat the entire family, both from a family-centered and a systemwide perspective.

The caregiver's goal is to enter "into the life situation of the individual, family, or group, to cushion the impact of stress that throws the person (or persons) off balance, and to help mobilize the resources of those affected directly" (Smith, 1983, p. 120). To be effective, however, helpers need to understand both the obvious and subtle ways in which disaster affects family dynamics and functioning (Ayalon & Lee, 1990).

TOUCHING REALITY

How Is Your Family?

Think of a time in your life as a child or a teenager when your family of origin was dealing with a highly stressful situation, one that, perhaps, caused a major change in your family's lifestyle, forced a change in your residence, or resulted in a major loss of property. Now, answer the following questions. (If you are working with someone, one of you can be the client and the other the facilitator; change roles after one of you has answered the questions. You may even compare your stories after you have both answered).

1. Who were the family members living under the same roof? How was your family just before the crisis, and what was the overall feeling in the family?
2. Was the change or crisis predictable? Did it happen by choice (If so, whose choice?), or was it imposed on the family from the outside?
3. How did your family talk (or not talk) about the crisis, before, during, and afterward?
4. Did you notice any changes in your parents' and siblings' behavior?
5. How did your own life change following the event? Did you feel better or worse than before?
6. Thinking back now, can you identify any particular changes in your family's routine—in the communication among family members, in the roles each of you fulfilled, in the daily rules and regulations—before and after the crisis?
7. Looking back, what have you learned about your family's pattern of coping with change or crisis?

First Aid for the Family System

Before considering what kind of help to offer a family under stress, it is important to acknowledge the spontaneous survival mechanisms and the acts of mutual caring that disasters often trigger in families. Certain aspects of emergency coping responses are generic to most disasters and are prevalent in the very first stages of the disaster. These responses cover the following needs:

- to save human life
- to provide water, first aid, food, shelter, or clothing in the aftermath
- to evacuate a dangerous space
- to get messages to family members to find out where and how safe they are
- to provide comforting support for victims; to survive economically
- to emerge in the aftermath in reasonable psychological shape.

Postdisaster Family Responsibility

I was living in Encino, California, 1.5 miles from the epicenter of the Northridge earthquake. Living in California, you're aware of little shakes and earthquakes, but right off, you knew this was not your typical earthquake. This one didn't stop after a few seconds. It was so strong that it knocked me to the floor. … The lights went off… pitch black. I felt my way, grabbed my jacket and I think I felt my head, which was bleeding. I grabbed a towel. Opened the door. The first thing I saw was that the emergency lights were on in the hallway and alarms were screaming. An elderly neighbor was on the floor in the hallway. She had started out of her apartment and fell down. I helped her up and helped her to the stairs, and down to the lobby to get outside.…

The only thing I could think of was that I had to get to my two brothers and their kids. … I was driving on Ventura Boulevard. … My friend was behind me in his car. His sister was alone in the same area that my brother lived.…

We got to my first brother's house because it was closer. He lived in a gated community, but there was no security guard and the gate was broken. It looked like a car had rammed it trying to get out. I remember pounding on the door, but there was no answer. The door was locked, but I didn't hear a single person. A neighbor came out and told me that my brother had just left to go to his mother-in-law's house. I asked if they were ok. The neighbor said that the kids were crying but they were okay. My brother had wrapped them in a blanket and they had jumped into the car.

I got back in the car. My friend had gone to his sister's house. You almost didn't want to be alone. But he had to go and check on his sister. So we decided to meet in exactly one hour at a certain location—one of our mutual friend's houses—close to both sets of relatives. I headed to my brother's house. He had two kids as well and his wife.

By the time I was on the road, there were more cars out. There were accidents. At least 20 accidents. There were hydrants blown left and right. There was water shooting in the air or gushing in the middle of the street. I remember seeing everyone out with blankets because it was the middle of the night and it was chilly. Not cold, but a little chilly for L.A.

When I got there, I saw my brother, his wife and two kids in the middle of the lawn. They were talking with neighbors. It was the same thing. You find a certain relief in groups and crowds. You just want to be together. I remember people having flashlights, candles, away from the houses, out in the middle of the lawn.

That gave me the chills.

Some researchers have found that although people exposed to a disaster may be temporarily stunned for a brief period they will soon pull together and start caring for their family members (Janis, 1985). In contrast to stereotyped description of families' reactions to disaster, such as panic, mass disorganization, or irrational behavior, most families act in controlled and adaptive ways. Once the intense impact is over, people soon show concern for loved ones, neighbors, and community members. The family is the major focal point and the main source of help to victims during this period (Quarantelli, 1985).

Activities to relieve the family's initial shock. To relieve the initial shock of a disaster, and to contribute to their gradual recovery, families engage in a variety of activities. Disaster workers need to respect and support the activities families engage in to restore some sense of order in their chaotic postdisaster situation: Family members participate in rescue efforts, care for their injured relatives, make an effort to gather the scattered family members and bring them all to a safe location, and assess the damages to their home and property.

Healing communication. The family can play an important role in helping an individual member adjust to new realities, such as an injury or the loss of a limb; family members can also help each other adjust to their altered family. Families move toward healing more quickly when they face the reality of death or severe injury together and encourage each other to work out their grief.

Family members need to talk among themselves and work though their traumatic experiences. This is not always feasible because parents and children may hide their distress from each other in an effort to spare the others' feelings. They can be greatly helped and comforted when encouraged to share their distress.

If the family home is destroyed in the disaster, finding an alternative place to live is of paramount importance, not only for safety reasons, but because the family members need a place where they can be together to grieve, to be angry, to be bitter, and to begin to heal together. Some members may present severe symptoms, such as brief emotional or psychosomatic disturbances, soon after the disaster's impact. The family will speed individual healing if it understands and expects reactions to be brief and transient. In addition, it will speed individual healing if it encourages family members to express their feelings and reactions in an accepting manner, without condemnation.

Although the family can offer an optimal stress-buffering environment, it does not always do so successfully. When the family cannot defuse serious disturbance in a family member, someone in the family should seek professional help.

Digging Family Members from the Rubble

In Turkey, after the 1999 earthquake, in the badly damaged town of Adapazaro, eight members of an extended family were buried under the rubble. The structure under which they disappeared was considered too dangerous even for rescue workers to dig for survivors. One son, whose life was saved by his absence from home that night, insisted on digging almost on his own for over 18 hours. He uncovered his parents' bodies, but did not stop there. His efforts, which almost cost him his life, were rewarded when he succeeded in rescuing his niece, bruised but alive.

Families will be more satisfied if they can keep some ties with their familiar neighborhood and friends, if possible. Families housed in temporary living quarters will fare better if they make the best of the situation, learn to be flexible, and rediscover their talents for living.

Evacuating children. In the period immediately following a disaster, there is often a tendency to protect children by sending them away to safer places. Since World War II psychologists have asked if it is better to have the children stay with their families and remain exposed to the danger or if it is better to evacuate them. This is complex, and presents a dilemma that reflects society's enormous personal and collective responsibility toward its children.

The practice of separating small children from their caretakers and evacuating them to a safer place was criticized as early as 1943 by Freud and Burlingham (1943), who observed that the separation added stress to the children's trauma. Recent findings by Shacham (2000) and Lahad, Shacham, and Niv (2000) corroborate Freud and Burlingham's observations. Shacham found that children evacuated without their families expressed a desire to stay with their families in a future emergency, even if it meant being exposed to mortal dangers. Lahad and colleagues found that during a one-week-long evacuation period, children reported more emotional, cognitive, physiological, and behavioral stress reactions than children who stayed in the danger zone with their families; being evacuated without their parents intensified the children's fears and worries.

The conclusion supported by research findings is this: If it is impossible to evacuate children with their families, it is advisable not to evacuate them at all.

Empowering Families

After the acute emergency period draws to its end, families struggling to cope with the aftereffects of a disaster need to anticipate recovery. Without a hopeful outlook, there is a danger of secondary responses of despair and demoralization (Erikson, 1995). It is important for the family to re-establish a home base as an initial step toward "seeing a light at the end of the tunnel" and as a step toward recovery. Families that take advantage of their natural desire to rebuild a shattered home, coupled with wise use of disaster relief resources, will more quickly restore a satisfactory environment in which to deal with their other problems.

Families that sustain substantial economic losses might try to cope by making a realistic assessment of their losses, and of any available insurance coverage and relief programs. They could then prioritize their needs and outline steps toward financial recovery. Ideally, the most functional way to cope would be to include an emergency disaster component in the family's overall financial management plan long before the crisis materializes. Sometimes even this foresight is not enough to cover losses in major disasters, however. Myers (1994) pointed out that disaster relief procedures have been called "the secondary disaster" because of red tape, hassles, and delays that cause disappointment for suffering survivors. Helpers at this stage may need to help family members find constructive channels for their anger. Mental health staff also may advocate with agencies on behalf of disaster clients (Myers).

If outside assistance is necessary, the family's predisaster concept of their competence and independence may be endangered. Seeing themselves now as dependent, they may be tempted to surrender and adopt a long-term role of learned helplessness

(Seligman, 1975). Family members, however, can be assertive, not passive, by identifying the guidance they need to assist them in their encounters with outside aid; this prevents them from falling into learned helplessness. Once motivated to regain their stability, family members should have a clear idea of their priorities, which will facilitate their work with relief personnel. In the end, by being flexible as they work with caregivers and by being tolerant of their temporary situation, family members adjust better to their necessary dependency on outside assistance. The motto of resilient and adaptive families in the United States seems to be, "problems are conquered, life goes on" (Smith, 1983).

Helping parents help their children. Although different families have different ways of coping with traumatic stress, one thing is certain: The way parents cope with the disaster, and the way they react to their children's trauma, are critical to the children. A strong link has been found between parents' felt distress and their children's symptomatology (Pynoos, Steinberg, & Goejian, 1996). Parents' emotional and behavioral responses to disaster mediate between the small child and the event and lend the event its special meaning, as either dreadful or endurable. For example, Almqvist (2000), working in refugee camps, found that when parents were overwhelmed by the disaster, they became emotionally unreachable for their children. Children were often forced to take on a parental role, for which they were not ready physically or psychologically.

Crisis intervention needs to respect adaptive family defense mechanisms at the impact stage, such as denial, even though they may rebound and later impede the family's rehabilitation. In situations of acute danger parents generally try to protect their children from recognizing the existence of a threat by denying or minimizing it for as long as possible. Children's ignoring, avoiding, or denying the threat, however, may contribute to their feeling of confusion in the aftermath. In addition, some parents and children, each trying to protect the other, avoid talking about traumatic events or hide their own pain and anxiety. Suppressing and denying traumatic feelings and memories thus becomes part of the parent–child relationship. Although this may have adaptive value as a survival strategy for both parent and child during the acute phase of a disaster, it may later obstruct family relationships and delay recovery. The helper must be sensitive to the timing of confronting the family with these issues. When denial is no longer adaptive, it may be helpful to reframe avoidance behaviors and attitudes as "great protectors" in the past, that have now become superfluous. By such reframing the caretaker contributes to the empowerment of the family and enhances its coping abilities.

Restoring family continuities. Rapid restoration of established parent–child and sibling interaction patterns provides children with security and comfort in the postdisaster period. Parents may find themselves caught up in trying to fulfill conflicting needs: their children's need for extra attention versus all the other urgent things that must be done to rehabilitate their lives. It is highly recommended that whenever possible parents should make an effort to spend more time with their children and involve them in the restoration activities.

Terr (1989) expressed doubt that frightened parents can "force" themselves to stay calm just for the sake of their children, but there is evidence to the contrary. Bergman and Cohen (1994) found that caring for and protecting their young children helped widowed mothers in their own recovery process, and professional support in their rehabilitative efforts succeeded in turning the mothers into the best "helping agents" for their own children. Parents are empowered when they are viewed as the preferred people to restore the historic sense of life in the family and the emotional continuity of love and trust that was disrupted by disaster.

Crisis intervention must, therefore, be geared to helping parents restore the sense of functional, emotional, cognitive, and historic continuity of the family system and of each individual family member (Ayalon & Lahad, 2000a). There are many activities that are helpful for restoring these continuities. For example:

- Families can make a list of things that need to be done to help to bring the house to its usual shape and function, hang the list in a central place, and ask each family member (adult and child) to choose a number of activities from the list; this activity helps restore functional continuity.
- Helpers can ask each member of the family to share a memory of the past that brings happy feelings and, if possible, have them write, draw, or enact the story; this activity helps restore emotional continuity.
- Family members can tell each other the sequence of events of the disaster, from before the disaster to the present time, step by step, making sure that each different story is respected and accepted by all; this activity helps restore a sense of cognitive continuity.
- Families can collect items, newspaper clippings, and other memorabilia connected with the disaster, then discuss and store the items for future reference; this activity helps restore a sense of historic continuity.

Family–to–family support. Crisis intervention for parents (and other family members), often conducted in groups because of the great demand for this counseling during and shortly after a disaster strikes, provides families with a very important resource for enhancing their coping resources. Group meetings create a buffer against the devastating feelings of isolation and loneliness that a disaster imposes, especially if it entails the loss of home, social status, dignity, and, as with complex disasters, basic trust in others (Ayalon, 1983b).

The Task Force on Families of Catastrophe recommends "shared fate families" interaction: "The concept which has emerged from the catastrophe treatment literature is the notion of defusing the trauma through contact with fellow survivors.... Thus, families affected by crisis will gain immeasurable benefits by talking with other families and discuss mutual concerns" (Figley & McCubbin, 1983, p. 197).

Methods and Techniques Parents May Use to Help Their Children

Parents who openly seek help after a disaster legitimize and model for their children the admission of a need for assistance (Hobfoll et al., 1991). Disaster relief professionals can help parents enhance their children's coping in a variety of ways. For example, they can give parents information about disaster-related stress, reduce their sense that they have to "have all the answers," and offer them information on available sources for help. These helpers can teach parents how to reassure their children without giving false assurance, how to encourage their children to ask questions and express their concerns, how to assure their children that their thoughts and feelings are not "bad," and how to mediate television news broadcasts by watching with their children and monitoring their responses. In addition, helpers should encourage parents to develop a family disaster plan in anticipation of a future disaster and to re-establish family rituals (Flynn & Nelson, 1998).

Disaster relief workers have found the concept of "parent as helper" to be very effective (Garbarino, Kostelny, & Dubrow, 1991). By delegating helping roles to parents, the helper empowers the family to work within its cultural, religious, and ethnic traditions to heal itself.

Interventions with parents that enlist them in the helping process are therapeutic and educational and, importantly, help parents develop the necessary attitude to help their children. Thus motivated, parents acquire a wide repertoire of specialized skills and practices, interchangeably fulfilling the roles of mediator, supporter, and guide as different needs arise (Hobfoll et al., 1991; Terr, 1989). Recruiting parents as helpers means

- teaching them to use therapeutic strategies, such as relaxation exercises and cognitive-behavioral reinforcements (Meichenbaum, 1985)
- training them to enhance their children's sense of control through guided imagery, make-believe, and metaphoric stories (Ayalon & Lahad, 1991)
- coaching them on how to get family members to make up stories together that break the vicious circle of fear, helplessness, and depression by constructing an empowering narrative from past memories and positive future expectations (White & Epston, 1990)
- guiding them in planning time for exercising the new techniques they learn
- instructing them to look for and understand their children's stress symptoms

and behavior, which also reduces the parents' anxiety, anger, and guilt and channels the motivation to overprotect their children into constructive actions (Hamblen, 2000)

- encouraging them to allow the traumatic event and trauma to be reconstructed according to each child's age, verbal capacity, and needs, which ensures that the family becomes the natural arena for sharing and processing grief over losses.

Advice from the National Association of School Psychologists

The following is an abbreviated example of a disaster guide for parents and teachers issued by the National Association of School Psychologists (2001) immediately after the attacks on the United States on September 11, 2001. These guidelines, titled *Helping Children Cope with Tuesday's Acts of Terrorism: Tips for Parents and Teachers*, and made available on the Internet, reflect the view of parents as the most available and efficient helpers to their children in disaster.

The first section details eight behaviors in which all adults should engage to help the children with whom they interact:

1. Because children take their cues from the adults around them, adults should *model calmness and control*.
2. Because children feared that the attack on the World Trade Center put their own neighborhoods at risk, adults should *reassure children that they are safe*, and that their neighborhoods are not at risk.
3. Because complex disasters reduce children's trust in adults, adults should *remind them that trustworthy people are in charge*, such as disaster workers, police officers, firefighters, doctors, and military personnel.

Disaster Relief Professionals and Parents as Co-helpers

The Dan family, a young couple with two daughters ages five and seven, lived on the fifth floor of a high-rise building. They awakened one night to the horrible noises of gunshots and screaming: Three armed men were raiding their building. Rushing out of their flat to run and hide, the family was separated and the parents lost sight of their daughters. Until they were reunited many hours later, each believed the others to be dead. They found out later that their next-door neighbors, a father and two daughters, had been brutally murdered.

Following the horrid event, each member of the family suffered severe stress reactions: The parents felt guilty and depressed, and the girls manifested phobic fears and catastrophic expectations of the ordeal repeating itself. They clung to their parents as they moved around the house, had nightmares, refused to sleep anywhere except in the parents' bedroom, and were afraid to leave the house.

The therapist paid a home visit and decided on crisis intervention strategies that engaged the parents as co-therapists in their daughters' treatment (Alon, 1985). This strategy was meant to empower the parents and to help them regain the parental accountability that was lost. The therapist assumed that the parents would gain from vicarious learning and guidance by helping the girls. In order to work in this manner, the therapist assumed different roles and modeled them to the parents, who were expected to carry on accordingly on a daily basis. The therapist, in guiding the parents, used a variety of behavioral, cognitive, and creative intervention techniques.

1. The girls were given "paradoxical instructions" that would confirm their clinging reactions as normal and implement a change at the same time: "It's absolutely impossible for you to leave your parents' bedroom at the moment. It will take a very long time before you'll be able to do so, maybe even a whole month!"

2. Behavioral and cognitive desensitization were used to reduce their fears and gain control:

   - The girls were asked to rate each room in the apartment according to how frightening it was, using a scale from 1 to 10.
   - The girls were asked to put signs on their door, reading: "The Room of Terrible Fear."
   - The girls were directed to write and draw a "Fear Diary" whenever nocturnal fears reoccurred.
   - The girls were asked to enact "jumping out of bed in a panic" to strange noises made by the therapist or parents.
   - After the girls returned to their own room they were urged to drill "emergency" escapes to the parents' bedroom on a designated night.

3. Creative methods:

   - The girls were asked to draw in detail frightening fantasies, with emphasis on small inappropriate details, such as a monster with a wristwatch.
   - The girls were taught to sing a "Song of Fear" composed by the therapist whenever they felt slightly afraid. The words of the song are: "I'm terribly afraid/I'm trembling a lot/There's no end to my suffering."

4. Changing the roles from "victim" to "caregiver": The girls were encouraged to "mother" and comfort their "frightened dolls."

5. Reframing: The therapist suggested that their "fear" was a sign of cleverness necessary for their survival.

In a period of two weeks, the girls' phobic reactions gradually subsided, and there were also marked decreases in the parents' fears.

4. Because the children feel angry and upset, adults should *let children know that it is okay to feel upset, angry, or feel other emotions.*

5. Because many children lack the ability to articulate how they feel, and express themselves nonverbally, adults should *observe children's emotional state* by noting changes in behavior, such as being aggressive, changes in appetite, such as eating more or less, and changes in sleep patterns, such as nightmares.

6. Because children know when someone is lying, and lies arouse suspicions that things are even worse than they might really be, adults should *tell children the truth.*

7. Because it is important for adults to tell the truth, adults should *stick to the facts*, avoid embellishing, or speculating on what happened or might happen.

8. Because children of different ages—at different developmental stages—need to be handled differently, adults should *keep their explanations developmentally appropriate.* For example, information for early elementary school children needs to be brief and simple, and information for upper elementary and early middle school children should help them separate reality from fantasy. By being good listeners, adults can encourage children to share their thoughts and feelings.

Nine recommendations for what parents can do to help their children put the parents squarely in the role of co–disaster–relief helpers. The recommendations are:

1. to focus on their children over the next day or so and tell them they are loved and that everything will be all right

2. to make time to talk with their children (or someone else will, and control over what is said is lost)

3. to stay close to their children both to reassure and to monitor them

4. to limit the amount of time their children watch the disaster on television

5. to maintain as normal a routine as possible, without being inflexible

6. to spend extra time with their children before the children go to bed

7. to ensure their children are eating, exercising, and sleeping well to reduce the effects of stress

8. to consider offering prayers, going to religious services, thinking hopeful thoughts for the victims and their families, and so on, to instill a sense that the family is being supportive

9. to find out what counseling plans their children's school have in place to help the children cope.

THE SCHOOL AS AN IMPORTANT INTERVENTION AGENT

A theme throughout this book is that schools play a central role in organizing and implementing rescue and early crisis interventions on all levels: the individual child, the classroom, school personnel, the family, and the community. In times of crisis, the importance of the school in re-establishing balance and continuity is paramount (Lerner, Volpe, & Lindell, 2003). This is an appropriate role for the school because schools are run by people who are professional educators, knowledgeable about child developmental needs in excess of the knowledge and expertise typically available to an individual family. School personnel have access to educational and psychological techniques and tools needed in times of emergency. Also, educational systems have access to national funds and community services for emergency intervention.

Key Role of School Personnel

An important argument for authorizing schools to deal with the traumatic effects of disasters is that such an intervention does not carry the stigma of pathology attached to mental health referrals. Although psychologists are pivotal to assessing needs and recommending appropriate interventions, they can transfer direct contact with children to school counselors and teachers. Only severely traumatized children need be referred to clinical specialists. School counseling services and in-system organizations, such as PTAs (Parent Teacher Associations), are the natural channel to provide disaster-related counseling to parents and families. However, even in a school, upheaval and a sense of urgency characterize the impact phase of a disaster.

Emergencies alter professionals' habitual functioning and call for broadening their scope of activity and responsibility of school staff. With the onset of the crisis a preassigned school emergency team should set up an ad hoc emergency center. This team is responsible for the following tasks, all of which are specific to crisis management:

1. Assess the danger; collect data from media, phone calls, and anecdotal observations by school personnel.
2. Take steps to curb panic and ensure the security of children and staff.
3. Assign roles, and guide teachers and other adults in how to deal with the pupils in their charge.
4. Screen the responses of the school population (children and adults).
5. Assign individuals to two subgroups. The first group is composed of the high-risk individuals who show signs of acute maladjustment. They are to be treated in small groups by the school psychologist or by other trained mental health workers. The second group contains all other students who are to be treated by school counselors and teachers trained to use crisis intervention methods, such as relaxation, cognitive-behavioral methods, reinforcement of coping skills, and creative work using art, writing, and play (Ayalon, 1997; Ayalon & Lahad, 2000a; Davis, 1995).

Helpers in Disasters in the Educational System

Disasters attract all kinds of helpers, such as natural helpers and nonprofessional volunteers, in addition to professional helpers who have been trained in disaster relief. When schools and children are involved, many people intervene who are not necessarily skilled and knowledgeable in working with schools and with children. Sometimes the school needs to coordinate and direct the goodwill of different "helpers" and make sure that the intervention takes into account the combined needs of the school and the type of help available.

The following list of potential helpers and their assigned target groups before and during a disaster may be helpful in planning disaster training for different groups.

- *Relatives, neighbors,* and *close friends* constitute a group of "natural" helpers who may provide the best immediate support for those exposed to a disaster.
- *Medical staff, social workers,* and *counselors* are able to offer direct support, information, and advice. They also are able to train potential helpers on how to provide disaster relief.
- *Teachers* are an important group for helping children who are not in need of medical attention and who are not so severely traumatized that they cannot

stay in a classroom. Importantly, teachers can provide children with a routine with which the children are familiar. In addition, they can listen actively to the children, attend to their emotional and social needs, and prepare them for post-disaster rituals, such as funerals and memorial services.

- *School counselors, school psychologists,* and *school social workers* can help teachers and school staff by providing counseling and attending to their needs, by sharing information on how to deal with children's distress, and by offering advice on school disaster management. In addition, this group can provide parents with information on normal reactions to traumatic situations, as well as advice and counseling.
- *Community leaders, the media,* and *community agencies* can provide the community with information, reassurance about action taken, and leadership.

SUMMARY

In this chapter, we focused on multidimensional strategies for crisis intervention, referring to the six coping channels presented in the BASIC-Ph model. We drew a distinction between immediate first aid during the impact phase of a disaster, and early crisis intervention conducted during the first six weeks after the event. Different methods of group crisis intervention are suited for different age groups. The discussions and examples in this chapter highlighted the needs of the individual child, the function of the family during and immediately after the disaster, and the value of working with groups. Schools can be a major agent for preparing intervention programs, training helpers, and helping both children and adults in disaster.

REFERENCES

Almqvist, K. (2000). Parent–child interaction and coping strategies in refugee children. In L. Van Willigen (Ed.), *Health hazards of organized violence in children: Coping and protective factors* (pp. 53–68). Utrecht, Netherlands: Stichting Pharos.

Alon, N. (1985). An Ericksonian approach to treatment of chronic posttraumatic patients. In J. K. Zeig (Ed.), *Ericksonian hypnotherapy* (pp. 307–326). New York: Brunner/Mazel.

Ayalon, O. (1978). *Emergency kit.* Haifa, Israel: Haifa University Press. (Hebrew)

Ayalon, O. (1983a). Coping with terrorism—The Israeli case. In D. Meichenbaum & M. Jaremko (Eds.), *Stress reduction and prevention* (pp. 293–339). Cambridge, MA: Perseus.

Ayalon, O. (1983b). *Precarious balance: Coping with stress in the family.* Tel Aviv, Israel: Sifriat Hapoalim. (Hebrew)

Ayalon, O. (1992). *Rescue! Community oriented preventive education handbook.* Ellicott City, MD: Chevron.

Ayalon, O. (1993a). Death in literature and bibliotherapy. In R. Malkinsom, S. Rubin, & E. Vitztum (Eds.), *Loss and bereavement in Israeli society* (pp. 155–175). Jerusalem: Ministry of Defense. (Hebrew)

Ayalon, O. (1993b). Posttraumatic stress recovery. In J. Wilson & B. Raphael (Eds.), *International handbook of traumatic stress syndromes* (pp. 855–866). New York: Plenum Press.

Ayalon, O. (1997). Creative methods offered to caregivers to prevent or deal with secondary traumatization. In D. Ajdukovic (Ed.), *Trauma recovery training: Lessons learned* (pp. 161–167). Zagreb, Croatia: Society for Psychological Assistance.

Ayalon, O., & Flasher, A. (1993). *Chain reaction: Children and divorce.* London: Jessica Kingsley.

Ayalon, O., & Lahad, M. (1991). *Life on the edge: Coping with stress of war and peace.* Haifa, Israel: Nord. (Hebrew)

Ayalon, O., & Lahad, M. (2000a). Coping with uncertainty. In O. Ayalon, & M. Lahad, *Life on the edge: Coping with stress, war, security hazards, violence* (pp. 327–347). Haifa, Israel: Nord. (Hebrew)

Ayalon, O., & Lahad, M. (2000b). *H.A.N.D.S.: Helpers Assisting Natural Disaster Survivors handbook* (limited ed.). Istanbul, Turkey: Bakish Treatment Center.

Ayalon, O., Lahad, M., & Cohen, A. (Eds.). (1998). *Community stress prevention 3.* Kiryat Shmona, Israel: Community Stress Prevention Center.

Ayalon, O., Lahad, M., & Cohen, A. (Eds.). (1999). *Community stress prevention 4.* Kiryat Shmona, Israel: Community Stress Prevention Center.

Ayalon, O., & Lee, M. S. (1990). Stresses and challenges in the family. *Chonnam Journal of Medical Sciences, 3,* 165–173.

Ayalon, O., & Soskis D. (1986). Survivors of terrorist victimization. In N. A. Milgram (Ed.), *Stress and coping in time of war: Generalizations from the Israeli experience* (pp. 257–274). Philadelphia: Brunner-Routledge.

Bandler, R. (1985). *Use your brain for a change.* Moab, UT: Real People Press.

Bergman, Z., & Cohen, E. (1994). *Toward the family's common ground.* Tel Aviv: Am Oved. (Hebrew)

Boatright, C. (1985). Children as victims of disaster. In J. Laub & S. Murphy (Eds.), *Perspectives on disaster recovery* (pp. 131–149). Stamford, CT: Appleton & Lange.

Breton, J. J., Valla, J. P., & Lambert, J. (1993). Industrial disaster and mental health of children and their parents. *Journal of the American Academy of Child and Adolescent Psychiatry, 32,* 438–445.

Brison, S. (1998). Trauma narratives and the remaking of the self. In M. Bal, J. Crewe, & L. Spitzer (Eds.), *Acts of memory: Cultural recall in the present* (pp. 39–54). Hanover, NH: University Press of New England.

Davis, C. B. (1995). The use of art therapy and group process with grieving children. In S. C. Smith & M. Pennells (Eds.), *Interventions with bereaved children* (pp. 321–331). Philadelphia: Taylor & Francis.

Dembert, M. L., & Simmer, E. D. (2000). When trauma affects a community: Group interventions and support after a disaster. In R. H. Klein (Ed.), *Group psychotherapy for psychological trauma* (pp. 239–264). New York: Guilford Press. Retrieved September 2, 2003, from http://psybc.com/pdfs/WhenTraumaEffects.pdf

Erikson, K. T. (1995). Notes on trauma and community. In C. Caruth (Ed), *Trauma: Explorations in memory* (pp. 183–199). Baltimore: Johns Hopkins University Press.

Figley, C. R., & McCubbin, H. I. (Eds.). (1983). *Stress and the family, 2: Coping with catastrophe.* New York: Brunner/Mazel.

Flynn, B. W., & Nelson, M. E. (1998). Understanding the needs of children following large-scale disasters and the role of government. *Child and Adolescent Psychiatric Clinics of North America, 7,* 211–227.

Freud, A., & Burlingham, D. T. (1943). *War and children.* New York: Medical War Books.

Gal, R. (1997). Colleagues in disaster: A personal perspective. In D. Ajdukovic (Ed.), *Trauma recovery training: Lessons learned* (pp. 113–125). Zagreb, Croatia: Society for Psychological Assistance.

Galliano, S., & Lahad, M. (2000). *Manual for practice of CIPR.* London: ICAS [Independent Counseling and Advisory Services].

Garbarino, J., Kostelny, K., & Dobrow, N. (1991). *No place to be a child: Growing up in a war zone*. San Francisco: Jossey-Bass.

Gardner, R. A. (1993). *Psychotherapy with children*. Northvale, NJ: Jason Aronson.

Gibbs, S. (1994). Post-war social reconstruction in Mozambique: Re-framing children's experience of trauma and healing. *Disaster, 18*, 268–276.

Hamblen, J. (2000). *Terrorist attacks and children*. Retrieved January 12, 2004, from http://www.ncptsd.org/facts/disasters/fschildrendisaster.html

Handford, H. A., Mayes, S. D., Mattison, R. E., Humphrey, F. J., Bagnato, S., Bixler, E. O., & Kales, J. D. (1986). Child and parent reactions to the Three Mile Island nuclear accident. *Journal of the American Academy of Child Psychiatry, 25*, 346–356.

Herman, J. L. (2000). *Trauma and recovery: The aftermath of violence, from domestic abuse to political terror*. New York: Basic Books.

Hobfoll, S. E., Spielberger, C. D., Breznitz, S., Figley, C., Folkman, S., Lepper-Green, B., Meichenbaum, D., Milgram, N. A., Sandler, L., Sarason, I., & van der Kolk, B. A. (1991). War-related-stress: Addressing the stress of war and traumatic events. *American Psychologist, 46*, 848–855.

Hoffman, S. (1994). Up from the embers: A disaster survivor's story. *National Center for Post-Traumatic Stress Disorder [NCP] Clinical Quarterly, 4*(2), 15–16.

Jagodic, G. K., Kontac, K., & Zubenko, W. N. (2002). Group interventions for children in crisis. In W. N. Zubenko & J. A. Capozzoli (Eds.), *Children and disasters: A practical guide to healing and recovery* (pp. 135-158). New York: Oxford University Press.

Janis, I. (1985). *Psychological stress*. New York: John Wiley & Sons.

Juul, J. (1997). How I happened to meet Plato and Aristotle on Ban Jelacic Square. In D. Ajdukovic (Ed.), *Trauma recovery training: Lessons learned* (pp. 13–26). Zagreb, Croatia: Society for Psychological Assistance.

Kirk, D. (1984). *Shared fate*. Brentwood Bay, British Columbia, Canada: Ben Simon.

Lahad, M. (1999). The use of drama therapy with crisis intervention groups, following mass evacuation. *The Arts in Psychotherapy, 26*, 27–33.

Lahad, M. (2000). *Creative supervision*. London: Jessica Kingsley.

Lahad, M., & Cohen, A. (1998). Eighteen years of community stress prevention. In O. Ayalon, M. Lahad, & A. Cohen (Eds.), *Community stress prevention 3* (pp. 1–9). Kiryat Shmona, Israel: Community Stress Prevention Center.

Lahad, M., Shacham, Y., & Niv, S. (2000). Coping and community resources in children facing disaster. In A. Y. Shalev, R. Yehuda, & A. C. McFarlane (Eds.), *International handbook of human response to trauma* (pp. 389–395). New York: Kluwer Academic/Plenum Press.

Lerner, M. D., Volpe, J. S., & Lindell, B. (2003). *A practical guide for crisis response in our schools* (5th ed.). New York: American Academy of Experts in Traumatic Stress.

Levine, P. A., & Frederick, A. (1997). *Waking the tiger, healing trauma: The innate capacity to transform overwhelming experiences*. Berkeley, CA: North Atlantic Books.

Lindy, J. D. (1989). Transference and posttraumatic stress disorder. *Journal of the American Academy of Psychoanalysis, 17*, 415–426.

McCubbin, H. I., & Patterson, J. M. (1983). The Family Stress Process: The Double ABCX Model of adjustment and adaptation. *Marriage and Family Review, 6*(1–2), 7–37.

Meichenbaum, D. (1985). *Stress inoculation training.* New York: Pergamon Press.

Monaco, N. M., & Gaier, E. L. (1987). Developmental level and children's responses to the explosion of the space shuttle Challenger. *Early Childhood Research Quarterly, 2*, 83–95.

Monahan, C. (1995). *Children trauma: A parent's guide to helping children heal.* San Francisco: Jossey-Bass.

Myers, D. (1994). Psychological recovery from disaster. *National Center for Post-Traumatic Stress Disorder [NCP] Clinical Quarterly, 4*(2), 1–5.

Myers, D., Zunin, H. S., & Zunin, L. M. (1990, November). Grief: The art of coping with tragedy. *Today's Supervisor, 6*, 14–15.

National Association of School Psychologists. (2001). *Helping children cope with Tuesday's acts of terrorism: Tips for parents and teachers.* Retrieved September 2, 2003, from http://www.naspoline.org/NEAT/terrorism.html

Oaklander, V. (1978). *Windows to our children: A gestalt therapy with children and adolescents.* Moab, UT: Real People Press.

Omer, H., & Alon, N. (1994). The continuity principle: A unified approach to treatment and management in disaster and trauma. *American Journal of Community Psychology, 22*, 273–287.

Overdorf, J., & Silverthorn, J. (1996). *Training trances: Multi-level communication in therapy and training.* Portland, OR: Metamorphous Press.

Parkes, M. C., & Weiss, R. S. (1995). *Recovery from bereavement.* Northvale, NJ: Jason Aronson.

Pen, A. (1997). The limits of the trauma paradigm. In D. Ajdukovic (Ed.), *Trauma recovery training: Lessons learned* (pp. 151–160). Zagreb, Croatia: Society for Psychological Assistance.

Pynoos, R. S., Goenjian, A. K., & Steinberg, A. M. (1998). A public mental health approach to the postdisaster treatment of children and adolescents. *Child and Adolescent Psychiatric Clinics of North America, 7*, 195–210.

Pynoos, R. S., Steinberg, A. M., & Goenjian, A. (1996). Traumatic stress in childhood and adolescence. In B. van der Kolk, A. McFarlane, & I. Weiaeth, (Eds.), *Traumatic stress: The effects of overwhelming experience on mind, body, and society* (pp. 331–358). New York: Guilford Press.

Quarantelli, E. L. (1985). An assessment of conflicting views on mental health: The consequences of traumatic events. In C. R. Figley (Ed.), *Trauma and its wake* (pp. 173–215). New York: Brunner/Mazel.

Rothchild, B. (1999). *Making trauma therapy safe: The body as resource for braking traumatic acceleration.* Retrieved January 12, 2004, from http://home.webuniverse.net/babette/artsafe.htm

Salmon, T. W. (1919). The war neuroses and their lessons. *New York Journal of Medicine, 59*, 993–994.

Seligman, M.E.P. (1975). *Helplessness on depression, development and death.* San Francisco: W. H. Freeman.

Shacham, M. (2000). *Stress reactions and coping resources mobilized by evacuees (adults and children) and the adults' perception of needed future preparatory measures.* Unpublished doctoral dissertation, Anglia Polytechnic University, Chelmsford, England.

Shapiro, F., & Forrest, M. S. (1997). *EMDR: The breakthrough therapy for overcoming anxiety, stress, and trauma.* New York: Basic Books.

Shaw, J. A., Applegate, B., Tanner, S., Perez, D., Rothe, E., Campo-Bowen, A. E., & Lahey, B. L. (1995). Psychological effects of Hurricane Andrew on an elementary school population. *Journal of the American Academy of Child and Adolescent Psychiatry, 34*, 1185–1192.

Slaikeu, K. A. (1990). *Crisis intervention: A handbook for practice and research* (2nd ed.). Boston: Allyn & Bacon.

Smith, S. M. (1983). Disaster: Family disruption in the wake of natural disaster. In C. R. Figley & H. I. McCubbin (Eds.), *Stress and the family, 2: Coping with catastrophe* (pp. 120–147). New York: Brunner/Mazel.

Speier, A. H. (2000). *Psychosocial issues for children and adolescents in disasters* (2nd ed.). Washington, DC: U.S. Department of Health and Human Services.

Terr, L. C. (1989). Treating psychic trauma in children: A preliminary discussion. *Journal of Traumatic Stress, 2*, 3–20.

Turner, A. L. (2000). Group treatment of trauma survivors following a fatal bus accident: Integrating theory and practice. *Group Dynamics: Theory, Research, and Practice, 4*(2), 139–149.

van der Kolk, B., McFarlane, A., & Weiseth, I. (Eds.). (1996). *Traumatic stress: The effects of overwhelming experience on mind, body, and society.* New York: Guilford Press.

White, M., & Epson, D. (1990). *Narrative means to therapeutic ends.* New York: W. W. Norton.

Yalom, I. D. (1985). *The theory and practice of group psychotherapy* (3rd ed.). New York: Basic Books.

Young, M. A. (1998). *The community crisis response team training manual* (2nd ed.). Washington, DC: National Organization for Victim Assistance. Retrieved September 2, 2003, from http://www.ojp.usdoj.gov/ovc/publications/infores/crt/welcome.html

Yule, W. (1992) Post-traumatic stress disorder in child survivors of shipping disasters: The sinking of the "Jupiter." *Psychotherapy and Psychosomatics, 57*, 200–205.

POSTDISASTER INTERVENTION

CHAPTER OVERVIEW

After studying the material in this chapter, you should

- understand the need for postdisaster intervention (tertiary prevention) for children and families
- understand the needs of traumatized children of different ages
- understand the role of the therapist of traumatized children
- be able to apply the BASIC-Ph model of coping resources to traumatized children
- understand methods to enhance recovery and healing
- be able to apply specific methods of postdisaster intervention
- understand the connections among trauma, loss, and grief in the family
- understand the needs of the different members of the bereaved or traumatized family.

IN THE AFTERMATH: TERTIARY INTERVENTION

The hurricane has blown past. The toxic waste has been cleaned up. The terrorists have been caught. Things will get "back to normal," right?

Not necessarily. For many, the postdisaster stage is characterized by mental and physical suffering that continues and sometimes escalates long after the trauma is over. In these cases, helpers need to apply postdisaster—"tertiary"—intervention.

The paradox is this: Although the disaster appears to be over, it is not over. One sufferer described this dilemma in a vivid metaphor: "When a person is drowning, she has no other choice but to make extreme efforts to swim and reach the beach. But when she finally arrives at the shore, totally exhausted, she is free of the struggle to survive. Only then does she realize how awful was her ordeal, and then she is flooded by unbearable feelings" (Noy, 2000, p. 162).

People who are "hidden victims" may live with their pain for years before seeking help, if they seek help at all. They are the family members, friends, teachers, and classmates of victims, the near-miss eyewitnesses, and the people who identify strongly with the victims. Postdisaster interventions need to be available for those presumably "unhurt" by the disaster, including those experiencing "survivor's guilt" (the tendency for a survivor to feel guilt for surviving although others have perished), and helpers who suffer from compassion fatigue (Figley, 1995). Special care also is required for vulnerable, high-risk individuals, such as the very young and very old, the physically and mentally challenged, the lonely and isolated, and those who have been repeatedly traumatized.

The aims of tertiary interventions are broad: to ameliorate the mental pain and social anguish underlying posttraumatic stress and to enhance better long-range coping. Interventions may specifically target prevention of posttraumatic symptoms, though outcome studies suggest that even when an intervention is effective in lessening immediate distress it is not always effective in preventing posttraumatic stress disorder (PTSD) (Wilson, 1989).

Tertiary interventions for children and for families presented in this chapter share the following assumptions about resilient people who experience a disaster (Ayalon, 1997a, 1997b):

- Resilient people will acknowledge their unfamiliar and overwhelming posttraumatic symptoms as "normal reactions to an abnormal situation." They will have a realistic expectation about the duration of their suffering. They will be able to change their self-perception from "victims" to "coping persons," and acquire some appropriate ways of dealing with the aftereffects of the trauma.
- Resilient people will learn to deal with their ordeal by using the six coping channels described in the BASIC-Ph model, even though one or more of their coping channels may have been blocked by the traumatic experience. These six channels (see chapters 2 and 8 for a more detailed discussion of the BASIC-Ph model) are *Belief* (value clarification), *Affect* (sharing feelings), *Social* (role-playing or engaging in a group activity), *Imagination* (fantasy and creativity), *Cognition* (information, rules, and planning), and *Physiology* (physical activity and relaxation).
- During the intervention process resilient people will rebuild trust in themselves and in the surrounding world, ventilate troubled emotions and regain emotional bal-

ance, resume social interactions and accept social support, and give and receive family care; free their imaginations from repetitive traumatic images and use their imagination creatively; learn cognitive skills for dealing with the trauma; and identify and desensitize the physical residues of the trauma and practice relaxation.

- Resilient people will accept help to regain a sense of continuity in the different areas that have been disrupted by the disaster. They will regain a sense of functional continuity that will enable them to fulfill a meaningful role in their family and in society; they will regain a sense of pre- and postdisaster historical continuity; they will re-establish their friendship networks; and they will be able to find their own personal meaning in their ordeal.

Reluctance to Accept Posttrauma Treatment

Psychologists who deal with posttraumatic stress have observed that many traumatized victims refuse to seek help. They may do this because of their tendency to repress memories of the ordeal in order to distance themselves from reminders of the trauma, their sense of inadequacy, or their sense of survivor's guilt. The tendency to refuse help may cause serious delay in the onset of tertiary interventions and reduce the chances of recovery from the posttraumatic symptoms (Christenson, Walker, Ross, & Maltbie, 1981; Weisaeth, 2001).

Terr's (1990) follow-up study of the kidnapped children of Chowchilla, California, showed families' and schools' reluctance to deal with their children's trauma: "Defenses go up fast after trauma strikes. People do not wish to think of themselves as abnormal, hurt or changed" (p. 289). This may account for the parents' refusal to acknowl-

edge their children's need for expert help. Two lessons are clear for trauma experts and other psychosocial caregivers: (1) they need to be proactive, especially when young children are concerned, and (2) they need to realize that older children and adolescents find posttraumatic services more acceptable if they are presented as "stress and crisis consultation" rather than as psychiatric services, which may suggest inadequacy (Raphael, 1986).

From Victim to Victor

How resilient are children? The answer to this question will determine the kind of posttraumatic services offered to them by the helping agents (see chapter 2 for descriptions of the PTSD model, the resiliency model, and the BASIC-Ph model, which falls within a resiliency framework.). At one end of the spectrum is the pathogenic model, which perceives children who have been touched by disaster as indelibly hurt unless they receive therapy; "Major personality shifts that come about as a result of childhood trauma require intensive treatment. The parents of a single blow psychic trauma will have to watch for symptoms" (Terr, 1990, p. 287). At the other end of the spectrum are the advocates for the salutogenic approach which is "health orientated" (Antonovsky, 1978; Violanti, 2000). This viewpoint stresses the natural resilience of children, which can be enhanced by appropriate educational guidance and psychological support.

Current research and clinical observations of many children who have suffered extreme traumatic experiences support the resilience model. The traumatized child and adolescent often emerge whole, without discounting the effect of the trauma on their lives (Ayalon & Soskis, 1986; Lahad,

1999; Lahad, Shacham, & Niv, 2000). They mourn the old self that was destroyed by the traumatic experience and are ready to nurture a new self. If past relationships were shattered, now it is time to build new ties, new hopes, and new values. In this process, the "victims" regain their world and become "victors."

It is well documented that existing coping resources may dwindle under the blow of a traumatic experience. Therefore, a careful assessment of the coping profile of the disaster client provides the blueprint for the most suitable, tailor-made intervention.

GUIDELINES FOR HELPERS

Posttrauma psychosocial support, counseling, or therapy, whether by clinical helpers or informal caretakers, needs to follow some fundamental guidelines. Helpers need to

- pay attention to and validate the disaster client's experiences
- accept each individual's own way of expressing her or his intense feelings of anxiety, distress, and agony
- assess any additional stress, reinforce adaptive coping, suggest methods of working through the trauma, facilitate the process of grief and mourning, and further the family's adaptation
- encourage the development of support networks and assist in the community's readjustment.

Rehabilitation in a disaster's aftermath includes ameliorating residual traumatic responses and behaviors, such as startle responses, phobic fears, and survivors' guilt. It also includes enhancing such coping resources and skills as accelerated maturity, flexibility, and positive self-image that may be triggered by survival of a crisis (Ayalon, 2000).

Assessing and Screening People Exposed to Disasters

Parson (1995a) suggested the need for a post-disaster assessment of all those exposed to a disaster in order to determine each one's specific, unique needs. To facilitate this assessment, Parson described a biopsychobehavioral approach to intervention for traumatic stress or PTSD symptoms that focuses on individuals' biological factors (for example, an assessment of overt symptoms, such as nausea and sweating), psychological factors (for example, short attention span, irritability, startle reactions, and anxious responses), and behavioral factors (for example, decreased interpersonal and social abilities, self-destructive tendencies, aggression, withdrawal behavior, clinging, and suspicion).

When dealing with a large number of children, helpers may be advised to group them according to their trauma exposure, as indicated by the circles of vulnerability (see chapter 2). For example, those who experienced direct impact may be put in one group, and those who had no personal injuries or property loss but who are affected by the suffering of family and friends may be put in another. It is also important to remember that individual children react differently to the same level of exposure, according to their age, previous experiences, level of trust, coping resources, and availability of support (Speier, 2000).

Postdisaster assessment tries to create a true client–service fit through systematic data gathering in the following areas:

- predisaster history of loss or trauma that may be triggered by the current event
- perceptions and behaviors during the critical event
- trauma-related deprivations following the event (for example, disruption of basic

needs, such as food, shelter, water, and medicines, and the loss of personal resources)

Systematic initial screening of children after a natural disaster is necessary to evaluate the severity of their traumatic experiences, their losses, their level of posttraumatic stress reactions, their grief reactions, their level of depression, and their level of separation anxiety disorder (Pynoos, Goenjian, & Steinberg, 1998). Periodic screening for potential secondary reactions in children should follow the initial screening. Helpers can use evaluation results to direct casework and treatment modalities. Children with posttraumatic stress reactions need early clinical intervention in order to prevent chronicity and secondary depression.

The Spotlight on Research "Postdisaster Assessment in New York City" describes a study of children in New York City five months after the September 11, 2001, attack on the World Trade Center.

Close observation of children's changing responses in the first two years after a critical incident led to Parson's developing the Self-Efficacy Adaptational Coping Model (SEAC) for children, which traces the process of coping and recovery in four post-disaster phases (Parson, 1995b).

The first phase is *turbulence and processing.* During this phase, which lasts from the onset of the incident to three months after it ends, some young children may suffer from general regressive symptoms, such as bed-wetting, soiling, and clinging to parents, or suffer from separation anxiety, school avoidance, disturbed sleep patterns, hyperarousal, and withdrawal from previously independent achievements.

The second phase is *stasis and reappraisal.* If there is no intervention, "frozen stasis" (meaning being locked up in the symptoms)

will continue and may last for another three to six months. Children who get no help may believe themselves to be trapped and lost in a new and strange world of fears, anxieties, and helplessness. A key characteristic of this period is the disruption of continuities: During this phase children commonly believe that "Yesterday does not predict tomorrow" and "Life will never be the same again." With appropriate help, children have the chance to think about their misfortune and to find some meaning in the chaos.

The third phase is *engagement and transition.* During this phase, which lasts from six to 18 months, people may still manifest posttraumatic symptoms, vulnerability, and intense rage. Some children will manifest withdrawal, difficulties in trusting, passive and numb reactions, and extreme mood shifts.

The fourth phase is *self-efficacy and adaptational coping.* This phase, which may last from 18 to 24 months, is marked by belief of a growing competence regarding the ability to manage events and deal with the environment. Spontaneous recovery, which is to be expected during this phase, is best reinforced by disengagement from the caretaker or therapist, investment in community projects, and by the client using his or her own experiences as the basis for helping others.

Parson's (1995b) list of 19 principles for posttrauma service delivery highlights the interdisciplinary and integrative nature of services. The first principle deals with the need to respect local customs, practices, and values. Other principles reinforce positive attitudes, enhance self-worth, facilitate self-help and social support groups in the community, and develop programs for taking care of the helper. There are ample recommendations by many experts who maintain that these principles should be translated into school activities for children (Johnson, 1998; Vernberg, 2002).

Postdisaster Assessment in New York City

On June 10, 2002, Dr. Christina Hoven (2002), a psychiatric epidemiologist in Columbia University's School of Public Health, gave public testimony regarding the mental health needs of New York City's public school children following the September 11, 2001, attack on the World Trade Center. She had surveyed more than 8,000 children in grades 4 through 12— ages about 9 to 17 years old—in late February and early March 2002.

Based on the results, she estimated that among the 1.1 million pupils in the New York City public school system, an estimated 75,000 had six or more symptoms of posttraumatic stress—enough to be diagnosed with the disorder. Children throughout the city, and not just those near the World Trade Center, showed symptoms of several psychiatric problems. In her testimony, she stated:

> According to our findings, one out of every seven children (15.0%) has agoraphobia [the fear of venturing outside the home, of being in open spaces—results of a 1996 study showed about 5% of children on average suffer from agoraphobia]. Rates of the other psychiatric disorders were as follows:

- 8% with major depressive disorder (MDD);
- 10% with generalized anxiety disorder (GAD);
- 12% with separation anxiety disorder (SAD);
- 9% with panic attacks;
- 11% with conduct disorder;
- 5% with alcohol abuse (grades 9-12 only).

All of these reported mental health problems were determined to be associated with impairment, that is, they were so severe as to indicate a need for immediate further assessment and appropriate intervention. Yet, at least two-thirds of children with probable PTSD following the 9/11 attacks have not sought any mental health services from school counselors or from mental health professionals outside of school. We expect to find similar rates of not seeking help for the remaining seven disorders we measured.

Results also indicated that 76 percent often thought about the terrorist attack, 24 percent had problems sleeping, and 17 percent had nightmares. The groups most likely to suffer from psychiatric disorders were younger children, girls, those who had experienced prior traumas, and those whose family members were at the World Trade Center (regardless whether they were killed, hurt, or unharmed).

Dr. Hoven concluded her testimony with several recommendations:

> I strongly believe that an effective and coherent response should be grounded within school based mental health services, which can utilize state-of-the-art screening, assessment, and evidence-based treatment approaches. Specifically, I recommend:

- The development of a flexible mental health system of care for children, based on a localized, coordinated system of clinical responsibility, ensuring that each school receives crisis intervention services and support immediately after any future threats or events.
- The development of a comprehensive school based mental health service system, developed in collaboration with all of the major medical centers as well as private and public mental health-providers in New York City, such that every single school and every individual child has ready access to quality clinical care.

cont'd

- Develop a permanent enhancement of school-based mental health resources, including screening and treatment for children and adolescents with persistent needs. It should be noted that this type of therapeutic service is specifically excluded from Project Liberty funding.
- Establishment of an ongoing research and monitoring agenda to further understand the nature of the effects of 9/11 on New York City public school children, to assess if optimal treatment is being provided to those most in need, both today and in the years to come, as the long term sequelae of 9/11 unfolds.

A report by Karla Gale (2002) for the *Journal of the American Medical Association* summarized research by William Schlenger of Duke University Medical Center in Durham, North Carolina. Schlenger and his colleagues surveyed people in large metropolitan areas, including New York and Washington, DC, between October 11 and November 11, 2001. They found that the prevalence of probable PTSD for New Yorkers was 11.2 percent; it was 4.3 percent for those in large metropolitan areas in the rest of the country.

Gale, K. (2002, August 6). High prevalence of PTSD symptoms seen in New York City after September 11. *JAMA, 288*, 581–588, 633–636.

Hoven, C. W. (2002, June 10). *Testimony presented at the United States Senate Field Hearing, Chair, Hillary Rodham Clinton, Held on Behalf of the Senate Health, Education, Labor and Pensions (HELP) Committee Regarding the Unmet Mental Health Needs of New York City Public School Children as a Result of the September 11th Attacks on the World Trade Center.* The hearing was held in the United States Customs House, New York City. Retrieved from http://chaos.cpmc.colum bia.edu/sph/Displayimage.asp?Event_No=309.

A Quick Reference Guide for Posttrauma Home and School Care

The following "quick reference guide" is adapted from Cynthia Monahon's (1997) book, *Children and Trauma: A Guide for Parents and Professionals.* As she pointed out, all traumas, whether a car accident or a hurricane, provoke common symptoms, such as fearfulness, nightmares, and even personality changes in a child (see chapter 3 for a discussion of the effects of disasters on children), and these changes in the child may be worsened by the parents' anxiety. However, if parents understand the effects of trauma and learn ways to respond to their children's symptoms, there is a greater likelihood that the children's sense of safety and balance will be restored.

Changes in behavior that signal the need for professional help. Changes in a child's behavior should diminish within a week or so, although some may need a few weeks to "bounce back." A few children, however, do not function well again without some type of therapeutic intervention. When a child's behavioral changes in the weeks or months after a disaster are extreme and remain extreme, professional help is probably necessary. Affirmative answers to the following questions (each of which highlights a warning sign to look for) signal that referral to a mental health agency is warranted.

When **exposure** is the criterion, consider the following questions:

- Did the child lose family members or friends in the event?
- Was the child physically injured in the event?
- Does the child consider herself or himself to have been in extreme danger during the event?

- Was the child present in a previous disaster?
- Is the child involved in another individual or family crisis?

When **experience** is the criterion, consider the following questions:

- Does the child talk about feeling detached from his or her body?
- Is the child *severely* depressed and withdrawn?
- Does the child seem *excessively* agitated and restless?
- Does the child talk *a lot* about death?
- Does the child complain of *significant* memory gaps?
- Does the child show *uncharacteristic* signs of self-neglect?
- Does the child engage in *obviously* self-destructive behavior, intentionally hurting herself or himself, or having repeated "accidents" that result in injury?
- Does the child demonstrate a *drastic* change of personality or temperament?
- Does the child hallucinate, appear disoriented, or otherwise show *obvious* signs of disturbed mental processes?
- Does the child evidence, for a month or longer, symptoms that are considered normal but that disrupt social, mental, or physical functioning?

Recommended responses to children of different ages. Children may be grouped into three broad categories based on their age: *early childhood*, approximately ages five through 11; *preadolescence*, approximately 11 through 14; and *adolescence*, approximately 14 through 18.

For children in early childhood, regressive behavior is the most typical postcrisis response; children in this age group may find it very difficult to deal with the loss of pets or prized objects. Helpers should:

- respond to regressive behaviors with patience and tolerance
- conduct individual or group play sessions
- relax expectations in school and at home (with a clear understanding that this change is temporary and that the normal routine will resume when the children are feeling better)
- provide opportunities for structured, but not demanding, chores and responsibilities at home and at school
- rehearse any safety measures to be taken in the event of a future disaster

For preadolescent children, peer reactions to the crisis are important. Preadolescents want to believe that their crisis reactions are similar to others'. Helpers should

- provide same–age group activities that continue known routines
- work in groups, and rehearse appropriate behaviors in the event of a future crisis
- allocate appropriate social roles and responsibilities

Because adolescents' activities and interests are focused primarily on their peers, youths between 14 and 18 years old are especially distressed by any disruption of their peer-group activities. Helpers should

- encourage participation in any community rehabilitation and reclamation work
- encourage the resumption of social activities (such as athletics, clubs, and school groups) when the children are ready
- encourage discussion of the crisis event and reactions with peers, extended family members, and significant others
- reduce expectations temporarily for performance both in and out of school.

METHODS TO ENHANCE RECOVERY AND HEALING

In her milestone book, *Trauma and Recovery*, Judith Lewis Herman (1992) stated that the first element of healing is to empower the traumatized by helping them regain control over their lives, their decisions, and their behavior. Therefore, it is important that the therapist or caregiver not play the "savior" role but, rather, support the child and delegate the management of healing to her or him.

Herman (1992) delineated three stages of trauma recovery and assigned clear therapeutic tasks to each stage. She also set boundaries for the therapist and described appropriate roles. Progress is never linear; rather, it evolves in a spiral. Old themes reappear and are managed in each stage. With a few modifications, these concepts work well with posttraumatic intervention with children, both in an individual and in a group setting.

The first stage involves establishing physical and psychological safety and security. The focus on safety begins with control of the body and moves outward to issues of control of the environment. Issues of bodily integrity include attention to basic health needs, regulation of bodily functions, such as sleep, eating, and exercise, and the control of self-destructive behaviors.

Environmental issues include establishing a safe living situation, with adequate attention to survival needs and a carefully considered plan for self-protection. The work of the first stage of recovery becomes increasingly complicated in proportion to the intensity, duration, and the early age of the child at the trauma's onset. For young children its application depends on their parents' or caretakers' cooperation.

The *second stage* of recovery is the phase of remembrance and mourning. It involves the client's work of exploring the traumatic experience, with the goal of having the client integrate the traumatic experience into the fabric of life. The helper, therefore, pays attention to dissociated or repressed sensations, memories, cognitions, and affect. The helper must pace and time the intervention to adjust to the child's tolerance so that the process represents a mastery experience rather than just a symbolic re-enactment of the trauma. The process may involve a period of grief and mourning over the losses accrued by the disaster.

What sustains the child through the second stage is the therapeutic alliance that supports the child's recovery, the child's hope of restoring or building new relationships, and his or her hope of finding some meaning in the traumatic experience. When major disasters destroy children's faith and trust, their sense of coherence may also be affected. Posttrauma intervention needs to address these issues, and to attempt to restore not only each child's somatic and social balance, but also his or her sense of coherence. This demands special attention to the issue of "finding meaning" by exploring the shattered meaning systems of the surviving children. Strategies of logotherapy may be very useful here (Frankl, 1969). Frankl developed the quest for meaning, which anchored him to life in a German concentration camp and enabled him to endure Nazi atrocities, into therapeutic methods that are especially suited for healing psychic trauma.

Frankl (1963) proposed a four-step procedure for logotherapy. The first step helps clients briefly divert their attention from the immediate problem, so they can relax and start to recuperate. The second step helps clients view their predicament from different perspectives, such as the broad context of their community, or their personal successes in helping themselves or others. The third step creates openness to new meanings, which may be connected to the client's family history (for example, "I'm a survivor like my grandmother," or "It is important to remember and tell the younger generations"). The fourth step helps clients make new commitments and pursue new goals (for example, "I'll follow the legacy of my father," "I'll move on and not look back," or "Together we will rebuild our shattered community").

The basic technique of logotherapy is Socratic dialogue, through which the counselor tries to make clients aware of *their own resources* and help them learn to use them to connect with the many sources of life's meaning or significance. Many additional techniques (such as values clarification, guided imagery, dream analysis, self-portrayal, and building a personal story) are used by logotherapists to further Socratic dialogue (Fabry, 1988). All techniques of logotherapy capitalize on the human capacity for objectively self-evaluating and transcending the personal story by giving it a broader universal connotation. According to Frankl, for a human to exist and survive hardships he or she needs to be guided by meaningful ideas or ideals (Das, 1998).

"Meaning" is not always what we expect when we think of "a rational solution" to a crisis. Sometimes it is a religious belief, sometimes it is an ideology of self-sacrifice for higher purposes or for the protection of others (Punamäki, 1996), and sometimes it is a metaphysical explanation, such as the popular metaphor of "superman." This universal story tells of an orphan who takes it upon himself to save others in order to find meaning for his own personal suffering. Meaning can also be a personal construction of a nonrational, imaginary narrative experience, as in the following example, "Finding Meaning."

Finding Meaning

Uri Orlev, (1960), as a child during the Holocaust, spent eight months hiding with his brother from the Nazis in a ruined house in Poland. The boys were seven and nine years old, the sole survivors of their family. What helped them sustain the harrowing experience of uncertainty, hunger, loneliness, and the perpetual threat to their lives was a fabricated story that the older boy told his younger brother. In this make-believe story they both were children of a king in exile, who swore them to be very quiet, conceal their real identity, and wait for the king to come to rescue them. The daily ritual of acting out the story gave meaning to their otherwise unbearable experience.

The *third stage* of recovery involves social reconnection as a way for regaining possession of one's image of the world and building positive future expectations. Peer-group support, important throughout the recovery process, is especially useful during this stage. Peer groups who have a shared fate allow resolution of issues of secrecy, shame, and stigma in a manner that cannot be duplicated in a one-to-one relationship with a therapist. Treatment of people recovering from a disaster is thus multimodal in that it uses physical, emotional, cognitive, social, and spiritual methods, and multiphasic in that it assesses the changing needs of the clients in each of the three recovery stages (Ayalon, 2000).

POSTTRAUMA INTERVENTIONS

The following strategies are grouped into the three stages of recovery and healing suggested by Herman (1992). Presented with each strategy are the BASIC-Ph coping channels that it activates.

First Stage of Recovery and Healing: Physical and Psychological Safety and Security

"Prior to sailing into the rough seas we need to ensure a harbor with a lighthouse or at least a memory of a lighthouse" (Lahad, 1985, p. 1).

Create your "safe space" in colors, shapes, and lines. The activity "Creating a Safe Space" is designed to help the disaster client create a "safe space," a harbor with a lighthouse, the consequence of which should be increased beliefs of safety and security. Adapted from Oaklander (1978), this experience activates and enhances the following coping channels: physiology (physical activity and relaxation), imagination (fantasy and creativity), and affect (sharing feelings).

Hypnotic storytelling: "Choose your dream." A hypnotic trance, a state of "focused concentration" in which a person is neither fully awake nor fully asleep, may be used therapeutically with traumatized children. Children in this state are deeply relaxed and are open to suggestions of letting go of their fears.

Children naturally use daydreaming to offset negative states, and this natural tendency can be used to abate sleeping disturbances, one of the most common difficulties of children following exposure to disaster. Intrusive pictures, sounds, and sensations repeatedly come back to them, especially when their world seems unsafe, and fear of the dark may bring back memories of the traumatic incident; falling asleep and staying asleep become problems. Because sleeplessness is a trigger of many other behavioral, cognitive and emotional symptoms, it is important for a helper to address this problem as soon as it has been identified.

Creating a Safe Space

Find a comfortable place, and sit or lie down. You may close your eyes or leave them open. Soon I'm going to take you on an imaginary trip to a very special safe and reassuring place. At the end of the trip you'll open your eyes and draw your impressions of this "safe place."

Now, imagine a place you like, a place where you feel good, where you feel reassured and comfortable—a place where you feel protected and loved, where you belong and where you can enjoy yourself. You may have been there before, or you may create this place in your fantasy. It can be outside or inside, in the woods, by the sea, in a house, in a castle—it can be anything and anywhere since it's your own private space.

Get a sense of that space—where your body is, the air that's around you. It's a nice place to be because it's yours.

Notice what's going on in your body. Notice any possible tension in your body. Don't try to relax these spots that feel tight or tense. Just notice them. Take notice of your body from head to toe. How are you breathing? Are you taking deep gulps of air or are you breathing with shallow, quick ones? Take a couple of very deep breaths now. Let the air out with some sound. Do it again.

In your mind's eye, look at where you are and notice the colors and shapes around you. Listen to any sounds you can hear. Is anyone else there?

Notice what it is that gives you this safe, comfortable and reassuring feeling.

Open your eyes. Draw a picture of your "safe place."

Young children go into a trancelike state as they become absorbed in an attractive story, and hypnotic stories are known to change their internal experience of an external event (Rosen, 1982). Relaxation

Choose Your Dream

Offer brief narratives on dreams (either known stories or made up ones) with embedded images of relaxation and coping. The child then chooses a dream that she or he would like to dream, paints the desired dream, and tucks it under the pillow. The following is an example of how to set up the "choosing a dream" situation, and is an an example of a hypnotic story that elicits healing dreams:

"A long time ago on a high mountain there was a very old man who was dreaming wonderful dreams. Before falling asleep he would take a deep breath, and another one, and yet another one ... Every morning when he woke up he used to put his beautiful, colorful and amazing dreams in a golden basket next to him. The old man never allowed anyone near that bag of dreams. However, children in the nearby village were told that the best dreams, the dreams that drive away all fears, were hidden in the golden basket. So one day—or maybe one night—when the old man was fast asleep, the kids came to his place and found the basket, but as they were about to take the dreams out, the basket fell and all the best dreams were scattered about. Now, everyone can choose one of these dreams—and so can you. So let's see which dream you would like to have tonight and we will draw it and put it under your pillow, and remember to breathe deeply three times before the dream starts.... The dreams are the ones that you paint, draw or write about."

and visualization, such as guided daydreaming, are both aspects of hypnosis that are safe, self-regulated techniques (Erickson, 1989).

The activity "Choose Your Dream" is designed to help young children gain control over frightening daydreams or dreams while they are asleep. By listening to the story, "The child can enter the haunted tunnel of anxiety, guilt, sadness and frustration, in order to emerge into the light and security awaiting at the end" (Ayalon & Schlesinger, 1991, p. 31). Adapted from Ayalon and Schlesinger, this method activates and enhances the following two coping channels: (1) physiology (activity and relaxation) and (2) imagination (fantasy and creativity).

Cognitive–behavioral tasks for unfreezing body–mind stress. When the disaster is over, the mind–body shock may stay on indefinitely. Some children may be fixated on one repetitive action; they may use a thought, movement, or play activity in an attempt to restore the familiar world that existed before the disaster or to gain a sense of control over the ordeal. In many cases, children also avoid previously comforting and safe behaviors. It is useful for helpers to ask children who are frozen in the shock of the trauma or who show compulsive–repetitive behavior to fulfill small tasks as "homework" (Kfir, 1989). Sometimes, according to Kfir, it is necessary to introduce a measure of external control by authoritative assignments, actions, and supervision. The parents or therapist reinforces achievements by marking each small task or assignment that is fulfilled. Foa, Hembree, and Dancu (2002) found that in vivo exposure to pretrauma, nonthreatening activities or places builds confidence in a person's ability to master traumatic avoidance behavior.

The activity "Unfreezing the Body–Mind with Cognitive–Behavioral Small Tasks" is designed to help children develop flexibility in their thoughts and actions and to find alternative modes of behaving that restore their sense of security. This activity triggers and enhances the following two coping channels: (1) physiology (physical activity and relaxation) and (2) cognition (information, rules, and planning).

Unfreezing the Body–Mind with Cognitive–Behavioral Small Tasks

I want you to choose an activity you used to like before the event, and that you find difficult to do now. When you recall that activity from the past, remember how comfortable it used to make you feel in your body or in your mind.

Choose a place to remember this activity, a place in which, now, you are uncomfortable—not very uncomfortable, but uncomfortable at a level 4 or 5 on a scale of 1 to 10, where 1 is minimum discomfort and 10 is extreme discomfort. Arrange for a parent or friend to be with you on your first attempt to remember the activity.

Keep going to this place and remembering the activity even if you feel the discomfort. The first time, stay for at least 10 minutes. The second time, increase the time you stay. Increase the amount of time you stay each time. Keep doing this for a whole week.

Report on changes in your feelings, thoughts, and behavior. Note how your discomfort goes down the scale with every trial. Try to reach 1 or zero discomfort, and to regain your past positive feelings for this place.

Eye movement desensitization and reprocessing (EMDR). The brain has an internal system that processes and sorts all our experiences, storing the memories in an accessible, useful form. A traumatic event can overwhelm the system, so that the experience is not processed. Instead, it seems to be locked in the nervous system. The various elements of the experience—the sounds, pictures, emotions, and thoughts—are often dissociated, disconnected fragments. This unprocessed material from the trauma is easily brought back to the conscious mind by similar situations, which results in emotional distress, flashbacks, nightmares, or unwanted thoughts and images of the trauma. Traumatic events also can result in the creation of negative beliefs about oneself or the world; for example, some think that they deserved what happened to them, or that they are a failure, or a bad person, either because of what happened or because of how they reacted during the trauma. This unprocessed material can connect with other similar experiences, creating a network or a chain of associated events. Trauma "eye movement desensitization and reprocessing" (EMDR) therapy works to process the experience, to integrate and resolve the elements of the traumatic experience so that it no longer results in distress.

The EMDR technique entails client visualization regarding a specific image of a past traumatic event. As the client visualizes the image, he or she is asked to think about the emotions associated with this particular mental picture. Then, on the therapist's cue, the client opens his or her eyes and is instructed to follow the therapist's hand while still thinking about the image and emotions associated with it. The therapist places his or her hand approximately 12 to 24 inches away from the client's face and repeatedly and quickly moves the hand back and forth. This rhythmical stimulation appears to activate the brain's information processing system, thereby enabling the client and therapist to desensitize the client to his or her traumatic memories and significantly reduce symptoms such as flashbacks, nightmares, emotional distress, and intrusive thoughts through cognitive restructuring (EMDR Institute, 1994). Over 30,000 clinicians have been trained worldwide; training is considered mandatory for appropriate use (Shapiro, 1999).

Research has found that EMDR helps people who have gone through a disaster (Shapiro, 1999; Shapiro & Maxfield, 2002; Silver & Rogers, 2002, Smith, 2003). For example, from her review of 12 controlled studies, Maxfield (2002) reported that civilian participants demonstrated a 70 percent to 90 percent decrease in PTSD diagnosis after three or four EMDR sessions. EMDR may also be useful with children: Chemtob, Nakashima, and Carlson (2002) studied the effects of EMDR on children ages six to 12 with disaster-related PTSD, and found significant reductions in anxiety, depression, intrusive re-experiencing of the disaster, avoidance of reminders, and arousal symptoms such as hypervigilance and irritability.

Some research, however, points out the limitations of EMDR. In a comparison of prolonged exposure therapy, relaxation training, and EMDR for reducing PTSD, Taylor and his colleagues (2003) found no differences in the incidence of symptom worsening or on numbing and hyperarousal symptoms, although exposure therapy produced significantly larger reductions in avoidance and re-experiencing symptoms. Rubin and his colleagues (2001) studied the effects of EMDR on children ages six to 15 in a guidance center and found no significant differences in Child Behavior Checklist scores between those who

received EMDR plus the center's routine treatment package and those who received only the routine treatment package. This finding raises doubts that EMDR produces rapid improvements with children whose emotional and behavioral problems are not narrowly connected to a specific trauma.

Second Stage of Recovery and Healing: Remembrance and Mourning

Trauma-induced beliefs distort a child's feelings of control over events: A child may be burdened by feeling too much—or too little—control. When faced with traumatic events that they are unable to comprehend or explain, children may develop irrational illusions of control, guilt feelings, and "traumatic beliefs," such as "If only I had done this or that, the disaster would not have happened." A "traumatic belief" may be created when a child's words or actions coincide with the occurrence of a traumatic incident. For example, if a young girl hits a lamppost at the same time that there is a citywide power outage, she may believe that she created the blackout, or if a young boy wishes a parent dead and the parent has an accident and dies, he may believe that he killed the parent.

Gaining control over posttraumatic issues with cognitive methods. An effective technique to reduce these trauma-induced beliefs is *cognitive reframing*. Albert Ellis developed this technique as part of his therapeutic rational–emotive method, which therapists often use to modify distorted beliefs. Ellis (1995) claimed that irrational beliefs usually are at the root of people's shattered self-esteem. The therapist helps the child to discover the irrational misinterpretations that underlie painful feelings, such as fear, guilt, humiliation, or helplessness, and grad-

Posttraumatic Intervention (EMDR) with Traumatized Children

In their book, *Light in the Heart of Darkness: EMDR and the Treatment of War and Terrorism Survivors*, Silver and Rogers (2002) reported a school-based EMDR short intervention following a group disaster that took place in Bet Shemesh, a small town between Jerusalem and Tel Aviv, Israel. In the spring of 1997, a class of 12-year-old girls on a school trip to "The Island of Peace" was attacked by a Jordanian soldier, who murdered seven girls and wounded many more by shooting them at short range.

Three months later, screening for traumatic reactions of all the school's teachers and students by local mental health workers revealed a number who manifestly suffered from symptoms of PTSD. Three teachers and five girls were offered a series of EMDR sessions by Alan Cohen, an EMDR trainer with the Community Stress Prevention Center. Each person in this high-risk group received three or four consecutive individual sessions of EMDR in a quiet room on the school ground. The following is a description of this process and outcomes.

The process for each participant focused on different traumatic imagery. One girl was troubled by the empty chair where her classmate, who had died, used to sit.

Another girl was plagued by acute anxiety. Not all those who received EMDR treatment were actually present at the disaster. Two girls who had missed the trip suffered from nightmares about what they imagined happened during the trauma, and from survivors' guilt at not having been there with their friends. The teachers suffered from guilt at thoughts that they could have done more to protect their students. The gory images of the massacre and her own feeling of utter helplessness haunted one teacher. One male teacher was completely distraught and guilt ridden, on top of being blamed by the bereaved parents. He could not benefit from the EMDR sessions in the given format (too short, too late, lack of time to develop rapport, lack of motivation to get well under the circumstances).

Reported results by participants and by the therapist were positive according to EMDR criteria, including a remarkable reduction in phobic, anxious, and guilt feelings. Two teachers were referred for further treatment, one for more EMDR and the other for traditional therapy. An informal follow-up conducted on the anniversary of the disaster corroborated the initial positive results.

---

ually tries to modify these misinterpretations by replacing self-defeating inner statements with more rational and benign ones. This reframing allows the child to see himself or herself in a more positive light. For example, if a boy who ran from the site of the catastrophe blames himself for cowardice, the therapist might reframe his flight as a heroic act that saved his life or a clever way of taking care of himself.

Touching Reality "Using Your Worry Box" is based on using reality-based, cognitive-sorting skills to control our worries by reframing them and creating an order of priority. It deals with issues of too little or too much feeling of control in the aftermath of disaster. This is a useful way of creating some order out of the chaotic feeling of being overwhelmed by uncontrollable experiences (Ayalon & Lahad, 1991). The "worry box" is a way of sorting worries, reframing them, and then assessing how to cope with them.

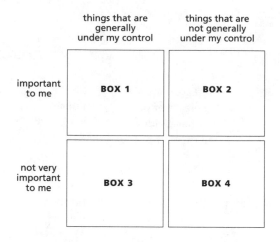

TOUCHING REALITY

Using Your Worry Box

In the aftermath of a disaster, our worries, large and small, may pile up, and we may believe that they ensnare us. The belief that there is "no way out" gets stronger and stronger until, finally, we encounter the "straw that breaks the camel's back." This "straw" could well be something small, meaningless, and insignificant; regardless, it is the trigger that finally defeats us.

A Worry Box helps you identify your worries, both large and small, and learn to distinguish between worries that you can control and those that are beyond your control. With this information, you will be able to change what can be changed and learn to accept what cannot be changed.

Begin by making a "worry list." List your personal worries, such as health, security, and family relationships. List worries associated with housing, school, work, and friends. List worries you have associated with a possible disaster—things you fear happening, things that upset you.

Now, sort your list of worries into the following four worry boxes.

Controlling painful memories by drawing visual images. The very act of giving a visual image to a physical or mental pain (by drawing or choosing from a pool of existing pictures) helps the child disconnect from the feeling of pain. Giving the pain a tangible image furnishes the child with a sense of knowing what she or he is dealing with—of moving from the unknown to the known. This is an important step in helping children gain a sense of control over their pain. Giving shape and color to something so amorphous as pain helps to control and "decatastrophize" it (Gregorian, Azarian, DeMaria, & McDonald, 1996; Kalmanowitz & Lloyd, 2002; Rossi, 1986). Another purpose of the drawings is a powerful one of implication. By asking the child to draw how the pain would look "all better," the therapist is implying that "all better" does exist. When the child agrees to draw the picture, it signifies that "all better" is a potential reality (Mills & Crowley, 1988).

The activity "Using Art to Make Pain 'All Better'" asks the child to make three drawings. Drawings help the child dissociate from the physical or mental pain by transforming it into an image on paper and, therefore, giving the child a sense of control

Using Art to Make Pain "All Better"

Children are instructed to draw on three pieces of paper (or on one piece of paper divided into three parts). On the first piece of paper, the child answers the question, "How does the pain look right now?"

On the second piece of paper, the child answers the question, "How does the pain look 'all better'?"

On the third piece of paper, the child answers the question, "What will help the first picture, picture 1, change into the second picture, picture 2?"

over it. The activity activates and enhances these three coping channels: (1) physiology (physical activity and relaxation), (2) imagination (fantasy and creativity), and (3) affect (sharing feelings).

Healing games. Although adults who have been through overwhelming trauma can suffer from psychic numbing, blocking out memories and feelings about the catastrophe, children often handle trauma differently. Because they use fantasy, play, and daydreams to recall and rethink their ordeals, they are less likely than adults to become numb to the trauma. Also, by voluntarily replaying the trauma, they avoid creating potent memories that can later burst through as flashbacks.

Terr (1990) first noted the usefulness of spontaneous healing games with traumatized children. She found such games among the children who were victims of the 1973 Chowchilla, California, bus kidnapping (kidnappers buried their school bus, with them inside it, in an ordeal that lasted 27 hours). Five years later, Terr found that the victims still re-enacted the kidnapping in their games. Girls, for example, played symbolic kidnapping games with their Barbie dolls. One girl, who had hated the feeling of other children's urine on her skin as they lay huddled together in terror, washed her Barbie over and over again. Another played Traveling Barbie, in which Barbie travels somewhere—it doesn't matter where—and returns safely, which is the point of the game. A third girl's game consisted of scenarios in which the doll is stuck in a hole and suffocates.

A very powerful method to deal with the second phase of trauma and recovery is the sand play method (Pabon, 2001; Steinhardt, 1998), particularly that technique of sand play known as "images of the self" (Weinrib, 1983). Sand play themes are defined as visual images in a sand play picture that represents the process of trauma and healing (Baum & Weinberg, 2002). The activity "Sand Play for Healing and Recovery" activates and enhances these coping channels: (1) physiology (physical activity and relaxation), (2) imagination (fantasy and creativity), and (3) cognition (information, rules, and planning).

Because exploration of the sand picture encourages the child to connect the picture with the real world, a world full of painful and frightening elements from the traumatic incident, it is essential to create a "safe space" for the child. Some children draw spontaneous connections between the sand images and their real life story; some use a too-quick connection to reality as a way of avoiding more significant parts of the trauma; some need to discuss reality after "testing the water" through the metaphor to ensure that it is safe enough to share the terrible events with a trustworthy and caring adult.

Children describe the scene, tell a story about it, tell what's happening, or what's going to happen. A child might say: "This tiger is going to eat everyone up" and then make it happen. Sometimes something new happens when an action is carried out. For example, the tiger may eat everyone up except a small rabbit that he feels sorry for. Younger children will often begin to play out something in the sand like a battle, while others will carefully and deliberately set items around the sand with no obvious plan. Older children seem to work out their scenes meticulously, choosing items with great care. The sand tray has no age limit. Adolescents may choose items from the shelves, which appeal to them, without too much planning, so that they build their world as they see it and feel it. (Oaklander, 1978, pp. 169–170)

Mourning process and rituals. In leave-taking rituals grief is shifted from the deceased to symbolic objects (van der Hart, 1983, 1988). Certain objects represent the loss and symbolize the broken connection with predisaster sources of safety; they become "transitional objects" that help the child gradually accept separation and loss (Winnicott, 1982). These linking objects—which can reflect both positive and negative emotions, a mixed bag that is so familiar in grieving—serve to maintain emotional contact with the deceased (Volkan & Searles, 1981).

Leave taking serves as a metaphorically corrective experience (van der Hart & Goossens, 1987). With older children, metaphoric stories enable projective identification with imaginary figures, animals, trees, and even objects (Ayalon, 1992), whereas the "farewell ritual" takes place within the metaphor, without further interpretation (Ayalon, 1993; Garuth & Ekstein, 1966).

The method of "guided leave-taking rituals" touches the fixated emotions that froze during the traumatic shock and sets them into motion again. It also activates and enhances the following five coping channels: (1) physiology (physical activity and relaxation), (2) imagination (fantasy and creativity), (3) affect (sharing feelings), (4) cognition (information, rules, and planning), and (5) social (role playing or engaging in a group activity).

During a guided leave-taking ritual, the child is encouraged to go back to the unresolved experiences of loss and grief. Then, different rituals may be enacted, with the child's full consent and participation. Rituals include, for example, painting a farewell picture or writing a farewell letter that will never be sent; creating small objects that symbolize the unwanted memories; acknowledging unwanted memories on paper, and then ceremonially burning them in a fire; throwing

Symbolic Burials

After the sudden death of a classmate in a car accident, a group of four-year-old preschool children began to compulsively bury objects in the sand. They also kept up a make-believe game of dying by command, saying to each other, "Now you die, now you live." The dismayed parents demanded that the teacher put an end to the morbid games. They also insisted that their children were too young to comprehend the meaning of death and would be better off if the tragedy were denied (by telling the children that the deceased boy was actually alive but had to move to another city). After listening to the parents and acknowledging their concerns, Ofra Ayalon (2001) showed them the French movie, *Forbidden Games*, which tells of a four-year-old girl whose parents, and the puppy she had been holding, were killed by a bomb while they were fleeing the Nazis. She survived and was taken into a French farmhouse by a boy about seven. The two children formed a secret alliance in which they engaged in a game of burying insects and little dead animals. When they fell short of corpses, they started killing animals so they could continue the burial obsession.

The story captured the imagination of the parents and gave them insight into the meaning of play as a child's language of processing loss and regaining a sense of control. Gradually, they could accept the children's right to grieve. The teacher was instructed to follow the burial games with "leave-taking rituals" appropriate to the children's age, such as pasting the missing child's photograph on a board and adorning the board with paintings and personal objects. The children's games receded within one week of this intervention.

little stones into the water, with a certain meaning attached to each one; and planting a tree to commemorate the dead.

The most effective element of these metaphoric activities is making a clear distinction between past and present, closing the past behind and opening a future perspective.

Third Stage of Recovery and Healing: Reconnection

When people exposed to a disaster show signs of reconciliation with the traumatic past, they face a new challenge, how to create a postdisaster future (Herman, 1992).

Touching Reality "Future Perception: Where Would You Like to Be in a Year?" offers a chance to create your future.

TOUCHING REALITY

Future Perception: Where Would You Like to Be in a Year?

Close your eyes and let your body relax. Let your mind drift with your imagination into the future. Try to imagine where you wish to be in a year. Is it where you are now? Is it different? Describe this place. Pay attention to the surrounding; observe it carefully: Is there anything unusual? What catches your attention? What is important for you? How do you feel there? Who is near you? How do you feel about that person or those persons being there?

What do you expect they will do? What do you do there? Are you still doing the same things as in the past? What makes you enthusiastic? Is it where you really want to be? Do you know how to get there?

What can you bring to the present from your vision of your future?

When the time comes to brighten up traumatized children's future perspective, helpers can use art materials with the following directive: *Draw a picture of the worst thing in your life and the best thing in your life* (Lahad & Ankor, 1994). This activates and enhances the following coping channels: imagination (fantasy and creativity), affect (sharing feelings), cognition (information, rules, and planning), and belief (value clarification).

Encouraging the child to create a dialogue between the "worst" and the "best" helps bring about a mutual recognition between these two otherwise antagonistic aspects of his or her life. The purpose of this exercise is to support and give permission for the re-entry of positive and enjoyable experiences back into the life of the traumatized child, who often develops "unhedonia," the inability to enjoy life in face of the endured loss and death. The idea that the "best" and the "worst" coexist is crucial for the integration of the traumatic experience into a new narrative of coping and hope.

Methods that use an intensive re-experiencing of the trauma, such as desensitization, operant shaping, "flooding" (implosion), prolonged exposure, and paradoxical intention aim to redeem the disaster client from emotionally stuck situations, repressed memories, and avoidant behaviors (Marks, 2002). Saigh (1992) recommended "flooding," and reports many cases of positive outcomes with children. Flooding is a powerful method, but not without risks (Keane & Kaloupel, 1982). For example, flooding as a method of trauma therapy may be inappropriate for children who use high levels of avoidance as their coping strategy (Brown & Fromm, 1986). Therefore, only highly experienced and supervised helpers should use flooding and other methods that focus on re-experiencing trauma.

The Dangers of Flooding

At the age of five, a girl survived a terrorist attack in which she witnessed the brutal murder of her parents and younger brother. She herself was badly wounded.

Thirteen years later, after a period of relative rehabilitation and normal functioning (during which she avoided memories of the traumatic event as well as her life before it), she approached a therapist to deal with the loss of a meaningful relationship. Her initial trauma was reactivated by exposure to gunshots. The girl, now an adolescent, withdrew into a severe depression.

Her situation was exacerbated as a result of a wrong choice of therapeutic method: She was flooded by repressed memories and encouraged to relive the initial circumstances of her traumatic event. She was overwhelmed with unbearable pain and guilt for having survived the trauma that killed her family (Levin-Bar-Yosef & Alon, 2000).

In his review of the therapeutic procedure, the therapist himself admitted that in this case the method of therapy was insensitive to the survivor's psychological defences and coping style. A corrective experience outside the clinical process, which involved a symbolic mourning and atonement ritual supported by her adoptive parents, helped the girl to regain her emotional balance.

Research on the effectiveness of posttraumatic therapies falls short of providing definitive information; therapists, therefore, must rely on clinical evidence in their choice and assessment of interventions (van der Kolk, McFarlane, van der Hart, & Rice-Smith, 1999). Sometimes, however, therapists and clients may report positive therapeutic outcomes and objective testing may show no effects of even negative outcomes (Solomon, Bleich, Shoham, & Nardi, 1992; Solomon, Shalev, Spiro, & Dolev, 1992; Solomon, Spiro, Shalev, & Bleich, 1992).

POSTTRAUMATIC FAMILY THERAPY

The family is the matrix in which the child grows up; thus, everything that affects the adults in the family affects the child, and vice versa. Disaster affects the family by disrupting its normal flow and upsetting its capacities to nurture and support its members. Disaster may sever the family from traditional sources of support, such as the extended family, friends, neighborhood, and community. The nuclear family, burdened by its losses, might then be left alone to fend for itself in the posttraumatic period; single-parent families are even more isolated and vulnerable than dual-parent families (Ayalon, 1983).

Postdisaster stress and loss may intensify the bonds among family members; however, they may also, paradoxically, have a destructive effect, shattering the precarious family structure and alienating its members. The family postdisaster response is largely determined by its history, level of predisaster conflict among family members, social status, educational level, economic and psychological resources available, and the degree of injury or loss it suffered in the disaster.

Raphael (1986) observed that the effect of the distress of some members on the functioning of the others may have considerable implications for family dynamics and stability. For example, one member may take the role of the "identified patient" by developing posttraumatic symptoms, and thus the rest of the family may appear untouched by the disaster.

Conflict of roles may create difficulties, as, for instance, in cases when a person who is supposed to be brave is afraid, and the one who is supposed to be sick is well. Similarly, children who take over adult roles during and after the disaster may be vulnerable. It is also difficult for others, especially those fulfilling adult roles, to have needs for regression and care met... Marital harmony and intimacy may be threatened, because of a need to avoid the topic of the disaster, or because of psychic numbing and other reactions or disturbances. (Raphael, 1986, p. 173)

Ensuing death and bereavement change the family's structure and development. When bereavement hits the family, the process of grief and the process of recovery from the trauma become intermingled. Families bereaved by the disaster go through two major processes in the postdisaster period. One is the mourning process, during which family members have to share the reality of death and the experience of loss; also, they need to allow mourning to take place according to each member's age and needs. The second process is the coping process, during which family members have to reorganize the family system, take on the roles and tasks of the deceased, and eventually invest themselves in other relationships and life pursuits. External circumstances—such as organized violence, an ongoing threat to life, violent and mutilating death, and multiple losses—may exacerbate a family's adverse reaction to death.

Suggestions for posttraumatic family intervention or therapy include an assessment phase followed by five distinct treatment phases: (1) building commitment to therapeutic objectives, (2) defining the main issues for treatment, (3) reframing the problem, (4) developing a healing approach, and (5) closure (Figley, 1988).

Family Assessment

A supportive, well-functioning family is the optimal group for healthy posttraumatic healing. In each case of posttraumatic distress, the therapist and the family members together decide whether family therapy is the desirable method of intervention. Both functional and dysfunctional families can benefit from intervention with the entire family group (Miller, 1999). However, dysfunctional families, who may be burdened with predisaster problems and lack inner and outer sources of support, may need a different therapeutic contract and specialized treatment methods that exceed the posttraumatic orientation and also may need socioeconomic assistance to help them deal with their posttraumatic distress.

For the sake of planning the required intervention mode, McCubbin, Cauble, and Patterson (1982) suggested several useful criteria for distinguishing between functional and dysfunctional families. A "yes" response to one of the following questions indicates the family is functional; a "no" indicates it is dysfunctional—although, admittedly, there are degrees of "yes" and "no," and families are very likely to have a mixture of "yes" and "no" responses to the nine questions:

1. Does the family acknowledge the traumatic stressor?
2. Does the family conceive the problem as family centered rather than assign it to a family member?
3. Does the family adopt a solution-oriented approach?
4. Is there an atmosphere of tolerance, commitment, and affection among family members?
5. Is family communication open?
6. Is family cohesion high?
7. Are there no reports of violence or of drug abuse among family members?
8. Are family roles and rules flexible rather than rigid?
9. Are supportive community resources available to the family?

The activity "Assessing Family Cohesiveness and Tolerance for Diversity" is an example of a creative way of assessing family cohesiveness and the tolerance for diversity among its members (Ayalon, 2004; Lahad & Ayalon, 1995). This nonthreatening activity, working with gamelike metaphors, helps overcome resistance against disclosure of sensitive information and enhances cooperation and participation of even very young or inarticulate family members.

Assessing Family Cohesiveness and Tolerance for Diversity

When the family is assembled in the therapist's room, the therapist may suggest that they all take part in a nonverbal gamelike activity that will help them understand their needs and plan desirable future help. The therapist puts a basket full of buttons of various colors and sizes in front of the family members and asks each member in turn to create an array of the buttons that represents the family as it was in the predisaster period.

Having done that, each member of the family creates a second array that portrays the family in the present (postdisaster) period. Each member, adults as well as children, describes his or her two images, while the others ask questions and offer comments.

Now, the family creates a "joint image" of the future, one that portrays where they would like to be in two or three months.

Family Treatment

Each family is different, so posttraumatic interventions must be tailor-made to suit the complexity and the variety of each unique family's responses to trauma, as well as its unique coping resources.

First treatment phase: Building commitment to therapeutic objectives. In cases when the clinician and the client agree that family therapy is indicated, the first treatment phase requires that family members disclose their individual ordeals, while the therapist recognizes their suffering (Figley, 1988). The therapist's sense of respect for each family member's reaction, coupled with her or his optimism and expertise, promotes trust and commitment to therapy. The therapist's acknowledgement and acceptance of the different individual responses leads to the next phase.

Second treatment phase: Defining the main issues for treatment. The therapist encourages each family member to tell her or his view of the traumatic event and how it affected her or him. The therapist encourages each member to listen as each family member speaks, and to try to understand each other's reactions to the trauma. When a family member mentions positive consequences of the ordeal (such as a greater appreciation of life after a close brush with death), the therapist encourages the others to listen in a positive way.

The activity "Creating a 'Traumatic Picture Story'" facilitates understanding of the traumatic event from each family member's point of view. This nonverbal, joint activity is appropriate for adults and children.

Third treatment phase: Reframing the problem. After family members share their individual experiences of the disaster and their personal interpretations and traumatic reac-

Creating a "Traumatic Picture Story"

Each family member creates a "traumatic picture story" that depicts—from her or his personal point of view—the problem that calls for intervention. To develop the picture-story, family members may paint, draw, or make a collage from journals and newspaper cuttings, photographs, and words and images.

After all of the picture-stories are complete, each member tells the traumatic story through her or his images and lets others comment. The therapist encourages exploration of feelings, memories, thoughts, fears, and hopes.

tions to it, they build a joint "family story" composed and accepted by all. The image created from their individual fragments is the metaphoric way of accepting a family story of the events, the family responses to their ordeal, the family's coping resources as a unit, and the family's mutual responsibility and support. The activity "Developing a Joint Family Story" provides an opportunity for the family to reach a common ground and to enhance its cohesiveness and mutual support.

Fourth treatment phase: Developing a healing approach. The goal of posttraumatic family therapy is to reach consensus regarding what happened in the past and to foster an optimistic expectation regarding the family's future capacity to cope. The activity "Developing a List of Tasks" helps the family make decisions about what needs to be done and who should assume responsibility for doing what.

Fifth treatment phase: Closure. The focus of this phase is on summing up therapeutic achievements, delineating further needs, and developing ways to map future progress. In addition, the therapist needs to prepare the family for common "anniversary reactions," and encourage family members to view the anniversary as an opportunity for another step toward healing and closure of the disaster experience. Anniversaries offer the family an opportunity to reflect on life changes since the disaster, to see the experience as something "then" and not "now," and to encourage a sense of mastery and survival.

The activity "Building Closure" uses photographs and rituals to achieve closure for the family and the therapeutic process.

Developing a Joint Family Story

Each family member is asked to give his or her "traumatic picture story" a name or a descriptive sentence and to write it on a large piece of paper (small children's contributions can be written for them by an older family member). The family is then encouraged to form a shared story, including the different aspects of their individual stories summarized by the names and descriptive sentences.

Developing a List of Tasks

Each family member is given the task of writing a list of things she or he would like to see happen in the family in the next three to four weeks. Then, each member presents her or his list and the therapist facilitates a family discussion of goals and objectives, the goal of which is to get to an agreed on list of priorities for the next few weeks.

When the family finally reaches agreement on at least five tasks, the following question is raised: "Who will be responsible for what?"

The session is closed after the family reaches agreement on the tasks of the family and each member's responsibility.

Building Closure

Family members choose photos from the family's album that are dear to them and are connected to the loss they have experienced (in cases where no pictures are available, pictures from magazines or newspapers can be used). Each member explains why he or she chose the photos or pictures and lets other family members react. (Sometimes, two family members pick the same photo but not always for the same reasons.) It is important for the therapist to be sensitive to photos that family members find very difficult to handle and to process these difficulties before moving to the final stage of creating a "commemoration photo album."

All of the photos and pictures family members select and discuss are organized into a commemoration album. Creating a family commemoration photo album provides an important teaching moment in the family's progress in dealing with the trauma, loss, and bereavement. It can serve, for example, as a memorial ritual that usually signs the ending of treatment and points toward future orientation of the family as a whole.

Mourning rituals do not stop in the therapy room at the closure of therapy. Rather, the family organizes itself to carry on the memories of its missing, dead, or injured members during the years following the disaster through anniversary rituals and memorials.

MOURNING AS A FAMILY PROCESS

Successful family coping depends on the ability of each member to work through his or her grief, both individually and as a group, a process made harder by the fact that members of a bereaved family may be going through different phases of mourning at the same time and be unaware of each other's struggles (Pynoos, 1992; Webb, 2002). Mourning as a family process demands that all family members participate—adults and children alike. When the family allows mutual mourning and the expression of a range of mixed feelings, it sends the message, "We all suffer—let's bear it together."

Specialized counseling is often recommended to protect the precarious balance of the posttraumatic family that is jeopardized by death. The process of working through the bereavement too often is impeded by misconceptions, denial, and social taboos, especially when death and trauma are intertwined (Ayalon, 1983).

Researchers have addressed the relationship of bereavement and trauma in recent studies. Some researchers have suggested a discrepancy between these two processes, indicating that the needs associated with coping with trauma may clash with the needs associated with coping with bereavement (Cohen, Mannarino, Greenberg, Padlo, & Shipley, 2003). Cohen and her colleagues distinguished *uncomplicated bereavement*, the normal mourning process "characterized by great sadness, feelings of anger, sleep problems, loss of appetite and weight, preoccupation with death, and difficulty concentrating" (p. 308); *childhood PTSD*, characterized by intense helplessness and fear, and reexperiencing, numbing, and avoidance symptoms after exposure to a traumatic event; and *childhood traumatic grief*, "the encroachment of trauma symptoms on the child's ability to grieve" (p. 311). Childhood traumatic grief presents in a similar way to PTSD symptoms, but in traumatic grief the symptoms impinge on the tasks of uncomplicated grief. "Impingement" is difficult to quantify, although a new instrument, the Expanded Grief Inventory (Layne, Savjak, Saltzman, & Pynoos, 2001), offers some help.

Two recent studies of people directly exposed to the 1995 bombing of the Murrah Building in Oklahoma City help clarify the relationship between trauma and bereavement. Pfefferbaum and her colleagues (1999) studied middle and high school students seven weeks after their exposure to the bombing and found that those bereaved were more likely than their peers who were not bereaved to report immediate symptoms of arousal and fear, changes in their home and school environment, and posttraumatic stress symptoms. Results of a later study of adults who were both traumatized and who suffered losses in the bombing indicated a strong association between posttraumatic stress symptoms and grief and that the relationship between grief and difficulty functioning was stronger at higher levels of posttraumatic stress than at lower levels. These results, the researchers posited, support the concept of "traumatic grief" (Pfefferbaum, Call, Lensgraf, Miller, & Flynn, 2001). In "The Traumatization of Grief?" Stroebe, Schut, and Finkenauer (2001) argued that both traumatic experiences and bereavement place individuals at high risk for developing a number of problems independent of PTSD and independent of pathological grief.

In cases where the traumatic incident involves loss, the processing of trauma or the dealing with acute grief does not automatically suggest successful resolution of both trauma and grief; indeed, strategies for dealing with one may clash with strategies for dealing with the other. "Working with Traumatic Grief," presented by Ayalon and Shacham (2000), highlights this problem.

Working with Traumatic Grief

Two Serb gunmen stormed into their Bosnian neighbors' apartment in Sarajevo on a February morning in 1993. They tied up the father, raped his wife and their nine-year-old daughter in front of him, and then shot him to death. Three years later, mother and daughter took part in a "war rape rehabilitation group" in their hometown.

The goals for the mother and daughter as they went through the five phases of rehabilitation, which included EMDR therapy, were to reduce their feelings of anxiety, helplessness, shame, and guilt that had overwhelmed them since the incident, and to restore their sense of dignity. The group encouraged memorial rituals for deceased family members. Both mother and daughter found any mention of the father to be devastating, because it brought back vividly the scene of their brutal rape. They were caught between their emerging abilities to cope with the trauma and their inability to mourn properly for the father.

Trauma processing involves the four phases of (1) reliving through the experience, (2) expressing feelings, (3) reconstructing a renewed world image, and (4) gradually coming to terms with the events and letting them fade in time. Grieving for a dear one who died follows the first three phases, but then there are continuing efforts to keep alive the memory of the deceased through photographs, memorabilia, and anniversary rituals. When the death occurred as a result of the traumatic experience, dealing with the grief reawakens traumatic memories and interferes with the client's rehabilitation and healing. These conflicting needs can seriously disrupt the family's capacity for coping and healing. The helpers must carefully consider other factors, such as the impact of culture, race, class, and religion on different modes of mourning (Doherty, 1999). Most of the research to date on this subject has been carried out in Western cultures, although there is now increasing awareness of the need to consider other cultures and nondominant cultures within populations (Newman, 2002).

Children's grief processes have been given special attention in research (Dyregrov 1991; Webb, 2002). The death of a parent or a sibling is a devastating experience to a child at any age and is perhaps the most stressful life event possible.

Family Members' Denial of Their Grief
Obviously, not all families deal with their grief in a constructive way. In many families, the mourning process is incomplete because children are hardly given the opportunity to grieve. Families with a closed communication system, for example, restrict members' expressions of feelings, fantasies, fears, and morbid thoughts, as well as topics such as death, perhaps as a way to protect members from each other's anxiety.

In the end, the child gets little chance of accurately reconstructing his or her shuttered world after a disaster. Incomplete mourning may produce an "emotional shock wave" after the disaster that runs through families; helpers may need to attend to this situation (Bowen, 1976).

Because verbal recollection of traumatic experiences reactivates the affect—such as the fear, helplessness, and rage—stored in their children's memory, some parents believe that it is not good for them (or themselves) to articulate these recollections. They may silence the children if they ask about the traumatic events and forbid them to play and reexperience what happened. They do not mention the disaster in front of the children. As a result, the children do not tell their parents about intrusive thoughts or nightmares of previous traumatic experiences, thus reinforcing the parents' denial of the effects of the loss on their child. Silence prevails as a mutual collusion between parents and children (Yule & Williamson, 1990). In the end, although parents "can do much to facilitate their children's coming to terms with traumatic events, their desire to shield their children from pain may lead to an initial resistance to intervention" (Gillis, 1993, p. 170), and it is crucial to the emotional needs of the parents and children to overcome their resistance to intervention. Family-oriented interventions are designed to help family members overcome their avoidance of their own trauma-related feelings.

The Spotlight on Research "Avoidance as a Coping Strategy after the Bombing of the Murrah Building" presents a study of some children's selection of avoidance as a way to cope with the bombing of Oklahoma City's Murrah Federal Building.

Narrative Techniques to Help Bereaved Families

One technique to help bereaved families uses the development of a family script. This may begin by having family members explore their extended family history of death and grief and creating a "family tree" that looks at past losses and the typical ways of mourning that have been learned through their past generations. Family scripts show how families fall back on learned patterns that may not be useful any more. The need becomes apparent to write a new and more adaptive "family story" (Byng-Hall, 1995).

Wall and Levy (1996; Levy & Wall, 2000) described the use of "narrative therapy" with families and children who suffer the death of a significant other because of homicide, or with children who witness a homicide. Although their specific focus was on helping clinicians apply narrative therapy as a way to mitigate the impact of homicides on children, families, and communities, their approach may be useful in other contexts. As defined by Wall and Levy (1996, p. 404):

Narratives are considered to be symbolized accounts of actions that have temporal dimensions. Narratives are not literal accounts of events, since they incorporate the narrator's perspective and evaluation ... Narratives are used to evaluate the past in the light of the present, as models to guide current behavior, as well as to anticipate future events and experiences.

Wall and Levy (1996) described an in-depth case study of how to use this intervention with a nine-year-old African American child who survived the death of his brother, a victim of gang violence. "Through constructive social action," such as using community resources to help the child cope

Avoidance as a Coping Strategy after the Bombing of the Murrah Building

Many families and children in Oklahoma City sought help after the 1995 bombing of the Alfred P. Murrah Federal Building. However, Suzanne Whittlesey and her colleagues (1999) noticed that a large percentage of those referred for crisis intervention and various types of therapy were canceling appointments, arriving late, or just not showing up at all. "Avoidance," it seemed, "was the primary coping mechanism used by these children and their families" (p. 304).

Whittlesey and her colleagues (1999) presented some of their clinical findings of five case reports from children six to 12 years old who came for evaluation during the two years after the bombing. All five lost a family member in the bombing and so were suffering from traumatic grief. "Most of the children and families we saw used avoidance to decrease intrusive thoughts, anxiety, and other emotions... Some avoid treatment because of painful memories. We also found some who did not want to recognize what might have been had the bombing not occurred" (p. 310).

Sometimes avoidance was a consciously selected coping strategy, and sometimes it was less conscious and reinforced by isolation, denial (of the problem or the importance of the problem), repression, and intellectualization.

Results of their analysis of the five clinical cases provided grounds for some recommendations to therapists. Because many of those who come for help will come only for symptom relief and only for a short time:

- recognize the need for brief therapy
- provide an educational component early in treatment that alerts children and their parents to the possibility that they may want to avoid therapy because they associate it with their trauma
- provide information on how children grieve, and how this process is different from what it is for adults
- let the family know that the trauma of the bombing may interfere with bereavement
- provide families with a face-saving way to drop out of therapy so that it is not associated with failure or shame.

Whittlesey, S. W., Allen, J. R., Bell, B. D., Lindsey, E. D., Speed, L. F., Lucas, A. F., Ware, M. M., Allen, S. F., & Pfefferbaum, B. (1999). Avoidance in trauma: Conscious and unconscious defense, pathology, and health. *Psychiatry: Interpersonal and Biological Processes, 62*, 303–312.

with the situation and reinforce the notion that the family is imbedded in a socially supportive environment, "clients can transform the homicide from a senseless event into one in which they imbue meaning. By engaging in constructive action, one can honor the memory of the victim and ensure the integrity of the survivors" (p. 412).

White and Epston (1990) developed a method of helping distressed children rewrite their own life story and change self-defeating beliefs about the self. Their narrative method involved a search for events that prove these self-defeating beliefs false. In this search, the therapist enlists the parents' help to find positive examples from the child's life that were ignored, played down, or forgotten. These can be used to "write a new story," one that separates the problem from the way the child sees himself or herself. Once the problem is found and named, it can be challenged. In the process, the child discovers a past, an identity, that was always there but that was hidden by the biases of the previous story of failure and pain. The new story liberates the child from the restraints of the problem.

Based on the narrative approach (White & Epston, 1990), professionals perceive parents as "helpers," collaborating in a joint effort to deal with the children's posttraumatic distress. It enhances the ability of parents and children alike to share their own disaster stories and to hear other people's stories (Greenberger, 2002). This approach respects and reinforces the continuity of the parental role within a process that emphasizes normalization of traumatic responses. Sometimes, direct work with parents is recommended, empowering them in their role as helpers for their children, and concurrently taking care of their own trauma-related difficulties. In addition, the therapist may interview the child in front of the parents, thus modeling to them the appropriate healing approach.

Traumatic loss and bereavement can lead to a concern with the ultimate issues of life and death, and a search for meaning. Such philosophic, religious, or spiritual questions can help the bereaved family accept the reality of their loss. Some survivors turn to a higher power whereas others lose their faith or turn against a Supreme Being. It is important to accept the bereaved person's choices without trying to cheer him or her up, offer platitudes, or impose a certain belief system.

SUMMARY

This chapter presents a variety of methods used to help people exposed to traumatic events in the long range, starting from one or two months after the disaster to years later. Posttraumatic services often come up against resistance either from the clients themselves or from their families. Posttraumatic therapy services need to be proactive, to use screening models applicable to children of different ages, and to monitor people for symptoms that require intervention. The therapeutic attitude proposed in this chapter is that all interventions need to respect natural resilience and enhance individual coping resources.

The chapter contains detailed descriptions of intervention methods for use with children and families, organized around three stages of recovery and healing: physical and psychological safety and security, remembrance and mourning, and reconnection.

Criteria that focus on the family are presented for distinguishing functional from dysfunctional families after a disaster. Once identified, treatment proceeds in five phases: (1) building commitment to therapeutic objectives, (2) defining the main issues for treatment, (3) reframing the problem, (4) developing a healing approach, and (5) closure. Examples of methods of working with families are presented within the context of each of the five phases.

The chapter concludes with a look at the relationship of bereavement and trauma, and the special issues that arise when a child or family is mourning the loss of a family member and simultaneously responding to the trauma of a disaster.

REFERENCES

Antonovsky, A. (1978). *Health, stress and coping.* San Francisco: Jossey-Bass.

Ayalon, O. (1983). *Precarious balance: Coping with stress in the family.* Tel Aviv: Sifriat Poalim.(Hebrew)

Ayalon, O. (1992). *Rescue! Community oriented preventive education handbook.* Ellicot City, MD: Chevron.

Ayalon, O. (1993). Death in literature and bibliotherapy. In R. Malkinsom, S. Rubin, & E. Vitztum (Eds.), *Loss and bereavement in Israeli society* (pp. 155–175). Jerusalem: Ministry of Defense. (Hebrew)

Ayalon, O. (1997a). *Listen to the child: A training manual for shelter workers* (limited ed.). Helsinki: Federation of Mother & Child.

Ayalon, O. (1997b). Creative methods offered to caregivers to prevent or deal with secondary traumatization. In D. Ajdukovic (Ed.), *Trauma recovery training: Lessons learned* (pp. 161–167). Zagreb, Croatia: Society for Psychological Assistance.

Ayalon, O. (2000). New strategies for enhancing coping resources in war-traumatized children. In L. V. Willigen (Ed.), *Health hazards of organized violence in children* (Vol. 2, pp. 121–128). Utrecht, Netherlands: Stichting Pharos.

Ayalon, O. (2001). *Clinical field notes*. Unpublished manuscript.

Ayalon, O. (2004). *Creative coping with death*. Haifa, Israel: Nord.

Ayalon, O., & Lahad, M. (1991). *Life on the edge: Coping with stress of war and peace*. Haifa, Israel: Nord Publications. (Hebrew)

Ayalon, O., & Schlesinger, D. T. (1991). *Dreams of joy and delight*. Haifa, Israel: Nord Publications. (Hebrew)

Ayalon, O., & Shacham, Y. (2000). Helping the helpers in war trauma. In A. Klingman, A. Raviv, & B. Stein (Eds.), *Children in stress and crisis situations* (pp. 159–251). Jerusalem: Ministry of Education. (Hebrew)

Ayalon, O., & Soskis D. (1986). Survivors of terrorist victimization. In N. A. Milgram (Ed.), *Stress and coping in time of war: Generalizations from the Israeli experience* (pp. 257–274). New York: Brunner/Mazel.

Baum, N., & Weinberg, B. (Eds.). (2002). *In the hands of creation: Sandplay images of birth and rebirth*. Toronto: Muki Baum Association.

Bowen, M. (1976). Family reaction to death.In P. J. Guerin (Ed.), *Family therapy: Theory and practice* (pp. 283–297). New York: Gardner.

Brown, D. P., & Fromm, E. (1986). *Hypnotherapy and hypnoanalysis*. Hillside, NJ: Lawrence Erlbaum.

Byng-Hall, J. (1995). *Rewriting family scripts: Improvisation and systems change*. New York: Guilford Press.

Chemtob, C. M., Nakashima, J., & Carlson, J. G. (2002). Brief treatment for elementary school children with disaster-related posttraumatic stress disorder: A field study. *Journal of Clinical Psychology, 58*, 99–112.

Christenson, R. M., Walker, J. I., Ross, D. R., & Maltbie, A. A. (1981). Reactivation of traumatic conflicts. *American Journal of Psychiatry, 138*, 984–985.

Cohen, J. A., Mannarino, A. P., Greenberg, T., Padlo, S., & Shipley, C. (2003). Childhood traumatic grief: Concepts and controversies. *Trauma, Violence, and Abuse, 3*, 307–327.

Das, A. K. (1998). Frankl and the realm of meaning. *Journal of Humanistic Education & Development, 36*, 199–211.

Doherty, G. W. (1999). Cross-cultural counseling in disaster settings. *Australasian Journal of Disaster and Trauma Studies, 3*(2).

Dyregrov, A. (1991) *Children and grief*. London: Jessica Kingsley.

Ellis, A. (1995). Rational-emotive therapy approaches to overcoming resistance. In W. Dryden (Ed.), *Rational emotive behavior therapy: A reader* (pp. 184–211). Thousand Oaks, CA: Sage Publications.

EMDR Institute. (1994). *Eye movement desensitization and reprocessing*. Retrieved September 4, 2003, from http://www. emdr.com/

Erickson, M. H. (1989). *Healing in hypnosis*. New York: Irvington.

Fabry, J. (1988). *Guideposts to meaning: Discovering what really matters*. Oakland, CA: New Habinger.

Figley, C. R. (1988). A five-phase treatment of post-traumatic stress disorder in families. *Journal of Traumatic Stress, 1*, 127–141.

Figley, C. R. (Ed.). (1995). *Compassion fatigue: Coping with secondary traumatic stress disorder in those who treat the traumatized.* New York: Brunner/Mazel.

Foa, E., Hembree, A., & Dancu, C. V. (2002). *Prolonged exposure (PE) manual* (rev. ed.). Unpublished manuscript, University of Pennsylvania, Philadelphia.

Frankl, V. E. (1963). *Man's search for meaning: An introduction to logotherapy.* New York: Washington Square Press.

Frankl, V. E. (1969). *The will to meaning: Foundations and applications of logotherapy.* New York: New American Library.

Gale, K. (2002). High prevalence of PTSD symptoms seen in New York City after September 11. *JAMA, 288,* 581–588, 633–636.

Garuth, E., & Ekstein, R. (1966). Interpretation within the metaphor: Further considerations. *American Academy of Child Psychiatry Journal, 5,* 35–45.

Gillis, H. M. (1993). Individual and small group psychotherapy. In C. F. Saylor (Ed.), *Children and disaster* (pp. 165–186). New York: Plenum Press.

Greenberger, I. (2002). *The therapeutic qualities of re-narrating life stories with Holocaust survivors.* Unpublished doctoral dissertation, University of Surrey, Guildford, Surrey, England.

Gregorian, V. S., Azarian, A., DeMaria, M. B., & McDonald, L. D. (1996). Colors of disaster: The psychology of the "black sun." *Arts in Psychotherapy, 23*(1), 1–14.

Herman, L. J. (1992). *Trauma and recovery.* New York: Basic Books.

Hoven, C. W. (2002). *Testimony presented at the United States Senate Field Hearing, Chair, Hillary Rodham Clinton, held on behalf of the Senate Health, Education, Labor and Pensions (HELP) Committee Regarding the Unmet Mental Health Needs of New York City Public School Children as a Result of the September 11th Attacks on the World Trade Center.* Hearing held in United States Customs House, New York City. Retrieved September 4, 2003, from http://chaos.cpmc.columbia.edu/sph/ Displayimage. asp?Event_No=309

Johnson, K. (1998). *Trauma in the lives of children: Crisis and stress management techniques for teachers, counselors, and student service professionals* (2nd ed.). Alameda, CA: Hunter House.

Kalmanowitz, D., & Lloyd, B. (2002). Inhabiting the uninhabitable: The use of art-making with teachers in Southwest Kosovo. *Arts in Psychotherapy, 29*(1), 41–52.

Keane, T. M., & Kaloupek, D. G. (1982). Imaginal flooding in the treatment of posttraumatic stress disorder. *Journal of Consulting and Clinical Psychology, 50,* 138–140.

Kfir, N. (1989). *Crisis intervention verbatim.* Philadelphia: Hemisphere.

Lahad, M. (1985). *No one is alone: Working with children following a critical incident.* Kiryat Shmona, Israel: Community Stress Prevention Center. (Hebrew)

Lahad, M. (1999). The use of drama therapy with crisis intervention groups, following mass evacuation. *The Arts in Psychotherapy, 26*(1), 27–33.

Lahad, M., & Ankor, H. (1994). *Once upon a fear.* Haifa, Israel: Ach. (Hebrew)

Lahad, M., & Ayalon, O. (1995). *On life and death.* Haifa, Israel: Nord. (Hebrew)

Lahad, M., Shacham, Y., & Niv, S. (2000). Coping and community resources in children facing disaster. In A. Y. Shalev, R. Yehuda, & A. C. McFarlane (Eds.), *International handbook of human response to trauma* (pp. 389–395). New York: Kluwer Academic/Plenum Press.

Layne, C. M., Savjak, N., Saltzman, W. R., & Pynoos, R. S. (2001). *UCLA/BYU Expanded Grief Inventory.* Unpublished instrument, Brigham Young University, Provo, UT.

Levin-Bar-Yosef, T., & Alon, N. (2000). Therapeutic approaches for PTSD. In A. Klingman, A. Raviv, & B. Stein (Eds.), *Children in stress and emergencies* (pp. 215–237). Jerusalem: Ministry of Education. (Hebrew)

Levy, A. J., & Wall, J. W. (2000). Children who have witnessed community homicide: Incorporating risk and resilience in clinical work. *Families in Society, 81,* 402–411.

Marks, I. M. (2002). Reduction of fear: Towards a unifying theory. *Psicoterapia Cognitiva e Comportamentale, 8*(1), 63–66.

Maxfield, L. (2002). Eye movement desensitization and reprocessing in the treatment of post-traumatic stress disorder. In C. R. Figley (Ed.), *Brief treatments for the traumatized: A project of the Green Cross Foundation* (pp. 148–169). Westport, CT: Greenwood Press.

McCubbin, H. I., Cauble, A. E., & Patterson, J. M. (1982). *Family stress, coping and social support.* Springfield, IL: Charles C Thomas.

Miller, L. (1999). Treating posttraumatic stress disorder in children and families: Basic principles and clinical applications. *American Journal of Family Therapy, 7,* 21–34.

Mills, J., & Crowley, R. (1988). A multidimensional approach to the utilization of therapeutic metaphors for children and adolescents. In J. K. Zeig & S. R. Lankton (Eds.), *Developing Ericksonian therapy: State of the art* (pp. 302–323). Philadelphia: Brunner/Mazel.

Monahon, C. (1997). *Children and trauma: A guide for parents and professionals.* New York: John Wiley & Sons.

Newman, M. (2002). Bereavement and trauma. *Bereavement Care, 21*(2), 27–29.

Noy, S. (2000). *Traumatic stress situations.* Jerusalem: Shoken. (Hebrew)

Oaklander, V. (1978). *Windows to our children.* Moab, UT: Real People Press.

Orlev, U. (1960). *Tin soldiers.* Tel Aviv, Israel: Am Oved. (Hebrew)

Pabon, A. J. (2001). Sandplay therapy in a time-limited school-based program. In A. A. Drewes, C. E. Schaefer, & L. Carey (Eds.), *School-based play therapy* (pp. 123–138). Hoboken, NJ: John Wiley & Sons.

Parson, E. (1995a). Mass traumatic terror in Oklahoma City and the phases of adaptational coping, part I: Possible effects of intentional injury/harm on victims' post-traumatic responses. *Journal of Contemporary Psychotherapy, 25,* 155–184.

Parson, E. (1995b). Mass traumatic terror in Oklahoma City and the phases of adaptational coping, part II: Integration of cognitive, behavioral, dynamic, existential and pharmacologic interventions. *Journal of Contemporary Psychotherapy, 25,* 267–309.

Pfefferbaum, B., Call, J. A., Lensgraf, S. J., Miller, P. D., & Flynn, B. W. (2001). Traumatic grief in a convenience sample of victims seeking support services after a terrorist incident. *Annals of Clinical Psychiatry, 13,* 19–24.

Pfefferbaum, B., Nixon, S. J., Tucker, P. M., Tivis, R. D., Moore, V. L., Gurwitch, R. H., Pynoos, R. S., & Geis, H. K. (1999). Posttraumatic stress responses in bereaved children after the Oklahoma City bombing. *Journal of the American Academy of Child and Adolescent Psychiatry, 38,* 1372–1379.

Punamäki, R.-L. (1996) Can ideological commitment protect children's psychosocial wellbeing in situations of political violence? *Child Development, 67*, 55–69.

Pynoos, R. S. (1992). Grief and trauma in children and adolescents. *Bereavement Care, 11*(1), 2–10.

Pynoos, R. S., Goenjian, A. K., & Steinberg, A. M. (1998). A public mental health approach to the postdisaster treatment of children and adolescents. *Child and Adolescent Psychiatric Clinics of North America, 7*, 195–210.

Raphael, B. (1986). *When disaster strikes: A handbook for the caring professions.* London: Hutchinson.

Rosen, S. (1982). *My voice will go with you.* New York: W. W. Norton.

Rossi, E (1986). *The psychobiology of mind-body healing.* New York: W. W. Norton.

Rubin, A., Bischofshausen, S., Conroy-Moore, K., Dennis, B., Hastie, M., Melnick, L., Reeves, D., & Smith, T. (2001). The effectiveness of EMDR in a child guidance center. *Research on Social Work Practice, 11*, 435–457.

Saigh, P. A. (1992). The behavioral treatment of child and adolescent post-traumatic stress disorder. *Advances in Behavioral Research and Therapy, 14*, 247–275.

Shapiro, F. (1999). *Eye movement desensitization and reprocessing: Level I training manual* (rev. ed.). Pacific Grove, CA: EMDR Institute.

Shapiro, F., & Maxfield, L. (2002). Eye movement desensitization and reprocessing (EMDR): Information processing in the treatment of trauma. *Journal of Clinical Psychology, 58*, 933–946.

Silver, S. M., & Rogers, S. (2002). *Light in the heart of darkness: EMDR and the treatment of war and terrorism survivors.* New York: W. W. Norton.

Smith, S. (2003). The effect of EMDR on the pathophysiology of PTSD. *International Journal of Emergency Mental Health, 5*, 85–91.

Solomon, Z., Bleich, A., Shoham, S., & Nardi, C. (1992). The "Koach" project for treatment of combat-related PTSD: Rationale, aims, and methodology. *Journal of Traumatic Stress, 5*, 175– 193.

Solomon, Z., Shalev, A., Spiro, S. E., & Dolev, A. (1992). Negative psychometric outcomes: Self-report measures and a follow-up telephone survey. *Journal of Traumatic Stress, 5*, 225–246.

Solomon, Z., Spiro, S. E., Shalev, A., & Bleich, A. (1992). Positive clinical impressions: II. Participants' evaluations. *Journal of Traumatic Stress, 5*, 217–223.

Speier, A. H. (2000). *Psychosocial issues for children and adolescents in disasters* (2nd ed.). Washington, DC: U.S. Department of Heath and Human Services.

Steinhardt, L. (1998). Sand, water, and universal form in sandplay and art therapy. *Art Therapy, 15*, 252–260.

Stroebe, M., Schut, H., & Finkenauer, C. (2001). The traumatization of grief? A conceptual framework for understanding the trauma-bereavement interface. *Israel Journal of Psychiatry and Related Sciences, 38*(3–4), 185–201.

Taylor, S., Thordarson, D. S., Maxfield, L., Fedoroff, I. C., Lovell, K., & Ogrodniczuk, J. (2003). Comparative efficacy, speed, and adverse effects of three PTSD treatments: Exposure therapy, EMDR, and relaxation training. *Journal of Consulting and Clinical Psychology, 71*, 330–338.

Terr, L. C. (1990). *Too scared to cry: Psychic trauma in childhood.* New York: Basic Books.

van der Hart, O. (1983). *Rituals in psychotherapy: Transition and continuity.* New York: Irvington.

van der Hart, O. (1988). *Coping with loss: The therapeutic use of leave-taking rituals.* New York: Irvington.

van der Hart, O., & Goossens, F. A. (1987). Leave-taking rituals in mourning therapy. *Israel Journal of Psychiatry and Related Sciences, 24*(1–2), 87–98.

van der Kolk, B. A., McFarlane, A. C., van der Hart, O., & Rice-Smith, E. (1999). Treatment of post-traumatic stress disorder and other trauma-related disorders. In S. Spiegel (Ed.), *Efficacy and cost-effectiveness of psychotherapy* (pp. 63–83). Washington, DC: American Psychiatric Publishing.

Vernberg, E. (2002). Intervention approaches following disasters. In A. M. La Greca, W. K. Silverman, E. M. Vernberg, & M. C. Roberts (Eds.), *Helping children cope with disasters and terrorism* (pp. 55–72). Washington, DC: American Psychological Association.

Violanti, J. M. (2000). Scripting trauma: The impact of pathogenic intervention. In J. M. Violanti, D. Paton, & C. Dunning (Eds.), *Posttraumatic stress intervention: Challenges, issues, and perspectives* (pp. 153–165). Springfield, IL: Charles C Thomas.

Volkan, V. D., & Searles, H. (1981). *Linking objects and linking phenomena.* New York: International University Press.

Wall, J. C., & Levy, A. J. (1996). Communities under fire: Empowering families and children in the aftermath of homicide. *Clinical Social Work Journal, 24,* 403–414.

Webb, N. B. (Ed.). (2002). *Helping bereaved children: A handbook for practitioners* (2nd ed.). New York: Guilford Press.

Weinrib, E. (1983). *Images of the self.* Boston: Sigo.

Weisaeth, L. (2001). Acute posttraumatic stress: Nonacceptance of early intervention. *Journal of Clinical Psychiatry, 62*(Suppl. 117), 35–40.

White, M., & Epston, D.(1990). *Narrative means to therapeutic ends.* New York: W. W. Norton.

Whittlesey, S. W., Allen, J. R., Bell, B. D., Lindsey, E. D., Speed, L. F., Lucas, A. F., Ware, M. M., Allen, S. F., & Pfefferbaum, B. (1999). Avoidance in trauma: Conscious and unconscious defense, pathology, and health. *Psychiatry: Interpersonal and Biological Processes, 62,* 303–312.

Wilson, J. P. (1989). *Trauma, transformation and healing.* New York: Brunner/Mazel.

Winnicott, D. W. (1982). *Playing and reality.* London: Tavistock.

Yule, W., & Williamson, R. M. (1990). Post-traumatic stress reactions in children. *Journal of Traumatic Stress, 3,* 279–295.

CHAPTER ELEVEN

DISASTER RECOVERY WITH VULNERABLE POPULATIONS

CHAPTER OVERVIEW

Chapter 11 presents the Trainer Notes and Participant Handbook for a one-day workshop to train disaster recovery workers and other interested individuals how to work with adult vulnerable populations—populations that are elderly, economically disadvantaged, hearing impaired, cognitively disabled, physically disabled, and sight impaired. The times given for each segment of the workshop are minimum recommendations. Indeed, it may be worthwhile to extend the one-day workshop to two days to allow for in-depth discussions.

The workshop is designed for approximately 25 participants, although it may be adapted for groups as small as 10 and for any number over 25.

The workshop takes place in two parts, following the opening remarks. The first part is designed to have participants reflect on what it is they do and why they use the methods they use in recovery work. The second part builds on the first and makes the transition to working with vulnerable populations. Participants make the transition from "helper with disaster clients *without* specific vulnerabilities" to "helper with disaster clients *with* specific vulnerabilities."

Disaster Recovery With Vulnerable Populations
TRAINER NOTES

OPENING (10 MINUTES)
1. Introduce the workshop and facilitator(s).

PART I
Have participants answer the following questions, to introduce themselves (35 minutes):

1. What is your name?
2. For what organization do you work?
3. What are the primary groups of people with whom you work? Consider those directly affected by the disaster and in a crisis state and those indirectly affected or who were directly affected but are no longer in a crisis state.

Hand Out Participant Worksheet 1 (15 minutes): *What I Do When Working with Clients Dealing with Disaster Recovery*
Instruct each participant to complete Worksheet 1 independently.

Hand Out Participant Worksheet 2 (25 minutes): *Common Helping Strategies for Working with Clients Dealing with Disaster Recovery*
Have participants form groups of four or five members each, and ask them to continue considering what they typically do and what they have done that was powerful. Have them create a longer list, if possible, with the theme, "The ways that we help anyone dealing with a disaster's impact."

Discuss the lists by asking for some examples of what seem to be *prevalent* common strategies for helping people who have experienced a disaster.

Hand Out Participant Worksheet 3 (20 minutes): *Expected and Desired Outcomes*
Remaining in their groups, ask participants to look back at their lists and use them to answer the questions on Worksheet 3. To facilitate completion of this worksheet, give an example of a connection between what a helper does and the overarching results she or he may hope to achieve. For example:

- *Action:* Arranging for a client to have her telephone service turned back on, so that she can call for assistance if she has a negative episode with her diabetes.
- *Result:* The client is able to continue living on her own and feels in control of the situation. The action has moved the client closer to normal living conditions.

Discuss the link between participants' strategies, methods, and techniques and their desired outcomes with the group. Ask:

- Who do you think will be most traumatized, or be traumatized for the longest time, following a disaster, such as a hurricane?

Professional support people working with persons who have experienced disasters found that it is possible to predict those people most likely to experience inordinate problems and, therefore, to need extended help. Predictions, in part, are based on consideration of four "circles of vulnerability," that is, four circles that help assess a person's risk (see chapter 2 for more discussion of the circles of vulnerability). The first circle considers an individual's physical proximity to the disaster, the second considers her or his psychological or social proximity, the third considers the extent to which she or he may be a member of a known at-risk population, and the fourth considers available support.

Hand Out Participant Worksheet 4 (20 minutes): *Circles of Vulnerability*

With participants working independently, review the worksheet and then ask:

- Considering the four circles of vulnerability, why is it that some people recover after a disaster but others do not? Why is it that two people may experience the same disaster, but one comes out of it satisfactorily and the other suffers inordinately from the trauma?
- What in some people's personal and psychological makeup, or their ecosystem, puts them at greater risk of suffering ill effects from a disaster? (What are some of the most common risk factors that you have encountered—factors that put clients at greater-than-usual risk from suffering ill effects from a disaster?)
- What in some people's personal and psychological makeup, or their ecosystem, serve to protect them from the ill effects of a disaster? (What are some of the most common protective factors—factors that put clients at less-than-usual risk from suffering ill effects from a disaster?)

Recently, research and professional attention have focused upon those individuals who prevail over great adversity. These individuals experience the same critical stressors as many others in their community, or survive a particular disaster, but they are able to return to functioning normally rather quickly, or can continue to cope amid tremendous hardship—these are individuals who are "resilient" in the face of risk and disaster.

Looking back at how helpers' strategies link to their desired outcomes, it is clear that what participants—helpers—are doing or trying to do with their many ways of helping is to reduce *the risks of those exposed to a disaster and enhance their protective factors.*

Hand Out Participant Worksheet 5 (25 minutes): *Risk Factors, Protective Factors, and Resiliency*

Have participants form groups, four or five members each. Ask them to consider what the particular vulnerabilities are associated with each of the circumstances that put people at heightened risk of suffering ill effects from a disaster. For example, why is "being an elderly person" a risk factor—what is there about being an older adult that increases one's vulnerability to the effects of a disaster? ·

Discuss what risk and protective factors are and how they "join" to create a resilient person. Discuss the dimensions of resiliency, the capacity to bounce back from or not succumb to traumatic events. Risk and protective factors listed on the handout come from three primary sources—summarizing research across a variety of types of disasters and considering data from interviews with survivors and clinicians:

Apfel, R. J., & Simon, B. (1996). Introduction. In R. J. Apfel & B. Simon (Eds.), *Minefields in their hearts: The mental health of children in war and communal violence* (pp. 1–17). New Haven, CT: Yale University Press.

Apfel, R. J., & Simon, B. (1996). *Psychosocial interventions for children of war: The value of a model resiliency.* Retrieved August 20, 2003, from http://www.ippnw. org/MGS/V3Apfel.html

Kirby, L. D., & Fraser, M. W. (1997). Risk and resilience in childhood. In M. W. Fraser (Ed.), *Risk and resilience in childhood: An ecological perspective* (pp. 10–33). Washington, DC: NASW Press.

When reviewing worksheet 5, consider the following.

Risk factors

- Being an older adult—There is a heightened risk of becoming disoriented.
- Having a cognitive disability—There is a heightened risk of not understanding early warnings or of not being able to understand and follow a helper's recommendations, which increases anxiety and disorientation.
- Having a hearing impairment—There is a heightened risk of missing early warnings, typically presented on television (without closed captions) or on radio.
- Being unable to resume one's usual routine in a reasonable amount of time.
- Being laid off or fired from employment.
- Having biomedical problems.
- Having a physical disability—There is a heightened risk of losing access to a social network if usual means of transportation become more difficult, such as not being able to use an elevator after the electricity has been cut off.
- Being economically disadvantaged—There is a heightened risk of not having access to medical care.
- Being illiterate in English—In the United States, English is the language in which most disaster-related material is printed.
- Being a victim of racial discrimination or injustice—There is a heightened risk of not receiving aid quickly or efficiently.
- Having a visual or auditory impairment—There is a heightened risk of becoming disoriented, especially if the usual environment is changed and the person needs to find the way to a shelter.

Protective factors

- Being in touch with a variety of feelings and emotions and not denying or suppressing them—This includes the ability to compartmentalize the pain and postpone affect until it is safe to express it, the ability to laugh, and the ability to stay calm in trying circumstances.
- Being able to remember and invoke images of good and sustaining figures—This factor offers standards and ideals that provide a sense of security and of order (with regard to Maslow's hierarchy).
- Responding actively to the disaster, rather than being a passive observer.
- Believing in one's own personal effectiveness.
- Having compassion for others.
- Having a conviction of one's right to survive.
- Having an easygoing temperament.
- Having a goal, something to live for.
- Helping others—Recognizing that helping others also helps oneself and that being helpless to stop the disaster does not mean being helpless to deal with its consequences.
- Having high intelligence.
- Having high self-esteem.
- Being near social support (including having the ability to recognize and access it).
- Being resourceful (which increases beliefs of power and competence)—This is the ability to find warmth and kindness in the worst of circumstances.
- Viewing the disaster as more than a personal struggle.

In addition to decreasing or responding to risk factors and increasing protective factors, recovery workers also help people fulfill a need as identified by Maslow's need hierarchy. Maslow, in a sense, tells recovery workers "what to do first."

To put the three perspectives we are looking at—risk and protection, vulnerable populations, and Maslow's need hierarchy—into a useable framework, consider that "risk and protection" gives us a way to assess people exposed to a disaster, "vulnerable populations" tells us who to work with first, and Maslow's need hierarchy tells us what to do first.

Hand Out Participant Worksheet 6 (40 Minutes): *Maslow's Need Hierarchy*

According to Maslow, our needs are hierarchical in the sense that lower needs tend to be satisfied before higher needs become very motivating. For example, if you are hungry enough, little else matters. However, this is not entirely how the hierarchy works; indeed, we can be motivated to satisfy needs at several levels simultaneously. For example, we can think about where we can find food to satisfy our hunger, while we fix our house and think about the safety of friends. The elements of the hierarchy are not separable; rather, the hierarchy is holistic and represents an integration of physical, mental, emotional, and spiritual needs (Young, 1998).

After discussion of each need, ask:

- What happens during a disaster to interfere with the fulfillment of these needs?

Ask participants:

- How is knowing about risk factors, protective factors, and Maslow's need hierarchy relevant to your job as a recovery worker?

Possible responses:

1. It helps provide direction when working with a client, keeping helpers from going off "half cocked."
2. It helps prevent burnout associated with having "ambiguous successes" by providing direction and a way to measure success.
3. It facilitates a vision of how the various ways of helping are integrated into a larger scheme, making sense of the "big picture" of providing help through recovery work.
4. It supports starting where the client is, not where the helper wants to be; that is, focusing on what the client needs and her or his risk and protective factors, influences the strategies the helper can use.

SHOW VIDEO SEGMENTS
(20 minutes)

For this section of the workshop, you will need to obtain a video of your choosing that demonstrates different responses to disaster. The Circles of Vulnerability indicate that people who are very close (physically and psychologically) to a traumatic occurrence often experience the disaster to a greater degree; also, persons who are more at risk—such as those in poverty, disabled in particular ways, isolated, and do not speak the major language—also are likely to experience a greater degree of disequilibrium. Consider a movie that would depicts these concepts. Some examples are segments from *Grapes of Wrath*, where people from different walks of life, especially the poor, are trying to survive a terrible drought. Some people in the movie show tremendous resilience, others wither and die. "Disaster movies" that might be useful (even though they may have stereotyped characters) include: *Dante's Peak* (natural disaster); *Inferno* (technological disaster); *Titanic* (technological disaster); and *Red Dawn* (complex disaster).

After showing one or more clips, lead a discussion about the ways a particular vulnerability increased the risk for trauma or death from the disaster (e.g., in *Titanic*, people in third class, who are poorer than those in the other classes, could not get to the lifeboats to be saved). Ask for examples from the participant's own knowledge or experience. Help participants think through the foundation for different responses from different people.

PART II

Hand Out Participant Worksheet 7 (10 Minutes): *What Is a "Vulnerable Population"?*

When working with members of vulnerable populations recovery workers have the same goals as when working with other populations. Those goals are to promote resiliency and to take care of needs as described by Maslow's need hierarchy. However, workers need to be sensitive to what strategies they may use that they use already, what adaptations need to be made to strategies already in use and what new strategies need to be used.

BEGIN ROLE ACTIVITY

(25 minutes)

Begin the role activity by forming participants into groups, assigning roles, and then presenting the guided imagery.

1. Have participants form groups of four to five members each, with each group representing a population with a particular vulnerability (a group made up with "elderly people," another group with "hearing impaired people," and so on); have an additional group representing a population of "helpers."

2. Hand each member of a "vulnerable population" group with a role describing her or his vulnerability plus a context within which the vulnerability exists. Below are five "elderly" roles, five "economically disadvantaged" roles, six "physically disabled" roles, five "cognitively impaired" roles, and four miscellaneous roles—25 roles in all. If you have fewer than 25 participants, make the groups smaller (for example, form groups with three members each, or form only a few groups, selecting the most relevant vulnerable populations for you); if you have more than 25, either write additional roles or have more than one person enacting each role. Have each group meet and decide on a group name or motto to create a sense of "groupness" and to give each person a moment to "get into" her or his role.

Elderly people

You are 79. You live alone with your three cats in a very small wood-frame, rural house. Your primary food source is what you grow in your garden. Your two children are grown and live several hundred miles away. Your partner has been deceased for about 10 years. Your children call you each week, but other than that, you pretty much stay to yourself. A farm family who lives about a mile away brings you sausage or chicken from their farm a few times a month. You have a 15-year-old car that you drive to the store periodically. Driving at night frightens you.

You are 87 and you live in an apartment in an assisted-living facility in a small city. Your sister, who is 90, lives next door. You have severe arthritis in your hands, and are somewhat limited in your abilities to do housework or cook. Without your medicine, you are in serious pain. Your sense of humor is keen, and your cognitive abilities quite sharp. As a result, you have a regular stream of visitors who come by to see you and chat. You have been single all your life, and have no children or pets. You no longer drive, and neither does your sister, so you sold your car.

You are 70. You live in a residence-care facility that has 34 beds. You walk with a walker and need assistance with eating and bathing due to acute circulation problems and high blood pressure. You expected to live out your older years with one of your three children and think often about what you must have done wrong to be living here instead. Two of your children live within 20 miles of the rest home you are in, and they come by a couple times a week to visit. Your partner left you many years ago, and you never divorced or remarried. At times, you remind people that you carried on and raised your kids by yourself, without your partner's help.

You are 77. You and your partner have a large home, are both quite active in various organizations, and like to travel whenever possible. You enjoy visiting your three grandchildren who live a few hours away, whenever it is possible. Slowly deteriorating vision has begun to curtail some of the things you are able to do, but so far, you have been able to obtain a strong enough prescription in your glasses that you can still move around pretty well. Your partner still drives with no problem.

You are 72 and still work as a housecleaner for a few families who have hired you for years. You cannot retire because you do not have enough social security paid in to be able to live off the pension. Your partner is older than you (84) and has no retirement benefits, either. You provide all the financial support for the family.

You have a daughter, 48, who has a substance-abuse problem and has been through detox about 10 times, to no avail. When she is around, you also try to support her.

Economically disadvantaged people

You are 20 and the parent of two children, ages five and three. You work in the Pantry Convenience store, making minimum wage. You spend a lot of your money paying for child care so you work second shift, which pays more. You live in a trailer in a large trailer park, and drive an old car to work, that you expect will give out very soon. The other parent of your children left about a year ago, and you want a divorce and to move on with your life. Right now, there is no money for either step. You asked your sister for money, and she berated you for staying with that "dirtbag" long enough to become pregnant twice. "You made your bed, now lie in it," she says.

You are 38 and live in town with your spouse of 20 years and two of your three children. You used to live on a farm, a life you liked very much, but you sold the farm to avoid foreclosure. You have a job at the poultry processing plant but have trouble getting to work now because your car's transmission failed. Two of your children are still at home (they go to high school), and the third lives about an hour's drive away and works in a fast-food restaurant. Your spouse works part-time as a janitor. You are constantly worried about money and what will happen if someone in the house gets sick or injured.

You are 28. You and your spouse and children came to the United States with your extended family two or three years ago, and have been working as a migrant laborer since then. Your spouse and eldest child work in the fields as well. You live in a tiny "cubby" on the farm. You send as much money as you can spare to your parents, in your home country. You speak some English, have no car, and work many hours each day. You are in debt to the local corner grocery store. Your younger son, age nine, is in school, and the teacher has called you to tell you that he seems to have a serious vision impairment, and needs to be evaluated by an eye doctor.

You are 50. You graduated from high school, and then were drafted into the war in Vietnam. You had a strong psychological reaction to the fighting and were sent home after having served for eight months. You spent some time in a Veteran's Hospital, but after discharge, discontinued counseling or medical visits partly due to the distance to the hospital from your hometown. You do not feel well, have vision difficulties, get dizzy, and have no energy. You have drifted from job to job, barely keeping a roof over your head. Now you work for a poultry processing plant as a packer. You receive no benefits, and are paid by the hour.

You and your spouse are 55. Your middle daughter became involved in drugs while she was working at a bar downtown. She disappeared about eight years ago, leaving her two children with you when she learned about a warrant for her arrest as an accomplice in a burglary. The father of the children is in prison for drug dealing. The children are 11 and 13 years old. You and your spouse adopted them about four years ago when you decided that their mother was probably not coming back. Your other grown children live nearby but have large families of their own and could not take in any more children. Shortly after you adopted the children, the older girl was diagnosed with juvenile diabetes. You work in the physical plant of a

large factory in town, and your spouse is a night security guard at the furniture factory.

Physically disabled people

You are 37. When you were 26, you were working in a dye plant when an explosion cost you your hearing. The company sent you through sign language school, and you are able to use American Sign Language (ASL) without difficulty. The insurance from the accident paid your medical bills and the company also sent you to the community college nearby to learn another aspect of the business, so you could continue to work there. You are married, and have two children, who are in high school. Your spouse is the administrative assistant to the director of nursing at the local hospital.

You are 29 years old. When you were two years old, your parents took you for a ride with them in the family pickup truck. You were not wearing your seat belt, and were flung out of the truck when the driver lost control of the vehicle going around a corner. Both your parents were killed, and your spine was severed, resulting in the loss of the use of your legs. You have been in a wheelchair, living with your grandparents since the accident. You did poorly in school, got involved in drugs, and in general took very poor care of your body. At 23, you checked yourself into a treatment center, where you were able to become clean and sober, and have remained so for the last six years. Last year you got married to a young woman with two children. You work at an auto detailing shop.

You claim to be around 60. You have been sight impaired since birth, due, the doctors believe, to some experimental medication your mother took while she was pregnant with you. Your family was not wealthy, but were able to send you to the State School for the Blind. You did well in school. You attended college, majored in communication studies, and were hired as a speechwriter by a local politician. Your research about working with people with physical impairments brought you to the attention of a university professor who has mentored you. You have worked for the university in a research consultant capacity for almost 30 years. You are planning to retire soon, although you have some concerns about the isolation of retirement. You are not married, and live at home alone. You have never had a large circle of friends.

You are 42. You were diagnosed with multiple sclerosis about five years ago. The disease has progressed somewhat rapidly, and you have regular weakness in your left leg and arm. You have trouble with vision more commonly now and may have to take medical retirement from your job with a publishing company. You are a graphics designer and need to be able to see clearly. You are recently separated because your partner is unable to come to terms with your disease and future dependence. You are an only child, born to your parents quite late in life. Your mother is deceased and your father, 87, lives in a nursing home.

You are 17. You live on a farm, and while driving a combine last year, you had a freak accident in which you lost both arms. Since then, you have been working with doctors and physical therapists to learn how to use prostheses on your stumps, which stop just above the elbow. You find the new arms difficult to manage; your stumps are not healing terribly well, and can be quite painful. You are very embarrassed about going to school, and your grades, which used to be very good, are slipping badly. Your parents are being as supportive as possible, but they must keep the farm going, care for your younger brother and

sister, and figure out how to pay the monumental medical bills this accident has created.

You are 22. You were in a car accident a year ago. You were driving too fast and hit a tree. Your legs were injured beyond repair. You worked with rehab for several weeks, learning how to transfer to the wheel chair that is now your legs. You are trying to come to terms with all the body changes, which has been very hard for you. Your health otherwise is very good. You are in good physical shape, you are becoming involved with sports again and are connecting with other paraplegic athletes. Psychologically you are "hanging on," trying to deal with this tremendous blow to your self-image. Your girlfriend has distanced herself from you, and your buddies are not sure how to deal with this new version of you. Your parents have been tremendously supportive, but they live several hundred miles away.

Cognitively impaired people

You are 31. When you were a teenager, you were involved in a house fire that burned you severely and caused the death of your older sister. As a result, your face was disfigured, and your arms and back received several skin grafts. Since the accident, you have experienced ongoing anxiety attacks, to the point that you are not able to work outside the home. At home, you earn money by stuffing envelopes and typing dissertations and papers for college students. Sometimes the anxiety attacks are so acute that you need short hospitalizations. You do not want people to see you and worry that people in your neighborhood talk about you because they think you look like a freak. You make the students who hire you pick up the papers in the hall, while you stand behind the door. You have heard that the students laugh about the "mad typist." You do not allow your parents to see you anymore.

You are 79 and have been diagnosed with Alzheimer's disease. You have grieved over the increasing loss of your memory. Your spouse cares for you deeply, but you have heard conversations in moments of clarity that let you know that your behavior is becoming more difficult to control at home. Sometimes you get very angry with your spouse or your neighbor who comes by because they are not acting the way you want them to. Other times you feel so guilty because you know you are swearing so much and yelling at your spouse. Sometimes you meet people that you are sure you should know, and you have to ask their names. You do not remember what people have told you, or if you have turned off the stove after fixing something to eat; once you accidentally started a fire. When you are clear headed, you know your condition will only get worse.

You are 42. You have Down syndrome. You are able to work at a grocery store as a bagger. You live with your aging parents a few miles away from the store. You learned how to take the bus to the store, and sometimes on a beautiful day, you walk home. You are glad that you can work and bring home money to your parents, because that is what people are supposed to do when they grow up. You have some friends at the store, but prefer to spend most of your time playing with your cat at home. Her name is Dogwood because "She is creamy white like dogwood flowers."

You are 15 and have been having trouble in school paying attention to what is being said, even though you are smart. Your parents took you to a doctor who said that you had attention deficit hyperactivity disorder (ADHD). What you have learned is that you have trouble focusing on what people tell you, almost as if you have a radio playing loud music in your ears while at the same time you are trying to hear what someone else is saying. Sometimes it is very difficult staying still, and you feel such a compulsion to move that you must get up out of your chair. As a result, your grades are not very good. You have several friends, but sometimes you think you are stupid when you cannot get things straight in your head (because of the "loud music"), or when you are given permission to take longer than anyone else to finish a test due to the ADHD. Routine is *very* important for you. Although you hate taking the medicine the doctor prescribed for you, when you do not take it, your struggles are much worse.

You are 47. When you were 22, you had a nervous breakdown. Since then, you take medicine regularly that makes it possible for you to work at a sheltered workshop and live a fairly "normal" life. When you stop taking your medicine regularly, auditory hallucinations start. Sometimes voices tell you to go outside with no clothes on. Other times they are loud, telling you that you are stupid and no good for anything. Occasionally, during these episodes, you temporarily lose touch with reality and need hospitalization. All this changed about 10 years ago. You started on a new medication that worked very well for you. Now you are living in a supervised apartment for persons with chronic mental illness. You are working at a photocopy center and paying your own way. You have not been hospitalized in four years. It is critical for you to take this medicine exactly as prescribed and to have your blood and liver checked at regular intervals. Sometimes you really want to stop taking all these drugs, but you remind yourself that each time you do, you have a psychotic episode, and you lose more functioning. You do not want that to happen.

Miscellaneous vulnerabilities

You are 29. You and your spouse live in a town house near the university. You are both graduate students. You moved very recently from a small town about 600 miles away, because the memories of your daughter, who died there, were too strong, and you had to get away. The plan, when you moved, was to start fresh. Your daughter was three years old when she was diagnosed with leukemia. She died two years later. You are your spouse both still feel pretty fragile, since your daughter's death was only eight months ago. You are still not sure if your marriage will tolerate the trauma, but you are trying hard.

You are 32 and have lived with your same-sex partner for seven years. You recently bought a home together and are thrilled with it. You put all your savings into the home, and borrowed a lot more than you had originally planned to. Your neighbors seem to be okay with you both as a couple and you are starting to relax. In the past, you both have experienced some strong discrimination, so you were worried about fitting into the neighborhood. You and your partner have recently taken in three cats from the shelter, who have quickly become central members of the family. You had gone to the shelter to adopt one cat, and took all three when you learned that any cat not adopted that day was to be euthanized, and you could not leave any behind to die!

You are 37. You and your spouse have been foster parents for about eight years. Now you have three foster children and your two birth children living with you. The children range in age from four to 12 years old. One of the foster children is new to your family. He is nine and very angry. He has been badly abused and has a very short temper with you or the other children. Another of the foster children has been with you several months, is very clingy and frightened, and has regressed a lot since the arrival of the new boy. They both take a tremendous amount of attention. You live on a small farm, which generates most of its money through raising chickens for a local chicken-packing plant.

You are 50 and a new minister to about six small rural congregations. You went through seminary somewhat later in life and were pleased that these parishes were willing to work with you. They are financially stretched for the most part and live far apart. On the weekends you spend your time traveling from church to church, helping in what ways you can and learning who the people are and what their needs may be. For their part, they are glad you are around and call and express their good wishes constantly. You want to do well, are glad that the Lord has sent you to a place where you are needed, and are just learning how to set boundaries so you will not burn out. You are single, do not know many other people in this area, and are just meeting the other ministers. You feel fairly isolated.

3. Next, read the following guided imagery, asking each participant to listen from the perspective of the role he or she has been given. Instruct members of the "helpers" group to listen to the guided imagery as if they are recovery workers who will be called upon to provide assistance. (Note: Insert the name of a local road that will be familiar to all participants where indicated.)

Even as we speak, a truck loaded with liquid chlorine is traveling south on _____ (insert the name of a local road). The truck's brakes have failed, and the driver is losing control. There are several other vehicles on the road, not far from the truck. As they realize that the driver is having difficulties, they give the truck more space.

The driver sideswipes some utility poles to see if he can start to decrease the truck's speed. The poles break off. Imagine that you are at home, unaware of the unfolding events.

Your electricity goes out. What is your reaction?

[Pause.]

The driver loses control of the truck, and wraps it around a pole. When it goes off the road, the truck tank ruptures. Liquid chlorine starts pouring out onto the road. As the chlorine meets the air, it goes through a chemical reaction, expanding into a gas 400 times greater than the volume of the liquid. The gas billows out from the truck, but because the gas is much heavier than air, it does not move quickly, even though there is a breeze.

When the truck hit the pole, it dug deep holes in the ground, and broke the telephone cables buried underground.

If you have phone service, it is unusable. Now, you have no electricity and no phone. What is your reaction?

[Pause.]

As the chlorine gas billows around the area, any vegetation it touches immediately dies. The driver is overcome quickly by the gas, and will die soon.

Birds start falling out of the sky when the gas reaches them. The drivers of the cars near the accident run away from their vehicles, coughing, and experiencing problems with their eyes, as they try to escape the gas. The outside finish of their cars begins to bubble where the gas is very thick.

Local businesses start shutting down as the gas begins to move toward the center of town.

Farmers fear for their crops. Their livestock are in mortal danger.

Officials realize now that when the truck crashed, chlorine spilled into the area's water supply. They make the decision to shut down the outlet valves that supply water to people in the city and nearby towns.

You are still in your home; you have no water. What is your reaction now?

[Pause.]

Someone has called law enforcement. Hazardous Material (Haz-Mat) personnel realize very quickly that this situation is life threatening and begin an immediate, mandatory evacuation of the area where the cloud of chlorine gas may float.

Your home is in that area. A law enforcement officer comes to your home and tells you that you have to leave in the next five to 10 minutes before you are overcome by chlorine gas, and that will kill you if you stay. You can take small animals but nothing else that you cannot fit in the car in the next five minutes.

Now you are hurrying to get to your car and move what you can. The officer cannot tell you how long you will be gone. You decide to look for a hotel because you do not know too many people in the area.

What is your reaction as you pack hurriedly to escape from the danger?

Where will you go?

[Pause.]

Town administrators do not have enough time to open shelters because the evacuation is so fast.

Officials realize that the cloud is heading for the area elementary and middle schools. They make the decision to line up busses and drive the children to a nearby safe community. Parents are not allowed to pick up their children from school, to ensure better control of their locations.

If you have children in school, what is your reaction now?

[Pause.]

Traffic out of town is backing up and no traffic is allowed into town. People are nervous. There is no solid information about what is happening.

[Pause.]

What is your reaction now?

[Pause.]

Before you open your eyes, consider these last questions:

1. What do you need from a helper, or a recovery worker?
2. What are the special ways the helper needs to attend to you to ensure that your needs are met?
3. What is the best way for you to get the help you need?
4. What are the problems you have that serve as barriers, obstructions, or impediments to receiving help? What are you worrying about?
5. What facilitates or makes possible or helps you receive help? What do you not worry about?

Instruct group members to discuss the final five questions together.

For "Vulnerability" Groups—Hand Out Participant Worksheet 8a (30 Minutes): *Special Needs of Vulnerable Populations*

For "Helper" Group—Hand Out Participant Worksheet 8b: *Specific Vulnerabilities of Vulnerable Populations*

Worksheet 8b provides each member of the helper group with information about vulnerable populations and the characteristics of his or her group's particular vulnerability (that is, the chart that crosses "vulnerable populations" with "vulnerabilities," and explains how a specific vulnerability applies to his or her group). Have helpers discuss this information and how it applies to their interacting with members of the group to which they are assigned.

After 15 minutes, have helpers (one or two, depending on the number of participants) join each group. Each helper's goals are:

- to assess the needs of the members of her or his group, and
- to consider what strategies she or he might best use to respond to group members' needs, as well as each member's needs.

After helpers complete their assessments, have participants "de-role," that is, assume they are no longer in their roles. Have them reintroduce themselves to one another using their real names.

Hand Out Participant Worksheet 9 (25 Minutes): *Special Needs of Vulnerable Populations: What Helpers Should Know*

Have group members discuss, in their groups, what they and the helpers discovered about "their" vulnerable population from the guided imagery activity and discussion.

Ask each group to present the results of their discussion to the other groups. As groups present, write their suggestions and comments on a flip chart.

Hand Out Participant Worksheet 10 (15 Minutes): *What All Helpers Need to Know When Dealing with Vulnerable Populations*

It is evident from the two worksheets—Worksheet 9, Special Needs of Vulnerable Populations: What Helpers Should Know, and Worksheet 10, What All Helpers Need to Know When Dealing with Vulnerable Populations—that there are ways to help people who are members of vulnerable populations that cut across types of vulnerabilities. You will notice on Table 11-2, in Worksheet 9, that "separation from social network" is the only vulnerability associated with all of the several vulnerable populations.

Hand Out Participant Worksheet 11 (25 Minutes): *How to Create a Social Support Network*

As a way of introducing Worksheet 11 without reading it all, indicate to participants:

- There are a variety of different types of support people need, even though what usually comes to mind is "emotional support." People need emotional support—knowing that someone is on their side—but they also need social support that challenges them to work harder, called "task support" or "technical challenge support," and social support that lets them know others see the world as they do, called "shared social reality support."
- Everyone needs support, and it is important for disaster recovery workers to

make an effort to check that their clients have social support networks, and to help them create them if they need to, and to strengthen them.

Conclusion (15 Minutes)

Ask participants:

- Of which vulnerable population would you least like to be a member? Why?
- As a recovery worker, has your perception changed of members of the various vulnerable populations? What is your perception now of members of the vulnerable populations we considered?

Hand Out Participant Worksheet 12: *Bibliography*

WORKSHEET 1

What I Do When Working with Clients Dealing With Disaster Recovery

What is the single most common or usual specific thing you do as a helper for those disaster clients with whom you work?

What is something specific you did in the last several weeks for a disaster client with whom you worked that was *powerful*?

WORKSHEET 2

Common Helping Strategies for Working with Clients Dealing with Disaster Recovery

1.

2.

3.

4.

5.

6.

7.

8.

9.

10.

Expected and Desired Outcomes

When recovery workers do something on your list of helping strategies, what are they trying to achieve? What are the overarching results that are desired when working with an individual or a family this particular way? How would a recovery worker like things to be for this family when she or he discontinues seeing that worker?

1.

2.

3.

4.

5.

6.

7.

Circles of Vulnerability *(1 of 4 pages)*

Circle of Vulnerability 1–Physical Proximity

1st Circle (most vulnerable): Victims—direct exposure

2nd Circle: Witnesses (near-miss experiences)

3rd Circle: People within hearing, feeling, or smelling, and so on of the disaster but who did not see it

4th Circle (least vulnerable): People outside the disaster area, in distant neighborhoods and communities (potentially the whole nation)

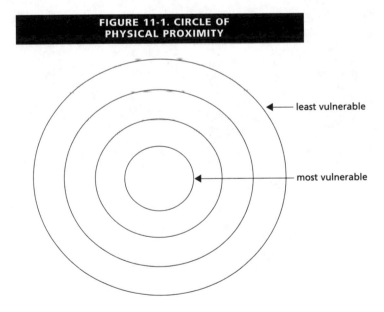

FIGURE 11-1. CIRCLE OF PHYSICAL PROXIMITY

least vulnerable

most vulnerable

WORKSHEET 4

Circles of Vulnerability *(2 of 4 pages)*

Circle of Vulnerability 2–Psychological or Social Proximity

1st Circle (most vulnerable): Those socially close to people who experienced the disaster, usually family, friends, and others who have a close personal relationship with victims

2nd Circle: People who know the victims socially, such as acquaintances or friends who are not considered "close"

3rd Circle (least vulnerable): People who identify with the victims, who see themselves as similar in some way to the victims

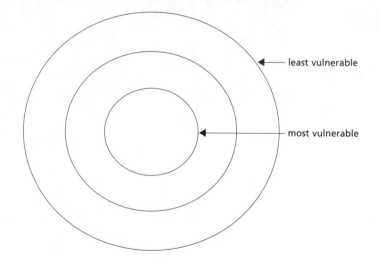

FIGURE 11-2. CIRCLE OF PSYCHOLOGICAL OR SOCIAL VULNERABLITY

least vulnerable

most vulnerable

WORKSHEET 4

Circles of Vulnerability *(3 of 4 pages)*

Circle of Vulnerability 3–Populations at Risk

1st Circle (most vulnerable): People who have experienced a similar trauma in the past, as well as, potentially, people who are elderly, economically disadvantaged, hearing impaired, cognitively disabled, physically disabled, or sight impaired

2nd Circle: People who experienced a significant loss over the past year

3rd Circle: People who are in the middle of a severe personal or social crisis

4th Circle (least vulnerable): People who are overly sensitive. (This may be an issue with adolescents, for example)

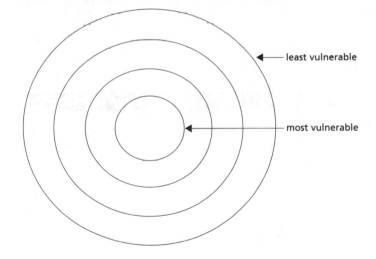

FIGURE 11-3. CIRCLE OF RISK ASSOCIATED WITH PRIOR EXPERIENCES

← least vulnerable

← most vulnerable

WORKSHEET 4

Circles of Vulnerability *(4 of 4 pages)*

Circle of Vulnerability 4–Circles of Support

1st Circle (least vulnerable): People in the first circle are those who are most familiar with the victim and available to provide the greatest degree of personalized and individualized support (such as family members and nearby friends and relatives).

2nd Circle: People in the second circle may know the victim personally, although not as closely as those in the most inner circle—these people can provide support and are readily accessible, although not as accessible as family members. (Examples are teachers, neighbors, mental health workers, and school counselors.)

3rd Circle: Members of the community who provide both direct and indirect support for the victim, and probably do not know the victim personally. (Examples are firefighters and police officers, school principals, the district superintendent, and the mayor.)

4th Circle (most vulnerable): Agencies outside the community that provide support for disaster victims (such as the American Red Cross, the Red Crescent Society, and the Federal Emergency Management Agency).

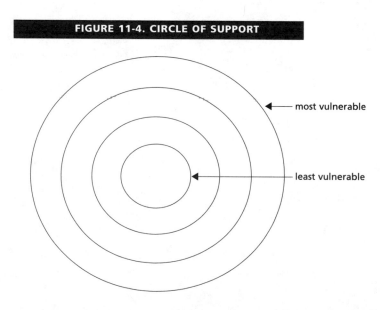

FIGURE 11-4. CIRCLE OF SUPPORT

most vulnerable

least vulnerable

WORSHEET 5

Risk Factors, Protective Factors, and Resiliency *(1 of 2 pages)*

Risk Factors: Circumstances that put people at heightened risk of suffering ill effects from a disaster

- Being an older adult
- Having a cognitive disability
- Having a hearing impairment
- Being unable to resume one's usual routine in a reasonable amount of time
- Being laid off or fired from employment
- Having biomedical problems
- Having a physical disability
- Being economically disadvantaged
- Being illiterate in English
- Being a victim of racial discrimination or injustice
- Having a visual or auditory impairment

Protective factors: Circumstances that protect people—put them at less-than-usual risk—from the ill effects of a disaster and that enhance their resiliency

- Being in touch with a variety of feelings and emotions, and not denying or suppressing them
- Being able to remember and invoke images of good and sustaining figures
- Responding actively to the disaster (rather than being a passive observer)
- Believing in one's own personal effectiveness
- Having compassion for others
- Having a conviction of one's right to survive
- Having an easygoing temperament
- Having a goal, something to live for
- Helping others
- Having high intelligence
- Having high self-esteem
- Being near social support (including having the ability to recognize and access it)
- Being resourceful (which increases beliefs of power and competence)
- Viewing the disaster as more than a personal struggle

Risk Factors, Protective Factors, and Resiliency *(2 of 2 pages)*

Resiliency is the "the power of recovery...the ability to return once again to those patterns of adaptation and competence that characterized the individual prior to the pre-stress period" (Garmezy, N. [1993]. Children in poverty: Resilience despite risk. *Psychiatry, 56,* 127–136; quote is on p. 129). In nontechnical language, *resiliency* is the ability to bounce back from a traumatic event.

In their Web site article, "Regaining Resiliency After Loss" (Hokanson, R. L. (1993). *Regaining resiliency after loss.* Minneapolis: Minnesota Extension Service. Retrieved August 20, 2003, from http://www.extension.umn.edu/distribution/familydevelopment/components/ITT-09.html), the Minnesota Extension Service defines common resilient characteristics of survivors of trauma:

- Almost without exception, those who survive a tragedy give credit to one person who stood by them, supported them, and offered them a sense of hope.
- Those who survive a tragedy understand the magnitude of what they have lost.
- Those who survive a tragedy learn to transcend their guilt (that is, to forgive themselves and define their own good qualities).
- Those who survive a tragedy have a reason to go on living (that is, they do not live solely in the past, and they see a real possibility of a future).

Maslow's Need Hierarchy

1. Physiological or survival needs

These needs refer to support and maintenance of basic body functions.
What happens during a disaster to interfere with the fulfillment of these needs?

2. Safety and security needs

Safety and security addresses our need to be free of fear, anxiety, chaos, and to have structure and order, such as establishing daily goals and knowing what needs to be done to fulfill them. Threats to our own lives as well as the lives of others in our families and communities make the fulfillment of this need of paramount importance.
What happens during a disaster to interfere with the fulfillment of these needs?

3. Love and belongingness needs

We need to have positive relationships with others, including family, friends, and the community as a whole.
What happens during a disaster to interfere with the fulfillment of these needs?

4. Self-esteem needs

Internally, self-esteem refers to having a sense of achievement and independence. With regard to others, it refers to status, recognition, attention, dignity, or appreciation.
What happens during a disaster to interfere with the fulfillment of these needs?

5. Self-actualization needs

Self-actualization needs are associated with being fully functioning, operating at "peak performance" in creative ways, and fulfilling all potential.
What happens during a disaster to interfere with the fulfillment of these needs?

6. Community actualization

Although not part of the elements of Maslow's hierarchy, there is evidence that he was heading in the direction of adding community actualization as an element. This need highlights altruism, the need to give back to one's community by helping others fulfill their own needs.
What happens during a disaster to interfere with the fulfillment of these needs?

What Is a "Vulnerable Population"?

People who, because of their particular challenges, are at greater risk than other people in the population to fail to recover from the effects of a disaster, or people who are likely to be affected to a greater degree than others.

People whose needs are not fully addressed by helpers trained to work with "usual" populations and who use nonadaptive methods of helping.

People who have less "easy" access to usual resources than others.

WORKSHEET 8a

Special Needs of Vulnerable Populations

With regard to the vulnerable population that you considered in the last exercise:

- What do its members need from a helper?
- What are the special ways the helper needs to attend to its members to ensure that their needs are met?
- What is the best way for its members to get the help they need?
- What are the problems its members have that serve as barriers, obstructions, or impediments to receiving help? What are these members worrying about?
- What facilitates, makes possible, or helps its members receive, access, or obtain help?
- What do they not worry about?

WORKSHEET 8b

Specific Vulnerabilites of Vulnerable Populations *(1 of 7 pages)*

TABLE 11-1. SPECIFIC VULNERABILITIES OF VULNERABLE POPULATIONS

	ELDERLY	POOR	DEAF & HARD OF HEARING	COGNITIVELY DISABLED	PHYSICALLY DISABLED	BLIND & VISUALLY IMPAIRED
Disorientation	X		X	X	X	X
Disease	X	X				
Electrical loss	X				X	
Standard forms of warning	X	X	X	X		
Displacement of and from familiar surroundings	X	X		X		X
Separation from social network	X	X	X	X	X	X
Closing of pharmacies	X			X		
Normal forms of communicating	X	X	X	X		X

Elderly people
Vulnerabilities:

Disorientation
- The elderly person's daily routine and familiar cues may be disrupted.
- Routine is needed for medication; disruption of this routine can lead to illness or even death for older adults dependent on medication.

Disease or sickness
- Elderly people are extremely temperature sensitive. Loss of air conditioning or heating can lead quickly to hyper- or hypothermia.
- Elderly people are susceptible to "shelter pneumonia" due to their lower immune systems and the unhealthy environments in some shelters.

Specific Vulnerabilites of Vulnerable Populations *(2 of 7 pages)*

Elderly people (continued)

Vulnerabilities:

Loss of electrical power

- This is dangerous for those older persons who are on life support machines and electrically powered respirators.

Standard forms of warning

- Television and radio transmissions may not help those elderly people who are hearing impaired.
- Many older adults have attenuated comprehension and cognitive processes, so if a message is not repeated several times, its meaning may not be completely or correctly processed.

Displacement of and from familiar surroundings

- This can cause anxiety, panic, and depression.
- Many elderly people limit their food intake at shelters because they fear or are uncomfortable with shelter facilities.
- Being uprooted from family and caregivers can cause older adults to feel helpless and can lower their self-esteem.

Separation from social network

- This can be devastating to elderly people because they are increasingly dependent on friends and loved ones not only to help with daily routines, but also to fill their need for human contact.

Closed pharmacies

- Closed pharmacies can hurt many elderly people who are dependent on medication for their survival and stabilization.
- The destruction of a pharmacy can mean the loss of vital prescriptions and medications.

Normal forms of communicating

- Normal communication, for some elderly people, may be impossible; an example is persons dependent on breathing apparatuses. They must therefore find other ways to communicate their needs to helpers.

Specific Vulnerabilites of Vulnerable Populations *(3 of 7 pages)*

Economically disadvantaged people
Vulnerabilities:

Disease and sickness
- Disease and sickness hits many impoverished societies, families, or individuals harder during and after a disaster than it hits those who have greater access to money. This is because most impoverished people go to relief camps when disaster hits and it is here, in these situations, where they are even more susceptible to common diseases.
- The poor pre-existing health and nutritional status of the impoverished population makes it vulnerable to stress and disease caused by disaster.

Standard forms of warning
- These may be ineffective in areas where people might not have access to working televisions and radios.

Displacement of and from familiar surroundings
- Housing not built to withstand a disaster may become uninhabitable after the passing of a hurricane or earthquake, for instance. Poor construction increases chances of death or injury during and after disasters, and increases the number of people who will be left homeless.
- Marginalized populations may live in vulnerable areas without basic amenities or infrastructure, necessitating their evacuation.

Separation from social network
- Disaster often separates impoverished people from their social networks; this might be, for example, because they do not have cars or other forms of transportation, or cell phones. Social networks are extremely important to impoverished people, as they are to all people, as a source of support and strength.

Normal forms of communicating
- Normal communication may be ineffective between impoverished people and helpers, especially when the helper does not speak the person's language, or if the person is illiterate.

—— **WORKSHEET 8b** ——

Specific Vulnerabilites of Vulnerable Populations *(4 of 7 pages)*

Hearing impaired people

Vulnerabilities:

Disorientation

- Although the disorientation experienced by those who are hearing impaired may not be as extensive as those who are vulnerable in other ways or have other disabilities, those who are hearing impaired still feel disoriented, confused, and lost when they are thrown into situations and places (such as shelters) where they are unable to communicate and understand what is going on.

Standard forms of warning

- Most first warnings, such as breaking news on the television, are not presented with closed captions, and are almost never interpreted for the hearing impaired.
- The hearing impaired are unable to hear warning sirens and public announcements.
- The hearing impaired cannot hear people knocking at their doors.

Separation from social network

- The hearing impaired need the people in their social network to inform them of what is going on and to translate what rescuers are asking.
- People in the hearing impaired person's social network help her or him feel less alone, disorientated, anxious, and panicked because they have developed methods for communicating with her or him.

Normal forms of communicating

- Unless the helper knows ASL, he or she might be unable to ask what the hearing impaired person needs or to understand his or her requests.

WORSHEET 8b

Specific Vulnerabilites of Vulnerable Populations *(5 of 7 pages)*

Cognitively disabled people
Vulnerabilities:

Disorientation
- The cognitively disabled may be unable to process what is going on. Some may forget why they no longer are in their homes, once they have been moved to a shelter, and could panic.
- They may also panic when disrupted from daily routines.

Standard forms of warning
- Many cognitively disabled people may not be able to comprehend warning reports.
- Many cognitively disabled people may need such warnings to be repeated several times and at a slow speed before comprehending.
- Cognitively disabled people may not be able to comprehend sequential directions.

Displacement of and from familiar surroundings
- This may cause additional confusion and anxiety for a cognitively disabled person.

Separation from social network
- Cognitively disabled people count on their social network for support and for help in understanding the situation.
- They also may depend on members of their social network to care for their medical needs.
- People from cognitively disabled persons' social network provide them with a familiarity that can alleviate some of the anxiety caused in disaster confusion.

Closed pharmacies
- Many cognitively disabled people depend on medication to keep then stable and functioning.
- The destruction of a pharmacy can mean the loss of vital prescriptions and medications.

Normal forms of communicating
- Many cognitively disabled people have difficulty understanding helpers if they speak too fast or use an extensive vocabulary.

Specific Vulnerabilites of Vulnerable Populations *(6 of 7 pages)*

Physically disabled people
Vulnerabilities:

Disorientation
- Disorientation can occur for the physically disabled when familiar exits or paths are blocked with debris.
- Physically disabled people who are unable to move may be unable to cover themselves or protect themselves from debris.
- The physically disabled person who is separated from her or his typical transportation mechanism, such as a wheelchair, may become disoriented.

Loss of electrical power
- Electrical loss may mean that the physically disabled person is no longer able to use elevators, escalators, and other forms of electricity-dependent forms of transportation.
- Machines that need to be electrically charged or recharged, such as battery-operated wheelchairs, may not function or may soon lose their ability to function.

Separation from social network
- This can cause serious problems when physically disabled individuals depend on these people to perform rudimentary or basic functions for them.

Specific Vulnerabilites of Vulnerable Populations *(7 of 7 pages)*

Sight impaired people
Vulnerabilities:

Disorientation

- By definition, sight impaired people are unable to clearly see what is going on around them.
- Familiar exits and routes might be blocked by debris.
- Sight impaired people may be unable to understand all the noises around them.
- Guide dogs may be fearful and unwilling or unable to assist the individual.

Displacement of and from familiar surroundings

- The disruption or movement of familiar objects can hinder the sight impaired individual's ability to seek shelter.
- If taken to a shelter, a sight impaired individual may be confused, disoriented, and even panicked in his or her new and unfamiliar surroundings.

Separation from social network

- Since they cannot drive a car, sight impaired individuals may be dependent on their social networks to get them to safety.
- The social network is there to be the "eyes" for sight impaired people who need it.
- The social network is there to familiarize the sight impaired individual with his or her new environment and help alleviate some of the anxiety caused by not knowing the new environment.

Normal forms of communicating

- All written forms that need to be completed by the sight impaired person need to be put on tape or read aloud.
- Sight impaired individuals must be read all written information that could be vital to them and their safety.
- All directions must be said to them, not pointed, or signed.

Special Needs of Vulnerable Populations:
What Helpers Should Know *(1 of 13 pages)*

TABLE 11-2. SPECIFIC VULNERABLE POPULATIONS: WHAT HELPERS SHOULD KNOW						
	ELDERLY	**POOR**	**DEAF & HARD OF HEARING**	**COGNITIVELY DISABLED**	**PHYSICALLY DISABLED**	**BLIND & VISUALLY IMPAIRED**
Disorientation	X		X	X	X	X
Disease	X	X				
Electrical loss	X				X	
Standard forms of warning	X	X	X	X		
Displacement of and from familiar surroundings	X	X		X		X
Separation from social network	X	X	X	X	X	X
Closing of pharmacies	X			X		
Normal forms of communicating	X	X	X	X		X

Elderly people
Vulnerabilities:

Disorientation
- The elderly person's daily routine and familiar cues may be disrupted.
- Routine is needed for medication; disruption of this routine can lead to illness or even death for older adults dependent on medication.

Disease or sickness
- Elderly people are extremely temperature sensitive. Loss of air conditioning or heating can lead quickly to hyper- or hypothermia.
- Elderly people are susceptible to "shelter pneumonia" due to their lower immune systems and the unhealthy environments in some shelters.

Special Needs of Vulnerable Populations:
What Helpers Should Know *(2 of 13 pages)*

Elderly people (continued)

Loss of electrical power
- This is dangerous for those older persons who are on life support machines and electrically powered respirators.

Standard forms of warning
- Television and radio transmissions may not help those elderly people who are hearing impaired.
- Many older adults have attenuated comprehension and cognitive processes, so if a message is not repeated several times, its meaning may not be completely or correctly processed.

Displacement of and from familiar surroundings
- This can cause anxiety, panic, and depression.
- Many elderly people limit their food intake at shelters because they fear or are uncomfortable with shelter facilities.
- Being uprooted from family and caregivers can cause older adults to feel helpless and lower their self-esteem.

Separation from social network
- This can be devastating to elderly people who live alone because they are increasingly dependent on friends and loved ones, not only to help with daily routines, but also to fill their need for human contact.

Closed pharmacies
- Closed pharmacies can hurt many elderly people who are dependent on medication for their survival and stabilization.
- The destruction of a pharmacy can mean the loss of vital prescriptions and medications.

Normal forms of communicating
- Normal communication, for some elderly people, may be impossible; an example is persons dependent on breathing apparatuses. They must therefore find other ways to communicate their needs to helpers.

WORKSHEET 9

Special Needs of Vulnerable Populations:
What Helpers Should Know
(3 of 13 pages)

Elderly people (continued)

Things to know (The first three are from Oriol, 1996).

- "Elders" is an extremely broad category that pertains to many different individuals at different stages in their lives.
- Many elders refuse help, believing that accepting help is admitting defeat and dependency, and bringing them one step closer to being put in a nursing home.
- Helpers need to remind those who need help that their tax dollars were used to fund these programs and that accepting help is just collecting on one's investment.
- Elders are also survivors, many bringing their experiences and wisdom to a disaster to show that "this too will pass."
- Elderly people are particularly sensitive to changes in their environment and routine.

Things to do (The first seven items are from Oriol, 1996).

- Provide strong and persistent spoken reassurance.
- Assist with recovery of physical possessions, make frequent home visits, and arrange for companions.
- Give special attention to suitable residential relocation, ideally in a familiar surrounding with friends or acquaintances.
- Help reestablish familiar social contacts.
- Assist in obtaining medical and financial assistance.
- Help reestablish medication regimes.
- Provide escort services.
- To ensure that the need for privacy is met, talk to each elderly person separately.
- Reinforce what the elderly person has said by repeating it or writing it down in simple and clear language.
- Identify elderly person's needs from her or his perspective—ask, do not assume, what is needed.
- Avoid acting as if the elderly person cannot hear or see (verify, first, if these senses are problematic), behaving in a bossy or intimidating manner, or sounding patronizing.
- Give assurance of continual care and help.
- Be persuasive with recommendations (for example, an elderly person may be highly reluctant to evacuate his or her home).
- Defer noncritical issues to a later discussion, but do not ignore them.
- Be sure to provide accurate information and a list of resources.

WORKSHEET 9

Special Needs of Vulnerable Populations:
What Helpers Should Know
(4 of 13 pages)

Economically disadvantaged people
Vulnerabilities:

Disease and sickness
- Disease and sickness hit many impoverished societies, families, or individuals harder during and after a disaster than they hit those who have greater access to money. This is because most impoverished people go to relief camps when disaster hits and it is here, in these situations, where they are even more susceptible to common diseases.
- The poor pre-existing health and nutritional status of the impoverished population makes it vulnerable to stress and disease caused by disaster.

Standard forms of warning
- These may be ineffective in areas where people might not have access to working televisions and radios.

Displacement of and from familiar surroundings
- Housing not built to withstand a disaster may become uninhabitable after the passing of a hurricane or earthquake, for instance. Poor construction increases chances of death or injury during and after disasters, and increases the number of people who will be left homeless.
- Marginalized populations may live in vulnerable areas without basic amenities or infra-structure, necessitating their evacuation.

Separation from social network
- Disaster often separates impoverished people from their social networks; this might be, for example, because they do not have cars or other forms of transportation, or cell phones. Social networks are extremely important to impoverished people, as they are to all peo-ple, as a source of support and strength.

Normal forms of communicating
- Normal communication may be ineffective between impoverished people and helpers, especially when the helper does not speak the person's language, or if the person is illiterate.

WORKSHEET 9

Special Needs of Vulnerable Populations:
What Helpers Should Know
(5 of 13 pages)

Economically disadvantaged people (continued)

Things to know

- Often, the economically disadvantaged person and members of impoverished societies receive help from all over the world in the wake of a disaster. In the United States, aid from other countries is rare.
- Helpers need to know the culture and custom of the people with whom they work to better serve and help them.
- Many impoverished and homeless people have a tendency to "slip through the cracks," their disappearance often going unnoticed.
- Impoverished people tend to believe that others do not recognize them as individuals and, with regard to receiving help, view them as if they were "two steps behind."

Things to do

- Learn what emergency support is available to provide needed money.
- Have interpreters available, if needed, and pamphlets in the impoverished person's language.
- Be sure to provide accurate information and a list of resources, particularly on available medical aid.
- Because it is likely that the economically disadvantaged person with whom you talk is distrustful of authority figures, explain your role to him or her.
- Be alert to people who are not asking for help (for example, illegal aliens).
- Identify the person's needs from her or his perspective—ask, do not assume, what is needed.

WORKSHEET 9

Special Needs of Vulnerable Populations:
What Helpers Should Know
(6 of 13 pages)

Hearing-impaired people
Vulnerabilities

Disorientation
• Although the disorientation experienced by those who are hearing impaired may not be as extensive as those who are vulnerable in other ways or have other disabilities, those who are hearing impaired still feel disoriented, confused, and lost when they are thrown into situations and places (such as shelters) where they are unable to communicate and understand what is going on.

Standard forms of warning
• Most first warnings, such as breaking news on the television, are not presented with closed captions and, usually, are not interpreted for the hearing impaired.
• The hearing impaired are unable to hear warning sirens and public announcements.
• The hearing impaired cannot hear people knocking at their doors.

Separation from social network
• The hearing impaired need the people in their social network to inform them of what is going on, and to translate what rescuers are asking.
• People in the hearing impaired person's social network help her or him feel less alone, disorientated, anxious, and panicked because they have developed methods for communicating with her or him.

Normal forms of communicating
• Unless the helper knows ASL, he or she might be unable to ask what the hearing impaired person needs or to understand his or her requests.

Special Needs of Vulnerable Populations:
What Helpers Should Know
(7 of 13 pages)

Hearing-impaired people (continued)

Things to know
- A hearing impaired person's disorientation and increased dependency "influences the level of emotional reactions which, in turn, may affect behavior and coping capacity" (American Psychiatric Association, n.d.).
- Hearing impaired people often believe themselves to be "a step behind" in getting information given in usual ways of communicating not available to them.

Things to Do
- Help the hearing impaired person adjust to his or her new surrounding.
- Identify the hearing impaired person's needs from her or his perspective—ask, do not assume, what is needed.
- Advocate getting interpreters on television warning reports.
- Always keep a pen and paper on hand.
- Be sure to provide accurate information and a list of resources, emphasizing those that are sensitive to hearing impaired persons' needs (for example, information that is written and resources that know ASL).
- It always helps to know a few important ASL signs.
- When talking to a hearing impaired person:
  Face the person
  Be aware of background noises
  Speak in a normal fashion
  Do not use hand gestures.

Special Needs of Vulnerable Populations:
What Helpers Should Know
(8 of 13 pages)

Cognitively disabled people

Vulnerabilities:

Disorientation
- The cognitively disabled may be unable to process what is going on. Some may forget why they no longer are in their homes, once they have been moved to a shelter, and panic.
- They may also panic when disrupted from daily routines.

Standard forms of warning
- Many cognitively disabled people may not be able to comprehend warning reports.
- Many cognitively disabled people may need such warnings to be repeated several times and at a slow speed before comprehending.
- Cognitively disabled people may not be able to comprehend sequential directions.

Displacement of and from familiar surroundings
- This may cause additional confusion and anxiety for a cognitively disabled person.

Separation from social network
- Cognitively disabled people count on their social network for support and for help in understanding the situation.
- They also may depend on members of their social network to care for their medical needs.
- People from cognitively disabled persons' social network provide them with a familiarity that can alleviate some of the anxiety caused in disaster confusion.

Closed pharmacies
- Many cognitively disabled people depend on medication to keep them stable and functioning.
- The destruction of a pharmacy can mean the loss of vital prescriptions and medications.

Normal forms of communicating
- Many cognitively disabled people have difficulty understanding helpers if they speak too fast or use an extensive vocabulary.

WORKSHEET 9

Special Needs of Vulnerable Populations:
What Helpers Should Know
(9 of 13 pages)

Cognitively disabled people (continued)

Things to know
- Remember that there are many different kinds of cognitive disabilities.
- What one person might need may be completely different from what another person might need.
- For some, forgetting might be a problem. Be sure to write instructions down. This group of individuals, similar to many others, needs to be comforted and reassured about their new surroundings.
- It is important to have some understanding of the person's particular cognitive disability.
- Touching and other forms of nonverbal behavior may scare or offend a cognitively disabled person, so it is important to be sensitive to what may and may not be appropriate behavior.
- It is likely that the cognitively disabled person will be afraid of you, so understand that anger, reticence, lack of trust, and so on, may be expressions of this fear.

Things to do
- Use very simple language to explain what has occurred and what usual reactions are to what has occurred, and repeat what you say several times.
- As much as possible, identify the cognitively disabled person's needs from her or his perspective—ask, do not assume, what is needed. It is likely that cognitively disabled clients will want to participate in the decisions affecting them, although they may be limited in their ability to do so.
- Focus on medication needs.
- Reassure the cognitively disabled person about her or his safety.
- Be patient.
- Be sure to provide accurate information and a list of resources, written in very simple language.
- Provide a great deal of reassurance and, if at all possible, consistency (for example, do not switch helpers).

Special Needs of Vulnerable Populations:
What Helpers Should Know
(10 of 13 pages)

Physically disabled people

Vulnerabilities:

Disorientation
- Disorientation can occur for the physically disabled when familiar exits or paths are blocked with debris.
- Physically disabled people who are unable to move may be unable to cover themselves or protect themselves from debris.
- The physically disabled person who is separated from her or his typical transportation mechanism, such as a wheelchair, may become disoriented.

Loss of electrical power
- Electrical loss may mean that the physically disabled person is no longer able to use elevators, escalators, and other forms of electricity-dependent forms of transportation.
- Machines that need to be electrically charged or recharged, such as battery-operated wheelchairs, may not function or may soon lose their ability to function.

Separation from social network
- This can cause serious problems when physically disabled individuals depend on these people to perform rudimentary or basic functions for them.

Special Needs of Vulnerable Populations:
What Helpers Should Know
(11 of 13 pages)

Physically disabled people (continued)

Things to know
- Helpers need to know how to safely transport physically disabled people, for example, how to place them safely in wheelchairs.
- Be familiar with community support available for physically disabled clients.
- Have a good working knowledge of the Americans with Disabilities Act, as well as other important laws (see http://janweb.icdi.wvu.edu/kinder/, a Web site developed and maintained by Duncan Kinder, for both information and links to other sources).

Things to do
- Learn what physical aids are available and how to use them.
- Focus on individual strengths (at least initially).
- Identify the physically disabled person's needs from her or his perspective—ask, do not assume, what is needed.
- Have access to people who know how to meet the mobility requirements of physically disabled people without hurting themselves or the physically disabled person.
- Be sure to provide accurate information and a list of resources.

—— **WORKSHEET 9** ——

Special Needs of Vulnerable Populations:
What Helpers Should Know
(12 of 13 pages)

Sight-impaired people
Vulnerabilities:

Disorientation
- By definition, sight-impaired people are unable to clearly see what is going on around them.
- Familiar exits and routes might be blocked by debris.
- Sight-impaired people may be unable to understand all the noises around them.
- Guide dogs may be fearful and unwilling or unable to assist the individual.

Displacement of and from familiar surroundings
- The disruption or movement of familiar objects can hinder the sight-impaired individual's ability to seek shelter.
- If taken to a shelter, a sight-impaired individual may be confused, disoriented, and even panicked in his or her new and unfamiliar surroundings.

Separation from social network
- Since they cannot drive a car, sight-impaired individuals may be dependent on their social networks to get them to safety.
- The social network is there to be the "eyes" for those sight-impaired people who need it.
- The social network is there to familiarize the sight-impaired individual with his or her new environment and help alleviate some of the anxiety caused by not knowing the new environment.

Normal forms of communicating
- All written forms that need to be completed by the sight-impaired person need to be put on tape or read aloud.
- Sight-impaired individuals must be read all written information that could be vital to them and their safety.
- All directions must be said to them, not pointed, or signed.

WORKSHEET 9

Special Needs of Vulnerable Populations:
What Helpers Should Know
(13 of 13 pages)

Sight-impaired people (continued)

Things to know
- Since they are used to the condition, these individuals can often help the sighted move in situations where the sighted are not able to see.

Things to do
- One of the first things helpers need to do is to familiarize the sight-impaired individual with his or her surroundings.
- Identify the sight-impaired person's needs from her or his perspective—ask, do not assume, what is needed.
- Help the sight impaired fill out important forms.
- Remember to care for the sight-impaired person's guide dog. (The dog is the person's eyes, and helps make the individual less dependent on others.)

WORKSHEET 10

What All Helpers Need to Know When Dealing With Vulnerable Populations

(1 of 2 pages)

- A helper is most effective when she or he understands the needs of the client and his or her culture. Therefore, have as much information as possible on the particular vulnerable population with which you are working, and on the culture and community in which the client is embedded.
- Have the facts concerning the disaster to share with your client—offering no information is better than offering incorrect information.
- Assess both needs and strengths (including available social support). Ask, do not assume, what is needed.
- Focus on strengths and what the client is able to do—at least initially.
- Let the client keep talking, and reflect what you hear. Use active listening to both gain information and provide support.
- Gain trust by listening first, not telling the client what to do.
- Help the client maintain a sense of control.
- Do not promise what you cannot deliver—do not offer false hope or reassurance.
- Know what is and is not your responsibility and authority.
- Have activities available for children to do.
- An important coping mechanism is to help others, so be alert to how your clients can help others.
- Know the people who might need special help evacuating their locations.
    - Help people who are members of vulnerable populations prepare for a disaster.
    - Create and know the emergency plan for your community if one does not already exist.
    - The best help comes when a plan already exists and is familiar.
    - Educate members of vulnerable populations on the importance of developing and maintaining social networks.
    - Make "Emergency Preparedness Tip Sheets" available to all.

What All Helpers Need to Know When Dealing With Vulnerable Populations
(2 of 2 pages)

- Keep in mind that different people have different needs.
- Do not focus on an individual's disability.
    - Do not portray successful people with disabilities as superhuman.
    - Do not sensationalize a disability.
    - Do not use a generic label for a disability.
    - Put people first.
    - Emphasize abilities.
- Show respect for people with disabilities.
- Avoid sudden changes in topic.
- Remember, the clients are under a lot of stress and have emotional needs, and may be overwhelmed by all that has happened.
- Know community resources and be ready to make referrals; also, provide the client with a list of resources.
- If possible, provide a timeline.
- All people need social networks.
    - They are personal support teams.
    - They can help prepare for a disaster.
    - They can help during a disaster.

WORKSHEET 11

How to Create a Social Support Network

See American Red Cross, 2003.

Recommendations a recovery worker can make to a client to help her or him develop a support network:

- ☑ Organize a support network for each location in which you spend a lot of time.*
- ☑ Make sure the people you choose for your support network are trustworthy.
- ☑ Do not depend on only one person. Make sure each area in which you spend a lot of time has a minimum of three support network people.
- ☑ Discuss your personal needs with support network people.
- ☑ Give support network members your emergency information, medical information, disability-related supplies and special equipment list, and evacuation plan.
- ☑ Ask support network members to inform you when there is a disaster, especially if you are hearing impaired and might not be able to receive the information from the news, or hear sirens.
- ☑ If needed, show support network members how to operate and safely move all your necessary equipment.
- ☑ Agree on how to contact each other if phones are not working.
- ☑ Give support network members all necessary keys.
- ☑ If you have guide animals, make sure they are familiar with the members of your support network.
- ☑ Label all your special equipment and include laminated information cards on how to use the equipment.
- ☑ Let support network members know if there is anywhere on your body where you have a reduction of feeling so they can check these areas for wounds after a disaster.
- ☑ Practice your plan with support network members.
- ☑ Choose an emergency meeting place.
- ☑ Agree upon a signal with your support network members that will let them know you are all right and have already evacuated.
- ☑ Review and revise your plan regularly.

---

* Clients who indicate they have no support may be asked why. For example, the client (1) may not recognize support that is available, (2) may not think that social support is important, (3) may be shy or lack skills necessary to access support, and so on. Each roadblock necessitates different intervention strategies.

WORKSHEET 12

Bibliography

For general sources that deal with a great many top-ics related to disaster recovery work, see:

DeWolfe, D. J. (2000). *Training manual for mental health and human service workers in major disasters* (DHHS Publication No. ADM 90-538). Washington, DC: Center for Mental Health Services. Retrieved September 9, 2003, from http://www. mentalhealth.org/publications/allpubs/ADM90-538

Lerner, M. D., Volpe, J. S., & Lindell, B. (2003). *A practical guide for crisis response in our schools* (5th ed.). New York: American Academy of Experts in Traumatic Stress.

Weaver, J. D. (1995). *Disasters: Mental health interventions.* Sarasota, FL: Professional Resource Press.

Young, M. A. (1998). *The community crisis response team training manual* (2nd ed.). Washington, DC: National Organization for Victim Assistance. Retrieved September 2, 2003, from http://www. ojp.usdoj.gov/ovc/publications/infores/crt/wel-come.html

For online sources on specific topics related to recov-ery work, such as working with pets, families, chil-dren, and people with different vulnerabilities, see:

American Academy of Child and Adolescent Psychiatry. (1998, November). *Children and grief.* Retrieved September 9, 2003, from http://www. aacap.org/publications/factsfam/grief.htm

American Psychiatric Association. [n.d.]. *Special pop-ulations.* Retrieved September 9, 2003, from http://www.psych.org/pract_of_psych/dpc_populations.cfm

American Red Cross. (2003). *Disaster preparedness for people with disabilities.* Retrieved September 9, 2003, from http://www.redcross.org/services/disaster/0,1082,0_603_,00.html.

American Red Cross. (1996). *Are you ready for a flood or a flash flood?* Retrieved September 9, 2003, from http://www.disasterrelief.org/Library/Prepare/flood.html. (Also available in Spanish.)

Coffman, S. (1996). Parents' struggles to rebuild fam-ily life after Hurricane Andrew. *Issues in Mental Health Nursing, 17,* 353–367.

Doherty, G. W. (1999). Cross-cultural counseling in disaster settings. *The Australasian Journal of Disaster and Trauma Studies, 1999–2,* 1–14. Retrieved September 9, 2003, from http://www.massey. ac.nz/~trauma/issues/1999-2/doherty.htm

Federal Emergency Management Agency. (2003, February 11). *Assisting people with disabilities in a disaster.* Retrieved September 9, 2003, from http://www.fema.gov/rrr/assistf.shtm

Federal Emergency Management Agency. (2003, February 12). *Disaster preparedness for people with disabilities.* Retrieved September 9, 2003, from http://www.fema.gov/library/disprepf.shtm

Federal Emergency Management Agency. (2003, February 11). *Helping children cope with disaster.* Retrieved September 9, 2003, from http://www. fema.gov/rrr/children.shtm

Federal Emergency Management Agency. (2003, February 12). *Pets and disasters.* Retrieved September 9, 2003, from http://www.fema.gov/library/petsf.shtm

Federal Emergency Management Agency. (2003, February 11). *Your family disaster plan*. Retrieved September 9, 2003, from http://www.fema.gov/rrr/displan.shtm.

Jackson, G., & Cook, C. G. (1999). *Disaster mental health: Crisis counseling programs for the rural community* (DHHS Publication No. SMA 99-3378). Washington, DC: U.S. Department of Health and Human Services. Retrieved September 9, 2003, from http://www.mentalhealth.org/publications/allpubs/sma99-3378/default.asp

Kansas State University Cooperative Extension Service. (1995, January). *Helping families in distress*. Retrieved September 9, 2003, from http://www.ag.uiuc.edu/~disaster/facts/famdist.html

Oriol, W. (1996). *Psychosocial issues for older adults in disasters*. Washington, DC: National Mental Health Services Knowledge Exchange Network. Retrieved September 9, 2003, from http://www.mentalhealth.org/cmhs/EmergencyServices/99-821.pdf

U.S. Department of Health and Human Services. (1996, December). *Self-care tips for emergency and disaster response workers*. Retrieved September 9, 2003, from http://www.mentalhealth.org/publications/allpubs/KEN-01-0098/

University of Illinois Extension Disaster Resources' recommended books (with short summaries) for preschool, kindergarten through grade 3, and grades 4 to 6: http://www.ag.uiuc.edu/~disaster/teacher/bib_pre.html; http://www.ag.uiuc.edu/~disaster/teacher/bib_k-3.html; and http://www.ag.uiuc.edu/~disaster/teacher/bib_4-6.html. Retrieved on September 9, 2003

The Community Disaster Plan

After studying the material in this chapter, you should

- understand the importance of disaster planning
- understand the major roadblocks to developing a community disaster plan
- be able to identify community hazards and their associated levels of risk
- be able to map your community with respect to identifiable groups in the community and to community resources
- be able to apply concepts of disaster planning and disaster education
- understand the various dimensions of a community disaster plan, and the role of testing the plan as part of its development
- be able to identify general characteristics of disaster warning and write a community warning
- understand the five phases of mobilizing community support and the necessity for integrative training of professionals
- be able to analyze disaster response efforts as the basis for revising a disaster plan
- understand the needs of those exposed to disasters and the importance of taking a culturally sensitive approach to their needs
- understand the circumstances under which a community's response to a disaster is likely to fail.

SUCCESSFUL INTERVENTION BEGINS WITH BEING PREPARED

On April 10, 1979, at 6:02 P.M., tornadoes leveled one-fifth of Wichita Falls, Texas. They destroyed 4,250 homes, injured 1,720 persons, and killed 46. More than half of those killed were in their cars, attempting to escape: They had not realized that cars are unsafe in a tornado. Others died in homes that were only slightly damaged: They had sought refuge in unsafe areas of the houses (not knowing that their basements offered the best protection). Those who escaped injury knew what to do when the tornado warning sounded: They were prepared (Scanlon, 1991).

Interestingly, within a week or so after a disaster, most unprepared communities—if they survive the first 10 days—get organized; that is, they achieve about the same level of performance as prepared communities. However, the question is whether any community can afford such a delay. In addition to the devastation caused by a disaster

during the first few days, there also may be a crisis of leadership: Will the citizens of an unprepared community that is hit by a disaster be able to sustain, or perhaps resume, their confidence in local leadership following such evidence of faulty planning?

Often, communities are inadequately prepared for a disaster because they do not realize they need to prepare. Emergency preparedness is rarely a priority for officials. Their thinking goes something like this: Disasters are uncommon, planning for one might "panic" community members, and predisaster planning costs a great deal of money. It is difficult to justify expensive preparedness planning when other more visible and immediate community issues need funding.

The lack of motivation to prepare is evident even in communities that have experienced a disaster. This may be due to the common belief that calamities never strike the same place twice, or that if the community made it through the last disaster without any special preparation, any investment in planning would be a waste. These are just some of the erroneous and dangerous positions community members and decision makers may take. But the reality tells a different story: Experience has shown and research has confirmed that disasters *do* repeat—floods and hurricanes strike the same place more than once, and bombs and shelling hit the same vicinity over and over again. Furthermore, a second disaster may be more devastating than the one that preceded it, such as occurs when floods and tidal waves follow an earthquake.

Scanlon (1991) suggested that reluctance to plan could be overcome if a leader in the community, such as the mayor or an appointed administrator, were to take the initiative. Leadership in preparedness manifests itself in four ways.

1. The community leader ensures that action is taken within the municipal structure to establish emergency plans that guarantee critical services during and after a disaster.
2. The community leader invests time and effort in gaining support for the community's political and informal leadership. Disasters may be rare, but they often have strong political impact, as was seen when New York City's Mayor Giuliani showed strong leadership in his use of that city's emergency system after of the September 11, 2001, attacks on the World Trade Center.
3. The leader supervises the development of a network of involved citizens and agencies.
4. The leader sets an example by attending key meetings, participating in exercises, and insisting that directives be followed and that plans be revised and developed according to lessons learned in other communities.

Community Hazard Analysis

Communities that plan to prepare an effective emergency contingency plan must first prepare a community hazard analysis. However, a plan that only fits a certain hazard or a specific scenario is not recommended since the purpose of a disaster plan is to be flexible enough to apply in a variety of possible events.

As a first step in hazard analysis, community planners must identify the hazards that face the community and assess the level of risk each represents (Scanlon, 1991). A hazard creates a potential for damage, and the risk associated with the hazard is determined by the way the damage is likely to be handled. For example, an unpaved road is a hazard because it creates the potential for a flat tire. The associated risk may be high if you are not prepared to handle the damage (that is, if you do not carry a spare tire and a tire jack), or it may be low if you are prepared to handle the damage (that is, if you have a spare tire and a tire jack). In a similar way, risks are greatest in an unprepared community (that is, does not have an emergency action plan) and lowest in a prepared community (that is, *does* have an effective emergency action plan).

The community members tasked with analysis begin by gathering material on potential hazards in and around the community. There are many useful techniques for gathering information, of which the following three are only examples.

First, staff members could start by gathering information on past incidents or disasters in the area. They could, for instance, look through archives of the local papers or municipality. In addition, there are numerous Web sites that offer historical accounts of a given city or location; in some cases these accounts provide expert analysis of disasters that occurred and the ways in which they were handled. Two such Web sites are the Federal Emergency Management Agency's site at www.fema.gov, and the Disaster Center's site at www.disastercenter.com.

Second, the staff members could consult experts as a source of information. They could, for instance, seek experts' advice on maps showing floodplains and high water levels, and charts that plot prevailing winds to identify potential hazards. This information could lead to an assessment of possible future incidents. The staff could also ask experts to forecast potential hazards and thereby cull useful information. Geologists, for example, can speculate on potential earthquakes, engineers can offer information on weak human-made structures, and public health officials can discuss wich immunizations people in the community have and which they need in the case of an incident.

Public awareness is a third source of information. As community members become familiar with information about potential hazards they may volunteer additional useful information. This might include information from the community on a local gas station that does not comply with rules governing the use of hazardous materials, a small chemical plant that operates illegally in a residential backyard, exposed gas cylinders, and support walls that are cracked. Information on potential hazards often provokes thought, raises awareness, and stimulates public involvement in disaster preparation—involvement that is vital for a successful preparedness plan. A clandestine community preparedness plan will not serve the community when disaster strikes.

Mapping the Community

In addition to listing hazards and evaluating risks, community leadership must map the community's diverse populations. For example, the community may contain groups of

Community Disaster Volunteer of Burbank, California

In Burbank, California, community members created the Community Disaster Volunteer (CDV), a volunteer service of the Burbank Fire Department Emergency Services Division. According to the CDV Web site (www.burbank. net/cdv), "Disaster service workers are any persons registered with the disaster council or state Office of Emergency Services (OES) to provide service without pay. Disaster service workers include public employees, registered volunteers, and persons pressed into service by persons authorized to command such services." Called into action when Burbank City is overwhelmed during and after a disaster, CDV "coordinates local volunteer CERT (Community Emergency Response Team) groups with Burbank City, LA County, and California State SEMS (Standardized Emergency Management System) organizations."

people who require special services to ensure they receive information in a timely fashion. Are there community members who speak a language other than the dominant one? If so, where do they find their information? Are there illiterate community members? How do they obtain their information? What are the sources of information for people who are hearing or sight impaired? The staff members may be able to access this information through local services. For example, officials in various departments, such as education and social and health services, should be familiar with the community's ethnic and language groups.

The staff members could gather information on community attitudes toward hazards, risk, and disasters through direct questionnaires, telephone surveys, and focus groups. These sources should provide the best information concerning how community members are likely to respond to emergencies, as well as information about the best available means for communicating with them and ensuring their cooperation in the event of a disaster.

In addition to mapping community groups, it is also important for staff to map community resources, both buildings and personnel. Where are public buildings, such as schools, that could be used for sheltering community members left homeless following a disaster? Where are voluntary humanitarian services and social clubs, and what are the best ways of contacting them? Which professionals in the community should be identified as important sources of aid (such as heavy machinery operators, health personnel, and social workers)? Not all of the potentially important community members who should be identified are part of the local services: Some might be, for example, retired social workers, military personnel, and physicians.

Developing a list of groups and individuals that could serve as resources, and knowing how to reach them, is only a first step. Community leaders must also reach out to these groups and individuals in the preparatory phase and get their agreement to participate in disaster exercises and to serve in the event of an actual disaster. To gain a wide consensus and willingness to take part in community efforts to prepare for disasters, community leaders must understand how the community perceives hazards and what the residents consider an appropriate response, should a threat develop. Scanlon (1991) recommended that large communities, which may already be using professional survey firms, piggyback a disaster study onto another project. Smaller communities may be able to use local volunteers to gather this information; for example, a high school class could take on the project of developing a questionnaire, distributing it to community members, and reporting the results.

Touching Reality "Mapping the Community" guides you in mapping your community.

Networking

Emergency planning requires broad community involvement. When planning interventions in response to disasters, large groups of people will always be involved in the decision-making process. This requires continual discussion in order to maintain agreement between the various organizations, such as school personnel, emergency teams, and government officials (Toubiana, Milgram, Strich, & Edelstein, 1988). Communities can carry out an intervention with the fewest complications when government, politicians, and organization administrators are all involved in the planning stages. Their cooperation and influence are needed to implement and direct public policy successfully.

According to FEMA Director James Witt (1997; cf. FEMA, 1996), private sector support is crucial to effective preparation. "Support from the private sector is often the weakest link in the emergency response chain for local governments....Businesses bring a wealth of experience and insight to the table, and inviting business leaders to participate in regular emergency planning meetings will give all parties a chance to get to know one another" (Witt, p. 27).

One way for community leaders to achieve community involvement is by networking. Networking has three distinct aspects. First, community leaders need to meet with rescue forces, such as the police and firefighters; local health services and psychosocial agencies; local media (television, newspaper, and radio outlets); and the education system. Second, community leaders need to break down the planning process into tasks. Third, community leaders need to assign the tasks to different groups—for example, a health committee, a social service committee, a transportation committee, and a

media relations committee. Each committee may begin work independently, but the committees eventually will need to work together (Scanlon, 1991). Burbank's CDV described above, for example, has eight committees, each of which is headed by a member of the CDV steering committee. These include a supplies committee, a safety committee, a coordinating committee, and a communications committee.

Community leaders need to build a network with adjacent authorities, because no community is immune to incidents that exceed its own resources. This process takes time but is not as complicated or difficult as might appear. It does, however, require coordination and commitment of all the communities involved and their local governments.

In some places, networking means building an interdisciplinary team with nongovernment organizations (NGOs). A good example is the emergency plan of the city of Kiryat Shmona, Israel (Kiryat Shmona Municipality Auditor, 1996). In Kiryat Shmona's plan, the emergency management team is composed of people representing psychosocial services, formal and informal education, health and sanitary services, and volunteer and humanitarian aid. Networking of this kind enables the limited human resources of the city to reach out to each of the 500 shelters, avoid duplication of services, and promote rapid response to the actual needs of the population.

Education and Public Awareness

The best emergency plan, if it is kept secret, will be very difficult to implement and operate in times of crisis. The question of public disaster education, however, has been the focal point of debates in various countries, focusing on the "frightening" issues such as biological, chemical, and nuclear warfare. The main arguments against informing and educating the public include the low probability of a disaster occurring, fear of irrational reactions, and damage to community businesses ("Who will want to do business with a community under such threats?"). Experience has shown that if prepared during times of peace and if prepared gradually, community members will respond to such information in a mature and responsible way, even to distressing information (Ben-Nesher, Lahad, & Shacham, 2002).

Disaster education, an essential part of community preparedness, aims to increase public awareness of what can happen and to enhance readiness to act according to the proposed disaster plan. In addition to using ongoing activities to educate community members, good public information planning seizes opportunities, such as unfortunate events in other places, to publicize local efforts. For example, Canada's Ontario Hydro, which runs several nuclear power plants, used the accident at the Chernobyl nuclear power plant to publicize its emergency plans.

Good public information planning also assesses the most efficient ways to reach community members. For example, APELL—a European program that, according to its Web site (www.uneptie.org/pc/apell), was "developed by UNEP [United Nations Environmental Programme] in conjunction with governments and industry with the purpose of minimizing the occurrence and harmful effects of technological accidents and environmental emergencies"—suggests that churches may be one effective way to reach community members.

Effective disaster education needs to target children, and not just with regard to issues directly related to them, such as fire drills or school evacuation, but also with regard to domestic and community hazards. Children will eventually be the community; providing disaster education for them today helps ensure a disaster-savvy community tomorrow. Children also can serve as a conduit to adults, especially to those who do not speak the community's dominant language. If children are given instruction in their classrooms, they can help educate other family members about impending hazards and the specific actions that can be taken to minimize risks. Such was the case before the 1991 Gulf War, when the Israel Ministry of Education, in collaboration with the Home Front Corps, taught schoolchildren how to use gas masks. Later, when the war started, they instructed other family members in how to use the masks (Lahad & Shacham, 1995).

Myths may be a barrier to local authorities' preparedness for disasters. Some common myths about disasters include the following:

- People exposed to disasters will be shocked, confused, and only think of themselves.
  People will panic.
- There will be looting.
- Given the size of the disaster and its potential to spread (for example, following a chemical or gas spill), or the large numbers of injured and dead, some rescue personnel will leave their posts to check on their families.
- Overall, organizations will perform better than individuals. (Dynes, Quarantelli, & Kreps, 1972; Gordon & Wraith, 1993)

The facts, based on 100 years of research (Dynes et al., 1972; Gordon & Wraith, 1993), do not support these myths:

- People exposed to disasters cope very well. Rather than being shocked and confused, the dominant immediate reaction is for people to help their families, their neighbors, and their coworkers (St. John & Fuchs, 2002).
- Panic is rare enough not to be a predictable problem. Panic is most likely when people do not have adequate information, when there is an immediate perceived threat of death or serious injury, and when there is a lack of leadership.
- Looting is rare. It is usually a phenomenon of public strife, not of disasters. Typically, crime rates fall after disasters.
- People with emergency responsibilities do not leave their posts in a disaster. In more than 500 field studies, the Disaster Research Center at the University of Delaware did not discover a single example of role abandonment (Granot, 1994).
- Organizations are at a disadvantage in disasters. Individuals can look around them, see what has to be done, and do it. Communication and transportation damage may make it impossible for organizations to act. Although ready and willing to help, organizations may not have adequate access to information or equipment (Scanlon, 1991).

These myths become dangerous when communities and organizations act on them. Fearing panic, radio stations may hesitate to issue warnings. Fearing criticism of "careless fund spending," authorities may delay the acquisition of new technology and methods. Fearing unnecessary public concern, the open exercises of emergency forces may be avoided. Fearing looting, police and armed forces may devote their resources to law and order activities. Presuming that people cannot cope, authorities may evacuate affected areas. Imagining people to be helpless, outsiders may rush to help, causing congestion. All of these actions put additional burdens on the affected community's already limited resources, resulting in wasted time, money, and human resources.

DEVELOPMENT OF A COMMUNITY DISASTER PLAN

The six initial steps in developing a community disaster plan are to

1. identify hazards and the risks associated with them
2. map the community's various populations and resources
3. assess the community's attitudes and needs
4. begin the planning process within the government
5. network to ensure broad community involvement
6. plan the public education program.

With these steps completed, work can begin on developing a community disaster plan—because, as Touching Reality "Without a Plan, Plan on Trouble" shows, "without a plan, plan on trouble."

Preparedness Options

Scanlon (1991) stated that preparedness can serve three goals: (1) to prevent disasters or their effects, (2) to warn people, and (3) to provide those exposed to disasters with an effective response. Therefore, "before undertaking a full-blown public education effort, a local government must decide which option or combination of them it will use" (Scanlon, p. 90).

To this end, Scanlon (1991) recommended that proposals should be made public before any decisions are made. The public can be told the advantages, disadvantages, and

Without a Plan, Plan on Trouble

Segment 6 on the CD, from the documentary *Hard Rain*, presents a portion of the section titled, "We're Third in Line—Main Street Tarboro." This segment was filmed at a town meeting with a representative of the Small Business Administration (SBA), who explains what the SBA can and cannot offer.

What problems do business executives in Tarboro face, and what are their main sources of confusion, frustration, and anger? How could a disaster plan have been designed to respond to their needs? How does this video segment reflect Reverend Cole's comment about Princeville: "We had no plan" (in segment 4 on the CD, "When Sorrows Come—Princeville," viewed in connection with chapter 5)?

costs of each choice, and be encouraged to come to their own conclusions. Of course, "this does not mean planning for the absurd. Although a Russian satellite has already landed in northern Canada and an American one in Australia, small communities need not plan for satellite crashes. However, genuine threats must not be ignored" (Scanlon, p. 90).

Warning the Public

For a warning to be effective, those within its range should understand it and be willing to respond accordingly. Although this seems straightforward enough, several steps are needed for those two eventualities to occur. First, the problem must be detected. Then, the danger must be calculated. Third, information must be gathered from alternative resources

and then decisions must be made about available responses. Finally, the recommended action should be activated—and only then is a public warning issued. For that process to be effective, disaster warnings must be:

- short and concise
- specific about the dangers
- specific about the steps to be taken
- specific about who is being warned
- issued by all possible sources
- based on previous education.

The following is an example of an effective warning that meets these criteria. The event is one in which people need to be warned about contaminated water resources:

Our water is contaminated. Please don't use tap water. Use only boiled water or bottled water. Water tanks will be in your neighborhood in the coming hour. Please get some containers in order to get fresh water from these water tanks. For water dispensing sites, please listen to our local radio on XYXY FM, or the community cable television, Channel XY. If you have any questions, call us at YXY-XYXY now. We will update you on any development.

For a warning to be effective it needs to be preceded by education: Community members must recognize the signs of impending threat, know what to do, know where to go, and know how to get there. This requires preplanning, exercises, and public awareness programs.

Communities often provide citizens with information about how to develop a family disaster plan, recognizing that when families are prepared for a disaster, this contributes to an effective community response. Touching Reality "How Prepared Are You for a

Disaster?" is based on a four–step disaster plan offered by the American Red Cross (2001). How prepared are you and your family for a disaster? (Chapter 8 presents a different approach to developing a family disaster plan.)

What happens when members of a community are told to evacuate. Why do some leave and some stay? The Spotlight on Research "Community Response to Warnings" describes a study of one community's reaction to being told to evacuate.

Little Red Riding Hood and the shepherd who cried "Wolf!" In fairy tales, a wolf— when there is one—symbolizes both a threat and the unknown (Lahad & Ayalon, 2002). The two predominant approaches fairy tale characters have to the wolf parallel those many community members have to the threat of a disaster. The first approach is the one taken by Little Red Riding Hood, and the second is the one taken by the shepherd who cried "Wolf!"

It is obvious that Little Red Riding Hood knows about the wolf (her mother warned her) and that she met the wolf on the way to visit her Granny. It is also clear that she knows Granny (Granny made the red hood for her, Little Red Riding Hood is going to bring Granny some food, and her familiarity is evident in her questions to the Granny-wolf). If all this is true, why does she question the wolf when she faces him, disguised as her Granny? That is, why does she not simply run away?

The Red Riding Hood approach to threats represents a common public approach to warnings: not paying attention, ignoring the danger, and playing innocent.

TOUCHING REALITY

How Prepared Are You for a Disaster?

Step 1: Find out what disasters could happen that would affect you
What are the most likely disasters to occur in your community?
What do your community's warning signals sound like?
What is the disaster plan at your workplace, at your children's school, and in your community?

Step 2: Create a disaster plan
Where will family members meet if there is a disaster?
Who is the contact person outside the family with whom everyone should "check in" if family members are separated?
How do you plan to handle family pets?

Step 3: Complete this checklist
☐ Are emergency telephone numbers listed near your phones (fire, police, ambulance, etc.)?
☐ Do the children know how and when to call 911 or the local emergency medical service?

☐ Does each family member know how and when to turn off the water, gas, and electricity at the main switches?
☐ Has each family member been trained on how to use the fire extinguisher (ABC type), and does each know where it is kept?
☐ Has a home hazard hunt been conducted?
☐ Is the disaster supplies kit stocked?
☐ Have safe places been located in the home for each type of potential disaster?

Step 4: Practice and maintain your plan
Do you quiz your children on the family disaster plan about every six months?
Do you practice fire and emergency evacuations?
Do you replace stored water and food every six months?
Do you test and recharge your fire extinguishers according to manufacturer's instructions?
Do you test smoke detectors monthly and change the batteries at least once a year?

Community Response to Warnings

Following a fire in a commercial gas farm, police, local authorities, and the media issued a warning to evacuate nearby houses. About 3,000 inhabitants evacuated the area, but 20 percent stayed in their homes. Alan Kirschenbaum (1992) studied both groups to understand the ways in which people receive a warning, accept it, and act upon it. He found that many, seeing the disaster in progress, evacuated the area before getting any official warning. The primary source of information was neighbors, who also provided support for immediate evacuation.

"The role played by immediate neighbors stresses how social networks act to selectively increase or restrict information crucial to an evacuation decision" (Kirschenbaum, p. 110). Information about the disaster and direct orders to evacuate are simply not sufficient. When official warning for evacuation is issued, a community network or community leadership must be actively involved. Neighborhood or community leaders can provide reliable information and confirm existing information about an evacuation. "They represent key figures in neighborhood social networks" (Kirschenbaum, p.111).

Kirschenbaum, A. (1992). Warning and evacuation during a mass disaster. *International Journal of Mass Emergencies and Disasters, 10*(1), 91–114.

In contrast, some members of the public cry "Wolf!" Similar to the shepherd in the story, they see shadows of sheep as wolves and are oversensitive, but when the danger is genuine, they fail to get help because they have exhausted everyone's willingness to see the threat.

The greatest problem is that Red Riding Hoods and "Cry Wolf" shepherds do not communicate very well with each other. In fact, the graver the threat the more each side competes for the approval of the "silent majority," who finds it difficult to determine the level of threat and the possibility of its realization.

Do you know any Little Red Riding Hoods? Can you point out the Cry Wolf shepherds in your community? Can you trace the ways each makes efforts to draw others to their side? Can you suggest a way to help them communicate with each other?

Volunteers

Ten months after the bombing of the Alfred P. Murrah Federal Building in Oklahoma City, data were collected on the role volunteers played in support of relief efforts immediately after the bombing. Craig St. John and Jesse Fuchs (2002) found that nearly 75 percent of those surveyed volunteered to support the relief effort in at least one way; the most common activities were giving money and donating nonprofessional goods or services. Who volunteered? The best predictors of volunteering were those who knew someone killed or injured in the bombing, those who belonged to voluntary organizations before the bombing, and those affiliated with a religious denomination. Although the outpouring of support was seen by the media as something unusual— indeed, something outstanding—St. John and Fuchs concluded that it was not extraordinary but was comparable to the levels of volunteering seen after other disasters.

The use of volunteers in disasters is of paramount importance for several reasons:

- The assumption is that there will never be enough professional helpers available so volunteers are an important part of the response capacity of the mental health teams.

- Often, the first to respond are local volunteers, due to practical setbacks such as roadblocks, curfews, or distance from the site.
- One of the factors of community resilience is the fact that "ordinary" people from the community have the knowledge and skill to help each other.
- The atmosphere of volunteering radiates a message of shared fate and responsibility from within the community and thus contributes to the community's sense of coherence.

Myers (1994) suggested that mental health agencies should integrate their disaster plans with the local emergency management plan. In particular, such agencies should identify which tasks (both disaster related and day-to-day) can be delegated to volunteers or mutual aid workers. Such jobs might include:

- clerical support, including record keeping and the compilation of statistics, typing grant applications, and answering phones
- development of educational materials, such as brochures and public service announcements
- assistance with coordinating services and logistical support for mental health staff in the field (If possible, the mental health agency should bring in a consultant or mental health disaster coordinator who has managed a large-scale disaster operation to assist the local mental health disaster coordinator.)
- assistance with grant writing
- outreach and crisis counseling at community sites
- conducting community support groups and debriefing groups for survivors and disaster workers

- training mental health and other professionals in mental health principles and interventions for disasters (An expert in the field who is experienced in disaster relief should provide this training.)

Planning and Implementing Aid for People Exposed to Disasters

Because disasters involve destruction of property, loss of life, and widespread injury, disasters cause suffering. Preparedness must take into account those who may lose their homes, loved ones, and livelihoods. Planners should pay special attention to populations with special needs and to ethnic minorities, providing for their rituals and customs. People exposed to disasters differ from those exposed to daily critical incidents in their number (there are many more exposed to a disaster than to a critical incident) and in their needs (many people may require complex help related to food, shelter, transportation, and so on). However, because so many people are sharing the same fate, the opportunity exists for people to share their problems and mutual aid.

An example of a good community plan that anticipates the many sudden needs of disaster victims is known as "one-stop shopping." Using this approach, all services are provided in one place. After the 1987 tornado in Edmonton, Alberta, local, provincial, and federal levels of the Canadian government joined forces with voluntary agencies and the private sector, took over a school, and established a service center within six hours of the disaster. In a single visit, people could collect car insurance, register for unemployment insurance, receive emotional counseling, find a new apartment, and arrange for utilities, including telephone service, for their temporary homes. The authorities were so well prepared that they let a local TV station

One-Stop Shopping: New York City's Response to the Attacks on the World Trade Center

Following the September 11, 2001, attacks on the World Trade Center, social services, such as counseling and crisis management, took place at the site of the attack, which was called Ground Zero. Because of the immense human services needs, New York City's Office of Emergency Management (OEM) brought all the city, state, federal, and private human services agencies under one roof by forming a Disaster Assistance Service Center. As the number of people seeking assistance increased, the city closed smaller assistance centers and replaced them with larger, more efficient, centers, such as the one on Pier 94.

Pier 94 became a one-stop shopping social services center, complete with people from the SBA, the Family Assistance Center, the New York State Worker's Compensation Board, the State Insurance Fund, various social services, and many insurance companies, including all of the country's largest.

"The Salvation Army was the last stop in the one-stop shopping. 'We did not want to jeopardize individuals' income or their ability to get financial assistance. By being at the end of the line The Salvation Army is able to help those people that fall through the cracks such as illegal immigrants, limousine drivers or unemployed airline workers,' said Major George Polarek, Incident Commander for The Salvation Army's World Trade Center Relief Effort" (www.salvationarmypendel.org/pr56.htm). The Salvation Army offered financial assistance for a variety of immediate needs, such as rent, utilities, insurance, and even moving and tuition costs.

follow the first family through the center. Ninety minutes later, that family left the center with the father happily displaying the key to his family's new apartment (Myers, 1994).

Homeless relief centers. Any preparedness plan should take into consideration the population likely to come to a Homeless Relief Center (HRC). HRCs should cater to all the necessities of foreseeable potential clients; thus, there should be arrangements for accommodation and care of infants, toddlers, preschool-age children, and school-age children. Similarly, there should be a special space for elderly persons and services for the special needs residents of the vicinity. The HRC staff should include, at least, food, health, education, and psychosocial services, as well as an information center and a public assistance bureau. Touching Reality "Planning a Homeless Relief Center" gives you the opportunity to plan a Homeless Relief Center.

TOUCHING REALITY

Planning a Homeless Relief Center

After reading the description of the HRC, consider this question: What needs to be planned to ensure that the HRC can handle a large number of evacuees? Then develop an outline of a plan for the following: primary health care, caring for populations with special needs, caring for young children, and meeting the needs of elderly people.

Think about activities that need to be planned for different target groups, such as young people and elderly people.

What can you do to encourage evacuees to actively participate in running the HRC?

Community Efforts to Unite Family Members

In the late 1940s, thousands of surviving Holocaust victims came to Israel from Europe. They came after years of being cut off from their loved ones and not knowing if anyone else from their family had survived. The Israeli Broadcasting Council (IBC) launched a daily radio program at to locate lost family members. Every day at the conclusion of the afternoon news, a long list of victims' names was read, with the hope of uniting them with their families. This is one of many efforts to unite family members, which now involves Web sites and other media (see: http://www.jewishgen.org/missing-identity/links.html).

Uniting family members. Because of the importance of keeping family members together and uniting those who have been separated (see chapter 9 for a discussion of interventions with families, including the importance of restoring family continuities), disaster plans need to include strategies for helping people contact relatives and find family members who may have been dispatched to different places. It may be difficult for helpers to unite family members, because most disasters knock out or temporarily disrupt transportation and communications. Movement of the injured to hospitals, the homeless to relatives, friends, and HRCs, and evacuees to shelters or, perhaps, to other countries, makes it hard for people to locate one another.

There are several simple strategies to include in a disaster plan to facilitate uniting family members:

- A disaster plan could specify centers where, after a disaster, community members could register their current location and where family members could go to learn about each other's whereabouts. Voter registration buildings, churches, HRCs, and schools could serve this purpose.
- A telephone message center could be set up where family members could leave recorded messages for family members and receive updates of their loved ones' whereabouts.
- Local TV and radio stations could broadcast a "locating missing relatives program" to help family members reunite.
- A Web site could publish pictures of missing family members with telephone numbers so that people who know of the missing person's location can contact either a family member or a central location that gathers the information.

Regardless of the specific strategy written into the disaster plan, it will work only to the extent that community members know what it is and how to use it. Therefore, for the first example, community members need to be taught that in the case of a disaster they should register at one of the predesignated locations, and, if looking for a family member, they should use the predesignated locations as places to get information.

Some victims may not be members of the community and, in planning for their needs, arrangements may need to be made to fly them to their homes. Similarly, some community members may need special care that is available only in a distant hospital. For example, when Cyclone Tracy hit Australia's northernmost city, Darwin, evacuees were flown to cities 1,800 to 2,500 miles away. In such situations, there may be technical difficulties, such as finding seats on planes, as well as misunderstandings due to different cultural expectations (Scanlon, 1991).

Testing and Updating the Plan

For a disaster plan to be effective, it is important to conduct real-life walk-throughs of emergency responses, to turn what Witt (1997) called "pencil plans" (plans that look good on paper) into reality, even if that reality is simulated. A plan works only if people become accustomed to it through exercises designed to train them and to increase their disaster awareness.

Simulations must be realistic—neither overwhelming, which conveys the message "No matter how we plan the odds are we won't be successful," nor simplistic, which conveys the message "This really isn't necessary." Disaster exercises are not games but opportunities to test the ability of local services to confront possible risks. An ideal simulation does not focus on horrible calamities; rather, it offers scenarios that could happen and that could be handled by local services or nearby communities.

The following four approaches to testing a disaster plan are effective and inexpensive.

1. A *reflective process* can be used by which individuals, services, or agencies think through their roles and functions in an incident. For example, for a test of school preparedness, a group of teachers can devise a scenario of a school disaster and "walk through" their role in different stages of the incident. In the discussions that follow, a school security attendant can review with the teachers their greatest concerns or hazards.

2. A *tabletop simulation* can be conducted in which a scenario is played out step-by-step to explore existing plans and possible developments. Participants can sit in their work groups and respond to the incident as it develops at each step. A group of disaster management leaders can conduct discussions based on responses from their respective services and the input provided by the simulation leader.

3. A *small-scale simulation* exercise can be used to expose disaster workers to a time-limited scenario (such as the first two hours after the disaster hits), an impact-limited scenario (dealing, for instance, only with injured community members), or a service-limited scenario (considering only police officers and firefighters, for example).

4. *Drills* are useful to test safety procedures. The most common are fire drills in public buildings. Fire drills work well only if they are carried out fully, for example, if buildings are actually evacuated and residents needing special help are identified.

Any of these approaches can be used to test on-site command posts and off-site emergency operations centers. Whatever approach is taken, knowledgeable and impartial outside observers must evaluate the process (Scanlon, 1991).

Putting a plan together, publicizing it, using simulations to test it, and even using it in a real disaster do not imply that the plan is finished. A plan must be revised and amended as lessons are learned from exercises, disasters, and other critical incidents. Without updating, any plan will become a "drawer plan," buried under piles of papers, and, in the end, will quickly become obsolete. Disaster plans and training need to reflect new methods that become available through development and testing; human resource changes that occur as people retire, leave the community, or join a volunteer group; and new technologies and programs. Even an excellent plan is only excellent for a particular moment in time; without testing and updating, it cannot remain excel-

Thinking about a Disaster Plan after the Disaster

In 1996, people living in Kiryat Shmona, a town in northern Israel, were evacuated to shelters because of shelling on their city. Only a small percentage of evacuees received adequate information regarding the length of their stay away from home, the equipment they had to take, or how the evacuation was going to be accomplished. Compounding the problem, no preparations were made before the evacuation—most guidance and preparation were done while the residents were in the shelters.

Upon their return home, Miri Shacham (2000) interviewed adults from the community regarding the preparations they thought necessary in their homes, schools (for their children), places of work, and shelters. Shacham also asked who they thought should be providing support.

Women and men differed in the order of their preferences for support. Women preferred support from, first, the municipality (local authority) to look after the shelters, provide information, and help them to evacuate. Second, they wanted support from the army to cater to their needs in the shelters, including preparing and maintaining the shelters and, if needed, providing food and other necessities.

Third was the government, which they said should compensate them for any losses, such as lost wages. Last, they saw themselves as a source of support.

The order for males was, as for women, the municipality first; after that, however, they preferred themselves, then the army, and, last, the government. This might reflect the men's greater confidence in their own ability to handle the situation. Importantly, the men had greater confidence in the ability of residents themselves to make the necessary preparations.

People of all ages indicated that the municipality comes first as a source of support. Those over 50 who were interviewed, compared with younger evacuees, preferred the government and the army as support sources. Shacham (2000) speculated that they may be adhering to the Israeli saying that "the State will take care of me."

The conclusion of this study points to two things: First, the important role of the local authority in the preparation for and mitigation of disasters and, second, the importance of public education to reduce dependency on local services.

Shacham, M. (2000). *Stress reactions and coping resources mobilized by evacuees (adults and children) and the adults' perception of needed future preparatory measures.* Unpublished doctoral dissertation, Anglia Polytechnic University.

lent. Spotlight on Research "Thinking about a Disaster Plan after the Disaster" presents the results of interviews with evacuees who were unprepared for their evacuation and their thoughts about what needed to be planned.

THE COMMUNITY MODEL

"In 1979, President Jimmy Carter ordered the creation of FEMA, the first major step toward implementing a coherent strategy, dubbed Comprehensive Emergency Management (CEM), recommended in an elaborate study by the National Governors' Association (NGA)" (Crichlow, 1997, paragraph 29). CEM deals with emergency management in four phases—(1) mitigation, (2) preparedness and planning, (3) response, and (4) recovery—and "views the process as a cycle, with all communities standing at some point in the process at any given time. Communities most often are in the mitigation and preparedness phases" (Crichlow, paragraph 39) The lynchpin in the process is the community: Without community mitigation and preparedness, help from federal agencies cannot be sufficient. As is true of politics, all disasters are (at least initially), local.

The first to respond to any disaster are normally inhabitants from the near vicinity (Quarantelli & Dynes, 1977). Regardless, helpers and officials from outside the community sometimes find it hard to accept the fact that the community has strengths, resources, and abilities; in short, that the local community is resilient. In the end, local forces usually are pushed aside. Surrendering control to people from outside the community, however, may make local people passive.

Results of a survey by Ben-Nesher, Lahad, and Shacham (2002) of several communities where armed conflict could occur at any moment, indicated that community members would like to be more actively involved in times of stress. With help, communities—including all their members—can develop resilience and the ability to cope with terrible events and their long-term effects.

Mobilizing Community Efforts

Figure 12-1 outlines several types of help needed after a disaster and the community groups that may serve as helpers.

This chart fails to stress, however, the variety of helpers and help groups that arise spontaneously, whether to provide financial

FIGURE 12-1. HELP NEEDED AND POTENTIAL HELPERS

Information	Media, local authorities, emergency services
Education	Teachers, informal education staff
Counseling	School counselors, school psychologists, religious representatives
Recreation	Community center staff, artists, sports instructors, youth organization staff, volunteers
Mental health	Clinical psychologists, school psychologists, religious representatives, nurses, help-lines
Social support	Social services, volunteer organizations, help-lines
Shelter	Local authorities, social services, volunteer organizations

help to the neighborhood family hardest hit by the hurricane, or to help with cleaning and repairing the local business destroyed by terrorists. For example, individuals from Oklahoma City and surrounding areas showed an immediate outpouring of support for victims of the 1995 bombing of the Murrah Building: People came to the area with food, to donate blood, and to offer free counseling services (St. John & Fuchs, 2002). People seemed to need, as well as want, to be part of the response to the disaster.

The problem is that it is impossible to predict, plan for, and rely on spontaneous action.

Terrorist Attack in Tel Aviv

An effective community support system evolved spontaneously within Israel's national bus company, Egged, following a terrorist attack on a tour bus near Tel Aviv in 1978. The bus was hijacked and a bomb detonated, killing or wounding 36 passengers, 18 of whom were the company's employees and family members.

Egged, which took full responsibility for the care of the victims as a reflection of the company's "community spirit," operated two support systems: a spontaneous, informal one and a professional one. The interventions reflected the special needs of the survivors:

- Volunteers maintained a vigil over the wounded and the bereaved for the first few days and nights.
- Professional helpers absorbed the psychological shock and contained all forms of the victims' and relatives' emotional expression, including outbursts of anger and grief.
- Egged management reassured survivors that in spite of any injuries and handicaps, their positions in the company were secure. This empowered the victims and reduced possible feelings of rejection and alienation.
- During the first week or two after the disaster, company volunteers performed several roles, as required by the size and suddenness of the disaster. They prepared lists of victims, identified bodies, notified the families and helped them through their mourning, sent the wounded to hospitals and followed up with their convalescence, mediated between family members and the wounded, and took care of their immediate financial needs. The volunteers served as a bridge between the victims and their families and wider social system, and later between the victims and the welfare and education agencies. (Ayalon, 1993)

- Professional expertise and humane devotion were evident in the care of the afflicted children. Supervised by the company psychologist, volunteers took on parental roles for children whose parents had been killed or wounded. In these roles, they helped to work through the agony of mourning, offering support and affection, fostering a sense of stability by spending time with the child, celebrating birthdays, and so forth. They tried to help children dissipate the trauma and distracted them by means of play, storytelling, and artistic expression. The volunteers also bridged the gap between the children and their families and between social and educational groups, a gap created by physical distance, the time of separation, and the traumatic experience.
- Posttraumatic intervention also was provided to those whose injuries were not physically apparent. Those who suffer "invisible wounds" are usually the most neglected among trauma victims. The individual and group posttraumatic interventions focused on dissipating survivors' guilt, accepting regressive behavior and increased dependency, and rechanneling aggression and anger. The bus company's therapy team reached out to other psychosocial agents (doctors and teachers) to explain concepts unfamiliar at that time, such as "survivor syndrome," which is the damage to personal, sexual, or professional identity. They tried to minimize the hazard of secondary victimization, which haunts victims of human tragedies.

The feeling among bus company employees was that, "It could have happened to me." Everyone felt vulnerable, so the support that they provided to the victims was also a form of self-aid, a means to overcome this latent threat.

It is risky to rely on spontaneous efforts; the better approach is to involve the community in preparing for a disaster. The Community Stress Prevention Center, located in northern Israel, developed a model useful for facilitating community involvement in preparing for disasters (Lahad & Shacham, 1995). The model has five phases.

Phase 1: During this phase, planners meet with local authorities and people in key community positions, from the mayor to the switchboard service operator. The goals of these meetings are to raise community awareness and to discuss basic training of local authorities. Contingency plans are developed that cover the knowledge and training are necessary, and what probable scenarios are likely to be most useful in simulations.

Phase 2: The second phase involves a synergic effort of all municipal services to develop their contingency plans and map possible human resources to assist them in times of disaster. During this phase, planners stress the notion that the public is a resource, not an opponent or an obstacle. Local services are encouraged to recruit volunteers to their emergency team.

Phase 3: The third phase focuses on interdisciplinary training of psychosocial and education teams. Planners form teams based on neighborhoods or quarters, and the head of each team is a school principal or a community center manager. Professional and nonprofessional team members are trained to handle acute stress reactions and, at the same time, to activate community resources, that is, to recruit and train local people for a variety of jobs, such as staffing an information center, dispensing food, and managing a shelter.

Phase 4: Using various in vivo exercises, planners in this phase focus on training teams and volunteers to work together. Discussions of lessons learned from the exercises, togeth-

er with briefings, help ensure effective team coordination. This phase also focuses on public education and readiness, and includes exercises with the public combined with meetings with specific groups, such as parents, hospital personnel, and elderly community members.

Phase 5: The final phase uses community meetings to raise community members' awareness (as in the first phase), to commend volunteers, and to raise public self-confidence as a "self-sufficient" community.

The Community Stress Prevention Center model stresses that no single service and no single team can provide all the help needed in the wake of a critical incident; coordination of teams and committees is essential. Therefore, the model requires psychosocial, educational, community, and medical services to operate under one coordinating committee. The community's director of social services usually heads this committee and serves as a consultant to the crisis management team with regard to the major psychosocial aspects of the disaster.

Emergency Intervention with Multidisciplinary Teams

When disaster strikes, the coordinating committee dispatches psychosocial and medical response teams to affected areas. The first teams on site assess the situation and provide immediate support to the affected population. This support may include providing food, shelter, and medical and psychological support; opening information and relief centers; taking charge of evacuation centers; and dispatching representatives to hospitals to help when patients or their relatives need assistance (for example, helping them secure lodging, find relatives, or obtain emergency funding). Psychosocial teams, working as part of this coordinating committee, also take charge of locating and providing help and support to people with special needs.

With the help of volunteers, the coordinating committee also supports people affected by the disaster, but who are less immediately vulnerable. Those in the center circles of vulnerability for physical, psychological or social, prior experience, or support vulnerability are most at risk—they may be hurt, or they may have witnessed death and destruction first hand. Nevertheless, those in peripheral circles—those who may know someone who was hurt or killed, or those who heard but did not see the destruction—also are vulnerable and require attention. (See chapter 2 for a discussion of the circles of vulnerability.)

Perhaps the most difficult jobs are to provide help and support at the site of the disaster and at a mortuary, in the event of casualties. Response team members—social workers, psychologists, and nurses—escort relatives throughout the terrible process of identifying the deceased and follow up during the mourning period, visiting at home and ensuring continuity of help from other local services.

Training Professionals

To ensure an effective response to a disaster, planners must provide special training for small groups of professionals. These professionals may be hospital social workers who will work with the families of the injured and deceased, response team personnel who deal with the process of identifying bodies, members of integrated teams that work for the mortuary, or psychosocial notification teams who inform families that their loved ones are dead.

Why do these professionals need integrated and specific training? Rosenfeld, Lahad, and Cohen (2001) suggested four answers to this question:

1. The disaster situation is extraordinary, and typical training for psychosocial professionals does not include working in the chaos following a disaster. Training that stresses psychological processes, such as insight and transference, is difficult to use in a crisis.
2. Integration among different psychosocial services is rare, presumably because each follows its own principles, models, and theories. It also is uncommon for the different services to be called upon to work together; it is more common for them to compete—which would interfere with disaster response efforts.
3. Disaster response requires being active, directive, and specific—similar to the battlefield medicine practiced in MASH units. The setting, pace, and need for interventions on the order of "triage" are alien to most community health and social work professionals.
4. When a professional works outside the familiar clinic and office—with its predictable "50-minute" hour—he or she can be overwhelmed by the forbidding experience, without prior training.

The training psychosocial professionals receive to help them respond effectively to a disaster depends on the community and the needs identified by local groups. Training topics may include mental first aid, nonpathological terminology, and insight into how individuals and families are likely to perceive the world during and after a disaster. Techniques taught might include pacing and leading, bridging continuities, information formulation, group interventions, identifying leadership in a crowd, and communicating with traumatized people. Other topics might include family crisis–intervention techniques, bereavement counseling, and the use of nonprofessionals and volunteers.

LEARNING FROM EXPERIENCE: REVISITING THE DISASTER PLAN

Certainly, experience is the best teacher. The best plans, the best predisaster simulated tests of those plans, and the most thoughtful reviews pale next to the information gleaned from experience. Therefore, after a disaster, the question that needs to be answered is, How well did the disaster plan work? With an answer to this question, adjustments can be made to the community's disaster plan to ensure a more effective response to the next crisis.

Consider the lessons learned from these experiences:

- In the summer of 1981, the northern Israeli town of Kiryat Shmona was under fire for 10 days. The attack that started just before the Jewish Sabbath. Many families in this traditional community had no food because their religious beliefs prohibit them from cooking on the Sabbath. Electricity was cut off by a direct hit and fresh food left in refrigerators was soon inedible in the summer heat.

  On Sunday (almost 48 hours later), local authorities planned to distribute food and mattresses to people who could not leave the shelters because they were still under attack. The distribution was made, albeit without suitable notification and without considering the distress of the inhabitants. Contrary to the authorities' expectations, nearly all the food and mattresses were taken by the inhabitants of the first few shelters at the beginning of the street, leaving those further away (at the other end of the street) with little food and no mattresses.

  Not only did the authorities fail to convey the message to those farther away that someone cared about them and that they would soon have food, they caused tension between those who received food and mattresses and those who did not, tcreating unrest in an otherwise cohesive neighborhood.

- In January 1992, local authorities in a large city in Israel received a warning from the National Meteorology Center that a hurricane was expected that night. After a brief discussion and contrary to experts' advice, the authorities decided not to warn the public of the possibility of heavy rains that might cause flooding. They supported this decision with claims that panic might follow such an announcement, as well as public embarrassment if the prediction was wrong. The result was flooded homes, people in search of help in the dark, loss of property, feelings of abandonment, and local authority services having to operate under extremely unfavorable conditions. In addition, authorities spent a huge sum of money for the victims' hotel accommodations, transportation, and loss of wages.

- On October 21, 1988, the cruise ship Jupiter set sail from Athens with about 400 British students—from 20 different schools—and their teachers. It was struck by an Italian tanker (chapter 3 presents a Spotlight on Research focused on this disaster). Without a group or person with the authority to coordinate responses to the traumatized children, some schools supported the quick organization of mental health teams, and other schools decided not to pursue help until nearly a year later. In his comparison of the different approaches, Yule (1992) found that children in the schools that pursued immediate help fared better than those in schools choosing to wait.

Moving a Communtiy from Crisis to Change

Following a series of disasters that hit one community in the north of Israel, in which authorities had noted a great deal of rivalry and overlapping among helping services, these authorities decided to examine the coordination among the different helping agents and services and to train for better coordination. Ofra Ayalon (1993) conducted a simulation as part of in-service disaster training for the disaster relief helpers.

Ayalon (1993) arranged a multidisciplinary meeting under the auspices of the Training Division of the National Insurance Institute. The purpose of the meeting was to examine the operations of the system in stress situations, identify the weak links in the system, and set up a model for interorganizational cooperation. The prerequisites for the implementation of this model were that there be motivation to change the set operational patterns and motiviation to develop trust among the workers among each service and among the various services. She chose two methods to achieve these objectives: (1) simulation of situations through role-playing and (2) group dynamics in mixed teams.

Simulation exercises create conditions for learning through experience and allow on-the-spot assessments of the results. Simulation exercises can serve as preparation for anticipated stress situations, as training for dealing with unusual situations, and as a way of relieving postdisaster stress.

The participants from the service agencies were presented with scenarios involving different victims of hostile action then and to present their programs for the care they would provide. Meeting facilitators posed the following questions:

1. What would be your reaction to the urgency of the situation?
2. According to the procedures of your service, who would be the object of assistance?
3. What would be your area of assistance and what would be your priorities?
4. Would you apply to another service for assistance? If so, under what conditions and at what stage of care?
5. Who should be responsible for assistance and for seeking possible assistance from the community?

The responses revealed diverse solutions and approaches among the different services. In addition, the varied approaches of the caregiving services stressed the assumed centrality of each representative's service. The facilitators then led discussions about conflict in implementation and lack of coordination to demonstrate the problematic nature of a situation involving a number of care-providing agencies who were all giving assistance to a family in an emergency situation.

This exercise showed the dangers inherent in the lack of cooperation and coordination among services. Accordingly, this community adopted a new policy to avoid overlapping services, contradictory plans, disagreements about the type of approach that be used (for example, clinical versus psychoeducational), and rivalries among the adults working together.

Ayalon, O. (1993). Posttraumatic stress recovery of terrorist survivors. In J. P. Wilson & B. Raphael (Eds.), *International handbook of traumatic stress syndromes* (pp. 855–866). New York: Plenum Press.

Spotlight on Research "Moving a Community from Crisis to Change" presents the results of one community's evaluation of its disaster plan after a series of disasters—an evaluation that revealed each response group's assumption of its own importance.

The Emergency Behavior Officer

Postdisaster analyses—what went right, what went wrong, and what needs to be changed next time—often highlight decision makers' lack of training in understanding the needs of the public when responding to a disaster. Sometimes decision makers, such as mayors and chiefs of police, think of community members as "helpless children" ("They'll just panic if we tell them about possible floods, so we'd better not tell them!"), or as unimportant to take into account ("Why bother telling them how we'll distribute mattresses and food? Let's just do it."), or perhaps as uninformed and unable to help ("Why bother getting information from child and school psychologists about whether help should be offered to the children immediately or later?").

Most, if not all, communities need to have an expert in the behavioral sciences to act as a consultant to decision makers. This consultant would serve as an emergency behavior officer, trained in the behavioral sciences and able to give advice to community leaders in predisaster intervention, as well as during and after the disaster. The emergency behavior officer can answer questions such as:

- How will community members—children, adults, and people with special needs—react to the disaster?
- What are alternative courses of action?
- How could we enhance community members' ability to cope?

- How should decision makers communicate with the public?
- How could the media be a source of support?

Each community is unique, and regardless of the training an emergency behavior officer receives, in the final analysis it must reflect the particular needs of the community. A manual for training emergency behavior officers by Lahad, Cohen, and Peled (1995), however, stressed that, while every community is distinct, much of what the emergency behavior officer needs to know about human behavior in disaster situations is applicable to every community.

The Disaster Media Consultant

Postdisaster analyses focus attention on one of the emergency behavior officer's important jobs: to work with the media. The requirements of this aspect of the job are large, and it may be necessary for someone in the community to work with the emergency behavior officer as a disaster media consultant. Research by Pfefferbaum (2001) and Morland (2000) provided empirical evidence—although the accumulation of anecdotal evidence is sufficient—that viewing a disaster on television can itself be traumatizing, especially to children.

It may be difficult, if not impossible, to influence national and international television stations to serve as a positive force in responding to a disaster (to cease repeated showings of disaster images, for instance), but this is not the case with local media. Local radio and cable television stations tend to focus on local news and issues, and so may be more sensitive and attentive to the community's needs. In a disaster situation, local media can help by providing specific information, answering questions from community members, broadcasting interviews with local people and disaster relief leaders, increasing confidence, and offering encouragement. (Chapter 13 presents an analysis of the media's role in disaster preparation and response, as well as how to work effectively with the various media.)

A disaster media consultant—trained in the behavioral sciences, as is the emergency behavior officer—can help local media present news in a way that facilitates disaster response. This could include offering advice on wording and programming, and assisting on-air personnel when terrible news is first disclosed (Lahad, 1996). The disaster media consultant also can train local television and radio personnel to develop programs for different target audiences, such as young children, adolescents, and adults, and how to present directions and information objectively. Impor-tantly, the disaster media consultant can help those who control local media to understand viewers' ability to cope with what the media present, how victims and their relatives are likely to think and feel after a disaster, and how people with different developmental needs and people of different ages comprehend messages.

Community Crisis Response

The U.S. Department of Justice Office for Victims of Crimes (OVC) established the Community Crisis Response (CCR) program to improve services for victims of violent crime in which there are multiple victims (Poland & McCormick, 1999). Direct assistance and training is available to communities that have been significantly affected by criminal incidents by funding "individuals or teams of trained responders to assist victims through debriefings and training in the aftermath of [severe crises]"

(Poland & McCormick, p. 142). For example, the CCR program provided assistance after the 1995 bombing of the Murrah Building in Oklahoma City by dispatching a nine-member CCR team the day of the blast. The CCR "funded crisis response teams that provided training and debriefings for thousands of [Oklahoma City] school children, teachers, and medical emergency personnel" (Poland & McCormick, p. 142).

Requests for CCR assistance can be obtained from the OVC Web site: http://www.ojp.usdoj.gov/ovc/publications/factshts/ccr/welcome.html.

Victims' Advocates

As discussed primarily in chapters 3 and 4, people exposed to disasters often are confused, bewildered, and emotionally and financially broken. To respond to these and other needs, a victims' advocate service is available in most U.S. communities, and is usually connected with the local prosecutor's office (Poland & McCormick, 1999). Although the specific services available vary by state, funding is available to assist the family members of victims in many ways.

A victims' advocate coordinates services for victims' families and explains their rights during a crisis or in situations where there is substantial crime. The victims' advocate supports families through any legal process and, if needed, takes care of practical issues, such as payment of medical bills, making mental health referrals, and assisting with day-to-day living concerns.

WHEN A COMMUNITY DISASTER PLAN FAILS

The double ABCX model (McCubbin & Patterson, 1983), described in chapter 4, emphasized that stressors rarely come one at a time, in a manageable and orderly fashion; they usually come in groups, causing a "pileup" of stressors. If the pileup continues, the family's resources are increasingly depleted and, finally, the family may cease to function. Although McCubbin and Patterson did not extend the model to the community level, the extension is an obvious one: The failure of a community to cope with a disaster is often caused by an accumulation of stressors—pileup at the community level. Ayalon (1983) described this process as the "snowball effect": Confronted by a disaster, a weak social system's resources for coping, insufficient from the outset, are depleted.

Prolonged economic, cultural, and social deprivation generates the characteristic traits of underprivileged communities: lack of leadership and cohesion, lack of community organization, insufficient communication within the group and with outside government agencies, and lack of autonomy in their approach to problem solving. Under these conditions, community disaster plans are likely to fail.

SUMMARY

This chapter focuses on community preparedness and organization as ways to mitigate disasters. By being well organized and well prepared—by having a community disaster plan—a community can help ensure that it will move from destruction to recovery. By no means, however, is this community plan meant to replace or underestimate the responsibility of every organization and family in the community to take an active part in disaster preparedness and the recovery efforts.

Authorities must test plans in a variety of simulations involving local services and the public. They must evaluate and revise these plans periodically, even if the plans are put to the test in a real disaster and are found to be effective.

Once disaster strikes, it is necessary to care for a variety of physical and emotional needs of the victims. When developing a plan to achieve this goal, it is important to keep in mind that communities have resources and capabilities to tap, and that overlooking them ignores a fundamental principle of community preparedness: to help community members to help themselves.

REFERENCES

American Red Cross. (2001). Family disaster planning. Retrieved September 13, 2003, from http://www.seattleredcross.org/disaster/familyplan/index.htm

Ayalon, O. (1983). Coping with terrorism. In D. Meichenbaum & M. Jaremko (Eds.) *Stress reduction and prevention* (pp. 293–339). New York: Plenum Press.

Ayalon, O. (1993). Posttraumatic stress recovery of terrorist survivors. In J. P. Wilson & B. Raphael (Eds.). *International handbook of traumatic stress syndromes* (pp. 855–866). New York: Plenum Press.

Ben-Nesher, U., Lahad, M., & Shacham, Y. (2002, August). *Study of community perception of resiliency: Hygienic and motivational factors.* Karmiel, Israel: Ministry of Welfare.

Crichlow, D. (1997, June 1). Taking a comprehensive approach to handling disasters. *American City & County.* Retrieved September 13, 2003, from http://americancityandcounty.com/ar/government_taking_comprehensive_approach

Dynes, R. R., Quarantelli, E. L., & Kreps, G. (1972, February). When disaster strikes (it isn't much like what you've heard and read about). *Psychology Today, 5,* 66–70.

Federal Emergency Management Agency. (1996). *Report on costs and benefits of natural hazard mitigation.* Washington, DC: Author. Retrieved September 13, 2003, from http://www.fema. gov/pdf/library/haz_cost.pdf

Gordon, R., & Wraith, R. (1993). Responses of children and adolescents to disaster. In J. P. Wilson & B. Raphael (Eds.), *International handbook of traumatic stress syndromes* (535–657). New York: Plenum Press.

Granot, H. (1994). *The golden hour: Individual and community in emergencies.* Tel Aviv, Israel: Dekel Academic Press.

Kirschenbaum, A. (1992). Warning and evacuation during a mass disaster. *International Journal of Mass Emergencies and Disasters, 10*(1), 91–114.

Kiryat Shmona Municipality Auditor. (1996). *Report on operation Grapes of Wrath: Lessons learned.* (Available from the Municipality Auditor, Kiryat Shmona, Israel.)

Lahad, M. (1996). Local media in disaster. *Da-Melach: The Journal of the Israeli High Commission for Emergency Planning 9*, 16–18, 37.

Lahad, M., & Ayalon, O. (2002). *A community from destruction to recovery.* Kiryat Shmona, Israel: Community Stress Prevention Center. (Hebrew)

Lahad, M., Cohen, A., & Peled, D. (1995). *Emergency Behaviour Officer training manual.* Ramart Gan, Israel: Defense Military Consultants.

Lahad, M., & Shacham, S. (1995, June). *A model for preparing a community to deal with disaster. A manual for MELACH (Israel Emergency Economy Authority).* Jerusalem: Ministry of the Interior. (Hebrew)

McCubbin, H. I., & Patterson, J. M. (1983). The Family Stress Process: The Double ABCX Model of adjustment and adaptation. *Marriage and Family Review, 6*, 7–37.

Morland, L. A. (2000). The Oklahoma City bombing: An examination of the relationship between exposure to bomb-related television and post-traumatic stress symptoms following a disaster. *Dissertation Abstracts International, 60*, 4239.

Myers, D. (1994). *Disaster response and recovery: A handbook for mental health professionals* (DHHS Publication 94-3010). Rockville, MD: U.S. Department of Health and Human Services, Center for Mental Health Services.

Pfefferbaum, B. (2001). The impact of the Oklahoma City bombing on children in the community. *Military Medicine, 166*(12, Suppl. 2), 49–50.

Poland, S., & McCormick, J. S. (1999). *Coping with crisis: Lessons learned.* Longmont, CO: Sopris West.

Quarantelli, E .L., & Dynes, R. R. (1977). Response to social crisis and disaster. *Annual Review of Sociology, 3*, 23–49.

Rosenfeld, L. B., Lahad, M., & Cohen, A. (2001). Disaster, trauma, and children's resilience: A community response perspective. In J. M. Richman & M. W. Fraser (Eds.), *Children, families and disasters: A risk and resiliency perspective* (pp. 133–185). Westport, CT: Greenwood Press.

Scanlon T. G. (1991). Reaching out: Getting the community involved in preparedness. In T. E. Drabek & G. J. Hoetmeter (Eds.), *Emergency management: Principals and practice for local government* (pp. 79–99). Washington DC: International City/County Management Association (ICMA).

Shacham, M. (2000). *Stress reactions and coping resources mobilized by evacuees (adults and children) and the adults' perception of needed future preparatory measures.* Unpublished doctoral dissertation, Anglia Polytechnic University, Chelmsford, UK.

St. John, C., & Fuchs, J. (2002). The heartland responds to terror: Volunteering after the bombing of the Murrah Federal Building. *Social Science Quarterly, 83*, 397–415.

Toubiana, Y. H., Milgram, N. A., Strich, Y., & Edelstein, A. (1988). Crisis intervention in a school community disaster: Principles and practices. *Journal of Community Psychology, 16,* 228–240.

Witt, J. L. (1997). Creating the disaster-resistant community. *American City & County, 112*(1), 23–28.

Yule, W. (1992). Post-traumatic stress disorder in child survivors of shipping disasters: The sinking of the "Jupiter." *Psychotherapy and Psychosomatics, 57,* 200–205.

DISASTERS AND THE MEDIA*

* Katherine T. Loflin contributed this chapter. She is the Content Program Officer for Civic Engagement, the John S. and James L. Knight Foundation, Miami, FL.

- understand the role of the media in disaster preparedness and response
- understand the principles and goals that guide the development and implementation of a crisis communication plan
- be able to describe the elements of a crisis communication plan
- understand how the media cover a disaster, including the activities they use to gather information
- recognize the importance of working with, not against, the media to ensure that the most accurate and timely information is communicated to the public
- understand the benefits and drawbacks of different interview situations, including live, taped, print, and radio interviews
- be able to anticipate the kinds of questions likely to be asked in an interview
- be able to develop a plan for responding to anticipated questions in an interview
- be able to speak in "sound bites" to facilitate a reporter's developing his or her story, and to ensure that the message you want to communicate is communicated
- understand and be able to implement a procedure for practicing for an interview.

Often, plans guiding crisis communication and media relations are overlooked and underdeveloped parts of a disaster response strategy. It may appear to be a misuse of finite resources for a disaster helper to expend efforts to interact with the media: Surely, workers' efforts should be directed to providing food to hungry people, shelter to homeless people, medical aid to hurt people, and counseling to traumatized people. However, given the power of the media to shape perceptions and to serve as an ally in recovery efforts, an integral part of a disaster response plan should be creating a crisis communication plan and developing media relations skills.

This chapter addresses the importance of working with the media during and after a disaster, establishing a useful crisis communication plan, developing media relations skills, and minimizing coverage that inflicts further damage on communities. Productive press relations are an important part of successful disaster recovery, and this chapter is a guide to developing and navigating that relationship.

THE MEDIA'S ROLE IN DISASTERS

The media are critical for facilitating predisaster preparedness, disseminating warning messages of pending disasters, providing information to citizens about a disaster, and facilitating recovery efforts (Elliot, 1980). A study by the Roper organization (Broadcasting & Cable Yearbook, 1995) indicated that more than 70 percent of the U.S. public relies on television as its primary source of news. During Hurricane Danny in 1997, for example, a survey of people in the affected area showed that the majority cited the local media as their primary source of information about the disaster (Piotrowski & Armstrong, 1998).

Moreover, the media can affect perceptions (Faberman, 1999; McCombs & Shaw, 1993), public opinion (Iyengar & Kinder, 1987; McCombs & Shaw), stress reactions (Morland, 2000; Pfefferbaum, 2001), depression and PTSD (Saylor, Cowart, Lipovsky, Jackson, & Finch, 2003; Ahern et al., 2002), and coping responses of communities (Lahad, 1997). The first few stories filed by the media set the tone for how they view a disaster plan's effectiveness and can affect the entire disaster and recovery effort (Berry, 1999). Media audiences learn more than facts from the news; they also learn about the importance of topics based on how the news media emphasize those topics (McCombs & Reynolds, 2002). If a disaster response team responds slowly or not at all to the media, their inaction may be viewed and reported as unpreparedness, incompetence, or a lack of responsibility (Moskovitz, 1999).

It is crucial for the disaster response team to provide information to a disaster-struck community to deescalate the crisis and reestablish calm (Barry McLoughlin Associates, 1996f; Ross, 2003). The team needs to disseminate timely and accurate information to save lives and minimize damage; the media play a key role in transmitting this information to the public (Hernandez, 1994). Furthermore, information may enhance coping (see the discussion of coping in chapter 2). Coping styles usually include a cognition component (information, rules, and planning), in which an increase in the amount of knowledge about a situation corresponds to improved coping (Lahad, 1997; Milgram, Sarason, Schoenpflug, Jackson & Schwarzer, 1995). In this sense, information is power. Therefore, proper information dissemination through the media should be a top priority for a disaster response team.

Regardless of the amount of information available, the media must report a disaster. Even though they know they should not report rumors, gossip, or hearsay, they have obligations and pressures from the community to report the story. Therefore, an official decision not to provide information or interviews does not stop media coverage or kill a story. Without factual accounts

Oklahoma City: Critique of Initial Media Coverage

On April 19, 1995, a bomb that shook the ground as far as 20 miles from the point of detonation destroyed the Alfred P. Murrah Federal Building in Oklahoma City, along with this country's sense of internal security. It was several days before the public knew definitively how many lives had been lost in the blast, and even longer for them to learn about the countless injured being treated at hospitals. However, the media had an obligation to begin reporting the story immediately, propelling this complex disaster into the national spotlight.

Later that year, at the conference of the Association for Education in Journalism and Mass Communication in Washington, DC, professionals, educators, and students attended a panel discussion of media coverage of the bombing. As part of the panel, Robert G. Picard, of the Department of Communication at California State University at Fullerton, specifically addressed initial news media coverage that not only characterized the disaster but also set the tone for recovery (Hernandez, 1995).

Picard praised the straightforward, event-oriented coverage of the bombing. However, he also pointed out that the media had primarily interviewed experts in Middle East terrorism, which fueled speculation that the bombing was a foreign terrorist act (Hernandez, 1995). In turn, there was a documented willingness nationwide to believe the speculation that the bombing was indeed a foreign terrorist act.

For the most part, however, Picard praised the coverage and told the conference that the media had emphasized the restoration of public order by reporting a strong, appropriate, and immediate response from officials, and by publicizing the establishment of security nets, they conveyed the message that the situation was under control (Hernandez, 1995). Media stories of heroism, poignant photos, and stories told by survivors suggested the message of "good emerging from bad," which helped the community and the nation recover.

from credible sources, the media become more reliant on speculation, rumors, unsubstantiated comments, and eyewitness accounts (Barry McLoughlin Associates, 1996b, 1996f), all of which are likely to hurt community recovery.

Cooperating with the media as soon as possible after a disaster creates the opportunity to fill airtime with accurate and reliable information—no matter how little information is available at first. Disaster response teams should provide reliable information to the media not only as soon as possible, but also in a concise and readily understandable form (Hernandez, 1994). By doing so, the relationship with the media is transformed from adversary to partner.

Through this partnership, the media can do many things before, during, and after a disaster. The media can

- assist in predisaster education
- enhance the credibility and perceived competence of the authorities and disaster response team
- warn the community of an impending disaster
- disseminate information to the public quickly
- reassure the public
- refute rumors
- provide evacuation information
- inform the public on how to access emergency funds and insurance benefits
- broadcast requests for volunteers, food, funds, and supplies. (Barry McLoughlin Associates, 1996f)

These services, which are primarily the responsibility of the disaster response team, could not be accomplished—or could not be accomplished as effectively—without the assistance of the media.

CRISIS COMMUNICATION PLAN

Communication is essential to any disaster response plan. A crisis communication plan provides a strategy for a disaster response team to deal with the media, including the steps that it must take, the rules it must follow, who should serve as spokesperson and other key experts, jobs to be carried out, and a chain of command. Similar to other components of a disaster response plan, the disaster response team must prepare the crisis communication plan before the disaster. It is too late to create such a plan after a disaster occurs, when emotions and stress are running high. The crisis communication plan enables the disaster response team to accomplish important tasks under the extreme stress of a disaster (Zoch & Duhé, 1997).

Most effective crisis communication plans are based on five principles, each of which has been established through the trial and error of developing and implementing plans in response to a variety of disasters (Barry McLoughlin Associates, 1996c). The five principles are as follows:

1. *Disseminate information responsibly.* Without information, situations deteriorate. The cornerstone to any crisis communication plan is the effective dissemination of accurate information to the public. Without this, disaster recovery is impeded and the disaster situation often worsens.
2. *Communicate early and often.* The response team has an ideal opportunity soon after the onset of a disaster to shape media coverage, develop credibility with the media and public, facilitate de-escalation of the crisis, and restore public order. By communicating early and often there is an increased probability of accurate reporting from the beginning. The creation of an

Facilitating Hurricane Preparedness
in South Florida

On August 21, 1992, Hurricane Andrew hit south Florida, devastating 1,000 square miles of Dade County, causing around $30 billion in property damage, and leaving approximately 200,000 homeless. With 61 fatalities, Hurricane Andrew was one of the most destructive and costly hurricanes in U.S. history. Before the hurricane hit, hurricane preparedness and recovery information was transmitted piecemeal from different media and government sources, with multiple, and sometimes conflicting, information being received by the public.

Hernando González, associate professor of journalism at Florida International University, and two of his graduate students became aware of this problem and subsequently studied public information on disaster preparedness and recovery available to south Floridians (González & Adams, 1997–1998). From interviews with journalists who covered Hurricane Andrew, they found that the media, the American Red Cross, the National Hurricane Center, and various state and local agencies had all produced guides or pamphlets on disaster preparedness. González and his team concluded that there was a need for one hurricane preparedness handbook containing the best advice and information from the experts, packaged in an easy-to-carry and easy-to-read format.

González released the first edition of the handbook in 1994, with sponsorship from Amoco; its release was publicized and praised by all four major network television affiliates as well as the Miami Herald. In 1995, students distributed a second edition of the handbook at major intersections in Dade and Broward Counties. The release of the second edition was also covered by local print and television news.

In 1996, the Public Relations Student Society of America (PRSSA) became involved in the project and created a hurricane superhero ("Hurricat"), developed hurricane worksheet lesson plans (in conjunction with the Dade County School Board), and distributed a third edition to all 25,000 Dade County fourth-grade students through their science teachers. For the release of the third edition, the project also secured a media partner, CBS affiliate WFOR-TV, along with the station's highly visible meteorologist, Bryan Norcross. Through this partnership, other sponsors were recruited and over 300,000 handbooks were printed, bringing the three-year distribution total to 500,000.

With additional funding from the International Hurricane Center in Florida, the fourth edition was distributed to over 100,000 Floridians in 1997. This time the handbook was available in English, Spanish, and Braille and included Red Cross disaster preparedness kits. The students also helped the Red Cross prepare public service announcements and news releases about the handbook.

information vacuum invariably results in the reporting of rumor, speculation, and sensational stories, all of which impede recovery.

3. *Be forthright and open with the media.* If the disaster response team withholds substantiated information from the media or is unresponsive, the media will use other mechanisms to obtain information. If the information they request is not yet available, say so, and let them know when you will have it to share with them. In other words, if the media are not welcomed through the front door, they will try to enter through the back door, and the team member who meets them there may not be the best spokesperson.

4. *Deal with the bad news.* Anticipate every bad news allegation. If there is bad news, the disaster response team should be proactive and announce it to the media. If there are a number of bad news points to convey, do so all together. However, always notify victims' families before public notification is made.

5. *Be organized and strategic in your dissemination.* Every aspect of the crisis communication plan must be deliberate, including establishing a well-equipped media room, having ready-made templates of fact sheets and press releases, and designing message strategies for interviews and press conferences. Realizing that disasters are stressful and scary for everyone, including team members, the "thinking" part of the plan should be done and practiced well before the disaster occurs. To some extent, the safety and recovery of the community depends on the information disseminated.

Because speaking to the press is the equivalent of speaking to the public, all communication should be based on a common strategic plan. The crisis communication plan has three goals: (1) to inform the public, (2) to anticipate and meet the needs of journalists, and (3) to establish and maintain credibility with the public and the media. To accomplish these three goals, the plan should contain information regarding the following objectives, each of which is discussed in detail below:

- identification of crisis communication team members and assignment of resources, roles, and responsibilities
- coordination with key departments and the larger disaster response team
- establishment of protocols, decision-making processes, and time frames
- definition of media relations activities and response strategies
- predisaster testing of the plan and postdisaster evaluation.

In addition, the plan must support media relations activities that facilitate reaching the public with key messages and must enable crisis communication managers to disseminate public information immediately after and throughout the disaster.

The crisis communication plan should be easily broken down and understood. It should be user-friendly and concise. Although everyone on the disaster response team should be familiar with the crisis communication plan before the onset of a disaster, this is often not possible. Therefore, the structure of the plan should be easy to understand and follow, even for those who first review it during a disaster.

Crisis Communication Team

Spokesperson. The disaster response team should designate one person to be responsible for communicating to the public through the media to ensure consistent messages. Since the spokesperson plays a crucial role in establishing the credibility of the response effort, he or she should have technical expertise, a position of authority, strong professional credentials, the ability to assimilate information quickly, an even temper, a reasonable tone, an honest presentation, an ability to offer good sound bites, and a propensity for getting along with reporters (Barry McLoughlin Associates, 1996c).

Media guide. Different from the spokesperson, the media guide's assignment is to facilitate communication by staying in constant contact with the media. His or her responsibilities include

- monitoring the media for errors
- keeping track of and distributing identification passes with the name and media outlet for each journalist
- taking requests for information, interviews, and comments
- providing the media with logistical support
- identifying, keeping track of, and suggesting appropriate locations where media personnel can videotape or photograph
- organizing and conducting a guided media tour of appropriately designated affected locations
- numbering and posting all news releases in the media center
- recording all briefings, conferences, and interviews
- arranging statements by others, such as technical experts, to the media
- releasing all preapproved background material and releases to the press (after first double checking all the facts)
- maintaining a log of all events, requests, and decisions

- continuously collecting information, evaluating it for potential release, recommending information for release, deciding with the crisis communication team how and when to release it, and then releasing it. (Barry McLoughlin Associates, 1996g)

The media guide does not give interviews per se. Content questions or comments should be addressed by the spokesperson. The media guide's role only concerns information dissemination (Barry McLoughlin Associates, 1996c).

Media center. The media center is a designated site from which information is disseminated to the media. In the media center, press conferences occur, press releases are posted, and key personnel, such as the media guide, are available to take information requests.

The necessary equipment and supplies for the media center include televisions and battery-powered radios; computers, modems, printers, and fax machines; an adequate number of power outlets; bulletin boards, flip charts, and markers; a photocopier; desks and chairs; and a large table at the front of the room capable of holding microphones and a speaker's lectern (Barry McLoughlin Associates, 1996e). In addition, because during and after some disasters there is no power supply, it is important to have power generators available to supply the media center's power.

A disaster response plan usually requires an emergency operations center or "war room." Since this and the media room serve distinct functions, they should be positioned in different places (Berry, 1999)—far enough away from each other so that internal decisions and discussions can take place in private.

Speakers bureau. Under some circumstances, it may be necessary for community leaders, experts, and other credible sources to collaborate to help respond to the demands for media interviews (Mitchell, 1993). The media guide coordinates the speakers bureau. The information disseminated through the speakers bureau should be known and approved by other members of the crisis communication team.

Where do reporters go for information? Spotlight on Research "Sources of Information Coverage of Disasters" provides some answers for two natural disasters.

Coordination with Key Departments and the Larger Disaster Response Team

The crisis communication team should develop and execute a crisis communication plan in conjunction with key departments, as well as with the larger disaster response team. Relationship building and other factors necessary for successful interorganizational relations need to be complete before a public crisis occurs. For representative and accurate external information to be disseminated there must be consistent and effective

---

SPOTLIGHT ON RESEARCH

Sources of Information for Television Coverage of Disasters

Who do reporters use as sources of information when there is a natural disaster? What are the implications of using particular sources of information for the social construction of disasters? Lynne Massel Walters and Susanna Hornig (1993) investigated who network television news reporters interviewed in their coverage of two natural disasters, Hurricane Hugo and the Loma Prieta earthquake, which occurred within weeks of each other in the fall of 1989.

The majority (40 percent) of interviewees in news stories were average citizens speaking of their experiences during the disaster. However, the media also used conventional news sources, such as government officials (16 percent) and experts (17 percent). This indicates that, "as with the day-to-day reporting process, news remains bureaucratically structured in times of emergency" (Walters & Hornig, 1993, p. 229).

Walters and Hornig (1993) also found that the sources used for stories were more likely to look for causes (71 percent) than solutions (29 percent) to problems resulting from the disaster. The majority (45 percent) named the government as the primary source of solutions to the disaster, and this was particularly true if the interviewee happened to be a government official.

The media sought people as sources for stories who could provide information on, or a context for, the disaster. This included expert interpretation and analysis, official information, and examples of positive citizen action. Therefore, broadcast journalists relied heavily on the traditional official or expert sources to provide information and an institutional response, and used everyday citizens for stories relating to personal experiences and perspectives to construct the reality of the disaster.

Walters, L. M., & Hornig, S. (1993). Faces in the news: Network television news coverage of Hurricane Hugo and the Loma Prieta earthquake. *Journal of Broadcasting and Electronic Media, 37*, 219–232.

internal communication. This requires coordination before, during, and after a disaster.

Establishment of Protocols, Decision-Making Processes, and Time Frames

By forming an effective crisis communication plan, the crisis communication team protects the public from conflicting official information. For this screening to take place, the crisis communication plan must include well-established protocols and decision-making processes. Therefore, a crisis communication plan must establish a hierarchy, which includes the criteria for designating the lead agency for the disaster (Barry McLoughlin Associates, 1996d).

The goal of protocols and clear decision-making processes that minimize "approvals" is to allow quick responses to media questions and quick dissemination of information to the public. To expedite the dissemination of resources and information, the development of a crisis communication plan should include evaluating existing clearance procedures for the release of resources and information in both normal times and during disasters (Berry, 1999).

Media Relations Activities and Response Strategies

The crisis communication team should develop working relationships with the media based on mutual understanding and respect for each other's characteristics, goals, and needs. Regular communication and reciprocity between the crisis communication team and the media before, during, and after disasters can facilitate a strong and mutually beneficial relationship (Hernandez, 1994).

The crisis communication plan should include message strategies and media relations activities. Knowing how to prepare for and participate in a media interview or press conference under normal circumstances can be nerve-wracking; the stress of a disaster requires special planning and practice of media relations techniques. Understanding how to speak with the media, the themes contained in the information disseminated, and the appropriate activities to engage in with the media are important aspects of the crisis communication plan.

Media relations activities. Response organizations dedicate 30 percent to 40 percent of their time to media relations activities during and after a crisis (Hall, 1993b). This includes direct interactions with the media, as well as activities that enable expedient information dissemination that, in turn, helps the media do their job.

Direct interactions with the media include:

- Media tours providing behind-the-scenes insights into disaster response (Barry McLoughlin Associates, 1996a)
- Media tours showing affected areas of the disaster (Hall, 1993b)
- Regular briefings corresponding to media deadlines and information requirements (Barry McLoughlin Associates, 1996a)
- Providing access to key disaster-management personnel and other credible sources that do not interfere with emergency response (Barry McLoughlin Associates, 1996a)
- Public outreach programs mobilizing the community in disaster preparation and recovery (Barry McLoughlin Associates, 1996a)
- Collaborating on stories that not only provide information on the disaster, but also are positive, featuring recovery, community resiliency, and survival (Mitchell, 1993).

Activities that enable expedient information dissemination include:

- Maintaining and continuously updating a comprehensive stand-by media kit (Barry McLoughlin Associates, 1996g)
- Developing template media tools such as ready-to-use news releases, media statements, fact sheets, and background materials in which pertinent information can be quickly inserted (Barry McLoughlin Associates, 1996d)
- Training key personnel on developing and practicing media messages (for example, what to say to the media in an interview or how to respond to media requests) (Berry, 1999).

These media activities create the foundation for easy and timesaving dissemination. To be most effective, however, media activities (and information) should be made available to all media outlets and reporters simultaneously. Offering "exclusive interviews" in the aftermath of a disaster, for example, creates resentment, accusations of favoritism, and overall bad media relationships (Barry McLoughlin Assoc-iates, 1996g).

Response strategies. Just as important as the media activities are the messages that are disseminated and how they are packaged. When a disaster first happens, the media are most interested in answering the following questions (Lazarus, Brock, & Feinberg, 1999): *When* [did the disaster begin or become known]? *Who* [was affected or is in charge of the recovery]? *What* [happened or what can we expect now, or what is being done to help]? *Where* [was the damage done, or where was something hit]? *Why* [was the damage extensive or recovery slow]? *How* [do we recover or help our

community]? The abstract and complex nature of these questions can make them difficult to answer succinctly. However, these questions must be answered quickly and concisely, which is why having a trained spokesperson is so important.

Although the media can play an invaluable role in disaster preparedness and warning, their need for information increases with the onset of a disaster. The following information should be provided to the media as soon as it is available after a disaster's onset:

1. Date and time the disaster began (such as when the hurricane hit the city), although this may be difficult in some disasters (for example, it may be difficult to say when toxic waste buildup reached a critical point)
2. Description of the disaster with as much detail as possible (for example, the kind of disaster, projected weather track, size of the storm, description of the storm, and so on)
3. Number of people affected or potentially affected
4. Extent of the injuries and confirmed deaths (after contacting next of kin)
5. Special security conditions at the disaster site (for example, live wires, unstable structures, flash floods, or looting)
6. Date and time of the next media briefing. (Berry, 1999)

Do not wait for the media to initiate reporting the recovery. Media center representatives should serve as a constant source of positive stories. Seek out these stories and provide enough evidence of their prevalence to justify the media shifting the focus of the coverage from damage to recovery (Mitchell, 1993).

The 1993 World Trade Center Bombing: Media Response Strategies and Lessons Learned

On February 26, 1993, the World Trade Center in New York was bombed, killing six people and injuring 1,000 more. Peter Yerkes, the media relations officer for the building's owner, was in the building at the time of the explosion. After feeling the building shake and seeing smoke reach his 68th floor office, he knew something terrible had happened. Communication systems were inoperable, and Yerkes had no idea that 40,000 people were trying to evacuate the building by the stairs, or that when they emerged disoriented, covered with soot, and injured, members of the press were there to capture it all.

When Yerkes and his media relations staff finally emerged, they had no information or instructions about what happened or how to proceed. They did not know if the disaster was complex or technological (that is, whether it was caused by a terrorist act or faulty construction). They also did not know that the story had already broken in the press and that the Port Authority, which constructed and operated the World Trade Center, faced a major loss of credibility.

The lessons Yerkes and his staff learned centered on what they did not do (Hall, 1993a). They did not control the flow of information—provide any context or "spin"— and so the media received the same information as the Port Authority. They also struggled with balancing knowing all they could about what happened and discussing these findings with their lawyers before they talked to the press— in a disaster the luxury of screening what is said to the media does not exist. By the afternoon, the Port Authority had set up a direct communication line with the emergency command center, which coordinated the activities of all the emergency response agencies.

Yerkes pointed out that it is important and a priority to supply the media with credible experts, and to do so quickly (Hall, 1993a). For example, he secured Port Authority Chief Engineer Gene Fasullo—dazed, exhausted, and still bloody—to do a live interview with WNBC-TV. And Yerkes himself—with four of his employees killed, a mystery surrounding what happened, and a building to repair—knew that the crisis demanded that he also participate in interviews.

The Port Authority disseminated information through formal communications, and held planning sessions and press conferences every morning, seven days a week, for six weeks, beginning the morning after the blast. The disaster response team set up an emergency communications center, staffed by 12 to 14 public relations professionals, on a visible spot on the concourse level of the World Trade Center to ensure a steady flow of information to the media.

Within 48 hours of the bomb's detonation, the disaster response team had given the media supervised access to the blast site. Once the media had seen the destruction, they expressed sympathy, understood why the situation was so chaotic, and no longer questioned why the emergency and communication systems had been knocked out. This supervised tour of the site, according to Yerkes, a former newspaper reporter, prevented the media from reporting conjecture, speculation, and rumor.

The disaster response team also took reporters to the temporary command center of the engineers responsible for repairing the World Trade Center. Though engineers voiced concerns about being photographed, Yerkes explained that it was necessary to turn the story around from disaster to recovery. As the coverage became routine, focus shifted from the event to rebuilding, recovery, safety precautions, security improvements, and the reopening of the World Trade Center.

The media also play a postimpact role. Therefore, when the media center is dispersed, provide the media with resources for obtaining postimpact information. These reports will contribute to shaping the final image of the disaster and recovery. It is at this point that perception becomes reality (Berry, 1999).

Disaster response teams and media organizations should seek opportunities to build positive relationships. This includes providing information to media personnel to enhance their reporting of disaster preparedness, mitigation, and relief efforts. Moreover, authorities can share information with the media on the importance of the timeliness, quality, responsibility, usefulness, and accuracy of reporting on disasters (Cate, 1994).

Predisaster Testing of the Plan and Postdisaster Evaluation

The disaster response team should test all aspects of the response plan before a disaster occurs, including the crisis communication plan. Although nothing can completely prepare people for a disaster when it actually occurs, this method at least may address glaring oversights.

Information recorded during the disaster and the recovery, such as the event log maintained by the media guide, can be a valuable resource in postdisaster and recovery debriefing, and crisis communication plan evaluation after the crisis. The disaster response team should evaluate the plan so it will evolve in its effectiveness, comprehensiveness, responsiveness, and usefulness.

NATURE OF MEDIA COVERAGE IN A DISASTER

Secondary Victimization and Sensational Coverage

Secondary victimization is defined as victimization that results from the response of the institutions and individuals to the victim, rather than from the traumatizing event (United Nations Commission on Crime Prevention and Criminal Justice, 2000). If they are aware of the potential for secondary victimization, especially through sensational coverage, disaster relief workers may have concerns about working with the media.

Touching Reality "The Media's Interference with Grieving" asks you to consider how the media might interfere with the grieving process.

The defining characteristics of sensational coverage include: (1) incorrectly reporting disaster impacts by skewing the significance of damage; (2) giving undue emphasis to dramatic, tragic, and wrenching scenes and stories; and (3) overrepresenting negative stories of disaster behavior, such as looting

---

TOUCHING REALITY

The Media's Interference with Grieving

Recall the ongoing news coverage about the families of those who lost their lives in the attack on the World Trade Center in New York City on September 11, 2001. What was your reaction to the journalists who visited people's homes, schools, and places of work to ask questions about the event? Some firefighters spoke of attending several funerals a day for weeks. Media representatives were always in attendance, taking pictures, and asking questions. How would your reaction to the media change depending on your place in the circle of vulnerabilty (see chapter 2 for a discussion of the circles of vulnerability)?

and price gouging (Kreps, 1980). Reporting that emphasizes these attributes may contribute to a public crisis by exacerbating panic, inactivity, and stress; paralyzing community members; and thwarting recovery. As a result, the community does not rebuild but further disintegrates (Lahad, 1997). Although experts have advocated for media organizations to create policies on disaster coverage to minimize the prevalence of irresponsible coverage, most of them have not done so (Deppa, 1994).

Despite criticism of the media for sensational coverage, such coverage continues. From the media's perspective, the reasons are obvious. Disaster coverage, including sensational disaster coverage, increases the audience (Walker, 1997). Moreover, the public demand for information immediately after a disaster, especially in an information vacuum, increases the likelihood of reporting accounts from unofficial sources and of seeking information any way possible. This, along with the fact that a lack of information can contribute to public panic and outcry (Deppa, 1994), reinforces the importance of consistent and reliable information being disseminated to the public by the media from the crisis communication team.

As already stated, an official decision not to provide information or interviews does not stop media coverage or kill a story. A reporter's job is to get the story, with or without official cooperation. Because reporters will find someone to talk to, especially after a disaster, the disaster response team should cooperate with them to influence the information reported and how it is presented.

How the Media Cover Disasters

If a crisis communication team knew what the media do to produce coverage of a disaster, it would give them insight into where the media may be, the sources they may be monitoring, and the information they may be seeking. By anticipating these activities, the crisis communication team can prepare for media activity and be responsive by being the primary source of what the media seek. Activities that the media can be expected to engage in include

- monitoring each other and emergency communication channels
- allocating extra resources and personnel for coverage
- allowing additional broadcast time and space for coverage
- going where they want to get a story, unless barricades are erected and monitored
- probing for details and uncovering information using all resources available (for example, confidential sources, public information officers, police or emergency response scanners, and other news outlets)
- using their own knowledge, experiences, and data sources, which may be unavailable to disaster response personnel
- reporting what they know and have discovered in a relentless and rapid way
- advancing the news coverage from the event to implications, next steps, and emergent issues
- going to where they have access to new information, expert opinions, and responses to their questions
- becoming suspicious and motivated when they are confronted with silence information vacuums or stonewalled by officials
- trying to get dramatic and interesting visual images and using whatever means they have to get them. (Barry McLoughlin Associates, 1996f)

Covering a Catastrophe: A View from the Inside

How does a disaster affect the operations of the local newspaper? This question guided Gypsy Hogan's (1995) case study of the *Daily Oklahoman* during the weeks after the April 19, 1995, bombing of the Alfred P. Murrah Federal Building in Oklahoma City. Staff at the newspaper, the state's largest, had to cope with personal loss and trauma while reporting the story.

Hogan (1995) found that the incident required journalists to produce more than usual to meet the public's demand for information—extra six-page sections for five days after the bombing and four-page extras for 10 days after that—and the paper to print 100,000 copies, twice as many as usual, the day after the bombing. Discovering that this many copies did not respond to the demand, on the second day postdisaster the paper produced 112,000 copies. Though decreasing as days went by, the demand for information remained high, with 7,000 extra copies of the paper included in the press run four weeks after the disaster. In the middle of this increased work, counselors assisted grieving staff members.

Several new news policies, which reflect the newspaper's adaptation to the situation, evolved as the disaster was reported:

- The bombing was never to be referred to as an "incident."
- The policy on profanity was relaxed to allow the printed page to reflect the anger people expressed.
- Funerals were not covered: The families were given their privacy and the reporters found other ways to tell the story.

- Photographs and artwork were given prominence in the newspaper's layout since visual images seemed more effective than words at conveying the story.
- Bomb coverage was divided among reporters based on issues rather than on traditional desk assignments, making it necessary for reporters to account to various editors based on the issue being covered. Because of this new reporting system, two extra news-planning meetings were scheduled each day to coordinate the information for dissemination.
- Artists for the paper produced final graphics on computer, but also were required to go to the scene with sketch-pads to document the actual scene.
- Families of those killed were allowed to run free classified obituaries. The classified department worked closely with the newsroom to secure permission from the families to run photographs of the deceased along with the obituary.
- To reduce confusion and the risk of incorrect reporting, one person was placed in charge of the highly sensitive injured, missing, and casualty lists.
- The newspaper set up a phone line for people to offer and receive help. This line allowed people to speak, and to hear others' thoughts about the bombing. This service fielded approximately 20,000 calls over the course of the recovery.(Hogan 1995)

This case study is a reminder that, although members of the media may themselves be exposed to a disaster, their jobs dictate that they continue to get the story. The media can help in postdisaster recovery by being sensitive and responsive to the community in its time of need.

Hogan, G. (1995). Covering the catastrophe: How the *Daily Oklahoman* covered the federal building bombing in their own backyard. *Editor and Publisher, 128*(23), 15–16.

Using these activities, local media can quickly turn a disaster into a national event, worthy of national coverage.

Because of their tenacity, the media sometimes are able to uncover information about a disaster before disaster response personnel are able to do so. The disaster response team should prepare for this, too. Crisis personnel, for example, should neither deny nor confirm information relayed to them until they have verified its accuracy. Though the media may report the information as "unconfirmed," the job of crisis personnel is to maintain the legitimacy and veracity of the information that is disseminated by the crisis communication team, as quickly as possible.

Disseminating information not only affects disaster recovery efforts, but the media organizations and the people who work for them. After all, many reporters live and work in the community that is reeling from the disaster. Spotlight on Research "Covering a Catastrophe: A View from the Inside" provides an opportunity to look at the effects of a disaster on one newspaper's operations.

MEDIA RELATIONS

Most human services workers have limited experience and training in working with the media (for example, preparing for media interviews, answering reporters' questions, knowing how to respond in different media formats). To help fill that gap, this section of the chapter introduces you to various topics related to dealing with the media. The information here comes from the media relations literature, and from the author's professional experience with the news media for the past eight years.[1]

When working with the media, it is essential for the disaster response team to recognize that the media seek assistance, not control. This means the disaster response team needs to assist them in collecting and managing the release of information provide logistical support, and, generally, see that their needs are met to facilitate their jobs.

Types of Media Venues

Different media venues present different challenges and offer different benefits. Therefore, each calls for a different type of preparation. In addition, the disaster response team should target each based on the kind of message to be disseminated, the amount of time available, and the urgency of the message.

Live interviews. Although most live interviews occur on television, there are also opportunities for radio interviews. These can occur in the newsroom or television studio or in the field. They can be in person or, if necessary, by phone. Live television and radio interviews usually are done for news broadcasts. Because they are live and occur during a news broadcast, these interviews are usually short and limited to two to five questions. Therefore, overall less information may be conveyed. The challenges of live interviews include the following:

- Live interviews can be the most nerve-racking type of interview because the interviewee does not normally know the questions to be asked in advance, and because of the unfamiliar process and format—all of which is compound-

---

[1] This experience includes doing more than 50 media interviews (both live and taped) on social issues for television, print, and radio; working with the media in social issue story development; completing a newsroom placement as a social worker; and developing and teaching a continuing education seminar on media relations and message strategies for nonprofit organizations.

ed by the increasing pressure not to misspeak.

- Live interviews are time limited, requiring the interviewee to be especially skilled in delivering information in an efficient, clear, and pithy way, as well as in an interesting and memorable way (typically known as "sound bites").
- There is no "take 2," so although you may have time to correct misspeaks, the interview cannot be redone.

Live interviews are challenging, but several benefits make them a good venue for disseminating information: (1) Because there is no possibility of editing or repackaging the message, the information disseminated is yours alone. (2) There is no waiting for the interview to air later—the information is disseminated immediately. (3) Because most people in this country get their information from television news (Broadcasting & Cable Yearbook, 1995; Center for Media and Public Affairs, 1997), this is the most efficient way to disseminate information to the most people.

Taped interviews. The media usually allot more time to taped interviews; they can occur either at the newsroom or in the field. Though the same number and kind of questions may be asked by the reporter as in a live interview, the time restraints typically are relaxed for responses. However, it remains important for the interviewee to be able to talk about the issue clearly, concisely, and in sound bites. Two challenges of taped interviews are important to consider when this type of interview is used:

- Part of the message in a taped interview, may be edited out which increases the likelihood of words being taken out of context. This can be counteracted by speaking in sound bites, making "answer chopping" difficult.
- Whenever more time is allotted for a media interview, the interviewee usually becomes more comfortable with the reporter, which can result in the interviewee getting too comfortable and saying something she or he should not.

Just as with live interviews, the challenges of taped interviews may be offset by two benefits: There is less time pressure on you; and you have more opportunity to clarify your message through the reporter's follow-up questions and to correct any misspeaks.

Print interviews. Print interviews, such as those found in newspapers, magazines, and specialty newsletters, consist of talking with a reporter who, in turn, relays the message in the printed word. These interviews can occur in person, over the phone, or by e-mail, and may be conducted over more than one meeting. The challenges of the print interviews include:

- With print interviews, the interviewee relies on the reporter to convey the intended message to the public, with the possibility of incorrect interpretations, misquotes, and out-of-context comments making it into print.
- Print interviews rarely allow the reader to receive your nonverbal messages, except when a word in a quote is emphasized with italics or boldface because, when speaking, you emphasized it, or when the reporter describes your behavior. Nonverbal messages, such as facial expression and tone of voice (which affect the extent to which you are perceived as

credible), are seen or heard only by the reporter and usually are not relayed through this form of media.

Two benefits of the print interview may make it a good choice for conveying information to the public. First, print interviews offer the opportunity to provide the reporter with pertinent written materials with background information, important statistics, significant facts, and so on, that the reporter may use for the story. Second, the print interview that often allows more time to speak with the reporter, which means that more information can be relayed and the interviewee's message or argument can be supported through examples and case histories, which provide more depth to the story.

Radio interviews. During and after a disaster, the radio interview may be the only (and, therefore, most used) form of media interview. These interviews can be conducted at the radio station, in the field, or over the phone and presented live or taped for later broadcast. Depending on the context which the interview occurs, there may be one or more call-in segments to allow the public to respond and ask questions of the interviewee. These interviews vary in length, depending on the context in which they occur. The challenges of the radio interviews are:

- Live radio interviews require all the skills necessary for a live television interview.
- Taped radio interviews require all the skills necessary for a taped television interview.
- If the radio interview includes a call-in segment, the interviewee will need to be able to respond appropriately and quickly to a wide range of questions. These questions may be more challeng-

ing than any posed by a reporter and, because they come directly from the public, they may require special thought and consideration.

Three benefits of the radio interview may make it a good choice for communicating with those interested in receiving information immediately after a disaster or during postdisaster recovery efforts. First, because of their immediacy (they can be made public faster than television or print interviews), radio interviews can serve as a lifeline to the community in disaster situations, and, therefore, can be an invaluable resource for the crisis communication team. Second, because there is no camera, the interviewee can refer to notes for facts, figures, dates, and other hard-to-remember pieces of information. And third, time constraints usually are less imposing with radio interviews than with other types of interviews, so they can go over their allotted time (both in live and taped interviews) to accommodate the importance, interest, or depth of the topic being discussed.

Anticipating Questions

One of the best ways to prepare for any media interview is to anticipate the questions that the reporter may ask. This includes the questions that are most likely to be asked as well as more controversial and offbeat ones. You have the opportunity to craft well-worded answers to anticipated questions.

By anticipating questions you can minimize the trepidation and "fear of the unknown" that many people feel before a media interview. This exercise is useful for all forms of media interviews and interactions. Therefore, it should be done before taped or live media interviews and press conferences. Touching Reality "Anticipating

Reporters' Questions" provides you with an opportunity to develop a list of likely questions.

TOUCHING REALITY

Anticipating Reporters' Questions

The purpose of this activity is to help anticipate questions from the media. The following prompts are designed to help you generate questions ahead of time; you can then prepare appropriate responses. Each prompt should identify multiple questions. Though this exercise may not result in a complete list of possible questions, it serves as a starting point for discussion among the crisis communication team members.

1. Given this disaster, the most logical questions a reporter would ask are:
2. Background questions most likely to be asked by a reporter are:
3. Information questions most likely to be asked by a reporter are:
4. The question potentially most damaging to our organization is:
5. The question that would be the most challenging to answer is:
6. The question to avoid or downplay is:
7. The question that would require the most research or time to be able to answer is:
8. The most difficult or delicate question that could be asked is:
9. A likely question about the most controversial aspect of the disaster, or disaster recovery activities, or disaster-related problem is:
10. A likely question to which it would be very difficult to formulate a good, concise answer is:

Creating *Priority Idea Points*

After anticipating the variety of questions that may be asked in a media interview, your next step is to develop main points to convey. These points go by several names, but the most descriptive is PIPs, "*Priority Idea Points*." PIPs should be created before any media interaction. PIP development includes four phases:

1. In conjunction with the other crisis communication team members, the spokesperson creates a complete list of points that should be communicated during the media interaction.
2. The spokesperson prioritizes the list, putting the most important or urgent points first, and the least important or urgent points last.
3. The spokesperson edits each point on the prioritized list to the briefest form, thereby creating a list that contains only trigger words to remind the spokesperson of the larger point to be communicated to the reporter.
4. The spokesperson memorizes these points.

In developing PIPs, the number of points to be conveyed should correspond to the allotted time of the interview or press conference. Although there are no absolutes, there are some rough guidelines for live and taped interviews or press conferences, in all formats: News interviews (two to three minutes of air time), no more than three PIPs; feature interviews (eight to 15 minutes of air time), four to seven PIPs; and in-depth interviews (30 minutes of air time), eight to 10 PIPs.

Touching Reality "Developing and Presenting Useful PIPs" provides you with an opportunity to develop some PIPs.

Developing and Presenting Useful PIPs

PART I:

For this exercise, imagine that a natural disaster has occurred in your community and you that have been designated as the media spokesperson by the disaster response and crisis communication team. The media guide has scheduled you to be interviewed by a local news organization about the disaster. The reporter states that the interview will take about 15 minutes, but will be edited down to a three-to-five-minute piece.

1. In conjunction with the other crisis communication team members, prioritize a list of points that should be relayed to the public. Remember, these points should reflect what you wish to convey during the interview by relating them to the questions that you anticipate you will be asked.
2. Prioritize the list, putting the most important or urgent points first, and the least important or urgent points last.

3. Reduce the list to "trigger words" that remind you of the larger point you wish to make in the interview. Memorize this trigger list.
4. Practice delivering these PIPs in a mock session with the "reporter," using the anticipated questions (from the previous Touching Reality) as well as other appropriate questions. The goal is to bridge the question asked back to a PIP you wish to deliver, making the response fluid, natural, and on target with the reporter's question.

PART II:

Repeat this exercise, imagining you have been contacted to discuss natural disaster preparedness when a disaster is not looming. (These requests usually happen at the beginning of a natural disaster season.) Repeat this exercise several times, imagining different circumstances in which the media may contact you to speak on various aspects of disasters and their impact on communities.

The Art of the Sound Bite

It is common for social workers and other human services providers to resist the notion of preparing sound bites. Feeling as if they are "cheapening" the problem by talking about it in sound bites, and fearing being labeled a "pop psychologist" or "pop social worker" by colleagues, human services providers may wonder, "How can I in good conscience talk about a problem such as [insert the type of disaster] in sound-bite form? It is far too complex; by using sound bites I'm minimizing the complexity and importance of the issue." The fact is, however, that working with the media presents an opportunity to publicize an issue or problem, mobilize the com-

munity, and be an influential voice about something important to the community.

As already emphasized, the media will find someone to talk to, and that someone is likely to be a person who has learned to speak in sound bites. This use of the media, gives these people an "unusual degree of power," simply because they are able to provide information in a "manageable and efficiently packaged form" (Goodell, 1977, p. 142). It is important to choose an experienced and capable spokesperson at all times, but especially during a disaster.

There are benefits for both the spokesperson and the reporter to use sound bites—messages that include information (such as one PIP), are pithy, uncomplicated, memorable, and last 10 to 15 seconds. First, for the spokesperson, using sound bites creates the opportunity to "feed" a desired message in a format preferred by the reporter, thereby increasing the probability of it being used in the story. In this sense, the spokesperson knows which responses will most likely reach the air or the printed page.

Second, usable quotes related in the interview may affect how the interviewee is used in the story or even the overall angle of the story. It is not uncommon to be told by a reporter the angle of a story before an interview only to see the angle shift by the time the story airs based on a spokesperson's responses.

For reporters, an interviewee who can provide usable sound bites is an asset, a truly useful source, and one they will use repeatedly. Unfortunately, many human services professionals are suspicious of the media and believe that reporters have their heart set on editing their responses in order to twist their words. The reality is that the majority of reporters do not have that kind of time and would much rather have an interviewee who can feed them good sound bites that will, in turn, minimize their editing time.

Practicing for the Interview

When the key proactive messages have been developed, they must be practiced. There is a big difference between silently and orally verbalizing PIPs and possible responses. Oral practice is the only way to determine if the selected PIPs are appropriate and concrete enough to be recalled and delivered in an interview format. Finally, practice enables the interviewee to be aware of and better able to estimate the time needed to make a point.

Because spokespersons may not have time to practice for an interview when a disaster hits, they should perform general practice and role-playing sessions regularly when no crisis is pressing. Regardless of whether the role-playing session is for general practice or for an upcoming media interview, the format of the session remains the same.

Each practice session should include role-playing questions and answers three or four times to sharpen the PIPs. Ideally, the spokesperson should videotape these sessions to self-evaluate and to get feedback on content and delivery. Seeing your interview on television is not the best time to discover a glaring distraction in a delivery style that was not picked up in the mock sessions. The following tips also can guide these practice sessions:

- Practice nonverbal behaviors that reinforce and add to the message. Do not engage in distracting hand behavior (such as hand wringing, face touching, and adjusting hair), facial expressions, or other gestures.
- Avoid using words and phrases that disrupt the fluency of your talk or, worse, distract from what you are saying, such as, saying "you know" at the end of sentences, and using "um," and "and-uh" as substitutes for pauses.
- Whenever possible, interject a positive perspective in your message, one that is hopeful and empowers people to action.
- Practice with your list of anticipated questions with the mock interviewer, mixing up the order and phrasing of the questions. In addition, the mock interviewer should digress from the anticipated questions and ask related questions that come to mind, just as a reporter would.

- When responding to a question, answer by bridging it back to the PIPs in a way that conveys the desired message while customizing the PIP to fit with the interviewer's question.
- Avoid overpreparing and developing "canned" answers—keep your responses natural by conveying the PIP in the context of the question asked.
- Set a time limit for the mock session that approximates the length expected for the actual interview.
- Never start the mock interview session over because of a misspeak; practice correcting the mistake and going ahead, just as you would in an actual interview.
- Hone the length and content of responses and practice speaking in quotes or sound bites.

Navigating the Media Interview or Press Conference

Anticipating questions, constructing PIPs, and practicing help you prepare for your interaction with the media (whether an interview, a press conference, or some other format). For all media interviews, your goal is to convey the desired points. You can accomplish this goal by responding to the questions in a way that bridges them back to the PIPs. Therefore, customizing the PIP to fit with the interviewer's question conveys the desired message. Following are some guidelines and techniques for navigating the interview or press conference.

- Never lie.
- Be yourself.
- Keep the message simple, memorable, relevant, and easily understood. Always strive to simplify points, explanations, and responses.
- Do not use jargon or acronyms unless you are certain they are well known. Replace technical and professional jargon with more commonly used words.
- Do not make too many complex points, especially in a television interview (whether live or taped).
- The tougher or more controversial the question, the shorter should be your answer.
- Once the question has been answered and the point has been made, stop talking. (Reporters sometimes let silence continue in hopes the interviewee will say more.)
- Read from prepared answers or statements only at a press conference.
- Do not allow distractions to undermine the interview. Other conversations, background motion, newsroom noises, and other diversions are easier to ignore if they are anticipated and you have practiced for them.
- It is fine (and sometimes even expected) for you to repeat the same key point, using different words.
- At the end of an interview, the reporter may ask if you would like to add anything. Use this opportunity to convey a PIP that has not yet been made. Do not be afraid to take advantage of the opportunity.
- Do not be intimidated by the camera or microphone; however, never forget that they are there! Direct answers to the reporter or interviewer, not to the camera. (The exception is a live television news interview where the questions are relayed to you from a reporter in another location; in that situation, the answer should be directed to the camera.)
- Throughout the interview process, concentrate on the desired points, the questions posed, and the message to be conveyed.
- If there is a difficult name or word to pronounce, make sure you can do so before the interview begins. Also, if your name is

difficult to pronounce, make sure the interviewer can pronounce it correctly before the interview begins.

- Always leave your business card with the reporter in the event there are follow-up questions.
- Remember that there is no such thing as "off the record."

SUMMARY

The key to dealing with the media during a disaster is preparation and the establishment of a relationship with the media before a disaster occurs. A well-developed and well-tested crisis communication plan can help ensure that the media play an effective role in preparing people for a disaster and in disaster recovery. Though working with the media requires planning, training, and patience, choosing not to work with them may cause additional hardships to communities trying to cope with and recover from a disaster. By working effectively with the media, the disaster response team can facilitate the recovery of a community by disseminating information to the public—information that enables the community to move from disaster to recovery, and foster hope for the future.

REFERENCES

Ahern, J., Galea, S., Resnick, H., Kilpatrick, D., Bucuvalas, M., Gold, J., & Vlahov, D. (2002). Television images and psychological symptoms after the September 11 terrorist attacks. *Psychiatry: Interpersonal and Biological Processes, 65*, 289–300.

Barry McLoughlin Associates. (1996a). Crisis communication series—Part 2: Emergency! Retrieved September 14, 2003, from http://www.mclomedia.com/cc2.htm

Barry McLoughlin Associates. (1996b). Crisis communication series—Part 3: Crisis. Retrieved September 14, 2003, from http://www.mclomedia.com/cc3.htm

Barry McLoughlin Associates. (1996c). Crisis communication series—Part 4: Goals and principles. Retrieved September 14, 2003, from http://www.mclomedia.com/cc4.htm

Barry McLoughlin Associates. (1996d). Crisis communication series—Part 5: Development of a crisis communications plan. Retrieved September 14, 2003, from http://www.mclomedia.com/cc5.htm

Barry McLoughlin Associates. (1996e). Crisis communication series—Part 6: Key planning elements. Retrieved September 14, 2003, from http://www.mclomedia.com/cc6.htm

Barry McLoughlin Associates. (1996f). Crisis communication series—Part 7: Executing a crisis communication plan. Retrieved September 14, 2003, from http://www.mclomedia.com/cc7.htm

Barry McLoughlin Associates. (1996g). Crisis communication series—Part 8: Key roles and responsibilities of the media guide in a crisis. Retrieved September 14, 2003, from http://www.mclomedia.com/cc8.htm

Berry, S. (1999). We have a problem: Call the press. *Public Management, 81*(4), 4–9.

Broadcasting & Cable Yearbook 1995 (Vol. 1, 1995). New Providence, NJ: R. R. Bowker.

Cate, F. (Ed.). (1994). *International disaster communications: Harnessing the power of communications to avert disasters and save lives.* Washington, DC: Annenberg Washington Program in Communications Policy Studies of Northwestern University.

Center for Media and Public Affairs. (1997). What do the people want from the press? Retrieved September 14, 2003, from http://www.cmpa.com/Mediamon/mm0506.htm

Deppa, J. (1994). *The media and disasters: Pan Am 103.* New York: New York University Press.

Elliot, D. (1980). Tales from the darkside: Ethical implications of disaster coverage. In D. Elliot (Ed.), *Disaster and the mass media* (pp. 9–33). Washington, DC: National Academy of Sciences.

Faberman, R. K. (1999). What the media need from news sources. In L. L. Schwartz (Ed.), *Psychology and the media: A second look* (Vol. 2, pp. 9–23). Washington, DC: American Psychological Association.

González, H., & Adams, W. C. (1997–1998). A life-saving public-private partnership: Amoco and Florida International University's hurricane preparedness program. *Public Relations Quarterly, 42*(4), 28–34.

Goodell, R. (1977). *The visible scientists.* Boston: Little, Brown.

Hall, B. (1993a). Terror in the Towers: A media relations pro tells his story. *Public Relations Journal, 49*(12), 12–13.

Hall, B. (1993b). Terrorism: The ultimate crisis. *Public Relations Journal, 49*(12), 6–8.

Hernandez, D. G. (1994). Covering disasters: Report defines role of media. *Editor and Publisher, 127*(41), 13–14.

Hernandez, D. G. (1995). Oklahoma disaster coverage: A look back. *Editor and Publisher, 128*(39), 24–25, 34.

Hogan, G. (1995). Covering the catastrophe: How the *Daily Oklahoman* covered the federal building bombing in their own backyard. *Editor and Publisher, 128*(23), 15–16.

Iyengar, S., & Kinder, D. R. (1987). *News that matters.* Chicago: University of Chicago Press.

Kreps, G. A. (1980). Research needs and policy issues on mass media disaster reporting. In D. Elliot (Ed.), *Disasters and the mass media* (pp. 35–74). Washington, DC: National Academy of Sciences.

Lahad, M. (1997). BASIC-Ph—The story of coping resources. In M. Lahad & A. Cohen (Eds.), *Community stress prevention 2* (pp. 117–145). Kiryat Shmona, Israel: Community Stress Prevention Center.

Lazarus, P. J., Brock, S., & Feinberg, T. (1999, September). Dealing with the media in the aftermath of school shootings. *National Association of School Psychologists Communiqué.* Retrieved September 14, 2003, from http://www.nasponline.org/publications/cq281 media.html

McCombs, M., & Reynolds, A. (2002). News influence on our pictures of the world. In J. Bryant & D. Zillmann (Eds.), *Media effects: Advances in theory and research* (2nd ed., pp. 1–18). Mahwah, NJ: Lawrence Erlbaum.

McCombs, M. E., & Shaw, D. L. (1993). The evolution of agenda-setting research: Twenty-five years in the marketplace of ideas. *Journal of Communication, 43*(2), 58–67.

Milgram, N., Sarason, B. R., Schoenpflug, U., Jackson, A., & Schwarzer, C. (1995). Catalyzing community support. In S. E. Stevan & M. W. deVries (Eds.), *Extreme stress and communities: Impact and intervention* (pp. 473–488). New York: Kluwer Academic/Plenum Press.

Mitchell, E. (1993). Weathering the storm. *Public Relations Journal, 49*(2), 11–13, 25.

Morland, L. A. (2000). The Oklahoma City bombing: An examination of the relationship between exposure to bomb-related television and post-traumatic stress symptoms following a disaster. *Dissertation Abstracts International, 60,* 4239.

Moskovitz, M. (1999). Managing the media. *American City and County, 14*(1), 54–58.

Pfefferbaum, B. (2001). The impact of the Oklahoma City bombing on children in the community. *Military Medicine, 166*(12, Suppl. 2), 49–50.

Piotrowski, C., & Armstrong, T. R. (1998). Mass media preferences in disaster: A study of Hurricane Danny. *Social Behavior and Personality, 26*, 341–345.

Ross, G. (2003). *Beyond the trauma vortex: The role of the media in healing fear, violence, and terror.* Berkeley, CA: North Atlantic Books.

Saylor, C. F., Cowart, B. L., Lipovsky, J. A., Jackson, C., & Finch, A. J., Jr. (2003). Media exposure to September 11: Elementary school students' experiences and posttraumatic symptoms. *American Behavioral Scientist, 46*, 1622–1642.

United Nations Commission on Crime Prevention and Criminal Justice. (2000). *Handbook on justice for victims: On the use and application of the United Nations Declaration of Basic Principles of Justice for Victims of Crime and Abuse of Power.* Retrieved September 14, 2003, from http://www.victimology.nl/onlpub/hb/hbook.html

Walker, D. (1997). No-show hurricane whips up storm. *Broadcasting and Cable, 127*(44), 70.

Walters, L. M., & Hornig, S. (1993). Faces in the news: Network television news coverage of Hurricane Hugo and the Loma Prieta earthquake. *Journal of Broadcasting and Electronic Media, 37*, 219–232.

Zoch, L. M., & Duhé, S. F. (1997). "Feeding the media" during a crisis: A nationwide look. *Public Relations Quarterly, 42*(3), 15–20.

HELPING THE HELPERS

PARTICIPANT HANDBOOK

HELPING THE HELPERS

Chapter 14 presents the Trainer Notes and Participant Handbook for a two-day workshop to train disaster recovery workers and other interested individuals on the topic of "helping the helper." The workshop is designed for approximately 25 participants, although it may be adapted for groups as small as 10 and for any number over 25.

The workshop consists of five parts, following the opening remarks. The first part introduces participants to the topic of stress and burnout, including typical sources of stress for disaster recovery workers and other caregivers or helpers. The second part builds on the first and invites participants to investigate their own verbal and nonverbal stress reactions, to increase self-awareness. This part also helps participants explore their usual ways of responding to stress—in other words, their coping mechanisms. The third part is brief and is related to the resiliency of disaster relief workers, serving as a transition to the fourth and fifth parts, both of which offer suggestions for self-care. In the fourth part of the workshop, participants learn several techniques that they can use alone to reduce their stress. Finally, in the fifth part of the workshop, participants learn three small-group techniques for responding to stress: (1) critical incident stress debriefing, (2) group defusing, and (3) multiple stressor debriefing.

Helping the Helper
TRAINER NOTES

OPENING (30 MINUTES)

Introduce the workshop and facilitator(s). Then, have participants answer the following questions to introduce themselves:

1. What is your name?
2. For what organization do you work?
3. What is your goal for participating in this workshop?

PART I: STRESS AND BURNOUT
The Effects of a Powerful Experience (40 minutes)

Hand Out Participant Worksheet 1:
The Effects of a Powerful Experience

Provide participants with Worksheet 1 and drawing pencils and ask them to "Draw a picture that depicts a powerful experience you had working as a disaster recovery worker during the past few months."

After they complete their drawings, have participants form small groups (three people each) and share their drawings.

Ask, volunteers to share how they felt during and after the *powerful experience.*

Some participants will choose to draw and discuss a positive experience, and some will focus on a negative experience. No matter whether the experience was positive (eustress) or negative (distress), these intense, powerful experiences, especially if ongoing and frequent (such as during disaster recovery), can cause burnout.

Stress and Burnout (20 minutes)

Stress is your body's reaction to any event that pushes it out of what you consider to be normal; it is the body's preparation to respond to the unusual. There is nothing in any event that in and of itself makes it a stressor. A person's perceptions of the event—such as defining it as "a powerful experience"—makes an event a stressor. As a result, every event and situation is a potential stressor.

Hand Out Participant Worksheet 2:
Stress and Burnout

Often, survivors of a stressful situation feel physically and mentally drained. They may want nothing more than to rest or escape. If exposure to a stressful situation is prolonged, burnout—physical, emotional, and mental exhaustion—results.

- Physical symptoms of burnout include fatigue, sleep disruptions, headaches, stomachaches, body aches, or susceptibility to colds or flu.
- Burnout may show up in work performance through absenteeism, tardiness, or declining productivity.
- Burnout may present as depersonalization in interactions with colleagues and clients.
- Emotional and behavioral symptoms of burnout include irritability, anxiety, depression, pessimism, cynicism, isolation, carelessness, or feelings of helplessness.

Factors Contributing to Burnout (70 minutes)

Note: The six factors contributing to burnout and the adaptation of Maslow's need hierarchy to the disaster–worker situation, are based on Young (1998). See chapter 11 for more on Maslow's need hierarchy.

Hand Out Participant Worksheet 3:
Factors Contributing to Burnout

Tell participants to read the six factors listed on Worksheet 3 that contribute to burnout. As they read, each participant should ask herself or himself, "Is this something I experience on a regular basis, or have ever experienced?" Ask participants to select those factors most relevant to their own experiences.

Ask participants to form small groups (three people each)—with people they do not know—and share with each other the most relevant factors contributing to their own stress and, perhaps, burnout. Allow 15 minutes for this part.

Then, ask those who found the first factor of particular relevance to indicate this by raising their hand; call on one of these participants to read the description of the factor aloud and then give his or her example. Then, ask each participant who raised her or his hand to give her or his example. If many participants indicate that the factor is particularly relevant, ask only a few to share their examples. Continue to process each factor in this way.

1. *Professional isolation.* Helpers may find that they have no one with whom they can talk about the nature of their work or its effect on their lives. Friends and family members may admire what they do, but may not want to hear "disaster stories." Even if some are willing to listen, helpers may find it difficult to talk about their experiences because friends or family cannot understand the effects of exposure to disaster and trauma.

Despite the fact that many helpers are trained in issues of trauma and caregiving, they often function in a work culture that values self-sufficiency, stoicism, and the repression of personal emotional reactions.

They may be reluctant to allow their colleagues to know how they are feeling and fear being ridiculed or censured if they reveal anxiety, tension, or turmoil over their encounter with traumatic events.

2. *Emotional and physical drain of providing continuing empathy.* Helpers are constantly faced with giving of themselves to others. They must listen with care to the stories of disaster clients and try to provide solace and reassurance. They often feel the need to be available for the people that they serve at all hours of the night and day. They are compelled by an ethical imperative to sacrifice themselves to help meet the needs of those exposed to disaster.

Many helpers also serve as caregivers to family and friends. They may function and be perceived as the source of strength when others falter. In part, this is because of their personalities and, in part, because they have the experience and knowledge to deal with difficult and stressful issues.

It is not unusual for strangers to relate tragic stories to helpers, once the helper's vocation has been revealed. Unless helpers have social support systems that can provide them with empathy and understanding, their emotional resources are constantly flowing toward other people while their own emotional reservoir is slowly depleted.

3. *Ambiguous successes.* Many helpers feel ambivalent in the aftermath of a crisis response. The coordination of the recovery effort, the teamwork, and the response of the community may have been extremely positive. People helped may have responded with gratitude and appreciation. Yet, no matter how successful the intervention was from these measures, the helper may become depressed.

Nothing can eradicate the effects of disaster—the number of dead or injured, the property lost, and the communitywide destruction. No matter how much is done in response, it may never seem to be enough. Helpers may particularly feel this void because they are rarely in direct contact with the community in the months or years that follow their intervention. They may never know if what was done was truly helpful or useful.

Although it is irrational for helpers to rush to a disaster scene, given the terrible sights and the overwhelming suffering, they do so because they believe, "My presence will make a difference." Of course, confronted with the disaster scene, the opposite and conflicting feeling may occur: "What can I do? I am impotent to help."

4. Erosion of idealism. Many helpers come to the field of disaster recovery or crisis counseling with strong beliefs in ideals such as the goodness of people, the ability to create a better world, the conviction that justice will prevail, and their own power to make a difference. Many of these ideals are challenged in disaster recovery work.

Crisis responders meet many good people among those exposed to disasters, but they also are confronted with the destructive and despicable behaviors (such as looting) that people sometimes display in the aftermath of disasters. Efforts to improve the lives of others after a tragedy are often undercut by countervailing forces, including bureaucracy, community divisiveness, and barriers to service.

5. Lack of expected rewards. Most helpers do not look to financial gain as their primary reward. Crisis helpers are notoriously underpaid, if paid at all, for their services. They may be compensated from their agency to cover the costs of being on call. Those who volunteer their services know that they will give up time with their families, time at their jobs, and time for themselves.

Sometimes helpers are frustrated by the lack of acknowledgment for their service and sometimes they are discouraged when they compare their work with the work of others and see others' rewards.

6. Helpers also may be survivors. Helpers often arrive on a disaster scene without recognizing or taking into account that they also may be victims, in the sense that they occupy one of the circles of vulnerability (they may, for example, share geographical proximity with survivors, or their friends and family may be victims, or they may identify with the victims). This increases the chances of experiencing burnout as they help others.

During a disaster, a helper's usual "ceremonies" cannot be conducted, creating an unfamiliar and often uncomfortable, anxiety-provoking situation for the helper. Three helper's ceremonies—which, perhaps, serve as anchors for the helper—cannot be conducted during a disaster. These three ceremonies are (1) the "intake ceremony," in which a history is taken in a logical sequence and the helper has time to learn about and reflect on the problem; (2) the "ceremony of place," in which the helper and client agree to meet in the helper's office; and (3) the "ceremony of time," in which the helper and client agree to meet for a specified amount of time. Following the first two dimensions of the PIE principle—proximity and immediacy—helpers work at the scene of the disaster (P), rather than in their offices and work quickly (I), often without anything approaching a detailed intake interview and time to determine "the problem." In addition, helpers may spend only a few minutes with some disaster clients and days with others, depending on survivors' needs (see Solomon & Benbenishty, 1986; Badenhorst & Van-Schalkwyk, 1992).

SHOW ONE VIDEO SEGMENT
(segment 7 on the CD; 25 minutes)

This video segment called "Lessons" shows several official and unofficial helpers who responded to Hurricane Floyd in North Carolina. There are political and agency officials, neighbors helping neighbors, people helping themselves, people finding strength in their spirituality, and several looking for ways to grow from this experience and to avoid another one like it in the future. With what stress and burnout issues might any of these helpers have to deal? What might they do to help themselves as they work with people who experienced the hurricane? It is clear that some of the people pictured are survivors of the hurricane as well as helpers. What kinds of support might need to be in place for them? In life situations when you have found yourself in a helper role, how have you provided self-care, as well as the nurturing needed by others?

Disaster Relief Work and Changes in Helpers' Beliefs (25 minutes)

Traumatization can cause caretakers to experience a lasting alteration in their belief systems that have a significant effect on their feelings, relationships, and life. Such alterations are similar to those that may occur among people exposed to a disaster. The difference for caretakers is that with repeated disaster interventions, these alterations can solidify, because the interventions confirm the validity of the changes in their beliefs. This is particularly

true if they have been victimized by trauma in their own lives.

Hand Out Participant Worksheet 4: *Disaster Relief Work and Changes in Helpers' Beliefs*

Confronted every day with death and the possibility of death, caregivers observe the consequences of sudden random disaster and live with the knowledge that their future is precarious.

Caretakers may become overly concerned with safety issues and become overly cautious, or deny their disaster realities and become more risk taking.

Caretakers may begin to feel out of control and powerless and react by seeking to impose order and control in their lives, or they might react by feeling overwhelmed with everyday tasks.

Constant work with disaster clients may result in caregivers speculating about similar tragedies happening in their own lives, leading to feelings of estrangement and isolation.

Four factors affect these belief changes most emphatically:

1. *Repeated exposure to sudden, random disaster.* Repeated re-exposure, inherent in the role of caretakers, repeatedly confirms the perception of alarm and danger.
2. *Repeated exposure to the impossible.* Many helpers find that one of the most disturbing aspects of their work is their repeated exposure to "impossible" events. What most ordinary people never experience in a lifetime is repeatedly experienced by the helpers.
3. *Lack of positive countervailing exposure to human good and world order.* This is critical: To stay healthy, caretakers need to have strong social connections and support, to view people as good, and to sustain their sense of spiritual connections.

4. *Lack of nurturing resources.* Helpers need to ask for help and be willing to receive it. Sometimes helpers try to take care of the "little child" inside by themselves. When that happens, the helper becomes lonely and frightened. It is crucial for helpers to seek and receive external care and nurturing, and it is also crucial for them to take care of themselves.

PART II: SELF–ASSESSMENT OF STRESS REACTIONS AND RESPONSES
Self–Assessment of Stress Reactions (30 minutes)

Hand Out Participant Worksheet 5:
Self–Assessment of Stress Reactions
Instruct participants to complete Worksheet 5, and ask them to think about how they behave when they feel stressed. After everyone has completed the checklist, ask:

- How many did you check? Do you have a few favorite ways to express your stress, or do you have a great many ways? How many items you checked is less important than how sure you are of the ones you checked.
- Ask participants to look at themselves from the perspective of a spouse, partner, or close friend and ask what he or she would have checked for them. Often, it is necessary to take another's perspective to get a clearer picture of the reality.
- How aware of your stress reactions are you—did you find it easy to respond to this activity, or did it take a lot of thought?

What Do You Do When You Feel Stressed? (80 minutes)

Hand Out Participant Worksheet 6:
What Do You Do When You Feel Stressed?

First, ask participants to write down their usual ways of coping with stress—the methods they use to deal with their stress. They should not write down only those methods that are successful, but all the methods they tend to use to reduce their stress, successful or not.

Second, have participants form groups of three or four members each and share with each other their usual methods for releasing, combating, and dealing with their stress. What methods did they have in common, and which were unique?

Third, have the different groups of participants share with the other groups the coping methods that they thought were most helpful or unusual. Invite participants to add methods to their own lists. As suggestions are shared, write them on a flipchart or on a slide for an overhead projector.

Danieli's Principles of Self–Healing (40 minutes)

Hand Out Participant Worksheet 7:
Danieli's Principles of Self–Healing
Danieli (1996) outlined several criteria to evaluate the usefulness of a particular coping method. Ask participants to read Worksheet 7, then to think about how their methods of coping with stress fit Danieli's principles.

- Self-healing is effective insofar as you recognize your own reactions

It is important for you to develop an awareness of somatic signals of distress—a chart of warning signs of potential reactions (for example, sleeplessness, headaches, and perspiration), such as in the "signs of stress" activity.

It is important for you to find words to name and articulate your inner experiences and feelings. What cannot be talked about can also not be put to rest; if these inner feelings are not resolved, they may not heal.

Ask participants:

1. What roadblocks have you encountered to recognizing your own reactions?
2. What encouragement have you experienced to recognizing your own reactions?

• Self-healing is effective insofar as you recognize and understand your reactions

It is important to identify your personal level of comfort in order to build openness, tolerance, and readiness to hear anything.

By knowing that every emotion has a beginning, middle, and end, you can learn to attenuate your fear of being overwhelmed by an emotion's intensity and to try to feel its full cycle without resorting to defensive reactions.

Ask participants:

1. What roadblocks have you encountered to containing your reactions and to recognizing that emotions have a beginning, middle, and end?
2. What encouragement have you encountered to containing your reactions and to recognizing that emotions have a beginning, middle, and end?

• Self-healing is effective insofar as you are able to heal and grow

You need to accept that nothing will ever be the same.

When you feel wounded, you need to take time to diagnose yourself accurately, to soothe yourself, and to heal yourself so you will be emotionally fit to continue to work.

Any of the affective reactions (including grief, mourning, or rage) that are triggered by victims' stories may interact with old, unresolved experiences. When this happens, it is important to seek consultation or counseling. Helpers are able to use their own professional work purposefully for their own growth.

It is essential to establish a network of people to create a holding environment within which you can share your trauma-related work.

It is essential to provide yourself with avenues outside your work for creative and relaxing self-expression in order to regenerate and re-energize yourself.

Ask participants:

1. What roadblocks have you encountered to healing and growing, to taking the time to heal yourself, to creating a network of people with whom you can share your disaster work, to regenerating and re-energizing yourself?
2. What encouragement have you encountered to healing and growing, to taking the time to heal yourself, to creating a network of people with whom you can share your disaster work, to regenerating and re-energizing yourself?

Have participants reform into their groups and evaluate their techniques (or, at least several techniques) for reducing their stress. If there is time, have each group report on one of the methods for coping it evaluated as meeting Danieli's criteria for a good coping method.

PART III: DISASTER WORKERS' RESILIENCE

Disaster Worker Resilience (30 minutes)

Disaster relief workers can be vulnerable to the same kinds of problems affecting disaster clients. In an American Psychological Association (APA) *Monitor* article, "Tapping Their Own Resilience," Michael O'Connor, chair of the APA's Advisory Committee on Colleague Assistance, pointed out that disasters intensify helpers' stress in obvious and subtle ways, and, as he puts it, helpers "must ensure that our own psychological needs are addressed, so we can continue to help those who require our professional services" (Clay, 2001).

They may not be invulnerable, but disaster relief workers are resilient. For example, a study of individuals who worked with human remains after the 1995 Oklahoma City bombing—including medical examiners, pathology residents, and students—found that they had few symptoms of post-traumatic stress and depression immediately after the disaster, and even fewer had symptoms a year later. The researchers speculated that they were resilient because of their social support, their ability to translate the unpleasant situation into a meaningful one, their participation in on-site critical stress management and debriefing, and their strong sense of community (Tucker et al., 2002).

Hand Out Participant Worksheet 8: *Disaster Workers' Resilience*

Protective factors—those things that protect people from the effects of stress and trauma—are internal and external influences that enhance resiliency and help people act in positive ways when coping with disasters. Protective factors fall into three broad areas:

1. *Qualities of the disaster helper*, such as a good sense of humor, resourcefulness, high self-esteem, altruism, and high intelligence.

Ask participants, "What personal qualities do you have that you feel serve as protective factors?"

2. *A strong sense of continuity*, including

- functional continuity—the ability to maintain usual routines during a disaster or after it
- historical continuity—the ability to maintain a sense of identity and a sense of history during a disaster or after it;
- interpersonal continuity—the ability to maintain a social network during a disaster or after it
- spiritual continuity—the ability to maintain faith in a stable and just world.

Ask participants, "What continuities do you have that you feel serve as protective factors?"

3. *Characteristics of her or his relationships*, such as warm and caring friends and support from inside and outside the family, such as religious affiliations and work. (Omer & Alon, 1994)

Ask participants: "What characteristics of your relationships do you feel serve as protective factors?"

An *APA Online* article (APA, 2001) pointed out that extraordinary demands "intensify the need for self-monitoring with an eye to self-care strategies that can help bolster professional resilience." The key to helping others as well as oneself is self-care that enhances resilience.

Now, we will take a look at self-help techniques in two categories: those that a helper can do alone and those that require others.

PART IV: SELF–HELP TECHNIQUES YOU CAN DO ALONE

Self–Help Techniques You Can Do Alone (60 minutes)

Begin this part of the workshop by noting all the useful coping methods discussed earlier in the day. Some may cover the several discussed below. Use information from participants to help provide examples as you discuss the several techniques.

Hand Out Participant Worksheet 9:
Self–Help Techniques You Can Do Alone

As part of the workshop, you may have the participants engage in either or both of the meditation techniques, as well as the guided imagery.

1. Exercise. Assume that you will need more sleep, exercise, and healthy foods—just as your clients and patients do. Exercise is an excellent way for someone to protect herself or himself from the negative effects of stress. Exercise serves at least two functions. First, once a person recognizes the occurrence of verbal and nonverbal indicators of stress, an exercise break may relieve initial stress reactions, refresh energies, and enable the person to get back to work. Second, an individual who has exercises will recover more quickly from stress than does a sedentary person. Physiological reactions to stress are similar to those experienced while exercising (for example, increased heart rate and muscle activity). If the body is well exercised, its ability to cope with changes and recover are increased.

To improve physical fitness as a coping behavior, an exercise program is needed. Often, it is possible to introduce exercise into your daily life without making any drastic changes in routine. For example, you can walk up stairs rather than take the elevator, park in the farthest lot rather than the closest, walk or bike to the store rather than drive, do isometric exercises while watching television in the evening, take an exercise class, or join a lunchtime exercise program at work.

2. Meditation. Another self-help technique is meditation—not spiritual meditation, but rather meditation as a practical tool to lessen stress. Meditation may block the stress mechanism that is related to different ailments.

Meditation is a useful activity for several reasons. First, it increases concentration, which facilitates problem solving. Second, meditation increases a person's ability to identify sources and effects of stress. Third, it teaches how to be quiet and calm.

There are, perhaps, as many meditation and relaxation techniques as there are people who meditate. Two techniques shown to be successful in dealing with stress are (1) repeating a word, sound, or phrase and (2) paying attention to one's breathing.

Repeating a word, sound, or phrase is one of the oldest and most common of all meditation procedures. The person selects a word, sound, or phrase with which she or he is comfortable, then repeats it over and over. The selected word, sound, or phrase can be a reflection of one's religious or cultural background. You might say the word *amen, shalom, om, one,* or *peace.*

This technique can control and still the mind. Our minds are usually very busy; we sometimes thrash around from idea to idea and thought to thought. In repeating the word, sound, or phrase, the mind quiets, and the person meditating feels calmer.

Paying attention to your breathing is slightly more involved than repeating a word, sound, or phrase, yet it too is thousands of years old. As the person moves through the steps of this technique, he or she should relax, calm down, and pay attention to the moment.

"Find a comfortable place to sit."

"Close your eyes to reduce distractions."

"Bring your focus and awareness to your body. Begin with your feet and work upward. Ask yourself how you feel. Are you comfortable? Tense? At ease?"

"Begin to pay attention to your breathing. Are you breathing too fast? Too slow? In an irregular fashion? Your breathing both mirrors your mental state and can transform it."

"Still paying close attention to your breathing, notice each time you inhale and exhale. As you monitor your breathing, you should mentally say the word 'rising' with each inhale and 'falling' with each exhale. Whenever your mind wander, bring it back by once again mentally saying 'rising, falling.' Over time, and with practice, this process becomes easier, more enjoyable, and an excellent means for coping with your stress."

3. Guided imagery. Ask participants to get comfortable, close their eyes, and relax. A simple relaxation exercise is to tell participants (with their eyes closed):

"Take in air through your nose, warm it up, and then circulate it through your body—beginning by moving the warm air over your forehead, the top of your head, down the back of your head, down your back, over the backs of your legs, across the bottoms of your feet, up the front of your legs, over your stomach, your chest, and out your mouth. With each breath—taking air

in, warming it, circulating it, and exhaling it—you become more relaxed."

Once participants are relaxed, read the following guided imagery, which is designed to reduce stress and to release hopelessness.

"Imagine that you are in a cocoon, surrounded by a soft strong shell that protects you from everything outside....Explore what it is like inside your safe cocoon.... what sounds are like....what the air feels like....what the colors look like.... what the smells smell like....Take a moment and explore your cocoon....

"Now, slowly, break out of your cocoon....Find your way out of your protective shell and be aware how you feel as you emerge into the light of the world.... The air is warm and the world seems lighted by a healing sun, a joyful light that penetrates everything, including you as you emerge from the cocoon....The light warms you and heals all your wounds.... The light energizes you and fills you with joy....You rejoice in how you feel."

Give participants a few moments to experience the guided imagery; then, ask them to open their eyes and reorient themselves to the room.

Form groups of approximately five members each and have participants consider the questions at the end of Worksheet 9:

- How do you think you could use the three self-help techniques (exercise, meditation, and guided imagery), or any one of them, in your work—for yourself, for other recovery workers, and for disaster clients?
- What could keep you from using any of these techniques in your work?
- When could you use these techniques, or any one of them, in your work—when would it be most appropriate?

- How do cultural differences among recovery workers and disaster clients affect your decision to use any of these techniques?

DAY 2, MORNING

Day 2 is divided into two parts. The morning consists of a discussion of debriefing and, specifically, Critical Incident Stress Debriefing. This is followed by an explication and example of Group Defusing. The afternoon is taken up mostly with an example of Multiple Stressor Debriefing.

PART V: SELF–HELP TECHNIQUES YOU DO WITH OTHERS

Self–Help Techniques You Do with Others (45minutes)

Hand Out Participant Worksheet 10: *Self–Care Strategies*

Review the advice from the APA (2001).

Research tells us that when recovery workers are in a safe and structured environment that is time limited, ventilating helps them reduce their stress. This workshop covers three ways of working in groups to provide this experience. The first is called Critical Incident Stress Debriefing (CISD), which is part of Critical Incident Stress Management. The second is called Group Defusing, and the third is called Multiple Stressor Debriefing (MSD).

Psychological debriefing. The term "debriefing," in the context of disaster, refers to a group procedure that takes place after a critical event. The aim is to protect the mental health of helpers such as rescue workers, social workers, ambulance and medical staff, firefighters, and police officers.

To understand what debriefing is, we can distinguish its *concept* from its *process* and *techniques* (Wraith, 2000). As a *concept*, debriefing provides an opportunity for the sequential recognition and validation of feelings and behaviors concerning the event. It is a structured way to elicit the personal story of the experience with an emphasis on sensory perceptions (sight, smell, sound, touch, and taste), thoughts, feelings, and behaviors experienced during and shortly after the event. These are shared with others in the "shared fate" small group, composed of people with similar roles as helpers, under the common conviction that any response to the disaster is accepted and normalized through the group sharing process.

As a *process*, debriefing is geared toward engaging helpers to integrate their bizarre and shattering experience into a cohesive cognitive, emotional, and social frame; in other words, the goal is to help group members find meaning and order in a chaotic and unexpected life experience. To do this requires exploring process issues in the group, which has to do, in large part, with finding ways to express the inexpressible, communicate, listen, and give and receive acceptance in the group (Dyregrov, 1999).

The debriefing *technique*, initially developed as a group-work protocol, "defines rules about leadership, venue, timing, confidentiality and the progression of stages within a complete session" (Wraith, 2000, p. 199). It relies on a chronological approach for addressing the crisis event step by step. The facilitator asks the participants to remember what happened to them at the time of the trauma, what happened in the aftermath, and what they expect to happen in the future. If the trauma is particularly severe, it is recommended to pace the group session slowly, as a protective device against the danger of flooding participants and overwhelming them with their intense feelings. To avoid premature exploration of trauma material, group facilitators may want to start group sessions with the question: "What was life like before the event happened?" thus creating an anchor in the continuity of the predisaster period.

Debriefing is neither counseling nor therapy. In other words, this procedure is not intended as a cure. Rather, debriefing is used to provide group members with an understanding of initial trauma reactions, to increase their sense of personal control, and to use the group for support (Mitchell, 2003). Thus, debriefing cannot always prevent posttraumatic symptoms, but it can help traumatized people accept and understand their meaning and take additional action if necessary (Ajdukovic & Ajdukovic, 2000).

Practical considerations in setting up debriefing. Following the PIE principle, the debriefing procedure should be carried out as near the disaster as possible (proximity); as soon as possible after the disaster (immediacy), before details of the incident fade away and become distorted; and with an active, positive, and hopeful orientation (expectancy). Although proximity to the site of the incident is often sought, safety is an overruling consideration. If the area of the disaster is not safe, debriefing needs to be conducted in a place removed from the dangerous area.

Those who conduct debriefing *must be well trained and skilled in group facilitation, interpersonal communication, and trauma management.* They need to be able to contain the stress, fear, anger, and mourning of the traumatized participants. It is best to have two facilitators, whatever the size of the group. The facilitators should be able to create an atmosphere of trust and support for all group members. They are expected to be able to identify participants who show excessive signs of suffering, either by expressing or by suppressing their feelings, and those who need individual attention and further treatment.

Critical Incident Stress Debriefing (45 minutes)

Hand Out Participant Worksheet 11: *Critical Incident Stress Debriefing*

CISD is a group crisis debriefing intervention developed by Jeffrey Mitchell (1983) to help *crisis response teams* (for example, firefighters, police, mental health workers, disaster relief workers, and social workers) to handle the psychosocial effects of the traumatic incidents they encounter in their work. It has been found that the death of children in disaster is the most difficult thing for rescue helpers handle and requires special support for the workers (Hodgkinson & Stewart, 1998).

CISD is a structured group intervention with seven phases that cover most aspects of the encounter with the disaster (Mitchell & Everly, 2001). The CISD process moves from cognitive ([1] introduction and [2] fact phase) to cognitive-moving-to-affective ([3] thought phase), to affective ([4] reaction phase) to affective-moving-to-cognitive ([5] symptoms phase), to cognitive ([6] teaching and [7] reentry phases).

1. Introduction. Introduce team members, explain the CISD process (for example, people do not have to speak if they choose not to), and set expectations, such as for confidentiality.

During the introduction, the facilitator will introduce herself or himself, tell about her or his role, and inform participants that CISD is not therapy. The goal is to help helpers get back to work without the consequences of the stress of the incident and to realize that their reactions are normal reactions to an abnormal event.

2. Fact phase. Collect information about the participants and about the event. Ask the following key questions—these are the only questions that require participants to speak in the group: "Who are you? What was your role (your job) at the time of the incident? Where were you and what did you see? What did you do?"

The goal of the fact phase is to have each participant describe the incident on a cognitive level, from her or his perspective.

3. Thought phase. The facilitator asks, "What went through your mind during the incident—what was the first thing you thought about? What is your most prominent thought about the event? What have your thoughts been concerning the incident since it happened?"

The goal of the thought phase is to have each participant describe his or her cognitive reactions to the incident, and to make the switch to his or her emotional reactions.

4. Reaction phase. The facilitator asks, "How did the incident affect you emotionally? What was the worst thing in this incident for you personally? How did you feel? How do you feel now? If you could change one part of the event, what would that be?"

The goal of the reaction phase—which takes as much as an hour of the group meeting—is to have each participant describe the most traumatic part of the incident and identify her or his emotional reactions.

5. Symptom phase. The facilitator asks, "How did you know this incident was having an effect on you? What symptoms—signals of distress—you did develop as a result of the incident, such as fears, startle reactions, feelings of dread, and intrusive thoughts?"

The goal of the symptom phase is to have each participant identify his or her symptoms of distress and begin the transition back to the cognitive level.

6. Teaching phase. Present information regarding expected physiological and psychological stress reactions and what to do about them.

The goal of the teaching phase is to normalize participants' reactions to the incident by presenting information on typical reactions and positive coping mechanisms.

7. Re-entry phase. Wrap-up questions. The facilitator asks, "What have you learned? What, if anything, have you gained from the experience that is positive? How can you help and be helped in the future?"

The facilitator provides information (handouts) about possible help, repeats reassurance, and announces the particulars of a follow-up meeting in approximately two weeks. The confidentiality agreement is reiterated as the final point.

The goal of the reentry phase is to facilitate closure by clarifying ambiguities and preparing participants for ending the group.

CISD original protocol yielded promising results helping rescue and other personnel deal with their preliminary reactions to traumatic events (Jordan, 2002; Pynoos, 1993; Robinson & Mitchell, 1993). (Jordan's study tested the usefulness of CISD and one-on-one crisis counseling in New York City after the September 11 terrorist attacks. She found that CISD helped those at a college in Manhattan deal with mild transitory symptoms and learn about normal reactions to a disaster. For more affected people, she offered one-on-one crisis counseling.) There may, however, be limitations to use of CISD. For example, an investigation by Tobin (2001) concluded that CISD is only effective when a major incident has occurred and there is a significant loss of life, and only when conducted by highly trained personnel who are peer supporters of the at-risk population. In addition, Humphries and Carr (2001) found that CISD is effective in the short term in reducing posttraumatic stress symptomatology, notably intrusive memories, following a critical incident, but it may be no more effective than a brief psychoeducational intervention.

CISD has generated much criticism, mainly because of its application to nonhelpers and its use by nonprofessionals—which is not a part of CISD procedures and training and is not sanctioned by the national CISD organization. For example, lack of appropriate training of nonprofessional facilitators was at the root of inadequate CISD, with 3 percent to 10 percent of participants rating it as unhelpful and even harmful (Dyregrove, 1999). Based on a study of a large database of CISD studies, reviewers concluded that most CISD criticism is based on practices that did not follow the rigorous procedures and criteria of the original Mitchell model; for example, single sessions were held with no follow up, encounters were too short, or groups were much larger than recommended were (Everly & Mitchell, 2000). In addition, misconceptions about CISD feed much of the criticism—for example, that all debriefings are the same as CISD, that CISD should erase all symptoms of traumatic stress, and that CISD is a cure for PTSD (Mitchell, 2003).

Although recent evidence points to the efficacy of CISD (Deahl, Srinivasan, Jones, Neblett, & Jolly, 2001; Irving & Long, 2001; Smith, 2001), the debate points to the need for a revised protocol suitable for disaster clients of all ages, and particularly for children. (See Bibliography for Trainers for documents discussing CISD.)

Group Defusing (90 minutes)

Group defusing is usually conducted at or near the site of the disaster for disaster workers who appear to be experiencing severe stress or need someone outside their work environment with whom to discuss recent events and personal well-being. It is purposefully short; typically not more than 30 to 45 minutes. Because of the time limit involved, the sessions do not attempt to address all elements of crisis intervention; rather, the focus is on immediate issues of safety, flash points of trauma reactions, and ideas about how to live through immediate re-exposure to the disaster or its aftermath.

Group defusing can take place at any time and is conducted with no more than eight group members. Whereas the primary purpose of MSD (see discussion below) is to provide group members time to take a break from their jobs and reflect on the positive and negative aspects of their work as a way of completing their experience of working as a helper, the primary purpose of group defusing is to provide helpers with a way to process strong feelings and reactions to a particularly troubling event, with the goal of returning to work as a helper. Group defusing also is useful for identifying helpers who may require additional aid.

Group defusing sessions are usually facilitated by a pair of facilitators who make the structure and the purpose of the group clear. Facilitators should obtain as much information as possible regarding the specific tasks in which group members are or were involved. Familiarity with worker's jobs during a disaster can aid in developing a better alliance with group members. As with any group of people exposed to traumatic events, members tend to look suspiciously at outsiders. By letting participants know that they are familiar with disaster work, leaders can speed the group process. This knowledge also can prepare group leaders to help group members to discuss what is troubling them rather than continue to avoid what is difficult.

Similar to many helping professionals, disaster recovery workers are comfortable identifying others who need help but may have a difficult time asking for assistance themselves. Consequently, it is important for group leaders to frame these groups and their workings in ways that can be received by workers. Members typically are receptive to a format that frames the group as one designed to help them process their experience and move on so that they can be better workers in the recovery effort.

Hand Out Participant Worksheet 12: *Group Defusing*

Review the four phases of the group defusing process.

Conduct a group defusing meeting as an example, using workshop participants.

DAY 2, AFTERNOON

Multiple Stressor Debriefing (150 minutes)

Hand Out Participant Worksheet 13: *Multiple Stressor Debriefing*

The primary purpose of MSD is to give recovery workers time to take a break and reflect on their work—both the positive and negative aspects—as a way of completing their experience as a recovery worker and preparing to return to their home life. Therefore, MSD, which may last as long as two hours and involve as many as 15 people, occurs at or near the conclusion of a disaster response.

MSD debriefings have four stages: The following outline of the four stages of MSD

summarizes Worksheet 13. The facilitator should cover this material before running a "sample" MSD group experience.

MSD sessions are conducted with people who have worked closely together during a highly stressful time and who may have worked together at other disasters. Group leaders should work in pairs and be trained about the procedures for facilitating a debriefing session. Leaders should be familiar with disaster recovery work and common reactions of workers to stress. In addition, facilitators should be closely linked to the existing mental health services for the workers.

Although individual debriefing is appropriate in certain circumstances, debriefing in a group format provides a cost effective and productive intervention. The advantages of group debriefing include an environment in which members listen to others and describe what was difficult and what they were proud of during the recovery effort; normalizing the stressors and the symptoms (for example, irritability, intrusive thoughts, emotional numbing, jumpiness, and guilt) that may accompany intensive recovery work; and encouraging members to share coping strategies. Because much of disaster recovery work is conducted in a group environment, group debriefing is a logical intervention.

Stage 1: Disclosure of Events

1. Leaders describe the parameters of the intervention, including the length (90 to 120 minutes) and purpose of the group (to take a break and reflect on your work, and to prepare for going home). They then outline the limitations of confidentiality in accordance with state law (for example, information about abuse of children or injury to self or others must be reported to the Department of Social Services).

2. Leaders communicate to participants that debriefing is neither psychotherapy nor primarily a critique of the past events. Instead, debriefing provides members of the group time to take a break from their jobs and reflect on the positive and negative aspects of their work.

3. Leaders encourage members to discuss one or two distressing events and positive events that occurred during their disaster work.

4. One of the leaders writes the events on a flipchart or chalkboard.

Stage 2: Feelings and Reactions

1. Group members discuss thoughts and feelings about the events written on the flip chart.

2. Group members are invited to vent their feelings about incidents in which they were involved. Group members and leaders give validation for their feelings.

3. Leaders emphasize that strong feelings are a normal response to a chronic stress experience, and that it is safe and helpful to talk about them. By establishing that their feelings and reactions are typical responses to the disaster recovery experience it is possible to create a supportive environment for group members to discuss the reactions that are bothering them.

Stage 3: Coping Strategies

1. Group leaders ask members to identify coping strategies they used during the disaster recovery operation and with similar past experiences.

2. Leaders help group participants in identifying numerous effective coping strategies, and encourage members to use these strategies.

3. It is important to identify ways that participants can care for themselves in the chronic stress environment of the disaster as well as what they can do as they prepare to return home.

4. Group leaders help assess whether members are expressing or exhibiting maladaptive and self-destructive coping behaviors.

5. By instructing group members about common stress responses, the leaders help normalize the members' experiences and decrease their anxiety.

Stage 4: Termination

1. Group members discuss the transition to their home lives and responsibilities.

2. Participants are asked to reflect on what they remember as positive from their disaster response work.

3. Members are encouraged to discuss what the process of leaving the disaster will be like for them—what difficulties they might encounter and what they are looking forward to. Leaders need to encourage members who have successfully coped with previous disaster work to help "first timers" with their upcoming transition home by telling them what to expect.

4. Leaders emphasize the importance for workers to continue to talk about their experience after returning home. Group leaders need to encourage the group members to discuss the troubling and positive aspects of the disaster work with their support systems after leaving the disaster site.

5. Group leaders identify workers who appear distressed and work with them respectfully to create a follow-up plan— individual, group, or family counseling, for example.

6. The MSD model does not assume that group members will finish processing their experience at the completion of the group session. Therefore, MSD

encourages members to continue to process the experience after they leave the debriefing.

Conduct an MSD group meeting as an example, using workshop participants.

After the MSD, have participants form groups with approximately four members each, and then turn to the last page of Participant Worksheet 13 and answer the questions as a group.

Finally, ask the participants, "How do CISD, group defusing, and MSD compare? What do you see as the advantages and disadvantages of each?"

Conclusion and Bibliography (30 Minutes)

Have participants brainstorm solutions to the following problem: "If this workshop—or any intervention with a disaster helper—has brought up a need for continued support or if support in general is needed (now or later), where do you get it?" Possible responses include:

- local mental health center
- religious leaders
- colleagues
- other mental health professionals.

Hand Out Participant Worksheet 14: *Bibliography*

Bibliography for Trainers
Sources cited in the discussion of CISD:

Ajdukovic, D., & Ajdukovic, M. (Eds.). (2000). *Mental health care of helpers*. Zagreb, Croatia: Society for Psychological Assistance.

Deahl, M. P., Srinivasan, M., Jones, N., Neblett, C., & Jolly, A. (2001). Commentary: Evaluating psychological debriefing: Are we measuring the right outcomes? *Journal of Traumatic Stress, 14*, 527–529.

Dyregrov A. (1999). Helpful and hurtful aspects of psychological debriefing groups. *International Journal of Emergency Mental Health, 1*, 175–181.

Everly, G. S., Jr., & Mitchell, J. T. (2000). The debriefing "controversy" and crisis intervention: A review of lexical and substantial issues. *International Journal of Emergency Mental Health, 2*, 211–225.

Hodgkinson, P. E. & Stewart, M. (1998). *A handbook of post-disaster psychosocial aftercare* (2nd ed.). New York: Routledge.

Humphries, C., & Carr, A. (2001). The short term effectiveness of critical incident stress debriefing. *Irish Journal of Psychology, 22*(3–4), 188–197.

Irving, P., & Long, A. (2001). Critical incident stress debriefing following traumatic life experiences. *Journal of Psychiatric and Mental Health Nursing, 8*, 307–314.

Jordan, K. (2002). Providing crisis counseling to New Yorkers after the terrorist attack on the World Trade Center. *Family Journal Counseling and Therapy for Couples and Families, 10*, 139–144.

Mitchell J. T. (1983). When disaster strikes: The critical incident stress debriefing process. *Journal of Emergency Medical Services, 8*(1), 36–39.

Mitchell, J. T. (2003). Major misconceptions in crisis intervention. *International Journal of Emergency Mental Health, 5*, 185-197.

Mitchell J. T., & Everly, G. S. (2001). *The basic critical incident stress management course: Basic group crisis intervention* (3rd ed.). Ellicott, MD: International Critical Incident Stress Foundation.

Pynoos, R. S. (1993). Traumatic stress and psychopathology in children and adolescents. In R. S. Pynoos (Ed.), *Posttraumatic stress disorder: A clinical review* (pp. 65–98). Baltimore: Sidran Press.

Robinson, R., & Mitchell, J. (1993) Evaluation of psychological debriefing. *Journal of Traumatic Stress, 6*, 367–382.

Smith, M. (2001). Critical incident debriefing in groups: A group analytic perspective. *Psychodynamic Counselling, 7*, 329–346.

Tobin, J. (2001). The limitations of critical incident stress debriefing. *Irish Journal of Psychological Medicine, 18*(4), 142.

Wraith, R. (2000). Children and debriefing: Theory, interventions and outcomes. In B. Raphael & J. P. Wilson (Eds.), *Psychological debriefing: Theory, practice, and evidence* (pp. 195–212). Cambridge, England: Cambridge University Press.

Other topics to explore

Clay, R. (2001, November) Tapping their own resilience. *Monitor on Psychology* (Online). Retrieved September 18, 2003, from http://www.apa.org/monitor/nov01/resilience. html

Omer, H., & Alon, N. (1994). The continuity principle: A unified approach to treatment and management in disaster and trauma. *American Journal of Community Psychology, 22*, 273–287.

Tucker, P., Pfefferbaum, B., Doughty, D. E., Jones, D. E., Jordan, F. B., & Nixon, S.-J. (2002). Body handlers after terrorism in Oklahoma City: Predictors of posttraumatic stress and other symptoms. *American Journal of Orthopsychiatry, 72*, 469–475.

WORKSHEET 1

The Effects of a Powerful Experience

Draw a picture that depicts a *powerful* experience you had working as a disaster recovery worker during the past few months.

WORKSHEET 2

Stress and Burnout

- Stress is your body's reaction to any event that pushes it out of what you consider to be normal; it is the body's preparation to respond to the unusual. Every event and situation is a potential stressor.

- If exposure to a stressful situation is prolonged, burnout—physical, emotional, and mental exhaustion—results.

--- **WORKSHEET 3** ---

Factors Contributing to Burnout

1. *Professional isolation*
   You may have no one with whom to talk about the nature of your work or its impact on your life. Sometimes you may find it difficult to talk about your experiences with friends or family who cannot seem to understand the effects of exposure to disaster and trauma.

2. *Emotional and physical drain of providing continuing empathy*
   Listening with care to the stories of people exposed to a disaster and trying to provide solace and reassurance—perhaps at all hours of the night and day—increases the risk of emotional and physical drain.

   This situation is exacerbated if you are a caregiver to, or the source of strength for, family and friends.

3. *Ambiguous successes*
   Even though the coordination of the recovery effort, the teamwork, and the response of the community may have been extremely positive, and disaster clients may have responded with gratitude and appreciation, you may feel a sense of depression in the face of the deaths, injuries, and communitywide destruction. No matter how much is done in response, it may never seem to be enough. You may never know if what was done was truly helpful or useful.

4. *Erosion of idealism*
   Strong beliefs in such ideals as the goodness of people, the ability to create a better world, the conviction that justice will prevail, and your own power to make a difference often are challenged in disaster recovery work.

5. *Lack of expected rewards*
   Crisis helpers are notoriously underpaid, if paid at all, for their services. They may be compensated from their agency to cover the costs of being on call. Those who volunteer their services know that they will give up time with their families, time at their jobs, and time for themselves. Sometimes, helpers are frustrated by the lack of acknowledgment for their service. And sometimes they are discouraged when they compare their work with the work of others and see others' rewards.

6. *Helpers also may be survivors*
   Sharing geographical proximity with survivors or identifying with them increases the chances of experiencing burnout as you help.

WORKSHEET 4

Disaster Relief Work and Changes in Helpers' Beliefs

Repeated disaster interventions can alter and solidify changes in helpers' beliefs, particularly if they have been victimized by trauma in their own lives. Four factors affect these belief changes most emphatically:

1. *Repeated exposure to sudden, random disaster.* Repeated exposure to trauma triggers the imprinting of traumatic responses in the brain and repeatedly confirms the perception of alarm and danger. Caretakers may become hyperalert and hypervigilant in their everyday life, or abdicate control assuming "nothing matters."

2. *Repeated exposure to the impossible.* *Repeated* exposure to "impossible" events alters belief in what is "normal."

3. *Lack of positive countervailing exposure to human good and world order.* Caretakers who are able to maintain their ability to function in a positive and healthy way are those who have strong social connections and support, who anchor themselves in the knowledge that people are good, and who are able to sustain themselves with their sense of spiritual connections.

4. *Lack of nurturing resources.* Helpers need to have people in their lives who will take care of them. They need to ask for help and be willing to receive it. Sometimes helpers try to take care of the "little child" inside by themselves. When that happens, the helper becomes lonely and frightened. It is crucial for helpers to seek and receive external care and nurturing, and it is also crucial for them to take care of themselves.

WORKSHEET 5

Self–Assessment of Your Stress Reactions
(1 of 2 pages)

Check each verbal behavior that you experience when you feel pressured or stressed.

_____ verbally attack people

_____ repeat the same words over and over without variation

_____ talk obsessively about the source of stress

_____ make errors in grammar and pronunciation

_____ encourage others to speak quickly

_____ experience lack of quick recall, resulting in pauses

_____ talk only if you can talk about the source of stress

_____ others:

Check each nonverbal behavior that you experience when you feel pressured or stressed.

_____ gritting teeth

_____ sweating palms

_____ tightened stomach muscles

_____ chewing on pencils

_____ hair twirling or twisting

_____ shifting position in a chair

_____ moving, walking, and eating rapidly

_____ finger drumming

_____ fist clenching

_____ jaw clenching

_____ head scratching

_____ nail biting

_____ leg bouncing

_____ repeatedly using nonverbal "tics," such as wetting the lips, clearing the throat, and wrinkling the forehead

_____ repeatedly using eye movements, such as rapid blinking, squinting, and looking away

_____ pacing

_____ shifting weight

_____ wiggling

Self–Assessment of Your Stress Reactions

(2 of 2 pages)

Check each nonverbal behavior that you experience when you feel pressured or stressed. (continued)

_____ eating too much or not at all

_____ drinking or smoking more than usual

_____ hands trembling

_____ sleeping too much or too little

_____ withdrawal—avoiding interaction

_____ using a sarcastic or nasty tone

_____ engaging in vocal explosiveness—accenting key words when there is no reason to do so

_____ speeding up at the ends of sentences

_____ using higher voice pitch than normal

_____ overarticulating—enunciating words so clearly and precisely that it draws attention

_____ headache

_____ rashes or hives

_____ muscle spasms

_____ others:

What Do You Do When You Feel Stressed?

Danieli's Principles of Self–Healing

- Self-healing is effective insofar as you recognize your own reactions

- Self-healing is effective insofar as you recognize and understand your reactions

- Self-healing is effective insofar as you are able to heal and grow:

  - Accept that nothing will ever be the same.
  - When you feel wounded, take time to diagnose accurately, to soothe yourself, and to heal yourself so you will be emotionally fit to continue to work.
  - Any of the affective reactions (including grief, mourning, or rage) you have that are triggered by victims' stories may interact with your old, unresolved experiences. Seek consultation or counseling for previously unexplored areas triggered by disaster clients' stories. You will thus be able to use your own professional work purposefully for your own growth.
  - Establish a network of people to create a holding environment within which you can share your trauma-related work.
  - Provide yourself with avenues outside your work for creative and relaxing self-expression to regenerate and re-energize yourself.

WORKSHEET 8

Disaster Workers' Resilience

Protective factors—those things that protect people from the effects of stress and trauma—are internal and external influences that enhance resiliency and help people act in positive ways when coping with disasters. Protective factors fall into three broad areas:

- *Qualities of the disaster helper*, such as a good sense of humor, resourcefulness, high self-esteem, altruism, and high intelligence.

- *A strong sense of continuity*, including
  - functional continuity—the ability to maintain usual routines during a disaster or after it
  - historical continuity—the ability to maintain a sense of identity and a sense of history during a disaster or after it
  - interpersonal continuity—the ability to maintain a social network during a disaster or after it
  - spiritual continuity—the ability to maintain faith in a stable and just world.

- *Characteristics of her or his relationships*, such as warm and caring friends and support from inside and outside the family, such as support from religious affiliations and work.

WORKSHEET 9

Self–Help Techniques You Can Do Alone
(1 of 2 pages)

1. Exercise

Assume that you will need more sleep, exercise, and healthy foods—just as your clients and patients do.
Exercise helps you relieve initial stress reactions, refresh energies, and get back to work.
An individual who exercises recovers more quickly from stress than does a sedentary
person: Physiological reactions to stress are similar to those experienced while exercising
(for example, increased heart rate and muscle activity), and if the body is well exercised,
its ability to cope with changes and recover is increased.

Exercise can be introduced into your daily life without making drastic changes in
routine. For example, you can walk up stairs rather than take the elevator, park in the
farthest lot rather than the closest, walk or bike to the store rather than drive, do isometric exercises while watching television in the evening, take an exercise class, or join a
lunchtime exercise program at work.

2. Meditation

Meditation increases concentration (which facilitates problem solving), increases your
ability to identify sources and effects of stress, and teaches you how to be quiet and to
calm your mind.

Repeating a word, sound, or phrase:
   select a word, sound, or phrase with which you are comfortable
   repeat the word over and over.

Paying attention to your breathing:
   find a comfortable place to sit
   close your eyes to reduce distractions
   bring your focus and awareness to your body
   pay attention to your breathing
   still paying close attention to your breathing, begin to notice each time you inhale
   and exhale—as you monitor your breathing you should mentally say the word "rising"
   with each inhale, and "falling" with each exhale. Whenever your mind begins to
   wander, bring it back by again mentally saying "rising, falling."

Self–Help Techniques You Can Do Alone
(2 of 2 pages)

3. Guided imagery

Imagine that you are in a cocoon, surrounded by a soft strong shell that protects you from everything outside.....Explore what it is like inside your safe cocoon....what sounds are like....what the air feels like....what the colors look like.....what the smells smell like..... Take a moment and explore your cocoon.....

Now, slowly, break out of your cocoon.....Find your way out of your protective shell and be aware how you feel as you emerge into the light of the world.....The air is warm and the world seems lighted by a healing sun, a joyful light that penetrates everything, including you as you emerge from the cocoon.....The light warms you and heals all your wounds..... The light energizes you and fills you with joy.....You rejoice in how you feel.

Consider:

- How do you think you could use the three self-help techniques (exercise, meditation, and guided imagery), or any one of them, in your work—for yourself, for other recovery workers, and for disaster clients?
- What could keep you from using any of these techniques in your work?
- When could you use these techniques, or any one of them, in your work—when would it be most appropriate?
- How do cultural differences among recovery workers and disaster clients affect your decision to use any of these techniques?

—— **WORKSHEET 10** ——

Self–Care Strategies

The following suggestions are from the APA (2001):

- Maintain contact with friends and family, and talk about your disaster-related experiences and feelings.

- Avoid enacting the role of a disaster recovery worker when not working with disaster clients.

- Connect with organizations in your community that are important to you.

- Attend to your spiritual needs, individually or within a spiritual community.

- Engage in activities that balance work and nonwork life: Pursue hobbies, don't attempt to do too much, and seek necessary time away from work.

- Write and talk about the disaster and its effects, recognizing that this may feel difficult to do under unusual circumstances.

- Increase interaction with other helpers (respected peers or a supervisor) in the forms of consultation or supervision—don't try to go it alone.

- Consider personal therapy.

WORKSHEET 11

Critical Incident Stress Debriefing

The critical incident stress debriefing (CISD) process moves from cognitive (Introduction and Fact phases), to cognitive-moving-to-affective (Thought phase), to affective (Reaction phase), to affective-moving-to-cognitive (Symptoms phase), to cognitive (Teaching and Re-entry phases).

1. *Introduction.* Introduce team members, explain the CISD process (for example, people do not have to speak if they choose not to), and set expectations (for example, confidentiality).
2. *Fact phase.* Collect information about the participants and about the event. Ask the following key questions: "What was your role (your job) at the time of the incident, where were you, what happened, what did you do?"
3. *Thought phase.* The facilitator asks, "What went through your mind during the incident? What is your most prominent thought about the event? What have your thoughts been concerning the incident since it happened?"
4. *Reaction phase.* The facilitator asks, "How did the incident affect you emotionally? What was the worst thing in this incident for you personally? How did you feel? How do you feel now? What was the worst part?"
5. *Symptom phase.* The facilitator asks, "How did you know this incident was having an effect on you? What are any symptoms that you may have developed as a result of the incident, such as fears, startle reactions, feelings of dread, and intrusive thoughts?"
6. *Teaching phase:* Present information regarding expected physiological and psychological stress reactions, and what to do about them.
7. *Re-entry phase:* Wrap-up questions. The facilitator asks, "What have you learned? What, if anything, have you gained from the experience that is positive? How can you help and be helped in the future?" The facilitator provides information about possible help, repeats reassurance, and sets a follow-up meeting in approximately two weeks.

WORKSHEET 12

Group Defusing Process

(1 of 3 pages)

The group defusing process can take place at any time, is typically not longer than 45 minutes, and is conducted with no more than eight group members. The primary purpose of group defusing is to provide helpers with a way to process strong feelings and reactions to a particularly troubling event, with the goal of returning to work as a helper. group defusing is also useful for identifying helpers who may require additional aid.

Group defusing usually is conducted at or near the site of the disaster for disaster workers who appear to be experiencing severe stress or need someone outside their particular work environment with whom to discuss how things are going. No attempt is made to address all elements of crisis intervention; the focus is on immediate issues of safety, flash points of trauma reactions, and ideas about how to live through immediate reexposure to the disaster or its aftermath.

Group defusing usually is facilitated by a pair of facilitators who make the structure and the purpose of the group clear. Facilitators should obtain as much information as possible regarding the specific tasks in which group members are or were involved. Familiarity with workers' jobs during a disaster can help in developing a better alliance with group members. As with any group of people exposed to traumatic events, members tend to look suspiciously at outsiders. By letting participants know that they are familiar with disaster work, leaders can speed the group process. This knowledge also can prepare group leaders to help group members to discuss what is troubling them rather than avoid what is difficult.

Similar to many helping professionals, disaster recovery workers are comfortable identifying others who need help but may have a difficult time asking for assistance themselves. Consequently, it is important for group leaders to frame these groups and their workings in ways that can be received by workers. Members typically are receptive to a format that frames the group as one designed to help them process their experience and move on so that they can be better workers in the recovery effort.

Phase 1: Introduction and Orientation (5 minutes)
Co-leaders introduce themselves and clearly describe the structure and the purpose of the group. This phase emphasizes safety and security for the group. It invites group members to decompress, get support, and get ready to return to their tasks. Co-leaders attempt to make group members comfortable and invite them to participate. Co-leaders should acknowledge the valuable work that workers have provided to people exposed to the disaster. Group members share their names and jobs at the disaster.

Group Defusing Process
(2 of 3 pages)

Phase 2: Ventilation and Validation (15 to 20 minutes)

This phase provides workers with an opportunity to express their reactions to their experience of working at the disaster site. Recognizing and expressing their reactions helps workers process and create distance between themselves and the incident. Having their reactions validated and normalized by other group members and the facilitators also allows them to accept and integrate their feelings. Many people who do emergency disaster work find that there is a specific incident during their immediate response that sticks in their minds or troubles them persistently. Facilitators should normalize the experience of these flash points. Facilitators might ask:

- Can you think of any specific incident during the last 24 hours that sticks in your mind or troubles you persistently?
- What do you remember seeing, hearing, smelling, touching, or tasting?
- What feelings or reactions do you have about that incident?

Co-leaders should acknowledge and validate for group members' experiences and reactions.

Phase 3: Prediction and Preparation (10 to 15 minutes)

This phase encourages group members to consider whether they will continue to be troubled by their experience. If so, they are encouraged to develop specific strategies to manage their situation. Facilitators might ask:

   As you go back to work, do you think that incident will continue to trouble you?
- What can you do to help yourself cope with such thoughts or reactions?
-

Facilitators should encourage group members to predict what kinds of things might trigger their reactions, for example, noises, smells, images that remind them of their troubling experiences. Help them to anticipate their experience. Then, facilitators should encourage the group members to brainstorm about the kinds of things they can do to cope with their troubling thoughts or reactions.

Group Defusing Process
(3 of 3 pages)

One of the facilitators could close this phase with a brief guided visualization. The guided visualization would start by helping group members move into a state of deep relaxation. Once in a relaxed state, the facilitator could have the group members visualize themselves successfully using the coping skills they have identified. The facilitator can encourage group members to remember this picture they have of themselves successfully coping with the thoughts and reactions that used to bother them. After a couple of minutes, the facilitator can reinforce this state of relaxed yet focused energy and gradually help group members to come back into the room.

Phase 4: Summary and Conclusion (5 minutes)
Facilitators should acknowledge the value of the work that group members have been performing with people exposed to the disaster. They should reassure workers about their competence. Finally, leaders should provide reassurance of continuing support for workers. When necessary, they can help workers contact other needed resources. Review the key phases of the model briefly and provide participants with the opportunity to ask questions.

Multiple Stressor Debriefing Process

(1 of 4 pages)

Helpers mobilized to assist with disaster relief are exposed to a multitude of stressors. The multiple stressor debriefing (MSD) process is designed to prevent or minimize the negative consequences of stress reactions in recovery helpers.

An MSD debriefing, which occurs near or at the conclusion of the disaster response, has four stages: (1) disclosure of events, (2) feelings and reactions, (3) coping strategies, and (4) termination.

The MSD model does not assume that group members will finish processing their experience at the completion of the group session. Therefore, MSD facilitators encourage members to continue to process the experience after they leave the debriefing. MSD was designed to facilitate the transition to the home environment.

MSD sessions function best when the size is limited to no more than 12 to 15 members, in recommended session lengths of 90 to 120 minutes. Group leaders should work in pairs and be trained about the procedures for facilitating a debriefing session. Leaders should be familiar with disaster relief work and common reactions of workers to stress, and be closely linked to the existing mental health services for the workers.

Guidelines for the Four–Stage Multiple Stressor Debriefing Process
Stage 1: Disclosure of Events
The first stage of MSD is disclosure of events. Leaders describe the parameters of the intervention, including the length (90 to 120 minutes) and purpose of the group, and outline the limitations of confidentiality in accordance with state law. The facilitators tell participants that debriefing is neither psychotherapy nor primarily a critique of the events. Instead, debriefing provides members of the group time to take a break from their jobs and reflect on the positive and negative aspects of their work. It is important to set clear rules for group participation so that participants understand what they can expect from leaders and other members, particularly because some of the material disclosed can be sensitive.

In the disclosure of events stage, the group leaders encourage members to discuss one or two distressing events that occurred during their disaster work. Group leaders also ask participants to identify positive events and experiences to enable group members to more fully integrate their experience.

Multiple Stressor Debriefing Process

(2 of 4 pages)

Stage 1: Disclosure of Events (continued)

One of the leaders writes the events on a flipchart or chalkboard. The visual aid enhances the educational component of the meeting. This technique is important for several reasons. First, it decreases participants' anxiety about being counseled or diagnosed during the debriefing process. Second, it communicates to the group members in a concrete way that their thoughts and feelings are important and significant. Third, it places the events outside the participants (on the flip chart), which creates some distance so they may put the event into perspective, and so their thoughts and feelings may be acknowledged by other group members.

Common events shared in this first phase are workers' experiences with aiding disaster clients, personality conflicts between workers, long hours, difficult work environment, recent exposure to other disasters or traumas, and being away from home. Positive events may include experience with people that seemed to be helpful, such as meals with coworkers after long hours and reunions with old acquaintances.

Stage 2: Feelings and Reactions

The second stage of the model focuses on feelings and reactions. Here the group members discuss thoughts and feelings about the events written on the flip chart. Facilitators help participants associate feelings with the troubling events. The use of the flip chart helps group members to explore and describe their feelings and reactions to the distressing events. Facilitators also set aside time for discussing feelings associated with positive events.

In this stage, group members are invited to vent their feelings about incidents in which they were involved. Group members and leaders validate their feelings. The leaders emphasize that strong feelings are a normal response to chronic stress experience and that it is safe and helpful to talk about them. By establishing that their feelings and reactions are typical responses to the disaster relief experience, it is possible to create a supportive environment for group members to discuss the reactions that are bothering them.

Negative feelings that are often expressed include guilt and inadequacy about not doing enough for people who are suffering, anger and disappointment with administrative disorganization, and frustration dealing with difficult workers. Positive themes include camaraderie, helping others, and a sense of belonging to the group.

Multiple Stressor Debriefing Process
(3 of 4 pages)

Stage 3: Coping Strategies

In the third stage of the model, the group discusses coping strategies. The group leaders ask members to identify coping strategies they used both during the disaster recovery operation and with similar past experiences. It is helpful for group members to talk with other group members about how they coped with other disasters so they can identify ways to cope with the current disaster. The leaders help group participants identify effective coping strategies and encourage members to use these strategies.

It is important to identify ways that participants can care for themselves in the chronic stress environment of the disaster as well as what they can do as they prepare to return home. During this stage, group leaders should observe carefully to assess whether members are expressing or exhibiting maladaptive and self-destructive coping behaviors. Since many groups of caregivers express reluctance and even guilt about taking care of themselves, leaders need to emphasize how much help workers could continue to provide if they were under less stress. Sometimes it is helpful to reframe getting help for oneself as a way to be a more effective worker.

Successful coping strategies that need to be identified include exercise, good nutrition, breaks from work, engaging in relaxing activities, sharing feelings with coworkers, participating in staff meetings or briefings, staying in touch with family and friends, setting realistic expectations for their work with disaster clients, and prayer. Leaders need to be ready to identify risks associated with unhealthy coping mechanisms, such as denial and substance abuse. By instructing group members about common stress responses, the leaders help normalize the members' experiences and reduce their anxiety.

Multiple Stressor Debriefing Process
(4 of 4 pages)

Stage 4: Termination

In the termination stage the group members discuss the transition to their home lives and responsibilities. Participants are asked to reflect on what they remember as positive from their disaster response work. This process can help workers assess their entire experience rather than amplify difficulties they encountered.

Members are encouraged to discuss what leaving the disaster will be like—what difficulties they might encounter and what they are looking forward to. Leaders need to encourage members who have successfully coped with previous disaster work to aid "first timers" with their upcoming transition home by telling them what to expect. Often, stress awaits workers as they return home. Most workers return home to numerous responsibilities at home and at their jobs. Leaders need to emphasize the importance for workers to continue to talk about their experience after returning home. Group leaders need to encourage the group members to discuss the troubling and positive aspects of the disaster work with their support systems after leaving the disaster site. Discussing positive aspects of teamwork and reviewing accomplishments helps instill hope for the future. In addition, encouraging members to say goodbye to those with whom they have grown close recognizes bonds that have formed during the disaster relief work. Discussing this bond openly can be important in helping workers with the transition home. One common mechanism group members use to deal with leaving is to discuss possible reunions in the near future.

Group leaders need to identify workers who appear distressed and work with them respectfully to create a follow-up plan. At the end of the group session, the group leaders should suggest individual, group, or family counseling for members who continue to have difficulties.

Consider:

- How do you think you could use MSD in your work—for yourself, for other recovery workers, and for survivors?
- What could keep you from using MSD in your work?
- When could you use MSD in your work—when would it be most appropriate?
- How do cultural differences among recovery workers and survivors affect your decision to use MSD?

───── **WORKSHEET 14** ─────

Bibliography for Participants
(1 of 1 pages)

American Psychological Association. (2001, October). *Tapping your resilience in the wake of terrorism: Pointers for practitioners.* Retrieved September 18, 2003, from http://www.apa.org/practice/practitionerhelp.html.

Armstrong, K. R., Lund, P. E., McWright, L. T., & Tichenor, V. (1995). Multiple stressor debriefing and the American Red Cross: The East Bay Hills fire experience. *Social Work, 40,* 83–90.

Badenhorst, J. C., & Van-Schalkwyk, S. J. (1992). Minimizing post traumatic stress in critical mining incidents. *Employee Assistance Quarterly, 7*(3), 79–90.

Bulkeley, K. (2003). *Dreams of healing: Transforming nightmares into visions of hope.* Mahwah, NJ: Paulist Press.

Cerney, M. S. (1995). Treating the "heroic treaters." In C. R. Figley (Ed), *Compassion fatigue: Coping with secondary traumatic stress disorder in those who treat the traumatized* (pp. 131–149). New York: Brunner/Mazel.

Danieli, Y. (1996). Who takes care of the caretakers? The emotional consequences of working with children traumatized by war and communal violence. In R. J. Apfel & B. Simon (Eds.), *Minefields in their hearts: The mental health of children in war and communal violence* (pp. 189–205). New Haven, CT: Yale University Press.

Everly, G. S., Jr., & Mitchell, J. T. (1995). Prevention of work-related posttraumatic stress: The critical incident stress debriefing process. In L. R. Murphy & J. J. Hurrell, Jr. (Eds), *Job stress interventions* (pp. 173–183). Washington, DC: American Psychological Association.

Figley, C. R. (1995). Compassion fatigue as secondary traumatic stress disorder: An overview. In C. R. Figley (Ed), *Compassion fatigue: Coping with secondary traumatic stress disorder in those who treat the traumatized* (pp. 1–20). New York: Brunner/Mazel.

La Greca, A. M., Silverman, W. K., Vernberg, E. M., & Roberts, M. C. (Eds.). (2002). *Helping children cope with disasters and terrorism.* Washington, DC: American Psychological Association.

Solomon, Z., & Benbenishty, R. (1986). The role of proximity, immediacy, and expectancy in frontline treatment of combat stress reaction among Israelis in the Lebanon War. *American Journal of Psychiatry, 143,* 613–617.

Weaver, J. D. (1995). *Defusing and debriefing.* Retrieved September 18, 2003, from http://ourworld.compuserve.com/homepages/johndweaver/debrief.htm

Young, M. A. (1998). *The community crisis response team training manual* (2nd ed.). Washington, DC: National Organization for Victim Assistance, Chapter 18, "Stress Reactions of Caregivers." Retrieved September 18, 2003, from http://www.ojp.usdoj.gov/ovc/publications/infores/crt/welcome.html

INDEX

COPE program. *See* Community Oriented Preventive Education (COPE) program
Coping. *See also specific topics*
    active, 210–211
    adaptational, 297
    in communities, 117–118
    competency in, 117–118
    with complex disasters, 209–213
    passive, 211–212
    phases of, 297
    resiliency models and, 50–51
    strategies for, 31, 320
Coping ability, age and, 67–68
Coping skills, activities for developing, 236–238
Coping styles, 137
Corrosive communities
    created by technological disasters, 165, 166
    explanation of, 116
Creating a Safe Space, 303
Creating a "Traumatic Picture Story" activity, 315, 316
Creative means for dealing with trauma, 275, 284
Crisis communication plan
    coordination elements of, 414–415
    explanation of, 410, 411
    media center for, 413
    media guide for, 413
    media relations and, 415–418
    predisaster testing of, 418
    protocols and decision-making processes for, 415
    speakers' bureau and, 413–414
    spokesperson for, 412–413
Crisis intervention
    body awareness in, 264–265
    early, 262–264
    explanation of, 224, 256–258
    with families, 274–285
    first aid stage of, 261
    group, 265–274. *See also* Group crisis intervention
    mending disrupted continuities in, 263–264
    prediction and preparation in, 260–261
    safety and security goals in, 258, 260
    in school, 285–287
    ventilation and validation in, 260
Critical incident stress debriefing (CISD), 443–445, 462
Croatia, postwar devastation in, 197
CROPS (Child Report of Post-Traumatic Symptoms), 43–44
Culture/cultural groups
    community integration of, 117
    disaster reactions and, 87–89
    in family systems, 101–102
    parent-child disaster-response relationship and, 108
    as risk factor, 89
    war trauma and, 76–77
Curiosity, 48
Cyclone Tracy, 392
Cyclones, 149

D

Dam disasters, 174–175
Dante's Peak, 106
Deaf individuals. *See* Hearing-impaired individuals
Death. *See also* Fatalities
    adolescent reactions to, 80–81
    culture as support for dealing with, 102
    fear of, 207
    of parents, 71
    from volcano eruptions, 132
Debriefing
    critical incident stress, 443–445, 462
    multiple stressor, 446–448, 466–469
    psychological, 442–443
Depression/depressive symptoms
    in children, 137
    coping with, 50–51
    following natural disasters, 137, 141
    following terrorism, 209
    in mothers, 109
Desert Storm. *See* Gulf War
Developing a List of Tasks activity, 315, 316
Developing countries
    natural disasters in, 133–135

predisaster prevention in, 154

Developmental levels
    in children, 67–68
    in preadolescents and adolescents, 79–81

Developmental stages
    explanation of, 68
    latency, 75, 77–79
    locomotor-genital, 73–75
    muscular-anal, 72–73
    oral-sensory stage and, 69–72

DeWolfe's disaster reaction model, 32–34

Diagnostic and Statistical Manual (DSM-I), 40

Diagnostic and Statistical Manual of Mental Disorders, Fourth Edition (DSM-IV-TR), 40

Diagnostic and Statistical Manual of Mental Disorders, Third Edition--Revised (DSM-III-R), 13, 40, 175

Diagnostic and Statistical Manual of Mental Disorders, Third Edition (DSM-IIl), 40

Disaster Center, 382

Disaster clients, defined, 20

Disaster education, 123, 384–386

Disaster movies, 332–333

Disaster plans. *See also* Community disaster plans
    considerations related to, 32–33
    development of family, 246–247
    education and public awareness and, 123, 384–386
    failure of, 402–403
    hazard analysis and, 381–382
    leadership in, 381
    lessons learned from, 399, 401
    networking and, 384
    overview of, 380–381
    planning and implementing, 390–392
    preparedness options for, 386–387
    in schools, 238
    testing and updating, 393–394
    victims' advocates and, 402
    volunteers and, 389–390
    warning the public and, 387–389

Disaster reaction models
    BASIC-Ph, 51–52, 56
    circles of vulnerability and support,

34–37, 39
    DeWolfe, 32–34
    explanation of, 30
    Gibson, 30
    posttraumatic stress disorder. *See* Posttraumatic stress disorder (PTSD)
    resiliency, 45–51
    Vernberg, La Greca, Silverman, Prinstein, 30–32

Disaster reactions. *See also* Posttraumatic recovery stages; *specific types of disasters*
    in adolescents, 14, 80, 81, 108–109
    in children, 12–16, 18, 30–39, 65–66, 75, 135–140, 176–177
    comprehension ability and, 84, 86–87, 108, 139
    culture and, 87–89
    in families, 106–109
    gender and, 83–84
    myths about, 385–386
    parent-child relationship and, 107–109, 204, 281
    in parents, 108–109
    prediction of, 33, 34, 65–66, 82–83
    in preschool-age children, 14, 42
    previous trauma and, 89–90, 103
    prior conditions and, 89–90
    secondhand, 177–179
    in toddlers, 14
    types of, 39
    underestimating, 176–177

Disaster Recovery with Vulnerable Populations Workshop. *See also* Vulnerability; Vulnerable populations
    Circles of Vulnerability Worksheet, 330, 345–348
    Common Strategies for Working with Clients Dealing with Disaster Recovery Worksheet, 329, 343
    Expected and Desired Outcomes Worksheet, 329–330, 344
    How to Create a Social Support Network Worksheet, 341, 376
    Maslow's Need Hierarchy Worksheet, 332–333, 351

Visually impaired individuals, 354, 360, 361, 372–373
Volcano eruptions, 132
Volunteers, 389–390, 398
Vulnerability
assessment of, 296
characteristics of, 352
circles of, 34–35, 329–330, 332, 345–348
physical, 34–35
psychological or social, 35
special needs related to, 353–373
Vulnerable populations
cognitively impaired individuals, 336–337, 354, 358, 361, 368–369
economically disadvantaged, 334–335, 354, 356, 361, 364–365
elderly individuals, 333–334, 354–355, 361–363
help knowledge for assisting, 374–375
miscellaneous, 338–340, 354
physically disabled individuals, 335–336, 354, 359, 361, 370–371

W

War. *See also* Complex disasters
adolescent responses to, 87
child soldiers in, 194
children as targets of, 64, 65, 194–196
children of prisoners of, 100
children's responses to, 49, 203–209
effects on families of, 196, 198–199, 318
family cohesion and adaptability during, 104–105
indirect exposure to, 195–196
interventions for, 18
ripple effects of, 196
sexual violence during, 195, 318
shell shock and, 40
statistics for victims of, 192
War trauma. *See also* Complex disasters
disaster reactions in individuals with, 31–32
family breakup and, 98
intensity, suddenness, and duration of, 77
intergenerational transmission of, 199, 201
processes involved in, 76–77
Warnings. *See also* Vulnerability, special needs

related to
community response to, 389
elements of effective, 387–388
Watt, James, 384
What All Helpers Need to Know Dealing with Vulnerable Populations Worksheet, 341, 374–375
What I Do When Working with Clients Dealing with Disaster Recovery Worksheet, 329, 342
What is a "Vulnerable Population?" Worksheet, 333–340, 352
When Disaster Strikes: A Handbook form the Caring Professions (Raphael), 5
Wichita Falls, Texas, tornadoes, 380
World Disasters Report 2001, The (International Federation of Red Cross and Red Crescent Societies), 131
World Food Programme (United Nations), 135
World Trade Center attacks. *See* Terrorist attacks of September 11, 2001
World War I, 192
World War II, 204, 280
Writing, free, 236–237

Y

Yerkes, Peter, World Trade Center bombing and, 417
Young children. *See* Children; Infants; Preschool-age children; Toddlers
Yuba County flood, 146
Yugoslavia, external help in, 193, 258